Fundamental Theology

Fundamental Theology

A Protestant Perspective

Matthew L. Becker

Afterword by Martin E. Marty

B L O O M S B U R Y

LONDON • NEW DELHI • NEW YORK • SYDNEY

Bloomsbury T&T Clark

An imprint of Bloomsbury Publishing Plc

50 Bedford Square
London
WC1B 3DP
UK

1385 Broadway
New York
NY 10018
USA

www.bloomsbury.com

Bloomsbury is a registered trade mark of Bloomsbury Publishing Plc

First published 2015

© Matthew L. Becker, 2015

British Library Cataloguing-in-Publication Data

A catalogue record for this book is available from the British Library.

ISBN: HB: 978-0-567-23005-8
PB: 978-0-567-56833-5
ePDF: 978-0-567-31525-0
ePUB: 978-0-567-55962-3

Library of Congress Cataloging-in-Publication Data

A catalogue record for this book is available from the Library of Congress.

Typeset by Fakenhm Prepress Solutions, Fakenham, Norfolk NR21 8NN

For Hans, Dick, and Chuck
And for Detra and Jacob, again

Contents

Preface

This book introduces college students to preliminary matters in the academic discipline of Christian theology. It serves as an orientation to theological prolegomena or fundamental theology since it addresses the issues that are foundational and basic to the discipline. The book also sets forth what has traditionally been called a theological encyclopedia because it describes the various branches of theology that together form it into a unified academic subject, one that intentionally seeks interdisciplinary engagement with all other university disciplines.

Fundamental theology should not be confused with Protestant Fundamentalism. In fact, the latter is typically quite uninterested in and often opposed to academic, interdisciplinary theology in a university setting. By contrast, fundamental theology, which is usually called "prolegomena" ("preliminary thoughts") within Protestant circles, makes use of human reasoning for the sake of investigating and understanding the basis or ground (Latin: *fundamentum*) of Christian faith in a meaningful and intellectually responsible manner. While fundamental theology cannot possibly hope to establish an irrefutable proof for that basis, given both the limitations of human beings and the nature of the subject that theologians seek to understand, it does want to respond intelligently to criticisms of that subject and to understand the central faith claims that are made by Christian theologians.

The genre of theological encyclopedia should not be confused with that of a general encyclopedia, as if it were providing an exhaustive and alphabetized summary of the various bits and pieces of theological knowledge. The goal of a theological encyclopedia is actually much more modest, if still somewhat challenging: to provide a rationale for the discipline of theology as a whole, to offer a brief introduction to its branches or sub-disciplines, and to highlight some of the ongoing problems within the discipline.

The few books that do address issues in fundamental theology and theological encyclopedia for an American audience seem to be oriented primarily toward graduate-level students and professors in seminaries and divinity schools. For example, the influential early writings by the Roman

Catholic scholar, David Tracy, which address issues in both fundamental theology and theological encyclopedia, were articulated within the context of a major North-American divinity school whose graduate students are often at a different academic level from those in undergraduate institutions.[1] The important works by another Roman Catholic scholar, Gerald O'Collins, also seem to be aimed primarily toward graduate-level seminary students, especially those who are already somewhat familiar with Roman Catholic themes and concerns.[2] This orientation also shapes the textbook by Fernando Ocáriz and Arturo Blanco.[3]

While some Protestant studies in fundamental theology have been published in America in recent decades, these are translations of German works that are likewise more suited to a seminary or divinity-school setting.[4] That same locale serves as the focus for Edward Farley's Theologia, which led to a fairly broad discussion about theological encyclopedia and the purpose of theological education in the United States near the end of the twentieth century.[5] A follow-up volume by Farley and two other books by another American divinity-school professor, David Kelsey, have furthered discussions in that context.[6]

All of the above works, each very important and significant in its own way, have shaped my understanding of fundamental theology and theological education. Nevertheless, those writings are not really directed toward the situation of an undergraduate institution in North America, where most students have never previously studied academic theology. In many colleges and universities, especially those that are church-related,

---

[1] David Tracy, Blessed Rage for Order: The New Pluralism in Theology (Minneapolis: Winston-Seabury, 1975); idem, The Analogical Imagination: Christian Theology and the Culture of Pluralism (New York: Crossroad, 1981).
[2] See Gerald O'Collins, Fundamental Theology (New York: Paulist, 1981); idem, Rethinking Fundamental Theology (New York: Oxford University Press, 2011).
[3] See Fernando Ocáriz and Arturo Blanco, Fundamental Theology (Woodridge, IL: Midwest Theological Forum, 2009).
[4] Wilfried Joest, Fundamentaltheologie: Theologische Grundlagen- und Methodenprobleme, 2nd edn (Stuttgart: Kohlhammer, 1981); Gerhard Ebeling, The Study of Theology, trans. Duane A. Priebe (Minneapolis: Fortress Press, 1978); and Wolfhart Pannenberg, Theology and the Philosophy of Science, trans. Francis McDonagh (Philadelphia: Westminster, 1976).
[5] See Edward Farley, Theologia: The Fragmentation and Unity of Theological Education (Minneapolis: Augsburg Fortress, 1983).
[6] Edward Farley, The Fragility of Knowledge: Theological Education in the Church and the University (Minneapolis: Fortress Press, 1988); David H. Kelsey, To Understand God Truly: What's Theological about a Theological School (Louisville: Westminster John Knox Press, 1992); and idem, Between Athens and Jerusalem: The Theological Education Debate (Grand Rapids: Eerdmans, 1993). This latter work provides a good summary of Farley's groundbreaking work and the main responses to it.

Christian theology may even be a curricular requirement in order to graduate within the arts and sciences, and yet very few theologians in America, especially in Protestant circles, have engaged matters of fundamental theology and theological encyclopedia in a way that is accessible to undergraduate students.

While most introductions to Christian theology include short descriptions of the nature and tasks of the discipline as a whole and some even offer additional analysis of its branches or sub-disciplines, these works, too, seem to have been targeted toward seminary and graduate students.[7] The same conclusion may be made about several shorter "invitations to theology" by seminary and divinity-school professors.[8] While two standard and widely-used introductions to Christian theology for college students include brief sections on the nature and place of theology in that setting, they do not address to any great depth specific issues within fundamental theology, theological encyclopedia, or the relation of Christian theology to other university disciplines. [9] It should be noted, too, that their respective approaches to the actual subject matter of Christian theology and the shape that it takes at the undergraduate level are different from the one set forth here.

Three fine collections of essays by scholars from around the world have appeared in recent years that also address religious studies, Christian theology, and the basic arguments about their relationship to each other at both the undergraduate and graduate level, but they do not explore issues within fundamental theology nor do they provide much of an indication

---

[7] Three representative examples of this approach by Protestant theologians (despite their significant substantive differences from one another) are the standard introductions by Daniel L. Migliore, *Faith Seeking Understanding: An Introduction to Christian Theology*, 2nd edn (Grand Rapids: Eerdmans, 2004), 1–19; Alister E. McGrath, *Christian Theology: An Introduction*, 5th edn (Oxford: Wiley-Blackwell, 2011), 101–19; and Peter C. Hodgson, *Christian Faith: A Brief Introduction* (Louisville: Westminster John Knox, 2001). For an excellent example of a Roman Catholic introduction to the tasks and methods of theology see the opening chapter by Francis Schüssler Fiorenza in the book he co-edited with John P. Galvin, *Systematic Theology: Roman Catholic Perspectives*, 2nd edn (Minneapolis: Fortress, 2011), 1–78.

[8] See, for example, Howard R. Stone and James O. Duke, *How to Think Theologically*, 3rd edn (Minneapolis: Fortress, 2013) and Stanley J. Grenz and Roger E. Olson, *Who Needs Theology? An Invitation to the Study of God* (Downers Grove: Intervarsity, 1996). W. Clark Gilpin's description of the practice of theology is largely shaped by what occurs at the graduate or professional level and by the use of methods within "religious studies." See W. Clark Gilpin, *A Preface to Theology* (Chicago: University of Chicago Press, 1996). This shaping is also evident in the essays on theological encyclopedia by Schubert M. Ogden that have been published as *On Theology* (Dallas: Southern Methodist University Press, 1992).

[9] See Richard J. Plantinga et al., *An Introduction to Christian Theology* (Cambridge: Cambridge University Press, 2010), 12–26; and Bradley C. Hanson, *An Introduction to Christian Theology* (Minneapolis: Fortress, 1997), 1–18.

about how theology might relate to other university disciplines at the undergraduate level.[10]

Christian theology in a liberal-arts college, whether church-related or not, takes a slightly different shape and has different goals from what it has in a seminary or divinity school, and thus I have tried to depict what that shape is within this other setting and to spell out its goals there. My main reason for doing so is that many American college students never seriously engage the nature of Christian theology as a university discipline. They typically do not understand the relationships among its branches, nor do they appreciate the desire that many academic theologians have for positively engaging other university disciplines. This book was written to encourage students to think about these matters. I have tried to keep in mind that not every undergraduate student, even in church-related institutions, is a Christian or is familiar with the principal traditions of Christian theology.

What is Christian theology? Why study it as an undergraduate student, especially if one is not preparing for service in a Christian church or if one is not even a Christian? Why does theology belong as an academic discipline within North-American universities? What is its subject? What are its sources and norm(s)? What knowledge and skills are necessary for a person to become competent in the discipline? What are its sub-disciplines and how do they relate to one another? How does Christian theology relate to the humanities, the arts, and the sciences in the university? These are the main questions addressed in this book. While the book focuses primarily upon formal questions within fundamental Christian theology and theological encyclopedia, including issues of theological method and hermeneutical principles, it also addresses on occasion several substantive issues regarding God and other Christian teachings.

Christian theology ought to lead people "to understand God more truly" (Kelsey), to liberate people from ignorance and unexamined prejudice, and to liberate them for critical and creative thinking and action in relation to God, other people and the world. It should assist individuals in becoming more appreciative of the religious dimensions of human experience, more knowledgeable about the varieties of Christian experience, more critical

[10] See Helen K. Bond et al. (eds), *Religious Studies and Theology: An Introduction* (Washington Square, New York: New York University Press, 2003); David F. Ford et al. (eds), *Fields of Faith: Theology and Religious Studies for the Twenty-first Century* (Cambridge: Cambridge University Press, 2004); and D. L. Bird and Simon G. Smith (eds), *Theology and Religious Studies in Higher Education* (New York: Continuum, 2009).

of the negative and destructive elements within all human institutions, including religious ones, more aware of the means and norms by which one might be able to discern a problematic element within a given religious tradition, and more comfortable about expressing an understanding of the nature of one's own religious faith or personal commitments.

Within my own university, I have sought to understand and teach the Christian tradition as a person of faith, indeed as one who publicly identifies himself as a confessional Lutheran Christian by conviction. Nevertheless, I have also tried to convey the benefits of allowing Christianity to be investigated critically through the same interpretive strategies that are brought to other human phenomena. In this respect I do not hesitate to indicate where and why the Christian tradition, its texts and institutions, have been criticized in the past and are still being criticized today. Richard Hughes' description of a Lutheran approach to "tradition" is helpful since it reminds us of the need always to reassess and rethink one's commitments and understandings. According to Hughes, the Lutheran tradition offers "a strategy of continual theological reflection." Embracing the notion of paradox that is near the heart of authentic Lutheran theology, he states:

> Lutherans can never absolutize their own perspectives, even their theological perspectives. They must always be reassessing and rethinking, and they must always be in dialogue with themselves and with others. But there is more, for if Lutherans *must* always be in dialogue with themselves and with others, it is equally true to say that they are *free* to be in dialogue with themselves and with others. For knowledge that one is justified by grace through faith grants the Christian scholar a profound sense of freedom to question his or her own best insights, to revise them, or to discard them and start again. This is the genius of the Lutheran tradition.[11]

Hughes' description parallels the epigraph to the published edition of the 1983 Jefferson Lecture by the most famous person to have taught at Valparaiso University, Jaroslav Pelikan (1923–2006), which is a quotation from Goethe's *Faust*: "*Was du ererbt von deinen Vätern hast, Erwirb es, um es zu besitzen.*" ("What you have inherited from your fathers, acquire it in order to make it your own.")[12]

---

[11] Richard T. Hughes, *How Christian Faith Can Sustain the Life of the Mind* (Grand Rapids: Eerdmans, 2001), 88 (emphasis is in the original).
[12] Jaroslav Pelikan, *The Vindication of Tradition: The 1983 Jefferson Lecture in the Humanities* (New Haven: Yale University Press, 1986), epigraph. The actual quotation is found in Goethe, *Faust (Part One)*, Night (Faust), lines 682–3.

While there are many challenges to the study of Christian theology in the complicated context of a modern liberal-arts university, such activity has a role to play there for reasons that will be set forth in the book. Not only does Christian theology address important questions of human self-understanding that are common to the academy, it also engages these and other questions on the basis of venerable intellectual traditions that provide a critical perspective on central issues within society, religious communities, and the university itself. Academic theology seeks to avoid "the victory of unexamined orthodoxies" (Migliore xiv), whether of the religious or of the secular kind, but it is finally also passionately concerned about the truth of God and about other matters of singular, "ultimate" importance. Christian theology, like other theologies, does not avoid articulating specific commitments or exploring the reasons for them.

As I wrote this book I tried to keep my gaze alternating between two different foci: the received traditions of the wider Christian community, on the one hand, and the contemporary situation of my university, on the other, a situation that includes people who are by nature without (explicit) faith or who come from a variety of non-Christian and non-religious backgrounds. Thus one task of the academic study of Christian theology, as it moves between these two foci, is to seek to understand the historical development of that faith, to discern how that faith is expressed today in a variety of conflicting ways, and to investigate where that faith overlaps with other religious and non-religious commitments, beliefs, and practices. Another such task is to place that development and the current expressions and understandings of that faith into a position of being questioned. That is, Christian academic theology must question both received Christian teaching and practice *and* engage the questions that are leveled against that complex tradition by its fiercest critics. Of course theology also has a responsibility to raise critical questions of its own about human beings, their beliefs and practices, their social institutions, and their most profound and persisting problems.

Although I have written the book for undergraduate students and in light of my own church tradition, I hope that all readers, regardless of their religious and educational background, will find the book useful for gaining entry into the study of Christian theology. I do not presume to present here a comprehensive treatment of the preliminary issues for all times and places. Nevertheless I have tried to summarize the problems of fundamental theology and theological encyclopedia, and several representative responses to them, in a way that is hopefully accessible for the beginning student and informative for the more seasoned learner. I have striven to keep footnotes to a minimum. Those who have some theological understanding will spot places in my presentation where this or that theologian or set of theologians has influenced my thinking. For those who are interested in pursuing deeper investigation into a particular topic, I have provided suggestions for further reading at the end of each chapter.

I need to underscore that the book is meant to be an introduction and thus I have deliberately chosen to focus primarily upon what I consider to be the major and classic figures within the mainstream Christian tradition. After teaching introductory courses in Christian theology to undergraduates for nearly twenty years, I continue to think that American college students today need to become more aware of the principal Christian theological voices from the past—the ones that still have an abiding influence on contemporary theological understandings—before they can enter meaningfully into conversations that are critical of those principal voices, and that offer contrary versions of Christian theology and its traditions from the one presented here. I have tried to be as broad as possible in what I present, and yet I realize my portrait is still quite narrow and necessarily incomplete. My hope is that students will take seriously the suggestions for further reading.

The book is divided into three parts. Part one leads students to reflect on the variety of ways in which human beings frequently enter into theological reflection and to consider the ways in which people, Christian and otherwise, have thought about "God." Chapter 1 indicates several representative situations in which theological reflection arises from human experiences. Chapter 2 provides a sketch of the historical development of the principal Christian groups and indicates their geographical spread in the contemporary world. Chapter 3 summarizes the origins of theology within ancient Greece and offers a very brief account of how representative Christian thinkers have thought about God. The final chapter of this first part sets forth my own definition of Christian theology as an academic discipline that invites critical and self-critical reflection on the revelation of God, the world, and human beings in the apostolic witness to Jesus of Nazareth.

While some may question why I begin the book in this fashion, I am convinced that within the pluralistic setting of a liberal-arts university it makes good sense first to highlight some common human experiences that lead in the direction of religion and theology and only then to proceed to offer a brief historical overview of the history of Christianity and a narrower description of the history of theology within that larger Christian framework. Only after fulfilling these tasks can one return to define more formally what Christian academic theology is today, what its subject matter entails, and where it fits within a modern university curriculum.

Part two of the book explores the subject of Christian theology. Chapter 5 explores the problem of talking about God today and the question of whether or not there is a universal awareness or knowledge of God that all (or nearly all) human beings have. The sixth chapter extends this discussion by analyzing what Christian theologians have traditionally called the natural knowledge of God (sometimes also called "general revelation"). This discussion extends into Chapter 7, which briefly summarizes some of the classic arguments for and against the reality of God. Chapter 7 concludes by describing the nature of Christian faith and its risk in view of "the hidden God." Chapter 8 turns to examine more directly the so-called "special" revelation of God, the world, and human beings in the witness of the Hebrew Scriptures and the writings of the New Testament. This chapter offers a typology of ways in which Christian theologians have understood the nature of God's "special" revelation. Chapter 9 then summarizes a few of the basic themes within that special revelation: God the Creator, the revelation of the divine law, and the revelation of the divine gospel. The result of this investigation is to identify the central theme in Christian theology, namely, the promise of the gospel within the prophetic and apostolic witness to Jesus Christ. Two final chapters round out this second part. Chapter 10 investigates the problem of sources and norms in Christian theology, focusing especially on the problem of biblical authority. Chapter 11 focuses more directly on the issue of biblical interpretation, less helpful ways for understanding the Bible, and some of the venerable principles for understanding the Bible theologically (hermeneutics).

Part three of the book examines the place of Christian theology within an undergraduate university. Chapter 12 describes how some have understood the place of Christian theology within universities and how they have divided theology into sub-disciplines. The next chapter sets forth my own understanding by describing theology's three sub-disciplines and their relationship to each other: systematic theology (inclusive of fundamental and doctrinal theology), historical theology (inclusive of biblical theology, the history of Christian theology, and the history of Christianity), and practical theology (inclusive of ecclesial studies and ethics). The final two chapters describe the relationship of Christian theology to other university disciplines. Together both chapters seek to highlight the ways in which theology assists human understanding within the humanities and the arts and the ways in which the discipline broadens human ways of knowing within the sciences. In short, these final two chapters seek to introduce the reader to the main ways in which Christian theologians have sought to relate Christian faith and knowledge to other forms of knowledge that have arisen within the academy. While Christian theology must take seriously the knowledge, truths, and insights disclosed through other academic disciplines, it also seeks to uphold the promise of the Christian gospel as integral to a Christian understanding of reality.

Upon reading the first chapters of the book some students may feel like they have entered a large, dark, and confusing forest. Unlike their experiences with other university subjects, which they have likely studied since elementary school (at least in a preliminary, foundational way), a student's initial experience with university-level theology may be challenging, disorienting, and even a bit uncomfortable. There will be a lot of new terms, many new names, and novel, unfamiliar ways of thinking. The beginner can easily get lost in the details. For these reasons I have tried to identify what is especially important in each chapter by putting key terms and names in bold print. I have also included review and discussion questions at the end of each chapter. Students might want to consult these as they move through a given chapter in order to have a clearer idea of what is most important. All key terms and names are also defined in the glossaries at the end of the book.

A classic essay on the study of Christian theology by Martin Luther (1483–1546) is included as an appendix. As will become evident, Luther's theology figures prominently throughout the book. It might be useful to know how this classic Protestant theologian thought about the academic study of theology.

In many ways, the writings about fundamental theology and theological encyclopedia by three German Protestant scholars have inspired this book. I hope I can honor the legacies of Wilfried Joest, Gerhard Ebeling, and Wolfhart Pannenberg, even while I write from the perspective of a later generation, in a different language, and for a different audience. My hope is that my Protestant account of fundamental theology and theological encyclopedia will contribute to the renewal of these sub-disciplines. I hope, as well, that the book can lead the reader into deeper reflection on God.

Matthew L. Becker
Valparaiso, IN.

Acknowledgments

I am grateful to Valparaiso University for supporting me as I wrote this book. In the first half of 2012 I was granted a sabbatical which allowed me to make substantial progress on the project.

Valparaiso's Provost, Mark Schwehn, has deeply influenced my thinking about the place of Christian theology in an undergraduate university and about the nature of higher education in general. While he undoubtedly disagrees with several of my statements in this book, he has been a gracious conversation partner for more than a decade. He kindly granted me permission to use the photo of a portion of a window in the Chapel of the Resurrection that appears on the cover. Gregg Hertzlieb, Curator and Director of the Brauer Museum of Art on Valparaiso's campus, was very helpful in providing me with the necessary information about that window.

My thanks go to several colleagues in the Theology Department at Valparaiso University: Jim Albers, Mark Bartusch, Richard DeMaris, Lisa Driver, George Heider, Jim Moore, Fred Niedner, and Ron Rittgers, who read portions of the manuscript and offered helpful comments toward improving it. I want to thank Pilar Domer for her help with creating the "circle of theology" that appears in Chapter thirteen.

My appreciation goes to those who read earlier drafts of chapters and offered their helpful suggestions for improvement: Michael Aune, Carl Braaten, Terry Cooper, Brian Gerrish, Ted Ludwig, Piotr Malysz, Mark Mattes, Jim Metcalf, Eric Moeller, Ross Moret, George Murphy, and Robert Sylwester. I am also grateful for the helpful suggestions that were given to me by six external readers whose identities are unknown to me and who encouraged my editor to go forward with this project. David Tracy helped me to think more carefully about my understanding of Rahner and the nature of fundamental theology within Roman Catholic circles.

My editor at Bloomsbury, Anna Turton, has been a joy to work with throughout the process of completing this project. I am grateful for the encouragement she gave me and for her persistence in seeing the project through to completion.

During the time that I wrote this book I served Immanuel Lutheran Church, Michigan City, Indiana, as its interim pastor. Because of my full-time responsibilities at the University, this was a part-time arrangement until the congregation could call a pastor. I am grateful to this congregation for its support between October 2010 and March 2014.

Martin E. Marty has been my teacher for more years than he and I would care to admit. When I was a college student and then a seminarian his books were a regular staple in my intellectual diet. I learned of him and his scholarly work initially through a few of my college professors who had been his students. Later I read his autobiography, *By Way of Response* (Abingdon 1981), which furthered my desire to study theology at the University of Chicago (1988–93). There he became a role model and, more significantly, a friend. While I do not pretend to have his gifts, I do aspire to the same kind of balance between church and academy that has been evident in his life and work. One would be hard-pressed to find someone more familiar with the promises and problems surrounding the nature and place of Christian theology in a university than he, so I am truly honored and thankful that he has written the Afterword.

I am grateful to the Public Religion Research Institute, NORC at the University of Chicago, and the Pew Research Center for their permission to cite material from their research. I also greatly appreciate that Fortress Press granted me permission to use copyrighted material from the American Edition of *Luther's Works* in Chapter fourteen and the appendix.

Hans Spalteholz, who was one of those who had studied with Marty, was my first undergraduate theology professor at Concordia College, Portland, OR. Over the past three decades that I have known him, he has taught me more about the Christian faith and discipleship than anyone else I know. He has been a principal mentor to me, first as my teacher (1980–4), then as a colleague, when he graciously made way for me to join that faculty (1994–2004), and now as a long-distance conversation partner. In many ways he has become a second father to me. I especially want to thank him for carefully reading most of the manuscript and for suggesting certain stylistic and substantive changes. Those who know him will recognize his influence throughout the book.

I wish to dedicate this book to him and to two other professors at Concordia who also were my teachers and then colleagues: Dick Hill, who has enriched my life in so many ways, who allowed me to team-teach courses with him in the humanities and theology, and with whom I have had innumerable significant conversations about life and other humane matters;

and Chuck Kunert, who has shaped my understanding of the sciences and their relationship to Christian theology and with whom I was privileged to have taught several undergraduate seminars in science and theology. I am grateful for the abiding friendship I have with each of these individuals.

Finally, I wish to express my deepest gratitude and love to my wife, Detra, and our son, Jacob. They have constantly supported my work, walked the extra mile, and made many sacrifices along the way. I dedicate this book to them, too.

Abbreviations

ABD   David Noel Freedman, ed., *The Anchor Bible Dictionary*, 6
            vols. (New York: Doubleday, 1992)

Althaus Paul Althaus, *The Theology of Martin Luther*, trans. Robert
            C. Schultz (Minneapolis: Fortress Press, 1966)

Aquinas Thomas Aquinas, *The Summa Theologica*, trans. Fathers
            of the English Dominican Province (New York: Benziger
            Brothers, 1947) [Bibliographical references always refer to
            the part, the question, and the article.]

Aulén   Gustav Aulén, *The Faith of the Christian Church*, 4th
            edn, trans. Eric H. Wahlstrom and G. Everett Arden
            (Philadelphia: Muhlenberg, 1948)

Barth   Karl Barth, *Church Dogmatics*, 13 vols, trans. G. W.
            Bromiley (Edinburgh: T & T Clark, 1936–69) [references
            will be to principal volume, I–IV, and their parts.]

Bayer-L Oswald Bayer, *Martin Luther's Theology: A Contemporary
            Interpretation*, trans. Thomas H. Trapp (Grand Rapids,
            Eerdmans, 2008)

Bayer   Oswald Bayer, *Theology the Lutheran Way*, ed. and trans.
            Jeffrey G. Silcock and Mark C. Mattes, Lutheran Quarterly
            Books (Grand Rapids: Eerdmans, 2007)

BC   Robert Kolb and Timothy J. Wengert (eds), *The Book
            of Concord: The Confessions of the Evangelical Lutheran
            Church*, trans. Charles Arand et al. (Minneapolis: Fortress,
            2000)

BCM   J. Kim and E. Susa (eds), *The Blackwell Companion to
            Metaphysics* (Oxford: Blackwell, 1995)

BCPR   Philip L. Quinn and Charles Taliaferro (eds), *The Blackwell*

	Companion to the Philosophy of Religion (Oxford: Blackwell, 1997)
BCSR	Robert A. Segal, ed., *The Blackwell Companion to the Study of Religion* (Oxford: Blackwell, 2006)
BDAG	Frederick William Danker, ed., *A Greek-English Lexicon of the New Testament and Other Early Christian Literature*, 3rd edn, based on Walter Bauer's *Greichischdeutsches Wörterbuch zu den Schriften des Neuen Testaments und der frühchristlichen Literatur*, 6th edn, trans. William F. Arndt, F. Wilbur Gingrich, and Frederick W. Danker (Chicago: University of Chicago Press, 2000)
BJ	Carl E. Braaten and Robert W. Jenson (eds), *Christian Dogmatics*, 2 vols (Minneapolis: Fortress Press, 1984)
Brunner	Emil Brunner, *Dogmatics*, 2 vols, trans. Olive Wyon (Philadelphia: Westminster, 1950, 1952)
Bultmann	Rudolf Bultmann, *What is Theology?*, Eberhard Jüngel and Klaus W. Müller (eds), trans. Roy A. Harrisville (Minneapolis: Fortress, 1997)
Calvin	John Calvin, *Institutes of the Christian Religion*, four books in two volumes, ed. John T. McNeill, trans. Ford Lewis Battles, The Library of Christian Classics (Philadelphia: Westminster, 1960). [References are to book, chapter and section.]
Denzinger	Henricus Denzinger and Peter Hunermann (eds), *Enchiridion Symbolorum: Definitionum et Declarationum De Rebus Fidei et Morum*, 43rd edn (Freiburg: Herder, 2010)
Ebeling	Gerhard Ebeling, *The Study of Theology*, trans. Duane A. Priebe (Minneapolis: Fortress Press, 1978)
EC	Erwin Fahlbusch et al. (eds), *The Encyclopedia of Christianity*, 5 vols, trans. Geoffrey W. Bromiley (Grand Rapids: Eerdmans, 1998–2008). (This is an English translation of the 3rd edn of *Evangelisches Kirchenlexikon* [Göttingen: Vandenhoeck & Ruprecht, 1986–1997])

ECT	William C. Placher, ed., *Essentials of Christian Theology* (Louisville: Westminster John Knox, 2003)
Elert	Werner Elert, *The Christian Faith: An Outline of Lutheran Dogmatics*, trans. Martin Bertram and Walter Bouman (Columbus: Lutheran Theological Seminary, 1974)
ER	Lindsay Jones, ed., *Encyclopedia of Religion*, 15 vols, 2nd edn (New York: Thomson Gale, 2004)
Gerhard	Johann Gerhard, *On the Nature of Theology and Scripture*, vol. 1 of *Theological Commonplaces*, trans. Richard Dinda (St. Louis: Concordia, 2006)
Gilkey	Langdon Gilkey, *Message and Existence* (New York: Seabury, 1981)
Grenz	Stanley J. Grenz, *Theology for the Community of God* (Grand Rapids: Eerdmans, 2000)
Hall	Douglas John Hall, *Thinking the Faith: Christian Theology in a North American Context* (Minneapolis: Fortress, 1991)
Harnack	Adolph von Harnack, *History of Dogma*, 7 vols, trans. Neil Buchanan (New York: Dover, 1961)
Hegel	Georg F. Hegel, *Lectures on the Philosophy of Religion*, 3 vols, ed. Peter C. Hodgson, trans. R. F. Brown et al. (Berkeley: University of California Press, 1984–5)
Heppe	Heinrich Heppe, *Reformed Dogmatics*, rev. and ed. Ernst Bizer, trans. G. T. Thomson (New York: Harper & Row, 1950)
HK	Peter C. Hodgson and Robert H. King (eds), *Christian Theology: An Introduction to Its Traditions and Tasks*, 2nd edn (Minneapolis: Fortress Press, 1985)
ICT	Richard J. Plantinga, Thomas R. Thompson, and Matthew D. Lundberg, *An Introduction to Christian Theology* (Cambridge: Cambridge University Press, 2010)
Jenson	Robert Jenson, *Systematic Theology*, 2 vols (New York: Oxford University Press, 1997–9)

Lohse	Bernhard Lohse, *Martin Luther's Theology: Its Historical and Systematic Development*, trans. Roy A. Harrisville (Minneapolis: Fortress, 1999)
LW	*Luther's Works* (American Edition), 55 vols, Jaroslav Pelikan and Helmut T. Lehmann (eds) (St. Louis and Philadelphia: Concordia and Fortress, 1955–)
Macquarrie	John Macquarrie, *Principles of Christian Theology*, 2nd edn (New York: Charles Scribner's Sons, 1977)
McGrath	Alister E. McGrath, *Christian Theology: An Introduction*, 5th edn (Oxford: Wiley-Blackwell, 2011)
Melanchthon	Philipp Melancthon, *Loci Communes* (1555), ed. and trans. Clyde Manschreck (New York: Oxford University Press, 1965)
Migliore	Daniel L. Migliore, *Faith Seeking Understanding: An Introduction to Christian Theology*, 2nd edn (Grand Rapids: Eerdmans, 2004)
NHCT	Donald W. Musser and Joseph L. Price (eds), *A New Handbook of Christian Theology* (Nashville: Abingdon, 1992)
NRSV	The Holy Bible, New Revised Standard Version (Washington, DC: Division of Education of the National Council of the Churches of Christ in the United States, 1989)
O'Collins	Gerald O'Collins, *Rethinking Fundamental Theology: Toward a New Fundamental Theology* (New York: Oxford University Press, 2011)
ODCC	F. L. Cross and E. A. Livingstone (eds), *The Oxford Dictionary of the Christian Church*, 3rd rev. edn (Oxford: Oxford University Press, 2005)
OED	J. A. Simpson and E. S. C. Weiner (eds), *The Compact Oxford English Dictionary*, 2nd edn (Oxford: Oxford University Press, 1991)
OHST	John Webster, Kathryn Tanner, and Iain Torrance (eds), *The Oxford Handbook of Systematic Theology* (Oxford: Oxford University Press, 2007)

Pannenberg   Wolfhart Pannenberg, *Systematic Theology*, 3 vols, trans. Geoffrey W. Bromiley (Grand Rapids: Eerdmans, 1991–8)

Pelikan   Jaroslav Pelikan, *The Christian Tradition: A History of the Development of Doctrine*, 5 vols (Chicago: University of Chicago Press, 1971–89)

Peters   Ted Peters, *God—The World's Future: Systematic Theology for a Postmodern Era* (Minneapolis: Fortress, 1992)

PTPS   Wolfhart Pannenberg, *Theology and the Philosophy of Science*, trans. Francis McDonagh (Philadelphia: Westminster, 1976)

Rahner   Karl Rahner, *Foundations of Christian Faith: An Introduction to the Idea of Christianity*, trans. William V. Dych (New York: Crossroad, 1978)

REP   Edward Craig, ed., *Routledge Encyclopedia of Philosophy*, 10 vols (New York: Routledge, 2000)

RPP   Hans Dieter Betz et al. (eds), *Religion Past and Present*, 13 vols (New York: Brill, 2009–13)

RSV   The Holy Bible, Revised Standard Version (Washington, DC: Division of Education of the National Council of the Churches of Christ in the United States, 1977)

SBO   Friedrich Schleiermacher, *Brief Outline of Theology as a Field of Study*, trans. Terrance N. Tice (Lewiston: Edwin Mellen, 1988)

SCF   Friedrich Schleiermacher, *The Christian Faith*, 2nd edn, trans. H. R. Mackintosh and J. S. Stewart (Edinburgh: T & T Clark, 1928)

Schmid   Heinrich Schmid, *Doctrinal Theology of the Evangelical Lutheran Church*, 3rd edn, trans. Charles A. Hay and Henry E. Jacobs (Minneapolis: Augsburg, 1889)

TDNT   Gerhard Kittel and Gerhard Friedrich (eds), *Theological Dictionary of the New Testament*, 10 vols, trans. Geoffrey W. Bromiley (Grand Rapids: Eerdmans, 1964)

Thielicke	Helmut Thielicke, *The Evangelical Faith*, 3 vols, ed. and trans. Geoffrey W. Bromiley (Grand Rapids: Eerdmans, 1974–81)
Tillich	Paul Tillich, *Systematic Theology*, 3 vols (Chicago: University of Chicago Press, 1951–63)
WA	*D. Martin Luthers Werke: kritische Gesamtausgabe* [Weimar Ausgabe], 65 vols in 127 (Weimar : Hermann Böhlaus Nachfolger, 1883–1993)
Weber	Otto Weber, *Foundations of Dogmatics*, 2 vols, trans. Darrell L. Guder (Grand Rapids: Eerdmans, 1981–3)

Part I

Theology

Ways into Theology

After providing a brief and simple definition of the term "theology" ("thinking about God"), this chapter explores several informal ways by which people enter into theological reflection. The chapter notes how some human questions, situations, and phenomena lead in this direction. The chapter then concludes by identifying academic theology as a more formal way for addressing these and other matters about God and religious faith.

How do people enter into theology? What prompts them to reflect that way? What draws them down that road? Before attempting to address these questions, one should probably have some idea of what **theology** is. Strictly speaking, it is "talking about **God**" or "thinking about God" (OED 2040). The term "theology" (*theologia*) comes from two Greek words: *theos*, which means "God" or "god," and *logos*, which means "word," "statement," "account," "thought," or "reason" (BDAG 599). "Speech about God," "reasoning about God," or "giving an account of God," would thus be other ways of rendering a simple definition of the word. Within a university context people often define "theology" as "the science of God" (ODCC 1616), or the scholarly study of God. Given the multiplicity of "gods/goddesses" spoken of by people, past and present, perhaps it would be more accurate to use the rather ugly-looking and strange-sounding word "theoilogy," the study of the gods (since the plural of *theos* is *theoi*). Nevertheless, despite the plurality of deities spoken about by human beings, scholars continue to use the traditional term "theology" for that kind of speaking and thinking. This preliminary definition of theology will do for the time being. Later in the book we will see that some people assert that "thinking about God" is too narrow of a definition. They want to broaden theology to include thinking about matters that go beyond God or the gods.

Perhaps the most common, informal way into theology is *through one's personal life*. Certain basic human experiences and questions lead one to reflect more deeply about one's life as a whole and upon matters that have the effect of calling one's life into question. The philosopher Karl Jaspers (1883–1969) has referred to these as **boundary questions** because they push one beyond trivial knowledge toward what he called "**the transcendent**."[1] Is my existence entirely an accident or is there a deeper purpose to it? Am I responsible to anyone or anything beyond myself? If there are authorities that I should heed, what are they and to what extent should I heed them? If I believe that certain ancient, venerable writings are among these authorities, how am I to understand them, especially in relation to today's problems and issues? These questions are not matters of indifference or instinct. They tend to move the self-conscious human being into an existential situation of anxiety about their solution. To the extent that a person addresses these issues in relation to God or gods or a Higher Power that person is engaged in a kind of informal theology.

Sometimes human beings find themselves in *extraordinary situations* that lead in the direction of the transcendent or God, and thus toward theology. Perhaps their conscience is troubled by a complex moral or ethical dilemma. "What should I do in this situation?" "What would God have me do now?" Or perhaps a person is overwhelmed by an experience that causes him or her to wonder about "the meaning of it all." That kind of experience can happen when an inexpressible joy and gratitude come upon a father after witnessing the birth of his first child, but it can happen in other, more frightening ways. A person is not the same as he was before he learned that his four-year-old nephew died from nerve cancer in the arms of his mother, with the whisper of "Jesus" as the last utterance from his tiny lips. In that circumstance one finds oneself wrestling with God and fears, known and unknown, with anger, grief, and a multitude of other emotions. Theology also occurs when one experiences the mystery of an unexpected medical outcome, as when one's four-year-old son did not die or suffer any ill effects from the 75 ml of blood that had pooled on his brain as a result of an accident that tore the artery under his cranium. Was this an answer to prayer? "Why, God, did this happen?" Other moments in life overwhelm one to the point that one can't help but think of God or the unknown that follows death, as when one is diagnosed with a life-threatening illness. Just

---

[1] Karl Jaspers, *Philosophy*, 3 vols, trans. E. B. Ashton (Chicago: University of Chicago Press, 1969–71).

what is one to make of those many people who have written about their mystical or near-death experiences and have drawn theological conclusions from them? Are they crazy or have they tapped into something akin to the divine?[2]

Some questions that lead toward God or the transcendent are a bit *more ordinary and mundane.* As that same four-year-old son grows, what should his dad and mom teach him about what is good, right, true, and worthy of pursuing in life? How should one respond when he asks where heaven is, the place where people had told him his dead cousin now was, the one who died from cancer? Or what do you say (or not say) when he blurts out in a fit of anger over the loss of his grandfather, cousin, and a beloved pet dog, "There is no God! There is no heaven! We die, and that's it! I hate God!"? How does one talk to anyone about terrible suffering, guilt, love, commitment or gratitude? Is the death of one's life and those of others the complete end, a "period," or are they but a "comma," after which there is another kind of life?[3]

Observations about the physical universe and *the course of human events* can also lead into an informal kind of theology. Why is there something and not nothing, and why is that "something" the way that it is? How does one account for the sense of awe and wonder that results from pondering the scope and grandeur of the universe, its apparent mathematical order, the predictability of particle physics, and the beauty detected in telescopic photos of deep space and in microscopic pictures of cellular organisms? Conversely, how does one make sense of the seemingly senseless range of suffering and death in the world and its natural history? Following the incomprehensible murders of 20 young children and six of their teachers at Sandy Hook Elementary School in Newtown, Connecticut, ten days before Christmas Eve 2012, there surfaced many public debates, in the media and

---

[2] See Hans Küng, *Eternal Life: Life after Death as a Medical, Philosophical, and Theological Problem*, trans. Edward Quinn (New York: Doubleday, 1984). Two recent, popular books have provided first-person accounts of "near-death experiences." Eben Alexander's *Proof of Heaven* (New York: Simon and Schuster, 2012) relates the experiences of an American neurosurgeon whose brain stopped functioning as a result of meningitis and who claims to have had an out-of-body experience of heaven that fundamentally altered his understanding of reality. *Heaven is for Real: A Little Boy's Astounding Story of his Trip to Heaven and Back* (Nashville: Thomas Nelson, 2010), by Todd Burpo and Lynne Vincent, recounts the claims of Burpo's four-year-old child to have had an out-of-body experience of heaven during emergency surgery for a burst appendix.
[3] The twentieth-century American comedienne, Gracie Allen, sent a note to her husband, George Burns, which he was to open only after her death. On the day of her funeral he read the note: "Never place a period where God has placed a comma."

on the internet, about "where God was" that day and "how could God allow such sickening death and suffering to occur." Such questions also were raised by those who gathered in their churches or synagogues to call upon God in mournful prayer, by those who wondered about the realities of sin and evil, and by those who undertook random acts of kindness, based on their religious faith, in the days and weeks that followed that catastrophe. Events like these also lead to questions about God or the transcendent or "the spiritual."

Still *other human experiences* may lead one in the direction of theological reflection. A person has an encounter with a work of art or a piece of music which leads that person to think about the meaning or absurdity of life or about matters of "ultimate concern," to use a famous phrase by the Christian theologian Paul Tillich (1886–1965). Classic works of art reveal aspects of "the depth dimension" (Jaspers) of human existence, and reflection on this revelation, insofar as it gives rise to thought about the transcendent or God or Being can properly be described as theological. Another person reads a novel, or a poem, such as Dante's *Divine Comedy*, which takes that individual through a kind of conversion process that leads the person to see himself or herself differently in the light of its theological themes. Still another person listens to a symphony by Beethoven (1770–1827) or engages the musical compositions of J. S. Bach (1685–1750), such as his profound Passions or the *B-Minor Mass*, and is led to contemplate the beautiful, mathematical order of music and to wonder about its mystical, theological dimensions.

Most people, even today, engage theological questions within the context of *a religion* or the vestiges of a religious tradition. "Religion," as a term and concept, is notoriously difficult to define, despite the fact that many people think they know it when they see it.[4] Is it "belief in God?" What then about those religions that believe in many gods, such as Hinduism, or those religions that have no concept of God or the divine, such as Confucianism and some forms of Buddhism? Is religion what "gives expression to an experience of the holy" (Rudolf Otto)? What then about ritual practices, beliefs, and concrete ethical behaviors, which Otto's definition seems to minimize? In that case, religion might best be defined as "living a moral life." But that also leaves out important aspects of religion such as specific beliefs,

---

[4]For a helpful overview of possible answers to the question, "What is religion?," see James C. Livingston, *Anatomy of the Sacred: An Introduction to Religion*, 5th edn (Upper Saddle River, New Jersey: Prentice Hall, 2005), 3–10. The examples given are from pages 5 and 9.

rituals, communal traditions, and the "feeling" dimension of religious experience.

A few have tried their hand at more formal definitions of "religion." For example, John Yinger asserts that religion is "a system of beliefs and practices by means of which a group of people struggles with the ultimate problems of human life."[5] Helpful here is the attention given to beliefs, practices, and communities of people. Yet this definition is not without its own problems. At face value it suggests that just about any human belief and practice could fit under the category of "religion." Perhaps a better definition that has gained wider currency among scholars of **religious studies** is the one by the anthropologist Clifford Geertz (1926–2006). Like Yinger's definition, it, too, focuses on the functional aspect of religion, but it is more specific with regard to the character of the objects of religious experience:

> Religion is (1) a system of symbols which acts to (2) establish powerful, pervasive, and long-lasting moods and motivations in [people] by (3) formulating conceptions of a general order of existence and (4) clothing these conceptions with such an aura of factuality that the moods and motivations seem uniquely realistic.[6]

As helpful as the above definition may be, it, too, seems to minimize the communal nature of the religions, that allows for the transmission of a particular system of symbols and helps to establish the mood and motivations and worldview of individuals within the religious community. That communal aspect reflects one possible etymology of the term "religion," namely, deriving it from the Latin word *religare*, which means "to bind together" or "to bring together" (OED 1552). That linkage would help to underscore the social and communal character of religion, which provides the content and context for reflection on those symbols, moods, motivations, behaviors, and overall worldview. It may also help to explain why many people in western cultures will say they are "spiritual" but not necessarily "religious." They may believe in God or a Higher Power or the spiritual, but they are not regular participants in any religious community, its rituals, customs, and ethos.

---

[5] John Milton Yinger, *Ethnicity: Source of Strength? Source of Conflict?* (Albany: State University of New York Press, 1994), 256. Yinger (1916–2011), an American sociologist who was also the son of Methodist ministers, wrote many works in the areas of sociology and anthropology.

[6] Clifford Geertz, "Religion as a Cultural System," in *Reader in Comparative Religion: An Anthropological Approach*, 4th edn, William A. Lessa and Evon Z. Vogt (eds) (New York: Harper and Row, 1979), 79–80.

For our purposes let's agree that most religions typically include specific language, symbols, myths/stories, rituals, patterns of behavior, claims to truth, and communal ways of transmitting all of these over the course of time. A good many of these religions (but not all) make reference to God or gods or some higher power(s) or some other transcendent reality (Atman, nirvana, etc.). To the extent that people think and speak about these matters in that context, they are engaged in theology, that is, thinking or speaking about God or Allah or whatever other name(s) is/are appropriate. The person so engaged in such thinking may even be described as a **theologian**, that is, as "one who speaks about God," at least in the broadest sense of the term. A **theist**, then, is one who believes in God or a god or a set of gods. An **atheist**, on the other hand, is one who rejects or denies the reality of any and all gods.

Certainly, *religious or spiritual practices* also lead in the direction of theology. "Why is this night different from all others?," asks the youngest child at the Passover meal. "Why do we wash ourselves and take off our shoes before entering our mosque," asks a young Muslim boy. Why does the university teacher of Hinduism tell her undergraduate students that this particular Hindu dance is the essence of Hinduism? "Why are the Jehovah's Witnesses opposed to blood transfusions?," asks the nurse at the hospital. "How will we raise our children?," wonder the Baptist husband and his Roman Catholic wife. "Do we baptize the children or not?" What constitutes "marriage" these days? Is homosexual behavior intrinsically sinful, against the eternal will of God, even within life-long, faithful, and loving partnerships? Do the names of Hindu deities refer to individual gods and goddesses, or are they merely names for "the unnamable One" behind and inclusive of all the sacred names?

Prayer may be one of the most basic ways people in effect "do" theology, since that practice makes assumptions about the One(s) so addressed. The way one prays gives clues about what one believes, and what one believes gives clues about what one prays. Within Christianity an ancient Latin phrase even highlights this connection: ***Lex orandi, lex credendi*** (literally, "the law of praying, the law of believing"). How you pray, to whom you pray, what you pray for—all these say a lot about what you believe regarding the nature of prayer, the nature of worship, the One(s) to whom you pray, and what you believe about the goal of such prayer. The same could be said about spiritual meditation and other spiritual practices that also make assumptions about oneself in relation to other realities, including the reality of the transcendent or the spiritual.

By now, one can probably detect a certain fuzziness about what theology actually studies since there are so many names for that object or set of objects. In this short chapter we've already identified a few of the common descriptors: God, gods/goddesses, the transcendent, transcendent reality, Higher Power(s), Being, the divine, the sacred, the holy, the spiritual, matters of ultimate concern, the depth dimension of human existence, the religions, religious experience. Theology is about all of these—and more.

"Although we have no way of knowing the mental and spiritual outlook of the earliest humans, we may at least assume that religious ideas and practices have been part of humankind's experience for as long as humans have had thinking, reflecting, and imagining capabilities."[7] To the extent that every religious tradition contains ordered reflection on its received stories (myths), rituals, behaviors, customs, and beliefs, that tradition is marked by theology, which many scholars of religion describe as thinking about "*the sacred*, the ground of all, the ultimate reality."[8] In this sense, the term "theology" may also be used loosely to describe reflection on "the holy," "the eternal," "the One," "nirvana," or whatever other name or term is used for "ultimate reality," even when such reflection occurs within non-theistic traditions or within a tradition that does not use the word "God." What should be clear by now is the fact that theology, broadly speaking, is always a distinct or particular kind of thinking and speaking of God or the transcendent, whether that speaking is Jewish, Christian, Muslim, Hindu, or some other way.

Within the three great western religions (Judaism, Christianity, Islam), which trace their respective heritages back to the single figure of **Abraham**, theology is undertaken within a context of **monotheism**, that is, a belief in one God.[9] Indeed, in each of these religions, God gives authentic theology or knowledge of God through **divine revelation** that makes knowledge of God possible for human beings. *God's own self-revelation* leads to distinct ways of thinking about God and formulating certain perennial problems and questions. Entry into these theological issues usually begins with careful study of the Scriptures in the tradition and how they have been understood over time. For example, what do the Jewish and Christian

---

[7] Theodore M. Ludwig, *The Sacred Paths: Understanding the Religions of the World*, 4th edn (Upper Saddle River, NJ: Pearson Prentice Hall, 2005), 27.

[8] Ludwig, *The Sacred Paths*, 13.

[9] Many scholars date the figure of Abraham to approximately 1800 BC, although the traditions about him are more recent.

Scriptures indicate about the nature of God's being and God's relation to the world? How are these understandings similar to or different from a Muslim understanding that develops from a close reading of the Quran? Is God involved in the way that the Jew or Muslim thinks or as the Christian thinks, or in some other way? Do Jews, Christians, and Muslims worship the *same* God (but in differing ways)? Or does each of these groups worship a different God?[10]

Sometimes people speak of God only *to question* that transcendent reality altogether or at least *to criticize* those who appeal to it for support of their beliefs and actions. In view of the incomprehensible deaths of millions in the genocides from just the past century alone, can one go on believing in a good and merciful God or must one give up that belief as faulty, wishful thinking? One can understand why the Jewish boy, who survived the Holocaust because his mother sent him to America to escape Nazi Germany in the mid-1930s, later lost his faith when he learned after the War that his mother, and all the rest of his family who could not leave, had died in the gas chambers at Auschwitz.

The towering atheistic, nineteenth-century anti-theologians, Ludwig Feuerbach (1804–72), Karl Marx (1818–83), and Friedrich Nietzsche (1844–1900), also criticized and rejected the object of religious conviction in favor of "this-worldliness" and secular, transformative action. Many contemporary atheists echo their concerns. Still, one notes that the reflections on religion and God by those who are opposed to these concepts involve these individuals, too, willy-nilly, in a form of theological discourse, albeit of a strictly negative kind. Even the atheist, the one who rejects altogether the reality of God or gods/goddesses or the transcendent, cannot help but also be a theologian of sorts. "God's unforgettableness means that He is present even in rejection."[11] The same is true of those who make

---

[10] See especially Miroslav Volf, ed., *Do We Worship the Same God: Jews, Christians, and Muslims in Dialogue* (Grand Rapids: Eerdmans, 2012). Volf himself provides a persuasive argument that the object of Jewish, Christian, and Islamic worship is the same, despite differing beliefs about this one God among Jews, Christians, and Muslims. See also Miroslav Volf, *Allah: A Christian Response* (New York: HarperOne, 2011).

[11] Leszek Kolakowski, "Concern about God in an Apparently Godless Age," in *My Correct Views on Everything*, ed. Zbigniew Janowski (South Bend: St. Augustine's Press, 2005), 183. Many western people use masculine pronouns to refer to God. Such usage reflects the patriarchal sociology and anthropology of ancient cultures. For example, the Greek word for God (*theos*) is masculine. The Jewish and Christian Scriptures use male language about God, although on occasion they also use female imagery. While Jesus taught his followers to pray to God as "our Father," he also alluded to 4 Esdras 1.30, where God is compared to a mother hen, when he lamented how he had tried to gather the children of Jerusalem like a hen with her brood (Lk. 13.34). At times masculine language

judgments about the behaviors of religious people that they find deeply troubling. How many engaged in theological reflection after witnessing the horrific events of September 11, 2001, events that clearly were at least partly motivated by religious conviction? Can one properly understand the medieval crusades or the post-Reformation "wars of religion" without some attention to the theological motivations of the participants in these conflicts? On the day that this paragraph was written 56 Shiite Muslims were killed in a suicide bombing by a Sunni Muslim in Kabul, Afghanistan. There have been so many such attacks in the past decade that one hardly pauses to consider the consequences of each one anymore, and yet thinking about the "God-dimension" of these actions involves one in theology, too, even if one rejects the reality of that dimension and/or criticizes the actions and the beliefs of those who appeal to it as justification for their behavior.

Given how "religion" and "thinking about God" impact major social and political conflicts in the Middle East, North Africa, China and Tibet, India, Pakistan, Iraq, the United States, France, Australia, Germany, Great Britain—to identify just a few of the more obvious locales—is it any wonder that some people would just as soon avoid discussing topics of religion and theology altogether? Not only do such topics often make people feel awkward and even uncomfortable, they can lead to fierce arguments and, sadly, even to violence—just as can happen with any deeply-held conviction about topics some parents teach their children to avoid discussing in public. (A few days after that bombing in Kabul several Greek Orthodox and Armenian priests, all supposedly Christian, got into a brawl with one another at the Church of the Nativity in Bethlehem. What is the theological dimension of that conflict?)

Sadly, even atheistic ideology (anti-theology) has also led to oppression, persecution, and violence. Witness what happened to religious people in the Communist Soviet Union, in Pol-Pot-led Cambodia, and in Maoist Communist China. Not only do people fight, suffer, and sacrifice because of their religious convictions; some also fight, suffer, and sacrifice because of anti-religious convictions. Such beliefs and values are perhaps the deepest feelings and ideas one can have about oneself and one's world, for they involve one's entire view of reality and how that view shapes individual and communal

---

for God will be used in this book (often in direct quotations), but it is important to note that mainstream Jewish and Christian theologians affirm that God is not to be understood as literally being male (or female, for that matter). When encountered, such masculine pronouns for God must be interpreted carefully and understood analogically.

belief and action in the world. One should not be surprised that such convictions, religious and otherwise, can become disastrously destructive.

Lest one conclude, however, that the best solution going forward is not to have any convictions at all, given how strongly-held religious and anti-religious principles can wreak such havoc upon society when they "go public," consider what our world would be like today if people of deep conviction had not been concerned about slavery, women's rights, child labor, civil rights, human rights, world peace, and other issues of social justice. People who study political movements, or who study the people who work for peace or who care for the poorest of the poor and the weakest of the weak, will also have to take note of the religious and theological dimensions of these movements and individuals. Several examples are worth highlighting: Can one fully understand and appreciate the civil rights movement without attention to the theology of the Reverend Dr. Martin Luther King Jr. (1929–68) and other civil rights leaders? Would the Peace Corps have become what it is were it not for the Christian convictions of its founding director, Sargent Shriver (1915–2011), who attended Mass daily before heading off to his work? How many social reformers have acted on the basis of deeply-held religious beliefs, as did Senator George McGovern (1922–2012), a Methodist, when he addressed the political issues of poverty and hunger, or as some Evangelical Christians are doing today in view of the threatening environmental crisis, or as Bono (b. 1960) did, when he successfully got religious conservatives to join him in working toward a solution to the global AIDS epidemic? Who else comes to mind when you think of the connection between religious conviction and public action? Even the person who is strongly opposed to "organized religion" has to acknowledge that people of strong religious faith have done, and continue to do, much public good because of that organized, communal faith, often in places where no one else will go and for people about whom many could not care less. *To understand these public actions* more fully invites one to enter into the theological understandings and motivations of those who do them.

Even in the face of obvious evil and suffering, people of religious conviction confess their sins and failures, they pray and work for a better world, and they have a sober hope in the ultimate goodness of God over against all evils. For example, despite what happened to the Jews under the regime of Hitler, many have continued to practice Judaism as a moral and theological necessity over against the evils perpetuated by the Nazis. One German-born rabbi, himself a Holocaust survivor who also lost family members in the death camps, has argued:

[Jews have the responsibility] to survive as Jews, lest the Jewish people perish, ...to remember in our very guts and bones the martyrs of the Holocaust, lest their memory perish, ...[to be forbidden] to deny or despair of God, however much we may have to contend with him or with belief in him, lest Judaism perish, ... [to be forbidden] to despair of the world as the place which is to become the kingdom of God, lest we help make it a meaningless place in which God is dead or irrelevant and everything is permitted. To abandon any of these imperatives, in response to Hitler's victory at Auschwitz, would be to hand him yet other, posthumous victories.[12]

Theology is not a hobby here, but a life-and-death struggle, a moral and religious necessity in the face of terrible events and disturbing mysteries. Other Jewish thinkers are critical of this kind of "negative" motivation for remaining Jewish; they insist that one should be Jewish for the sake of Judaism alone, not as a protest against Hitler and the Holocaust. But that, too, is just another way of entering into theology, when one disagrees with a theological understanding set forth by another. (It should be noted that many Jews refrain from using the term "theology," largely because of its Greek and Christian etymology, and yet they, too, interpret their practices, laws, and beliefs and seek to understand them.)

Finally, **academic theology** can itself be a significant entry point into the topic of theology. This may be the most formal manner by which people think about God, spiritual beliefs and practices. Indeed, for many university students, this entry might provide them with their first opportunity to undertake a sustained effort at thinking critically and systematically about their own beliefs and commitments and those of others. What is more, they can do so in ways that are related to the history of theological reflection and to knowledge discovered and transmitted in the other university disciplines. Such an entry could help to avoid one of Ernest Boyer's fears about undergraduate education in America: "At a time in life when values should be shaped and personal priorities sharply probed, what a tragedy it would be if the most deeply felt issues, the most haunting questions, the most creative moments were pushed to the fringes of our institutional life."[13]

---

[12] Emil Fackenheim, *The Jewish Return into History: Reflections in the Age of Auschwitz and a New Jerusalem* (New York: Schocken Books, 1978), 23–4. Fackenheim, a Reform rabbi, was born in 1916; he died in 2003.

[13] Ernest Boyer, *College: The Undergraduate Experience in America* (New York: Harper and Row, 1987), 283–4.

Thankfully, many university students today do want to explore "the big questions" of life, of meaning, purpose, and faith.[14] These have to do with intensely personal questions: "Who am I?" "What do I believe about myself and the world around me?" "What am I to do with my life?" Yet these types of questions also lead toward broader, more public issues, such as global peace, justice, the common good, the environmental crisis, the future of the planet and of human beings on it. These questions are not inherently secular; they are often wrapped up with religious convictions and commitments. For example, within a North American context, students of theology might be asked to think critically about the theological assumptions that American citizens make about their country as exceptional in the eyes of God. Since nearly two-thirds of all Americans today fully or mostly agree with the questionable assertion that God has granted America a special role in human history, one might wonder, what is the basis for this commonly held belief in American "exceptionalism"?[15] What role does this belief about "God and America" play in Americans' perceptions of U.S. foreign policy and how does this theological assumption affect other people and countries in the world? "If U.S. foreign and domestic policy is in fact based on theological beliefs regarding God, the U.S., the world, and human history, then it is vital that such beliefs be brought out fully into the open and articulated clearly so that they can be discussed and analyzed. If we theologians do not do this, who will?"[16]

One university student, who is of nominal Christian background, feels compelled to study academic Christian theology when she becomes embarrassed that a non-Christian student knows more about her Christian tradition than she does. As she goes deeper into the Christian tradition she wonders why women have not been allowed to serve as priests or pastors in the major church groups (Eastern Orthodox, Roman Catholic, conservative Protestant) and why Christians have oppressed women and others over the centuries. She also begins to question certain beliefs and practices that seem in her judgment to contribute to major global problems of overpopulation and environmental degradation. Thus she begins to think theologically.

---

[14] See especially Sharon Daloz Parks, *Big Questions, Worthy Dreams: Mentoring Young Adults in Their Search for Meaning, Purpose, and Faith* (San Francisco: Jossey-Bass, 2000).

[15] Public Religion Research Institute, "PRRI-RNS Religion News Survey," (May 2011). This survey was conducted by the Public Religion Research Institute in partnership with Religion News Service. (http://www.publicreligion.org) [accessed January 8, 2011]

[16] David A. Brondos, "On the vital role of theology today," *Dialog* 50 (Fall 2011), 222.

Theology pops up in other university contexts, too, often within a broader argument for the importance of the humanities, philosophy, and the arts in higher education. Since the history of human culture contains theological symbols and ideas, attention to academic theology can help one to uncover the meaning(s) these symbols and ideas have had and might continue to have. The history of western art and literature, for example, cannot be fully appreciated without some theological understanding of Judaism and Christianity.[17]

Certainly theology will be an aspect of any *investigation into the world's religions*, the study of which ought to be "a necessary part of any quality program of higher learning."[18] While the scholarly analysis of any given religion should strive for objective description and analysis, questions about normative judgments and theological criticism do frequently arise, especially when scholars ask whether or not one is justified in making at least some critical judgments about specific beliefs and practices within the religions, say when one is convinced such beliefs and practices are harmful to others or unjust. There might very well be good reasons for being critical of some beliefs, practices, and theological understandings.[19] One thinks, in particular, of certain exclusivist beliefs and practices in some of the world's religions that have fomented nationalism, fanaticism, racism, sexism, conflict, and violence. As was noted above, the pressing and significant global problems that are compounded, if not actually caused, by (false?) theological understandings and practices, lead many to conclude that the study of the religions is incomplete without at least some attention to rigorous theological inquiry. The faith dimension of many of the most troubling of problems in the contemporary world cannot be avoided: the growing gap between rich and the poor; the population explosion; ongoing violent conflicts between different racial, cultural, and religious groups (the arming of which no one seems able to stop); the global environmental crisis.

---

[17] For a high-school textbook that emphasizes this point, see Cullen Schippe and Chuck Stetson, *The Bible and Its Influence*, 2nd edn (New York: BLP, 2011).

[18] Douglas Jacobsen and Rhonda Hustedt Jacobsen, *No Longer Invisible: Religion in University Education* (New York: Oxford University Press, 2012), 153. The Jacobsens organize the second part of their book around six key questions that lead in the direction of theological reflection: What should an educated person know about the world's religions? What are appropriate ways to interact with those of other faiths? What assumptions and rationalities—secular or religious—shape the way we think? What values and practices—religious or secular—shape civic engagement? In what ways are personal convictions related to the teaching and learning process? How might colleges and universities point students toward lives of meaning and purpose?

[19] This point is made by Robert S. Ellwood and Barbara A. McGraw, *Many Peoples, Many Faiths: Women and Men in the World Religions*, 7th edn (Upper Saddle River, NJ: Prentice Hall, 2002), 12.

Many students within religious studies also often ask about normative, theological issues: Are all religions true? Are all false? Are some truer than others? If all religions cannot be equally true in every respect, do all contain truthful elements? Do the religions of the world have anything good in common with each other? If so, what is this? Conversely, can one identify when a given theological understanding is false or harmful or worse than another? Are religions generally a force for evil in the world or a force for good? How does one articulate a "norm" for discerning a theological truth or at least identifying a theological harm, if not a theological falsity? Recent textbooks on religious studies indicate an abiding interest in these questions, even if the questions themselves are problematic for a discipline whose many practitioners eschew such normative issues in favor of the ideal of scholarly neutrality and careful, objective description.[20] Perhaps less problematic are questions about why religious fundamentalisms and nationalisms are flourishing in the world today, often seemingly in response to perceived threats from secularizing forces. These questions, too, call for a scholarly sensitivity to the theological content of these religious movements and the shared convictions of those within them.

While some might want to relegate Jewish studies or Islamic studies or Buddhist studies or Christian studies to private schools or institutions, or study religious ideas merely in the context of the history of world religions or in religious studies, there seem to be no legitimate grounds for excluding from a university the scholarly study of specific religions, their teachings and practices, as long as such inquiry is consistent with the scholarly canons of the university and the intellectual virtues that are fostered there. This form of study also gives rise to theological understanding and criticism. Such scholarly investigation, even within state colleges and universities, should not be understood as providing legitimacy or state sponsorship to a specific religious tradition, its practices, and beliefs, but as giving mature students the opportunity to gain cultural insight and self-understanding within a situation of religious pluralism. In that context the student honors the specificity of the religious tradition, examines its claims to reality critically, uncovers its impact on people and their societies, and explores the potential illumination it provides for the interpretation of reality and the deepening of self-understanding.[21] While the Jacobsens also underscore that

---

[20] For example, see Chapter 6, "The Comparisons of Religions," in Walter Capps, *Religious Studies: The Making of a Discipline* (Minneapolis: Augsburg Fortress Press, 1995), 267–330.
[21] For a recent argument on the importance of studying specific religious traditions within public

the distinction between "teaching about a religion" and "teaching religion itself" is often difficult to maintain in a university setting, especially when students raise questions in class about their own and others' spiritual and religious convictions, those who teach the theology of a specific religious tradition in that setting do so best when they "present a variety of perspectives on a given religious doctrine and tell students that ultimately what they believe is theirs to decide."[22]

Investigations in the natural and human sciences also raise theological questions about human beings, their self-understandings, and their relation to the cosmos in which they live, as when a biologist confidently makes the statement that the entire universe is meaningless or that evolution in nature is entirely a random process. Don Browning (1934–2010) and others have shown that humanist psychologists have sometimes made assertions that imply a kind of theological understanding, as when Carl Rogers "implicitly assumed that human beings are acceptable not simply before a therapist, or even a community of acceptance, but instead, acceptable before the very source of life."[23] Such a view that "life or ultimate reality accepts the client [has] smuggled in a quasi-theological assumption about Divine acceptance."[24] Of late, some neuroscientists have developed empirical models for investigating the relation between human brain activity and religious experience and behavior. What are the theological implications of these recent scientific investigations into the neuropsychology of spirituality? Other university scholars are involved in interdisciplinary studies on a multitude of topics relating to theology: the connection between religious practices and health, the role of religious traditions in the articulation of virtue and ethical principles, the supposed evolution of religion in the context of human evolution, and so on.

Unfortunately, however, many criticize academic theology as too complex, too speculative, too impractical, and too esoteric. It is viewed as a "sectarian intruder" within a fully secular institution.[25] A large number of Americans understand religion primarily as a set of behaviors rather than a set of overarching beliefs, and thus they tend to be skeptical about

---

universities, see Martin E. Marty, *Education, Religion, and the Common Good: Advancing a Distinctly American Conversation about Religion's Role in Our Shared Life* (San Francisco: Jossey-Bass, 2000), 103–40.

[22] Jacobson and Jacobson, *No Longer Invisible*, 41.

[23] Terry Cooper, *Don Browning and Psychology* (Macon, GA: Mercer University Press, 2011), 7.

[24] Ibid.

[25] Farley, *Theologia*, 133.

theological reflection altogether.[26] These attitudes continue to be expressed in the United States, where experience and activity are frequently valued more highly than academic theology.[27] This skepticism about academic theology has been prevalent in America since at least the eighteenth century, when people like Thomas Jefferson (1743–1826) and Benjamin Franklin (1706–90) expressed significant criticism against some religions and their attendant theologies, which they understood to be superstition and coercive "priestcraft," and yet one notes that even these specific critics engaged in theological reflection. Jefferson's library contains dozens of books on the New Testament and Christian theology, he spent many evenings trying to discern what the historical Jesus actually said and did, and he wrote a document that includes the words, "all men… are endowed by their Creator with certain unalienable rights." Even Jefferson knew that most human actions have underlying assumptions, motivations, and goals that are theoretical, religious, and even perhaps theological, or at least metaphysical and ethical, in nature.[28] Engaging in practical action without giving any attention to the thought that accompanies that action will likely be viewed by many as rather impoverishing for the doer, even as attending to thinking alone apart from practical action will be deemed short-sighted. It needs to be noted, too, that while some theologians uncritically defend and protect the teachings of their particular religious community, academic theologians often criticize traditional understandings and practices within their own religious communities and look for fruitful dialogue with scholars across the university. In this latter context they might also defend some religious traditions that have been wrongly understood or unfairly rejected.

---

[26] Martin Marty, *A Nation of Behaviors* (Chicago: University of Chicago Press, 1977).

[27] Robert D. Putnam and David E. Campbell, *American Grace: How Religion Divides and Unites Us* (New York: Simon and Schuster, 2010).

[28] It is significant to note the importance of the Declaration's appeal to the Creator, especially within important public speeches by American presidents and public leaders. The second inaugural address by President Obama is an excellent example of this American "civic religion": "…What makes us exceptional, what makes us America is our allegiance to an idea articulated in a declaration made more than two centuries ago. We hold these truths to be self-evident, that all men are created equal. That they are endowed by their creator with certain unalienable rights, and among these are life, liberty, and the pursuit of happiness. Today we continue a never ending journey to bridge the meaning of those words with the realities of our time. For history tells us that while these truths may be self-evident, they've never been self-executing. That while freedom is a gift from God, it must be secured by his people here on earth." The speech, which was given on Martin Luther King Day, echoed themes touched upon by Dr. King, whose "I have a Dream" speech also grounded such "self-evident truths" in the transcendent Creator above and beyond all human categories and conditions.

To be sure, poor academic theology—the kind that avoids serious, critical and self-critical reflection, that allows bias and prejudice to interfere with a careful examination of all relevant data, that belittles opposing arguments, and that does not seek to instill basic academic virtues—is indeed contrary to the best and highest ideals of a university community. There is no room in a university classroom for "using the lecture podium as a pulpit." But that same concern arises regarding any poorly taught university course in a host of other human-focused academic areas. Sociology, political science, economics, courses on race and gender, come quickly to mind, as also liable to bias and prejudice.

Despite the dangers, critical reflection on religious convictions, practices, and values, which could be another way of describing theology, is too important to leave out of a university curriculum. The study of these phenomena, which indeed gives rise to theological reflection, should be undertaken as fairly, as objectively (fact-oriented), and as carefully as possible, and not left unstudied. The point that Douglas Jacobsen and Rhonda Hustedt Jacobsen make about "religion" in university education applies equally well to the place of academic theology within that same context: "When the subject is handled well, discussed intelligently, and reflected upon seriously, religion (broadly construed) has the potential to enhance higher learning and open up a range of questions about the world and the human condition that otherwise might never be asked."[29]

Since the encounter with religious questions and wisdom is an integral dimension of what it means to be an educated human being, academic theology assists in that engagement by inviting students to think critically about their own faith and its tradition(s), to sift their tradition in light of other knowledge uncovered and transmitted within the university, and to hunt for helpful, considered understanding and wisdom from that tradition.[30] Students not only are encouraged to pursue their own quests for transcendent or ultimate reality, whether theistic or not, they are also asked to consider carefully which skills and attitudes are most helpful for engaging in theological dialogue with people of differing faiths and with those of no apparent faith. Given that a professionally-oriented university degree is no guarantee today that one will easily find employment after gradu-

---

[29] Jacobsen and Jacobsen, *No Longer Invisible*, 154.
[30] Edward Farley, "The place of theology in the study of religion," *Religious Studies and Theology* 5 (September 1985), 16. Professor Farley's essay has significantly informed my own understanding of the positive, critical role that theological inquiry can have in modern universities of all types.

ation, a student ought to use the university to sharpen and define his or her own self-understanding, including its religious dimension, to cultivate the virtues of character and intellect, also with respect to the theological content of religious and philosophical traditions, and to improve the skills and attitudes that are necessary for truly understanding the religious practices and theological ideas of others. While the task of **comparative theology** (that is, comparing theological understandings within the various world religions) is daunting and, some will argue, really impossible to fulfill, since no one has a complete understanding of multiple religious traditions or, perhaps, of even one tradition, the need for interreligious understanding is great today, given how religious differences so often lead to conflict and violence, and thus the task is worth pursuing. One has to start somewhere. Hopefully academic exercises in comparative theology, undertaken according to the strict standards of universal scholarship, can help to ward off theological prejudice and serious misunderstandings.

Perhaps because academic theologians often raise difficult, complicated questions about received religious traditions, beliefs, and practices, many who live within those traditions are uncomfortable with scholarly theology. They would rather live with a simple faith that relies on unexamined or uncritical readings of sacred writings or on an appeal to religious institutional authority. Still others might be uncomfortable because the examination of religious traditions might call their faith, whether secular or religious, into question. They might even fear that critical inquiry into theology might lead them to revise or even reject their previously-held convictions and beliefs. The death of one's god(s) or the loss of a previously believed certainty, whether of the atheistic or theistic variety, can be painful. But is an unexamined faith worth holding? Is such a faith legitimate, if it cannot risk careful scrutiny and the possibility of its loss?

Too often contemporary people do not realize that others have also addressed themselves carefully to personal faith, to theological issues and problems, and to questions that many find so fascinating and perplexing in the present. Could it be that studying academic theology might actually benefit the individual's own attempt to make sense of his or her world and to interpret it for others? Perhaps by attending to the wisdom and knowledge of those who have "done theology" well in the past, one might hope "to do theology" better in the present. At least some who do take the risk of examining their beliefs critically in the university are gratefully surprised when they find clarity for their faith and helpful language for expressing their deepest understandings of themselves and the world around them. In this way, academic theology assists people in the Socratic examination of their life. It leads them to reflect critically and constructively on the ideals, convictions, values, and practices that ground them as human beings and make their lives meaningful. Such an approach is especially consistent with student-centered learning that has become a norm for higher education in recent decades. Perhaps after moving through doubt and criticism about their faith, they enter into a kind of "second naïveté," to use the helpful notion developed by the philosopher Paul Ricoeur (1913–2005); that is, a critical understanding of their faith and its symbols that nevertheless allows them in a new way to believe truthfully and live fruitfully within the symbols of their faith.[31]

Key Words

theology	atheist
God	prayer
boundary questions	lex orandi lex credendi
the transcendent	Abraham
religion	monotheism
religious studies	divine revelation
theologian	academic theology
theist	comparative theology

Reference literature

For a general orientation to theology

BCSR 193–210 ("Theology," [Markham]); EC 5:363–70 ("Theology" [Owen]); ER 13:9125–34 ("Theology: Comparative Theology" [Tracy]); OHST 1–15 ("Introduction: Systematic Theology" [Webster]); RPP 12:608–10 ("Theologia" [Cancik]); RPP 12:617–46 ("Theology" [Schwöbel])

---

[31] Paul Ricoeur, *The Symbolism of Evil*, trans. Emerson Buchanan (Boston: Beacon Press, 1969), 351.

Questions for review and discussion

1   What are three possible ways of defining the term "theology"?
2   What did Karl Jaspers mean by "boundary questions?" Can you provide an example of such a question? How are such questions related to theology?
3   Can you identify at least four specific examples of informal ways into theology? Which of these ways have led you into theological reflection? Which of these informal ways do you think is the most commonly traveled?
4   Why is the concept of "religion" so difficult to define?
5   The chapter uses several terms to describe the object that theology studies (God, the sacred, religious experience, the transcendent, etc.). Which terms describe this object most accurately? Are there terms that you think are less helpful? Why?
6   What does *lex orandi, lex credendi* mean? How does that phrase relate to theology?
7   What does an atheist believe? Why does the author think that even atheists are "theologians"? Do you agree with this assertion?
8   Why do some think that the study of specific religious traditions (for example, Christian theology) does not belong in a university curriculum? Do you think these concerns and criticisms about teaching a specific religious tradition within a university are justified? What might be some arguments and evidence that would counter this view?
9   How do the Jacobsens think Christian theology should be taught in a university context?
10 What goals or outcomes do you hope to achieve as a result of the academic study of Christian theology?

Suggestions for further reading

All of the suggestions for further reading in this chapter and subsequent ones are just that: recommendations. One cannot avoid the problems of subjectivity and bias in devising such selections for further reading. Many more titles could have been given at the end of each chapter. But these are perhaps sufficient to get the student's attention and to direct him or her to works that will themselves point in further directions. I tried to select works that are substantive and significant and that will likely have an abiding importance in the undergraduate discipline of Christian theology. The sequence of titles is alphabetical and not chronological or in order of importance. Normally, each bibliographic reference is indicated only once.

Reference works in religious studies and Christian theology

Hans Dieter Betz et al. (eds), *Religion Past and Present*, 13 vols (New York: Brill, 2009–13) [This is an English translation of the fourth edition of *Religion in Geschichte und Gegenwart*. It is the standard reference work for the academic disciplines of religious studies and theology. Students are well advised to begin their research here. Helpful bibliographies accompany each entry.]

Lindsay Jones, ed., *Encyclopedia of Religion*, 15 vols, 2nd edn (New York: Thomson Gale, 2004) [Updated edition of the standard English-language encyclopedia of religious studies.]

Oxford Scholarship Online: Religion and Theology [Regularly updated three times a year, this online resource grants access to over 1,000 key titles in religion, all peer-reviewed.]

Mark Juergensmeyer et al. (eds), *Oxford Handbooks Online: Religion* [This major online reference work makes tracking down peer-reviewed articles in religion fast and easy.]

Oxford Bibliographies: Religion [This online resource combines the best features of an annotated bibliography with a high-level encyclopedia to offer an unparalleled entry into the best scholarship on a wide range of topics in religious studies and theology. This is a great place to go after examining RPP and ER.]

Religious studies

Walter Capps, *Religious Studies: The Making of a Discipline* (Minneapolis: Fortress, 1995) [Provides a nice overview of the discipline of religious studies, including a chapter on theological approaches to the comparative study of world religions.]

Peter Connolly, *Approaches to the Study of Religion* (New York: Continuum, 2001) [Written for undergraduate students, this book provides an overview of the principal approaches to the academic study of religion. These include feminist studies, phenomenology, psychology of religion, philosophy of religion, sociology of religion, and theology.]

Lawrence S. Cunningham and John Kelsay, *The Sacred Quest: An Invitation to the Study of Religion*, 3rd edn (Upper Saddle River, NJ: Prentice Hall, 2002) [A good undergraduate-level introduction to the study of religion.]

Bradley L. Herling, *Beginner's Guide to the Study of Religion* (New York: Continuum, 2008) [Describes several classic theories for interpreting "religion" and summarizes the most pressing current issues in the discipline of religious studies.]

James C. Livingston, *Anatomy of the Sacred: An Introduction to Religion*, 5th edn (Upper Saddle River, NJ: Prentice Hall, 2005) [Comprehensive introduction to the nature and variety of religious beliefs and practices. It provides a helpful overview of various definitions of "religion" and the myriad ways in which religions have been studied.]

Robert A. Segal, ed., *The Blackwell Companion to the Study of Religion* (Oxford: Blackwell, 2006) [Helpful articles on all of the central issues in religious studies by leading scholars.]

The relationship between Christian theology and religious studies

D. L. Bird and Simon G. Smith (eds), *Theology and Religious Studies in Higher Education* (New York: Continuum, 2009) [This set of essays by scholars from around the world sets forth some of the current issues and debates regarding the tensions, conflicts, and agreements between the academic disciplines of "religious studies" and "theology."]

David F. Ford, Ben Quash, and Janet Martin Soskice (eds), *Fields of Faith: Theology and Religious Studies for the Twenty-first Century* (Cambridge: Cambridge University Press, 2004) [This collection of essays by mostly British scholars explores conflicting positions on the relationship between Christian theology and religious studies. The second part of the book includes essays that explore themes that overlap the two scholarly disciplines: God, love, scripture, worship, argument, reconciliation, friendship, and justice.]

2

Traditions of Christianity

Tradition is the living faith of the dead; traditionalism is the dead faith of the living. (Pelikan 1.9)

This chapter presents a broad overview of the historical development of the main traditions of Christianity. It introduces several key terms and movements and provides some important contemporary statistical and demographic information about the variety of Christian church groups and their distribution throughout the world today.

Where did Christianity arise? How has it become the most populous religion in human history? Where are its main centers? Who have been the key figures in the historical development of Christian theology?

Before turning to other important preliminary matters in Christian theology, one should have a basic understanding of the larger contexts, both temporal and spatial, in which Christian theology has arisen. To understand the temporal context better, this chapter refers to some of the principal terms, historical turning points, and key groupings in the development of Christianity. To understand the spatial context better, the present chapter includes data that provides an overall picture of the geographical and demographical spread of Christian traditions in the early twenty-first century. The next chapter introduces several significant figures within the history of theology, both pre-Christian and Christian. Altogether, this information should help to make one more aware of the complexity of Christian traditions in the world today.

"**Tradition**" is a tricky matter. The word itself comes from the Latin word *traditio*, which can refer to a delivery or to something that is surrendered, or handed down, as in a saying or a teaching that is delivered (OED 2092; ODCC 1546). The English word "traitor" derives from this same Latin term, referring as it does to someone who hands over secret things to an enemy. The Latin verb *tradere* ("to hand over" or "to pass on") was itself a rendering of the Greek word *paradidomi*, which has the same meaning. Thus, tradition can refer both to the process of handing over someone or something and to the content of that which is transmitted. For example, the Christian apostle Paul (sometimes called Paul of Tarsus or Saint Paul) used the verbal form of this word in both senses when he defended the tradition of the resurrection of Jesus:

> Now I would remind you, brothers and sisters, in what terms I preached to you the gospel, which you received, in which you stand, by which you are saved, if you hold it firm—unless you have believed in vain. For I *handed over* to you as of first importance what I also received, that Christ died for our sins in accordance with the Scriptures, that he was buried, that he was raised on the third day in accordance with the Scriptures, and that he appeared to Cephas, then to the twelve... (1 Cor. 15.1–5, emphasis added)[1]

A number of scholars note that a given theological tradition, consisting broadly of beliefs and practices, is never a static, unchanged object that is already well defined and merely something to be passed on in total. Rather, every tradition is always something that is contested, debated, defined, and re-defined in ever new and changing situations, often over against competing traditions and views that are deemed contrary to "the tradition" as one understands it. For example, Irenaeus of Lyons (c. 130–c. 200) defended his understanding of Christian tradition in the second century, over against others who also claimed to be Christians. He did this by appealing to authoritative traditions that were taught and passed on publicly in the principal Christian cities of that time. Yet Irenaeus' own theological understandings furthered the tradition precisely by critiquing these other claims. (Irenaeus' opponents are today usually called "Gnostic" Christians because they emphasized a secret "knowledge" [Greek: *gnosis*] that Jesus had supposedly taught his followers privately.) In the process of defending received tradition, Irenaeus caused the tradition itself to undergo further refinement.

Alisdair MacIntyre (b. 1929) has thus defined a tradition as "an argument extended through time in which certain fundamental agreements are defined and redefined."[2] If the argument comes to an end, then the

---

[1] All Bible translations are my own, unless otherwise noted. I have frequently used terms and phrasing from the *Revised Standard Version* (Washington, DC: Division of Education of the National Council of the Churches of Christ in the United States, 1977) and the *New Revised Standard Version* (Washington, DC: Division of Education of the National Council of the Churches of Christ in the United States, 1989). As with Jesus, the years of Paul's birth and death are unknown. Scholars generally date Paul's life between AD 10 and AD 65.

[2] Alasdair MacIntyre, *Whose Justice? Which Rationality?* (Notre Dame, IN: University of Notre Dame Press, 1988), 12.

tradition(s) come(s) to an end as well. Hans-Georg Gadamer (1900–2002) made a similar point: "Every tradition is as such not an organic event but depends on the conscious effort to preserve what has been passed [on]."[3] These definitions stress the fact that traditions are dynamic in nature and involve ongoing discussions and debate in the present about what constitutes "the tradition."

The history of every religious tradition demonstrates that such traditions have frequently undergone change and revision over time. Sometimes that change seems geologic in nature—very, very slow and almost imperceptible—as has been the case with many Eastern Orthodox beliefs and practices, which have remained remarkably stable over the centuries. In other instances, a tradition undergoes very rapid change, as happened when leaders in the Roman Catholic Church re-examined that church's entire range of beliefs and practices over the course of three years in the 1960s and changed some of them in rather remarkable ways.[4] Whether a tradition changes rapidly or slowly, every tradition is in some measure a product of historical development, even as almost every tradition seeks some kind of normative character that persists through time and social circumstance.[5] Of course, the challenge for anyone interested in the integrity and truth of a given theological tradition is to articulate a way of distinguishing authentic development from inauthentic, of identifying artificial and arbitrary continuities within and among the traditions of theology and distinguishing them over against real and significant connections and developments.

Traditions within religions are often questioned, criticized, defended, and even sometimes replaced by alternative traditions. Such processes have certainly been ongoing within the history of Christianity. The common examples are rather obvious, but they serve to demonstrate the point: (1) The enslavement of some human beings by others had been an accepted Christian tradition for centuries, but so, too, had been the teaching that all human beings are equal before God, that they deserve to be protected from harm, and treated with respect; (2) The view that children are totally

---

[3] Hans-Georg Gadamer, "The Future of the European Humanities," in *Hans-Georg Gadamer on Education, Poetry, and History: Applied Hermeneutics,* Dieter Misgeld and Graeme Nicholson (eds), trans. Lawrence Schmidt and Monica Reuss (Albany: State University of New York Press, 1992), 197.

[4] For example, the bishops authorized the use of vernacular languages in the celebration of the Mass, they stressed the collegial character of church leadership, and they opened the door for deeper, positive engagement with other Christians and people from other world religions.

[5] See Dale T. Irvin, *Christian Histories, Christian Traditioning: Rendering Accounts* (Maryknoll: Orbis, 1998).

the property of their parent(s) has also been a long-standing Christian tradition, which has allowed for the forced labor of children to earn money for their family, but there are also other theological traditions which assert that children, too, ought to be protected from oppression and abuse by others, including even their parents; and (3) Still another common Christian tradition has been the subordination of women to men, which has often been asserted to be an abiding social arrangement or order in God's creation. Even in our own day, people argue about whether women can serve as priests or pastors or bishops in the Christian churches, just as others argue that elements within the Christian biblical tradition teach and support the full equality of men and women before God and that both men and women are gifted by God's Spirit for service in the world. One could provide many other common examples of contested Christian traditions, but these few are sufficient to make the point that such traditions are often debated, defended, modified, and sometimes even rejected in view of other aspects of "the tradition."

Clearly, Christianity consists of a dynamic complex of theological traditions, which are always embodied and transmitted in church communities of faith and practice, both large and small. As such, Christianity and its traditions have an historical context, a temporal dimension, and, at any given period of time, so embodied, they can be spatially depicted. We need now to gain an overview of both dimensions, the temporal and the spatial, as preliminary to this introduction to Christian theology.

An historical overview

The history of Christianity could be described as a history of arguments about Christian tradition. Such conflicts had begun already within the parent tradition of Christianity, **Judaism**, because of disagreements about the identity of **Jesus of Nazareth**, who was born around 5 or 6 BC and who died around AD 30.[6] Was he the fulfillment of Hebrew prophecies regarding

---

[6] Throughout this book the traditional abbreviations "BC" ("Before Christ") and "AD" (Latin: *Anno Domini* = "In the Year of the Lord") will be used. These are Christian abbreviations that attempt to order time in reference to the birth of Jesus. They were invented by the sixth-century Christian monk, Dionysius Exiguus, whose chronological calculations, based on earlier figures by Julius Africanus (160–240), included reference to the supposed incarnation of the Word in Jesus. Dionysius' dating system was officially adopted in England in the seventh century and was widely used later by Europeans and then in the Americas. Unfortunately, Julius miscalculated the year in

"the **Messiah**" (Hebrew: *Masiach* = "anointed") or wasn't he? In other words, was he "**the Christ**" (Greek: *Christianos*; Latin: *Christianus* = "anointed") who had been promised by the ancient Hebrew prophets, or wasn't he?

The label "**Christian**" was initially applied to first-century disciples ("followers") of Jesus because they were convinced that he was indeed the Christ. The Greek form of the word "Christian" occurs in three places in the **New Testament** (NT): in the Acts of the Apostles (11.26 and 26.28) and in First Peter (4.16). The references in Acts indicate that followers of Jesus were first called "Christians" in Antioch a decade or so after the death of Jesus. Like Jesus himself, most of these followers were Jews, although by the end of the first century many Christians were non-Jews ("Gentiles").

The earliest Christian theology can be found already in the authoritative writings that have been collected in the NT, the central sacred writings of Christians. While undoubtedly many teachings that are found in the NT go back to Jesus himself, he did not write anything down for posterity, and perspectives that reflect historical situations that came after Jesus' earthly life have shaped each NT writing. Most of the writings in the NT were completed several decades after his death. Because first-century Christians primarily used the Jewish Scriptures to make their case that Jesus is the Christ, these Scriptures, too, are understood by Christians to contain Christian theology, although Christians throughout the centuries have disagreed among themselves about how best to understand the theological content of what has traditionally been called the **Old Testament** (OT; "the **Hebrew Bible**" for Jews). Nevertheless, a central claim in the NT is that Jesus is the Christ or the Messiah (see Mk 8.27–30 and parallels; Jn 1.41), terms that mean the same thing: "the anointed one." According to commonly held first-century Jewish expectations, when the Christ came, he was to be anointed in order to bring in God's new age or kingdom. Thus, "Christ" is not a proper name, but a title, like "president" or "king." Whether Jesus himself accepted this title has been debated among scholars, but it is clear that the NT writings themselves attach it to Jesus (approximately 350 times).

---

which Herod the Great died (he was off by about four years). Since Herod the Great died in 4 BC and the Gospel of Matthew indicates that Herod was still alive when Jesus was around two years old, Jesus could have been born six or seven years earlier than Julius and Dionysius figured. In other literature one will encounter the more neutral abbreviations "BCE" ("Before the Common Era") and "CE" ("Common Era"), despite the fact that the actual numerical figure beside them is based on a Christian ordering of time. For an examination of Julius' calculations, see A. A. Mosshammer, *Easter Computus and the Origins of the Christian Era* (Oxford: Oxford University Press, 2008).

While many priests and kings had been anointed with oil in ancient Israel, there developed within ancient Israelite religion the expectation of a final Anointed One, especially after the destruction of the last tribes of Israel and the end of kingship in the Davidic dynasty (after 586 BC). During the time after this terrible event, many Jews expected this new Messiah to arrive with the new kingdom of God that would replace the old world and its subjugation of the Jews to hated foreign powers. This Christ was to be God's agent in establishing a new world order and to serve as God's representative within the new age. While first-century Jewish groups differed among themselves about this coming Messiah (the Essenes, for example, apparently expected two of them, one political and the other priestly; the Sadducees seemed not to have expected any Messiah), mainstream Jewish expectations (including those of the Pharisees or "separate ones") centered on one coming figure who would be like **King David** of old.[7]

A central issue in the NT is to assert that Jesus is this Messiah, a descendent of David, and to clarify the messianic character of his life, death, and resurrection as the true fulfillment of these Jewish expectations about the Messiah. All later traditions of Christian theology have their starting-point in the theological reflections that are found already in the NT itself and, by extension, in early Christian interpretations of the OT, especially its prophetic writings and the Psalms. (It should be noted that Paul of Tarsus, whose writings form a large and central portion of the NT, had been a Pharisee and an opponent of early Christians, but then, according to his own testimony, he had an encounter with the risen Christ that led him to become a disciple of Jesus and an apostle.)[8]

All trajectories of Christian tradition can be traced back to apostolic

---

[7] Scholars are divided about the historical figure of David, whose exploits are recounted in the books of First and Second Samuel, the first part of First Kings, and First Chronicles. Some doubt he actually existed, while others date his reign to around 1000 BC.

[8] Whereas earlier generations of Christians understood Paul to have turned his back on Judaism after his encounter with the risen Jesus (and thus become an early progenitor of Christian anti-Semitism), more recently several New Testament scholars criticize the notion that Paul "converted" from Judaism to Christianity. These scholars have set forth a "new perspective" on Paul which stresses Paul's vocation and mission within Judaism and that his real concern is to bring Gentiles into God's original covenant with the Jews. For this "new perspective," see Krister Stendahl, "The Apostle Paul and the Introspective Conscience of the West," *Harvard Theological Review* 56 (1963), 199–215; E. P. Sanders, *Paul and Palestinian Judaism: A Comparison of Patterns of Religion* (Minneapolis: Fortress Press, 1977); James D. G. Dunn, "The New Perspective on Paul," *Bulletin of the John Rylands University Library of Manchester* 65 (1983), 95–122; and N. T. Wright, "New Perspectives on Paul," 10th Edinburgh Dogmatics Conference (August 25–28, 2003), http://ntwrightpage.com/Wright_New_Perspectives.pdf [accessed February 3, 2014].

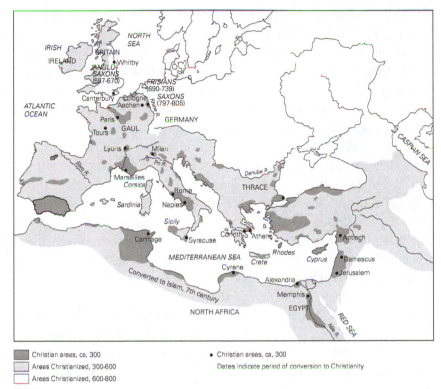

Christian areas, ca. 300
Areas Christianized, 300-600
Areas Christianized, 600-800

● Christian areas, ca, 300
Dates indicate period of conversion to Christianity

Figure 2.1 Map of the spread of Christianity in the first eight centuries.

sources in the NT and through them to Jesus, who is confessed to be "Lord" and "Messiah," along with many other titles that are given him. The NT itself contains a variety of theological perspectives about Jesus and the communities that followed him. For example, if one compares the descriptions of Jesus' words and actions in the **synoptic gospels** (Matthew, Mark, and Luke) with those in the Gospel of John, one might wonder if they are talking of the same person, since the descriptions are so different from one another. The NT also points to a multiplicity of models of church order, none of which is dominant. Within the so-called Pauline mission (the missionary work begun and maintained by the apostle Paul), there was a more dynamic structure than what one finds mentioned in NT documents that date from the late first century or early second (e.g. 1 Tim.). In the missionary activities connected to Paul, both men and women participated as leaders and the Spirit equipped individuals for specific ministries or functions within local congregations. Within this dynamic, charismatic structure there was room for a variety of services or gifts (*charismata*): **apostles** ("sent ones"), who had a unique and authoritative role within earliest Christianity;

traveling prophets and prophetesses; deacons and deaconesses; teachers; workers of miracles; pastors; and several others.

That dynamic structure in Paul's missionary work eventually gave way to certain basic institutional forms of church order that included the specific offices of **bishop** ("overseer"), **elder** or **pastor** ("shepherd"), and **deacon** ("minister"). Already, by the end of the first century, several key cities in the pagan Roman Empire had Christian overseers or bishops whose spiritual authority for their city and region became more and more important over time. These key places were: *Jerusalem* (where Jesus was crucified and was reported to have risen from the dead and where the outpouring of the Holy Spirit upon Jesus' followers initially occurred); *Antioch* (the starting-point for the Pauline mission); *Alexandria* (the center for the Egyptian churches); *Byzantium* (the eastern capital of the Roman empire, which was renamed Constantinople in the fourth century for Constantine the Great, the first Christian emperor of the Roman Empire); and *Rome* (the western capital city). While the first four of those cities were all centers of *eastern Christianity*, Rome eventually became the center for *western Christendom*, largely as a result of a legend that the apostle Peter had been bishop there and that his bones and those of the apostle Paul are buried there. By the end of the fourth century, the bishop of Rome was understood by western priests and bishops to be the head of the western, Latin-speaking church (Italy, Gaul, North Africa), whereas the bishops in the four principal centers of eastern, Greek-speaking Christianity understood the five bishops (themselves and the bishop of Rome) to be "equals" in authority and responsible for the spiritual oversight of their respective locales (dioceses) and/or regions. Nevertheless, the eastern bishops showed great respect for the bishop of Rome and occasionally appealed to him to settle theological disputes among the eastern churches (as when the bishop of Constantinople and the bishop of Jerusalem became embroiled in controversy regarding the person of Christ). A chief duty of a bishop was to interpret the Scriptures truthfully and faithfully. Indeed, the formation of the Christian Bible went hand in glove with the authoritative duty of bishops and priests to proclaim and teach the Christian Scriptures correctly and, in some cases, to identify which Scriptures were in fact "Christian" and which ones were not.

Eventually, over the course of several centuries, the governing structure of the Latin-speaking, western church became solidified under the authority of the bishop of Rome, who had also been called "**pope**" (Latin: *papa* = "father"), as had other bishops in the ancient church. After the eleventh century he was called this in an exclusive sense by western Christians. For this reason many prefer to speak of the post-eleventh-century western church as the *Roman* **Catholic Church**, since what is "**catholic**" ("according to the whole [church]" or "according to the universal [church]"), was further qualified by what was authoritatively taught by the bishop of Rome (ODCC 1422–3). When referring to this western church prior to the eleventh century it is more accurate to speak of "the western church of the Latin rite" rather than "the Roman Catholic Church."[9]

During these same early centuries, the governing structure of the Greek-speaking eastern churches continued to be centered on the bishop or **patriarch** (Greek: *patriarchus* = "father") in each of the four principal cities, although the patriarch of Constantinople, the chief city in the eastern empire, was said to be "first among equals." Collectively, these eastern churches became known as the **Orthodox Church** and their traditions identified as **Eastern Orthodoxy** (Greek: *orthodoxia* = "right opinion," "correct teaching"), since these churches are said to preserve the traditions of the faith in their true and proper form from the earliest days of the apostles. Particularly important in the definition of what is "orthodox" were the decrees and decisions of the first seven **Ecumenical Councils**, which addressed various theological conflicts regarding the right teaching about ·God and the person of Christ. The term "**ecumenical**" is based on a Greek word that refers to the management of a household (OED 495). The first seven councils are called "ecumenical" or "universal" because most of them drew bishops from all parts of the Roman empire and because they sought to affirm what should be taught and believed within "the whole household of God" (the *oikoume*), that is, all the churches throughout the empire. Eastern Orthodox Christians especially desire to maintain fixed worship forms because of their conviction that authentic church teaching has been handed down in these authoritative ways.

A central element within those worship forms is the authoritative **creed** (Latin: *credo* = "I believe") that was initially articulated at the first ecumenical council in Nicaea (AD 325) and then expanded at another such council that convened in Constantinople (AD 381). This creed is usually called "the Nicene Creed," although a more accurate designation is the "Niceno-Constantinopolitan Creed" (a mouthful!). Used regularly in the divine services of all churches that affirm the decrees of the first seven ecumenical councils, it sets forth the basic contours of the orthodox

---

[9]See Diarmaid MacCulloch, *Christianity: The First Three Thousand Years* (New York: Penguin, 2011), 289.

teaching about God, Jesus, and the Holy Spirit, over against the theological error of Arianism:

> We believe in one God the Father all-powerful, maker of heaven and of earth, and of all things both seen and unseen. And [we believe] in one Lord Jesus Christ, the only-begotten Son of God, begotten from the Father before all the ages, light from light, true God from true God, begotten not made, consubstantial with the Father, through whom all things came to be; for us humans and for our salvation he came down from the heavens and became incarnate from the Holy Spirit and the virgin Mary, became human and was crucified on our behalf under Pontius Pilate; he suffered and was buried and rose up on the third day in accordance with the Scriptures; and he went up into the heavens and is seated at the Father's right hand; he is coming again with glory to judge the living and the dead; his kingdom will have no end.
>
> And [we believe] in the Spirit, the holy, the lordly and life-giving one, proceeding forth from the Father, co-worshipped and co-glorified with the Father and the Son, the one who spoke through the prophets. [We believe] in one, holy, catholic and apostolic church. We confess one baptism for the forgiving of sins. We look forward to a resurrection of the dead and life in the age to come. Amen.[10]

Another example of an authoritative decree from an ecumenical council is the dogmatic "Definition of the Faith" from the Council of Chalcedon (AD 451) that sets forth teaching about the person of Christ over against understandings that were also deemed heretical:

> Following the saintly fathers, we all with one voice teach the confession of one and the same Son, our Lord Jesus Christ: the same perfect in divinity and perfect in humanity, the same truly God and truly man, of a rational soul and a body; consubstantial with the Father as regards his divinity, and the same consubstantial with us as regards his humanity; like us in all

---

[10] Norman P. Tanner, ed., *Decrees of the Ecumenical Councils*, 2 vols (Georgetown: Georgetown University Press, 1990 [Burns and Oates by permission of Bloomsbury Publishing Plc.]), 1.4 (slightly modified). Arius (256–336), a priest from Alexandria, was condemned as a heretic for teaching and preaching that "there once was when the Word [the *Logos*] was not" and "before the *Logos* was begotten he was not." These statements were condemned at the first Council of Nicaea. Arianism held that the *Logos* was the first creature of God and thus not fully divine or eternal as the Father was. (The use of the masculine term "Father" to refer to God is traditional in Christian theology, stemming primarily from Jesus' own teaching about God. More recently some scholars have recognized how ancient patriarchal language and assumptions have negatively influenced the development of Christian theology and have led to the marginalization and subordination of women within Christian communities. When encountered, such masculine language for God must be interpreted carefully and understood analogically. See footnote 11 in Chapter 1.)

respects except for sin; begotten before the ages from the Father as regards his divinity, and in the last days the same for us and for our salvation from Mary, the virgin God-bearer, as regards his humanity; one and the same Christ, Son, Lord, only-begotten, acknowledged in two natures which undergo no confusion, no change, no division, no separation; at no point was the difference between the natures taken away through the union, but rather the property of both natures is preserved and comes together into a single person and a single subsistent being; he is not parted or divided into two persons, but is one and the same only-begotten Son, God, Word, Lord Jesus Christ, just as the prophets taught from the beginning about him, and as the Lord Jesus Christ instructed us, and as the creed of the fathers handed it down to us.[11]

The historical background to these dogmatic decisions in early Christianity involved much argument, debate, political actions, frequent misunderstanding, but also repeated attempts at coming to a right understanding of the prophetic and apostolic witness to Jesus Christ. The language and phrasing in each of the above-quoted ecumenical decrees were intended to condemn **heresy** ("false teaching") and **heretics** ("false teachers"), to ward off false understandings of God and Christ, and to set forth right teaching ("orthodoxy"). Nevertheless, this very process of coming to an official, orthodox dogmatic decision contributed to the further clarification (and thus development) of the Christian doctrinal tradition.

Despite the fact that both the western Catholic Church and the eastern Orthodox churches recognize the decrees and decisions of the first seven Ecumenical Councils (fourth through seventh centuries), several factors, both theological and cultural, led to the eventual **schism** (separation) in AD 1054 between these two main branches of early Christianity. A chief theological disagreement centered on the western innovation (after AD 589) of inserting "and the Son" into the original Niceno-Constantinopolitan Creed, thus unilaterally modifying that creed's assertion that the Holy Spirit proceeds solely "from [God] the Father" and not, as the later western version has it, "from the Father and the Son." While this innovation may today strike many as rather trivial, it is not so viewed by eastern theologians, who insist that the unity of God is thereby undermined by the western innovation and that the ancient Tradition of the Orthodox Church was

---

[11] Tanner, ed., *Decrees of the Ecumenical Councils*, 1.86–7.

thereby inappropriately and errantly changed.[12] Still other conflicts arose between east and west, including whether the bishop of Rome is the head of only the western churches (the Orthodox view) or of the whole church on earth (the medieval Roman Catholic view), whether priests may marry (in the Orthodox Church priests may marry, but usually not bishops; in the Roman Church, no clergy may marry, apart from a few exceptions), and whether additional councils beyond the first seven have theological authority (the Orthodox recognize only the first seven, whereas Rome holds to many more, right up to Vatican II).

Unlike the eastern churches, which have generally been able to avoid major schism in their history (aside from conflicts with Syriac, Ethiopian, and Coptic churches, and the major schism with Rome in 1054), *the western church has undergone serious and complicated divisions since medieval times.* Chief among these is the cluster of divisions that occurred in the sixteenth century in the wake of reforms that **Martin Luther** (1483–1546) inaugurated in Germany, that **John Calvin** (1509–64) established in Switzerland, and that **Henry VIII** (1491–1547) and his Protestant successors set forth in England. While each of these reform movements had its distinctive characteristics, all were united in their rejection of the Pope's supreme authority over the whole church and in their insistence, contra Rome, on the following teachings and practices:

- that a human being receives the forgiveness of sins solely by faith alone in Christ alone (apart from human religious behaviors);
- that the OT and NT Scriptures alone are the sole authority in matters of faith and life;
- that there are only two **sacraments** (**Baptism** and **the Lord's Supper** [also called **the Eucharist**]);
- that both the consecrated bread and wine should be distributed in the Lord's Supper;
- that priests may marry;
- that the liturgy should be spoken in the language of the local people (and not in Latin);
- that some traditional Roman Catholic beliefs and practices are biblically unsupportable (for example, the sale of indulgences, belief in

---

[12] Because of their reverence for sacred tradition as a stable body of authoritative teaching and practice, the Eastern Orthodox churches typically capitalize the word "Tradition."

purgatory; intercession of the saints; and veneration of the Virgin Mary, the mother of Jesus).

Each of the main reform movements that began within the western Catholic Church stressed its continuity with the apostles and early Christian theologians and appropriated the label "catholic" for its teachings and church practices. However, a succession of Roman popes and the hierarchy beneath each one took actions against these changes and judged the reformers and their followers to be heretics who were guilty of teaching heresy. After 1529 many of these reform movements were grouped together under the label "**Protestant**," a term that referred to their "protest" against the halting of reform efforts by the Holy Roman Emperor at the time. While Luther did not want his followers to be called "Lutheran" or "Protestant" (he preferred the term "**Evangelical**," from the Greek word for "**gospel**" or "good news"), much less to establish a new sect, his excommunication from the Roman Catholic Church in 1521 can be understood as the event that most directly led to the formation of distinct "Lutheran" churches. The excommunication of Henry VIII similarly led to the formation of the distinct Anglican Church. Its spiritual authority is connected to the Archbishop of Canterbury and its history has been marked by internal movements or groups that have been oriented either toward reunion with Rome or against Roman influence within the Church of England, as it is sometimes also called.

Each of *the principal Protestant churches* (**Evangelical-Lutheran**, **Reformed**, and **Anglican**) developed its own confessional statements that defined its understanding of the Christian faith and church practices based on the teachings of Holy Scripture and that criticized errant beliefs and practices in the Roman Church and others. In the case of the Lutherans, the *Augsburg Confession* (1530) and the *Small Catechism* of Luther (1529) are the central documents. (These documents were later collected together with other central confessional writings from sixteenth-century Lutheran reformers and published as the *Book of Concord* in 1580.) For the Reformed, the *Heidelberg Catechism* (1562) and the *Westminster Confession* (1647) are especially important, as are the *Thirty-Nine Articles* (1563, later modified) and the *Book of Common Prayer* (initially published in 1549 and later revised) for the Anglican Church. Within the perspective of these Protestant churches and their heirs, the post-sixteenth-century Roman Catholic Church, which solidified its specific teachings and practices at the Council of Trent (1545–63) and the First Vatican Council (1869–70), was viewed as a more or less flawed church body that had adopted theological positions at odds with the clear teaching of apostolic Scripture: papal primacy/ supremacy and infallibility, the immaculate conception of Mary and her bodily assumption into heaven, forced clerical celibacy, seven sacraments, the use of indulgences, and so on.[13]

Within the Roman Catholic Church, however, theologians argued against Protestant views and defended their own theological teachings as legitimate developments of both Scripture and church tradition. It is important to note that, since the Second Vatican Council (1962–5), the Roman Catholic hierarchy has re-examined and, in some cases, reformed its teachings and practices. For example, it authorized the Mass to be celebrated in the language of the local people and it called for greater unity among the divided churches. Subsequent to that ground-breaking council, Catholic leaders have pursued ways to foster ecumenical dialogue with Lutherans, Reformed, Anglican and other Protestant churches, as well as with representatives of the Orthodox churches (and other non-Christian religions). The Roman Catholic Church remains the single largest Christian church group in the world.

In the twentieth century a number of smaller national Catholic churches (for example, the Church of Utrecht) broke away from the Roman Catholic Church and formed what is called "The Old Catholic Church," which holds to the first seven ecumenical councils and the dogmatic decisions of the Eastern Orthodox Church and rejects the primacy and infallibility of the Pope. Clergy and bishops are permitted to marry, the consecrated bread and wine are both given in Holy Communion, and the words of the liturgy are in the vernacular. These churches are now in fellowship with the Anglican Church.

Several *other churches* or **denominations**, as they are sometimes called, received their start in the sixteenth century, either by breaking away from the Roman Catholic Church or by splitting off from one of the main Protestant churches (Lutheran, Reformed, Anglican), which were viewed as corrupt in one way or another. Anabaptists ("re-baptizers") refused to baptize infants and young children and insisted that only believing older children and adults should be baptized. They teach that only the baptism of believers is authentic baptism. Many Anabaptists criticize secular forms of government, most insist upon strict pacifism, and some want to return

---

[13] A classic example of a Lutheran critique of the decrees from the Council of Trent is Martin Chemnitz (1522–86), *An Examination of the Council of Trent*, 4 vols, trans. Fred Kramer (St. Louis: Concordia, 1986).

to OT laws (such as allowing for polygamy). Luther, Calvin, and Roman Catholic authorities rejected these ideas. Those who held them were often persecuted in the sixteenth, seventeenth, and eighteenth centuries.

One set of Protestant churches traces its spiritual heritage back to the fifteenth century, a century before the time of Luther and Calvin. This set of traditions centers on *the Moravian Church*, whose key figure was the important fifteenth-century reformer, **John Hus** (c. 1372–1415). He insisted that Christians should receive both the consecrated bread and the wine in the Lord's Supper. Later, under the strong influence of Nikolaus von Zinzendorf (1700–60), this church stressed personal re-birth or conversion and individual piety as key features of the Christian life. Because of this focus, pious experience and missionary service were viewed as more important than intellectual understanding of the faith, although several key academic theologians have come from this church body.

Likewise, the Moravian understanding of piety has influenced other churches, such as the **Methodist** churches. Charles Wesley (1707–88) and his brother, **John Wesley** (1703–91), who were originally clergymen in the Anglican Church, promoted a particular method of religious faith and piety that had a close resemblance to the spiritual emphases coming from the Moravian Brethren, as did George Whitefield (1714–70), the other founder of the Methodist movement. (John Wesley had visited the Moravian community at Herrnhut, where Zinzendorf had been the major figure.) These Methodist emphases also included a strong sense of missionary zeal to spread the love of God in the gospel of Jesus to people who do not know it. Most Methodist churches reject the Lutheran and Reformed teaching about the slavery of the human will to sin (Luther and Calvin held that human beings are incapable of turning to God or cooperating with divine grace) as well as the Calvinist teaching about predestination (that from all eternity God has decreed who will be saved and who will be damned). Methodists insist that individuals have a free will that can either accept or reject God's universal offer of divine mercy.

Many of the individual churches that developed within the broad Reformed theological tradition differ from one another with respect to church government. The founders of the *Presbyterian* churches in the sixteenth and seventeenth centuries insisted that their form of church polity, in which a council of elders or **presbyters** (Greek: *presbyterus* = "elder") governs the local church, returned the church to an authentically apostolic form of government. *Congregational* churches, on the other hand, developed a more democratic form of church polity and insisted upon "the priesthood of all believers" under Christ, an idea also taught by Luther. Congregationalism developed in England in the sixteenth century as a protest movement against "Catholic" influences within the Church of England. Gradually "separatist" or "puritan" movements (also labeled "Non-conformists" or "Independents") developed, and some of these groups left old England for the new colonies in North America. While these groups had complexities of their own, they, too, generally reflected the theology and practices of Calvin.

Ecumenical relations among Protestant churches led to the formation of so-called "*union*" or "*uniting*" churches in the twentieth century. One such church is the Church of South India, a "uniting" church that formed from the merger of Presbyterian, Methodist, and Anglican churches. In America the United Church of Christ formed from the merger of several Congregational churches and the Evangelical and Reformed Church.

Many, many other Protestant churches have begun during the past four centuries. Scholars estimate that there may be more than 35,000 separate Christian church groups or denominations in the world today. Some of these are individual **non-denominational** "evangelical"[14] churches that are unaffiliated with any other congregation or association, although their teachings are often related to other Protestant traditions.[15]

---

[14] The term "evangelical" in this contemporary American context means something different from what it meant in sixteenth-century Lutheranism. Martin Luther used the term "*evangelisch*" to refer to the gospel about Jesus and the forgiveness of sins through his death and resurrection. Since the sixteenth century, many Lutheran churches and some other Protestant churches have understood the term "evangelical" to be synonymous with "Protestant" or "Lutheran," especially in Germany. Many Lutheran churches that follow the teachings of Luther also use the word "evangelical" in the sense that he gave it. But after 1942, with the founding of the National Association of Evangelicals, this word began to take on a different meaning. It now was used to define those American Protestants and their denominations which opposed the "modernist," liberal, and ecumenical Federal Council of Churches (later called the National Council of Churches). In this context an "evangelical" is a conservative Protestant Christian who has undergone a conversion experience ("being born again") and who affirms the inerrancy of the Bible, the miracles it reports, the blood atonement of Jesus, his physical resurrection, and his Second Coming. Most evangelicals also oppose the theory of evolution and, at least since the 1950s, have generally supported conservative, Republican political causes.

[15] The 2008 American Religious Identification Survey, conducted by Barry A. Kosmin and Ariela Keysar through Trinity College, Hartford, Conn., indicates that 14 percent of Americans identify themselves as "just Christian," suggesting no strong connection to a specific church group or denomination. (Of those surveyed, 4 percent called themselves "non-denominational.") See American Religious Identification Survey [ARIS 2008], http://commons.trincoll.edu/aris/publica-tions/aris-2008-summary-report/ (internet) [accessed January 26, 2014]. The General Social Survey between 1972 and 2010, conducted by NORC at the University of Chicago, indicates that, among those who identified themselves as "Protestant," the percentage which claims "no denomination" has been on the rise (3.5 percent of all Protestants in 1972; 15.3 percent in 2006). See http://www3.norc.org/GSS+Website/Download/ (internet) [accessed January 26, 2014].

Among these larger Protestant traditions, especially in the United States, is the so-called **Baptist**, whose origins lie with sixteenth-century "separatists" in the Netherlands and later in old England, but also among the Anabaptists in Switzerland (who also rejected infant baptism). Unlike the Calvinists and more like the Methodists, the Baptists stress the free will of human beings to accept or to reject God's grace. This idea was classically articulated by Jacobus Arminius (1560–1609), a sixteenth-century Dutch Reformed theologian, who doubted, and then rejected, the Calvinist teaching about predestination. Arminius insisted that Christ desires everyone to be saved and to respond freely to the salvation he offers. This view eventually led Baptists (and most Methodists, too), to emphasize "revival" meetings in order to bring about a personal conversion experience ("being born again") that is then followed by baptism as the external symbol of this inward conversion to Christ ("Believers Baptism"). Baptists insist on the full immersion of believers in baptism.

In spite of their tremendous institutional variety and strong individualism, Baptist churches are perhaps the most visible example in North America of what Americans mean when they speak of "**Protestant Evangelicalism**." Like Methodists, Baptists, too, have a strong sense of Christian mission and evangelism and they want to convince non-Christians of the truths about God, sinful human beings, and the salvation offered in Christ. The Baptist tradition in America includes such specific denominations as the Southern Baptist Convention, the Disciples of Christ, the Churches of Christ, and many independent "Fundamentalist" and "non-denominational" churches.

The *Adventist* movement, which attracted large numbers of Baptists after the 1830s, must also be understood within the Baptist tradition. Begun by William Miller (1782–1849), who had predicted the Second Advent or "Coming" of Christ in 1843–4, the chief group today is the Seventh-Day Adventists. They insist on keeping many of the OT laws, including especially the law not to work on the Sabbath, that is, from Friday evening to Saturday evening. (The Restorationist churches, which believe that the contemporary churches need to return to a "purer" form of apostolic Christianity, strive to keep all or most of the OT laws and they desire to reform the United States into a theocracy that is based on those laws.)

Also emerging from the Reformed theological tradition are the so-called **Dispensational churches**. They teach that history can be divided into seven periods or "dispensations" and that the final dispensation will be a future literal "millennial" or thousand-year reign of Christ on earth. Many well-known American Christians have defended dispensationalism, including the evangelist Billy Graham, the authors of the popular *Left Behind* series, the public commentator Pat Robertson, and theologians at Dallas Theological Seminary and the Moody Bible Institute. Dispensational or millennial Christians fall into two groups, those who believe that the millennium will follow the Second Coming of Christ ("pre-millennialists") and those who think it will precede Christ's return to earth ("post-millennialists"). It should be acknowledged, however, that Christians in several other denominations (Adventist, Plymouth Brethren, Baptist, Methodist) also have millenarian beliefs. All of these are convinced that people today are living in the final days of the earth and that the literal return of the risen Jesus is imminent.

While millenarian beliefs have frequently popped up in the history of Christianity since the second century, the Roman Catholic, Orthodox, Lutheran, and liberal Protestant churches do not interpret Chapter 20 in Revelation to teach a literal millennial reign of Christ on earth. They maintain that the 1,000 years should be understood figuratively to refer to the perfect reign of Christ that has begun with his resurrection and ascension.

Two other American Protestant groups are the *Society of Friends*, commonly known also as the "Quakers," which was begun by George Fox (1624–91), and the numerous **Holiness-Pentecostal churches** that have developed since the beginning of the twentieth century. The Society of Friends emphasize the immediacy of Christ's truth and the "Inner Light" that can be known directly within each individual, thus making superfluous the need for ordained ministers or any formal, pre-arranged structure for worship. The Holiness churches, which developed from the Wesleyan-Methodist tradition and its influence on Protestant revivals, stress the centrality of sanctification, growth in holiness through the gifts of the Holy Spirit and personal obedience to righteousness. The Church of the Nazarene is the best-known example of a holiness church in the United States.

Pentecostalism is closely related to the holiness churches, since its modern form grew out of the latter near the end of the nineteenth century. Many of the Pentecostal churches have either a Methodist (holiness) or a Baptist background. The Pentecostal label comes from the experience that followed fifty days after Christ's resurrection, on the Day of Pentecost, described in the second chapter of the Acts of the Apostles. There the disciples of Jesus are depicted as having received the gift of the Holy Spirit so as to speak in unfamiliar languages (see also 1 Cor. 14). Whereas the Roman Catholic, Orthodox, Lutheran, Reformed, and Anglican churches generally teach that

Major Groupings of Christian Tradition
(The arrows indicate the direction of theological influence from one group to another.)

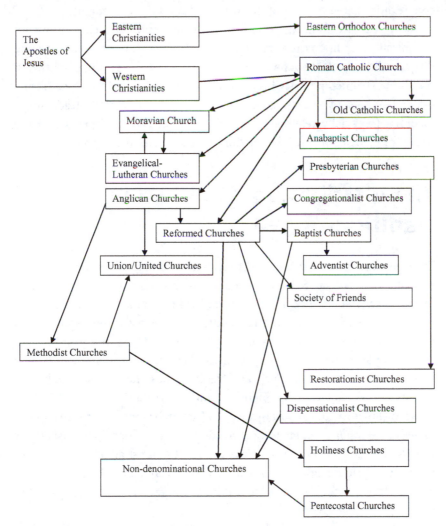

Figure 2.2 Major groupings of Christian tradition

this special gift was limited to the time of the original apostolic church and merely equipped them to carry the gospel message to foreign-speaking lands, modern Pentecostal Christians insist that yearning for and receiving the gift of "tongues" (understood as a "spiritual," non-worldly language) directly from the Holy Spirit is a sign of (non-water) "baptism in the Holy Spirit." These Christians teach that other "charismatic" gifts of the Spirit, such as miraculous healing, are also essential marks of the true church of Christ. In the United States the Assemblies of God and most of the Church of God congregations are examples of this form of Protestant Christianity.

As we can see from just this brief and incomplete sketch, the history of Christian traditions is very complicated. (See also the accompanying diagram that depicts the general relationship of the main groups of Christian traditions.) Contemporary Christianity continues to be marked by differing understandings of church government (polity and church leadership), theology (especially relating to teachings about the sacraments and the nature of the church), and the relation of faith to cultural expression.

The distribution of Christian traditions

The transmission of Christian traditions is not only a temporal phenomenon of history; it is also reflected spatially. Before narrowing our focus in the next chapter to specific key figures within mainstream traditions of Christian theology, we should take note of some basic geographical and demographical information about contemporary Christian groups. How many people in the world today identify themselves as "Christian" of one type or another? Which Christian tradition has the largest number of adherents? Which locales are predominantly Christian?

According to a 2011 report by the Pew Research Center, there are *approximately 2.184 billion people* in the world today who identify themselves as *Christian*.[16] This means that Christianity has the most adherents of any of the major world religions. A 2012 report by the same Pew Research Center provides the most recent data (2010) for the largest religious groups in the world (see Figure 2.3).

This report also reveals that major shifts have occurred since 1910, when nearly two-thirds of all Christians lived in Europe. Today only one-fourth lives there. The rest are located in the Americas (37 percent), sub-Saharan Africa (24 percent) and the Asia-Pacific region (13 percent). Two-thirds of all countries in the world have Christian majorities. That is about one-third

---

[16] See "Global Christianity: A Report on the Size and Distribution of the World's Christian Population," The Pew Forum on Religion and Public Life" (December 19, 2011), Pew Research Center, Washington, DC, www.pewforum.org (internet) [accessed January 26, 2014].

Religion	Approximate Number of Adherents	Principal Geographical Center(s)
Christianity	**2.18 billion**	Africa, the Americas, Europe
Islam	**1.6 billion**	Central Asia, North Africa, Indonesia
Hinduism	**1 billion**	India
Buddhism	**500 million**	Africa, Australia, Asia
Folk/Indigenous Religions	**400 million**	Asia, Africa, Australia, the Americas
Other Religions	**58 million**	Asia, the Americas
Judaism	**14 million**	Israel, North America

Figure 2.3 Data on World Religions

of the world's total population. By contrast, Islam is about 23 percent of the world's population.

So where is Christianity growing the fastest? Over the past century the answer to that question has been *sub-Saharan Africa*. In 1910 only about 9 percent of the African population was Christian, whereas today that figure is about 63 percent. Ironically, only about 4 percent of people living in the Middle East and North Africa identify themselves as Christian, despite the fact that early Christianity first developed in these regions.

The Pew Research Center report also indicates that the largest sub-group of Christians in the world is Roman Catholic (more than 1 billion adherents), the next largest is Protestant (over 800 million), and the third largest is the Orthodox (around 260 million). A fourth category, "other Christian" (just over 28 million), refers to smaller groups which have a more tenuous connection to the name "Christian" because of their specific teachings and practices which many view as inconsistent with historic Christian doctrine (for example, the Mormons and Jehovah's Witnesses). The Roman Catholic Church thus comprises nearly 16 percent of the world's population and makes up close to 50 percent of the total population of Christians in the world. Protestant groups together comprise nearly 12 percent of the world's population and slightly fewer than 37 percent of all Christians in the world.

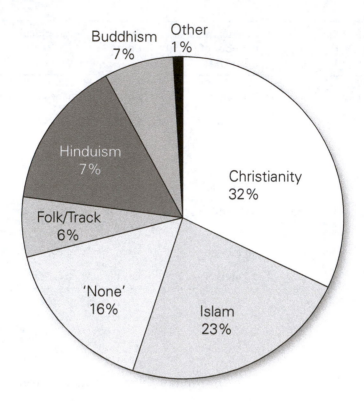

Figure 2.4 Adherents within the religions as a percentage of world population

These figures are based on a 2012 report by the Pew Research Center on the state of religious belief in 2010. See "The Global Religious Landscape," December 18, 2012 (www. pewforum.org [accessed January 27, 2013]). This report indicates that 5.8 billion of the world's total population in 2010 (6.9 billion), that is, approximately 84 percent, have some kind of religious affiliation. The report also indicates that of the 1.1 billion who are religiously "unaffiliated" or who say that have "no religion," or "none", many will still affirm belief in some kind of "Higher Power." Most of the "nones" live in Asia, although that figure might be misleading, since many Chinese are reluctant to tell their actual religious views in a situation of state-sponsored atheism within their country. (44 percent of Chinese stated they had worshipped at a graveside or tomb in the previous year. Likewise, estimates of the number of Christians in China vary between 60 million and 130 million. For the latter statistic, see "Underground Christianity," *The Economist* [August 24, 2013], 42.)

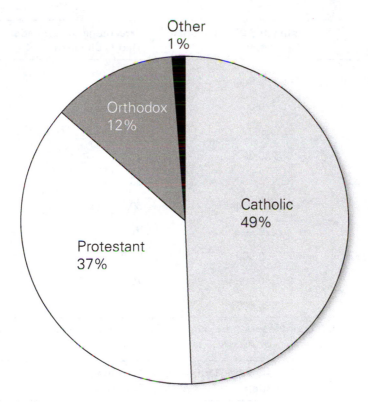

Figure 2.5 Size of Christian traditions in the world

The Orthodox, about 12 percent of all Christians, embody approximately 4 percent of the world's population. Mormons, Jehovah's Witnesses, and "other Christians," total less than 0.5 percent of the world's population and less than 2 percent of all Christians.

Clearly, of all the countries in the world, the United States has the most citizens who identify themselves as Christian (nearly 246 million), and Brazil has the second highest number (175 million). Within the United States, approximately 80 percent of all people identify themselves as some form of Christian. Of these, most are Protestant (approximately 160 million), although the Roman Catholic Church remains the single largest religious group or denomination in the U.S., with around 75 million adherents. Research on the structure and organization of Protestants in this country indicates that the denominational groupings that have historically been significant are in numerical decline, that loyalty to denominations is generally not as strong as it used to be, and that within traditional

	Estimated 2010 Christian Population	Percentage of Population That Is Christian
United States	246,780,000	79.5%
Brazil	175,770,000	90.2
Mexico	107,780,000	95.0
Russia	105,220,000	73.6
Philippines	86,790,000	93.1
Nigeria	80,510,000	50.8
China[1]	67,070,000	5.0
DR Congo	63,150,000	95.7
Germany	58,240,000	70.8
Ethiopia	52,580,000	63.4

Figure 2.6 Ten countries with the largest number of Christians[17]
[1] This is a conservative estimate. The actual number is likely higher.

	Estimated 2010 Orthodox Population	Percentage of Population That Is Orthodox
Russia	101,450,000	71.0%
Ethiopia	36,060,000	43.5
Ukraine	34,850,000	76.7
Romania	18,750,000	87.3
Greece	10,030,000	88.3
Serbia	6,730,000	86.6
Bulgaria	6,220,000	83.0
Belarus	5,900,000	61.5
Egypt	3,860,000	4.8
Georgia	3,820,000	87.8

Figure 2.7 Ten countries with the largest number of Orthodox Christians

[17] The following four tables are based on data from "Global Christianity: A Report on the Size and Distribution of the World's Christian Population," The Pew Forum on Religion and Public Life" (December 19, 2011), Pew Research Center, Washington, DC, www.pewforum.org [accessed January 28, 2013].

	Estimated 2010 Catholic Population	Percentage of Population That Is Catholic
Brazil	133,660,000	68.6%
Mexico	96,330,000	84.9
Philippines	75,940,000	81.4
United States	74,470,000	24.0
Italy	50,250,000	83.0
Colombia	38,100,000	82.3
France	37,930,000	60.4
Poland	35,290,000	92.4
Spain	34,670,000	75.2
DR Congo	31,180,000	47.3

Figure 2.8 Ten countries with the largest number of Roman Catholic Christians

	Estimated 2010 Protestant Population	Percentage of Population That Is Protestant
United States	159,850,000	51.5%
Nigeria	59,680,000	37.7
China[1]	58,040,000	4.3
Brazil	40,500,000	20.8
South Africa	36,550,000	72.9
United Kingdom	33,820,000	54.5
DR Congo	31,700,000	48.1
Germany	28,640,000	34.8
Kenya	24,160,000	59.6
India	18,860,000	1.5

[1] This is a conservative estimate. The actual number of Protestants in China is likely higher.

Figure 2.9 Ten countries with the largest number of Protestant Christians

denominations there are divisions between those who are more politically liberal and those who are more conservative.[18]

The following pie chart, based on recent data from the Pew Research Center and the Gallup polling organization, shows the breakdown of all the major religious groups in the United States:

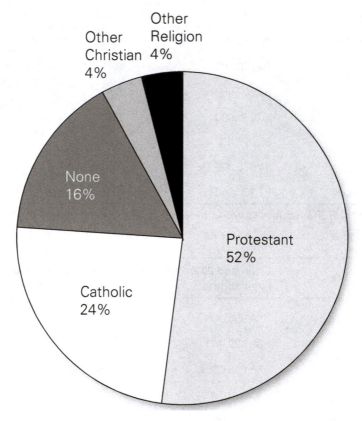

Figure 2.10 Size of religious groups in the U.S.

According to data collected for the 2011 *Yearbook of American and Canadian Churches*, the nine largest Protestant denominations or church groups in the United States are the following:[19]

---

[18] See especially, Robert Wuthnow, *The Re-structuring of American Religion* (Princeton: Princeton University Press, 1990). More recently, Wuthnow's basic conclusions have been further verified by Robert D. Putnam and David E. Campbell, *American Grace: How Religion Divides and Unites Us* (New York: Simon and Schuster, 2010).

[19] Eileen W. Lindner, ed., *2011 Yearbook of American and Canadian Churches* (Nashville: Abingdon,

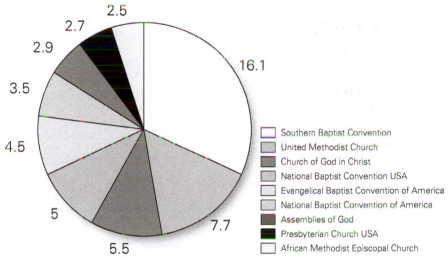

Figure 2.11 Largest Protestant groups in the U.S. (millions)

- Southern Baptist Convention
- United Methodist Church
- Church of God in Christ
- National Baptist Convention USA
- Evangelical Baptist Convention of America
- National Baptist Convention of America
- Assemblies of God
- Presbyterian Church USA
- African Methodist Episcopal Church

A recent survey by the Gallup Organization indicates that about 40 percent of Americans say they attend religious services at least once a week, or almost weekly. This percentage has remained relatively constant over the past five decades, despite the ongoing decline in denominational loyalty that has occurred since the end of the Second World War.[20] Only 15 percent say they never attend religious services. While a higher number of Americans today refuse to give a religious identity when asked than was the case 50 years ago, slightly more than nine out of ten continue to answer "yes" when asked, "Do you believe in God?" Even with the rise of the "nones" (those who say they have no religion), Americans, especially American women, remain remarkably religious. Frank Newport's analysis of the Gallup data suggests that this high level of religiosity will likely continue for the foreseeable future.[21]

2011), 12. Not included in the above chart is the Church of Jesus Christ of Latter-Day Saints (6 million adherents).

[20] Frank Newport, *God is Alive and Well: The Future of Religion in America* (Berkeley: Gallup, Inc., 2012), 11.

[21] Newport, *God is Alive and Well*, 70, 196, 234–5, 237–44.

Key Words

tradition	heretic
Judaism	schism
Jesus of Nazareth	Martin Luther
Before Christ (BC)	John Calvin
Anno Domini (AD)	Henry VIII
Messiah	sacraments
Christ	Baptism
Christian	Lord's Supper
New Testament	The Eucharist
Old Testament	Protestant
Hebrew Bible	evangelical
King David	gospel
synoptic gospels	Evangelical-Lutheran Church
apostles	Reformed Church
bishop/elder	Anglican Church
pastor/deacon	denominations
pope/Catholic	John Hus
Roman Catholic Church	Methodist Church
patriarch	John Wesley
Orthodox Church	presbyter
Eastern Orthodoxy	non-denominational churches
Ecumenical Councils	Baptist Church
ecumenical	Protestant Evangelicalism
creed	Dispensational churches
heresy	Holiness-Pentecostal churches

Reference literature

For a general orientation to traditions of Christianity

ABD 1:925–6 ("Christian" [Wilkins]); ABD 1:926–79 ("Christianity" [White et al.]); EC 5:517–19 ("Tradition" [Gassmann]); ER 3:1660–741 ("Christianity" [Pelikan et al.]); ER 13:9267–81 ("Tradition" [Valliere]); ODCC 336 ("Christian"); ODCC 1646–7 ("Tradition"); RPP 2:570–606 ("Christianity" [Stolz et al.]); RPP 13:41–50 ("Tradition" [Baumann et al.]).

For a general orientation to Jesus of Nazareth

ABD 1:914–21 ("Christ" [de Jonge]); ABD 3:773–820 ("Jesus" [Meyer et al.]); EC 3:24–8 ("Jesus" [Holtz]); ER 7:4843–52 ("Jesus" [Allison]); ODCC 335 ("Christ"); ODCC 877–80 ("Jesus Christ"); RPP 2:549–60 ("Christ" [Stock, Frenschkowski]); RPP 6:698–723 ("Jesus Christ" [Roloff et al.]).

For introductions to specific traditions of Christianity

EC 3:860–6 ("Orthodox Christianity" [Meyendorff]); EC 3:866–72 ("Orthodox Church" [Kallis]); EC 4:713–23 ("Roman Catholic Church" [Kennedy]); EC 4:394–9 ("Protestantism" [Raiser]); ER 4:2286–91 ("Denominationalism" [Hudson]); ER 4:2580–95 ("Eastern Christianity" [FitzGerald]); ER 11:7446–59 ("Protestantism" [Marty]); ER 11:7656–65 ("Reformation" [Hillerbrand]); ER 12:7873–92 ("Roman Catholicism" [McBrien, Schuck]); ODCC 1205–6 ("Orthodox Church"); ODCC 1347–9 ("Protestantism"); ODCC 1418–19 ("Roman Catholicism"); RPP 2:442–50 ("Catholicism" [Beinert et al.]); RPP 7:676–83 ("Lutheranism" [Schubert et al.]); RPP 9:393–404 ("Orthodox Churches" [Hauptmann et al.]); RPP 9:404–13 ("Orthodoxy I: Terminology" and "Orthodoxy II: Christianity" [Slenczka et al.]); RPP 10:461–70 ("Protestantism" [Wallmann et al.]); RPP 10:700–9 ("Reformation" [Köpf]); RPP 10:710–21 ("Reformed Churches" [Busch et al.]).

Questions for review and discussion

1 How have MacIntyre and Gadamer defined "tradition"? Why are many traditions contested? Which religious tradition(s) has or have most influenced you? What roles do community and ritual play in the preservation and transmission of tradition?

2 Based on your understanding of Christianity, what are some Christian traditions that have changed over time? Which traditions have remained central?

3 What is a "Christ"? Who invented the term "Christian"?

4 Roughly when was Jesus of Nazareth born? Why do scholars think Jesus was born before 4 BC? Roughly when did he die? Do you find it problematic that we do not know for sure when Jesus was born or when he died?

5   What were the five main centers of early Christianity? Which city became the center of western Christianity? Which city became the center of eastern Christianity?

6   What was one theological factor that led to schism between eastern Orthodoxy and western Catholicism?

7   What were two reasons most Protestants were critical of the Roman Catholic Church in the sixteenth century?

8   Approximately how many different Christian church groups are in the world today? Do you think this large number of differing groups is a problem or weakness to the presence of Christianity in the world today or do you think it is a strength?

9   Which Christian groups are the largest ones today in the United States? Which countries today have the largest Christian populations?

10   Where is Christianity growing the fastest? Why do you think it is growing fastest there?

Suggestions for further reading

Reference works on Christianity

General

David Barrett et al. (eds), *World Christian Encyclopedia*, 2nd edn, 2 vols (New York: Oxford University Press, 2001) [This interesting resource provides a comparative survey of churches and Christian groups in the world.]

F. L. Cross and E. A. Livingstone (eds), *The Oxford Dictionary of the Christian Church*, 3rd rev. edn (Oxford: Oxford University Press, 2005) [The standard one-volume dictionary of Christianity. Helpful bibliographies accompany each entry.]

Erwin Fahlbusch et al. (eds), *The Encyclopedia of Christianity*, 5 vols, trans. Geoffrey W. Bromiley (Grand Rapids: Eerdmans, 1998–2008). [This is an English translation of the third edition of *Evangelisches Kirchenlexikon*. It provides useful entries on all aspects of the Christian tradition.]

More specialized

Everette Ferguson, ed., *Encyclopedia of Early Christianity* (New York: Garland, 1990)

Hans Hillerbrand, ed., *Oxford Encyclopedia of the Reformation*, 4 vols (New

York: Oxford University Press, 1996) [Standard reference work for
Reformation studies.]

Daniel Reid et al. (eds), *Dictionary of Christianity in America* (Downer's
Grove: InterVarsity, 1990)

Scott Sunquist, ed., *Dictionary of Asian Christianity* (Grand Rapids: Eerdmans,
2001)

Christianity among the world religions.

Robert S. Ellwood and Barbara A. McGraw, *Many Peoples, Many Faiths: Women
and Men in the World Religions*, 9th edn (Upper Saddle River, NJ: Prentice
Hall, 2008) [Standard college textbook in world religions. Provides good
overviews of the main religions and has sections on women and politics.]

Duncan S. Ferguson, *Exploring the Spirituality of the World Religions: The
Quest for Personal, Spiritual, and Social Transformation* (New York:
Continuum, 2010) [Helpful introduction to the ways in which religion and
spirituality are actually practiced.]

Theodore M. Ludwig, *The Sacred Paths: Understanding the Religions of the
World*, 4th edn (Upper Saddle River, NJ: Prentice Hall, 2005) [Another
standard university textbook. Provides an historical orientation coupled to
thematic comparisons.]

The history of Christianity

Adrian Hastings, ed., *A World History of Christianity* (Grand Rapids:
Eerdmans, 1999) [Provides a complimentary perspective on the
developments of global Christianity to earlier European-centered accounts,
such as the McManners-edited volume listed below.]

Philip Jenkins, *The Lost History of Christianity* (San Francisco: HarperOne,
2008) [An engaging and insightful, revisionist account of traditional
European-centered histories of Christianity. Jenkins stresses Christian
developments in Central Asia, India, Armenia, Ethiopia, Nubia, and
Persia.]

Diarmaid MacCulloch, *Christianity: The First Three Thousand Years* (New
York: Penguin, 2009) [The single best one-volume historical analysis of the
principal traditions of Christianity in the world. A very readable account of
very complex developments.]

John McManners, ed., *The Oxford Illustrated History of Christianity* (New
York: Oxford University Press, 1990) [Important European-centered
account of Christian origins and developments to the mid-twentieth
century.]

Jaroslav Pelikan, *The Christian Tradition: A History of the Development of Doctrine*, 5 vols (Chicago: University of Chicago Press, 1971–89) [The last great attempt at writing a synthetic overview of the development of Christian teaching from the apostles through the Second Vatican Council.]

Histories of specific Christian traditions

Thomas Bokenkotter, *A Concise History of the Catholic Church*, rev. edn (New York: Doubleday, 2004) [The best one-volume history of the Roman Catholic Church by a Roman Catholic scholar.]

Peter Brown, *The Rise of Western Christendom*, 2nd edn (New York: Wiley-Blackwell, 2003) [The single best examination of western, Latin-speaking traditions of Christianity by a leading scholar in the field.]

Diarmaid MacCulloch, *The Reformation* (New York: Penguin, 2005) [Excellent account of the historical development of Protestant complexity in the western Catholic Church in the sixteenth century.]

Martin E. Marty, *Protestantism* (New York: Doubleday, 1995) [A helpful historical overview of Protestantism in the world with special attention on the variety of teachings and rituals among the principal Protestant church groups.]

Arthur Carl Piepkorn, *Profiles in Belief*, 3 vols (New York: Harper and Row, 1977–9) [An important, if unfinished, summary of the main traditions of Christian belief. Volume 1 focuses on eastern traditions, Volume 2 on Roman Catholicism and Volume 3 on Protestantism.]

Timothy Ware, *The Orthodox Church*, rev. edn (New York: Penguin, 1993) [Informative to the traditions of Eastern Orthodoxy.]

Creeds and confessions

Robert Kolb and Timothy J. Wengert (eds), *The Book of Concord: The Confessions of the Evangelical Lutheran Church*, trans. Charles Arand et al. (Minneapolis: Fortress, 2000) [The standard collection of sixteenth-century confessional documents of the Evangelical-Lutheran Church.]

Jaroslav Pelikan, ed., *Creeds and Confessions of Faith in the Christian Tradition*, 4 vols/CD-ROM (New Haven: Yale University Press, 2003) [Standard reference work in the English language.]

Norman P. Tanner, S. J., ed., *Decrees of the Ecumenical Councils*, 2 vols (Washington, DC: Georgetown University Press, 1990) [This reference work contains the original texts and English translations of all decrees of the twenty-one councils that the Roman Catholic Church recognizes as "ecumenical" (from the first Nicene Council in AD 325 to the Second

Vatican Council, 1962–5). Only the first seven of these councils are recognized as truly "ecumenical" by the Eastern Orthodox Church and many Protestant churches.]

Sociology of Christianity

Afe Adogame et al. (eds), *Christianity in Africa and the African Diaspora: The Appropriation of a Scattered Heritage* (New York: Continuum, 2011) [Provides an extensive analysis of key issues in the rapid expansion of Christianity in Africa.]

Sidney Ahlstrom, *A Religious History of the American People*, 2nd edn (New Haven: Yale University Press, 2004) [Still the best one-volume historical survey of the history of religions in North America.]

Edwin Gaustad and Philip L. Barlow, *New Historical Atlas of Religion in America* (New York: Oxford University Press, 2001) [Major reference work for understanding the distribution of Christian traditions and populations within the United States.]

Douglas Jacobsen, *The World's Christians: Who They Are, Where They Are, and How They Got There* (Oxford: Wiley-Blackwell, 2012) [Helpful overview of where Christian populations are located in the world.]

Frank S. Mead et al., *Handbook of Denominations in the United States*, 13th edn (Nashville: Abingdon, 2010) [Standard reference work that contains statistical information on most Christian church groups and denominations in the United States.]

Robert D. Putnam and David E. Campbell, *American Grace: How Religion Divides and Unites Us* (New York: Simon and Schuster, 2010) [A very interesting sociological study of religions, especially Christianity, in contemporary America.]

3

Traditions of Christian Theology

This chapter introduces several key thinkers in the history of Christian theology by examining how they have defined the nature and task of theology. After briefly examining the origins of theology in ancient Greece, the chapter summarizes some of the ways in which Christians have described theology. The chapter gives special attention to important figures from the past century.

Now that we have some idea of the historical and spatial development of Christian traditions in the world, we can turn to look more closely at how Christians have understood the nature and task of theology. How have Christians thought about God? What do Christians think they are doing when they "do theology"? What is the best way to do Christian theology?

Before we can answer these questions, however, we need to focus some attention on ancient Greek theology and metaphysics, since Greek ways of thinking have had an influence on the origin of Christian theology. Christians were not the first to think theologically, nor have they remained unaffected by traditions of theology beyond their own circles. Because Christians have more or less always made use of non-Christian, western philosophical traditions, no description of Christian theology and its task can avoid these other traditions and their impact on Christianity. Among those traditions, none was more influential than Greek philosophy.

Ancient Greek theology

"We see with the eyes of the Greeks and use their phrases when we speak."[1] Not only did ancient, pre-Christian Greeks first use the word "theology" (*theologia*), but they were also among the first to wrestle with questions about the nature of reality as a whole, that is, with **metaphysics** (*ta meta ta physika*, literally, "the things after nature") or the knowledge that arises from reflection on "being" or nature (*physis*) itself (ODCC 1083). Their ideas about these matters affected early Christian thinkers, and they still affect people today. Greek philosophers, the first "lovers of wisdom," wondered about "the one and the many," about the origin and ground of everything, about the divine, about being, about what is good, true, and beautiful. For example, **Parmenides** (c. 515-c. 445 BC), often called the "father of western metaphysics," viewed differences in nature as illusory. He held that true reality is unchanging, invisible, indivisible, and intelligible. He was thus the first to insist on a distinction between the world as it *appears* to human beings and reality as it *really is*. His ideas seem to suggest a kind of pantheism ("God is all") in which God is identical to nature.

The Greek metaphysical tradition, which explores not only the nature of being but how human beings know what they know, also raised critical questions about received religious traditions. **Xenophanes** (c. 570–480 BC), for example, attacked those who "attributed to the gods everything that is a shame and a reproach among men," such as stealing, committing adultery, and deceiving one another (BCPR 74). He maintained that there is "one God, greatest among both gods and men," who is "in no way similar to mortals either in body or in mind... He always remains in the same place, not moving at all. Nor does it befit him to move about at different times to different places."[2]

This "critical" aspect of Greek **philosophical theology** is perhaps its most important and influential feature. **Plato** (c. 428–347 BC) thus engaged in theology (*theologia*) when he criticized the fictional, immoral stories (*muthos* = "story" or "**myth**") about the gods that he deemed inappropriate for society and contrary to the nature of the highest good.[3] Most of the

---

[1] Jacob Burckhardt, *The Greeks and Greek Civilization*, ed. Oswyn Murray, trans. Sheila Stern (New York: St. Martin's, 1998), 12.
[2] Xenophanes of Colophon, *Fragments*, trans. J. H. Lesher (Toronto: University of Toronto Press, 2001), Fragments 11, 23, 26 (translation slightly modified).
[3] Allan Jay Silverman, *The Dialectics of Essence: A Study of Plato's Metaphysics* (Princeton: Princeton University Press, 2002).

theological expressions of the poets, he thought, seemed to be false. Still, he held out the possibility that there could be true speech about "the God" (*ho theos*). This view is reflected in the words of Socrates in *The Republic*:

> But the claim that God, who is good, is the cause of evil to anyone, we must oppose in every way. We must not allow anyone to make this claim in our city, if it is to be well governed, nor should we let anyone hear it, whether that one is young or old, and whether or not the myth-maker tells his story in verse. These claims, if they are said, would not be holy or beneficial for us nor consistent with one another... This, then, said I, will be one of the laws and patterns about the gods to which speakers and poets will be required to conform, that God is not the cause of all things, but only of the good.[4]

In the tenth book of *Laws*, Plato has the Athenian Stranger defend against religious impiety, atheism (insisting that there is no god at all), and materialism.

In the *Timaeus*, Plato's one strictly cosmological dialogue, Socrates speaks about the highest good in relation to a myth about a demiurgic Craftsman who has fashioned the universe into an intelligible, mathematical order. This creation story was particularly influential among later Platonists, such as Plotinus (205–270), who referred to God as "the One beyond Being," and Proclus (c. 412–85), the last head of Plato's Academy, who was also influenced by Christian theology. This last thinker brought together elements of Platonic thought and other philosophical traditions into a single metaphysical system that he outlined in his book, *Elements of Theology*.[5] Here he tried to explain rationally the relation of "one God" to "many gods," of "one Spirit/Intellect" to "many spirits/intellects," of one "Soul" to "many souls." Sorting out these religious, metaphysical, and theological issues remains an unfinished task today.

Plato's most famous student, **Aristotle** (384–322 BC), also criticized the ancient stories (*muthoi*) about the gods that he thought were implausible:

> The school of Hesiod and all the theologians thought only of what was plausible to themselves, and had no regard for us. For, asserting the first principles to be gods and born of gods, they say that the beings which did not taste of nectar and ambrosia became mortal; and clearly they are using

---

[4] Plato, *The Republic*, Book 2, 380b, trans. Tom Griffith (slightly revised), in *Plato: The Republic*, ed. G. R. F. Ferrari, Cambridge Texts in the History of Political Thought (Cambridge: Cambridge University Press, 2000), 66.
[5] Proclus, *Elements of Theology*, trans. Thomas Taylor (Wiltshire, England: Prometheus Trust, 1994).

words which are familiar to themselves, yet what they have said about the very application of these causes does not make sense. For if the gods taste of nectar and ambrosia for their pleasure, these are in no way the causes of their existence; and if they taste them to maintain their existence, how can gods who need food be eternal? But into the subtleties of the mythologists it is not worth our while to inquire seriously...[6]

While Aristotle rejected the **anthropomorphisms** of Homer and Hesiod, that is, their depictions of the gods in human forms, and criticized other implausible elements in the ancient Greek myths, he did not reject theology altogether. In his *Metaphysics* he developed what he called "the first philosophy" or "the science of being as being" ("ontology," literally, "thinking about being"), which he also called "theology" (*theologia*). This form of thinking raises questions about the nature of being itself:

But if there is something which is eternal and immovable and separable, clearly the knowledge of it belongs to a theoretical science—not however to physics (for physics deals with certain movable things) nor to mathematics, but to a science prior to both... There must, then, be three theoretical philosophies: mathematics, physics, and what we may call theology, since it is obvious that if the divine is present anywhere, it is present in things of this sort. ...If there is no substance other than those which are formed by nature, natural science will be the first science; but if there is an immovable substance, the science of this must be prior and must be first philosophy, and universal in this way, because it is the first. And it will belong to this to consider being *qua* being [being *as* being]—both what it is and the attributes which belong to it *qua* being [*as* being].[7]

Aristotle thus furthered the view that one God is the basis for order (*cosmos*) in the universe, the "unmoved mover" who affects the world by drawing all things toward itself. In this view, God is both "an impelling force within the universe" and "an object of desire" that draws human beings beyond the universe toward God.

By the end of the second century BC in the Roman world, theology had been divided into three branches: (1) mythological theology, which maintained and interpreted the stories about the gods from ancient Greece; (2) natural theology (rational or philosophical theology), which reasoned about God or the gods on the basis of the world or universe (and was

[6] Aristotle, *Metaphysics*, Book 3, Chapter 4, 1000a9, trans. W. D. Ross (slightly revised), in *The Basic Works of Aristotle*, ed. Richard McKeon (New York: Random House, 1941), 725–6.
[7] Aristotle, *Metaphysics*, Book 6, Chapter 1, 1026a.10–33 (McKeon, 779).

often critical of the ancient myths as fictional and immoral); and (3) civil theology, which served to understand and perform the rites and ceremonies in the cult of the Caesars (and often to justify whatever political regime was ruling at the time). This three-fold way of understanding theology was first set forth by the Stoic philosopher, Panaetius of Rhodes (c. 185–110 BC). Some Christian thinkers, such as Tertullian (c. 160–c. 225) and Augustine of Hippo (354–430), later used this same three-fold distinction in their own writings.

For our purposes we need not trace the rest of the trajectory of western, Greek-based metaphysics. Suffice it to say that over the past millennium many western thinkers have taken a more and more negative position against the possibility of metaphysics and philosophical theology. In so doing they have furthered the critical aspect of *theologia* toward the ancient stories or myths and rejected the positive aspect as understood by Plato and Aristotle. Nevertheless, despite the serious criticisms that have been leveled against the possibility of philosophical theology, certain basic *metaphysical questions* that first arose with those ancient Greeks still surface today:

Is there proof or solid evidence for the existence of God?
Is there proof or solid evidence for the non-existence of God?
Are religious beliefs in general rational?
How are we to understand the ancient religious stories and myths?
How does God act within the world?
How should one understand the so-called problem of evil?
Is there life after death?

It is fascinating to note that each of the principal religious traditions in the world has had to engage these and other philosophical questions, too, both as they relate to that given religious tradition and as they overlap with other broad areas of human knowing, such as epistemology (how do we know what we know), ethics, the philosophy of language, anthropology, the human sciences, history, and the natural sciences.[8]

The long tradition of western philosophical theology, which began with the Greeks, was furthered by Christian, Jewish, and Muslim thinkers in later centuries, who examined metaphysical issues within the context of their respective religious traditions and, going beyond strictly metaphysical

---

[8] A helpful introduction to these and other metaphysical problems, as analyzed within philosophy, is the little book by Earl Conee and Theodore Sider, *Riddles of Existence: A Guided Tour of Metaphysics* (Oxford: Clarendon, 2005).

questions, asked about "the meaning and truth of ultimate reality, not only in itself but also as it relates existentially to human beings" (ER 13.9131). Many of these later thinkers defended the notion that theology is possible only because of an initiating address ("revelation") from God or ultimate reality that then gives rise to theological reflection.

Early and Medieval Christian theology

While the Greek words that form the term "theology" (*theologia*) appear in the NT (*logia tou theou*, Rom. 3.2; *logia theou*, 1 Pet. 4.11; *logion tou theou*, Heb. 5.12), the term itself does not occur. It was actually understood negatively by the earliest Christians, since it had traditionally been associated with pagan religions and philosophical criticism of the Greek myths. Thus, "*theologia*" was not favorably used by Christians to refer to what they did when they spoke or thought of God, Jesus, or the Holy Spirit. Prior to the third century, Christians described their way of thinking about God as devotion to "sacred Scripture", or "sacred knowledge", or "sacred wisdom" (inclusive of both the OT and the NT). Later, in the medieval west, Thomas Aquinas (1224/5–74) gave currency to the expression "sacred teaching" (*sacra doctrina*), which he also called "the science of God" (see Aquinas 1a.1.2–6).

The first Christian thinker to use the term "theology" favorably to describe the knowledge of God revealed in the history of ancient Israel and Jesus was likely **Clement** (c. 150–c. 215), who lived in Alexandria and later in Palestine. He spoke of the "theology of the ever-living Word" [*Logos*] that is taught by the theologian.[9] For Clement and his most important student, **Origen** (c. 185–c. 254), all of the biblical writers, especially the prophets and the apostles, were theologians who bore witness to the divine *Logos* or "Word" in Jesus. Others could also be called theologians, in a derived sense, if they believed in the divine Word, were apt to teach the mysteries of the faith to others, and were equipped by the Spirit of God to defend the truth of Christian wisdom and to refute error.

---

[9] Clement of Alexandria, *The Stromata* [Miscellanies], 1.13.57.6, in Schaff, Philip and Henry Wace (eds), *Nicene and Post-Nicene Fathers of the Christian Church*, 2nd series, 14 vols (Peabody, MA: Hendrickson, 1995), 673. See also ODCC 998.

While later Christians more than a century after his death condemned some of Origen's teachings, during his lifetime he tried to reconcile Hellenistic learning, especially the ideas of Platonism, and Christian biblical teaching. He and other eastern Greek-speaking Christians understood the God revealed in the Hebrew and Christian Scriptures to be identical to the Intelligible One who transcends the material, sensible world and who alone can be truly known. While faith in God is grounded in Scriptural authority, the individual Christian is called to love and know God above all things in this earthly life and to long for the vision of God that will be more complete in the life to come after death.

Origen wrote hundreds of Bible commentaries, sermons, and other theological works, but his greatest theological work, *On Divine Principles*, which survives only in unreliable forms, systematically examines God and heavenly beings, human beings and the material world, human freedom and its consequences in human life, and the Holy Scriptures of the OT and NT. Following a practice for reading the Bible that was developed by the Alexandrian Jewish scholar, Philo (c. 20 BC–c. AD 50), Origen recognized that biblical verses typically have three levels of meaning: (1) the literal meaning, which is the sense that the words and sentences have on the surface; (2) the moral meaning, which is the ethical teaching of the verses; and (3) the allegorical meaning, which is the spiritual and mystical meaning that leads the Christian thinker to ascend beyond the visible world to the contemplation of the divine Word who dwells eternally with God. For Origen, this latter figurative meaning is the most important. It was this "deeper," "spiritual" meaning that allowed him to fit the biblical texts more closely with truths discovered through philosophical reasoning. With Origen one has for the first time in the history of Christian doctrine a complete theological system that is linked to the reigning philosophical understandings of his day. For him, true philosophy and true theology form a single whole. For this reason, too, he coveted dialogue with Jews and non-Christian philosophers, since they also might have something to contribute to divine and human understanding.

Clement and Origen were not alone in their work of defending the truth and wisdom of Christian theology and of demonstrating its continuity with important aspects of Greek philosophy. Half a century earlier **Justin Martyr** (c. 100–c. 165), who was perhaps the most significant of the second-century "apologists," strove to defend (Greek: *apologia* = "defense") Christian teaching and practices over against those who were critical of Christianity and who persecuted Christians. Justin's *First Apology* stresses that "seeds" or elements of Christian truth can be found among the writings of non-Christian pagans who wrote long before the coming of Jesus. Whatever is true in those sources has an important continuity with Christian truth. Indeed, according to Justin, these other truths prepared the way for the fullest manifestation of truth, which has occurred in God's final revelation of the Word (*Logos*) that became incarnate in Jesus. As a theologian, Justin desired to highlight these important continuities.

But not every Christian apologist of the second century looked favorably upon Greek philosophy or secular learning. Some, like **Tertullian**, who converted to the Christian religion around AD 197, argued that the revelation of God given in the Hebrew and Christian Scriptures has nothing in common with the "god" of the Greek, pagan philosophers. For Tertullian, Christian theology is entirely a matter of faithful understanding of the sacred Scriptures and strict, moral obedience to God. It is interesting to note that Tertullian, like Origen, was also condemned as a false teacher. This occurred after he had joined a group of Christians known for their strict and rigorous morality and their concentration on new prophecies of the Holy Spirit. While Tertullian himself was a highly educated Latin rhetorician and essayist, his conservative form of theology was anti-cultural.

In the aftermath of Origen's phenomenal work, the verb *theologein* ("to theologize") was used by Greek Christians to ascribe a divine nature to the person of Jesus Christ and to think of him in relation to the divine being of God. Christian thinkers in these early centuries did not always agree with one another about how best to understand the being of God in relation to the person of Christ, or even how best to understand the Scriptural witness to the divine and human natures of Jesus Christ. For example, some theologians stressed that, because God is the creator, ground, and goal of all being, God must transcend all creaturely categories, including the category of "being." God is said to be "beyond being" and unity. Other theologians, such as Irenaeus, stressed that God's eternal identity unfolds historically though the revealing acts of God in history that culminated in the incarnation of the Word (*Logos*) and the outpouring of the Holy Spirit. According to Irenaeus, the actions of the incarnate Word transform human history itself and redeem humankind.

Despite these differences in emphasis and focus, all major Christian theologians in these early centuries wrestled with the problem of how best to understand the relationship between God's *oikonomia* ("the economy or plan of God for human salvation"), which addresses the incarnation of the Word (see Jn 1.14), the church, and the sacraments, and God's *theologia* ("the essence or nature of God" as understood by human beings), which involves metaphysical reflection upon "the account of God, or the record of God's ways, as given in the Bible" (OED 2040).[10] Later, both eastern Greek and western Latin Christians began to use the word "theology" to refer simply to the Scriptures themselves, while also maintaining the belief that the best form of theology is *prayer*, since only through prayer can God be known most fully. Not surprisingly, most Christian theologians in the first six hundred years of Christianity were actively involved in the worship and everyday life of the church as bishops.

During these early centuries of Christianity, the "correct prayer and praise" ("orthodoxy") of God led many to reflect more deeply upon the object of faith, especially when they were confronted with teaching, praying, and preaching that they considered to be false or heretical. Theological reflection also occurred when bishops had to address the problem of apostasy in times of persecution. For example, the most influential North-African bishop in the third century, **Cyprian of Carthage** (c. 200–58), wrote several theological treatises in which he defended the notion that there is only one catholic and orthodox church and that the person who purposely severs his or her ties with that church is guilty of "schism," an offense that is just as bad as heresy. In Cyprian's view, anyone who breaks away from the church can no longer receive the benefits of Christ's salvation. He thus criticized those Christian bishops who had committed apostasy ("falling away") through their renunciation of Christ and his church in a time of persecution.

While Cyprian himself seems to have recognized that a lapsed bishop could repent later of his sinful actions, receive the forgiveness of Christ, and thus be restored to his office as bishop, other Christians in North Africa at the time argued that such "traitors" (those who had "handed over" Christian Scriptures to be burned by the pagan Romans) were incapable of ever being bishops again and their sacramental actions were invalid. That controversy between the Donatists (who took the more rigorous line against the traitorous bishops) and the Catholics, as they came to be known, was not resolved until nearly a century later through the argumentation of Augustine of Hippo, who defended the notion that the validity of the sacraments depends solely on the Word and not on the moral character of the priest administering them. Even then, Donatist traditions continued to

---

[10] See also Jaroslav Pelikan, *Christianity and Classical Culture* (New Haven: Yale University Press, 1993), 329, 332.

rub against Catholic ones and members of the two groups sometimes took violent actions against each other.

Over time, some expressions of faith and interpretations of Scripture, even ones that had been popular in earlier centuries, were eventually deemed by bishops and church councils to be contrary to essential aspects of the object of faith. For example, Donatism was eventually deemed a heresy, since it made the validity of the church's sacraments depend upon the moral character of the priest and bishop rather than on the power and efficacy of the Word itself. As other heresies were condemned, more orthodox ways of understanding God and Christ took hold. For example, as we noted in the second chapter, orthodox Christians confessed the *Logos* of God to be "of the same being" as the Father, not of "like being" or "different being." Similarly, the two natures in the one person of Christ were understood to be distinct yet share a personal union. With the gradual clarification of orthodox teaching, there developed "the beginnings of a reflection on faith and in faith or, in other words, something of a theology" (ER 13.9135). The most important figures in this development of orthodoxy are usually called the principal **doctors of the church**. Among them are Athanasius (d. 373), Basil of Caesarea (d. 379), Gregory of Nazianzus (d. c. 390), Gregory of Nyssa (d. c. 394), Chrysostom (d. 407), and Cyril of Alexandria (d. 444), in the East; and Hilary (d. 367), Ambrose (d. 397), Jerome (d. 419), Augustine (d. 430), and Leo I (d. 461), in the West.[11]

While it is inaccurate to think that eastern traditions of Christian theology have been without innovation—since those traditions were indeed defined partly through novel theological formulations and by tinkering with liturgies (forms of worship) and prayers—one can state as a generalization, and without too many qualifications, that Greek, Syriac, and Ethiopian traditions have been more resistant to theological change than western theological traditions. These eastern forms of theology have tended to reject rationalization within theology in favor of mystical and monastic devotion upon the incarnation of the Word (about which eastern theologians had often disagreed), the holy Trinity, and the divinization of human beings. While the last of the most important Greek theologians, John of Damascus

---

[11] For an introduction to those who are recognized by the Roman Catholic Church to be pre-eminent theologians or "doctors of the church," see Bernard McGinn, *The Doctors of the Church: Thirty-three Men and Women Who Shaped Christianity*, 2nd edn (New York: Crossroad, 2009). Basil, his brother (Gregory of Nyssa), their sister (Macrina), who was an excellent theologian in her own right, and their friend Gregory of Nazianzus, are sometimes also called collectively "the Cappadocians," since they lived in that region of Asia Minor (Turkey).

(c. 655–c. 750), occasionally set forth creative insights into theology, he, too, merely wanted to set forth an exact reproduction of the orthodox faith as it had been handed down in the Divine Liturgy.

The most important theologian in the western catholic tradition has been **Augustine of Hippo** who, like the earliest Greek theologians, sought to reconcile the best in Platonic philosophy with the central teachings of Christianity. To be sure, Augustine came to recognize the limitations of some Platonic themes (such as the notion that if one knows "the good" one can do it) and the usefulness of secular knowledge, but he nevertheless yearned to find unity between his Christian faith and the abiding truths in Platonic philosophy and secular learning. True thinking and speaking about God, he believed, were most truthfully set forth within the Holy Scriptures as taught by the Catholic Church. Once one recognized this, one could use Platonic philosophy to articulate and defend the truths of Catholic teaching. Augustine himself did so in biblical commentaries, letters, and treatises that became standard resources for medieval theology for well over a millennium. One of his most important works to define the nature of theology is *On Christian Doctrine*, which helps the beginning student to know how best to interpret the Scriptures, to mine them for theological truths, and to communicate them faithfully and winsomely.[12]

For Augustine, theology is both *introspective*, since it leads one to discover the presence of God within one's soul, and *biblical*, since it directs the soul to contemplate the God who is revealed through the Scriptures. The goal of theology is to lead the restless individual to find his or her ultimate "rest" in God. Augustine himself wrote about his own conversion to the Catholic faith in his *Confessions*, a long prayer that recounts many experiences through which, in retrospect, God had led him back to God.[13] In Augustine's view, a theologian is called to assist other human beings in their pilgrimage back to God, to help them find their eternal satisfaction in God. The role of a bishop in this regard is to interpret Scripture rightly and learnedly for the sake of the faithful. Such a one must pay careful attention to the clarification of the ambiguities and apparent problems in the biblical texts, often by means of figurative and allegorical ("spiritual")

---

[12] Augustine, *On Christian Teaching*, trans. R. H. P. Green (New York: Oxford University Press, 2008).

[13] Augustine of Hippo, *Confessions*, trans. Henry Chadwick (New York: Oxford University Press, 1991).

interpretation, as Philo and Origin and Augustine's own bishop, Ambrose, had as well. As we will see, Augustine's focus on interiority, on God and the soul, will be a hallmark of later forms of Christian theology, both Catholic and Protestant.

During the centuries between AD 600 to the late medieval period (c. 1500), new modes of thinking and understanding reality gradually developed. In this period most Christian theologians were **monks** and **nuns** who lived in monastic communities. For them theology was primarily *contemplative* as they prayed and thought and worked—and prayed again. One of the most influential theologians in this period was **Anselm of Canterbury** (1033–1109), a monk who became an archbishop. He helped to develop this new way of doing theology, which we usually call "**scholasticism**." It is a highly intellectual, philosophical form of theology that shares important affinities with earlier Greek philosophical theology. Instead of merely quoting from Scripture or ancient Christian doctors of the church, Anselm preferred to defend the truth of Christian faith by means of intellectual reasoning "apart from Scripture." For example, he thought he could rationally demonstrate the reality of God apart from an appeal to Scriptural authority. While he understood faith to be the crucial presupposition for right thinking about God and divine matters, a position that had earlier been set forth by Augustine and others, he also thought that theology included the responsibility to use one's mind as best one could to comprehend the truths of God's revelation. Anselm thus stated, "I believe in order to understand" (*credo ut intelligam*). But it should be noted that he also maintained that our critical faculties should be used in service to that faith. Here the motto was "**faith seeking understanding**" (*fides quaerens intellectum*), an approach also consistent with that of Augustine, who devised a similar formula: "Do not seek to understand in order to believe, but believe that you may understand."[14] This same idea is expressed in the Septuagint version of the prophet Isaiah 7.9: "Unless you believe, you shall not understand." If there is a difference between Augustine's and Anselm's respective understandings of theology, it is that Anselm

---

[14] Augustine, *Tractate 29 on the Gospel according to John 7:14–18*, 6, in *Nicene and Post-Nicene Fathers of the Christian Church*, 2nd series, 14 vols, Philip Schaff and Henry Wace (eds) (Peabody, MA: Hendrickson, 1995), 7.185 (translation slightly modified). See also Augustine *Sermon 43.7, 9* in *Patrologia Latina*, 221 vols, ed. J. P. Migne (Paris, 1844–64), 38.257–8, where he uses the Latin formula, *Intelligere ut credas meum verbum; crede ut intelligas verbum Dei* ("understand my word, in order to believe; believe the word of God in order to understand"). This is often shortened to: "understand that you may believe, believe that you may understand."

thought human reason itself to be fully capable of discovering on its own the rational coherence of the truth of the faith, apart from any appeal to divine revelation or the Scriptures, "as though we knew nothing of Christ." Augustine, on the other hand, stressed the mutual interaction of faith and understanding in the interpretation of the Scriptures for the sake of true knowledge of God.

Another medieval monk, **Peter Abelard** (1079–1142/3), understood theology in a way similar to Anselm, that is, as an orderly discipline of critical reflection on the revealed truths of the Christian faith. He hoped that by questioning the content of that faith he could set forth for himself and others a deeper and more complete understanding of it. One immediately detects here continuity with the ancient Greek practice of criticizing the traditional "myths" in search of philosophical truth, but also continuity with Origen's practice of looking for deeper, spiritual truths beneath the literal statements in the Bible. Abelard was particularly concerned to resolve the apparent contradictions in sacred Scripture and the doctrinal traditions of the western Christian church. To do this he developed a dialectical approach of "yes" and "no" (*sic et non*) that affirmed and negated these seemingly contradictory statements in order to bring about a more satisfactory intellectual resolution.

Yet another form of theology that developed in this medieval period resulted from reflection on mystical experience. Both men and women engaged in such mystical theology. We'll focus here on only two mystics, both of them women: **Hildegard of Bingen** (1098–1179) and **Julian of Norwich** (c. 1342–c. 1416). Hildegard was an **abbess** (female head of a monastery) who claimed to have received spiritual revelations from God that she then interpreted as instructions from the Spirit to know "the ways of God." Her devotion to spiritual singing led her to use music as a way of conveying theological truth and wisdom. Much of her writing, like that of other medieval mystics, is metaphorical and highly symbolic. Julian of Norwich, who was an English **anchorite** (she lived her later life almost entirely secluded in a small hut), wrote about the revelations or "showings" of Christ that she received while she was gravely ill and on the point of death. These visions and her reflections upon them led her to a profound understanding of the nature of Christ's incarnation as the manifestation of God's love for the world. This understanding led her to speak of God and Christ in feminine terms, for example, of Christ as "loving Mother," who nourishes her child, the church. Her understanding of Christ contrasted with the masculine and martial images of God that male theologians typically used at the time. Both Hildegard and Julian remind us of the imaginative, creative, and emotional aspects of Christian theology. Their work and that of other women in the Christian tradition raise the question as to whether women "do theology" differently from men.

Before he himself received a mystical vision that apparently led him to quit writing theology altogether, **Thomas Aquinas** brought the scholastic form of theology to its pinnacle. For him, theology or "sacred teaching" is about God and everything else in relation to God. "In sacred doctrine all things are treated under the aspect of God, either because they are God himself, or because they are ordered to God as their beginning and end. Hence it follows that God is truly the subject of this science" (Aquinas 1a.1.7). While Christian theology indeed treats all things "under the aspect of God," it "does not treat of God and creatures equally, but of God primarily; and of creatures only so far as they refer to God as their beginning or end" (Aquinas 1a.1.3). In contrast to other scholarly disciplines, whose sole basis is human reasoning, Christian theology proceeds on the basis of "principles made known by the light of a higher science, namely, the science of God and the blessed" (Aquinas 1a.1.2). In other words, God's own self-revelation is the starting point of sacred science, which for Thomas included what today is narrowly meant by "Christian doctrine" as well as all other learning. Thus, in a way different from all other scholarly disciplines that do not study things in relation to God as their beginning and end, sacred science studies the light which God's self-revelation sheds on all created things in their relation to God as their origin and goal. The purpose of such study is to make human beings "wise unto salvation" (2 Tim. 3.15 [RSV]), whereas all other scholarly disciplines tend to focus merely on knowledge of, and for, this world. While divine *revelation* provides the starting point of Christian theology, Aquinas thought that the theologian is able to use his or her God-given *reason* to seek insight and rigorous argumentation to disclose the unity and truth of sacred doctrine. For him, the revealed truths of God, properly understood, are fully consistent with truths that can be discovered by human reasoning. In his brilliant reconciliation of the perennial tension between revelation and reason, he made extensive use of Aristotelian principles to explicate and defend the various teachings within sacred doctrine. Thus, he agreed that while the truths of the faith, including the reality of God, cannot be "proved" by reason, they can be shown to be consistent with matters proved by reason. This scholastic form of academic theology became firmly established in medieval universities, and it persisted well into the Reformation era. Many Catholic theologians today continue to seek to articulate a kind of Thomistic synthesis between faith and philosophy.[15]

Reformation and post-Reformation theology

Martin Luther (1483–1546), who had been trained as an Augustinian monk and scholar in this broad tradition of scholastic theology (though he seems not to have studied Aquinas' theology to any great depth), underwent a serious personal crisis of faith which led him eventually to reformulate the nature and basis of theology. He sharply criticized the use of Aristotle's philosophy or any other form of human reasoning in the discipline of theology. He thought philosophy easily led theologians down a wrong path when it came to understanding God. A true theologian takes his or her cues solely from God's Scriptural word of promise about Christ, the crucified and risen Savior. Such a word, Luther held, can only be received by faith (which he understood primarily as "trust"). Either one trusts the promise of forgiveness through Christ or one doesn't. While Luther, too, held that "every Christian is a theologian" (WA 41.11), academic theology is oriented toward Scripture alone in service to faith alone to bring praise and honor to Christ alone. Such theology occurs not merely in the classroom, where Luther excelled as a university professor of the Bible, but in the weal and woe of a human life that is lived always "before God," through prayer, the liturgy of the church, meditation on Scripture, one's secular vocation in life, through spiritual crisis, doubt, suffering, and the awareness of death. All of these experiences "make the theologian," in Luther's view. "It is by living, no—more—by dying and being damned to hell that one becomes a theologian, not by knowing, reading, or speculating" (WA 5.163.28). His own conflict-ridden life testifies to the crucible in which "the theologian of the cross" studies Scripture so as to teach and preach the good news about Christ crucified that alone can lead the sinner to trust in Christ for

---

[15] Thomas was not the only medieval theologian to use Aristotle's philosophy as a handmaid to theology. The Persian philosopher Avicenna (980–1037) and the Spanish thinker Averroes (1126–98) also used Aristotle's philosophy to articulate their respective understandings of truth, given by divine revelation to the Prophet Mohammed (c. 570–c. 632). Similarly, Maimonides (1135–1204), a Spanish-Jewish rabbi, attempted to reconcile Aristotle's metaphysics with the teachings of Judaism.

salvation. Like Augustine, Luther, too, wanted to assist fellow pilgrims in their faith before God.

While Luther engaged theology in a wide variety of contexts and genres (sermons, polemical treatises, catechisms, letters), the majority of his theological writings are commentaries on biblical books in which he endeavored to illuminate God's word of graceful promise in distinction from God's word of judgment against sinners. He not only used all of the available scholarly methods and resources for the formal study of Scripture but held that the goal of such study, even in the university classroom, is always the cultivation of faith. The theologian's chief task is to minister the word of promise to troubled souls like one's own.

Luther thus emphasized that Christian theology is about both God *and* human beings. According to him, Psalm 51 teaches "the unique object of theology is the human being who is lost and condemned in his sins and God as the God who justifies and rescues the sinner" (WA 40/2.327, 11ff.). Here Luther shows his continuity with older definitions, which also insisted that theology is about God, but he stressed that the discipline cannot speculate about how God is "in God," who remains hidden from human beings and ultimately unknowable by them. For Luther, one can think of God only on the basis of how God gives God to be known in relation to human beings. This knowledge of God comes through God's address to human beings in the divine law and the gospel about Christ. This two-fold address of law and gospel forms the essential content of Luther's theology.

John Calvin (1509–64), the other great Protestant reformer, also thought that theology is about both God and human beings: "Nearly all the wisdom we possess, that is to say, true and sound wisdom, consists in two parts: the knowledge of God and of ourselves" (Calvin 1.1.1). For Calvin these two parts form an indivisible whole, since the knowledge of God and one's self-knowledge are interrelated and depend upon each other: "Without knowledge of self, there is no knowledge of God; . . .without knowledge of God, there is no knowledge of self" (ibid.). Such a view goes back at least to Augustine, who said that theology consists of "a knowledge of God and of ourselves." He supposedly prayed daily, "O Lord, allow me to know you and myself." That is a prayer that Calvin could have prayed as well. He, too, desired to know nothing but God and his own soul.

Since the days of Luther and Calvin most Christian theologians have been university professors. Luther's colleague at the University of Wittenberg, **Philip Melanchthon** (1497–1560), wrote the first topical exposition of the Christian faith that reflected the new "evangelical" teaching.[16] Unlike Luther, who tended not to use philosophical categories and methods to explicate Christian doctrine, Melanchthon made frequent use of Aristotle and the writings of humanist scholars to articulate and defend Scriptural teaching on the various theological topics (*Loci*). His way of doing theology harkens back to Aquinas. Nevertheless, Melanchthon agreed with Luther's view that the gospel is distinct from philosophy, which he defined as "the teaching of human reason." "The Gospel is not a philosophy or a law, but it is the forgiveness of sins and the promise of reconciliation and eternal life for the sake of Christ, and human reason by itself cannot apprehend any of these things."[17] Theology, properly speaking, is all about the gospel.

But Melanchthon also acknowledged that theologians do have some knowledge of God apart from that gospel. Other Evangelical (Lutheran) and Reformed (Calvinist) theologians have agreed. Melanchthon thus maintained the medieval distinction between "natural theology," which comes from what human beings can know of God on the basis of their reasoning and experience, and "revealed theology," the knowledge of God that comes from Holy Scripture (Schmid 17; see also Heppe 1–11). In the words of Melanchthon:

> [All human beings] by nature know that there is an eternal omnipotent being, full of wisdom, goodness, and righteousness, that created and preserves all creatures, and also, by natural understanding, that this same omnipotent, wise, good, and just Lord is called God. Many wise people, therefore, such as Socrates, Xenophon, Plato, Aristotle, and Cicero, have said that there is such an almighty, wise, good, just God, and that we must serve this one Lord in obedience to the light that he has built into our nature concerning the distinction between virtue and vice. (Melanchthon 5)

While the "innate" knowledge of God through human reason and conscience does not mean that finite human beings have perfect knowledge of the nature and essence of God—the infinite majesty of God alone refutes such a notion (see Isa. 40.28)—the knowledge they do have is sufficient to provide them with the consciousness of God's reality and the need to worship

---

[16] Philip Melancthon, *Loci Communes* (1521), ed. and trans. Charles Leander Hill (Boston: Meador, 1944). Quotations here from Melanchthon's *Loci*, however, are from the 1555 edn, ed. and trans. Clyde Manschreck (New York: Oxford University Press, 1965). In this context "evangelical" means "oriented to the good news about Jesus."

[17] Philip Melanchthon, "On the Distinction between the Gospel and Philosophy," *Philip Melanchthon: Orations on Philosophy and Education*, ed. Sachiko Kusukawa, trans. Christine F. Salazar, Cambridge Texts in the History of Philosophy (Cambridge: Cambridge University Press, 1999), 24.

God, although not with the knowledge of who God is or how God is to be worshipped rightly. Although human beings have within their minds, "and indeed by natural instinct, an awareness of divinity" (Calvin 1.3.1; altered), and although they know that God is to be honored, worshipped, and obeyed, this natural knowledge of God is insufficient since human beings "do not find peace in this natural understanding, as one can see, for all wise people have grave doubts about whether God wants to help" them, "and in all times many gods are invented" (Melanchthon 6). Such natural understanding of God speaks only of divine law, the uncertainty about God's intentions toward human beings, and about God's judgment. It does not speak of God on the basis of God's specific revelation of grace and mercy through Jesus Christ.

Despite their disagreements about other matters, Lutheran and Reformed theologians in this post-Reformation period were united in stressing that theology is not "mere outward knowledge, by which the understanding alone is enriched," but an "eminently practical wisdom" about "God and divine matters." The purpose of theology is to teach sinful human beings what they need to know and do from Holy Scripture "in order to attain true faith in Christ and holiness of life" (Schmid 15; see also Heppe 3). The seventeenth-century Lutheran theologian **Johann Gerhard** (1582–1637) captures this focus in a classic and representative definition:

> Theology... is a divinely given discipline, bestowed upon human beings by the Holy Spirit through the Word, whereby they are not only instructed in the knowledge of the divine mysteries, by the illumination of their minds, so that what they understand produces a salutary effect upon the disposition of their hearts and the actions of their lives, but so that they are also qualified to inform others concerning these divine mysteries and the way of salvation, and to vindicate heavenly truth from the aspersions of its foes; so that human beings, abounding in true faith and good works, are led to the kingdom of heaven. (Schmid 18)

This definition clearly reflects a position similar to Aquinas, since Gerhard also defined theology on the basis of its unique object, and he made use of Aristotelian philosophy to explicate its content. For Gerhard Christian theology "deals with God the creator, redeemer, and sanctifier. It continually occupies itself with God and teaches how everything has its basis in him, how everything has received its origin from him and how everything finds its goal in him, in order finally to rest in him" (Gerhard 1: Preface, §29). Gerhard even favorably quoted Aquinas: "Theology is taught by

God, it teaches God, and it leads to God" (Gerhard 1: §2). Nevertheless, Gerhard also emphasized that theology is "practical instruction" which teaches human beings about "true faith and pious living for eternal life" (Gerhard 1: Preface, §§28, 31). Once again we hear echoes of Augustine: the object of theology includes "the human being" who is "to be led to eternal blessedness" (ibid., §28). Gerhard's approach to theology thus focuses upon "the created and corrupted nature" of human beings and "the means that lead to the goal of theology, namely, the restoration and salvation" of human beings. "These means are the true and salutary knowledge of God, true faith in Christ, and whatever else serves these means" (ibid.).

Christian theology in the Enlightenment and post-Enlightenment periods

While Gerhard and several other Protestant theologians of the seventeenth and eighteenth centuries utilized Aristotelian philosophy to articulate the content of Christian doctrine, so-called **Pietist theologians** understood theology to be mostly a matter of the "regenerated heart" of the Christian. They emphasized the practical, experiential aspect of theology and were generally critical of "theoretical" academic theology that was seemingly uninterested in matters of "practical theology" and the Christian moral life. Such a view of theology has come over into American circles of Christianity influenced by Puritan traditions of Reformed theology (e.g. American Evangelicalism).

Toward the end of the seventeenth century some individuals who had been raised as Lutheran Pietists developed once again a more rational, critical approach to religion in general and to Christian theology in particular. A good illustration of this approach appears in the work of **Johann Semler** (1725–91), also a university professor. He was totally uninterested in the liturgical and spiritual life of the church and focused almost all his attention on historical and philological problems in the development of doctrine in Christianity. He was among the first to use critical-historical tools for studying the Bible like any other ancient text. As did many others of his day and later, he more or less bracketed out of his research any actual reference to the object of Christian faith. He demonstrated that the Bible is a set of primitive religious writings that had been written by different human beings and that contained as many problems and errors as just about any other ancient, human text. With the emergence of critical tools for biblical study, scholars tended to reject the supernatural, miraculous elements within the Bible and to restate the content of Christian faith exclusively in rational and moral terms.

A further classic example of this rationalist way of understanding theology appears in the writings of **Immanuel Kant** (1724–1804). His book, *Religion within the Limits of Reason Alone*, largely reduced the content of Christianity to a matter of moral teaching.[18] Kant put sharp limits on human knowledge, wherein all knowledge arises from a synthesis of sense, experience of reality and the mind's own ability to shape that experience into the form in which all experiences are received and understood. A major outcome of Kant's metaphysics—which also included strong criticism of traditional arguments for the reality of God as understood in western philosophical theology—was his rejection of the possibility of establishing any metaphysical truths. He thus prevented human access to ultimate reality as an object of knowledge, although he did "posit" God, freedom, and immortality as postulates of "practical," moral reason, that is, as necessary for the conduct of one's life in this evil world.

In America, **Jonathan Edwards** (1703–58) renewed the Calvinist tradition and sparked a great revival ("The Great Awakening" in the 1730s and 1740s) about what he called "the great things of the eternal world." He opposed vanity, defended the vitality of religious experience, and shepherded people who came in droves to hear him preach. While some American high-school students might recall having read his most famous sermon, "Sinners in the Hands of an Angry God," Edwards' Puritan theology is about more than God's damnation, hell-fire, and brimstone. His theological perspective was one that brought together both an intellectual, even philosophical, accounting of Christian truth and what he called "the Christian affections" (which was the title of one of his more popular books). Like the medieval mystics mentioned above, Edwards, too, wanted people to strive for a life of holiness. With some justification he has been called "America's greatest theologian."[19]

Friedrich Schleiermacher (1768–1834), a theologian from the same Calvinist tradition as Edwards, had been a Pietist as a young boy but then

[18] Immanuel Kant, *Religion within the Limits of Reason Alone*, trans. Theodore M. Greene and Hoyt H. Hudson (New York: Harper and Row, 1960).
[19] See Robert Jenson, *America's Theologian: A Recommendation of Jonathan Edwards* (New York: Oxford University Press, 1992).

as a university student came under the influence of Kant's moral theology and his critique of metaphysics. We know from letters to his father that he went through a crisis of faith in the university. Later he broke away from the rationalist approach to Christianity and defined theology as reflection on a given sense or feeling of the Infinite or, more broadly, as reflection on various states of religious self-consciousness. He sometimes defined this as a feeling of absolute dependence upon God. This religious sense or feeling is both prior to and distinct from human knowing and moral action. According to Schleiermacher, theology is not metaphysics or science. It is not ethics or morality, nor is it grounded any longer in a divinely inspired, inerrant Bible. Instead, Christian theology is reflection on religious feeling or states of consciousness, as these are shaped and modified within a given, particular, historical church community. In other words, Christian theology critically describes "a way of believing" that is common to a Christian community. In Schleiermacher's view, the primary purpose of academic theology is to prepare leaders for their practical tasks as teachers and preachers in these specific church communities.

Schleiermacher's re-visioning of Christian theology as an academic discipline is so important that we should look at his position more closely. Because theology is partly dependent upon non-theological academic disciplines, a question arose in the late eighteenth century regarding its place within higher education. Does it really belong within a European university? Wanting still to be a full participant within German and American universities, Christian theology found itself nevertheless constantly giving way to those who studied it non-theologically, that is, who studied it historically, psychologically, and sociologically. The question of its properly theological character, including the issue of its truthfulness, was either bracketed out or deemed unimportant. In this way theology became more and more marginalized in the university in relation to the natural, social, and human sciences.[20]

When Schleiermacher helped to found the University of Berlin in 1810, he argued for the inclusion of theology as an academic discipline. For him theology was necessary to the mission of a German university since it educated and equipped future Protestant ministers with a scholarly understanding of Christianity. Only in this way would they be properly outfitted for public service in the Prussian (German) Protestant Church. Such a scholarly

---

[20] For the history of this marginalization, see Thomas Albert Howard, *Protestant Theology and the Making of the Modern German University* (New York: Oxford University Press, 2006).

understanding of Christianity is the result of the critical investigation of its historic sources and norms. For Schleiermacher, theology is "a positive scholarly discipline [*Wissenschaft*]" (SBO §1) because it gathers together the knowledge that is "requisite for carrying out a practical task" (ibid.), that is, for preaching, teaching, engaging in ethics, caring for individuals, and leading Christian communities.[21] "Christian theology, accordingly, is that assemblage of scholarly knowledge and practical instruction without the possession and application of which a united leadership of the Christian Church, that is, a government of the Church in the fullest sense, is not possible" (SBO §5, translation slightly modified).

Later, when he wrote his dogmatics, Schleiermacher defined theology more concretely in terms of the content of Christian faith. In this way he turned more directly toward the object of theology and somewhat away from its practical goal. In his later years he stressed that the content of theology could not be "God as God is *in se*" (how God is "in God") but only statements that the believing Christian could assert about his or her faith in God. For this reason, Schleiermacher's dogmatics has been called a "*Glaubenslehre*," that is, a "teaching about faith." Instead of focusing on the transcendent God and God's self-revelation, the concern of the theologian is the way in which specific religious people *believe* within their religious communities of faith. Christian theology explicates the pious self-consciousness of contemporary believing Christians in relation to the historical investigation of the development of Christian theological understanding for the sake of the present practical needs of Christian leaders and the communities they serve. "Christian doctrines are accounts of the pious Christian affections set forth in speech" (SCF §15). The self-consciousness of faith, not God's self-revelation as attested to in Scripture, marks the starting-point of Schleiermacher's theological project. It is an essential aspect of the broad nineteenth-century liberal Protestant tradition that he helped to inaugurate.

Georg Hegel (1770–1831), a German-Lutheran philosopher and contemporary of Schleiermacher, rejected the latter's understanding of theology and his call for the peaceful independence of religion from the sciences. He thought that Christianity represents the highest form of religion and contains within its doctrinal traditions the symbols which, if properly understood and philosophically explicated, bear the deepest universal truth.

---

[21] In this context the German term "*Wissenschaft*" has a broader meaning than merely "empirical science." It refers to "scholarly discipline" or "scholarship."

"The goal of philosophy is the cognition of the truth—the cognition of God because he is the absolute truth. In that context nothing else is worth troubling about compared with God and his explication" (Hegel 3.246). By explicating "the rational content in the Christian religion" and showing "that the witness of the Spirit, the truth in the most all-embracing sense of the term, is deposited in religion," he hoped to reconcile "reason with religion in its manifold forms" and "to rediscover truth and the idea in the revelatory religion" (Hegel 3.247). Hegel thus endeavored to uncover the kernel of philosophical truth in the historical development of the religions of the world. In a way, he was doing what Plato and Aristotle had done to criticize the Greek myths and to uncover the philosophical truths that they contained. Just as all religions and specifically Christianity contain the genuine content of philosophical truth, so Hegel thought the philosophy of religion must necessarily change the form of religious symbols and teachings into a more adequate, rational form. His system of philosophy, borrowing heavily from the Christian tradition, is among the grandest of human efforts to express the fundamental unity of apparent paradoxes and contradictions in life and thought, religion and philosophy, God and world. Still, it was just a matter of time before some of Hegel's students, notably Feuerbach and Marx, turned their teacher's theological philosophy on its head and transformed it into philosophical atheism and materialism. Nevertheless, the abiding significance of Hegel's philosophy is to raise continually the question of truth in religious studies and Christian theology. That concern shows his continuity with ancient Greek philosophers.

The last century of Christian theology

The liberal tradition of Protestant theology, that began with Kant, Schleiermacher, and Hegel, came to an end with the First World War (1914–18) and the cultural crisis that it unleashed in Europe. Already, as a parish pastor and then later as a professor in Germany and Switzerland, the Reformed theologian **Karl Barth** (1886–1968) rejected central aspects of that liberal tradition in which he had been educated. The new theological movement that he and a few others established is best described by the label **"dialectical theology"**—rather than "neo-orthodoxy," a label many also give it—because it wants to affirm and deny certain theological statements on the basis of the qualitative difference between God and creation. Barth explicitly rejected Schleiermacher's understanding of theology, especially the view that it concerned the devout self-consciousness and religious experience of the believer. Barth wanted to return theology to what he considered its proper grounding in the self-revelation of God. According to Barth and his followers, theology is not about the self-description of the Christian's religious affections or devout self-consciousness, nor is it about "the Christian faith" as a human way of believing; it is solely about the word of God, the address of God, which the theologian is merely to speak faithfully again and again in the present situation. For Barth, theology begins and ends with the self-giving of God in God's own revelation in Jesus Christ as the living Word of God, to which the biblical writings attest:

> Theology is one among those human undertakings traditionally described as "scholarly disciplines" [*Wissenschaften*]. Not only the natural sciences [*Naturwissenschaften*] are "scholarly disciplines." Humanistic disciplines [*Geisteswissenschaften*] also seek to apprehend a specific *object* and its environment in the manner *directed* by the phenomenon itself; they seek to understand it on its own terms and to speak of it along with all the implications of its *existence*. The word "theology" seems to signify a special scholarly discipline, a very special discipline, whose task is to apprehend, understand, and speak of "God." . . . Such theology intends to apprehend, to understand, and to speak of the God of the gospel, in the midst of the variety of all other theologies and (without any value-judgment being implied) in distinction from them. This is the God who reveals himself in the gospel, who himself speaks to men and acts among and upon them. Wherever he becomes the object of human scholarship, both its source and its norm, there is *evangelical* theology.[22]

Such a theology is, however, also guided by what the theologian discovers in the local newspaper, since the theologian/preacher needs to discern "the signs of the times" in order to understand how the word of God needs to be proclaimed faithfully in that set of circumstances. Barth once said that a Christian preacher steps into the pulpit with the Bible in one hand and the newspaper in the other!

In that situation, Barth argued, theologians and preachers need to resist the adaptation of Christian theology to modern, western, scientific culture. Like Tertullian before him, Barth asserted that Christian theology is about

---

[22] Karl Barth, *Evangelical Theology: An Introduction*, trans. Grover Foley (Grand Rapids: Eerdmans, 1979), 3 (translation slightly modified).

the triune God who is revealed in the person of Jesus Christ through "the strange new world of the Bible."[23] Christian theology is not about human beings, their religious experience, or their religious ideas. It certainly is not about human optimism, technological achievement, and so-called "advances" in western civilization. The First World War had called all of that into question, but so, too, had the Bible's teaching about human depravity and sin. According to Barth, one cannot talk about God by talking about human beings in a loud voice!

For him, all Christian theology is revealed vertically "from above" and solely grounded in that divine revelation. This position is reflected in the so-called *Barmen Declaration*, which Barth, as principal author, wrote in opposition to the Nazification of the German Protestant Church during the dictatorship of Hitler. The first thesis of that document underscores a Barthian understanding of Christian theology:

> Jesus Christ, as he is attested for us in Holy Scripture, is the one Word of God which we have to hear and which we have to trust and obey in life and in death. We reject the false doctrine, as though the church could and would have to acknowledge as a source of its proclamation, apart from and besides this one Word of God, still other events and powers, figures and truths, as God's revelation.[24]

Rudolf Bultmann (1884–1976), who was another key figure in the early movement of dialectical theology, agreed with Barth that "the object of theology is *God*." He thought that "the chief charge to be brought against liberal theology is that it has dealt not with God but with man." Nevertheless, he also stressed, in a way that Barth did not, that theology "speaks of God because it speaks of man as he stands before God. That is, theology speaks out of faith."[25] In other words, God can only be spoken of in relation to human existence "before God:"

> If we are actually speaking of God, then the mode of access appropriate to him must be conformable to him as the object of experience, the mode we call faith. If God is the object of faith and accessible only to faith, then a

---

[23] Karl Barth, "The Strange New World within the Bible," in *The Word of God and the Word of Man*, trans. Douglas Horton (New York: Harper & Row, 1957), 28–50.

[24] *Die Barmer Theologische Erklärung: Einführung und Dokumentation*, Martin Heimbucher and Rudolf Weth (eds), 7th edn (Neukirchen-Vluyn: Neukirchener, 2009), 37.

[25] Rudolf Bultmann, "Liberal Theology and the Latest Theological Movement," in *Faith and Understanding*, ed. Robert W. Funk, trans. Louise Pettibone Smith (Minneapolis: Fortress Press, 1987), 29, 52. "Man" here, of course, refers to humankind or human beings as a totality.

scholarly discipline apart from faith or alongside it can see neither God nor faith, which is what it is only by means of its object. . . The task, therefore, is to define the nature of theology on the basis of its object, and within its only possible mode of access, on the basis of the *fides quae* [the faith that believes] and *qua creditur* [the faith that is believed]. What God is cannot be understood if faith is not understood, and vice versa. Theology is thus scholarly discipline about God, since it is scholarly discipline about faith, and vice versa. (Bultmann 37, 49, translation slightly modified)

Bultmann likewise differed from Barth by insisting on the central importance of critical-historical investigation of the NT and by arguing that modern Christians needed to re-think (and perhaps even reject) the supposedly "mythological" elements within the apostolic proclamation (the three-storied universe, the intervention of supernatural powers, Satan, demons, pre-existence of the Son of God, the virgin birth, the resurrection and ascension of Jesus) so as not to confuse "authentic faith" with an outmoded worldview.[26] Bultmann and those influenced by him, such as Gerhard Ebeling (1912–2001), thought that the best means for doing this necessary reinterpreting was an **existentialist** philosophy and theology that helped to clarify the conditions of human existence, the present self-understandings of human beings, and the future possibilities of human existence. Once again, the ancient Greek critical-philosophical spirit shows itself here. While the word of God is still central for Bultmann and his followers, that word lays claim to human beings and the totality of their existence:

We cannot talk about our existence since we cannot talk about God. And we cannot talk about God since we cannot talk about our existence. We could only do the one along with the other. If we could talk of God from God, then we could talk of our existence, or vice versa. In any case, talking of God, if it were possible, would necessarily be talking at the same time of ourselves. Therefore the truth holds that when the question is raised of how any speaking of God can be possible, the answer must be, it is only possible as talk of ourselves.[27]

The key to understanding this statement is the difference between the prepositions "about" and "of." Following Luther, Bultmann thought that all talk "about" God is sinful, since God "can never be seen from without, can never be something at our disposal, can never be a 'something in respect

---

[26] Rudolf Bultmann, "New Testament and Mythology," in *Kerygma and Myth*, vol. 1, ed. Hans Werner Bartsch, trans. Reginald H. Fuller (London: SPCK, 1957), 1–44.
[27] Rudolf Bultmann, "What Does It Mean to Speak of God?," in *Faith and Understanding*, 60–1.

of which.'"[28] God is not an "object" for human manipulation, which is what Bultmann thought occurred as soon as people began talking "about" God. Human beings are sinners who are wholly other from God, who stand under the God who is "Wholly Other" (a phrase first used by Kierkegaard and then by Barth), and yet they must speak *of* God, if they are to know their own true human existence "under God" through faith, which is itself created only by the speaking *of* God.

> Faith can be only the affirmation of God's action upon us, the answer to his word directed to us. For if the realization of our own existence is involved in faith and if our existence is grounded in God and is non-existent outside God, then to apprehend our existence means to apprehend God... We can speak of him only in so far as we are speaking of his word spoken to us, of his act done to us.[29]

Here Schleiermacher's liberal Protestant understanding of theology as a "teaching about faith" again comes into view, despite Bultmann's earlier criticism of the liberal tradition.

Many have noted that the line of thinking set forth by Schleiermacher and then revised by Bultmann—that one can only speak of God by speaking at the same time about human beings—could lead to the conclusion that theology is really only anthropology. Might it be that God is not really "Wholly Other", or "over against", or even "for" human beings in "the word of faith," and that theology is involved in a grand deception or illusion? Bultmann's understanding of the theological task seems to lead in the direction of the radical critique of the traditional object of theology, its transformation into something other, and even the revision of theology into atheistic theology ("a-theology"). This concern that theology might become something other than what it is and ought to be was behind Barth's criticism of Bultmann's existentialist approach and his program of "de-mythologizing" the NT. Barth concluded that Bultmann's translation of the message of the NT had lost the gospel of God's condescension into the world, God's self-revelation through the ministry, death, and actual resurrection of Jesus from the dead, and his lordship over the church. Barth accused Bultmann

---

[28] Ibid., 60.

[29] Ibid., 63. Bultmann then quotes his own liberal Protestant teacher, Wilhelm Herrmann (1846–1922): "Of God we can only tell what he does to us." This position is reminiscent of the famous statement by Philip Melanchthon: "...to know Christ [is] to know his benefits [to us]" (Melanchthon, *Loci Communes* [1521], 68).

of replacing the proper subject of theology—God—with something of the modern theologian's own making.[30]

Another important German Protestant theologian, **Werner Elert** (1883–1954), criticized both Barth and Bultmann because they seemed to have forgotten the long-standing distinctions between the divine law and the divine gospel, between natural theology and revealed theology, and between the way in which God works, on the one hand, coercively through secular governments, law, and conscience, and non-coercively, and on the other hand, through the Scriptural word of promise and the means of grace for the sake of faith. For Elert and other confessional Lutherans God relates to sinful human beings, albeit negatively, through the divine law that is revealed apart from Christ, through the human conscience, through the human experience of guilt, suffering, and death, and through the consciousness of sin and the divine retribution for sin. These areas of human experience are also open to scholarly investigation by Christian theologians. Clearly, Elert's own understanding of the nature of Christian theology and its (partial) orientation toward human religious experience is indebted to both Luther and Schleiermacher.

That same indebtedness is evident in the theology of another twentieth-century German Lutheran theologian, **Paul Tillich**, whose "method of correlation" provides "answers" to "questions" formulated by philosophical reflection on human existence, its problems, and challenges:

> Philosophy formulates the questions implied in human existence and theology formulates the answers implied in divine self-manifestation under the guidance of the questions implied in human existence. This is a circle which drives man to a point where question and answer are not separated. (Tillich 1.61)

Tillich's "answering theology" represents a creative effort to restate traditional Lutheran confessional Christian theology into modern terms and concepts that correspond to his own understanding of philosophical metaphysics. He thought this was necessary in order to articulate and defend the truths of Christian faith for modern human beings who live in "this world that has come of age," to use the phrase made famous by the Lutheran theologian Dietrich Bonhoeffer (1906–45).[31] Like other existentialist theologians, such

---

[30] See Karl Barth, "Rudolf Bultmann: An Attempt to Understand Him," in *Kerygma and Myth*, vol. 2, ed. Hans Werner Bartsch, trans. Reginald H. Fuller (London: SPCK, 1962), 83–132.

[31] Dietrich Bonhoeffer, *Letters and Papers from Prison*, ed. John W. De Gruchy, trans. Isabel Best,

as Bultmann, Tillich thought the revelation of God cannot be properly understood apart from the self-understanding of modern human beings. Without attention to contemporary intellectual currents and modes of thought, the Christian message of God will be deemed irrelevant and unintelligible. In this view the task of theology entails the need for existential analysis of human existence and careful attention to the proclamation of the word of God for the sake of creating faith in the present moment.

One may detect a similar "existential" approach to theology in the work of the Roman Catholic theologian **Karl Rahner** (1904–84), who wrote many essays on a variety of theological topics. He was especially concerned to address the contemporary intellectual challenges to the Christian faith. His "theological investigations" take seriously the centrality of the human experience of God (a sense of the transcendent that Rahner thought had been lost in the modern world) and the biblical witness to the mystery of God's decisive act of salvation in Jesus. He found insights from Augustine and Aquinas particularly useful for contemporary theology. According to Rahner, one's thinking about God has its starting point in the human experience of the mystery of salvation in Christ.[32]

Since the days of Barth, Elert, Tillich, and Rahner, both Protestant and Roman Catholic theologians have become much more aware of their social and cultural contexts, and this awareness has in turn led to transformations of traditional definitions of Christian theology. Over the past half century many theologians, themselves critical of Barth's own seeming lack of attention toward a theology of nature and the future of the whole cosmos, have attacked the existentialist theologians for their excessive individualism and for their neglect of the larger social and universal horizons of cosmic history and creation. Among the most important of these theologians is **Jürgen Moltmann** (b. 1926), who questioned Bultmann's focus on the self-understanding of human beings:

Is any self-understanding of man conceivable at all which is not determined by his relation to the world, to history, to society? Can human life have subsistence and duration without outgoing and objectification, and without

---

Lisa Dahill et al., vol. 8 of Dietrich Bonhoeffer Works, Victoria J. Barnett and Barbara Wojhoski (eds) (Minneapolis: Fortress, 2010), 426 *et passim*.

[32] Another very influential Catholic theologian in the second half of the twentieth century, Hans Urs von Balthasar (1905–88), who himself was influenced significantly by Barth, emphasized that Christian theology is always a faithful response to God's own self-revelation, which he stressed is best understood as the revelation of divine beauty or "the glory of the Lord." The connection with Barth's understanding of theology is unmistakable here.

this does it not evaporate into nothingness in endless reflection? It is the task of theology to expound the knowledge of God in a correlation between understanding of the world and self-understanding.[33]

Still other theologians, influenced by Moltmann's global and political concerns, want to renew the practical orientation of theology by stressing how it ought to interpret critically contemporary situations of political and social oppression and to reflect theologically upon the actions of human beings in service to the practical goal of social, economic, and political justice. These concerns have been especially highlighted by the various forms of **liberation theology** (Latin American, African, Asian), whose practitioners have argued that Christian theology cannot merely be theoretical but must also involve actual "praxis" (behavior, specific practices, actual deeds), and the critique of social injustice, poverty, and oppression.

Among the more central voices of liberation theology has been **Gustavo Gutiérrez** (b. 1928), whose Latin-American theology of liberation exposes the oppression of poor and despised people and confesses the transforming love and grace of God to bring about true human liberation.[34] Indeed liberation theologians speak of God as being revealed within the history of the poor, of coming among us as one who is poor and who suffers. God's work among the poor is to bring about true transformation and liberation of the poor, the forgotten, the despised, and the oppressed. This revelation of God fundamentally alters the nature of theology itself, which is no longer a privileged activity of wealthy "first-world" university and seminary professors, but is now a concrete praxis and reflection in relation to specific structures of oppression, with actual grass-roots communities of faith, and in light of "God's preferential option for the poor." Such a theology, which clearly has also influenced **Pope Francis I** (b. 1935), desires to understand the Christian faith on the basis of a commitment to the poor and the marginalized "from a point of departure in real, effective solidarity with the exploited and the vulnerable" (OHST 635). In this way, too, liberation theology once again defines Christian theology primarily in relation to its practical end, similar to earlier definitions that stress theology as the study of practical, divine wisdom, or that stress, as did Schleiermacher, its practical orientation toward the leadership of Christian communities.

---

[33] Jürgen Moltmann, *Theology of Hope*, trans. James W. Leitch (London: SCM Press, 1967), 65.
[34] See especially Gustavo Gutiérrez, *A Theology of Liberation* (London: SCM Press, 1973).

There are many other forms of **contextual theology**, including feminist, womanist, gay and lesbian theologies that yearn to awaken people to the need for social and sexual justice, to uncover systems of oppression and repression, and to envision a new and better human, global community. These forms of theology are often grouped together as "**revisionist theologies**," since they desire to re-vision God and reality in ways that will be beneficial to the world and to oppressed communities in it. Such theologies are critical of those biblical images for God and Christ that are perceived as contributing to Christian triumphalism and to the exploitation of people and the world. Revisionist theologians hope to find ways of lifting up biblical images and meanings that contribute to more humane patterns of life and toward healing, love, and justice in the world.[35]

Another significant example of revisionist theology is that of so-called "feminist theologians." **Feminist theology** stresses the importance of listening to non-traditional voices—especially those of women—which have been suppressed, oppressed, and often ignored in the history of Christianity.[36] Feminist theologians argue that women bring a unique perspective to the theological task, one that is concerned with the role of women in church and society (for example, by making arguments for the ordination of women to the priesthood or pastoral office), with gender, and with the transformation of theology itself to become truly liberating. Many of these theologians draw upon earlier theological reflections by medieval mystics who also offered a contrasting understanding of God from male forms of thinking.

While there is a great diversity of voices within feminist theology—that is one of its emphases, the welcoming of diversity—we will note just two: **Rosemary Radford Ruether** (b. 1936) and **Elisabeth Schüssler Fiorenza** (b. 1938), who, along with many others, speak from within the church and

---

[35] Gordon Kaufman (1925–2011) is a further example of a "revisionist" theologian. He wanted to reform Christian theology to become more beneficial to human communities and to the global environment. Kaufman's work underscores theology as a revisionist, imaginative, philosophical, constructive enterprise. Like Sallie McFague (b. 1933), who has acknowledged Kaufman's influence upon her own work, Kaufman has striven to set forth a conception of God that moves beyond the biblical models and metaphors of "judge" and "king" to develop the notion of God as the ordered "creativity" that undergirds the universe. See, for example, Gordon Kaufman, *God-Mystery-Diversity: Christian Theology in a Pluralistic World* (Minneapolis: Fortress, 1996) and idem, *Theology for a Nuclear Age* (Philadelphia: Westminster John Knox, 1985).

[36] For an introduction to the history and complexity of Christian feminist theology, see especially Rebecca Chopp and Sheila Davaney (eds), *Horizons in Feminist Theology: Identity, Tradition and Norms* (Minneapolis: Fortress Press, 1997).

who seek to renew and re-vision it as a true spiritual "community of equals." These theologians also highlight practices that will make for justice in both the church and the world. Like other theologians, they have been critical of traditional language about God as "Father" and about some theological categories that they view as demeaning to human beings (especially to women) and as contributing to the degradation of human community and the destruction of the planet.[37]

Within the North American context, the last half-century has also witnessed theologians who have more or less reflected positions of the principal theologians from the first half of the century. Some generally reflect the positions of Tillich and Bultmann, namely, that academic theology must entail critical and self-critical reflection on the key symbols of the Christian faith. Other theologians generally reflect the position of Barth.

Among those influenced by Tillich, or who share his concern to relate theology to contemporary thought forms, one needs to note the important Roman Catholic thinkers, Bernard Lonergan (1904–84), Hans Küng (b. 1928), and **David Tracy** (b. 1939). For them, if theology is to be an academic discipline in a university setting, it must adhere to well-established criteria for evidence, rational argumentation, and intelligibility, and to the position that truth corresponds to reality. These are the same criteria that are used elsewhere in the university, especially in the modern natural and social sciences. The use of these criteria, external to Christian theology and its subject matter, does not necessarily provide theologians with a set of rules to follow but with a basic and normative "pattern of recurrent and related operations" (sensing, inquiring, imagining, understanding, formulating, judging, speaking, writing) that yield "cumulative and progressive results."[38] The challenge of this so-called "transcendental" or "metaphysical" method in theology is for the theologian to be "attentive, intelligent, reasonable, responsible," and open to change.[39] Within this approach, one's understandings of the Bible and church traditions are always open to criticism from external sources and to the possibility that one's theological understandings will have to be revised in light of other knowledge and experience. So these theologies, too, may properly be described with the label "revisionist."

---

[37] See, for example, Sallie McFague, *Models of God: Theology for an Ecological, Nuclear Age* (Minneapolis: Fortress Press, 1987).
[38] Bernard Lonergan, *Method in Theology* (New York: Seabury, 1972), 13–14.
[39] Ibid., 14.

Tracy's modification of Tillich's method of correlation allows for the "mutual-critical correlation" between theology and the three main "publics" with which the theologian interacts (the church, society, and the academy). For Tracy, who has been especially influenced by Schleiermacher, Tillich, and Lonergan, the challenge of the modern theologian, who is also informed by postmodern critiques of modernity, is to demonstrate the meaningful relevance of Christian theology for these publics, even while he or she acknowledges the possibility of revising theology when such revision is called for in the light of new knowledge and insights. Whatever good reasons the theologian has for setting forth the truth of Christian theology, those reasons must accord with norms that can be publicly verified. Truth must correspond to reality, it must be confirmed by experience and critical reflection; it cannot be purely subjective. Theologians cannot simply appeal to traditional theological sources, especially the Bible, that are only accepted by the theologians themselves and their fellow believers. If theologians cannot provide persuasive reasons for their theological truth claims which will stand up to public scrutiny, then the claims cannot be maintained, at least not in the public realm, that is, the "shared rational space where all participants, whatever their particular differences, can meet to discuss any claim that is rationally redeemable."[40]

By contrast, other theologians stress the need for theology to have closer ties to traditional sources of theology and the church communities in which those theologies have originated and to be suspicious of "modern," universal claims to truth. We may loosely label this other way of doing theology as "**post-liberal**," since theologians in this group want to overcome the modern approaches to metaphysics and theology that have been classically defined by Kant and Schleiermacher. Post-liberal theologians, despite their differences, tend to stress the need to take the particularities of Christianity more seriously than has been the case in Protestant liberalism and other forms of revisionist theology. Many of the post-liberal theologians have been significantly influenced by Barth and, like him, they want the overall shape of the biblical narrative to have a priority in the theological task. Furthermore, they emphasize the intimate relationship between the biblical texts and the specific communities that read those sacred texts. So these theologians tend to understand Christian theology completely (or mostly)

---

[40] David Tracy, "Theology, Critical Social Theory, and the Public Realm," in *Habermas, Modernity, and Public Theology*, Don S. Browning and Francis Schüssler Fiorenza (eds) (Chicago: University of Chicago Press, 1992), 19.

within the cultural or semiotic system that constitutes Christianity as a distinct religion. They articulate theology entirely (or mostly) according to the "grammar" or "internal logic" of "the Christian narrative" as it is authoritatively given in the Bible and summarized in the classic creeds and confessions of the Christian churches. The method followed here is not transcendental or "universal," but quite specific to the internal "language" and "grammar" of the Christian faith that together form the self-description of Christian faith and practice.

A fairly recent instance of this approach appears in "the cultural-linguistic model" of theology defended by **George Lindbeck** (b. 1923). He used Geertz's theory of culture to argue for the "absorption" of the universe by the overarching "Scriptural world."[41] For Lindbeck and other post-liberal theologians, influenced especially by the theology of Barth, the challenge of a Christian theologian is to maintain the orthodox identity and integrity of Christian teaching, especially in view of what he or she perceives to be false ways of knowing and living within other religious and secular worldviews. Of special concern is the need to articulate and defend the particular Christian narrative and how that narrative shapes the life of the Christian within the church and the academy. Some of Lindbeck's students have thus modified his model so as to emphasize that the Scriptures, creeds, and authoritative doctrinal statements have a priority over all other forms of knowledge within the Christian worldview.[42] Within the approach of Lindbeck and his followers, Christian truth is entirely a matter of "coherence" within the world of the Bible, of how Christian beliefs and practices are interconnected into an integrated and coherent whole that provides the overarching framework of meaning for the individual Christian and his or her community of faith.

Those who follow the post-liberal approach are less concerned to be *relevant* to the contemporary situation than they are to be *faithful* to what they perceive to be the true and correct understanding of God as it is

---

[41] George Lindbeck, *The Nature of Doctrine: Religion and Theology in a Postliberal Age* (Philadelphia: Westminster, 1984).

[42] See Bruce Marshall, *Trinity and Truth* (Cambridge: Cambridge University Press, 2000). As another post-liberal theologian, Stanley Hauerwas (b. 1940) has argued, if the Christian theologian is going to engage any contemporary culture, it is best to know first what Christian doctrine and practices actually are and what they entail within the community of Christian faith. "The apologist of the past stood in the church and its tradition and sought relationship with those outside. Apologetic theology was a secondary endeavor because the apologist never assumed that one could let the questions of unbelief order the theological agenda" (Stanley Hauerwas, *Against the Nations: War and Survival in a Liberal Society* [Minneapolis: Winston, 1985], 24).

given within the Christian Bible and orthodox tradition. The challenge of the theologian is to describe this particular "Christian worldview" that "shapes the entirety of life and thought."[43] One must first be clear about the Christian subject matter, its claims and assertions, and what these mean for one's understanding of reality and reasoning, before one is in a right position to engage theology within an academic setting of mutual inter- action. The theologian must be concerned to understand and articulate a coherent Christian identity—one that is to be kept free from the influence of external criteria of rationality, evidence, and argumentation—before doing theology within any context, university or otherwise.

Finally, we may note two theologians who do not line up with either the revisionists or the post-liberals: **Wolfhart Pannenberg** (b. 1928) and **Oswald Bayer** (b. 1939). Pannenberg wants to return Christian theology to earlier, classical understandings that focus strictly on "talking of God" and "thinking of God." For this reason Pannenberg has called upon all Christian theologians to be concerned with theology's proper object, namely, "God." Hearkening back to classic definitions articulated by Aquinas and Gerhard, he has defined theology as "the science of God," which he insists must first and foremost be about "the truth" regarding the reality of God on the basis of language that God himself has authorized within Scripture.[44] "Talk about God that is grounded in humanity, in human needs and interests, or as an expression of human ideas about divine reality, would not be theology. It would simply be a product of human imagination" (Pannenberg 1.7). The truth of Christian teaching must be the theme of Christian theology. He has thus been critical of all contextual theologies that take their cues from human experience and needs, including human desires for political and social justice. He has also been critical of what he perceives to be wrong notions of social and political utopianism that have entered into the theologies of some liberation, feminist, and revisionist theologians. For Pannenberg human political and social liberation/freedom cannot be conflated with divine redemption, and human beings cannot be reduced to mere political and social creatures. In the view of Pannenberg, to under- stand theology as an imaginative enterprise plays right into the criticism of the atheist Feuerbach who judged all theologies to be instances of mere

---

[43] Lindbeck, *The Nature of Doctrine*, 33.
[44] Pannenberg had already made this point clear in his essay, "What Is a Dogmatic Statement?", in *Basic Questions in Theology*, vol. 1, trans. George H. Kehm (Philadelphia: Westminster, 1983), 182–210, esp. 201–2, 206–7.

projection of human needs onto God and thus merely matters of creative illusion. If that were the case, then all human talk of God is merely just that, human talk. For this reason, Pannenberg has insisted that Christian theology must maintain the Greek theological ideal of criticism, especially when one detects false thinking within the discipline. In this way, too, theology is not primarily a practical discipline but a theoretical one that aspires to give a truthful, faithful, coherent, and comprehensive understanding of God and other theological topics.

Oswald Bayer has also been critical of the recent transformation of theology into a human-centered, political and social enterprise, but he resists Pannenberg's position that theology is only oriented to "true discourse about God" rather than also to human existence and the world. Bayer argues that Luther's modification of Aquinas' definition more adequately encompasses the fullness of theological reflection. Christian theology is not merely about how the revelation of God's mercy and love are revealed in and through the gospel concerning Jesus but also about how (sinful) human beings are revealed and exposed for who they are in the revelations of God's law and gospel. Christian theology cannot speculate about how God is "in God," who remains hidden from human beings, but it can examine God on the basis of how God is self-giving and known in relation to human beings through the divine revelations of law and gospel that lead to repentance and faith in Jesus Christ. Bayer thus insists, as did Luther, on the priority and externality of God's "mighty acts" in history for us, and our salvation, in relation to the apostolic witness to Christ. He also insists, in a way reminiscent of Bultmann, that Christian theology is also about human beings in light of the word of God, about divine speech and faith, and not merely about God. In this way, too, Bayer's theology shares similarities with the concerns of all contextual theologies (liberation theology, feminist theology), namely, that theology is never merely talking of God in isolation from reality, or even social reality, but always speaking of God in relation to other matters, such as creation, human beings, human communities, and the world as a whole. Bayer stresses Luther's point that Christian theology is never just about God: It is about the God who justifies sinful humanity through the cross of Christ *and* about sinful human beings who need to be so justified.

As one can hopefully detect from the above sketch, Christians have disagreed among themselves about what theology is and how it should be undertaken. What is the best way to define Christian theology as an academic discipline within the context of an undergraduate liberal-arts university? That is the question we will address in the next chapter.

First Century	Apostles of Jesus
Second Century	Justin Martyr Irenaeus
Second/Third Centuries	Origen Tertullian Cyprian
Fourth Century	Athanasius Augustine The Cappadocians
Seventh/Eighth Centuries	John of Damascus
Eleventh/Twelfth Centuries	Anselm of Canterbury Peter Abelard Bernard of Clairvaux
Thirteenth Century	Hildegard of Bingen Thomas Aquinas
Fourteenth/Fifteenth Centuries	Julian of Norwich Catherine of Siena
Sixteenth Century	Martin Luther Philip Melanchthon John Calvin Teresa of Ávila
Seventeenth Century	Johann Gerhard
Eighteenth Century	Jonathan Edwards
Nineteenth Century	Friedrich Schleiermacher Georg Hegel
Twentieth Century	Karl Barth Rudolf Bultmann Paul Tillich Dietrich Bonhoeffer Karl Rahner Gustavo Gutiérrez Rosemary Radford Ruether Wolfhart Pannenberg

Figure 3.1 Key Christian Theologians

Key Words

metaphysics
Parmenides
Xenophanes
philosophical theology
Plato
myth
Aristotle
anthropomorphism
Clement of Alexandria
Origen
Logos (the Word)
Justin Martyr
Tertullian
Cyprian of Carthage
doctors of the church
Augustine
monk
nun
Anselm of Canterbury
scholasticism
"faith seeking
    understanding"
Peter Abelard
Hildegard of Bingen
Julian of Norwich
abbess
anchorite
Thomas Aquinas
Martin Luther
John Calvin

Philip Melanchthon
Johann Gerhard
Pietist theologians
Johann Semler
Immanuel Kant
Jonathan Edwards
Friedrich Schleiermacher
Georg Hegel
Karl Barth
dialectical theology
Rudolf Bultmann
existentialist theology
Werner Elert
Paul Tillich
Karl Rahner
Jürgen Moltmann
liberation theology
Gustavo Gutiérrez
Pope Francis 1
contextual theology
revisionist theologies
feminist theology
Rosemary R. Ruether
Elisabeth Schüssler Fiorenza
David Tracy
post-liberal theology
George Lindbeck
Wolfhart Pannenberg
Oswald Bayer

Reference literature

For a general orientation to ancient Greek theology
and philosophical theology

BCPR 73–9 ("Ancient Philosophical Theology" [Flannery]); ER 13:9125–34

("Theology: Comparative Theology" [Tracy]); OHST 653–69
   ("Comparative Theology" [Clooney]); REP 6:338–41 ("Metaphysics"
   [Craig]); RPP 8:307–10 ("Metaphysics" [Enskat]); RPP 12:608–10
   ("Theologia" [Cancik]).

For a general orientation to traditions of Christian theology

BCSR 193–210 ("Theology" [Markham]); EC 5:363–70 ("Theology"
   [Owen]); ER 13:9134–42 ("Theology: Christian Theology" [Congar]);
   OCCT 700–2 ("Theology" [Hastings]); ODCC 1616 ("Theology"); RPP
   2:592–602 ("Christianity IV: Systematic Theology" [Schwöbel]); RPP
   4:141–52 ("Dogmatics I–II: History and Systematic Theology" [Herms];
   "Dogmatics III: Glaubenslehre [Doctrine of the Faith]" [Lange]); RPP
   12:617–46 ("Theology" [Schwöbel]); RPP 12:646–50 ("Theology, History/
   Historiography of" [Köpf]).

Questions for review and discussion

1   Which culture invented the term "theology"? What did the term origi-
    nally mean? How did Plato and Aristotle differ regarding the purpose
    of theology? How were their respective views of theology similar?
    Who are those Christian theologians who most closely reflect the
    critical spirit of Plato and Aristotle?
2   Why were most early Christians opposed to the use of the term
    "*theologia*?" Who was the first Christian to use the term favorably?
    How did he understand the term "*Logos*" in relation to Greek
    philosophy?"
3   Tertullian and Origen understood theology very differently. What
    are the strengths and weaknesses of their respective approaches to
    theology?
4   How did Anselm of Canterbury define the nature of Christian
    theology? How is his definition similar to Augustine's? How are their
    respective understandings different? Do you think a person must be
    a believer in Christ in order to do theology in the way of Anselm and
    Augustine ("faith seeking understanding")? Why or why not?
5   The chapter identifies several female theologians within the Christian
    tradition. How are their respective ways of doing theology different
    from some of the other theologians discussed in the chapter? Do you

think men and women do theology differently from each other? Why or why not?

6   Why was Martin Luther critical of medieval scholastic theology? What did he think the proper goal of theology is? Do you agree with Luther that Christian theology is very different from philosophical theology? Or are you more inclined to agree with Aquinas and Johann Gerhard that philosophy ought to assist the Christian theologian? What might be some weaknesses of each of these approaches?

7   How did later theologians change the nature of academic theology from the definition that was given to it by Johann Gerhard? More specifically, how are Aquinas' and Gerhard's definitions of theology different from Schleiermacher's initial practical understanding? How did Schleiermacher's later understanding return to a position closer to Aquinas and Gerhard?

8   What is the basis of theology, according to Barth? What was Elert's principal criticism of Barth's theology? How might his criticism of Barth reflect similar concerns by Rahner and Tillich? For example, where does each of these theologians see the starting point of Christian theology?

9   Based on the brief descriptions of Tillichian "revisionist" theology (Tracy) and Barthian "post-liberal" theology (Lindbeck), which approach do you think is better suited to a college context today? What are the strengths and weaknesses of these two differing approaches to theology?

10   Pannenberg has been critical of feminist theologians and all others who see theology as including also "talk about human beings." Contextual theologians have been critical of Pannenberg's approach, since he wants to limit theology strictly to "the science of God" (hearkening back to Aquinas). Which side of this argument do you support? Why?

Suggestions for further reading

Reference works in the philosophy of religion

Frederick Copleston, *A History of Philosophy*, 9 vols (New York: Image, 2005) [Exhaustive historical narrative of the principal figures and movements—and many less well-known ones—by an Oxford Jesuit scholar.]

Edward Craig, ed., *Routledge Encyclopedia of Philosophy*, 10 vols (New York: Routledge, 2000) [Standard reference work for the discipline of philosophy.]

William Lane Craig, ed., *The Blackwell Companion to Natural Theology* (New York: Wiley-Blackwell, 2012) [This is a major reference work that contains essays on each of the principal arguments for and against the reality of God. This provides a good picture of the state of this issue within both Christian theology and the philosophy of religion.]

Philip L. Quinn and Charles Taliaferro (eds), *The Blackwell Companion to the Philosophy of Religion* (Oxford: Blackwell, 1997) [Provides introductory articles on central issues in the philosophy of religion. Helpful bibliographies.]

Philosophy for theology students

Diogenes Allen and Eric O. Springsted, *Philosophy for Understanding Theology*, 2nd edn (Louisville: Westminster John Knox, 2007) [Engaging analysis from Plato to Postmodernism by two theologians who favor a postmodern approach to Christian theology.]

Colin Brown, *Philosophy and the Christian Faith* (Downers Grove, IL: InterVarsity, 1968). [Despite its author's rather narrowly conservative Reformed perspective, this book provides a good overview of how Christian theologians from the medieval period through the mid-twentieth century have engaged philosophical systems (from Aristotle through Existentialism)].

Derek Johnston, *A Brief History of Philosophy: From Socrates to Derrida* (New York: Continuum, 2006) [This is a very good place for the beginning student to start.]

Bertrand Russell, *The History of Western Philosophy* (New York: Simon & Schuster, 1945) [A classic one-volume analytical survey by a major twentieth-century philosopher.]

William A. Wallace, *The Elements of Philosophy: A Compendium for*

Philosophers and Theologians (New York: Alba House, 1977) [An engaging overview of Thomistic philosophy by a major Roman Catholic scholar.]

Metaphysics and philosophical theology

Earl Conee and Theodore Sider, *Riddles of Existence: A Guided Tour of Metaphysics* (Oxford: Clarendon, 2005) [A very readable introduction to the difficult questions of metaphysics. Good bibliographies.]

Ed. L. Miller, *God and Reason: An Invitation to Philosophical Theology*, 2nd edn (New York: Pearson, 1994) [A very readable introduction to the principal issues in the philosophy of religion.]

On the history of Christian theology

David Ford, ed., *The Modern Theologians: An Introduction to Christian Theology in the Twentieth Century*, 2nd edn (Oxford: Blackwell, 1997) [Major survey of relatively recent theologians and theological movements. Includes sections on European, British, American, African, and Asian theologians, as well as sections on various theological movements (liberation theology, feminist theology, Black theology, etc.).]

Justo L. Gonzalez, *A History of Christian Thought*, 2nd edn, 3 vols (Nashville: Abingdon, 1987) [Helpful, easy-to-read account of the history of Christian theology from the time of the apostles until the end of the twentieth century by a Methodist scholar. A good place to turn after reading Johnston or McGrath.]

Adolph von Harnack, *History of Dogma*, 7 vols, trans. Neil Buchanan (New York: Dover, 1961) [The classic "liberal Protestant" treatment of the development of Christian teaching in the early centuries of Christianity. Harnack was the major twentieth-century scholar of early Christianity. He has set the standard for subsequent scholars.]

Derek Johnston, *A Brief History of Theology: From the New Testament to Feminist Theology* (New York: Continuum, 2009) [This is a good place to start before trying to tackle any of the multi-volumes listed here.]

Gareth Jones, ed., *The Blackwell Companion to Modern Theology* (New York: Wiley-Blackwell, 2007) [An excellent reference work that provides overviews and analysis of the principal figures and movements in modern Christian systematic theology.]

Alister E. McGrath, *Historical Theology: An Introduction to the History of Christian Thought* (Oxford: Blackwell, 1998) [A good one-volume survey of the main Christian theologians and theological movements by a major Protestant theologian from Britain.]

Jaroslav Pelikan, *The Christian Tradition: A History of the Development of Doctrine*, 5 vols (Chicago: The University of Chicago Press, 1971–89) [The last major work of its kind so far. Pelikan was a Lutheran scholar for most of his professorial life—he co-edited the American Edition of Luther's works—and then became a member of the Orthodox Church near the end of his life. His work helps to correct Harnack's lack of attention to the liturgical life of early Christian communities and their spiritual traditions.]

Linwood Urban, *A Short History of Christian Thought*, 2nd edn (New York: Oxford University Press, 1995) [Succinct, well-written account of key issues in the history of Christian thinking. A good intermediate text after Johnston or McGrath.]

4

What is Christian Theology?

This chapter defines the nature and purpose of Christian theology as an academic discipline in an undergraduate university setting. Christian theology is a discipline that invites critical and self-critical reflection on the revelation of God, the world, and human beings in the apostolic witness to Jesus Christ. Such reflection takes into account how this revelation has been understood and believed by Christian communities over the past two millennia, and how it ought to be understood in light of contemporary knowledge from other disciplines in the university. The goal of this reflection is four-fold: (1) to understand the content of this witness clearly in light of the history of Christianity and the knowledge from other university disciplines; (2) to consider the nature of Christian faith as trust in the gospel promise given within this witness; (3) to identify weak or faulty understandings of the witness; and (4) to appropriate the truth and wisdom in the witness.

As Chapter 1 has suggested, perhaps the most common form of Christian theology occurs within an individual's life and immediate relationships. This type of informal theology is often, though not always, connected to activities within specific Christian communities or churches, such as praying, preaching, singing, and meditating. A person's "confession of faith" or "practice of faith" is also a kind of rudimentary theology that might occasionally issue forth in deeper reflection. In this religious context such thinking tends to be more informal than the kind that pays scholarly attention to academic theology and its history. While some Christians might be skeptical about the latter because they perceive that it could call their faith into question and make them uncomfortable, non-academic Christians still tend to hold some reflective understandings of their faith, even if these are generally guided by deference to external authorities, such as the Bible and/or church leaders. To the extent that such individuals investigate academic theology, they do so primarily for the sake of discerning whatever practical wisdom it might provide them for living their lives. In general, however, many Christians get their theology from non-academic sources. One thinks, for example, of all those who have completely bought into the nineteenth-century millennialism of John Nelson Darby (1800–82), which informs the very popular "Left Behind" stories by Tim F. LaHaye and Jerry B. Jenkins.[1]

There is another kind of Christian theology, however, which the previous chapter has surveyed, that is more formal. We will identify this as **academic theology**. While people have defined this discipline differently over the past two millennia, a common concern among these representative theologians has been to offer an ordered account of Christian teachings, usually for the sake of educating church leaders or for the purpose of serving as a resource for those who practice the arts of ministry. In this context, students typically study theology as a formal discipline within an academic institution that is often, although not always, operated by a particular church body or consortium of churches. Here, theology tends to be primarily practical and parochial. In other words, it is an activity *of* and *for* the church, since it examines the church's actual proclamation and teaching against the original authorities for Christian proclamation (the apostolic writings found in the NT and the prophetic writings of the OT) and in the light of human knowledge and experience.

While Schleiermacher's practical rationale for Christian theology as a university discipline has had a tremendous impact on the development of theological education over the past two centuries, it has been used by some Christians to defend the position that Christian theology cannot really be done well or faithfully within a modern university and thus should be located only within church-related, private, praxis-oriented academic institutions, such as Bible colleges and seminaries. Others agree, but for different reasons. Some hold that a university should only include those disciplines that are able to study data empirically through mathematical models of inquiry that quantify their results. In this view, theology (not to mention the other disciplines in the humanities and the arts) does not fit such an empirical model and so it should be excluded or at least marginalized in the pursuit of truth and understanding. Certainly such a secular position

---

[1] See Tim F. LaHaye and Jerry B. Jenkins, *Left Behind: A Novel of the Earth's Last Days* (Wheaton, IL: Tyndale, 1995) and subsequent stories in the series.

toward theology has contributed to its marginalization in many universities, and even its full exclusion, over the past four hundred years.[2]

Both the sectarian view, namely, that Christian theology can only be properly done within a church-related school or seminary, and the secularist view, namely, that Christian theology does not belong among the university disciplines, are inadequate to the nature of academic theology itself. Certainly, this form of theology is different from physics or even other disciplines within the humanities, but it has an abiding part to play in the pursuit of truth and understanding, and thus it belongs within a university. To dismiss academic theology, merely because its object of study and the means of studying that object are different from that which the natural and social sciences are able to investigate, is shortsighted. Such a dismissal neglects or at least diminishes the contribution that the study of Christian theology could make to the cultivation of wisdom and understanding among all university students, even among those who might have serious questions and doubts about the object of Christian theology. Likewise, many will argue that the truth regarding the subject investigated by academic theology remains an open question, the answer to which is already presupposed by many in their various views toward reality, knowledge, and "truth."

Moreover, academic theology is too important to relegate solely to a seminary or church-related school and its education of future church leaders. Within the setting of a liberal-arts university, Christian theology invites Christian and non-Christian undergraduate students alike to examine Christian ideas, institutions, and history more accurately in a properly theological manner. What is Christian faith? How has it informed people's actions over the past two millennia? What does it mean to investigate that faith critically in relation to other academic disciplines? Might one be able to appropriate its possible truth, wisdom, and insights?

In an undergraduate setting, theology relates more broadly to the human sciences and more specifically to the philosophy of religion, the philosophy of science, and religious studies, without necessarily being completely

---

[2] For earlier accounts of the secularization of American institutions of higher education, see especially George Marsden, *The Soul of the American University: From Protestant Establishment to Established Nonbelief* (New York: Oxford University Press, 1994); and James T. Burtchaell, *The Dying of the Light: The Disengagement of Colleges and Universities from their Christian Churches* (Grand Rapids: Eerdmans, 1998). Both of these studies show how many American colleges and universities, which were founded by Christians and had historically propagated Christian teaching, eventually abandoned their connections to Christianity in favor of a purely Enlightenment-based quest for truth.

subsumed under any one of these other disciplines or their methods of investigation. Thus theology strives to articulate and understand the unique character of that which it studies and the manner in which that object remains open to investigation.

Undergraduate students of theology will also pursue interdisciplinary work, research, and dialogue with other fields of study, something that is taking place in nearly all academic areas today—from physics, law, medicine, biology, and ecology to history, education, and the humanities. Study of theology in a university setting can inspire and equip students to participate more fully in such interdisciplinary study, whatever their primary academic field may be. In this same context, Christian theology wants to make a contribution to the human search for truth and the human pursuit of social and global justice. The possibility of such wisdom and truth within specific religions, including Christianity, must remain an open question within the liberal education of all human beings.

Certainly, the place where Christian theology occurs affects the nature and task of theology in that place. How one undertakes theology in a Bible college or a church-related seminary will be different from how it is undertaken in the context of a modern, western, liberal-arts university (either church-related or not) or in a state college or university (whose faculty's academic freedom is limited constitutionally on matters relating to the study of religions and religious ideas) or in an ecumenical divinity school. One may thus define the academic discipline of theology in an undergraduate context as follows:

> Christian theology is (1) a university discipline that invites (2) critical and self-critical reflection (3) on the revelation of God, the world, and human beings in the apostolic witness to Jesus Christ, (4) as that revelation has been understood and believed in the churches over time, (5) in order (a) to understand the content of that witness clearly within the ecumenical and intellectual situation of the present, (b) to consider the nature of Christian faith as trust in the gospel promise given within this witness, (c) to identify weak or even faulty understandings of the witness itself or within later developments, and (d) to appropriate the possible truth and wisdom within the witness.

Because this definition is open to misunderstanding, a few comments about each main part of it are in order.

(1) Christian theology is *a university discipline*. As such, it does not belong exclusively within the province of the church or institutions operated by Christians, but neither is it unrelated to communities of Christian faith that

are located outside of the academy. Christian theology as a university discipline overlaps both the academy and communities of Christians. Usually located in the arts-and-sciences faculty of a university, it is a sub-discipline in the humanities, either alongside or within religious studies, although it also has an important relation to all other academic disciplines. Indeed, Christian theology is most vital when it is in dialogue with philosophy, the humanities, and the sciences in the common pursuit of clarifying the goods of human life.

As suggested above, some insist that Christian faith or any other religious belief is unworthy of scholarly investigation, especially because the truth regarding its object is open to question. This introduction contends that Christian theology deserves careful, critical attention within the broad discipline of the humanities. The question of religious truth remains an important question for billions of people today, and the impact of the Christian tradition and Christian humanism on the development of human culture, including its theological dimension, is worthy of continued study. Furthermore, Christian theology deserves to be better understood than it currently is throughout academia and in the larger western culture, precisely because of its huge influence on the development of that culture. "We should study this Christian heritage because it is in our bones—even the bones of the unbeliever—in ways we often do not understand. It comes down to this: we cannot understand ourselves unless we understand what historical forces have shaped us, and Christianity is certainly one of those central influences."[3]

Aside from the historical influence, the theologian will continually inquire about the truth of theology. There might very well be more to "what is" than "what is known."[4] The question regarding religious truth, moreover, will be better addressed if one attends closely to past and present theological and philosophical understandings within the academy. Insofar as members of the university community are concerned with knowledge as an end in itself, "the university is at the very least obliged to pay attention also to the knowledge of [the theological] dimension of its subject matter."[5]

---

[3] Don S. Browning, *Reviving Christian Humanism: The New Conversation on Spirituality, Theology, and Psychology* (Minneapolis: Fortress, 2010), 2.

[4] A similar point is made by the philosopher Roy Bhaskar and other "critical realists." See Andrew Collier, *Critical Realism* (London: Verso, 1993).

[5] Jaroslav Pelikan, *The Idea of the University: A Reexamination* (New Haven: Yale University Press, 1992), 40.

To be sure, some might agree that Christian theology is an academic discipline, but insist that it should be studied only in a graduate or professional school or seminary whose principal purpose is the cultivation of practical knowledge and vocational skills for "the already-committed religious believer." This introduction, however, contends that Christian theology ought to be studied also by undergraduate students, even by those who are not Christian, since knowledge of human life, history, culture, and society will be radically incomplete without explicit attention to the religious dimension of these realities and the equally necessary task of understanding this dimension *theologically* and not merely in reductionist ways and categories that lead to the bracketing out of theology and questions about the truth of its subject matter. Thus, the above definition of theology broadens the circle in which the Christian faith is examined critically, beyond the specific communities in which is primarily a church-related practical activity.

Likewise, contrary to those who insist that theology must be protected from "godless" academic disciplines in the university and relegated only to a strictly church-controlled setting, such as a Bible college or church university, this introduction contends that Christian theology must take into account knowledge and research from the wider academic community, especially knowledge that overlaps with matters that are also studied in Christian theology, in order to avoid falsehood and ignorance, but also in order to provide a theological perspective on these same matters that is relevant, informed, and self-critical. In this way, Christian theology looks for conceptual clarity through rational methods of inquiry, invites critical dialogue with the other university disciplines, and avoids being sectarian and isolated from the larger academic community and its intellectual ideals. In this respect, too, the issue of academic freedom is also important to theology.

So Christian theology invites comparison with other theological and religious traditions, it endeavors to foster intentional theological dialogue between people of different religions about the basic questions that religious traditions address: What is the nature of reality? What, if anything, is wrong with human beings and their situation in the world? How does this religious tradition address, or respond to, that problem or set of problems? Dialogue about these and other basic questions of theology need not necessarily presuppose "that all religions are basically the same" (thus flattening them out and shaping them into something of one's own making), or that "my religion is the only one that has all the truth," or that "we can never understand the truth claims asserted by someone from a religion different from our own." Real interreligious dialogue presupposes a respectful openness toward people who believe and behave differently from oneself, a readiness to share one's own convictions about theological truth, and a willingness to learn from the other. One can listen to and even understand the truth claims of others, risking that one's own theological understanding might grow and change as a result of conversation with the other, even if one might think at the outset that, at least for the time being, one's own present understanding is closer to "the real truth."

(2) Christian theology is a university discipline *that invites critical and self-critical reflection.* The use of the term "critical" here implies the full range of meanings that the original Greek word (*krino*) had, from which the English word derives (OED 364). "**Critical reflection**" involves "thinking about" and "considering" the Christian faith and its traditions, "passing judgment upon" and "criticizing" it, if necessary, and repeatedly "coming to a conclusion" in light of one's ongoing considerations (see BDAG 567–8). Such an understanding hearkens back to the ideals of Plato and Aristotle, whose philosophical criticism of Greek religion was undertaken in service to truth about God and reality, but is also consistent with classic forms of Christian theology.

Despite differences in definition, nearly all Christian theologians agree that theology involves critical inquiry into Christian origins, contemporary theological reflection on human beings and their experiences, analysis of the Christian confession of faith in God, and the articulation of practical wisdom. As noted in the previous chapter, a key way of capturing this intimate connection between faith and critical inquiry is the phrase, "faith seeking understanding," an approach that has been given classic form in the writings of Augustine and Anselm and that has been defended by many theologians throughout the history of Christianity. In the words of Barth, "the special task of theology is a *critical* one... Theology has to reconsider the confession of the community, testing and rethinking it in the light of its enduring foundation, object, and content... What distinguishes faith from blind assent is just its special character as 'faith seeking understanding.'"[6] More recently still, Daniel Migliore rightly asks, "How could we ever be finished with the quest for a deeper understanding of God? What would be the likely result if we lacked the courage to ask, Do I rightly know who God is and what God wills?" (Migliore 2).

---

[6] Barth, *Evangelical Theology*, 42–3.

Christian theology thus invites people to question, investigate, explain, and perhaps criticize the Christian faith and/or Christian traditions. Clearly, the discipline is thus inherently **hermeneutical** (from a Greek word meaning "to interpret"); that is, it concerns the processes by which one understands and interprets its subject matter, whose primary sources, specialized language and conceptuality, and historical development comprise material that is temporally distant. To assist in this process of understanding, theology makes use of the best scholarly tools for the scholarly investigation of the Christian faith and Christian traditions, it gives serious attention to the claims to truth and wisdom that are made within those traditions, it engages the most serious criticisms of those traditions, and it fosters an openness toward dialogue on matters of mutual concern with the other university disciplines, especially the humanities and the social and natural sciences.

Such hermeneutical, critical reflection may involve the "**demystification**" (Max Weber) of that which is studied and even its total negation (atheism), although one ought to be aware that many who engage in critical reflection upon their faith and that of others often discover that their own faith has deepened as a result of their inquiries. Still, one needs to acknowledge from the start that theology involves risk to one's self-understanding. Precisely because of this threat, some students might experience anxiety about the discipline, especially if they are fearful that they might lose their own faith or be disturbed by knowledge that might call their particular understanding of faith into question. This risk makes theology similar to philosophy but perhaps different from most other academic subjects whose object does not directly impact one's self-knowledge and worldview. The existential relationship between the student and the object of Christian theological study can be uncomfortable, especially in light of the possibility that one's faith or worldview, whether secular or religious, might need to be revised. This reflection on one's worldview or faith, one's own and that of others, which the study of theology initiates, may threaten, even shatter, one's personal equilibrium, but the promise of theology is that those who engage in such reflection again and again discover that their own earlier understanding or faith has deepened into a new equilibrium, in what **Paul Ricoeur** calls "a second naiveté."[7]

Christian theology thus invites students to be self-critical in light of the subject matter of theology, to be open to new insights and criticisms that

---

[7] Ricoeur, *The Symbolism of Evil*, 351.

theology itself might present to the student and to others, to be more aware of one's religious presuppositions and prejudices and how they themselves might be in need of revision in light of what is uncovered in the discipline and in related scholarly fields.

> By its very nature, of course, the knowledge and scholarly study of faith can be not only controversial but contagious: it can lead lifelong believers to surrender cherished tenets of faith, or it can engage students existentially in such a way that, having come to observe and criticize, they remain to pray. The university must not pretend that either of these outcomes cannot happen within its walls; nor should it, in its care for its members as human beings, dismiss such concerns as trivial.[8]

Moreover, the study of Christian traditions and faith need not necessarily be undertaken by one who is a scholarly outsider to that tradition and faith, as if only a non-Christian or non-religious person or one who is not committed to a given tradition could provide careful, accurate description and objective analysis of the Christian tradition. In fact, scholars of differing religions who lack any religious convictions cannot avoid being committed to *some* kind of tradition, perhaps the Enlightenment tradition that aspires to scholarly neutrality and objectivity, and yet this tradition, too, has been shown to be prone to illusion and distortion.[9] Commitment to the religious tradition one is studying need not disqualify one from engaging that tradition critically, carefully, and rigorously.

Christian theology holds out the promise that the student of theology might even be surprised that his or her critical inquiry into the Christian faith and traditions results in a deeper understanding of God, a greater appreciation of one's considered faith, and a posture in which one is grateful for new insights into divine wisdom.

(3) Christian theology is a university discipline that invites critical and self-critical reflection *on the revelation of God, the world, and human beings in the apostolic witness to Jesus Christ*. A key presupposition of Christian theology is the **self-revelation of God** in and through the traditions of ancient Israel and the prophetic and apostolic witness to Jesus of Nazareth. The "knowledge of God that is made possible by God, and therefore by revelation, is one of the basic conditions of the concept of theology as such. Otherwise the possibility

---

[8] Pelikan, *The Idea of the University*, 40.
[9] One of the abiding claims of post-modern critiques of "modernity" is that all scholars are biased and prejudiced, often in ways they themselves do not perceive.

of the knowledge of God is logically inconceivable; it would contradict the very idea of God" (Pannenberg 1.2). According to the central figures within the Christian theological tradition, divine revelation is the principal source of all Christian theological knowledge and provides the basis for the response of faith. Thus the revelation of God, which both non-Christians (at least in a fragmentary manner) and Christians have received, serves as the subject of theology, since God cannot be studied directly or unambiguously. The basis for knowledge of God is God's own self-giving.

Yet God's own self-giving is properly received only in *faith* ("trust," "confidence"). Such faith is indeed an actual phenomenon that could be studied critically by examining Christian biblical documents, Christian confessions of faith, the history of Christian theological reflection, Christian accounts of basic human experiences, and Christian engagement with other religions, their documents and confessional writings. Nevertheless, while Christian theology investigates the nature and basis of Christian faith and seeks to clarify its meaning for people today, faith in and of itself is not the proper object of theological investigation. The proper object of theological study—as Bultmann and Pannenberg have rightly stressed in their differing ways—must be faith *in God*, as it is properly grounded in the witness to the gospel in the preaching of the word of God. Thus the question and meaning of *God* must remain central to the critical inquiry of Christian theology, even if theology cannot avoid paying attention to the nature, form, and content of the Christian *faith* in God as revealed in and through ancient Israel and Jesus.

Theology, if it is *Christian* theology, examines the claims that are made about Jesus of Nazareth, especially the claim that he is the promised Christ or Messiah of God in whom there is salvation. Such an inquiry begins with the questions, "Who or what is a 'Christ?'" What does it mean to call Jesus "the Christ of God?" What does it mean to speak of God on the basis of Jesus? What does Jesus reveal about God? What is the salvation to which the revelation of God in and through Jesus bears witness? These are the fundamental presuppositional questions that make theology "Christian." These questions have their starting point in the apostolic witness to Jesus as the Christ.

But Christian theology is not merely about the revelation of God in and through Jesus; it is also about how the world and human beings in the world are revealed and exposed for who they are in and through the revelation of God in Jesus. Following Luther, Schleiermacher, Bultmann, and Bayer, one needs to underscore that Christian theology is also about (sinful) human beings who are the object of God's forgiveness, love, and redemption in and through Jesus of Nazareth. Given this two-fold focus, on sinful human beings and on God who addresses sinful human beings in Christ, Christian theology examines such additional questions as: What does Jesus reveal about human beings? Who am I in light of the witness to Jesus the Christ? What do I believe about myself and other human beings on the basis of the witness to Jesus?

Because the revelation of God in Jesus Christ is understood by Christians to imply a comprehensive understanding of reality, Christian theology must also address itself to understanding "the world" on the basis of the Christian understanding of God. For example, what does the revelation of God and human beings in Jesus Christ imply about non-human creatures and creation as a whole? "Inasmuch as we understand God as Creator, Redeemer, and Consummator, and hence as the ground, measure, and end of all reality, all aspects of the Christian faith's understanding of reality come together, rooted in the Christian understanding of God" (RPP 5.468 [Schwöbel]). Aquinas is quite right to state that Christian theology is about God and about all other things "under the aspect of God" or in relation to God.

In both directions, whether toward the revelation of God or toward the revelation of human beings and the world within the revelation of God, theology is a critical-historical-systematic discipline that inquires into the basis and nature of Christian faith in God. Traditionally, this faith is partially informed by "**natural theology**," subject to the critical faculties of human reasoning, and partially by "**revealed theology**," which is given through the originating events (and witnesses to the events), and which has been, and is being, transmitted through church traditions. Hence, theology has historically involved the interplay of reason and revelation, of philosophy and theology, even if some theologians, notably Luther, Bultmann, and Barth, stressed that so-called "natural theologies" have little or nothing to do with God as "Wholly Other" (completely transcendent to created reality) who addresses sinful human beings with a word that can be received and understood only by faith.

This part of the definition has a negative and a positive aim. It desires to resist the separation of the historical-critical investigation of the Christian faith from the critical-theological inquiry into the truth and essence of that faith. Just as historical investigation cannot be isolated from a metaphysical or theological understanding of one kind or another, so theological investigation cannot be kept in isolation from historical understanding. This part of the definition also resists the notion, defended especially by Schleiermacher, that Christian theology is grounded in the university merely or primarily because of its practical goal of teaching the skills necessary for church leadership. Rather, this third part of the definition helps to keep open the question of theological truth and illusion and to return again and again to the distinctive *theological* dimension of that which is investigated within this academic discipline. While theology must continue to learn from those academic disciplines devoted to the history, phenomenology, philosophy, sociology, and psychology of religion, it will seek to identify and make explicit its uniquely theological perspective on the meaning and truth of Christian faith in the revelation of God, and on the possibility of understanding and responding to the self-revelation of God in the present intellectual situation. No, one, academic discipline has a purchase on the entirety of knowledge or the totality of reality; but theology, unlike many other disciplines, desires to understand the final and total meaning of the whole of reality by means of hermeneutical inquiry. In this regard, too, Christian theology is distinct from religious studies and the philosophy of religion, which approach the Christian faith, if at all, on the basis of a different perspective, in view of different goals, and through different methods of inquiry. Theology nevertheless desires critical engagement with these other disciplines for the sake of greater clarity about its own subject matter.

This third part of the definition also implies the historical-critical and hermeneutical character of academic theology. Because the revelation of God in Jesus is given within the apostolic and prophetic witness, this witness itself calls for critical, historical, and theological investigation. Such investigation of the originating sources of Christian faith (**Sacred Scripture** or **the Bible**) involves careful attention to the variety of literary genres and modes of thought within those writings. The student of the biblical writings must be concerned both for the archeology of the biblical texts and for the dynamic trajectories of their interpretation.

(4) Christian theology is a university discipline that invites critical and self-critical reflection on the revelation of God and human beings in the apostolic witness to Jesus Christ, *as this revelation has been understood and believed in the churches over time.* Theology, if it is *Christian* theology, examines the witness to the self-revelation of God in Jesus that is embedded in the apostolic writings of the early Christian Church, yet that witness has never been alone or isolated from the long tradition of Christian believing and practicing. Theology cannot be merely about Christian *faith*, but includes

investigation of the basis or bases for that faith and the trajectories in which that faith has been held and transmitted. To be sure, Christian theology is primarily oriented to the person of Jesus, as he is testified to by the apostles and prophets (both the OT and NT), yet it also engages the historic witness of the Christian churches through the centuries. Likewise, theology explores the nature and content of Christian faith as it has been debated and defined through the ages and within many different cultural settings.

There is a kind of balancing act that occurs in Christian theology, as one moves from the originating, core witness that Jesus is the Christ to contemporary understandings of that witness in the various global, cultural contexts and to questions about the present meaning of Christian faith. Clearly, Christian theology is not something that is constructed out of thin air. Rather, much like the study of civic law, the study of Christian theology involves critical inquiry into the historical and cultural traditions of theology and how those traditions have been understood over time. Is there a "core" to the Christian tradition? Assuming there is a basic or elemental content to the Christian faith, how have Christians disagreed with one another about what constitutes that core? How has the Christian faith been understood and believed over time? How has the Christian faith been understood similarly and differently by peoples from differing cultures? What is Christian faith? What is the nature of the trust and confidence in God that Christian believers receive because of the self-revelation of God in Jesus the Christ? How should that faith or trust/confidence be understood in light of contemporary challenges to that faith, some of them novel? Once again, the hermeneutical (interpretive) nature of Christian theology is apparent, as soon as one begins to wrestle with the challenge of retrieving and reformulating the content of Christian faith for today.

(5) Christian theology as a university discipline, thus defined, has a four-fold goal:

> (a) to understand the content of the apostolic witness clearly within the ecumenical and intellectual situation of the present;
> (b) to consider the nature of Christian faith as trust in the gospel promise given within the apostolic witness;
> (c) to identify weak or faulty understandings of the Christian faith, either in the witness itself or in later developments;
> (d) to appropriate the possible truth and wisdom in the witness.

These four aims should not be understood as being separated from one another, as if they were separate steps in the theological process. They are intimately related to each another in the process of understanding that which academic theology investigates.

(a) The first aim is toward understanding the apostolic witness within the intellectual situation of the present. Included in this process of understanding is the awareness that contemporary Christians have not originated or invented their faith, but that it is related to an originating tradition or set of traditions that have come down to them in authoritative ways that are complex and partly conflicting. Thus, one aspect of the contemporary process of understanding is *ecumenical* in nature; that is, it is oriented toward the world-wide diversity and divisions among the living communities of Christians, toward understanding and endeavoring to reconcile those differences theologically by returning again and again to the originating sources of the faith and their relation to the living communities of faith: both the Jewish communities, with respect to the Hebrew Scriptures that as OT are also treated as Sacred Scripture by Christians, and the multiplicity of Christian communities. The process of understanding includes humility and openness to learn from Christians and other religious people beyond one's immediate church tradition and confessional circle. Contemporary theology must also address how the originating apostolic tradition has undergone transformation over time, how it has been challenged through the centuries, how it has been defended in view of criticisms, and how it is currently being debated and discussed. Thus it is only in the fact that Christian theology must be oriented toward historical claims, and the interpretation of those claims through the course of history, that it can faithfully be oriented toward the present intellectual situation. That orientation is the other aspect of the contemporary process of understanding the apostolic witness.

The *present situation* will necessarily involve all that Tillich referred to when he spoke of "the situation," that is, "all the various cultural forms" (Tillich 1.5) that express the self-understanding of contemporary human beings such as scientific, economic, religious, philosophical, literary, and artistic understandings. Christian theology, at least as it is undertaken within modern, western universities, cannot merely repeat prophetic and apostolic expressions and modes of thought without giving some attention to how those expressions and modes of thought are being retrieved and reformulated (and perhaps distorted) in present cultural expressions and ought thus to be understood in the present intellectual situation. While Christian theologians disagree among themselves as to the degree to which the Christian faith can be adapted to the "modern mind" without losing its essential and unique character, even most who stress the contrast between modernity and Christianity acknowledge the need for contemporary translation of the Christian tradition. In short, the "present ecumenical and intellectual situation" includes a variety of overlapping realities: the diverse communities of Christians around the world, their beliefs and practices; the results of the scholarly investigation of Christian origins and the historical development of Christian traditions and practices; the academic and cultural milieu of one's university; and modern society, one's national and global life, our common human problems, crises, and challenges.

Thus, there is the need for Christian theology to engage in responsible dialogue with other academic disciplines, to encourage interdisciplinary collaboration and research, and to test theological positions and assertions in the light of knowledge that arises from the other disciplines. The fulfillment of this need will help to improve the clarity of theological expression and the articulation of Christian theological understandings in relation to the current state of knowledge about matters that overlap with theological concerns. That dialogue may invite such questions as: Can one speak of God meaningfully and carefully within the context of the sciences within the university? Is God real or an illusion? How does my experience of God relate to the experiences of which others speak? How is one to understand the Christian doctrine of creation in light of contemporary scientific knowledge? What is the contemporary meaning of the apostolic witness to the resurrection of Jesus and the consummation of creation?

(b) As will become clearer in subsequent chapters, the promise of the good news or gospel about Jesus Christ is at the center of the apostolic witness to him. So a second aim of academic theology is to explore the nature of the gospel and nature of Christian faith. What is the nature of this gospel promise? What is its content? What is the relation of faith to the gospel promise? What is the nature of faith in the promise? Christian theology, if it is to be faithful to its basis, will be primarily oriented toward faith in the gospel promise as this is articulated within the apostolic witness to Jesus, his death and resurrection. But that ancient promise is itself aimed toward contemporary people today. So it challenges one to ask, is it still valid and trustworthy today, and, if so, how and on what basis? Christian theology thus strives to make clear the character of the gospel as promise and the character of Christian faith as trust in that promise.

(c) Identifying weak, or even faulty, theological understandings in the witness itself or in later developments of Christian theology is a third aim of academic theology. This aim directly relates to the critical character of

Christian theology. The goal is to develop appropriate understandings of the Christian witness and to criticize understandings that are contrary to authentic Christian faith. The history of the Christian tradition demonstrates how Christian theology has sought to understand its object aright, "to understand God truly," and to avoid false understandings, self-deception, and illusions.

The Christian tradition has thus historically maintained a distinction between "false teaching" ("**heresy**") and "correct teaching" ("**orthodoxy**"), between behaviors and practices that are consistent with Christian faith, hope, and love, and those that are not. Within the early church, an overseer or bishop, "as stewards of God," "must be faithful to the reliable word as taught, so that he is able to give instruction in sound teaching and also to refute those who speak against it" (Titus 1.9). Throughout the history of Christianity, people have raised critical questions regarding the right formulation of teachings about God and Jesus Christ, about sin and salvation, about the church and its ministry. Some beliefs and practices were eventually deemed to fall outside of "sound doctrine." For example, was the lopping off of "infidel" heads by medieval Christian crusaders consistent with orthodox Christian beliefs and practices, or contrary to these ideals? Was the transformation of Christian symbols and beliefs by German Nazi Christians legitimate or illegitimate? What about the insistence of some Christians that the first chapters of the Bible must be understood as literal, straight-forward historical descriptions of how God has created the universe or the first human beings? Or the insistence of other Christians regarding the inherent incompatibility between economic capitalism and Christian social teaching? Or between the latter and the production and maintenance of nuclear weapons?

Through critical, hermeneutical investigation of the Christian faith, its sources, and traditions of interpretation—including the interaction with the social and natural sciences and other academic disciplines—Christian theology seeks to expose elements within its own tradition that need to be critically understood and even resisted on both theological and moral grounds (for example, how the Christian tradition has supported and even sanctioned the exploitation of poor people, people of color, and women). Such testing, critiquing, and revising are aspects of the process of interpreting the Christian tradition so as to expose injustice and detect bias. This process surely need not, and should not, lead to the complete rejection of the tradition or the suppression of its influences within the academy and the larger western culture, which some positivistic philosophers are inclined to do. It can lead, through critical reflection, to a re-appropriation of the ancient tradition and its wisdom and truth, refined, for example, through the critical process of "alienating distanciation," explanation, "diagnosis," and understanding, to use Ricoeur's conceptual language for describing the critical moments in the dialectical process of understanding a given tradition.

In the modern period some people have critically rejected all religious beliefs, including Christian ones, as being illusory. These critics use the term "theology" in a pejorative manner, to dismiss the discipline as impractical or as foolish nonsense. Proponents of such a negative view of theology will typically call to mind the pointless speculations of medieval theologians about how many angels can dance on the head of a pin. Such critics of theology might also appeal to Kant's critique of theological speculation and his insistence that humans can have no knowledge of "the noumenal world" (the world as it really is in itself) and that real knowledge can only arise from reflection on "the phenomenal world" (the world as it appears to us through sense experience). In view of modern criticisms of Christian theology, academic theology has had to wrestle with the nature of the object(s) it investigates and with the proper understanding of the relation between faith and reason: Is a given understanding of Christian faith free from illusion? Is such a faith well grounded? In what ways have specific understandings and articulations of Christian faith been blind to evidence that rubs against those understandings and cherished beliefs? There is no room for such blind faith in any academic discipline, least of all in theology. Still, theology has also needed to examine critically the claims of those who oppose theology and reject that which theology investigates. Christian theology is concerned to identify where the natural and social sciences and the humanities might be blind to the accomplishments within human culture and religious traditions, specifically the tradition of Christianity, critically appropriated, when they attempt to ground all human value and wisdom solely within their own academic disciplines.

Academic theology cannot avoid engagement with both of these activities, both the concern to evaluate internal understandings of the Christian faith within the Christian churches themselves (what used to be called "**polemics**") and the concern to address external criticisms of the Christian faith by those who are antithetical toward it (what used to be called "**apologetics**"). For example, theology will address itself critically to the claims and actions of Christians and others who insist on defending and propagating interpretations of the Bible that are out of touch with basic scientific understandings, and assess those claims and practices in light of the sources and norm of Christian faith. Theology will also attend itself critically to the claims of those who are completely dismissive of central assertions within the Christian tradition, or whose positions otherwise conflict with the essential content of the gospel promise, to assess them in light of the sources and norm of Christian faith. By addressing all theological and atheological "fronts," theology can perhaps set forth an alternative position, which Don Browning has rightly called "a revived Christian humanism," namely, a position that is more faithful to the complexities of reality, more attendant to the problems of evil and injustice in the world, and more consistent with the Christian-humanist pursuit of truth, justice, and wisdom.

(d) A final aim of academic theology is to hold open the possibility that the student of theology might be able to appropriate truth and wisdom from the Christian tradition. This last aim might be the most foreign to many university students, since they are acutely aware of the plurality and relativity of all human knowledge and are skeptical about claims to "truth," especially a claim to universal truth on the part of a specific religion. For many people religion is merely a matter of taste, not a matter of truth and wisdom. In our time, scientific knowledge is held to be the epitome of truth and the only reliable guide to what is real. While university theology must take seriously the evidence and argumentation of other academic disciplines, it will want to make the case that scientific knowledge is not the only form of knowledge worth pursuing in the academy, that there are matters that properly fall into the domains of wisdom and folly, and that matters of faith—of what one ultimately believes about one's self in relation to the total of what is real— take one beyond the capability of empirical verification but not thereby beyond what is worth knowing and even treasuring. In this way, theology joins those who defend the importance of the humanities in the academic pursuit of truth, virtue, and wisdom. This pursuit should not be understood as being inherently in conflict with the knowledge that is produced in the natural, human, and social sciences, based as they are on mathematics and empirical observation, but as complementing that knowledge and allowing that knowledge to complement the investigations and pursuits of theology, despite the fact that obvious tensions and contradictions will likely continue to exist between the sciences and the humanities (the arts, literature, philosophy, religious studies, history, theology, and other disciplines that resist merely mathematical and statistical methods).

Unlike those who think that all forms of metaphysics and theology have become outdated, Christian theologians and some philosophers will point out "that the propensity for metaphysics in humans is not so easily suppressed."[10] Is it not part of being human to ask questions about the meaning of the whole and the possibility of lasting truth, virtue, and wisdom? These questions take one near the center of Christian theology. To partially paraphrase Ricoeur: "the wager" of Christian academic theology is that critical engagement with the revelation of God in Jesus Christ, its historical transmission, and the trajectories of its interpretation, will give rise to a deeper understanding of God, the world, and human beings, as given within the Christian tradition, that is, a deeper understanding of Christian faith and Christian wisdom.[11]

Key Words

academic theology	revealed theology
critical reflection	sacred Scripture
hermeneutical	the Bible
demystification	ecumenical
Paul Ricoeur	heresy
self-revelation of God	orthodoxy
faith	polemics
natural theology	apologetics

Reference literature

See the listings for "theology" in Chapter 1.

---

[10] Gadamer, "The Future of the European Humanities," 198.

[11] See Ricoeur, *The Symbolism of Evil*, 355–7. "I wager that I shall have a better understanding of man and of the bond between the being of man and the being of all beings if I follow the *indication* of symbolic thought. That wager then becomes the task of *verifying* my wager and saturating it, so to speak, with intelligibility. In return, the task transforms my wager: in betting *on* the significance of the symbolic world, I bet at the same time *that* my wager will be restored to me in power of reflection, in the element of coherent discourse" (ibid., 355).

For introductions to the nature and task of Christian theology in the more important textbooks of dogmatics

SBO §§ 1–5; SCF § 15; Aulen 3–30; Barth 1/1 § 1; Brunner 1:3–21; Tillich
1:3–68; Weber–1:3–69; Macquarrie 1–40; BJ (Braaten) 1:5–60; Migliore
1–19; Pannenberg 1:1–61; Peters 3–78; Grenz 1–25; Hall 1:17–56, 247–324;
Jenson 1:3–22; ICT 3–26; McGrath 101–4

For older understandings of the nature and task of Christian theology

Aquinas 1a.1; on Luther (Bayer 15–82); on Lutheran Orthodoxy (Schmid
15–25); on Reformed Orthodoxy (Heppe 1–11)

Questions for review and discussion

1   Does the place in which Christian theology is undertaken make a difference for how it is undertaken? The author is critical of Schleiermacher's practical orientation. Why? Do you agree with the author's concern?

2   Do you agree that even non-Christian and non-religious people should study Christian theology as an academic subject? If not, why not? If so, for what reason(s) should they study theology?

3   Is Christian theology a credible academic discipline in a university? Does it deal with an actual reality, or is it merely a matter of human illusion and imagination? How is theology different from other academic disciplines? How is it similar?

4   The author also uses the terms "ecumenical" and "hermeneutical" to describe the nature of Christian theology. What do these terms imply about how Christian theology is done?

5   What does it mean to say that Christian theology has "a critical task"? What gets criticized? Do you think it is appropriate for Christian theologians to keep re-thinking about God, the world, and human beings?

6   Why does theology involve risk to one's self-understanding? How would you describe your current comfort level in relation to academic theology?

7   To what degree should Christians pay attention to scholarly knowledge from non-theological disciplines? What is/are the risk(s) here? Conversely, should the non-theological disciplines pay any attention to the claims made within Christian theology? What is/are the risk(s) here?

8   What is the importance of "revelation" in Christian theology? What does that concept imply about God? In other words, what is it about God that requires revelation? What gets revealed in the apostolic witness to Jesus?

9   What is faith? The chapter uses several other terms to describe faith: knowledge, trust, confidence. Which of these three terms is more central to the concept of faith, if any, and why or why not? Do you agree that faith can be subject to critical investigation? Why, or why not? What is the relation between God and faith?

10   Review the author's definition of Christian theology. How, if at all, would you modify it? Why?

Suggestions for further reading

On the nature and tasks of Christian theology

Karl Barth, *Evangelical Theology: An Introduction* (Grand Rapids: Eerdmans, 1963) [Chapter 1 in this brief book addresses the purposes of Protestant theology. This is one of the more accessible routes into Barth's theology.]

Karl Barth, "The Word of God as the Task of Theology," *The Beginnings of Dialectical Theology*, ed. James M. Robinson, trans. Keith R. Crim and Louis De Grazia (Richmond: John Knox, 1968) [This 1922 essay helped to define the character of "Dialectical Theology" over against the liberal Protestant tradition that had been established by Schleiermacher and furthered by later German Protestants. The essay stresses the revelation of God from above as the proper starting point of theology.]

Oswald Bayer, *Theology the Lutheran Way*, ed. and trans. Jeffrey G. Silcock and Mark C. Mattes (Grand Rapids: Eerdmans, 2007) [A truncated version of Bayer's original introduction to theology. He identifies its subject according to Luther's definition, namely, the God who justifies sinners and sinners who need to be justified.]

Rudolf Bultmann, *What Is Theology?*, Eberhard Jüngel and Klaus W. Müller (eds), trans. Roy A. Harrisville (Minneapolis: Fortress, 1997) [An excellent English translation of Bultmann's 1926 lectures on theological encyclopedia. His opening chapter underscores "the risk" of faith and the impossibility of speaking "of God."]

Rebecca S. Chopp and Mark Lewis Taylor, "Introduction: Crisis, Hope, and Contemporary Theology," in *Reconstructing Christian Theology*, Rebecca S. Chopp and Mark Lewis Taylor (eds) (Minneapolis: Fortress, 1994), 1–24 [A helpful overview of the varieties of theological options in the academy near the end of the previous century.]

Gerhard Ebeling, "Discussion Theses for a Course of Introductory Lectures on the Study of Theology," *Word and Faith*, trans. James W. Leitch (London: SCM Press, 1963), 424–33 [This essay sets forth an understanding of Christian theology by one of the leading existentialist theologians of the past century.]

Gerhard Ebeling, *The Study of Theology*, trans. Duane A. Priebe (Minneapolis: Fortress Press, 1978) [This is Ebeling's set of lectures on theological encyclopedia for the German university scene in the late 1960s and early 1970s. Though dated, his account of the orientation of theology as a whole in Chapter 1 provides a helpful description of the discipline within a university context. Throughout his discussion of the multiple branches of theology in the rest of the book he continually reminds us of the hermeneutical nature of Christian theology.]

Francis Schüssler Fiorenza and John P. Galvin (eds), *Systematic Theology: Roman Catholic Perspectives*, 2nd edn (Minneapolis: Fortress, 2011), 1–78. [The introduction by Fiorenza provides an excellent, recent orientation to the tasks and methods of theology as seen by a leading Roman Catholic theologian in America.]

Bradley C. Hanson, *Introduction to Christian Theology* (Minneapolis: Augsburg Fortress, 1997) [A popular college-level textbook that is written from the perspective of a mainstream American Lutheran influenced by post-liberal theology.]

Gareth Jones, *Critical Theology: Questions of Truth and Method* (New York: Paragon House, 1998) [The first part of this book examines several of the figures introduced here in this chapter. The second part sets forth Jones' own understanding of the method of Christian theology in terms of mystery, event, and rhetoric.]

Alister E. McGrath, *Christian Theology: An Introduction*, 5th edn (Oxford: Wiley-Blackwell, 2011) [Popular introduction to systematic theology by an important British-Evangelical scholar.]

Daniel L. Migliore, *Faith Seeking Understanding: An Introduction to Christian Theology*, 2nd edn (Grand Rapids: Eerdmans, 2004), 1–19 [This is a major seminary-level textbook by a principal Reformed theologian in the U.S. Chapter 1 extends elements that have been made in the present chapter.]

Schubert Ogden, *On Theology* (Dallas: Southern Methodist University Press, 1986) [A set of essays on the nature and task of Christian theology as viewed by one of the leading Protestant revisionist theologians in America during the past 50 years.]

Richard J. Plantinga, Thomas R. Thompson, and Matthew D. Lundberg, *An Introduction to Christian Theology* (Cambridge: Cambridge University Press, 2010) [Chapter 1 in this widely-used college textbook provides a helpful introduction to the nature of Christian theology from a Reformed Protestant perspective.]

Dorothee Sölle, *Thinking about God: An Introduction to Theology* (Philadelphia: Trinity Press International, 1990) [An English translation of introductory lectures to Christian theology by a leading German feminist theologian from the second half of the last century. Sölle delivered these lectures to large audiences of non-experts. She covers a wide swath of theological territory in a very accessible way, although some of her illustrations are oriented more to her European context.]

David Tracy, *The Analogical Imagination: Christian Theology and the Culture of Pluralism* (New York: Crossroad, 1981), 3–98 [This is the major work in fundamental theology and theological encyclopedia by the leading American Roman Catholic revisionist theologian of the past half century. The first 95 pages explore the nature and tasks of Christian theology. He further develops his Tillichian understanding of theology as a critical process of correlation between the symbols of Christian faith, on the one hand, and one's contemporary culture, on the other. One of the most discussed books in Christian theology during the past 30 years.]

Part II

The Subject of Christian Theology

5

The Problem of God

Before turning to examine the nature and basis of Christian faith in God, one needs to acknowledge the problems that attend talking about God in our contemporary western culture. What is meant by this term "God"? The chapter explores some of the ways in which the concept of God has been criticized and why the concept nevertheless persists in being discussed by modern people. The chapter gives special attention to the nature of "religious experience" and how it gives rise to "talk of God."

To what are Christians referring when they speak of "God"? What are atheists rejecting when they confidently assert they do not believe in "God"? To speak of God is not without its problems, even among those who use the term in the singular ("one God"). What does the monotheist mean when he or she uses the word "God"? Given the plethora of names for the one God within the monotheistic religions (Judaism, Christianity, Islam), and the accompanying understandings that are attached to those names, are there not numerous contrasting conceptions of God? Is God personal and thus addressable, as traditional Jews, Christians, and Muslims believe? Or is God impersonal, as Spinoza and others have thought? Or is God merely an abstract principle or relationship, the Ultimate Principle or Primordial Unity? Or does God best equate to the notion of "the supreme Being?" If so, what does that expression mean? Is God distinct from the universe, the ultimate that is not dependent on anything else for its existence and upon which all other things so depend? Or is God in some way identical to nature or reality (as in forms of pantheism, wherein all is understood to be God)? Both Aquinas and Spinoza used the expression "the Supreme Being," and yet each understood this notion differently from the other.

What do people mean by the term "God"? Does it signify "that than which nothing greater can be thought," as Anselm and Aquinas thought (see Aquinas 1a.2.1)? Or is God "the One who Is" or "Being Itself," as

Augustine confessed on the basis of his interpretation of Exodus 3.14?[1] What about Aristotle's views on "the unmoved Mover" or Hegel's reflections on God as the "world-spirit"? Is God best understood in the categories of so-called classical philosophical **theism**, wherein God is said to be omnipotent (all-powerful), omniscient (all-knowing), immutable (changeless), omnipresent (present everywhere), eternal (timeless), and unconditioned?[2] Or is God better understood in the categories of **process theology**, wherein God or the Ultimate Reality is not omnipotent, omniscient, immutable or timeless, but is dynamic, changing, ever responding to created beings and their actions, standing in a reciprocal relation to the world of constant change, and thus totally conditioned? Or maybe God just does not exist in any sense whatsoever.

What do people mean by the term "God"? For example, what do American atheists (who make up about 5 percent of the total U.S. population) reject when they tell pollsters that they do not believe in "God"?[3] What do they understand by the term "God," whose reality they reject? What are the remaining 95 percent affirming when they use the term? Does the word "God" refer to an actual reality, or is God merely the subjective projection of an individual's wishes and opinions, as **Sigmund Freud** (1856–1939) suggested in his psychological explanation for the origins of all religions in infantile wish fulfillments (discovered in dreams and neurotic symptoms), or the result of some other merely materialistic, naturalistic mechanism or process?[4]

If God is understood by Christians to be transcendent to all that is real, how does one know that God is in fact really real and not an illusion?

---

[1] Augustine of Hippo, *The City of God*, trans. Henry Bettenson (New York: Penguin, 1984), Book VIII, Chapter 11, *et passim*.
[2] The term "theism" is also related to the Greek term "*theos*" ("god"). Theism within philosophy refers to rational discussion about the nature of God. "Classical theism" is built upon Greek philosophical reflection on the nature and attributes of God (often apart from any consideration of the special revelation of God in Israel and Jesus).
[3] The term "atheist" is open to misunderstanding; also by people who are asked if they are "atheists." Nevertheless, the term is often understood to describe a person who denies the reality of God or a Higher Power and insists on a materialistic-positivistic worldview. For statistical information on "atheism," see Tom W. Smith, "Belief About God Across Time and Countries," NORC at the University of Chicago (April 18, 2012), http://www.norc.org [accessed January 26, 2013]. This report indicates that belief in God is highest among older people and increases with age, even among populations with high percentages of atheists. For the 5 percent figure on atheists in America, see the 2009 Pew survey and recent WIN-Gallup International polling data.
[4] See Sigmund Freud, *The Future of an Illusion*, trans. W. D. Robson-Scott, rev. by J. Strachey (Garden City, NY: Doubleday Anchor Books, 1964); and idem, *Moses and Monotheism* (New York: Vintage, 1967).

Could it be that God does not really "exist" in any sense of the term? Some Christian theologians, such as Tillich, insist that God does *not* exist, since "existence" implies that God is a "thing" that exists as an object alongside other objects. For these theologians, God is beyond existence or finite being and essence (See Tillich 1.205). They prefer to say that God is "real" or that God is "the really real" who transcends finite reality. But even then others might ask, "If God is said to be 'beyond existence' and even 'beyond being,' is God in any sense 'real?'"

The rejection of God

This latter question, of course, pushes one to consider the various forms of **atheism**, disbelief in God(s), that have arisen since at least the fifth century BC, when certain skeptical individuals leveled criticism against the traditional gods in the ancient cultures of India, China, and Greece, and when some non-theistic religions emerged as well (such as Buddhism and Confucianism). During the Enlightenment, European philosophers and scholars also developed arguments that attacked traditional religious belief in God and that explained all religions as purely human phenomena without recourse to God or the divine. For example, **David Hume** (1711–76) was deeply skeptical of all religious beliefs. Despite his own uncertainty about the possibility of a divine cause or causes for the apparent order in the universe, he thought that all religions could best be explained naturally as the result of human fears of the unknown, principally their fear of death, and of their hope for life after death.[5] He thought that, as more and more matters that had formerly been mysterious became more fully understandable through scientific explanation, religions and their beliefs/superstitions would gradually disappear. He predicted that such a disappearance would occur after about 300 years of scientific advance.[6]

---

[5] David Hume, "The Natural History of Religion," in David Hume, *Writings on Religion*, ed. Antony Flew (La Salle, IL: Open Court, 1992), 114. Hume's basic position is also reflected in the philosophy of Bertrand Russell (1872–1970): "Religion is based, I think, primarily and mainly upon fear. It is partly the terror of the unknown and partly, as I have said, the wish to feel that you have a kind of elder brother who will stand by you in all your troubles and disputes. Fear is the basis of the whole thing—fear of the mysterious, fear of defeat, fear of death" (Bertrand Russell, "Why I am Not a Christian," in *Why I am Not a Christian and Other Essays on Religion and Related Subjects* [New York: Simon and Schuster, 1957], 22).

[6] Hume died in 1776.

Ironically, modern atheism was itself propelled by the arguments of seventeenth-century French Roman Catholic theologians who appealed to philosophical and scientific arguments, and not primarily to biblical revelation, to defend their belief in God. When these arguments were themselves attacked by later thinkers and found seriously wanting, many in France and elsewhere concluded that belief in God is entirely irrational, and that atheism is the more defensible, rational position.[7]

Subsequent developments of atheism were influenced especially by **Immanuel Kant**, who subjected traditional "rational proofs" for God's existence to careful critique; by **Ludwig Feuerbach**, who argued that Christian belief in God is an illusion and a "projection" of human wishes and ideals (humankind is really "the essence of Christianity"); by **Karl Marx**, who also asserted that Christian belief is an illusion and that religion in general has functioned historically like an opiate to keep the proletarian masses numbed in their places of subordination within society by social elites (including the clergy); and by **Friedrich Nietzsche**, who proclaimed "the death of God" and called for the complete eradication of God from human life and the world since the notion is stifling and based on false conjecture.[8]

Others point to natural and human evils to reject belief in an all-good, all-powerful deity. For example, in view of the mass murder of Jews by the Nazis, the radical Jewish rabbi Richard L. Rubenstein Jr. (b. 1924) could no longer believe in God's providential direction of history and God's special relation to the Jewish people.[9] He asserted that these beliefs must be rejected "after Auschwitz" and that people must face the stark reality that they live in an absurd, blind, and indifferent universe. For Rubenstein human beings must create their own religious rituals "in a world without God." Then, too, many Christian believers are aware of the element of doubt within their own faith, even as they are tempted by the faith of the atheist or at least that of the self-sufficient "secular humanist." The possibility of functional atheism

---

[7] Michael J. Buckley, *At the Origins of Modern Atheism* (New Haven: Yale University Press, 1990).

[8] Immanuel Kant, *The Critique of Pure Reason*, trans. Norman Kemp Smith (New York: St. Martin's Press, 1965), 454–531; Ludwig Feuerbach, *The Essence of Christianity*, trans. George Eliot (New York: Harper & Row, 1957); Karl Marx and Friedrich Engels, *Marx and Engels on Religion*, intr. Reinhold Niebuhr (New York: Schocken, 1964), 13–87; Friedrich Nietzsche, *The Gay Science*, trans. Walter Kaufmann (New York: Random House Vintage Books, 1974); and idem, *Thus Spoke Zarathustra*, trans. Walter Kaufmann (New York: Viking, 1966).

[9] Richard L. Rubenstein Jr., *After Auschwitz* (Indianapolis: Bobbs-Merrill, 1966).

dwells in every human being. (How many believe in the reality of God, but live their lives as if God does not exist?)

Over the past 400 years many western thinkers have taken an altogether negative position against the possibility of belief in God. Although he remained a faithful Catholic Christian throughout his life, the philosopher **René Descartes** (1596–1650), who claimed to have had a religious-mystical experience of the mathematical order of the universe, nevertheless set forth a method of inquiry that cast doubt upon all metaphysical assertions. He defended his method of radical doubt (rejecting everything that can be doubted in the least) so as to arrive at an unshakeable philosophical foundation, namely, himself as a doubter. Such a turn to the individual knowing/doubting subject, however, created a crisis in western metaphysics when British empiricists, especially Hume, questioned the distinction between ideas of objects and the sense experience of objects that cause those ideas, thus casting doubt upon the reality of material substance altogether. As we have already noted, Hume's skepticism led Immanuel Kant to articulate the limits of human knowledge and to bar the door to any legitimate metaphysical knowledge. By the beginning of the twentieth century many practicing philosophers had rejected the idea of God altogether as a fanciful human invention. Despite the fact that the twentieth-century German philosopher Martin Heidegger (1889–1976) had once studied for the Catholic priesthood, he later claimed to have completely destroyed the western metaphysical tradition, including its theological dimension. More recently, artists and dramatists—such as the Czech writer and politician, **Vaclav Havel** (1936–2011), responding to this post-Kantian situation—depict the modern self in "a state of crisis," as having "lost his fundamental metaphysical certainty, the experience of the absolute, his relationship to eternity, the sensation of meaning—in other words, having lost the ground under his feet."[10] Lost, too, is God.

Underlying these suspicions about metaphysics and the reality of God is a corresponding lack of confidence for making sense of life and the universe in any systematic manner. Typical is the confession one finds in the preface to a well-regarded three-volume history of Europe that was written shortly after the end of the First World War:

---

[10] Vaclav Havel, *Disturbing the Peace: A Conversation with Karel Hvizdala*, trans. Paul Wilson (New York: Random House, 1990), 53. Havel was commenting on "the theater of the absurd," which he held to be "the most significant theatrical phenomenon of the twentieth century" (ibid.).

Men wiser and more learned than I have discerned in history a plot, a
rhythm, a predetermined pattern. These harmonies are concealed from me.
I can see only one emergency following upon another as wave follows upon
wave.[11]

In the recent period of western intellectual life, often given the label "the
postmodern," many underscore this sense of the seeming pointlessness
to human history and the absence of any divine presence. They echo
Rubenstein's lament that there is no rhyme or reason to reality, that it lacks
a plot, and that one cannot make any overarching sense of it as a whole.
People are thus suspicious of what Jean Francois Lyotard (1924–98) has
called grand, overarching "**meta-narratives**" that attempt to situate one's life
or family or religion or nation in the context of a larger historical narrative
that has a clear plot and progressive development.[12] This suspicion is
especially prevalent in universities today, where scholars demonstrate how
self-serving most such meta-narratives are and have been, how they tend to
construct a vision of reality that favors the powerful over against the weak
and the marginalized, and how there are other ways of construing history,
ways that take into greater account the fragmentary, arbitrary nature of
human experience. In this view "God" is often merely a construct to justify
one's own selfish desires and parochial, tribal agendas.

But there are other ways, too, in which the reality of God gets questioned.
Within the scholarly study of the religions, which includes attention to the
history, sociology, and psychology of religion, and which tends to bracket
out questions about the ultimate truth or illusion of religious beliefs and
practices, all religions are interpreted as humanly-constructed phenomena,
and this, too, often results in a kind of implicitly atheistic position.[13]
Within the social sciences there is a long-standing tendency to reduce
all theological concepts and experiences into categories of anthropology,
psychology, and sociology.

More recently, in America, a few individuals have also articulated
arguments that defend atheism, that expose perceived intellectual
weaknesses and defects in religions, and that elevate scientific materialism

---

[11] H. A. L. Fisher, *A History of Europe*, 3 vols (Boston: Houghton Mifflin, 1935–6), 1.vii.

[12] Jean François Lyotard, *The Postmodern Condition: A Report on Knowledge*, trans. Geoff Benington
and Brian Massumi (Minneapolis: University of Minnesota Press, 1984).

[13] See, for example, Peter Berger, *The Sacred Canopy: Elements of a Sociological Theory of Religion*
(Garden City, New York: Doubleday & Company Inc., 1967), whose "methodological atheism"
suggests that all religions are the result of human projections of meaning onto the universe, even
though Berger himself is not an atheist.

and humanism as the best and most accurate world view.[14] In the view of these "**new atheists**," supposedly rational "science" is pitted against supposedly irrational "religion." Their arguments are often noticeably marked by an emotional hostility toward religions and religious beliefs, which itself betrays a kind of passionate, deep concern about religion and God, albeit a negative passion. A principal target of these atheists is organized religion of any type and religious supernaturalism, which they equate with superstition. All religion is attacked on the basis of several well-known abuses and evils that have occurred in the history of the religions, especially Christianity.

Some people are not so sure, of course, about either the varieties of theism or the varieties of atheism. These individuals do not know for certain if God is real or not, one way or the other, and thus they appropriate for themselves the cautious term "**agnostic**" (literally, "one who does not know"), which was invented by Thomas Huxley (1825–95) in the late nineteenth century to describe a kind of middle, respectful way between traditional (Christian) belief and committed atheism.[15] Included here, too, would be people who might believe in a Higher Power but are critical of all religions as corrupt, impure, illusory ways of relating to such a Being. Individuals who hold this view might affirm that they themselves are "spiritual" but not "religious." They might believe in some kind of deity or goddess, but steadfastly refrain from participating in any religious institution or group, even though they might in fact hold elements of one or more religious traditions, often without even knowing that religious institutions have shaped their beliefs and spiritual practices.

---

[14] The proponents of the so-called "new atheism" do not all make the same arguments or make them with the same precision, but in general see Sam Harris, *The End of Faith: Religion, Terror, and the Future of Reason* (New York: W. W. Norton & Company, 2004); Richard Dawkins, *The God Delusion* (Boston: Houghton Mifflin, 2006); Daniel Dennett, *Breaking the Spell: Religion as a Natural Phenomenon* (New York: Viking, 2006); Lewis Wolpert, *Six Impossible Things before Breakfast: The Evolutionary Origins of Belief* (New York: W. W. Norton & Company, 2006); Victor Stenger, *The Comprehensible Cosmos: Where Do the Laws of Physics Come From?* (Amherst: Prometheus Books, 2006); Christopher Hitchens, *God is Not Great: How Religion Poisons Everything* (New York: Twelve, 2007); and idem, *The Portable Atheist: Essential Readings for the Nonbeliever* (Philadelphia: Da Capo Press, 2007). Dawkins and the former Anglican Archbishop of Canterbury, Rowan Williams, have debated with each other publicly about God and religious belief. One may view these debates easily on the internet. It is significant that Dawkins now admits he is not entirely sure there is no God, although he is nearly certain about this position.

[15] Thomas Henry Huxley, *Agnosticism and Christianity and Other Essays* (Amherst, NY: Prometheus Books, 1992).

Skepticism about the skeptics

The criticisms that atheists and agnostics level against "God" and "religions" need to be taken seriously. This is especially true of the older, classic forms of atheistic critique (Marx, Feuerbach, Nietzsche, Heidegger). But are they entirely convincing?

The arguments of the so-called "new atheists" seem especially prone to criticism. Mark Johnston, for instance, contends that none of the "new atheists" presents careful engagement with philosophical and scholarly arguments for the reality of God. The evils that have occurred within the history of religion are profoundly lamentable, but they have a limited bearing on the question of the truth about God.[16] While Johnston's own theological position denies the Christian's hope in a new creation and a new heaven beyond this present world, he does expose the serious flaws in the arguments by these "undergraduate atheists," as he calls them.[17] What they attack are caricatures and straw men, as if religious superstitions and appeals to supernatural, interventionist deities fully exhaust the nature of religion and of every theological understanding of God. Missing in their polemical attacks is any awareness of the nuanced, sophisticated discussions of God by such classical, rational theists as Kant or Spinoza.[18]

---

[16] This same point is made by Roy Abraham Varghese in his introduction to the book he co-authored with Antony Flew, *There is a God: How the World's Most Notorious Atheist Changed His Mind* (New York: HarperOne, 2007). See also the appendix by Varghese in the same book, which provides a biting analysis and assessment of the main proponents in "the new atheism" (ibid., 159–83).

[17] See Mark Johnston, *Saving God: Religion after Idolatry* (Princeton: Princeton University Press, 2009), 37–52.

[18] While Christopher Hitchens (1947–2011) and Richard Dawkins (b. 1941) appeal to Spinoza, they wrongly interpret him as an atheist after their own hearts. It is clear they have not studied his writings very carefully. Spinoza, a "God-intoxicated man," was a rational theist, one who fully accepted naturalistic and rational explanations for worldly phenomena, but who also believed that Jesus Christ had a mind that was in tune with the mind of God. "Therefore I do not believe that anyone has attained such a degree of perfection surpassing all others, except Christ. To him God's ordinance leading men to salvation were revealed not by words or by visions, but directly, so that God manifested himself to the Apostles through the mind of Christ as he once did to Moses through an audible voice. The Voice of Christ can thus be called the Voice of God in the same way as that which Moses heard. In that sense it can also be said that the Wisdom of God—that is, wisdom that is more than human—took on human nature in Christ, and that Christ was the way of salvation" (Benedict Spinoza, "The Theological-Political Tractate," in *Spinoza: Complete Works*, ed. Michael L. Morgan, trans. Samuel Shirley [Indianapolis: Hackett, 2002], 398). For further analysis of Spinoza's complex theology on the basis of all of his writings, see Richard Mason, *The God of Spinoza: A Philosophical Study* (Cambridge: Cambridge University Press, 1997). While Spinoza was not an orthodox Christian or a member of any Christian group, he himself rejected the label of atheist as an accurate term for his view toward God.

More seriously, the new atheists, to a person, assume that every religion and every theology is essentially supernaturalistic, as if creationism (the belief in a literal six-day supernatural creation by God) is the only option for a Christian theological understanding of the universe, and as if the facts of Darwinian evolution fully exclude every form of theism. The new atheists do not recognize that both scientists and theologians are constantly questioning and revising their understandings of reality, including the reality of God, to accord better with what is known to be true, at least at a given time. As will be noted in the final chapter, there are many practicing Christians today who are also well-regarded scientists in their field and who endeavor to articulate points of agreement between scientific knowledge and Christian faith in God, just as there are several academic theologians today who seek to do the same thing.

Contemporary scientists do not discount the legitimate findings of Isaac Newton because those findings happened within a worldview that became outdated after Einstein. Many thoughtful religious believers today have no difficulty affirming naturalistic explanations for natural phenomena *and* robust theological understandings that are consistent with those explanations. What science is incapable of disproving is the source of that theological understanding and commitment that many believers find fully consonant with the very possibility of scientific investigation in the first place, namely, the seemingly rational, mathematical order of the universe. "The very idea of a refutation of religion by science is thus a misplaced generality. It would have to involve the singular scientific result that there is no authentic source of existential strength. Which subfields of science are working on that question, and with what methods?"[19]

What about the more rigorous arguments of the classic atheists, Feuerbach, Marx, Nietzsche, and Freud? How do they stand up against their critics? Certainly their arguments have been able to raise serious doubts about the reality of God, but they, too, have not been able "to make God's non-existence unquestionable."[20] None of the classic atheist theories about religion and God has been able to demonstrate conclusively that God is merely an infantile illusion (Freud), a projection of human needs (Feuerbach), or an opiate to console people in a cruel world (Marx). Each of these anti-theistic views presupposes the non-reality of God and the

---

[19] Johnston, *Saving God*, 44.
[20] Hans Küng, *Does God Exist? An Answer for Today*, trans. Edward Quinn (New York: Crossroad, 1991), 329.

falsity of religious belief, including specifically Christian belief. A recent analysis of the development of modern secular social theories points to the same dynamic. Such theories are themselves "theologies or anti-theologies in disguise" which have within them certain theological and anti-theological assumptions.[21] Many have rightly noted that atheism, too, is an indemonstrable faith, which means that it also remains open to question, similarly to questions about the reality of God.[22] Precisely because there are competing and contradictory truth claims about reality as a whole, "competing narratives," so to speak, there is the need to weigh alternative understandings critically and to strive for clarity about the basic questions of truth with respect to nature, history, language, the religions, and, ultimately, "God."[23]

Likewise, the evil realities of the Holocaust and other injustices in history have not led to the complete rejection of God or religion, even after Auschwitz. Over against Rubenstein's rejection of divine transcendence stands Fackenheim's summons, which was noted in Chapter 1, namely, to believe in God's transcendent judgment as a protest against the evils freely created by human beings. Still another survivor of Auschwitz, Elie Wiesel (b. 1928), agrees. This famous scholar and recipient of the Nobel Peace Prize has repeatedly given voice to theological protest:

> I have never renounced my faith in God. I have risen against His justice, protested His silence and sometimes His absence, but my anger rises up within faith and not outside it. I admit that this is hardly an original position. It is part of Jewish tradition... I will never cease to rebel against those who committed or permitted Auschwitz, including God. The questions I once asked myself about God's silence remain open. If they have an answer, I do not know it. More than that, I refuse to know it. But I maintain that the death of six million human beings poses a question to which no answer will ever be forthcoming. My Talmudist master Rabbi Saul Lieberman has pointed out another way to look at it. One can—and must—love God. One can challenge Him and even be angry with Him, but one must also pity Him. "Do you know which of all the characters in the Bible is most tragic?" he asked me.

---

[21] John Milbank, *Theology and Social Theory: Beyond Secular Reason* (Oxford: Blackwell, 1990).
[22] Küng, *Does God Exist?*, 329–30. See also Swinburne and Plantinga in Chapter 7. They, too, attempt to demonstrate the failure of a range of objections to theism in general and to Christian theism in particular.
[23] Wolfhart Pannenberg, *An Introduction to Systematic Theology*, trans. Philip Clayton (Grand Rapids: Eerdmans, 1991), 6. See also Dianne L. Oliver, "Religion as 'Truth-Claims,'" in *Introduction to Religious Studies*, ed. Paul O. Myhre (Winona, MH: Anselm Academic, 2009), 51.

"It is God, blessed be His name, God whose creatures so often disappoint and betray Him."[24]

What about the more modest claims of the agnostic? To be sure, the person who says that he or she is unsure about knowing God is partly right. Many Jews, Christians, and Muslims also affirm that God is ultimately unknowable. This is partly what makes God, "God." But agnostics do in fact have *some* knowledge of God, sufficient to make them reject belief in God (or what they think is "God"), or at least to make them wonder about the reality of God. Agnostics have presuppositions about God that lead them to question God's reality. Those presuppositions involve at least some knowledge. For example, some agnostics might presume that God has not given any revelation, thus implying that God is incapable of giving revelation or of providing human beings with any divine knowledge. Other agnostics are genuinely doubtful about the truthfulness of the data of Christian divine revelation and are unconvinced of the divine reality that others affirm on the basis of the same evidence. Or they think it an impossible task to judge the truth and falsity of competing claims to "divine revelation" within the multiplicity of the world's religions. Still others, perhaps more confident than the typical agnostic and thus closer toward the position of atheism, seem to assume that any claim to divine revelation, either general or specific, is an illusion.

But could it be that atheists and agnostics are themselves relying on wishful thinking? If so, could it be that such individuals are hoping that God is not real, since that reality, if it were true, might call into question some of their cherished assumptions about themselves and their world? Or could it be that atheists and agnostics have not fully investigated that which rational theists point to as the basis for their knowledge of God, in which case they are rejecting as unreal a figment of their own imagination? It could be that what the atheist and agnostic reject as "God" is what the theist will reject as well, since such a conception does not fit the data on which the theist affirms his or her faith.

Conversely, the theist might respond to both the atheist and the agnostic with the metaphysical question of why they trust reality at all. What is the ultimate basis for their confidence in the trustworthiness of the reality that they encounter? Of the meaningfulness and trusting character of their life as a whole? What is the ground of their individual life-purpose? To many

---

[24] Elie Wiesel, *All Rivers Run to the Sea: Memoirs* (New York: Schocken, 1995), 84–5.

theists, such as the Roman Catholic theologian **Hans Küng**, the denial of God seems to involve the one making such a denial in a contradiction: On the one hand the person is clearly attempting to live a meaningful, purposeful, moral life, often in view of suffering, setback, and death, and yet on the other hand the person gives vocal commitment to the lack of any basic, meaningful grounds for such a life. To the theist, such a denial of God seems to imply the rejection of an ultimate basis for the meaningfulness of reality as a whole, including the meaningfulness and purposefulness of one's individual human life.

> No, it is not a matter of indifference whether we affirm or deny God. The price paid by atheism for its denial is obvious. It is exposed by an ultimate groundlessness... aimlessness, [and exposed] to the danger of possible disunion, meaninglessness, worthlessness, hollowness of reality as a whole. When we become aware of this, the atheist is exposed also quite personally to the danger of an ultimate abandonment, menace and decay, resulting in doubt, fear, even despair. All this is true, of course, only if atheism is quite serious and not an intellectual pose, snobbish caprice or thoughtless superficiality.[25]

Is the atheist or the agnostic really able to provide lasting, satisfying, positive answers to the ultimate, metaphysical questions that were raised in the first pages of Chapter 1? Perhaps they can, but the sufficient reasons for their responses to those boundary questions would be worth examining: Who am I? What or who can I trust? On what basis? Why am I living under these specific and relative conditions of my life and not others? What is the purpose of my life? Where am I going? How shall I live? To whom am I responsible? What is the meaning of friendship, love, personal sacrifice, courage, suffering? How shall I address my mistakes, my faults, my failures, and those of others? What is the meaning of my death? Why can the universe be understood rationally, at least in part? Can I count upon an unconditioned in the midst of all the conditions of my life?

The atheist and the agnostic respond to these questions very differently, if they respond to them at all, from the one who affirms God as the basis of reality as a whole and thus as the basis for his or her life and all others. At the very least, the theist is able to offer reasons for his or her ultimate trust in the meaningfulness of reality as a whole and for the positive answers that he or she gives in response to those boundary questions. That trust

---

[25] Küng, *Does God Exist?*, 571 (translation modified).

and those answers are grounded in an ultimate, trans-personal source and oriented toward an ultimate goal that supports one's life in the midst of all the uncertainties and absurdities of life and gives it meaning, direction, and stability.[26]

The persistence of God in human experience

Despite atheistic critiques of God and religion, and despite agnostic reluctance to come to a committed position, one way or the other, belief in God persists in the modern, secular age for good reasons.[27] Would not Hume be surprised that people still confess religious faith and act upon it in the modern world, a world that has been marked by wonderful advances in science and technology but also a world wherein modern science and technology have led to weapons of mass destruction and have contributed to the conditions that made the Holocaust possible to such a terrible scale? Would Hume not be surprised that religious faith is affirmed today, even by people who have suffered radical evil? Would he not be surprised that religious faith continues to attract people, even people who were formerly convinced atheists, such as Peter Hitchens (the brother of the late Christopher Hitchens), Francis Collins (formerly the director of the human genome project and currently the director of the National Institutes of Health), Alastair McGrath, A. N. Wilson, and Antony Flew (at one time a foremost proponent of philosophical atheism in the twentieth century)?[28]

---

[26] Ibid., 572. Küng's position here is quite similar to that of Schubert Ogden (b. 1928), an American Protestant theologian, who stresses that Christian theology needs to begin by analyzing common human experiences that give rise to the general revelation of God. See the title essay in his book, *The Reality of God and Other Essays* (New York: Harper and Row, 1963), 21–43. Ogden, too, defines "faith" as a basic confidence in the meaningfulness of life. Ogden's approach to God, however, is critical of classical theism and supportive of a form of process theology.

[27] For the fullest and most remarkable critical appraisal of the rise of "secularization" in the western world, see Charles Taylor, *A Secular Age* (Cambridge: Harvard University Press, 2007). Contrary to other theorists of secularism, Taylor does not think that "the human aspiration to religion" is in serious decline in western societies. There continues to be a serious desire on the part of most human beings to respond to the transcendent, however it is further specified and defined.

[28] Peter Hitchens, *The Rage against God: How Atheism Led Me to Faith* (Grand Rapids: Zondervan, 2010); A. N. Wilson, "Why I Believe Again," *New Statesmen* (April 2, 2009); Antony Flew and Gary R. Habermas, "Exclusive Interview with Antony Flew," *Philosophia Christi*, vol. 6, no. 2 (Winter 2004), 197–212; and Flew, *There is a God*. After describing his journey from atheism to Christian faith, Peter Hitchens refutes three typical atheistic complaints against the religions by arguing that

Could it be that atheistic critiques of religion and God do not necessarily lead to the destruction and elimination of religion, including Christianity, or to the destruction of religious faith and commitment, but can lead to the legitimate critique of false understandings, false idols, and evil practices within the religions so as to clear the ground for a new understanding of religious faith and practice?[29] Havel himself left open the possibility of new meaning that might surprise one in the midst of the crisis of meaning.

As people today know too well, religious faith and openness to transcendence can be dangerous, as can the strong ideals and ideologies of the anti-religious. Idolatry of any kind tends to breed violence. Is it any wonder that the prophetic texts of the Hebrew Scriptures are most concerned to speak against every idolatry and to proclaim that God alone is the Lord of all creation and that everyone is accountable to God? The apostolic Scriptures in the NT teach the same when they appeal to the transcendent Lordship of the risen Jesus Christ and reject all other gods as idols. Jesus, too, was critical of the ideologically rigid religious institutions of his day. (Marx failed to acknowledge this prophetic strain within biblical religion, as if the biblical writings were in fact merely concerned to keep the poor and working classes drugged and deluded beneath the rich and the powerful.)

Moreover, when so-called materialistic positivists reject metaphysics and theology as "meaningless," they themselves seem to be engaging in metaphysical reflection in order to be able to make this assertion. In other words they, too, are attempting to speak meaningfully about the nature of being as a totality, even if in doing so they call into question the ultimate

---

conflicts fought in the name of religion are often not about God or religion (he freely acknowledges the terrible history of cruelties in Christianity), that the determination of what is morally right cannot occur without a transcendent, objective source of all good, and that officially atheist states have shown a consistent tendency to commit mass murders in the name of a greater good. He and others have drawn attention to the "religious" zeal and absolutist-fundamentalist spirit that many proponents of the "new atheism" exhibit in their writings and public comments. Wilson was a believer, then an atheist, and now a believer again. He has been critical of the fanatical anti-religionists, such as Christopher Hitchens, Richard Dawkins, and Poly Toynbee, who "ignore all the benign aspects of religion and see it purely as a sinister agent of control" (A. N. Wilson, "Religion of hatred: Why we should no longer be cowed by the chattering classes ruling Britain who sneer at Christianity," *The Daily Mail* [April 10, 2009]). "Materialist atheism says we are just a collection of chemicals. It has no answer whatsoever to the question of how we should be capable of love or heroism or poetry if we are simply animated pieces of meat" (Ibid.). The change in thinking by Flew will be summarized in the next chapter.
[29] This is the thesis developed by the Christian philosopher, Paul Ricoeur, in his 1969 Bampton lecture, "Religion, Atheism, and Faith," in *The Religious Significance of Atheism*, Alasdair MacIntyre and Paul Ricoeur (New York: Columbia University Press, 1969).

meaning of that about which they are attempting to speak meaningfully. We need not point out that the very act of raising critical questions against metaphysics, including its theological dimension, is itself a product of this metaphysical tradition—for the spirit of critical inquiry over against traditional religious understandings is one of the abiding contributions of the Greeks to philosophical theology.

Perhaps the persistence of religious faith, including Christian faith, is due, not to a nasty virus-like quality that religious people possess, as Dawkins would have people believe, but to the apparent fact that the modern sciences are incapable of fully explaining **religious experience**, of eliminating all sense of wonder and awe that often arise in human life, and of replacing a basic and fundamental religious trust in the "worthwhileness" of human existence before God, the sacred, the holy, the transcendent ground of all that is (assuming for the moment that these terms are nearly synonymous). Basic metaphysical questions keep surfacing in human lives that direct them toward the transcendent, the sacred, the holy, in short, toward what many people call "God."

Certainly, many people from many different religious traditions have told others about their extraordinary visions of heaven or the afterlife, such as the American neurosurgeon, Eben Alexander, whose skepticism about the afterlife was radically changed after his own brain stopped functioning as a result of meningitis and he had an out-of-body experience about which he wrote later.[30] But a strong word of caution is in order at precisely this point: Others have made claims to divine revelation that have put them in a mental ward at a state psychiatric hospital! People are thus right to be skeptical about specific claims to divine revelation, but they should be equally skeptical about those who want to dismiss all discussion of religious experience out-of-hand, simply because it does not fit totally into their conception of reality.

One does not need to have had such a special mystical, ecstatic (literally "standing outside of oneself") experience for one to sense "the sacred" or "the holy" or "the divine presence." Many people simply become aware, often gradually, of a wondrous reality or "Other" "behind" or "above" everything that occurs in human life.[31] The Roman Catholic theologian Bernard Lonergan insightfully outlines four paths that lead to the question of God:

[30] Eben Alexander, *Proof of Heaven* (New York: Simon and Schuster, 2012).
[31] Hywell David Lewis, *Our Experience of God* (New York, Macmillan 1959).

The question of God is epistemological, when we ask how the universe can be intelligible. It is philosophic when we ask why we should bow to the principle of sufficient reason, where there is no sufficient reason for the existence of contingent things. It is moral when we ask whether the universe has a moral ground and so a moral goal. It finally is religious when we ask whether there is anyone for us to love with all our heart and all our soul and all our mind and all our strength.[32]

The idea of "an objective Ideal of supreme goodness and beauty, toward which human life is oriented at its most basic level, and which is discernible in the intelligibility of the world, in the beauties of nature and art, in the demand and attraction of morality, and in the sense of personal presence that can be felt in prayer and contemplation," is one that most people continue to find persuasive.[33]

Historical and ethnological investigations into the world's religions certainly indicate that religions have undergone a process of development over time, but many ethnological researchers today are critical of attempts to explain all religions on the basis of an overarching theory of their historical genesis, whether within a larger evolutionary framework or in a framework that assumes a stage of perfection at the beginning and only subsequent degeneration in all later forms.[34] Thus the claim that all religions are based on fear or on superstitious beliefs in spirits or souls ("animism"), or on magic and taboo and religious rites connected with a totem (sacred object for a clan or group), or in various combinations of these, has generally not been supported by actual ethnological investigations into so-called "primitive" religions and other religions. What is remarkable is that all human cultures seem to have been connected to practices and beliefs that one may properly call "religious." Such a fact ought to give one pause when addressing the important question as to whether or not so-called modern

---

[32] Bernard Lonergan, *Philosophy of God and Theology* (London: Darton, Longman & Todd, 1973), 54–5. This quote provides an amplification on Kant's three basic metaphysical questions: What can we know? What ought we to do? For what may we hope?

[33] Keith Ward, *Why There Almost Certainly is a God: Doubting Dawkins* (Oxford: Lion Books, 2008), 142.

[34] See, for example, Brian Morris, *Anthropological Studies of Religion* (New York: Cambridge University Press, 1987); Robin Horton, *Patterns of Thought in Africa and the West* (New York: Cambridge University Press, 1993); Benson Saler, *Conceptualizing Religion* (Leiden: Brill, 1993); Daniel L. Pals, *Seven Theories of Religion* (New York: Oxford University Press, 1995); Morton Klass, *Ordered Universes* (Boulder: Westview, 1995); and Stephen D. Glazier, ed., *Anthropology of Religion* (Westport, CT: Greenwood, 1997). For an impressive, recent attempt at accounting for religion within an overarching evolutionary framework, see Robert Bellah, *Religion in Human Evolution* (Cambridge: Harvard University Press, 2011).

materialism, with its confident assertions about the nature of reality and atheism, is a more adequate worldview than those that remain open to the transcendent, to mystery, to the sacred, and to venerable religious traditions from the past. How can one be so certain that there is no reality at all behind the religions? Even Nietzsche noted that interest in metaphysics and religion has the tendency of persisting in human culture and individual experience:

> How strong the metaphysical need is, and how hard nature makes it to bid it a final farewell can be seen from the fact that even when the free spirit has divested himself of everything metaphysical, the highest effects of art can easily set the metaphysical strings, which have long been silent or indeed snapped apart, vibrating in sympathy... He feels a profound stab in the heart and sighs for the man who will lead him back to his lost love, whether she be called religion or metaphysics.[35]

Contrary to Hume's prediction, religion and belief in God have not disappeared, even among many practicing scientists and philosophers, although secularism does pervade huge portions of western universities. Charles Taylor (b. 1931) points to extraordinary events, such as the death of Princess Diana, and to extraordinary individuals (Dorothy Day [1897–1980], Mother Teresa [1910–97], Pope John XXIII [1881–1963], Pope John Paul II [1920–2005]) as traces or premonitions of the sacred in our midst, however fragmentary and arguable they are. Moreover, he highlights the legacy of certain artifacts within the Christian tradition (the music of Bach, the writings of Dante and Dostoevsky, medieval cathedrals) that hint at the transcendent or the divine in our present world. How many people have become believers in God or had their faith in God renewed due to their perception of sublime beauty in art or music?

This legacy of the power and beauty in art as it relates to religious experience calls for a brief detour. While the complete unity of religious experience and the experience of beauty in art cannot be supported, since they are not identical, religion and beauty "are parallel lines, which intersect only at infinity and meet in God."[36] This intersection, from a Christian theological perspective, is marked by both the disturbance of human beings,

---

[35] Friedrich W. Nietzsche, *Human, All Too Human: A Book for Free Spirits*, trans. R. J. Hollingdale, intro. Erich Heller (Cambridge: Cambridge University Press, 1986), 153.

[36] Gerardus van der Leeuw, *Sacred and Profane Beauty: The Holy in Art*, trans. David A. Green (New York: Oxford University Press, 2006), 333. See also Jaroslav Pelikan's valuable, accessible, and fascinating study of "the Holy" in relation to the True, the Good, and the Beautiful: *Fools for Christ: Essays on the True, the Good, and the Beautiful* (Minneapolis: Fortress Press, 1995).

often in the grip of depravity or the demonic, before the mystery of the sacred and by the power of beauty to reveal the goodness and surprising grace of God. In this way art can serve as a locus of "the general revelation of God" (which we will explore in Chapters 6 and 7) and provide illumination on human beings and their condition before this general revelation. Such art need not be explicitly "religious," or even intended by the artist as conveying religious meaning and truth, but it may allow the one who is impacted by its sublime beauty to be given insight into the sacred, the holy, and one's condition before the mystery of God. Art that is not religious may be of religious significance.[37] Truly great, imaginative art has a way of becoming "religiously significant," of creating variety in religious aesthetic experience, of manifesting "the truth and goodness of the depths of reality," of manifesting the depths of human longing for the divine—all of which invite further theological reflection upon human beings, their experiences, and their world.[38] Some art may reveal "the absence that makes presence possible," to quote the French philosopher, Jacques Derrida (1930–2004), whose postmodern idea of *différence*, the "radical alterity" that underlies the intelligible world, has been used by some theologians as a signal of transcendence, as a pointer to "the Wholly Other" (EC 1.76).[39]

More than 40 years ago, **Peter Berger** (b. 1929) identified certain common occurrences in contemporary societies that serve as yet another set of "**signals of transcendence**."[40] Such pointers to the divine are still worth pondering today. One such signal occurs when human beings act to restore *order* in situations of disorder: a mother comforts her troubled child ("Everything's going to be alright..."), a medic soothes a gravely-wounded person, first-responders clear rubble after a bombing attack and begin to rebuild. Such actions seem to tap into an underlying order within the universe that points in the direction of a transcendent cause for that order. Berger also draws attention to the presence of *play* among human beings that draws them beyond ordinary time toward a kind of extraordinary transcendence of time, which likewise points toward an order

---

[37] Frank Burch Brown, *Religious Aesthetics* (Princeton: Princeton University Press, 1989), 8.

[38] Brown, *Religious Aesthetics*, 111; Hans Urs von Balthasar, *The Glory of the Lord: A Theological Aesthetics*, 7 vols, various translators (New York: Crossroad, 1982), 1:117–18. See also the chapter on "The Taste for Art and the Thirst for God," in Frank Burch Brown, *Good Taste, Bad Taste, and Christian Taste: Aesthetics in Religious Life* (New York: Oxford University Press, 2000), 95–127.

[39] Jacques Derrida, *Aporias*, trans. D. Dutoit (Stanford: Stanford University Press, 1993).

[40] Peter Berger, *A Rumor of Angels: Modern Society and the Rediscovery of the Supernatural* (New York: Anchor, 1970).

beyond normal time, toward eternity. Moreover, Berger notes the persistence of *hope* in hopeless circumstances and the reality of gallows *humor*, which makes light of death and suggests the possibility of a larger, transcendent order beyond one's immediate, dire straits. Finally he describes how outraged people call for the *damnation* of those whose deeds cry out to heaven. This, too, he argues, is a kind of pointer toward the transcendent or what many other people (not Berger himself, it should be added, at least not here) will label "God."

The classic **phenomenological** studies by such diverse scholars of religion as William James (1842–1910), **Rudolf Otto** (1869–1937), Gerardus van der Leeuw (1890–1950), and **Mircea Eliade** (1907–86) also support the position that "the sacred" or "the holy" has persisted into the modern age.[41] The aim of these studies is to describe "meanings" and to avoid making critical judgments about their validity or truthfulness.[42] Otto referred to "the holy" as a uniquely religious and primal phenomenon that he thought was best described as "*mysterium tremendum et fascinans*," that which is beyond our human ability to comprehend or conceptualize, the extraordinary and mysterious, and thus that which leads to a sense of awe and even dread. Otto characterized all such experiences of "the holy" as "numinous" (from the Latin term for "divine"), since they result from the manifestation of divine majesty and power and lead to the awareness of one's creaturely condition before the "wholly Other."[43]

Eliade built on Otto's exploration of religious experience and concluded similarly that human beings become aware of "the sacred" because it continually manifests itself in human experience, "shows itself as something wholly different from the profane," the ordinary.[44] This understanding of religious experience is similar to the phenomenological position of Tillich, who held that "the object of theology" is a matter of "ultimate, unconditional, total, infinite concern," that which "can become a matter of being or not-being for us" (Tillich 1.12, 14). "Man is infinitely concerned about the

---

[41] William James, *The Varieties of Religious Experience* (New York: Collier Books, 1961); Rudolf Otto, *The Idea of the Holy*, trans. John W. Harvey (London: Oxford University Press, 1923); Mircea Eliade, *The Sacred and the Profane: The Nature of Religion*, trans. Willard Trask (New York: Harcourt Brace Jovanovich, 1959); Gerardus Van Der Leeuw, *Religion in Essence and Manifestation*, 2 vols (New York: Harper and Row, 1963).

[42] See Edmund Husserl, *Ideas*, trans. Boyce Gibson (New York: Macmillan Company, 1931).

[43] Otto, *The Idea of the Holy*, 27

[44] Eliade, *The Sacred and the Profane*, 11.

infinity to which he belongs, from which he is separated, and for which he is longing" (ibid.).

A similar phenomenological approach to theological discourse was set forth by **Langdon Gilkey** (1919–2004). His analysis of the disjunction between people's secular understandings of themselves and "the felt character" of their actual existence indicates that modern human beings have not outgrown their need for religious symbols and that these symbols can in turn be explicated by the Christian theologian.[45] For example, Gilkey draws attention to the tension between the modern sense of the relativity of everything and the ongoing search for abiding meanings and values and the affirmation of one's own contingent being:

> A nonsecular dimension in our experience appears in the lived character of secular life, despite the fact that the forms of our modern self-understanding have no capacity for dealing with it. This strange interloper into our secularity appears not so much as a new reality or being, as rather the ultimate presupposition for dealing with the ordinary relative realities we meet; not so much a presence—though it may be—as a final limit and a demand; not so much an answer as an ultimate question. But what this presupposition entails, what the demand is about, and what the questions ask for is radically and qualitatively different from the rest. It has the character of ultimacy, of finality, of the unconditioned which transcends, undergirds, and even threatens our experience of the ordinary passage of things and our dealings with the entities in that passage. It is, therefore, sacred as well as ultimate, the region where value as well as existence is grounded.[46]

David Tracy has also focused on the concept of "limit" in "ordinary" human experience (for example, human finitude and contingency), which he has borrowed from the philosopher Jaspers, whom we quoted near the beginning of Chapter 1. Tracy identifies these "boundary situations" as those that create certain limits within human experience which at the same time point beyond (or ground) such ordinary experiences. For example, he notes that people exhibit a basic or fundamental trust in the worthwhileness of their existence or a basic belief in order and value, whether in the common culture or a subculture. This insight is similar to Berger's detection of a basic "order" within human cultures that serves as a signal toward transcendence. These boundary situations and signals of transcendence, as Tracy insists,

---

[45] Landon Gilkey, *Naming the Whirlwind: The Renewal of God-Language* (Indianapolis: Bobbs-Merrill, 1969).

[46] Ibid., 253. The influence of Tillich here is obvious.

point to the abiding religious dimension of human life—which then, in turn, he further rightly insists, must be seen as pointing to God.[47] These signals appear within life's "limit questions," for instance, within science, such questions as: Is scientific investigation possible if the universe is not intelligible? Can the world be intelligible if it does not have an intelligent ground? Are there ethical limits to scientific research? Those signals also appear in life's "limit situations" such as: sickness, guilt, fear, anxiety, death, and the "ecstatic experiences" of love, joy, the creative act, and other profound reassurances of the importance and meaningfulness of one's life.

How is it that these basic human questions and common human experiences suggest that human beings are inherently religious, and what do we mean by "religious"? We humans continually encounter those boundary questions. We are forever acting, thinking, and speaking in ways that provide subtle and not-so-subtle clues about what we in fact believe about ourselves and others in the context of the larger scheme of things. Since that scheme always contains (what Ricoeur calls) "a surplus of meaning," we face the mystery of the world and its being without ever being able to comprehend it fully. Our secular *Weltanschauung* (worldview) has no ready point of reference for this depth experience—scientific academia invariably uses reductive categories and terms. But these encounters with life's "transcendent mystery" can jolt (or may lead) people to seek answers to life's "existential" questions of meaning and purpose and to develop ways of addressing these experiences of guilt, shame, suffering, love, and death. These common, "ordinary" experiences push people in the direction of "the infinite" (Schleiermacher), "the ultimate" or "the unconditioned" (Tillich, Gilkey), "the holy" (Otto), "the sacred" (Eliade), or "the transcendent" (Jaspers, Rahner). It is this depth experience that is meant by the necessarily religious dimension of human life; and as this experience presents people with that which addresses them from beyond themselves the Western tradition insists on the necessarily *theistic* interpretation of human existence. To do so, it uses symbols that also point beyond themselves, principally, of course, the term "God." Thus the general revelation of God in Christian theology normally refers to this ultimate, sacred, transcendent reality, "the powerful ground of man's world and the source of power to overcome the experiences of evil and suffering which occur in that world" (PTPS 346).

---

[47] Tracy, *Blessed Rage for Order*, esp. 92ff.

According to those who study the religions phenomenologically—that is, those who try to uncover the concrete and actual forms of the religions, their rituals and symbols, and the meaningfulness of their discourse—religious experience cannot be explained away as either the product of the unconscious, or as social processes, or the result of a medical pathology. Their scholarly work shows that the complexity of religious experience alone ought to caution one to attempt a restatement of all religious experience into non-religious categories, for instance. For Eliade, the sacred is more basic, more elemental, and a permanent aspect of the experience of human beings, both primitive and modern.

While the phenomenological study of the religions has made indisputably clear that religious experience is always culturally conditioned, some scholars, such as Wayne Proudfoot and Stephen Katz, have argued that religious experience is entirely the result of cultural expectations in the communities in which the religious experience occurs.[48] This argument, however, that all religious experience can be reduced merely to forms of cultural expression, has met with serious criticism. Significant research indicates that religious experience is not culturally *determined* or simply reducible to matters of language and culture. William P. Alston's phenomenological study into mystical experience indicates that for the subjects of the experience "something," namely, "God," has been *presented* or *given* to their consciousness, in generically the same way as that in which objects in the environment are (apparently) presented to one's consciousness in sense perception, and that this *appearance* or *presentation* is "essentially nonconceptual and nonjudgmental."[49] Against Proudfoot and Katz, Alston rejects the notion that religious experience is entirely a matter of subjective experience that is then followed by a causal explanation. Religious experience cannot be reduced to linguistic and cultural expression, just as emotional states cannot be fully grasped through explanatory description. This same research would seem to call into question those who insist on a cultural-linguistic interpretation of specific religions, such as Christianity.[50]

---

[48] Wayne Proudfoot, *Religious Experience* (Berkeley: University of California Press, 1985); Stephen Katz, *Mysticism and Language* (New York: Oxford University Press, 1992).

[49] William P. Alston, *Perceiving God: The Epistemology of Religious Experience* (Ithaca: Cornell University Press, 1991), 11, 16, 39–40. See also Gregory R. Peterson, *Minding God: Theology and the Cognitive Sciences* (Minneapolis: Fortress, 2003), 103–4.

[50] The key work that makes an argument for a "cultural-linguistic" approach to Christian teaching is George Lindbeck, *The Nature of Doctrine: Religion and Theology in a Postliberal Age* (Philadelphia: Westminster, 1984).

The phenomenological understanding of religious experience also finds tentative, if ambiguous, support in recent work in the cognitive sciences, still in its infancy stages. This research desires to uncover and explain the neural basis for such experience, while bracketing out any concern for a possible trans-individual source ("God") for the experience. For example, d'Aquili and Newberg have investigated the parietal lobe and brain states during religious meditation and prayer and have concluded that religion is an integral aspect of human experience, that it has a biological basis, and that this biological basis is at least part of the reason why religions have not disappeared in scientifically informed cultures.[51] Other scholars have begun to integrate a neuroscientific understanding of human behavior with a spiritual/religious/theological perspective and to allow neuroscientific knowledge and methodology to shed light on a wide variety of religious experiences and concepts. Many within this burgeoning scholarly field of "**neurotheology**" conclude that human beings seem to be biologically oriented toward religion.[52] Thus the "biology of belief" may be a principal reason for "why God won't go away."[53] Lest one conclude, however, that such biological insights into religious experience eliminate or at least discredit the object of the experience, Alvin Plantinga (b. 1932) cautions: "To show that there are natural processes that produce religious belief does nothing to discredit it; perhaps God designed us in such a way that it is by virtue of those processes that we come to have knowledge of him."[54]

It needs to be stressed that phenomenological approaches to the study of religion, wherein the terms "wholly Other" or "the sacred" or "ultimate concern" could be used interchangeably with the term "God," do not necessarily establish an actual reality behind the terms. This same assertion applies to neurotheological investigations of religious experience, which remain neutral regarding the actual cause of the experience. While such investigations and approaches undermine the claim that religious experiences are merely cultural and linguistic in nature, they do not provide any real insight into the actual external source of the experiences. Does

---

[51] Eugene G. d'Aquili and Andrew B. Newberg, *The Mystical Mind: Probing the Biology of Religious Experience* (Minneapolis: Fortress, 1999). See also Andrew B. Newberg, *Principles of Neurotheology* (Surrey: Ashgate, 2010).

[52] James Ashbrook and C. R. Albright, *The Humanizing Brain: Where Religion and Neuroscience Meet* (Cleveland: Pilgrim, 1997). For a review of the recent literature, see Newberg, *Principles of Neurotheology*, 12–13.

[53] Andrew Newberg et al., *Why God Won't Go Away: Brain Science and the Biology of Belief* (New York: Ballantine, 2001).

[54] Alvin Plantinga, *Warranted Christian Belief* (New York: Oxford University Press, 2000), 145.

the concept of "the Holy" or "the sacred" or "ultimate concern" within culturally-shaped religious experience—marked as it is by reference to a plurality of "gods" and divine beings in the world religions—actually refer to a single reality? How can one know for sure that one's religious sense or experience is actually "of God?" Which god(s)?

In order to gain insight into the question of the actual source of the religious experience, external to the person experiencing it, we need to move from the phenomenological inquiry into religious experience to the field of philosophical theology proper, primarily classical theism and process theology. As Peterson has rightly noted, while the theologian is convinced that the actual external cause of individual religious experience is indeed God, we cannot know this for certain, and so "once again we are thrown back onto a larger theological framework in order to interpret such experiences."[55] Pannenberg points out that those scholars who completely suspend judgment regarding the reality or illusory character of the object of religious experience have already made a prejudiced decision in favor of an Enlightenment perspective that interprets religious experience solely in anthropological, this-worldly, naturalistic and even atheistic terms (PTPS 363).

If we place the exclusively anthropological Enlightenment view of God-talk at one end of the spectrum of kinds of philosophical theology, at the other end lies the mystical view. Certainly, the religious mystic claims to have a knowledge of God that comes from an immediate, nonrational, noninferential experience of the Holy, one that is self-authenticating and often beyond the ability of language to describe (at least rationally). Yet that very claim places the mystical outside the field of philosophical theology, which by definition talks about "God" rationally and inferentially. Within that field we now narrow our focus to the value and limitations of the relatively recent, renowned process theology in relation to the still dominant classical theism.

Despite the importance of emphases within process theology and its metaphysics (for example, its emphasis upon the temporality of God to engage the world in love and to respond to the world), which can serve as correctives to misleading metaphysical concepts, classical theism is still the dominant position within the western Christian theological (and philosophical) tradition. Such a position has good reasons for remaining

---

[55] Peterson, *Minding God*, 116.

the preferred understanding. To speak of a "becoming" God, as occurs in most forms of process theology, "subjects God to a process which has the character of a fate or which is completely open to the future and has the character of an absolute accident. In both cases the divinity of God is undercut" (Tillich 1.247). There is no real possibility for hope within process theology, since it merely affirms God as One who shares our suffering, but offers no compelling reason for why God could ever overcome evil and sin. Within classical theism, however, the transcendent infinity, immutability, and actuality of God, beyond all finite categories, are maintained. In this view the all-powerful, all-knowing, all-good, unconditioned God is the "One" cause and goal of all things (in contrast to the plurality of gods in the world's religions), "the one origin of the unity of the cosmos" (Pannenberg 1.70). Here God is in a position to overcome evil and death and redeem and renew the fallen creation. Charles Hartshorne (1897–2000), who was himself a process theologian, nevertheless rightly underscored the superlative quality of God that classical theism seeks to affirm as well:

> God is a name for the uniquely good, admirable, great, worship-eliciting being. Worship, moreover, is not just an unusually high degree of respect or admiration; and the excellence of deity is not just an unusually high degree of merit. There is a difference in kind. God is "Perfect," and between the perfect and anything as little imperfect as you please is no merely finite, but an infinite step. The superiority of deity to all others cannot (in accordance with established word usage) be expressed by indefinite descriptions, such as "immensely good," "very powerful," or even "best" or "most powerful," but must be a superiority of principle, a definite conceptual divergence from every other being, actual or so much as possible. We may call this divergence "categorical supremacy."[56]

The term "God," at least as it is commonly understood within classical philosophical theology, also makes possible an ultimate understanding of the being of the universe as an ordered totality ("cosmos") and that supports the understanding of human beings as a single "human community." Once "the plurality of the gods was reduced to the concept of the one God as the origin of the one world, the word 'God' did in fact

---

[56] Charles Hartshorne, "Introduction," *Philosophers Speak of God*, Charles Hartshorne and William L. Reese (eds) (Chicago: University of Chicago Press, 1953), 7. (This quote is also used by Paul Sponheim [BJ I:199–200].) Ironically, Hartshorne himself proceeded to define God's "perfection" as implying God's mutability and "becoming."

become a key word for the awareness of the totality of the world and of human life" (Pannenberg 1.71; see also the similar point that Tillich makes about "the world" as "cosmos," Tillich 1.170–1). In contrast to the multiplicity of gods in the world religions—who are understood as individual "beings" who can be spoken of in terms of finite categories— God is the One who transcends all categories, including, even, numbers, and is the unconditioned to all things.

Pioneering in this movement toward the one God was the development of Israel's faith from **henotheism**, its tribal belief in the one true god, *YHWH* (the Hebrew word that is translated as "LORD"), alongside other (false) gods, to **monotheism**, the belief that there is only one true God, the LORD, the Creator of heaven and earth.[57] Greek philosophical theology (see especially the *Fragments* from Xenophanes of Colophon [d. c. 480 BC]) also contributed to the further development of this understanding of God, and helped to make the Christian message about the revelation of God in Jesus intelligible to non-Jews and to those who had difficulty in comprehending the Christian understanding of God. Both Judaism and Greek Platonism refer to the immateriality, infinity, and creative providential ordering of the one God as the source of all that is (of the "universe" = the whole of created beings viewed as one [OED 2175]), who is the basis for the reality of truth and for the reliability of the knowledge of created beings. Within the NT itself, there is an indication that the one God worshipped by Jews and Christians (and later, Muslims) is in some measure "known" by all people, even those who worship other (false) gods, and that this "natural knowledge of God," albeit incomplete and imperfect, serves as common ground between non-Christians and Christians when they want to talk further about God on the basis of the revelation given in and through Jesus Christ. The so-called "natural knowledge of God" or "general revelation of God" is the focus of the next chapter.

---

[57] The Hebrew proper name for God is comprised of four consonants that are transliterated into English as "YHWH." It seems to be based on the Hebrew verb, "to be" (see Exod. 3.14), but no Jew would ever try to pronounce it, out of respect for this special, holy name and for fear of breaking the divine commandment ("Do not take the name of the LORD your God in vain," Exod. 20.7). Whenever Jews came across the proper name of God in their Bible, they substituted another Hebrew word for it, most often the word "*Adonai*," which in English means "Lord." Some Jews also refer to "Ha-Shem" ("The Name"). In most modern English Bibles, the divine name is rendered "LORD" in all capital letters.

Key Words

theism	agnostic
process theology	Hans Küng
Sigmund Freud	religious experience
atheism	Peter Berger
David Hume	signals of transcendence
Immanuel Kant	phenomenology
Ludwig Feuerbach	Rudolf Otto
Karl Marx	Mircea Eliade
Friedrich Nietzsche	Langdon Gilkey
René Descartes	David Tracy
Vaclav Havel	neurotheology
meta-narrative	henotheism
"new atheists"	monotheism

Reference literature

For a general orientation to the problem of God and atheism

RPP 1:478–80 ("Atheism II–III: Church History and Philosophy of Religion" [Dietz, Clayton]); RPP 5:459–75 ("God" [Zinser et al.])

Questions for review and discussion

1   Why is the concept of "God" a problem in the contemporary world? Is "God" a problem only in western cultures, or is "God" a worldwide problem?

2   What are the principal attributes of God as affirmed within classical philosophical theism? How does this understanding differ from process theology? The author favors classical theism over process theology. Which do you favor? Why?

3   What is "atheism?" What are its assumptions about reality? Identify the strongest arguments in favor of atheism. What is your assessment of the arguments put forward by the so-called "new atheists"? Do you

agree that their arguments are not as strong as the classical proponents of atheism (Marx, Feuerbach, Nietzsche, Freud)?

4   How is atheism different from agnosticism? How are they related?

5   The author repeats and supports the basic criticism that Hans Küng, Langdon Gilkey, and David Tracy have leveled against atheism and agnosticism. Do you agree with this critique? Why or why not?

6   Is it not possible that some atheists and agnostics will simply affirm the meaning of their life merely on the basis that the world in which they live is relatively stable and reliable and that they need no recourse to "God" who transcends the universe? What do you make of this affirmation?

7   Describe how phenomenologists study religions. How might recent work in the cognitive sciences support a phenomenological under-standing of religious experience? Do you think all religious experiences are "tapping into" the same reality? Why or why not?

8   What is "neurotheology"? Do you see the findings in this new scholarly field threatening to your faith? Why or why not?

9   Do you agree with Pannenberg's claim that scholars who completely suspend judgment regarding the reality or illusory character of the object of religious experience (for example, "God") have already made a prejudiced decision in favor of an Enlightenment perspective that interprets religious experience solely in anthropological, this-worldly, naturalistic and even atheistic terms?

10 What is the difference between "monotheism" and "henotheism"?

Suggestions for further reading

The problem of God and God-language

Langdon Gilkey, *Naming the Whirlwind: The Renewal of God-Language* (Indianapolis: The Bobbs-Merrill Company, 1969) [An important examination of the nature of religious experience and language by the foremost interpreter of Tillich's theology in the second half of the twentieth century. Gilkey's book provides a major defense of the need for "God-talk" in contemporary discourse about human experience and offers a careful critique of those who think that language about God is meaningless and empty.]

Gordon D. Kaufman, *God the Problem* (Cambridge, MA: Harvard University Press, 1972) [This is another attempt to speak meaningfully about "God" within the context of interpreting human/religious experience. Like Gilkey, he does not offer an argument for the reality of God, but he does demonstrate the meaningfulness of language about God.]

Schubert Ogden, *The Reality of God and Other Essays* (New York: Harper and Row, 1963) [The essay in the title affirms the basic approach to general revelation set forth here, namely, that there is a basic, common religious experience of God that serves as the context for the special revelation that is given in and through Jesus. Ogden also provides a strong critique of classical theism and offers a form of process theology. So his position on theism differs from the one favored here.]

Mark I. Wallace, "Can God be named without being known? the problem of revelation in Thiemann, Ogden, and Ricoeur," *Journal of the American Academy of Religion* 59/2 (Summer 1991), 281–308. [This essay argues that "God" cannot really be known in a general way but only in and through the particularities of a given faith. The essay reflects Barthian, post-liberal concerns and offers a counter-point to the positions set forth by Ogden, Kaufman, and Gilkey.]

Atheism

In addition to the classic works that espouse atheism (listed in footnotes 4, 5, and 8 above), see the following:

Eberhard Jüngel, *God as the Mystery of the World*, trans. Darrell L. Guder (Grand Rapids: Eerdmans, 1983) [A major engagement with philosophical atheism by one of the leading Lutheran theologians of the second half of the twentieth century.]

Hans Küng, *Does God Exist? An Answer for Today*, trans. Edward Quinn (New York: Crossroad, 1991) [This is a fair examination of the major proponents of atheism by a leading Roman Catholic theologian of the second half of the twentieth century. His affirmation of God shares important similarities to that of Ogden and Tracy, but without buying into their process-oriented metaphysics.]

Marcel Neusch, *The Sources of Modern Atheism: One Hundred Years of Debate over God*, trans. Matthew J. O'Connell (New York: Paulist, 1982) [A very helpful and readable analysis of the classic proponents of atheism: Feuerbach, Marx, Nietzsche, Freud, Sartre, Garaudy, and Bloch.]

6

The Natural Knowledge of God

This chapter discusses the general revelation of God on the basis of the natural knowledge of God which the New Testament asserts is generally or universally available to all human beings. The chapter describes the principal positions that Christian theologians have taken regarding the possibility of a natural knowledge of God.

What is the object of Christian theology? What does the discipline study? According to the definition given in Chapter 4, the object of theology is not "God" (as God is in essence), nor is it mere Christian "faith" (believing in God through Christ). Rather, the object is the *revelation of God, the world, and of human beings in the apostolic witness to Jesus Christ*. This definition presupposes that God is not an empirical object like any other object in the world. God is beyond human observation. God "resides in unapproachable light" (1 Tim. 6.16). God is such that God cannot be seen or known as an object of human perception. "No one has ever seen God" (Jn 1.18). Because God is the creator and source of all things, God is not one more "thing" in the universe. While human beings may try to raise themselves to the place of God, God is beyond their reach. They cannot raise themselves to the level or dimension of God, and all attempts to do so end in failure and sin. (Surely this is one of the theological conclusions that one may legitimately draw from the story of the Tower of Babel in Gen. 11) God transcends all things, even numbers. God is certainly not open to scientific verification or human manipulation. While Christians believe that God is real, they do not believe God is real in the same way that created reality is real.

Moreover, Christians believe that no mortal creature can know God directly in God's essential being. God remains ultimately incomprehensible, also for the Christian believer, whose knowledge is always finite, limited, time-bound, and imperfect. As the psalmist put the matter, the knowledge that God has "is too wonderful for me; it is high, I cannot attain it" (Ps. 139.6 [RSV]). The **Apostle Paul** echoed that claim: "No one comprehends the mind of God except the Spirit of God" (1 Cor. 2.11). "We now see dimly in a mirror, but then face to face. Now I know only a little; then I shall understand, even as I have been understood" (1 Cor. 13.12). "O the depth of the riches and wisdom and knowledge of God! How unsearchable are his judgments and how inscrutable his ways. 'For who has known the mind of the Lord?...'" (Rom. 11.33–4a [RSV]). Even for the Christian, God remains a mystery which is hidden, whose **hiddenness** persists despite the mystery that is unveiled through the manifestation of the glory of God in Jesus Christ.

This emphasis on the hiddenness and mystery of God runs like a red thread through the history of Christian thought. "No created intellect can comprehend God wholly" (Aquinas 1a.12.8). Again, the biblical story of the Tower of Babel is instructive, since God dwells beyond where the efforts of human beings to reach God can go. Even Moses, who desired to see God's glory (Exod. 33.18–23), was prohibited, since no mortal sinner can see God's "face" and live. Moses was allowed only to see God's "backside," God's posterior. Even then, God remained a mystery beyond the comprehension of mere mortals. Of course there is a paradox here, since something more of the mystery is known through the unveiling, but it is not fully known. The mystery resists full resolution.

While God cannot be studied like real objects are studied, most Christians believe that God can be sufficiently, if incompletely, known on the basis of God's own unveiling or self-revelation. "Our access to God is thus really understood as God bringing us to himself."[1] It may help to remember that the word "**revelation**" comes from the Latin verb "*revelare*" ("to uncover," "to unveil"), which itself is a translation of the Greek verb "*apokalypto*" ("to cause something to be fully known, reveal, disclose, bring to light," BDAG 112; see also ODCC 1402–3). Through "revelation" (Greek: "*apokalypsis*") what was hidden or covered gets unveiled. Although the concept of revelation as God's self-disclosure has assumed a dominant position within Christian theology only since the seventeenth century, it does express an important biblical insight, namely, that God alone can make God known

---

[1] Eberhard Jüngel, *God as the Mystery of the World*, trans. Darrell L. Guder (Grand Rapids: Eerdmans, 1983), 155.

to human beings, and thus the term has been fruitfully used by Christian theologians within the past century (see Thielicke 2.6).

According to Christian theology, the self-revelation of God is truly "of God," originating and coming solely from God, not something produced by human beings. Moreover, it is given both through "nature" ("**natural knowledge of God**") and "history" ("**special revelation of God**"), and principally, Christians believe, through Jesus of Nazareth, an historic individual. He not only reveals God to human beings and acts as God's means for accomplishing the **salvation** of the world, but he also reveals human beings to be the objects of God's redemptive love. For Christians, God remains more hidden, veiled, and incomprehensible apart from Jesus. "For God, the one who has spoken, 'Let light shine out of darkness,' is the one who has shown in our hearts to give the illumination of the knowledge of the glory of God in the face of Christ" (2 Cor. 4.6). Jesus reveals "the glory" of God, even as the resurrection of Jesus reveals the power of God and the vindication of Jesus, God's servant. In this way the revelation of God in and through Jesus continues and fulfills God's self-disclosure in the history of Israel and Israelite traditions, especially in the promises to Abram (Gen. 12.1–3) and David (2 Sam. 7.16), but also in the rescue and vindication of Israel from slavery in Egypt and in the prophetic hope that God's glory would be manifested to the nations in the final event of God's salvation.[2] Christian faith "lives on the gospel's assurance that in Jesus Christ there has appeared the ultimate salvation of God the Creator for the world" (RPP 5.468 [Schwöbel]).

While traditionally the Christian doctrine of God has taken its point of departure in the so-called natural knowledge of God, which is sometimes also called "**general revelation**," Christian faith *as faith* trusts in God solely on the basis of the historical revelation of God in Jesus, who reveals God as the loving Creator and Redeemer of the world. This historical revelation of God is sometimes also called "**special revelation**." Thus the Christian doctrine of God is centered Christologically, that is, in the person and work of Jesus the Christ. This center leads to the development of the teaching about the **Trinity**, namely, that God is triune: God the eternal **Father** sends forth the Word (also referred to as "**the Son**") into the world, who redeems the world, and sends **the Holy Spirit**, who leads people to receive this salvation accomplished by the Son to the glory of the Father. In this sense,

---

[2] This latter aspect is especially emphasized in the essays in *Revelation as History*, ed. Wolfhart Pannenberg, trans. David Granskou (London: The Macmillan Company, 1968).

God is not the "object" of theology, but its "Subject" who addresses human beings, who alone judges them rightly, and yet ultimately acts to save them.

It is worth emphasizing that the revelation of God also includes the revelation of the world and of human beings in the world and of God's relationship to them. Contrary to those Christian thinkers, such as the medieval philosopher, Duns Scotus (c. 1265–1308), who have thought that the triune God alone is the object of theology, Christian theology does in fact speak of more than God. It also speaks of human beings, as creatures made in the image of God, who are "fallen" and alienated from God, but redeemed by Christ. Christian theology, as Thomas Aquinas rightly noted, also speaks of everything else in relation to God through Jesus Christ and the working of the Holy Spirit. The claim of Christian theology is that human understanding of the universe, and of the place of human beings within the universe, remains incomplete apart from the revelation of the universe as the created object of God's redeeming love. The announcement of the gospel is that sinful human beings are loved and forgiven by God and are called by the Spirit to find the source and goal of their being in God and in God's love for them and for others. In some sense Christians maintain that human beings cannot truly know themselves for who they ultimately are, as they are created and intended to be, unless they know themselves to be loved by God and intended for relationship with God. As Augustine famously wrote in his *Confessions*, "You [Lord] stir man to take pleasure in praising you, because you have made us for yourself, and our heart is restless until it rests in you."[3]

This dual focus has remained important within Christian theology down to the present. Centuries after Augustine, John Calvin echoed this Augustinian position when he began his *Institutes of the Christian Religion* with two inter-related propositions: "Without knowledge of self, there is no knowledge of God... Without knowledge of God there is no knowledge of self" (Calvin 1.1. 1–2). One of the great Christian preachers of the twentieth century made the same point: "We find our humanity in the humanity of Jesus Christ. We see in him the original of humanity. We perceive our goal in a living person. We cannot say of ourselves who we are, for we cannot say of ourselves who God is. In this sense anthropology is always for Christians a part of theology."[4] This claim of Christian teaching, namely, that human

---

[3] Augustine of Hippo, *Confessions*, Book 1. i. 3.
[4] Helmut Thielicke, *Modern Faith and Thought*, trans. Geoffrey W. Bromiley (Grand Rapids: Eerdmans, 1990), 53.

beings do not really know themselves aright until they know themselves to be known and loved by God, is a basic element within Christian **theological anthropology** (the theological understanding of human beings).

According to key documents within the NT, all human beings, even those who worship other gods, have some knowledge of the one, true God and are thus without excuse when they do not worship or serve God and instead serve other gods. This so-called natural knowledge of God has traditionally been called general revelation, because it is a knowledge of God that has been given to everyone. In the words of the apostle Paul:

> For the anger of God is being revealed from heaven against every impiety and injustice of human beings who by their injustice suppress the truth. For what can be known of God is apparent to them, because God has manifested it to them. For ever since the creation of the world God's invisible nature, namely, God's eternal power and deity, has been clearly perceived in the things that have been made. So they are without excuse; for although they knew God they did not honor God as God or give thanks to God, but they became futile in their thinking and their senseless minds were darkened. Claiming to be wise, they became fools, and exchanged the glory of the immortal God for images resembling mortal human beings or birds or animals or reptiles. (Rom. 1.18–23)

A Jewish precursor to Paul also complained that people in his day worshipped as gods "fire, wind, . . . rushing water, or the great lights in heaven that rule the world":

> If it was through delight in the beauty of these things that people supposed them gods, they ought to have understood how much better is the Lord and master of them all; for it was by the prime author of all beauty they were created. If it was through astonishment at their power and influence, people should have learned from these how much more powerful is he who made them. For the greatness and beauty of created things give us a corresponding idea of their Creator. (Wisdom of Solomon 13.2ff. [NRSV])

According to Paul, even people who do not know the Jewish and Christian Scriptures know the moral law of God, which is "written on their hearts" and active within their conscience (Rom. 2.15). Similarly, the Gospel of John asserts that the Word (*Logos*) by which the entire universe was made is "the true light that enlightens everyone" (Jn 1.9). Both Paul and the author of the Fourth Gospel (whose contents are traditionally linked to the **Apostle John**) are reflecting earlier Greek philosophical theology, especially Stoicism, with its ideas of universal reason throughout an orderly cosmos and the divine law that is intrinsic to every human being. Such concepts are implicit in other parts of the NT as well (see Acts 14.16–17; 17.22–31). In the NT book of Acts Paul is depicted as preaching to non-Christian philosophers in Athens, where he tells them that what they worship "as unknown" and in "ignorance" he will make clear to them, namely, that "the God who made the world and everything in it, being Lord of heaven and earth," does not live *in* anything or have human needs but is the source of all that is. Paul even quotes favorably a pagan statement: "In [God] we live and move and have our being."

From these Scriptural passages early Christians affirmed the idea of a natural knowledge of God. This idea holds that God's eternal power and deity are manifest to all human beings from creation and, as Acts 17.27ff. indicates, that every being receives its being from God. This means that every human being has some awareness, however dim, of a Higher Power, who is the source of human being and of all being. The claim of Paul is that since God is self-revealing through God's creation, all human beings can indeed know something of God, but because of human finitude and sin people frequently choose to ignore or distort this general, natural revelation. Although every human being could know and ought to know the living Creator, Paul states that they do not know the true God and that they worship idols rather than the Creator.

This line of thinking about a natural knowledge of God was extended in the second century by the Greek apologists, such as Clement of Alexandria, who wrote that even non-Christians have some knowledge of God, albeit fragmentary and distorted, by means of the *Logos*, the divine reason, that enlightens every human being (Jn 1.9). Complementing the knowledge of God that comes from the sensible evidence of the external world, there is also an innate, though imperfect, knowledge of God within every human person. This latter idea has been common, though controversial in the history of Christian thought. Tertullian, who had been trained in Stoicism, taught this, despite his otherwise strong criticism of paganism and the sharp contrast he made between Christian teaching and all pagan philosophy. Although Tertullian famously quipped that Athens (symbol for pagan philosophy and learning) had nothing in common with Jerusalem (symbol for God's special revelation in Israel and Jesus), he nonetheless held that one could receive a natural knowledge of God that derived from the order and beauty of the sensible cosmos and from the immediate witness of the soul.[5]

---

[5] On the natural knowledge of God via the soul, see Tertullian, *Apology* 17, 6. "[Paul] had been at Athens, and had in his interviews (with its philosophers) become acquainted with that human

The principal Greek theologians in the East defended similar claims about the order of the universe, as did Augustine in the West.[6] According to the latter, every human being is capable of contemplating God, in whose image he or she has been created (Gen. 1.26–7), and of receiving the gift of wisdom that comes from God, yet all human beings fall short of truly understanding God and acquiring wisdom because of their finite, sinful condition.[7] For Augustine, the thinkers who approached closest to this truth were the Platonist philosophers, when they "conceived of God, the supreme and true God, as the author of all created things, the light of knowledge, the Final Good of all activity, and who have recognized him as being for us the origin of existence, the truth of doctrine and the blessedness of life."[8]

Several centuries after Augustine, the medieval theologian Bonaventure (who died in the same year as Aquinas) echoed his intellectual ancestor when he underscored that human beings may contemplate God within themselves because God's image is imprinted upon their soul and the light of God's eternal Word (*Logos*) illumines their minds with the "the light of eternal Truth, since the mind itself is immediately formed by Truth itself."[9] Going beyond what Augustine taught about the image of God imprinted on the human soul, however, Bonaventure seems to have thought that even the non-Christian—who is also created in the image of the only true and living God, the Father, the Son, and the Holy Spirit—could have some knowledge of this divine mystery, though he denied that they could know God as "the Father, the Son, and the Holy Spirit" (Pelikan 3.282–3, 287).

Aquinas, too, emphasized the mediation of the natural knowledge of God through sensory experience of things in the world, but he also

---

wisdom which pretends to know the truth, while it only corrupts it, and is itself divided into its own manifold heresies, by the variety of its mutually repugnant sects. What indeed has Athens to do with Jerusalem? What concord is there between the Academy and the Church? Between heretics and Christians? Our instruction comes from 'the porch of Solomon,' who had himself taught that 'the Lord should be sought in simplicity of heart.' Away with all attempts to produce a mottled Christianity of Stoic, Platonic, and dialectic composition! We want no curious disputation after possessing Christ Jesus..." (Tertullian, *On the Prescription of Heretics*, 7).

[6] For an insightful analysis of "natural theology" among the Cappadocians (Basil of Caesarea, Gregory of Nazianzus, Gregory of Nyssa, and Macrina), see the 1992–3 Gifford Lectures by Jaroslav Pelikan, published as *Christianity and Classical Culture: The Metamorphosis of Natural Theology in the Christian Encounter with Hellenism* (New Haven: Yale University Press, 1993).

[7] Augustine of Hippo, *The Trinity*, trans. Edmund Hill (Brooklyn: New City, 1991), Book XV, Chapters 2–3, 399–411.

[8] Augustine, *City of God*, Book VIII, Chapter 9.

[9] Bonaventure, *The Mind's Road to God*, trans. George Boas (Upper Saddle River, NJ: Prentice Hall, 1953), Chapter 5, sec. 1.

acknowledged, as did his teacher, Albert the Great (c. 1195–1280), that all humans have an implicit, if incomplete and confused, knowledge of one, true God: "To know that God exists in a general and confused way is implanted in us by nature, since God is man's Happiness" (Aquinas 1a.2.1). In this Augustinian-Platonic view, God is the goal of human goodness and happiness, and to the extent that every human strives for goodness and happiness he or she is striving toward God, the highest good. Thomas, however, made a sharper distinction between the knowledge of God that is "natural" and that which is "supernatural" than did Bonaventure. Aquinas taught that the supernatural knowledge comes from God's grace and is "above reason," though not contrary to it, and that it is necessary for one to have this supernatural grace in order for one's mind to be divinely illuminated about the mysteries of God. Natural reason is limited to what it can perceive through the senses, but it also recognizes the reliability of the prophetic and apostolic witnesses to be the means of special, divine revelation. Aquinas thus emphasized a synthesis between natural reason and supernatural grace:

> ...[S]acred doctrine makes use even of human reason, not, indeed, to prove faith (for thereby the merit of faith would come to an end), but to make clear other things that are put forward in this doctrine. Since therefore grace does not destroy nature, but perfects it, natural reason should minister to faith as the natural bent of the will ministers to charity... Hence sacred doctrine makes use also of the authority of philosophers in those questions in which they were able to know the truth by natural reason, as Paul quotes a saying of Aratus: *As some also of your own poets said; For we are also His offspring.* (Acts 17.28) (Aquinas 1a.1.8)

This Thomistic attitude toward a natural knowledge of God has been quite influential in the history of Christian theology and it received official sanction in the Roman Catholic Church at the First Vatican Council (1869–70): "The same Holy Mother Church holds and teaches that God, the beginning and end of all things, can be known with certitude by the natural light of human reason from created things..." (Denzinger 588, para. 3004). Nevertheless, many Protestant theologians criticize this position since it seems to suggest that human beings, through their own rational efforts, can achieve knowledge of God on their own, and that such knowledge is a human possibility rather than the result of God's own self-disclosure through the works of creation (Barth 2/1.79ff.; Pannenberg 1.75–6).

One needs to note, however, that Luther and Calvin also taught that God provides the basis or ground for knowledge of God to all people through the light of their reasoning about the works of creation. Despite Luther's strong criticism of those who think they can know God truly on the basis of a natural knowledge through their reason, he nevertheless agreed with Paul's assertion that all people, even people in other religions, have some knowledge of the true God and are thus without excuse when they do not worship God faithfully. On the basis of his understanding of Romans 1.20 Luther argued that this natural knowledge that God gives everyone includes an awareness of God's power, righteousness, immortality, and goodness.

> Reason knows that there is a God. However, it knows neither who the true God is nor what he is like. Reason plays blind man's buff with God; it makes all kinds of attempts to grasp him but always without success. It invariably misses him. For this reason it always identifies as God something that is not God and denies that the real God is God at all. It would do none of these things if it did not know that there is a God—or if it knew who God is and what he is like. Therefore it simply jumps in and gives divine titles and honor to what it thinks is God, while actually never hitting upon the true God... So there is a great difference between knowing that there is a God and knowing who he is and what he is like. Nature knows the first and it is written in all hearts. The second is taught by the Holy Spirit. (Luther, "Lectures on Jonah," LW 19.54–5 [slightly revised])

Calvin developed a nearly identical position, as did Melanchthon, at least in his mature years, and both of these thinkers influenced later articulations of the same basic position in the Protestant theologians of the seventeenth and eighteenth centuries.[10] According to Calvin, God has provided human beings with an innate "sense of the divine," "a certain understanding of his divine majesty," "a sense of deity inscribed in the hearts of all" (Calvin 1.3.1). While all humans are truly aware of the divine, this sense is inchoate and unclear. Because of sin and the tendency toward idolatry, all human beings "degenerate from a true knowledge of him" (ibid., 1.4.1). According to Melanchthon, "God built into our human nature an understanding of

---

[10] In his 1521 *Loci*, Melanchthon asserted that "the reality of God, the wrath of God, and the mercy of God are spiritual things, and therefore cannot be known by the flesh." For Calvin's understanding of natural theology, see B. A. Gerrish, "'To the Unknown God': Luther and Calvin on the Hiddenness of God," and "The Mirror of God's Goodness: A Key Metaphor in Calvin's View of Man," in *The Old Protestantism and the New* (Edinburgh: T & T Clark, 1982), 131–59.

number and order and other distinctions, so that we might learn something about him, so that we might distinguish the only eternal Being from all the many created things" (Melanchthon 11). While Melanchthon spoke of this knowledge as "the first article of faith," clearly he thought natural human reason could arrive at the correct conclusion "that there is one unified eternal omnipotent Being" and not additional deities (ibid.). Reformed theologians in the tradition of Calvin referred to this innate and acquired knowledge of God as "natural religion."

Later Protestant theologians, both Lutheran and Reformed, referred to this preliminary, natural knowledge of God as "general revelation," which they held to be theologically subordinate to, and preliminary to, God's "special revelation" in the history of Israel and the words and actions of Jesus and the Spirit. John Gerhard referred to this two-fold revelation using a distinction that goes back at least as far as Augustine: God discloses the divine Self not only "from the **book of Scripture**" but even earlier "from the **book of nature**" (Gerhard 2, §59 ["On the Nature of God"]), that is, not only through "the light of grace," but also through "the light of nature" (Gerhard 1, Preface, §17). Gerhard further distinguished "the light of nature" into two parts: the knowledge of God that comes from the inner nature of human beings, including especially the conscience that relates to God's moral law within the individual, and the knowledge of God that comes from the external world, through the works of creation.

This natural knowledge of God is not saving knowledge, since it does not really help people before God, but it does serve as an important, preliminary knowledge of God that is only clarified and fulfilled (and surpassed) with the special revelation of God in Jesus through the Spirit. As an important Reformed confession puts the matter: "Although the light of nature, and the works of creation and providence, do so far manifest the goodness, wisdom, and power of God, as to leave men inexcusable; yet they are not sufficient to give that knowledge of God, and of his will, which is necessary unto salvation."[11] Because of the reality of sin that adversely affects all aspects of human creaturely being, including their reasoning, human beings are incapable of freeing themselves from sin and its corrupting influence on their knowledge of God. In themselves, even with their natural knowledge of God, they are incapable of trusting God for their every good, and thus

---

[11] *Westminster Confession of Faith* (1646), Art. 1/1, in *Creeds of the Churches*, 3rd edn, ed. John H. Leith (Atlanta: John Knox, 1982), 193.

they stand under God's criticizing judgment but also under God's promising grace.

While human reason is a gift of the Creator and fully capable of arriving at accurate knowledge of the universe vouchsafed by the Creator, it is incapable of arriving at accurate, saving knowledge of God. On the one hand, Luther's *Small Catechism* affirms human reason and the senses as gifts from the Creator: "I believe...God has given me and still preserves my body and soul: eyes, ears, and all limbs and senses; reason and all mental faculties" (*Small Catechism*, BC 354); on the other hand, it affirms that only the truth of the gospel, as attested in Holy Scripture, gives true and saving knowledge of God and that this knowledge is given as a divine promise that can only be received by faith: "I believe that by my own reason or strength I cannot believe in Jesus Christ my Lord or come to him, but instead the Holy Spirit has called me through the gospel, enlightened me with his gifts, made me holy, and kept me in the true faith..." (ibid., 355 [slightly revised]). Such a theological position is consistent with Paul's teaching in 1 Cor. 2.14ff.: "Those who are natural [or unspiritual] do not receive the gifts of God's Spirit, for they are foolishness to them, and they are unable to understand them because they are spiritually discerned. Those who are spiritual discern all things, and they are themselves subject to no one else's scrutiny. 'For who has known the mind of the Lord so as to instruct him?' But we have the mind of Christ."

With the emergence of the modern period, philosophy, the natural sciences, and jurisprudence became more and more liberated from the authority of Christian theology, and this emancipation had significant implications for understandings of a so-called natural knowledge of God. **René Descartes**, who was born 50 years after the death of Luther, made radical doubt his methodological principle for establishing legitimate knowledge. As a result, the traditional, pre-modern Christian way of relating natural reason to supernatural revelation, wherein "faith" is prior to "understanding," became gradually reversed. Now the thinking person's reason, as it strove to be certain about actual knowledge, was prior to and above divine revelation and faith. The Cartesian "thinking I" stands over against the world as an independent (epistemological) norm, and this gives rise to significant doubts about the objective reality of God and even the world, both of which could in fact be illusions or projections of the thinking self—or the deceptive product of an evil and untrustworthy deity. Only by first establishing himself as a thinker, as a "thinking I," could Descartes then take the next step of asking how he could have knowledge of that which is outside of him, the world and God.[12] Descartes was himself convinced that the idea of God was innate, that "God is no deceiver," and that in fact the concept of God—which he thought must be produced by the perfect, eternal, and almighty Supreme Being—is the inherent principle of all philosophical certainty, including the certainty that the world itself exists and that it can be understood rationally. While Descartes thus held that the concept of God is the normative basis for the structure of human thought—and that the nonexistence of God is an impossible thought— later thinkers became less and less certain of the conceivability of God.

The transition from seventeenth-century Protestant Orthodoxy to seventeenth- and eighteenth-century **Deism** (based on "*deus*," the Latin word for "God") was made easier by the fact that both movements were highly rationalistic and sought to make logical deductions from "first principles" (ODCC 468). Whereas orthodox Protestant theologians at least tried to maintain the medieval unity between "the Book of Nature" and "the Book of Scripture," Deism made a sharp separation between the two and insisted that human reason is always the normative criterion of truth, also with respect to any supposed divine revelation. The desire to find a universal, rational criterion of religious truth was, in part, meant to move the various actual, historical religions and their adherents away from their religious differences—and the religious wars of the sixteenth and seventeenth centuries that resulted in part from those contradictory religious claims—toward that upon which all rational people could agree.

After carefully examining many of the known religions of the world, Lord Herbert of Cherbury (1582–1648), the father of English Deism, concluded that God "has bestowed common notions upon men in all ages as media of his divine universal providence."[13] These "common notions" included the belief that one God exists, that this God is to be worshipped, that the chief way to worship God is by practicing virtue, that evil is to be avoided and repentance of sins to be done, and that God will reward the good people and punish the wicked after death.[14] The next major philosophical voice,

---

[12] René Descartes, *Meditations on First Philosophy* [1641], Cambridge Texts in the History of Philosophy, ed. John Cottingham (Cambridge: Cambridge University Press, 1996). While the famous phrase "*cogito ergo sum*" ("I think, therefore I am") never appears in any of his published writings, it does represent his concern to ground philosophical reflection in the certain self-consciousness of the thinker.

[13] Lord Herbert of Cherbury, *De Veritate*, 3rd edn, trans. Meyrick H. Carré (Bristol: J. W. Arrowsmith, 1937), 117–18.

[14] For a summary of Cherbury's thought, see James C. Livingston, *Modern Christian Thought*, 2 vols, 2nd edn (Upper Saddle River, NJ: Pentice-Hall, 1997–2000), 1.15–16.

John Locke (1632–1704), rejected as contrary to reason any proposition that is inconsistent with, or irreconcilable to clear and distinct ideas, and argued that genuine religious knowledge can be uncovered by human reason and in those propositions that are "above" reason but not contrary to it. Similarly to Aquinas, he thought Christian teaching about the Trinity and the resurrection of the dead were not necessarily contrary to reason but above it and, once revealed, capable of being understood rationally. Locke's near contemporary, John Toland (1670–1722), however, disagreed. He did not think that there are any truths which are "above reason." Later Deists, such as Matthew Tindal (1655–1733), endeavored to set forth the thesis that the gospel is simply a reiteration of the original, natural religion that is common to all human beings of every time and place. In this view, "rational religion" is "moral religion," whose goal is the cultivation of virtue. In this way the theological content of Deism is rather slim. The content of revelation becomes wholly rationalized and limited to the notion of God as the impersonal first cause of the universe and the moral arbiter in the afterlife, who thus remains more or less uninvolved with the world, and limited to the articulation of certain moral principles. For most Deists God is a rather absent, uncaring deity.

The theological content of **David Hume**'s philosophical skepticism was even slimmer: If there is any natural knowledge of God, it can only amount to a vague, ambiguous sense that the apparent order in the universe has been caused by an intelligence that bears some analogy to human intelligence, but humans have no way of knowing this for certain. Against Deists and other rationalists, he asserted that all perceptions of the human mind are either impressions of sense experience or ideas that have come from these sense impressions, which the mind has received in a purely passive manner. There are no innate ideas, certainly not the innate idea of God; all knowledge comes from empirical experience. Because what is sensed as occurring in reality cannot be established beyond the appearance of a probability, "causality" is merely the result of habit and inference and there is no real knowledge, certainly not of anything metaphysical or of God. Hume concluded that even the "self" and objects in the external world cannot be established with certainty, that they are merely the result of habits of sense perception, and that they could easily be vain illusions.

While **Immanuel Kant** overcame Hume's radical skepticism by analyzing how the human mind in some respects imposes its own form of cognition (space, time, causality, etc.) *a priori* upon the materials of experience that are sensed and thus makes possible a real knowledge of "phenomena" in the empirical world, he nevertheless maintained that one cannot truly know anything that transcends the sensible world. All attempts to prove (or disprove, for that matter) the reality and attributes of God are thus completely fruitless. According to Kant, all of the traditional rational "proofs" for the existence of God (which will be examined in the next chapter) are wrongheaded. The only approach to God, according to him, is through "practical reason," wherein God, the freedom of the individual, and the immortality of the soul are "postulates" of human reason, necessary for the fulfillment of moral duty and the attainment of the highest good. In Kant's view, God must be a kind of guarantor that the free moral agent will receive in the afterlife the just consequence of his or her actions. Only an omnipotent and omniscient Being can do this.

Following Hume and Kant, Protestant theologians have tended to be skeptical about the possibility of a natural knowledge of God based on the revelation of God through the natural world. While agreeing with Kant that the traditional natural knowledge of God was no longer possible, **Friedrich Schleiermacher** nevertheless did allow for a kind of "natural experience" of God, which he located in the individual's "sense and taste for the infinite," an "intuition and feeling of the infinite," that arises from one's relation to "the world" or "the whole" of reality. For Schleiermacher "God" and "the world" are not without each other, but neither are they identical to each other. He later referred to this experience of "intuition and feeling of the infinite" as one's immediate self-consciousness that one is in relation to God as creature to Creator, which he also described as "the feeling of utter dependence upon God" (SCF §4 [slightly altered]). According to Schleiermacher, Christian theology is not based on metaphysics, as in the older forms of natural theology, or on moral experience, as in Kant's postulation of the reality of God, but upon the more elemental religious sense or feeling that undergirds all thought and action and that is itself determined by a particular "way of believing" in God, of being in relation to God, within a given historical religious community. "Christian faith," this particular way of believing in God, is distinct from "knowing" (metaphysics and the philosophy of religion) and from "doing" (morality, ethics). For Schleiermacher, the essence of religion or piety, as the feeling of utter dependence upon God, can only be an abstraction from the Christian way of having "faith."[15] In this view of religion, God is immediately present to the human being but cannot

---

[15] I am grateful to Brian Gerrish for making this point clear to me.

be isolated as an object of direct thought. Moreover, contrary to the Deists, who reduced all religions to a kind of universal common denominator and whose ideas conflicted with the individual's experience of utter dependence upon God (since for them "God" is "*a* being" that is external to the universe), Schleiermacher held that religion is uniquely particular and historical, quite varied and distinct, and that the variety of religions in the world is the result of the manifold response to the feeling of utter dependence upon God. It is no exaggeration to say that for him religion refers to that human situation or event—traditional Christian theology had called it "revelation"—which has its origin within the inner dispositions of the believing individual and its determination within a specific religious-social group, but which cannot be described as knowledge per se. He did think that this religious disposition, which he even identified as revelation, is divinely caused, but he was "unwilling to accept the further definition that it operates upon man as a cognitive being" (SCF §10, postscript). In this way, too, Schleiermacher defended both the independence (and integrity) of religious experience, which is grounded in the very structure of human existence, *and* the theological assertions of the modern Christian consciousness that reflect this experience (here "religious knowledge" comes back into view), while at the same time acknowledging the legitimacy of the modern sciences to uncover accurate knowledge of the universe. He further acknowledged that contemporary theologians must also take into account and reflect upon such knowledge, insofar as it overlaps with their theological concerns. With respect to God and God's attributes, on the basis of the awareness of one's being utterly dependent upon God, the Christian theologian can speak of God as eternal, omnipresent, omnipotent, omniscient, unconditioned, and undivided; but all such discussion is limited to how God is apprehended in the religious self-consciousness, which for the Christian is entirely shaped by the redemption accomplished by Jesus Christ (SCF §11) and which cannot be understood as objective knowledge of God as God is "in himself," as even earlier theologians (Augustine, Luther, Melanchthon, Calvin) had maintained as well. Half a century after the death of Schleiermacher, Albrecht Ritschl (1822–89) stressed the same point when he argued that God can only be known in the specific act of salvation through Jesus Christ by which humans receive God's self-revelation. God is "known" in no other way.

Karl Barth has been the one major theologian in the Christian tradition to reject entirely any natural knowledge of God that precedes the revelation of God in Christ and prepares for it. Barth's criticism of all natural theologies led him to be critical of all religions, including Christianity, as human phenomena that reflect human sin and idolatry. For Barth, who desired to break completely with the liberal Protestant tradition in which he had been educated, the revelation of God is exclusively a revelation from God and centers entirely upon the Word of God that is revealed in and through Jesus Christ—"the one Word of God which we are to hear and which we have to trust and obey in life and in death," to quote from the *Theological Declaration of Barmen* that Barth co-authored.[16] In this view, there is no general revelation of God that all people share. Over against Schleiermacher's interpretation of religious experience, Barth held that human religiosity stands in sharp opposition to the subject of Christian faith. All attempts to understand God "from below"—whether from human experience, philosophical reflection, or any kind of natural knowledge of God that might be innate to human beings or derived from the world as creation—only end up with an idol god of human imagination, not the living God who addresses human beings in the single Word of God. Not surprisingly, Barth quoted favorably from the writings of atheist philosophers like Feuerbach and Nietzsche, who attacked all religions as the product of illusory human wish-fulfillments.

Barth's total rejection of natural theology became most clear in his debate with **Emil Brunner** (1889–1966) over the starting point of Christian theology, a debate that led to their estrangement from one another for several decades.[17] Whereas Barth maintained that theology can only begin from its own starting point in the one divine revelation of the Word of God from above, Brunner argued that the NT itself refers to a revelation of God apart from Christ, namely, the revelation of the anger (or wrath) of God (Rom. 1.18), and that this revelation is preparatory to the full and clear revelation of God in Christ. The general revelation of God serves as the presupposition to God's saving, special revelation in Jesus Christ. According to Brunner, all human beings possess rationality and language, grounded in the image of God, which, though damaged by sin, still provide them a "point of contact" (*Anknüpfungspunkt*) for the general revelation of God. Within this general revelation of God, God is experienced as judge,

---

[16] *The Theological Declaration of Barmen* (http://matthewlbecker.blogspot.com/2012/10/pericope-of-week-theological.html [accessed 3 May 2014]).

[17] For the principal documents in the debate, see John Baillie, ed., *Natural Theology: Comprising "Nature and Grace" by Professor Dr. Emil Brunner and the reply "No!" by Dr. Karl Barth*, trans. Peter Fraenkel (Eugene, OR: Wipf & Stock, 2002).

from whose judgments sinners need to be liberated. While both Barth and Brunner agreed that divine revelation comes totally from God, from above, Brunner held that human beings have within them the creaturely conditions for the reception of that revelation.

Barth totally rejected this view and denounced Brunner's position with a sharply worded "*Nein!*" For Barth divine revelation itself creates the conditions for its reception. Every attempt to find a point of contact in sinful human beings for divine revelation ends up repudiating the uniqueness of Christ as God's Word to creatures. In the view of Barth—who wrote during a time when Christians in Germany were re-defining and distorting Christian belief and practice to fit with the racist National Socialism of Hitler—every natural theology is a theology of the Anti-Christ that supports idolatry. For Barth the sole task of Christian theology is to proclaim the one Word of God to sinful human beings, who have totally lost the image of God in the "original creation" of Gen. 1.26–7. Barth's reading of Rom. 1.19–20 led him to the conclusion that God is hidden and inaccessible apart from the divine self-giving in Christ alone.

Barth's rejection of all forms of a natural knowledge of God has met with some acceptance (see Weber 1.199–218), but generally with widespread criticism. Most Christian theologians, even among Protestants, do not think that the image of God has been totally lost and corrupted because of human sin. Chief among those who have been critical of Barth's position (aside from Brunner) have been confessional Protestant theologians, such as Werner Elert; Roman Catholic theologians, such as Rahner; conservative Protestants who maintain the traditional position of Luther and Calvin on this question; and more liberal Protestants, such as Bultmann and Tillich.

In the case of **Elert**, there is an experience of God apart from Christ that is sharply different from the mercy of God given in Christ. Apart from Christ, God is partially known as moral Judge through the conscience, but is directly experienced as divine threat through the experience of "fate" (that which is sent you in life, such as your biological parents, your genes, your gender, IQ, and so on), religious anxiety, suffering, and death in human life and history.[18]

In the case of **Rahner**, there is "a more original, unthematic and unreflexive knowledge of God" that is the result of "man's basic and original orientation towards absolute mystery, which constitutes his fundamental

---

[18] See Matthew Becker, "Werner Elert in retrospect," *Lutheran Quarterly* 20 (Autumn 2006), 249–302.

experience of God," the human being's "transcendental orientation toward mystery" (Rahner 52). "The unthematic and ever-present experience, this knowledge of God which we always have even when we are thinking of and concerned with anything but God, is the permanent ground from out of which the thematic knowledge of God emerges which we have in explicitly religious activity and philosophical reflection" (ibid., 53). In his book, *Spirit in the World*, Rahner strove to overcome the Kantian position that human beings can have no metaphysical knowledge, and to articulate an Augustinian-Thomist position that real "world-transcending knowledge" is in fact possible, even though all human knowledge is tied up with sense experience of this world.[19] Human beings have a "pre-apprehension" of God which is a real knowledge of God, but it is a knowledge of God as the undefined and absolute mystery of the world that is tied to human experience of the world. This knowledge leads beyond this world and summons human beings toward the transcendent, namely, God. It is this "pre-apprehension" of the transcendent, of God, that serves as the condition for the possibility that a human being may be open to hearing God's revelation in Jesus, which is the revelation (to use Tillich's language) of "the ground of one's being" and the being of all other beings.[20]

In the case of **Bultmann**, human beings are able to receive and understand God's revelation in Christ only because they first have a "pre-understanding" of it apart from Christ.[21] Because the Christian message is a message of the forgiveness of sins, the message implies continuity between "the old human being," who is trapped by sin (curved in on oneself, to cite Luther's image for sin), and "the new human being," who is a forgiven sinner. While Bultmann agreed with Barth against Brunner that there is no point of contact within a human being that makes possible the reception of God's revelation, he did think, against Barth, that the human sinner had a pre-understanding of himself apart from the gospel that makes possible the reception of the gospel message and which becomes radically changed with the acceptance of the gospel in faith. Through Christian faith a person comes to a new understanding of himself or herself. The natural self-understanding of the sinner comes to be questioned and changed for the better through the revelation of God's mercy in Jesus Christ. With respect to this natural knowledge of the sinner, Bultmann had in mind a theological understanding of conscience, to

---

[19] See Karl Rahner and J. B. Metz, *Spirit in the World* (New York: Continuum, 1994).

[20] See Karl Rahner, *Hearer of the Word*, trans. Joseph Donceel (New York: Continuum, 1994).

[21] Rudolf Bultmann, "The Problem of 'Natural Theology,'" in *Faith and Understanding*, 313–31.

which the Christian message is addressed (2 Cor. 4.2). He also had in mind the human experience of being beset by one's "own desires and fears," of being "helpless before the unknown, before the enigma." This, too, prepares one to hear the Christian message and to respond decisively in faith, which overcomes one's natural knowledge of self and the enigma of God as threat and judge.[22]

In a similar way, **Tillich** argued that natural knowledge about one's self and about the world can lead to "the question of the ground of our being," to a set of questions to which revelation, "the manifestation of that which concerns us ultimately," namely, the ground of our being or "God," is the proper response (Tillich 1.119, 110). While he, like Barth, rejected the terms and purposes of natural revelation and natural theology, he nonetheless interpreted revelation as that which "points to the mystery of existence and to our ultimate concern" (ibid., 117), in a way that is reminiscent of Schleiermacher's "sense of the infinite." Why something, not nothing? Am I not jolted by the threat of "non-being" to my "being," by "the shock and stigma of nonbeing?" (ibid., 120). These are human questions that give rise to an openness to the manifestation of "the ground and abyss of our being"; in other words, the religious dimension of human life. Like Jaspers, Tillich called this "the depth dimension" of human existence, that points to what is ultimate and unconditioned in life, namely, to that which sustains one's being and gives the fullest meaning of one's life. Thus, "the object of theology is what concerns us ultimately. Only those propositions are theological which deal with their object in so far as it can become a matter of ultimate concern for us" (ibid., 12). Following Paul and Luther, Tillich held that human beings tend to put their unconditional trust in finite, temporal and thus mutable objects in this world, as if they were the ultimate, infinite source of one's meaning and existential security and truly able to save human beings. Humans are inherently religious beings who inveterately worship idols and not that which truly determines their being or nonbeing. Here, Tillich and Barth approximate one another in their respective criticisms of human idol-making.

Other theologians who rejected Barth's complete rejection of a natural knowledge of God include Edmund Schlink (1903–84) and Schlink's most famous student, Wolfhart Pannenberg (b. 1928). For Schlink—who had studied under Barth and had also opposed the Nazification of the Protestant

---

[22] Ibid., 319.

churches in Germany—the human creature has knowledge of God as Creator and law-giver, which is experienced in the conscience but also in one's familial-social-political community. Thus one becomes aware of God's judgment and wrath through the experiences of sin, anxiety, guilt, suffering, and death.[23]

For **Pannenberg** the revelation of Christ "presupposes the fact that the world and humanity belong to, and know, the God who is proclaimed by the gospel," even though an entirely new light is shed on this fact by the revelation of God in Christ (Pannenberg 1.75). Precisely because the *Logos* came "to his own" (Jn 1.11), though his own did not receive him, "the ones who did not receive him were not strangers but from the very first they were his own people. If this is so, then it cannot have been totally alien to their being or their knowledge, for the being of creatures, even of sinners, is constituted by the creative presence of God, his *Logos*, and his Spirit among them" (ibid.). Through the creation God discloses the knowledge of his deity (Rom. 1.20), something that has occurred long before the coming of Jesus. But this revelation of God is not a human possibility (here Barth was correct); it is a revelation *of* God *from* God through God's creation. It exposes human beings as sinners when they worship false gods, "beings that by nature are not gods" (Gal. 4.8). This statement by Paul implies, of course, that the God revealed in the gospel proclaimed by Paul is the only true God, the Creator of the cosmos. Here Pannenberg agrees with Barth: the God revealed in the gospel is "the only God who is God by nature" (Pannenberg 1.79).

In view of the above representative positions on the natural knowledge of God, what conclusions can we draw about a Christian understanding of the natural knowledge of God? Contrary to Barth, and in keeping with the mainstream currents of Christian thought that come forth from the apostles Paul and John and that were flowing already in the witness of the Hebrew prophets and psalmists, Christian theology must continue to affirm a natural knowledge of God, if only in a very limited way as a sense or an awareness of the divine. While some cognitive scientists boldly assert that such a sense is merely the illusory result of hidden cognitive mechanisms, others point out that the evolution of such a human cognitive faculty by natural processes does not (and could not) demonstrate the divine to be an illusion. It could well be that there is a

[23] Edmund Schlink, *The Theology of the Lutheran Confessions*, trans. Paul F. Koehneke and Herbert J. A. Bouman (Minneapolis: Fortress Press Press, 1961), 37–66.

completely natural explanation for the awareness of the divine *and* that the divine also exists.[24]

The sense of the divine reality stands as the "unconditioned" behind the multiplicity of gods, idols, and religions in the world, as Paul seems to suggest in Rom. 1.19–20. By the very nature of the case, all definitions of "the essence" of "religion" are inadequate, since the experience of the Other in the religions cannot be fully fathomed; but those by Schleiermacher, Tillich, Otto, Eliade, and Gilkey do justice to the fact that religion has to do with Someone, or something, beyond the individual to whom the individual stands in a necessary relationship, who confronts the individual with a total claim, and whose ultimate, holy mystery remains elusive to human beings. To Otto's notions of "dread" and "fascination" must be added the additional element of "trust," as Luther stressed:

> A "god" is the term for that to which we are to look for all good and in which we are to find refuge in all need. Therefore, to have a god is nothing else than to trust and believe in that one with your whole heart. As I have often said, it is the trust and faith of the heart alone that make both God and an idol. If your faith and trust are right, then your God is the true one. Conversely, where your trust is false and wrong, there you do not have the true God. For these two belong together, faith and God. Anything on which your heart relies and depends, I say, is really your God. (*Large Catechism*, BC 386)

So Luther acknowledged that (to use Otto's key concept) "the Holy" need not be a supernatural or transcendent object, or even a personal deity. It could be anything of "ultimate concern" (the phrase which Tillich thought also captured Luther's basic view), namely, that which makes a total claim upon the individual and invites an ultimate, total commitment. In this sense, even the atheistic humanist has "faith" and a "god," as perhaps does the non-theist as well. Of course, following the teaching of the apostle Paul, Tillich pointed out that many people place their ultimate trust in that which is not truly ultimate. They put their complete confidence in that which is

---

[24] There might be "a perfectly good natural explanation of the god-faculty and the beliefs it produces...but it might also be true that a personal God providentially guided these natural processes so that people would acquire true belief in God. Both the natural and supernatural explanations may be true" (Kelly James Clark and Justin L. Barrett, "Reidian Religious Epistemology and the Cognitive Science of Religion," *Journal of the American Academy of Religion* 79/3 [September 2011], 655). By "god-faculty" they are referring to a cognitive mechanism in the human mind that produces beliefs in spiritual agencies and powers such as gods or God.

a finite thing, and not the infinite, true God, who alone is "categorically supreme."[25]

Christian theology must continue to wrestle both with the apostles' and early Christians' criticisms of non-Christian religions and with the apostles' and early-Christian apologists' attempts to build bridges between non-Christian religious experience and the proclamation of the gospel of God in Jesus Christ. This wrestling will take seriously the psalmist's statement that "the heavens declare the glory of God and the firmament proclaims his handiwork" (Ps. 19.1), the biblical assertion that human beings have been created in the image and likeness of God (Gen. 1.26–7), the apostle's statements about the plain knowledge of God that can be "clearly perceived" (Rom. 1.20), and his argument that God is near to everyone (Acts 17). According to the apostles and early Christian theologians, the world religions may be correct in the questions which they ask about the Holy or the sacred, but they are incorrect in the answers which they have discovered. Sinful people have turned from the true and living God, whose invisible nature can be perceived through the things that have been made, in order to put their ultimate trust in finite gods of their own making and in religious answers of their own devising. True answers about the Holy, however, cannot be discovered through human action or thinking; they are known only in the self-revelation of the Holy One in Jesus Christ. While God's "eternal power and divine nature" (Rom. 1.20) are indeed implicit in creation, their full import becomes explicit only in special revelation.

Before we turn to consider that special revelation, however, we need to devote more attention to the philosophical arguments for the reality of God that have been provided within the broad Christian tradition. That will be the subject of the next chapter.

---

[25] Charles Hartshorne, "Introduction," in *Philosophers Speak of God*, 7.

Key Words

The Apostle Paul
hiddenness of God
revelation
natural knowledge of God
special revelation of God
salvation
general revelation
Trinity
God the Father
the Son of God
the Holy Spirit
theological anthropology
The Apostle John

two books (nature/Scripture)
René Descartes
Deism
David Hume
Immanuel Kant
Friedrich Schleiermacher
Karl Barth
Emil Brunner
Werner Elert
Rudolf Bultmann
Karl Rahner
Paul Tillich
Wolfhart Pannenberg

Reference literature

On divine revelation as understood in Christian theology

ABD 2:1041–55 ("God" [Scullion, Bassler]); EC 4:672–77 ("Revelation" [Antes, Sykes]); ER 5:3537–60 ("God" [Sperling et al.]); ODCC 688–91 ("God"); OHPT 30–53 ("Revelation and Inspiration" [Davis]); OHST 325–44 ("Revelation" [Quash]; RPP 5:459–75 ("God" [Zinser et al.]); RPP 11:165–75 ("Revelation III–V: Old Testament, New Testament, Christianity" [Kaiser et al.]).

For recent analysis of divine revelation in the more important textbooks of dogmatics

SCF §§ 3–11; Aulén 30–65; Barth 1/2 §17; Elert §§2–5, 8, 22–5; Brunner 1:117–36; Tillich 1:106–59; Weber 1:199–227; Macquarrie 43–58; Rahner 44–71, 138–321; BJ 1:197–264 (Sponheim); Thielicke 2:1–258; Gilkey 39–107; Hall 1:402–27; 2:43–72; Pannenberg 1:63–257; Migliore 20–43; Jenson 1:42–60; ICT 49–76.

For older understandings of the subject of theology and divine revelation

Aquinas 1a.2; 12.12; 2b.92–4; on Luther (Althaus 15–24; Lohse 196–218); Calvin 1.43–69; on Lutheran Orthodoxy (Schmidt 21–38); on Reformed Orthodoxy (Heppe 1–11).

Questions for review and discussion

1 Why do Christians insist that God is not real in the same way that created reality is real? Why do some Christian theologians stress that God is a Subject but not an object? Do you agree with Tillich's argument that God does not exist?

2 For Christians, what is the difference between general revelation and special revelation?

3 According to the Apostle Paul, what does "nature" reveal about God?

4 What do Christian theologians mean by the expression "natural knowledge of God?" What are the contents of this knowledge?

5 How did Descartes change the traditional Christian relationship between "reason" and "faith" (in contrast to how Augustine and Anselm understood this relationship)?

6 How did the Deists understand the relationship between "the two books of God" (nature and the Bible)? Which of these books was more important to them? Do you agree with their position on this issue?

7 Be familiar with the basic understanding of natural theology by Schleiermacher, Barth, Brunner, Elert, Rahner, Bultmann, Tillich, and Pannenberg.

8 Why was Barth critical of all natural theologies? Who had the stronger argument, Barth or Brunner?

9 Of the theologians analyzed here, which one, if any, best reflects your own understanding about the possibility of a natural knowledge of God?

10 What is your "ultimate concern"? To what or toward whom do you look "for all good" and in which you "find refuge in every need"?

Suggestions for further reading

Reference works in systematic theology

William Lane Craig and J. P. Moreland (eds), *The Blackwell Companion to Natural Theology* (Oxford: Blackwell, 2009) [A standard reference work that contains sections on general revelation, religious experience, and the possibility of a Christian natural theology.]

Donald W. Musser and Joseph L. Price (eds), *A New Handbook of Christian Theology* (Nashville: Abingdon, 1992) [A useful reference work that provides brief entries on central topics within Christian theology, including the issues relating to natural theology.]

John Webster, Kathryn Tanner, and Iain Torrance (eds), *The Oxford Handbook of Systematic Theology* (Oxford: Oxford University Press, 2007) [Provides historical and systematic overviews of key issues, figures, and movements within contemporary Christian systematic theology.]

The natural knowledge of God

Emil Brunner and Karl Barth, *Natural Theology: Comprising "Nature and Grace" by Professor Dr. Emil Brunner and the Reply "No!" by Dr. Karl Barth*, trans. Peter Fraenkel (London: Centenary, 1946) [A translation of the classic exchange between Barth and Brunner over the possibility of natural theology.]

Rudolf Bultmann, "The Problem of 'Natural Theology,'" *Faith and Understanding*, ed. Robert W. Funk, trans. Louise Pettibone Smith (Minneapolis: Fortress Press, 1987), 313–31 [Bultmann's criticism of Barth's basic position.]

7

Natural and Philosophical Theology

This chapter describes several of the more important rational arguments for the reality of God and the main criticisms against them. Included are Anselm's ontological argument, Kant's moral argument, Aquinas's "five ways," and more recent versions of the teleological argument by Swinburne and Flew. The chapter's second section highlights some of the problems that surface in all attempts to relate "reason" and "revelation." This section focuses especially on Luther's conviction that human beings can reasonably conclude that God is real, but they cannot say for certain who God is. God remains "hidden" to human beings. For human beings to know God requires God to reveal God. Christian faith trusts that this has happened in the history of ancient Israel and especially through the person of Jesus. Such trust involves risk, since there is no absolute proof for this faithful conclusion.

The concern to clarify the nature and basis of the natural knowledge of God has led some Christian theologians to develop what they consider to be rational arguments and even "proofs" for the existence of God. The perennial possibility of atheism has also contributed to the articulation of these arguments. They are often presented under the label of **natural theology**, since many of them proceed from reflection on the natural world and involve mere natural human reason apart from special revelation.

Such arguments for the reality of God have largely developed in dialogue with philosophical reflection on God as the creating and preserving cause of all things and the source of all wisdom. It may help to remember that the classical meaning of the term "philosophy" is "love of wisdom," and that Greeks (such as Pythagoras) and Christians (such as Augustine) have held that wisdom itself is the proper possession of God alone, toward which humans are only able to strive and never fully attain.

Sometimes, however, arguments for the reality of God do not proceed from observation on nature but arise from philosophical reflection on a given concept of God, and thus some refer to these arguments as **philosophical theology**. While philosophical theology entails more than just metaphysics (what is real) and epistemology (how do we know what we know) to include axiology (what should we value), ethics (how should we live), aesthetics (what is beauty), and logic (how should we think correctly), it has historically focused on rational arguments for and against the reality of God. The long history of philosophical theology demonstrates that belief in God is not "blind faith" or a matter of irrational belief. Faith in God "has usually been expounded by the best-known philosophers as the most rational view of the world... It lies at the very basis of acceptance of the intelligibility of the universe, of the importance of morality, and of a deep understanding of the nature of human existence."[1]

The goal of natural theology or philosophical theology within the Christian tradition has been to clarify the reality and nature of God as the object of the natural knowledge of God (albeit knowledge that also is understood to agree with the special revelation of God), to understand the divine in accord with its own nature, and "to bring out the unity and uniqueness of the deity in contrast to the multiplicity of gods" (RPP 9.55 [Link]). In other words, natural and philosophical theology strives to come to a true understanding of the divine or the Holy, in contrast to false understandings. It should be noted, however, that while these rational approaches to God involve human observation, inference, reflection, and interpretation that are supposedly unaided by special divine revelation and that rely entirely on the natural light of human reason, within the Christian tradition such argumentation tends to be informed by special revelation.

Arguments for God

Augustine's intellectual discovery of the explanatory power of God as the immaterial and infinite source of all that exists—notions that come from both the OT and Greek philosophical traditions, especially Neo-Platonism and Stoicism—is a good example of how philosophical reflection on God helped an individual to leave behind his earlier materialistic and dualistic

---

[1] Keith Ward, *God and the Philosophers* (Minneapolis: Fortress, 2009), 1.

understandings of God that he came to see as deficient and wrongheaded. He no longer believed that God was an extended and infinitely diffused material substance, an idea that to his mind implied that God could be divided and limited by his "materiality." Rather, for Augustine, God is immaterial and eternal. God is the source of all perfections and truth, and distinct from all that exists. God is perfect Being and knowable only within an individual, through one's soul. God is also the key to understanding the nature, order, and purpose of the cosmos. Augustine emphasized that God is the perfectly good and rational source of all being, who has creatively ordered all things toward himself—their highest good.

Unlike Augustine, who did not develop any kind of rational "proof" for God and who understood God not as an "object" but always as a "Subject," other theologians within the Christian tradition have, however, developed rational arguments (often through syllogisms) or demonstrations (through reflection on empirical reality) to defend the proposition "that God is." Many theologians thus have agreed with the basic position of Aquinas who held that theology cannot proceed without first establishing that God exists. "For if we do not demonstrate that God exists, every investigation of divine matters is impossible."[2]

Among the more interesting, if enigmatic, arguments for the existence of God has been the one developed by **Anselm**. Since it is not based on sense experience and begins solely with the concept of God, it is a type of *a priori* ("from the prior") argument, one that is based on the very notion of the term "God." One needs to note that Anselm did not try to prove the reality of God to non-believers, but merely to provide a rational explication of the concept of God from within the perspective of believing faith. "For I do not seek to understand that I may believe, but I believe in order to understand."[3] He thus located his argument within an extended prayer to God, in which he asked for divine illumination. In this context he famously defined God as "that than which a greater cannot be conceived," that is, the

---

[2] Thomas Aquinas, *Summa contra Gentiles*, trans. Anton Pegis (South Bend: University of Notre Dame Press, 2001), Book 1.9 (translation slightly altered).

[3] Anselm of Canterbury, *Proslogium*, Chapter 1, in St. Anselm, *Basic Writings*, 2nd edn, trans. S. N. Deane, intro. Charles Hartshorne (La Salle, IL: Open Court Classics, 1962), 53. My summary of Anselm's argument has been guided by the helpful analysis of Eddie LeRoy Miller, *God and Reason: An Invitation to Philosophical Theology*, 2nd edn (Englewood Cliffs, NJ: Prentice-Hall, 1995), 25–43. Other thinkers in the Christian tradition have also noted that normally people who already believe in the reality of God proceed to give reasons for their faith. Such people reflect the statement that Blaise Pascal put in the mouth of God: "You would not seek me if you had not found me" (Blaise Pascal, *Pensees*, trans. A. J. Krailsheimer [New York: Penguin, 1966], 314; see also O'Collins 29).

most perfect being.[4] Because his argument is based on the concept of God's being (Greek: "*own, ontes*" = "being"), it is usually called the **ontological argument**. Drawing attention to Psalm 14.1 ("The fool says in his heart, 'There is no God.'"), Anselm argued that even the atheist can accept the definition of God as "that than which nothing greater can be conceived," though he will deny that such a being actually exists. But this puts the atheist in the position of being a "fool," since it is "greater" for a thing to exist in actuality than for it to be a mere idea in one's head. God must necessarily exist in actuality, and not merely as a concept in the mind, for if God only existed as an idea in one's head then God would not be God. Something "greater" than this mere idea could still then be conceived, namely, God as existing in reality.

> Therefore, if that, than which nothing greater can be conceived, exists in the understanding alone, the very being, than which nothing greater can be conceived, is one than which a greater can be conceived. But obviously this is impossible. Hence, there is no doubt that there exists a being, than which nothing greater can be conceived, and it exists both in the understanding and in reality.[5]

While many additional Christian thinkers have agreed with Anselm's basic position, such as Descartes (who understood the idea of God as "the most perfect being" bound up with the idea of "the infinite" that is implanted within human beings) and, more recently, Norman Malcolm (1911–90) and Charles Hartshorne (1897–2000), others have concluded that the argument is muddled. Just because one has the idea of "that than which nothing greater can be conceived" in one's mind does not make it so in reality. Even if one could conceive of "the most perfect island," one's thought does not make the island necessarily real. This criticism was already leveled against Anselm's argument by one of his contemporaries, a fellow Christian monk named Gaunilon.[6]

But Anselm and Descartes and those influenced by them might respond: We are not talking about perfect islands, the existence of which cannot be deduced from its concept, since the idea of a perfect island does not involve "existence" as one of its essential properties. We are talking solely about "God," who alone is that than which nothing greater can be conceived. It is "greater" or "more perfect" for something to exist than not to exist, so if God

---

[4] Anselm of Canterbury, *Proslogium*, Chapter 2, in St. Anselm, *Basic Writings*, 54.
[5] Ibid., Chapter 2, St. Anselm, *Basic Writings*, 54.
[6] See Gaunilon, *In Behalf of the Fool*, in St. Anselm, *Basic Writings*, 308–9.

does not exist then God cannot be what the concept says God is, namely the greatest or most perfect being. God *must* exist since *existence* is a necessary property or perfection of the most perfect being, without which God is not God. The very notion of "God," entailing all perfections (as Descartes thought), thus includes the existence of God, the nonexistence of which is inconceivable.

The ontological argument has met with mixed reviews in the centuries subsequent to Anselm. Some, such as the nineteenth-century Lutheran philosopher Hegel, have concluded that it is the most perfect argument for the existence of God, since the idea of God is a necessary thought of human reason. Others judge this argument and later versions of it to involve more smoke and mirrors than careful reasoning. Still others completely reject every *a priori* argument, including ones for the existence of God, since they argue that real knowledge, including knowledge of God, can only come from inductive reasoning about the world as humans perceive it through their five senses. While God's existence can be inferred from the world of sense experience, *who* God ultimately and essentially is remains beyond human comprehension.

More significantly, both Hume and Kant have argued that "existence" cannot properly be attributed to the concept of anything:

> By whatever and by however many predicates we may think a thing—even if we completely determine it—we do not make the least addition to the thing when we further declare that this thing is. Otherwise, it would not be exactly the same thing that exists, but something more than we had thought in the concept; and we could not, therefore, say that the exact object of my concept exists.[7]

In other words, the ontological argument cannot demonstrate the actual existence of God.

Despite recent attempts to reformulate this argument in a more convincing way (for example, by eliminating the assertion that "existence" is a predicate of "God"), the basic argument remains open to serious philosophical objection.[8] Many conclude that the argument merely demonstrates that, if God does in fact exist, God is not a contingent being. Thus, the argument is

---

[7] Kant, *Critique of Pure Reason*, 505.
[8] For twentieth-century articulations of the ontological argument, see especially Charles Hartshorne, *Man's Vision of God* (New York: Harper and Row, 1941); idem, *Anselm's Discovery* (La Salle, IL: Open Court Publishing, 1965); and Norman Malcolm, "Anselm's ontological arguments," *Philosophical Review* 69 (1960), 41–62.

helpful for the one who already believes in God and who seeks conceptual clarification about the being of God. What is not proved is that God exists.[9]

Another argument for the reality of God that is also *a priori*, one that does not proceed from sensible experience, is the so-called **moral argument** that **Kant** devised in the eighteenth century. While he rejected all arguments for the existence of God that proceed from sensible experience, he was not an atheist but a rational theist—despite the label "God-destroyer" that was given to him by his detractors. Although the mind can conceive of God and assert the realities of God, freedom, and the immorality of the soul as postulates of "practical reason" (whereby God functions as the ultimate guarantor of justice in the afterlife by rewarding the virtuous and punishing the wicked), there can be no actual philosophical knowledge of God as a supersensible object, since human beings lack the means by which to know this object. As Kant wrote in the preface to the second edition of the *Critique of Pure Reason* (1787), "I had to deny knowledge in order to make room for faith."[10] In other words, he denied a theoretical knowledge of God and criticized the traditional rational arguments for God, but he maintained the idea of God as a regulative concept for practical reason, that is, for the moral life.

Kant was convinced that most human beings sense the world in which they live to be a moral world: "Two things fill the mind with ever new and increasing admiration and awe, the oftener and the more steadily we reflect on them: the starry heavens above me and the moral law within me."[11] For him, moral duty and responsibility are given in the moral law that is just as objective and external to oneself as the stars in the sky. While he refrained from articulating a specific set of particular duties and responsibilities that are universally correct, he did insist that the moral sense of right and wrong is universal and thus the moral consciousness is an *a priori* concept. While specific moral responsibilities and individual customs and laws are defined differently from culture to culture, what does not vary is the sense of moral duty itself, which points to an underlying moral order to the universe. Moreover, he insisted that one is perfectly rational to think that every human being ought to pursue the highest good, which entails perfect virtue and the happiness that is proportional to virtue. Getting to the highest good must be possible if the idea of moral responsibility is not

---

[9] John Hick, *Arguments for the Existence of God* (New York: Seabury Press, 1971), 90.

[10] Kant, "Preface to the Second Edition," *The Critique of Pure Reason*, 29.

[11] Immanuel Kant, *Critique of Practical Reason*, trans. Lewis White Beck (New York: Macmillan, 1956), 166.

to be completely empty. Nevertheless, because of the presence of evil in the world, not everyone receives in this life the happiness that ought to accord with his or her virtue. In other words, there is not always agreement between one's virtuous actions and the achievement of the highest good. Thus, God must be postulated so that each person can receive the just dessert of their actions in life and receive happiness in proportion to their degree of virtue.

According to Kant, it is "morally necessary to assume the existence of God" because in this life one frequently observes a disconnection between a life of virtue and a lack of happiness. Innocent individuals suffer at the hands of evil people, and the wicked often get away with murder and other injustices. Such a disparity between virtue and happiness in this world is an affront to moral reason and requires the existence of God as an omnipotent and omniscient cosmic Judge, who can ensure in the afterlife the correct proportion of ultimate happiness to the level of virtue in each individual's life. Because there must be an afterlife in order for this apportionment to work justly, the immortality of the soul is also a postulate of moral reason. In this Kantian view, God is the object of moral faith, and "religion within the limits of reason alone" is entirely a matter of morality, of recognizing moral duties as divine commands, and of wanting to clarify universal moral principles that accord with human reason.[12] Without the existence of God and the other postulates of practical reason (i.e. individual freedom to pursue virtue, the immortality of the soul), moral faith collapses.

Kant is not the only one to have argued for the reality of God on the basis of a universal sense of right and wrong. More recently C. S. Lewis (1898–1963) and Francis Collins (b. 1950) have argued in similar ways. They have criticized those who try to derive moral obligation (what ought to be done) purely from nature (what *is* the case) and the subjective emotional states of human beings.[13] If morality is purely a matter of subjective taste and human emotion, could one ever be wrong about one's moral decisions or ever be in a position to criticize the actions of others as immoral?

---

[12] See Chapter 3 above, p. 78.

[13] For a classic restatement of the moral argument for God, see C. S. Lewis, *Mere Christianity*, rev. edn (New York: Macmillan, 1952). For his criticism of moral relativism and subjectivism, see C. S. Lewis, *The Abolition of Man* (New York: Macmillan, 1947). Francis Collins indicates that he became a Christian believer after acknowledging the forcefulness of Lewis' arguments about the universal moral law, reflections that are clearly partially dependent upon Kant's basic position. See Francis Collins, *The Language of God: A Scientist Presents Evidence for Belief* (New York: Free Press, 2006), 21ff.

As one can probably surmise, Kant's argument has also not been immune to criticism. For example, some have argued that there can be human morality without the need for postulating God as its cause. Who is to say that what one knows of God and of morals is not merely the result of hearsay from others, including especially one's parents and family? Or maybe there are many gods (polytheism) that have given rise to many different positions on what is "right" and "wrong." Many reject the idea of an objective moral law and insist that the sense of moral responsibility, which they believe is always relative, has its sole origin in nature, subjective human feelings and emotions, and is not the result of some divine Mind acting to create moral consciousness within each human being. More importantly, might Kant have simply succumbed to wishful thinking? Postulating God for the sake of one's understanding of universal moral consciousness is not the same as proving or demonstrating the reality of God. For the person who does not accept the initial, *a priori* idea of an objective moral world order, Kant's argument and later restatements of it will remain unconvincing.

Precisely because of the dubious nature of *a priori* arguments for the reality of God, many have tried to arrive at "God" rationally by another route, namely, on the basis of sense experience. Despite their own set of problems, these arguments continue to be defended. Many thinkers, such as Aquinas in the thirteenth century, Gottfried Leibniz (1646–1716) in the seventeenth, Paley in the nineteenth, and still others in the twentieth, have found this latter kind of argument much more persuasive than the kind of *a priori* arguments put forth by Anselm and Kant, since they think real knowledge can only arise through sense experience. This kind of argument is called **a posteriori** ("from what comes after") or **empirical**, since it arises as a result of inductive reasoning about observed facts in nature. This line of thinking draws attention to some feature of things that is known to us on the basis of our experience and then moves from this feature to conclude that God is real.

Already in the fourth century, Gregory of Nazianzen taught that human perception of the cosmos and of the law of nature teaches that God "is" and that God is the cause and preserver of all things.[14] In a way similar to Gregory's position, **Aquinas** held that "the natural light of the intellect" is able to derive the existence of God from the world of sense experience, but

---

[14] See Gregory Nazianzen, "Oration 28 ('The Second Theological Oration')," sec. VI, *Nicene and Post-Nicene Fathers*, Second Series, vol. 7, Philip Schaff and Henry Wace (eds) (Peabody, MA: Hendrickson, 1995), 290.

it is incapable of coming to a true and proper understanding of God's nature as triune (God the eternal Father, the eternal Son, the eternal Holy Spirit). Aquinas thus sharply distinguished what is accessible to rational knowledge from what is an article of faith. While he held that the triune nature of God is an article of faith that is based solely on God's supernatural revelation, he thought that the reality of God could be rationally demonstrated through **five ways** of reflecting on sensible experience of the world. His own reflections were themselves guided by Aristotle's philosophical speculations about God and by theological reflections of Jewish and Muslim scholars. They too discussed the reality of God on the basis of specific knowledge of the empirical world.

What Gregory of Nazianzen kept together side-by-side as a two-fold argument for the reality of God, Aquinas broke down into three related arguments. He then added two additional ones (for a total of five). He called each of these five arguments a "way" to God.[15] The first is usually called the **argument from motion**. Influenced by Aristotle's similar argument, Aquinas concluded from common observation that an object that is in motion (e.g. the planets, a rolling stone) must be put in motion by some other object or force. While Aquinas acknowledged that some objects, such as people and animals, can move themselves or change themselves, he argued that nothing is completely the source of its own movement or change. From this, Aquinas believed that ultimately there must have been an unmoved Mover ("God") who put the first thing in motion. This argument proceeds on the basis of the observation that nothing can move itself. If every object that is in motion had a mover, then the first object in motion itself needed a mover. This first mover is the unmoved Mover, "and this is what everybody understands by God" (Aquinas 1a.2.3).

The second way to God is usually called the **argument from causation**. Aquinas concluded that common sense observation tells us that no object creates itself. In other words, some previous object had to create it. Aquinas believed that ultimately there must have been an uncaused First Cause ("God") who began the chain of existence for all things. This argument proceeds on the basis of the observation that things are caused or created by other things. Nothing can be the cause of itself. Since there cannot be an

---

[15] For a more complete historical analysis of Aquinas' "five ways," see Brian Davies, *The Thought of Thomas Aquinas* (Oxford: Clarendon, 1992), 28–39. Before Kant's critiques of the traditional arguments for God no one spoke of "proofs" for God's existence. Aquinas certainly did not use that term.

endless string of objects causing other objects to exist, there must then be an uncaused First Cause, which everyone understands to be God. This is Aquinas' response to the questions, "why is there something, not nothing? Why is there change at all? What keeps the process of 'change' going at all?" As he stated the matter later in the *Summa Theologiae*, "We are bound to conclude that everything that is at all real is from God... All things other than God are not their own existence but share in existence" (Aquinas 1a.44.1). God is the reason there is something, not nothing. God alone exists by nature; all other things depend upon God for their existence.

The third way to God is usually called the **argument from contingency**. This way defines two types of objects in the universe: contingent beings and necessary beings. A *contingent being* is an object that can perish (for example, plants and animals). A *necessary being* is imperishable; it "must be." A contingent being cannot exist without a necessary being causing its existence. Aquinas believed that the existence of contingent beings would ultimately necessitate a being which must exist for all of the contingent beings to exist. This being, called a necessary being, is what we call God. This argument proceeds on the basis of the observation that contingent beings are caused. Yet not every being can be contingent. There must exist a being which is necessary to cause all contingent beings. This necessary being is God.

Aquinas also set forth two additional "ways" that take him beyond Gregory's two-fold argument. The fourth way is often called the **argument from degrees of perfection**. It is based on the observation of the differing qualities of things in the world. Following Plato, Augustine, and many other thinkers, Aquinas held that the idea of "perfection" implies varying degrees of perfection. For example one may say that of two paintings one is more beautiful than the other. So, for these two objects, one has a greater degree of beauty than the other. This is referred to as degrees or gradation of a quality. From this fact Aquinas concluded that for any given quality (for example, goodness, beauty, and knowledge) there must be a perfect standard by which all such qualities are measured, something that has maximum perfection. This maximal perfection is the source of all perfections, namely, God.

The final, fifth way is the **argument from design**. This is based on the detection of order in nature and the universe. Aquinas held that one can observe in nature that all things operate toward some end or purpose, even when the thing seems to lack consciousness. The operation of the thing observed hardly ever varies and typically tends to turn out well, in such a way that it suggests a purpose, not a chance accident. Here Aquinas was again making use of Aristotle's philosophy, in this case, his notion of a "final cause," that is, a goal or purpose toward which an action is undertaken. Aquinas stated that common sense tells us that everything in nature works in such a way that it is directed toward its goal by Someone with intelligence, namely, "God." In other words, all physical laws and the order of nature and life were designed and ordered by God, the Designer. This basic position was given later support by **William Paley** (1743–1805), who scoured the scientific literature of his day for evidence of design in nature. He compared nature to the discovery of a clock watch, whose intricate design gives rise to the rational inference that the watch had a maker, "that there must have existed, at sometime, and at some place or other, an artificer or artificers, who formed it for the purpose which we find it actually to answer; who comprehended its construction, and designed its use."[16] In Paley's view, the observation that objects in nature act for a purposeful end suggests that these objects are directed toward that end by an intelligent being, "by whom all natural things are directed to their end."

What are we to make of Aquinas' five ways? We should probably note right away that each of the five ways follows the same pattern of argument, which indicates that his arguments are not entirely *a posteriori*. In other words, they involve some understanding of God that is *a priori*. By stating at the end of each of the arguments, "and this is what everybody understands by God," Aquinas gave a hint that he was already operating with some understanding of who God is. His arguments thus help one to find the God that one already knows in some other fashion. This observation is important, as it would suggest that Aquinas' arguments are not "proofs," per se, but merely his attempts at giving reasons for the faith in God that he already has. Once again we see here examples of a "faith seeking understanding."

We should also point out that each of the five ways to God, and their further elaboration and defense by later thinkers, has received significant criticism over the centuries. For example, many have argued that a First Cause of the universe is not necessary. The universe could simply be an everlasting phenomenon, something that is temporally uncaused. The concept of God is no longer necessary in a universe that is viewed as an eternal entity. Some scientists—with very little evidence, one should add— have speculated that the universe has had multiple "big bangs" and multiple "big crunches," the so-called "oscillating universe" of repeated expansions

---

[16] William Paley, *Natural Theology: Selections*, ed. and intro. F. Ferré (Indianapolis: Bobbs-Merrill, 1963), 4.

and collapses. Such a speculative view could be used to reject the idea of a First Cause of the universe.

While some have indeed spoken of God as the temporal cause of the universe and have appealed to the scientific theory of the Big Bang and the Second Law of Thermodynamics to support the argument that the universe has had an actual temporal beginning roughly 13.7 billion years ago and to argue that God is the cause of the Big Bang (Francis Collins supports this view), this line of thinking is not what Aquinas had in mind when he spoke of God as the **uncaused Cause** or the **unmoved Mover**. According to Aquinas, one could grant the philosophical point that the universe *could* be eternal, but to acknowledge this as a possibility would still not answer the question, "why is there a universe rather than nothing?" While Aquinas believed as an article of faith, given through divine revelation (Gen. 1.1), that God created the universe "out of nothing" (*ex nihilo*), he nevertheless agreed with Aristotle that the Unmoved Mover need not be thought of as a first cause in *time*, but as the first cause in *Being*. In other words, God is not the cause that sets the universe in motion at a particular point in time in the past, but, rather, God is the ultimate cause of the temporal processes of the universe at every moment. For Aquinas, there must exist an ultimate and self-existent "necessary being" (that is, necessary in itself) upon which all other beings depend for their existence.[17] Unlike all beings that come into being and then pass away, the eternal and necessary God is the eternal and necessary Being, upon whom all other beings depend. This means, too, that God is uncaused, since God transcends space and time, and since the necessary cause of all sensible things cannot itself be one of those "things."

Of course, for the person who is convinced that the universe "just is," this argument will be unconvincing. Any argument for the reality of God that is based on causation will also be rejected by the person who is uncertain about all causality and deeply skeptical about the necessity of metaphysical causation (as was Hume), or even by the one who is more certain about the universality of causality but who limits the concept of causality strictly to this world of sense experience and thus concludes that God, who transcends space and time, cannot be the cause of anything (as Kant argued).

Aquinas' fifth way, the argument from design (or order and purpose), which is also called **the teleological argument** (the Greek word, *telos*, means "end," "goal," or "purpose"), has also received significant criticism.

---

[17] Miller, *God and Reason*, 60.

For example, Hume (through the voice of his character, Philo) argued that one cannot infer a cosmic Designer from the apparently designed character of the universe.[18] For Hume and others influenced by his thought (including Kant), all human analogies between the universe as a whole and some human product are weak and unverifiable. The nature of God remains unknowable, and thus any analogy that compares the mind of human beings with the mind of God is flawed. Material objects could themselves be possessed of their own faculty of order and purpose; there is no need to posit a cosmic Designer for such apparent order, since the order could have come about in purely naturalistic ways. Moreover, there is much imperfection and chaos in nature that can easily lead one to conclude that humans live in a blindly indifferent universe that is governed, if at all, by "blind chance" and destructive, amoral forces. Darwinian evolutionary theory further underscores the philosophical position of Hume that apparent "order" in nature can be completely explained through naturalistic causes.[19] One cannot rationally infer a perfect and infinite Creator from an imperfect and finite universe. Even if this fifth way, the argument from design, were convincing, there is little in the universe that reflects the perfection, infinity, and unity of God. Given the nature of the universe, one could just as easily conclude from the evidence that the cause of the universe is imperfect, not all-powerful, finite, and possibly involves more than one cause.

Despite the criticisms by Hume and Kant and later thinkers, others have defended rational approaches to God on the basis of inductive reasoning about natural phenomena. **Frederick Tennant** (1866–1957), for example, took seriously the above philosophical criticisms and acknowledged the basic facts explained by Darwinian evolution, while also arguing that nature as a whole is intelligible and open to a purposive, meaningful explanation. Not only does nature as a whole give rise to an overwhelming sense of beauty, providing a forcible suggestion that it is the outcome of intelligent design, it has also led to the evolution of human beings, who are moral and spiritual beings. For Tennant, evidence for divine design is not to be found

---

[18] David Hume, *Dialogues concerning Natural Religion*, ed. and with an introduction by Norman Kemp Smith (Indianapolis: Bobbs-Merrill, 1977). Smith's judgment that Philo reflects the skeptical views of Hume is persuasive. "Philo, from start to finish represents Hume; Cleanthes can be regarded as Hume's mouthpiece only in those passages in which he is explicitly agreeing with Philo or... while refuting Demea, he is also being used to prepare the way for one or other of Philo's independent conclusions" (Smith, "Introduction," David Hume, *Dialogues concerning Natural Religion*, 59).

[19] So Richard Dawkins, *The Blind Watchmaker: Why the Evidence of Evolution Reveals a Universe without Design* (New York: W. W. Norton & Company, 1994).

"in the gaps between the explanatory achievements of natural science, which are apt to get scientifically closed up," but in reference to the whole of nature, its interwoven and dovetailing parts.[20]

Darwin himself articulated a similar position. He could not think of "the world as we see it" as "the result of chance," but neither could he "look at each separate thing as the result of design."[21]

> [Reason tells me of the] extreme difficulty or rather impossibility of conceiving this immense and wonderful universe, including man with his capability of looking far backwards and far into futurity, as the result of blind chance or necessity. When thus reflecting I feel compelled to look to a First Cause having an intelligent mind in some degree analogous to that of a man; and I deserve to be called a Theist.[22]

Many have further noted that the Darwinian explanation for the evolution of species, accurate as far as it goes, does not sufficiently account for the regularity of the actual laws of nature, for example, of chemistry and physics, upon which the laws of evolution are based, nor does it address the obvious question as to why these particular, regular, orderly laws are actually there, which regularities very narrowly allow for the emergence of life and the evolutionary potential of species in the first place.

More recent thinkers highlight these and similar issues in support of a modified version of the teleological argument.[23] Following the basic procedures of scientists, historians, and police detectives, the Oxford philosopher **Richard Swinburne** (b. 1934), perhaps the most well-known supporter of rational theism today, argues that the reality of God (as generally affirmed in the three great western religions, Judaism, Christianity, and Islam) is the best and simplest explanation for *everything* we observe in the universe, "the ultimate brute fact that explains everything else."[24]

> [God] explains the fact that there is a universe at all, that scientific laws operate within it, that it contains conscious animals and humans with very

---

[20] Frederick R. Tennant, *Philosophical Theology*, 2 vols (Cambridge: Cambridge University Press, 1928–30), 2.104.

[21] Charles Darwin, *Life and Letters*, 2 vols, ed. Francis Darwin (London: Murray, 1888), 2.353ff.

[22] Charles Darwin, *The Autobiography of Charles Darwin 1809–1882*, ed. Nora Barlow (London: Collins, 1958), 92–3.

[23] For a very helpful overview and analysis of recent thinking regarding the teleological argument, see Robin Collins, "The Teleological Argument," in *The Blackwell Companion to Natural Theology*, William Lane Craig and J. P. Moreland (eds) (Oxford: Blackwell, 2009), 202–81.

[24] See Richard Swinburne, *The Existence of God*, 2nd edn (Oxford: Oxford University Press, 2004); and idem, *The Coherence of God*, rev. edn (Oxford: Oxford University Press, 1993).

complex intricately organized bodies, that we have abundant opportunities for developing ourselves and the world, as well as the more particular data that humans report miracles and have religious experiences. In so far as scientific causes and laws explain some of these things (and in part they do), these very causes and laws need explaining, and God's action explains them. The very same criteria, which scientists use to reach their own theories, lead us to move beyond those theories to a creator God who sustains everything in existence.[25]

"The very success of science in showing us how deeply orderly the natural world is provides strong grounds for believing that there is an even deeper cause of that order."[26]

The growing amount of scientific evidence for an underlying "order" in nature eventually led "the world's most notorious atheist," the British philosopher **Antony Flew** (1923–2010), to change his mind about the reality of God.[27] An atheist for more than six decades, Flew eventually rejected that philosophical position and publicly acknowledged that the evidence in the universe, especially the fine-tuning evident in the laws of nature and the complex arrangements in DNA that are needed to produce life, had led him to accept the existence of an infinite, super-intelligent Creator:

> I now believe that the universe was brought into existence by an infinite Intelligence. I believe that this universe's intricate laws manifest what scientists have called the Mind of God. I believe that life and reproduction originate in a divine Source. Why do I believe this, given that I expounded and defended atheism for more than half a century? The short answer is this: this is the world picture, as I see it, that has emerged from modern science. Science spotlights three dimensions of nature that point to God. The first is the fact that nature obeys laws. The second is the dimension of life, of intelligently organized and purpose-driven beings, which arose from matter. The third is the very existence of nature.[28]

To restate these dimensions into the form of questions: How did the laws of nature come to be? How did life as a phenomenon originate from nonlife? How did the physical universe come into existence? In each case, Flew thought the evidence and rational argumentation about the evidence point

---

[25] Richard Swinburne, *Is There a God?* 2nd edn (Oxford: Oxford University Press, 2010), 2.
[26] Ibid., 62.
[27] See Flew and Varghese, *There is a God*. While Varghese wrote much of this book, Flew himself confirmed that it reflected his basic position. Already in the late 1990s Flew was moving toward theism, long before his thinking became affected by dementia near the end of his life.
[28] Ibid., 88–9. It is important to underscore that Flew became a theist, not a Christian theist.

overwhelmingly in the direction of an omnipotent divine Intelligence. The more we know about the chemical basis for life and the intricacy of the genetic code, coupled with what we know about the laws of physics and chemistry, the more unbelievable is the standard materialist, mechanistic account of the origins of life and the emergence of mind/spirit as purely chemical accidents.[29]

Several scientists have also raised doubts about the standard materialist, atheist account of nature and have endeavored to keep open the question of God's relationship to the natural world. These scholars generally agree with Darwin's rejection of "blind chance" and are compelled by natural evidence to conclude there is a First Cause ("God") to all that is and that the idea of God is compatible with what we know to be true in the sciences.[30] Here the approach is not to try to prove the existence of God on the basis of scientific observations about nature, but to show that theism resonates with what is observed in nature by rational human beings.[31] "Where an earlier generation might have thought it could 'prove' the existence of God by reflection on nature, this approach to natural theology holds that nature reinforces an existing belief in God through the resonance between observation and theory."[32]

---

[29] Even the atheist philosopher, Thomas Nagel, acknowledges that Dawkins' materialist account for the origin of life is unbelievable. See Thomas Nagel, *Mind and Cosmos: Why the Materialist Neo-Darwinian Conception of Nature is Almost Certainly False* (New York: Oxford University Press, 2012). Nagel's skepticism about materialist, "blind chance" accounts of the origin of life "is not based on religious belief, or on a belief in any definite alternative. It is just a belief that the available scientific evidence, in spite of the consensus of scientific opinion, does not in this matter rationally require us to subordinate the incredulity of common sense. That is especially true with regard to the origin of life" (ibid., 7). That some scientists estimate the fraction of stuff in the visible universe to be in living form as approximately 0.000000000000001 percent (one millionth of one billionth of one percent) does not necessarily mean that "life would seem to have been only an afterthought" of the divine creator, as Alan Lightman and others would interpret it. That statistic could be viewed the other way: look how astonishingly rare—and thus precious—life truly is in the universe! See Alan Lightman, "Our Place in the Universe," *Harper's* (December 2012), 38.

[30] The list of such scientists is long, but see especially Paul Davies, *The Mind of God* (New York: Touchstone, 1993); John Polkinghorne, *Faith of a Physicist* (Minneapolis: Augsburg Fortress, 1996), idem, *Belief in God in an Age of Science* (New Haven: Yale University Press, 1998); Collins, *The Language of God*; and Owen Gingerich, *God's Universe* (Cambridge: Harvard University Press, 2006). These books make clear that the notion of a permanent state of warfare between science and religion is unsupportable.

[31] This is also the approach of yet another scientifically-informed atheist who became a believer in God, namely, Alister E. McGrath, *The Open Secret: A New Vision for Natural Theology* (Oxford: Blackwell, 2008). See also Alister E. McGrath, *A Fine-Tuned Universe: The Quest for God in Science and Theology* (Louisville: Westminster John Knox, 2009). See also O'Collins, 32.

[32] McGrath, *The Open Secret*, 18.

The question of the reality of God continues to be explored and debated by philosophers of religion, scientists, and theologians. More recently a number of books have appeared by philosophers of religion that support the position of atheism and are critical of all forms of theism. Among the more important of these are works by **Jordan Howard Sobel** (1929–2010) and **Graham Oppy** (b. 1960). They are much more persuasive than any of the works that have been written by "the new atheists," precisely because they take seriously the arguments of those with whom they disagree, and give them a fair hearing. For example, Sobel's massive work, *Logic and Theism*, provides careful, exhaustive analysis and criticism of the basic arguments for the reality of God (ontological, cosmological, and teleological), and concludes that each of the arguments in support of "God" is unpersuasive.[33] The Anselmian ontological argument, premised on the notion of God as "that than which nothing greater can be conceived," does not necessarily establish the existence of the thing that is thought nor does "existence" contribute to "greatness." Against the cosmological ways of Aquinas, Sobel stressed that the universe could have had multiple "first" causes, perhaps an infinite regress of such causes, and, even if the universe had just one efficient cause, there is no obvious reason why it should still exist.[34] In his view, other cosmological arguments and all arguments for design fail for Humean and Darwinian reasons.[35] The book concludes with a lengthy analysis of the principal argument against the reality of God, namely, that which is based on a rational consideration of evil: evil exists; evil is incompatible with the existence of a perfect being; therefore, a perfect being does not exist.

For his part, Oppy, also, concludes that there are no successful arguments that could persuade a non-theist to change his or her mind about the reality of God.[36] Oppy runs through versions of the ontological argument, several cosmological arguments, and many teleological arguments, and finds them all wanting for one reason or another. All versions of Anselm's ontological argument fail to be successful in persuading the non-theist to change his or her mind because such arguments inherently conflate the concept of God in human understanding with God's reality. (This was Kant's criticism as well.) Cosmological arguments are not persuasive to non-theists because the latter

---

[33] Jordan Howard Sobel, *Logic and Theism: Arguments For and Against Beliefs in God* (Cambridge: Cambridge University Press, 2004).

[34] Ibid., 194–9. "First sustaining-cause arguments are 'nonstarters'" (ibid., 200).

[35] Ibid., 277.

[36] Graham Oppy, *Arguing about Gods* (Cambridge: Cambridge University Press, 2006), xv.

think they are able to offer their own non-theistic rationalizations for the evidence upon which theists build their arguments. Teleological arguments fail for the reasons Hume set forth. Like Sobel, Oppy also thinks that the argument from evil makes a persuasive case against the reality of God.

But not everyone is persuaded by these arguments in favor of atheism. Other philosophers and scientists defend arguments in favor of theism and, more specifically, Christian theism. In addition to Swinburne, one should note the important work of **Alvin Plantinga** (b. 1932). He argues that there are "warrants" for Christian theism, that is, a sufficient quantity of argued reasons that count as "knowledge" and not "mere belief."[37] Taking his main cues from Aquinas and Calvin, he begins by noting that there is a sort of natural yet confused knowledge of God that God has implanted in all (or nearly all) human beings, which Calvin called "a sense of divinity," that is "natural, widespread, and not easy to forget, ignore, or destroy."[38] Human beings have a basic capacity for this sense of divinity, which must develop and mature over time. It is often triggered or occasioned and deepened by natural grandeur and beauty that reveal the glory of God. While this sense has been adversely affected by sin and its consequences, it is "partly healed and restored to proper function by faith and the concomitant work of the Holy Spirit in one's heart."[39] This sense of divinity is produced by cognitive processes that aim at giving us true beliefs about God. God who has created us would want us to know our Creator, so God has given us faculties by which to do so. Thus, belief in God is "a basic belief" that requires no argument:

> And here we see the ontological or metaphysical or ultimately religious roots of the question as to the rationality or warrant or lack thereof for belief in God. What you properly take to be rational, at least in the sense of warranted, depends on what sort of metaphysical and religious stance you adopt. It depends on what kind of beings you think human beings are, what sorts of beliefs you think their noetic faculties will produce when they are functioning properly, and which of their faculties or cognitive mechanisms are aimed at the truth. Your view as to what sort of creature a human being is will determine or at any rate heavily influence your views as to whether theistic belief is warranted or not warranted, rational or irrational for

---

[37] See especially Alvin Plantinga, *Warrant: The Current Debate* (New York: Oxford University Press, 1993); idem, *Warrant and Proper Function* (New York: Oxford University Press, 1993); and idem, *Warranted Christian Belief*.

[38] Plantinga, *Warranted Christian Belief*, 171–3.

[39] Ibid., 186.

human beings. And so the dispute as to whether theistic belief is rational (warranted)... is at bottom not merely an epistemological dispute, but an ontological and theological dispute.[40]

Just as Plantinga begins his reflections on the reality of God from the presupposition of the truth of Christian faith and its assumptions about reality and human beings, so he asserts that philosophical criticisms against rational theism presuppose that theism is false. Those who argue in favor of atheism presuppose the premise for which they are arguing, namely, the falsity of theism. Yet, if those criticisms really depend upon atheism and do not provide a rational critique that is independent of that atheism, then they should not have any force for one who does not share the presuppositions of atheism.[41] Such a view may also help to explain why Plantinga's own philosophical position on God or the reality of evil has not been persuasive to atheistic philosophers of religion.[42]

Given the ambiguities surrounding arguments for and against the reality of God, some thinkers have taken routes similar to **Blaise Pascal** (1623–62), who thought that people must either believe in God or not. He wagered that it is a safer bet to believe in God. Weighing what gains and losses would occur if one staked all one had on God's existence, he concluded that one would gain eternal blessing if the wager turned out to be correct and, if it did not, one would lose nothing. Conversely, one could potentially receive eternal damnation if one wagered against the reality of God and in the end that bet turned out to be wrong. We can chart Pascal's "wager" like this:

	God exists	God does not exist
Wager to believe in God	Temporal good and eternal blessings	Temporal good
Wager not to believe in God	Potential damnation	Temporal good

Figure 7.1

[40] Ibid., 190.
[41] Ibid., 198.
[42] With respect to the problem of evil, Plantinga has defended the possibility that an all-powerful God could not create a world in which human beings never choose evil. He also develops the view that an all-good God would desire to create a world that contains evil if moral goodness requires free moral creatures (who are able to choose between good and evil).

Obviously for the person who is already inclined to believe in God as revealed through the western religious tradition, in which the possibility of divine damnation by almighty God is real, this line of thinking could be persuasive. But for the person who is not already predisposed to think of faith in reference to a single Almighty and just Creator, Pascal's argument is probably unconvincing. Such a person might be led to think that God could be different from what Pascal thought.

For many religious people, what counts is not so much *a rational basis* for their belief in God, but the *practical goods* that result from that belief. In their view the life that comes from theistic faith is fuller, happier, and healthier than the life they perceive the non-believer to have. In the face of suffering and death, they will insist that the promise of their faith helps them to live better. Many Christians will conclude that their faith gives them meaning, purpose, and a more hopeful framework within which to address life's challenges, perplexities, and set-backs, even as it deepens their sense of joy and gratitude for the blessings they experience in this world.[43] It gives them a personal, addressable, loving, graceful, transcendent referent for their wonder at surprising beauty, love, and the sublime in the world, and a basis for their ethical responsibilities. This "will to believe" in God makes God the "center of gravity" for all their attempts "to solve the riddle of life."[44] These practical outcomes are often the main reasons people give for holding the faith that they do. While such faith is indeed a risk—it would not be faith otherwise—they think it is a risk worth taking, given the One in whom they trust and the potential benefits that result from that faith. They point to the healing and consolation that they believe come from God, the source of every blessing. Like Kierkegaard and other theologians, these believers stress that God can be grasped only *by faith*, that God's immediacy is only given in this way, which then alters one's entire existence, way of thinking, course of action, and view of the world.

While no human argument can prove—or disprove—the reality of God beyond the shadow of a doubt, philosophical arguments about God and natural theology assist in highlighting the abiding nature of the idea of God in human self-understanding and the ways in which many human beings have sought to make rational sense of this idea, even if those ways are not

---

[43] As an example of this line of thinking, see Ann Voskamp, *One Thousand Gifts* (Grand Rapids: Zondervan, 2010).

[44] William James, *The Will to Believe and Other Essays in Popular Philosophy* (Cambridge, MA: Harvard University Press, 1979), 116.

finally persuasive to committed non-theistic or atheistic thinkers. For the committed theist, the arguments in support of theism serve to point toward the mystery of God that transcends human beings and their world. Such arguments thus help to keep open the question of that transcendent, infinite reality. They can assist in helping people to think more carefully about the concept of God and the contingent, finite realities of this world, that lead some people to be persuaded that the reality of God is indeed real.

"Lo, these are but the outskirts of [God's] ways; and how small a whisper do we hear of him! But the thunder of his power who can understand?" (Job 26.14) This verse captures nicely the tension between "the whisper" that God gives through the general, natural knowledge of God, received either *a priori* or *a posteriori*, and "the thunder" of God's power that remains hidden and ultimately incomprehensible to finite, sinful human beings.

The hidden God and the risk of faith

As we have already noted in Chapters 3 and 6, there have developed within the history of Christian thought two major positions with respect to the relation between the so-called "general" knowledge of God, which could be developed on the basis of natural reason, and the so-called "special" knowledge, which is given through God's special revelation. The first of these ways maintains that the "special" supplements and fulfills the "general," and that they each are comparable and continuous. This view was classically articulated in the theology of Aquinas and other medieval scholastic theologians, who held that the special revelation of God surpasses but does not contradict the general, natural knowledge of God that could be gained through philosophical reflection. In this way, "reason" and "revelation" are harmonious, and revelation merely adds truths to philosophy that could be obtained in no other way, such as the truth that God is Triune or that the world is created with time.

The second way of relating reason and revelation is marked by tension and conflict, if not outright rupture, between the two. When, for example, Tertullian raised the question, "What has Athens to do with Jerusalem?," he answered with the simple word, "nothing." Natural philosophy has absolutely nothing to do with the specific acts of divine revelation in the history of Israel and in Jesus. For Tertullian there can be no accurate knowledge of God apart from God's special revelation. This position is also quite similar to Barth's complete rejection of any natural knowledge of God.

While post-Humean and post-Kantian Protestant theology has generally been dismissive of rational attempts to demonstrate the reality of God, one needs to note that both Luther and Calvin concluded that human reason could rightly conclude *that God is*, but not surmise correctly *who God is* or what God's ultimate attitude is toward oneself and the rest of creation. This conclusion is not as far removed from the theological position of Aquinas as some might imagine, at least with respect to a natural knowledge of God, although these principal sixteenth-century Protestant Reformers agreed with the basic conclusion of Nominalism, namely, that the natural knowledge of God is utterly deficient and that the particular, special revelation of God is all the more necessary. There are, after all, clues in both Luther and Calvin that they did not completely reject every form of metaphysical knowledge of God. Nevertheless, the various "natural" ways of pointing to the reality of God, whether in philosophical theology or even the cognitive sciences, can at best only indicate (but not prove) *that* God exists. They cannot give a full account of *who* God is or what God's nature is, or what this means for one's understanding of the world, the place of human beings in it, and of one's standing before God. This is also a conclusion one can come to after reading through the intricate dialectics in Hume's *Dialogues*: human reason is impotent to uncover the nature of God and yet one is left with the existential and practical problem of living before the question of God in this strange, awesome, sometimes orderly, and disturbing world.

While the Protestant tradition is right to warn against the dangers of a strictly rational approach to the reality of God, since such an approach often ends up with an idol in place of God or a faulty idea of God that is the result of the philosopher's own making, Protestant theology cannot dismiss every attempt to speak reasonably about the reality of God, at least if it wants to maintain continuity with the Pauline and Johannine statements about the natural knowledge of God that is available to all human beings. Thus some continuity must be affirmed between the so-called "natural knowledge of God" and "the revealed knowledge." The latter allows the former to be put in a new light. "A Christian natural theology is thus about seeing nature in a specific manner, which enables the truth, beauty, and goodness of God to be discerned, and which acknowledges nature as a legitimate, authorized, and limited pointer to the divine."[45]

---

[45] McGrath, *The Open Secret*, 5. McGrath acknowledges that natural theology cannot "prove" the reality of God on the basis of observing nature, but can understand nature in such a way as to comprehend within a Christian framework what is observed in nature and to make sense of it on

Against a strictly rational approach to God, however, one must underscore the prophetic and apostolic teaching that human beings on their own cannot know the nature of God, which remains hidden to human beings and only knowable in God's own self-giving, unveiling or revelation that is received by faith. While early Christian theologians acknowledged the importance of natural theology and even the importance of philosophical theology, they stressed that human beings are incapable of coming to a true knowledge of God on their own. The world of nature is too ambiguous in this regard. For them, God the Creator can only be known as God acts to make the divine reality known. Revelation is thus something that God does as an act of God's judgment and **grace** (God's "favor," "mercy," and the forgiveness of sins). Apart from **the self-revelation of God** and its reception by faith, God is "truly a God who hides himself" (Isa. 45.13). Yet even in the revelation of God's name to Moses (Exod. 3.12) there was the concealment of God's reality, since God's name "eludes every human attempt to grasp him, possess him, and pin him down. God's name will always remain a mystery, forever."[46]

The claim of Christian teaching about God is that apart from faith in Jesus Christ, God is **hidden** or "naked," a "strange, terrifying, indeterminate presence."[47] The "hidden God" is God in the mystery and variability and arbitrariness of fate, in accidents, in the awesome power of nature, in the ambiguities of history, in the vision of the Western world's great tragic literature, utterly inscrutable and incomprehensible in majesty. There are realities, such as birth and illness and death, about which human beings are not first asked if they would like to experience or avoid them. Contrary to the notion of Karma, which attempts to rationalize suffering on the basis of a supposed connection between one's present life and the morality, good or bad, of one's previous life, Christian theology teaches that there is only one biological existence that is given to each creature, and that birth and

---

that basis. Nature is understood as an "open secret," that is, "a publicly accessible entity, whose true meaning is known only from the standpoint of the Christian faith... The explanatory fecundity of Christianity is affirmed, in that it is seen to resonate with what is observed" (ibid., 16–17). While McGrath does not thereby mean to suggest that scientific investigation of nature, apart from any reference to Christian faith and theology, is misleading or unimportant, his position could easily be twisted by fundamentalist Christians who attack legitimate scientific knowledge of nature on the basis of their faith. They would need to be shown McGrath's strong support for the empirical investigation of nature and for "an enriched and deepened engagement between the natural sciences and Christian faith" (ibid., 20).

[46] Oswald Bayer, "A Public Mystery," *Lutheran Quarterly* 26 (Summer 2012), 133.

[47] B. A. Gerrish, "To the Unknown God," in *The Old Protestantism and the New*, 133.

death are the two boundaries that mark the fixity of that existence. Time is irreversible. These are realities over which human beings ultimately have no control, which determine them and shape them in all sorts of ways, realities that they must ultimately suffer and accept, perhaps in protest. "Why? Why here and now and not another time and place or a different set of circumstances? Why this body? These genes? That mother and father? This family? This nation and its history? Why this way today and that way tomorrow? Why must I deal with my fate, my 'lot in life?'"[48] With one hand God gives life, and with the other life is taken away. As Job asked God, "Why have I become your target?" (Job 7.20).

The Scriptures also point to this experience of divine uncertainty when they make reference to the almighty and holy God, whose ways are mysterious and hidden from the reasoning and control of human beings. The biblical prophets dislodge human beings from being the center of the world and starkly proclaim that God has "hidden his face" from them and that God cannot be called forth from the divine hiddenness at their whim. In view of this divine hiddenness human beings have no claim upon God. God is not beholden to them. Almighty God cannot be manipulated or controlled, as if God were "the Big Guy in the sky" and not the sovereign Lord and majestic Creator. "I am the first and the last; besides me there is no god. Who is like me? Let them proclaim it, let them declare and set it forth before me" (Isa. 44.6–7 [RSV]). "I am God, and also henceforth I am He; there is no one who can deliver from my hand; I work and who can hinder it?" (Isa. 43.13 [RSV]). Everyone who questions after God "with reservations," namely, from a position of a supposedly secure existence, or for the sake of establishing such a secure existence, is an act of opposition over against God. The words of God addressed to Job are ones that apply to everyone:

---

[48] For profound Christian theological reflection on the realities of "fate," see Elert 60–8. The German term that is translated as "fate" in English is *Schicksal*. As he employed it, the term denotes something different from "fate" and "destiny," in the usual sense of these two terms. Whereas "destiny" implies an inescapable future goal, "fate" conjures up Greek tragedy and the notion of fatalism, that is, a belief in a teleological concatenation of circumstance that hopelessly also cancels human freedom. For Elert *Schicksal* refers primarily to one's "lot" in life and includes reference to finitude and location. Thus *Schicksal* refers to all the factors that constitute human existence, over which human beings have no say, about which they are not asked, into which they find themselves "thrown": e.g. one's body, gender, family, sibling constellation, race, nation, era, etc., which together become an inescapable dynamic entity and power, that delimit human freedom and with which human beings must come to terms and which can finally exercise power over them, as is most singularly evident in their death. *Schicksal* is literally that which is "sent to us," *was uns geschickt ist*. It is this concept that is behind the term "fate" as it is used here.

Where were you when I laid the foundation of the earth? Tell me, if you have understanding. Who determined its measurements—surely you know! Or who stretched the line upon it? On what were its bases sunk, or who laid its cornerstone, when the morning stars sang together, and all the sons of God shouted for joy? (Job 30.4–7 [RSV])

Luther thus spoke of the ***deus absconditus***, "the God who is hidden," whose majesty and unfathomable power are concealed to all of creation. This is the God who forms light and creates darkness, who makes weal and creates woe (Isa. 45.7), who causes fear to arise in human hearts, who fills them with wonder and perhaps dread in the face of the Wholly Other, who suddenly comes upon human beings when they least expect. How quickly life can change and thrust one into a kind of wilderness: a terrifying accident, a sudden illness, a mysterious death, a terrorist attack, terrible suffering. One is bewildered, in unfamiliar surroundings, out in the region of the Jabbok (Gen. 32), so to speak, wrestling with God. "Why?" "Why now?" "How do we move on?" "What will happen next?" Like Job, people in such circumstances want to have answers, but so much remains an inscrutable mystery. "Why, O LORD, do you stand far off? Why do you hide yourself in times of trouble?" (Ps. 10.1 [RSV]). "Why do you hide your face and forget our misery and oppression?" (Ps. 44.24). According to the Gospel of Mark, even Jesus died with a terrifying question on his lips, "My God, my God, why have you abandoned me?" (Mk 15.34).

To slightly modify the famous expression of Pascal: God has God's own reasons that human reason knows not. The counsels of the Lord are not human counsels. "For as the heavens are higher than the earth, so are my ways higher than your ways and my thoughts than your thoughts, says the LORD" (Isa. 55.9 [RSV]). Because God is so different from human beings, humans can never reach God on their own power or reason, or attain to God from their own resources. In view of the divine mystery, human beings remain in the dark, groping for some kind of light, some kind of under-standing. Sometimes the divine and the demonic seem identical, when God is absent and human life takes on the characteristics of the tragic, the absurd, and the empty.

The experience of the hidden God is also the experience of God in righteous anger and judgment, whose jealousy is absolute, whose ways are not our ways. The divine claim on each individual is total, the claim of the Creator on the creature: "Hear, O Israel: The LORD is our God, the LORD alone. You shall love the LORD your God with all your heart, and with all your soul, and with all your might" (Deut. 6.4–5 [RSV]). Jesus affirms and adds: "You shall love the LORD your God with all your heart, and with all your soul, and with all your mind... And you shall love your neighbor as yourself" (Mt. 22.37–9). In reality, human beings do not love God with *all* their heart, *all* their soul, *all* their mind, nor do they love their neighbor as themselves. In the presence of almighty God, their consciences accuse them as having fallen short of what God demands. This experience of the alarmed conscience occurred to Francis Collins when he realized the existential, divine threat posed by the Moral Law within his own heart:

> Judging by the incredibly high standards of the Moral Law, one that I had to admit I was in the practice of regularly violating, this was a God who was holy and righteous. He would have to be the embodiment of goodness. He would have to hate evil. And there was no reason to suspect that this God would be kindly or indulgent. The gradual dawning of my realization of God's plausible existence brought conflicted feelings: comfort at the breadth and depth of the existence of such a Mind, and yet profound dismay at the realization of my own imperfections when viewed in His light.[49]

This is similar to Isaiah's sense of dread and dismay in the presence of the holy and righteous God: "Woe is me! For I am lost; for I am a man of unclean lips, and I live in the midst of a people of unclean lips; for my eyes have seen the King, the LORD of hosts!" (Isa. 6.5). This was also Luther's experience of "*Anfechtungen*" (spiritual crises, trials, and religious anxieties), the mystics' experience of "the dark night of the soul," Mother Teresa's experiences of spiritual darkness and desolation, and Tillich's experience of anxiety about the existential threat to one's being and the fear of non-being.[50] Then, too, one realizes that there is not always a one-to-one correspondence in this life between the proper proportion of justice to one's actions: Innocent people often suffer an unjust fate, even as people who are guilty of terrible injustices (but perhaps experience no personal guilt whatsoever) often get away with their crimes and prosper along the way (Ps. 73.3). There seems to be no immanent equivalence between one's virtue and one's lot in life, despite every rationalistic ethic to argue otherwise. No wonder Kant thought it necessary to posit God for the sake of supporting a rational, moral faith!

Humans experience "the hidden God" both as God's numinous, tremendous presence (Otto) that confronts the sinner (how God is a consuming, devouring, raging fire that makes of us dust and ashes) and

---

[49] Collins, *The Language of God*, 30.
[50] Mother Teresa and Brian Kolodiejchuk, *Come Be My Light: The Private Reflections of the Saint of Calcutta* (New York: Doubleday, 2007).

as God's absence (how God seems distant, cold, uncaring, mixed up with irrational fate and evil). In both ways the hidden God cannot be loved. Luther thought that in such situations God and the devil seem to be one and the same: "God indeed uses the devil to afflict and kill us. But the devil cannot do this if God does not want sin to be punished in this way" (LW 13.97). God's wrath against sinners is thus bound up with Satan's accusations against sinners. The works of God and the devil appear to be one and the same, despite the fact that the devil remains an enemy of God. "The devil is 'God's devil'" (Althaus 165). Such a conclusion is one that Scripture makes as well when, for example, what happened to Job is attributed to both Satan and God (Job 2.3). Viewed in this way, the hidden God and the devil have a lot in common (see LW 12.373ff.).

This hidden God is the inscrutable God who works weal and woe and whose thoughts are not human thoughts. The majesty of God is a "consuming fire" (Heb. 12.29). God brings people to ruin, smites and hammers people and seemingly pays no attention to their cries for mercy and justice. Moreover, time waits for no one; it always has more breath than the creature has. An honorable death? What if that too is not allowed the individual? "After this Job opened his mouth and cursed the day of his birth" (Job 3.1). Is that not to hate fate? "If I sin, what is that to you, you watcher of men?" (Job 7.20). That is contempt both for one's own lot in life and the final rejection of God the Creator (Elert 68). It is a common human experience, more common than those who sing the praises of God will often acknowledge.

Luther understood this experience of the hiddenness of God as God taking on certain "masks" within creation. God uses human beings and other things as instruments behind and through which God accomplishes God's own purposes. "All creatures are God's larvae and mummery that he will let work with him and help in all sorts of creating, but that he otherwise can and does do without their help, so that we can cling only to his word" (WA 17/2.192.28–31).[51] While Luther rejected the notion that human beings are capable of cooperating with God in their salvation, he did think human beings cooperated with the Creator in the activities of daily, secular life. But even there, it is always God alone who is ultimately acting omnipotently and omnipresently to bring about God's own purposes and ends. "[God] is present everywhere, in death, in hell, in the midst of our foes, yes,

---

[51] This quote is taken from Lohse, 213.

also in their hearts. For he has created all things, and he also governs them, and they must do as he wills" (Luther, "Lectures on Jonah," LW 19.68).

Luther and Protestantism in general hold that rational approaches to God are problematic because they desire to know God on their own terms. In this way God becomes an object whose possibility is determined by the one questing and questioning after the divine reality. The end result is that the quester/questioner tends to stand somewhat aloof from that which he or she is trying to demonstrate or prove, and this is an affront to God's total claim upon the individual as Creator to creature. That is why Bultmann labeled all "talk *about* God" as sin and idolatry.

In similar fashion, the Christian view maintains that every effort on the part of human beings to establish a proper relationship with God ends in failure, since it is grounded in the desire of the human being for self-perfection and self-security over against God. In contrast to every human approach to the reality of God, the proper, trusting relationship with God cannot be the result of the aspirations of human beings, either mentally or morally or religiously, but only the product of God's own condescension in Jesus Christ, his suffering, and his death on the cross. For the apostles, his is "the only name under heaven given among mortals by which we must be saved" (Acts 4.12 [NRSV]).

Moreover, the proper relationship to God takes one beyond a purely objective and rational basis to the perspective of **faith**, trust, love and other dimensions of human existence that transcend the rational. While we have noted that Christian faith "seeks understanding," that it pursues intellectual coherence and an accurate understanding of the divine, the personal faith of the one seeking is never "certain"; it is always "actively at risk."[52]

Such faith involves wonder, humility, vulnerability, repentance, personal commitment, and the human responses of love, joy, and the other "fruits of the Spirit," to use Paul's language (Gal. 5). Unlike trivial or ultimately unimportant questions that can be neatly set aside, questions of faith and existence, of life and death, of God and the complexity of reality, are "fraught with doubt, confusion, uncertainty, risk—and passion."[53] They are a matter of "ultimate concern," namely, "that which determines our being or not-being" (Tillich 1.14). These questions of faith and existence invite a "change of thinking" (the Greek word for **repentance**, *metanoia*, literally

---

[52] Christian Wiman, *My Bright Abyss: Meditation of a Modern Believer* (New York: Farrer, Strauss, Giroux, 2013), 75.

[53] Miller, *God and Reason*, 239.

means "a change of mind" [BDAG 640]), dying to one's sinful self, being "reborn" into the image and likeness of Christ, and entrusting one's future entirely to God.

Such faith is the result of God's grace (God's favor or merciful presence), a grace that becomes all the more surprising and remarkable as it breaks through the experiences of God's hiddenness and absence. There is therefore surprise and gratefulness on the part of the faithful when God makes divine grace and the divine presence known once again. The same psalmist who lamented God's absence could also note with thanksgiving when God did see trouble and grief and considered it "to take it in hand" (Ps. 10.14). Psalm 22, from which come the words that Jesus used from the cross in his time of God-forsakenness, is immediately followed by a Psalm that speaks of the Lord as "my shepherd who... restores my life" (Ps. 23.1–2). "Even though I walk through the valley of the shadow of death, I fear no evil; for you are with me; your rod and your staff—they comfort me" (v. 4 [RSV]).

But how can one have such faith in God without first knowing who God really is? "How are people to call upon One in whom they have not believed? And how are they to believe in One of whom they have never heard? And how are they to hear without a preacher?" (Rom. 10.14). How are they to give praise to God's grace if they do not know God? Ironically, while the general revelation of God is real, it fails to reveal God, as God wants to be known and trusted by human beings. Instead of providing human beings with a path to God, the general revelation of God reveals the inability of human beings to listen to God and their creative ability to devise their own convenient ways of reaching the divine. "Because human beings are in revolt against God, general revelation gives them just enough knowledge to befuddle them, confuse them, and lead them astray. This is not God's fault, for he wants to reveal himself. It is our fault... even God's general revelation is perverted by human beings to hide God."[54] This perversion of God's general revelation makes necessary the special revelation of God in Jesus Christ. The Christian claim is that the only way one can believe/trust in God is on the basis of God's own special self-revelation, a revelation that invites one to trust in God through faith in Jesus Christ. This faith alone provides the proper relationship of human beings to God. It is this faith that allows God's promise in Christ to come to its completion in the life of believer.

---

[54] George Forell, *The Protestant Faith* (Minneapolis: Fortress Press, 1962), 50.

Key Words

natural theology
philosophical theology
a priori
Anselm of Canterbury
ontological argument
moral argument
Immanuel Kant
a posteriori
empirical
Thomas Aquinas
Aquinas' five ways to God
argument from motion
argument from causation
argument from contingency
argument from degrees of
  perfection
teleological argument
  (argument from design)
William Paley

uncaused Cause
unmoved Mover
Frederick Tennant
Richard Swinburne
Antony Flew
Jordan Howard Sobel
Graham Oppy
Alvin Plantinga
Blaise Pascal
grace
self-revelation of God
Martin Luther
The hidden God (*deus
  absconditus*)
faith
Anfechtungen (spiritual
  crises)
repentance

Reference literature

For a general orientation to natural and philosophical theology

ER 5:3537–60 ("God" [Sperling et al.]); RPP 1:478–80 ("Atheism II–III: Church History and Philosophy of Religion" [Dietz, Clayton]); RPP 5:459–75 ("God" [Zinser et al.]); RPP 9:55–7 ("Natural Theology" [Link; cf. EC 3:709–11]).

For recent analysis of the problem of God and natural theology in the more important textbooks of dogmatics

SCF §§ 3–11; Aulén 30–65; Barth 1/2 §17; Elert §§2–5, 8, 22–5; Brunner

1:117–36; Tillich 1:106–59; Weber 1:199–227; Macquarrie 43–58; Rahner 44–71, 138–321; BJ 1:197–264 (Sponheim); Thielicke 2:1–258; Gilkey 39–107; Hall 1:402–27; 2:43–72; Pannenberg 1:63–257; Migliore 20–43; Jenson 1:42–60; ICT 49–76.

For older understandings of the subject of natural theology

Aquinas 1a.2; 1a.12.12; 2b.92–4; on Luther (Althaus 15–24; Lohse 196–218); Calvin 1.43–69; on Lutheran Orthodoxy (Schmidt 21–38); on Reformed Orthodoxy (Heppe 1–11).

Questions for review and discussion

1   What is the goal of philosophical theology in Christian theology? How did philosophical theology help Augustine? Do you agree with Aquinas that theology cannot proceed without first establishing that God is?

2   What are the main elements in Anselm's "ontological" argument for the reality of God? Do you agree with him and other supporters of the ontological argument that "existence" is implied in the notion of "God," namely, "that than which nothing greater can be conceived?" Why or why not?

3   What are the strengths and weaknesses of Kant's "moral" argument? Who are two other individuals mentioned in the chapter who make a similar argument based on a moral order of the universe?

4   Be familiar with Aquinas's "five ways" to the reality of God. Which "way" do you think has the most merit? Why? Which one is least persuasive? Why?

5   Swinburne thinks the very "success of science in showing us how deeply orderly the natural world is provides strong grounds for believing that there is an even deeper cause of that order." Do you agree? Why or why not?

6   What led Flew to change his mind about theism? Does his change of mind itself lend any weight to the probability that God exists? Why or why not?

7   The chapter identifies two basic positions regarding the relationship between "general revelation" (natural knowledge of God) and "special

revelation," that of Aquinas and the one articulated by Luther. If you had to pick one of these as more persuasive, which one would it be? Why?

8   Why has the Protestant theological tradition generally warned against basing Christian theology on a strictly rational approach to the reality of God? Do you agree or disagree with this concern?

9   What "risks" are involved in any religious faith? How does Pascal's "wager" relate to "the risk" of faith?

10   Why do you believe or not believe in the reality of God? Of all of the arguments presented in the chapter regarding the reality of God, which one do you think is most convincing? What additional physical evidence or philosophical argumentation would you put forth in favor of the reality of God? Which evidence or philosophical argumentation is most convincing in favor of God's non-existence?

Suggestions for further reading

Arguments for and against the reality of God

In addition to the suggested works at the end of Chapters 3 and 6, see the following:

William Lane Craig, ed., *The Blackwell Companion to Natural Theology* (New York: Wiley-Blackwell, 2012) [This is a major reference work that contains essays on each of the principal arguments for and against the reality of God. This provides a good picture of the state of this issue within both Christian theology and the philosophy of religion.]

Antony Flew, *There is a God: How the World's Most Notorious Atheist Changed His Mind* (New York: HarperOne, 2007). [Flew was one of the most important philosophers of atheism in the twentieth century. Near the end of his life he adopted a position of non-Christian theism. This book explains his shift in thinking.]

Graham Oppy, *Arguing about Gods* (Cambridge: Cambridge University Press, 2009) [Provides philosophical analysis of classic and recent arguments for the existence of God and concludes that atheism is more supportable than theism. Provides counter arguments and analysis to those made by Swinburne, Plantinga, and Ward.]

Alvin Plantinga, *God and Other Minds: A Study of the Rational Justification of Belief in God* (Ithaca, NY: Cornell University Press, 1990) [This is one of many books by Plantinga that address arguments for and against belief in God. Plantinga has been a leading American philosopher of religion over the past half century who is convinced that theism is rationally justified.]

Alvin Plantinga, *Warranted Christian Belief* (New York: Oxford University Press, 2000) [Chapter 6 provides a good summary of the "warranted" beliefs for theism that Plantinga thinks are significant.]

Jordan Howard Sobel, *Logic and Theism: Arguments for and against Beliefs in God* (Cambridge: Cambridge University Press, 2009) [An accessible, expansive account of the principal figures and arguments on this issue in the philosophy of religion. Sobel's conclusion is that God does not exist.]

Richard Swinburne, *The Existence of God*, 2nd edn (Oxford: Oxford University Press, 2004) [Updated edition of Swinburne's most important book. Many consider it to be the strongest case for the probability of God's reality, based on analysis of the nature of the universe, the finely tuned laws of nature, human consciousness, and the sense of a moral order.]

Keith Ward, *God and the Philosophers* (Minneapolis: Fortress, 2009) [This professor of Christian theology at Oxford University provides an engaging historical and theological analysis of several key thinkers who have thought about the existence of God. Ward stresses that western philosophy has tended to support a spiritual, theistic understanding of reality over against recent efforts to put forth atheism and materialism as more defensible.]

8

Special Revelation

This chapter summarizes what Christians mean by "special revelation." This form of revelation centers upon the disclosure of God the Creator within ancient Israelite and apostolic traditions, the manifestation of the gospel or good news about Jesus in the apostolic witness to him, and the gift of the Holy Spirit. Because theologians have disagreed among themselves about the character of God's special revelation, the chapter analyzes five distinct ways in which people have understood its form.

For Christians, the **special revelation of God** in the history and traditions of ancient Israel, and its culmination in **Jesus of Nazareth** and the gift of **the Holy Spirit**, does not merely confirm or complete the general revelation of God. Rather it "repeatedly challenges, corrects, and transforms all of our earlier knowledge of God, from whatever source," as well as underscores whatever is good and true in it (Migliore 32). While most Christians acknowledge that God is known, at least in part, beyond God's revelation in ancient Israel, in Jesus of Nazareth, and in the gift of the Holy Spirit, Christian faith centers on Jesus as the Christ. As such, faith grows from the historic communities and traditions that led to the coming of Christ and that developed from the outpouring of the Spirit. Thus for Christian faith and theology, the one God, the Creator of all things, has been revealed freely and progressively in many ways, especially in the divine call and promise of blessing to Abram (Gen. 12.1–3), but also in these other ways:

- the **theophanies** ("divine manifestations") to the **patriarchs** and **matriarchs**;
- the further revelation of God's name to Moses ("I am who I am" or "I will be what I will be," Exod. 3.14);
- the giving of **the law** to those Israelites liberated from slavery (Exod. 15ff.);
- the promise of an eternal kingdom to David (2 Sam. 7.16);

- the preaching and symbolic actions of the biblical prophets, and their visions and predictions about the future;
- and ultimately the incarnation of the Word of God (the *Logos*) in the person of Jesus, who is confessed to be the eternal Son of God, God's final word to all people (Mt. 1.1; Mk 1.1; Heb. 1.1ff. *et passim*).

Christians maintain that the clearest and fullest understanding of God that is available to human beings comes from the revelation of God in the good news about Jesus. According to the Gospel of Matthew, "all things have been handed over" to Jesus by his "Father" (Mt. 28.18). "No one knows the Son except the Father, and no one knows the Father except the Son and anyone to whom the Son chooses to reveal him" (Mt. 11.27; cf. Lk. 10.22).

The basic claim of the apostolic writings in the NT is that Jesus is the revelation of God's love and mercy for sinful humankind, that his self-giving life, his sacrificial death, and his resurrection from the dead have brought eternal life to light for mortal humankind. His life has inaugurated a new creation for the old one marked by sin, death, and evil. Christians believe that "God was in Christ reconciling the cosmos to God, not counting people's sins against them" (2 Cor. 5.19). An early sermon in the NT nicely summarizes this understanding of the significance of Jesus:

> What was from the beginning, what we have heard, what we have seen with our eyes, what we have gazed upon and our hands have touched, concerning the word of life—and the life has appeared, and we have seen it, and bear witness to it, and proclaim to you the eternal life which was with the Father and appeared to us. (1 Jn 1.1–2)

According to the biblical witness of **the prophets** and **the apostles**, the special revelation of God is not a divine showering of eternal, abstract truths "from above," as if divine revelation were merely a matter of disseminating divine ideas or propositional statements in the Bible, nor is it the direct unveiling of God in the fullness of God's glory. Rather, the special revelation of God is a self-giving of God that has taken place in particular spaces and times, in the muck and mire of history itself. Still, this revelation involves some specific content. As the Apostles' Creed states, Jesus "was crucified under **Pontius Pilate**," a rather insignificant Roman official, whom Christians nonetheless remember as a way of pin-pointing Jesus in history and of remembering that he was himself a flesh and blood individual who lived in a certain time and place. Thus time and history are themselves significant for understanding the divine self-giving in God's special revelation, according to Christian teaching.

God has created time and space, and yet God has freely and lovingly entered into time and space through God's eternal Word (the *Logos*) that has ultimately become incarnate in Jesus. "And the Word became flesh and dwelt among us... No one has ever seen God. It is God the only Son, who is close to the Father's heart, who has made him known" (Jn 1.14, 18). "In many and various ways long ago, God spoke to our forebears by the prophets, but in these last days he has spoken to us by a Son, whom he appointed heir of all things, through whom he also made the world order. Being the radiance of God's glory and the full expression of God's being, he sustains all things by his powerful word" (Heb. 1.1–3).

In view of these testimonies, Jesus is not a mere teacher about God, as if he were on the same level as a divine messenger (an angel) or a human prophet. In a basic way he was understood by the early witnesses to his life and actions to have incarnated the very being of God in the world and to have manifested that being for what it truly is: "God was revealed in the flesh, vindicated in the Spirit, seen by the angels, proclaimed among the Gentiles, believed in throughout the world, taken up in glory" (1 Tim. 3.16). The divine plan or "mystery" became manifest in the flesh of Jesus (Rom. 16.25; Col. 1.26; Eph. 3.9). "He who has seen me has seen the Father" (Jn 14.7). Is it any wonder that the biblical gospels present religious leaders who accuse Jesus of committing blasphemy and of making claims that no mere human being should ever make?

According to this apostolic witness, the Word of God has entered human history and has revealed himself in the forgiveness of sins as the Giver and Lord of life and salvation. The self-revelation of God in Jesus discloses the self-giving of God for human beings, their salvation, and the salvation of the world. This divine self-disclosure reveals to those who receive it in faith God's character, nature, attributes, and intention toward them. The claim of the message invites a response, either rejection or acceptance. Revelation is not really mere factual knowledge, although Christians will insist that the self-giving of God in history has truly occurred; instead, the purpose of the self-giving of God is to invite a trusting response ("**faith**") from the one who hears the message. By so trusting the message about God in Christ, one's understanding of God, oneself, others, and the world changes. Everything is now viewed in a new light, in the light of God's love and grace that are revealed in the person of Jesus Christ.

The shorthand term that Christians use to label this message of salvation in and through Jesus is the word **gospel**, based on an old English word that means "good message" or "good report" (see BDAG 402–3; TDNT 2.721).

Christians call each of the first four books in the NT a "gospel" (the **four canonical gospels** of Matthew, Mark, Luke, and John) because they tell of "the good news" that has come through Jesus. Mark's gospel begins with these words: "The beginning of the good news of Jesus Christ, the Son of God" (Mk. 1.1). Jesus himself is depicted there as announcing "the good news of God," namely, that "the time is fulfilled, and the kingdom of God has come near; repent, and believe in the good news" (Mk. 1.14–15). Luke's gospel, which begins very differently from Mark's, contains a message of an angel to shepherds who were tending their sheep near Bethlehem, where Luke indicates Jesus was born. On that occasion the angel announces: "Do not be afraid; for see—I am bringing you good news of great joy for all the people: to you is born this day in the city of David a Savior, who is the Messiah, the Lord" (Lk. 2.10–11). Much later, when Jesus began to proclaim the kingdom of God, he quoted from the OT prophet Isaiah to interpret his own ministry: "The Spirit of the Lord is upon me, because he has anointed me to bring good news to the poor. He has sent me to proclaim liberation to the captives and the restoration of sight to the blind, to let the oppressed go free, to proclaim the year of the Lord's favor" (Lk. 4.18–19; cf. Isa. 61.1–2). So prior to the written gospels of Mark, Matthew, Luke, and John, there was an oral gospel that was proclaimed by Jesus himself.

Whereas for Jesus the gospel or good news is all about the coming kingdom of God, the apostle Paul, who wrote a letter to some Christians in the ancient city of Corinth more than two decades after the death of Jesus (c. AD 53–55), identified the gospel with the death and resurrection of Jesus:

> Now I would remind you, brothers and sisters, of the good news that I proclaimed to you, which you in turn received, in which you also stand, through which you also are being saved, if you hold firmly to the message that I proclaimed to you—unless you have come to believe in vain. For I handed on to you as of first importance what I in turn had received: that Christ died for our sins in accordance with the scriptures, and that he was buried, and that he was raised on the third day in accordance with the scriptures, and that he appeared to Cephas [Peter], then to the twelve [apostles]. Then he appeared to more than five hundred brothers and sisters at one time, most of whom are still alive, though some have died. Then he appeared to James, then to all the apostles. Last of all, as to one untimely born, he appeared also to me." (1 Cor. 15.1–8 [NRSV]).

According to Paul, the gospel is the good message about the death and resurrection of Jesus for the forgiveness of sins. Elsewhere, in another letter he wrote later in his life, he calls this gospel "the power of God for salvation to everyone who has faith, to the Jew first and also to the Greek. For in it the righteousness of God is revealed through faith for faith; as it is written, 'The one who is righteous will live by faith'" (Rom. 1.15–17). This passage would have repercussions throughout the history of the Christian church, but especially at the time of the Protestant Reformation, since Luther interpreted these verses as the key to the teaching that salvation is received by human beings "by faith alone" (*sola fide*).

Within the Lutheran and Reformed traditions of Protestantism, the gospel, strictly speaking, is "nothing else than a proclamation of comfort and a joyous message which does not rebuke nor terrify but comforts consciences against the terror of the law, directs them solely to Christ's merit, and lifts them up again through the delightful proclamation of the **grace** and favor of God, won through Christ's merit" (*Formula of Concord*, Epitome, Art. 5, BC 501). Thus the gospel is always a message about the cross and suffering of Jesus the Messiah. It is a message that conveys the forgiveness of people's sins. Its goal is to provide consolation to troubled consciences. For this reason, the gospel message, for it to be truly *good news*, includes the words "for you." The gospel is directed in a very specific way to individuals and their circumstances: "Christ died to forgive *you* your sins..." Likewise, for the message to be heard as a message for oneself, it is best conveyed through oral proclamation that has the quality of being "the living voice of the gospel" (RPP 5.532–3). In short, the gospel proclaims God's sovereign act in Jesus to be gracious and merciful to sinners.

The gospel is not a new law or demand, but a divine gift of forgiveness, life, and salvation. For Luther especially, the gospel is sharply different from the divine law. The gospel should not be made into a new divine law. "For this obscures the merit of Christ and robs troubled consciences of the comfort that they otherwise have in the holy gospel when it is preached clearly and purely. With the help of this distinction [between the law and the gospel] these consciences can sustain themselves in their greatest spiritual struggles against the terror of the law" (*Formula of Concord*, Solid Declaration, Art. 5, BC 581). This distinction between the law and the gospel makes clear that salvation is entirely an unconditional gift of God's mercy and favor for the sake of Jesus Christ.

Types of understanding special revelation in Christian theology

Despite the simplicity of this basic gospel message, the prophetic and apostolic witness to God's revelation is rich in form and content. Not only is the witness to God's self-giving something that is conditioned by human speech, (for example, the languages of ancient Hebrew, Aramaic, and Greek), historic cultures, and ambiguous historical events, but also it involves a number of different literary forms and genres, each of which must be engaged carefully for the sake of theological understanding. Included within that historical witness are figures, metaphors, and symbols that can appear initially opaque and uncertain. As will be discussed further in Chapter 11, the challenge of uncovering theological understanding within the special divine revelation—relating the historic meaning(s) to contemporary significance—can be met only with the assistance of basic principles of interpretation (hermeneutics).

In the history of the Christian church the idea of special revelation has received significant attention only since the sixteenth century, when both Protestant and Roman Catholic theologians desired to defend their respective confessional positions on the basis of their understanding of the Bible as the deposit of divine revelation. Since the sixteenth century, others have set forth the idea of special, divine, biblical revelation over against perceived theological errors, notably Deism, and other errors, such as naturalism, positivism, and materialistic atheism. While all contemporary Christian theologians agree on the centrality of divine revelation for faith and theology, they disagree among themselves regarding the nature of revelation. Since the special self-revelation of God in history is rich and complex, given the multiplicity of prophetic and apostolic witnesses, their historical circumstances, and their use of language, it is not surprising that differing types of understanding divine revelation would emerge in the history of Christian theology.

Avery Dulles (1918–2008), an important Roman Catholic theologian, has helpfully categorized some of these basic **models of understanding revelation** into five different types and has further identified their respective strengths and weaknesses.[1] One may list them as follows:

---

[1] Avery Dulles, *Models of Revelation*, rev. edn (Garden City, New York: Doubleday, 1985).

1 Revelation as propositional truth;
2 Revelation as the biblical witness to divine acts in history;
3 Revelation as divine address in the present moment of proclamation;
4 Revelation as interior experience of God's grace or communion with God; and
5 Revelation as imaginative vision.

We shall take a look at each of these five types and summarize their respective strengths and weaknesses in the light of Dulles' own analyses.

(1) *Revelation as propositional truth.* The first type of understanding divine revelation stresses that revelation is to be found in clear propositional statements that can be drawn from the divinely inspired Bible and defined by church leaders. This model views divine revelation as "inspired communication" from God, that is, knowledge that can only be given by God, which people then collect and organize in the official teachings of a church body. While Roman Catholic scholastics and Protestant Fundamentalists disagree about the specific content of divine revelation, both insist that revelation comes in the form of words that have propositional content.

Those who work with this model define faith as intellectual assent to the propositional content of revelation, whether it is located in an infallible and inerrant Bible (as Protestant Fundamentalists maintain) or in an infallible teaching office (as the Roman Catholic Church asserts). Some conservative Protestant church bodies, which give lip service to the authority of the divinely inspired and inerrant Bible, allow church leaders (for example, a church body's commission on theology and its convention decisions and resolutions) to define the propositional content of divine revelation. Many theologians, including Origen in the third century, Gerhard in the seventeenth-century, and conservative Protestants today, have thus limited divine revelation to the propositional content that is drawn from the inspired biblical writings.

If a strength of this type of understanding is its emphasis upon clear doctrinal teaching, as drawn from the Bible and articulated in the context of the church, a key weakness is its assumption that the verbally inspired Bible is mainly a collection of doctrinal propositions that need only be organized by theologians and defined as divine revelation through a church's official teachers, its commission on theology, or its conventions and official assemblies. To be sure, against those who deny that divine revelation involves any propositional content, one must affirm with Dulles that if "we had no confidence in the propositional teaching of the Bible, we could hardly put our trust in the persons or events of biblical history, or even in the God to whom the Bible bears witness."[2] Yet, one must also acknowledge that not every statement in the Bible, especially as literally taken, expresses a revealed truth of God. As soon as one detects even minor errors in the Bible, such as errors of cosmology or history, this model of revelation suffers.

This same conclusion can be made about a supposed infallible teaching authority, as in Roman Catholicism or some Protestant churches, whose commission on theology typically functions like a church body's **magisterium** (its authoritative teachers). Missing here is the historical-critical task of theology that always seeks to investigate anew the sources of divine revelation, including its cognitive content (which it surely has), and to test contemporary theological understandings against that normative content in the prophetic and apostolic witness to God.

(2) *Revelation as the biblical witness to divine acts in history*. A second type of understanding revelation stresses that the self-manifestation of God has occurred through specific acts in history, to which the Bible and church teaching bear witness. While the first type maintains this basic position as well, the second stresses that revelation is God's own self-disclosure, which only later leads to the articulation of statements and doctrines about God. A number of theologians have held this type of understanding, including the nineteenth-century Johannes von Hofmann (the so-called "father of salvation history") and the twentieth-century theologians, Oscar Cullmann (1902–99), H. Richard Niebuhr (1894–1962), and Wolfhart Pannenberg. Despite their great differences from one another, these theologians insist that divine revelation is not a collection of infallible teachings about God, but rather the historic witness within the Scriptures to God's acts of salvation in history. This type of understanding views divine revelation as "progressive," since God discloses who God is over time and not all at once. Here divine revelation is identical to a series of historical events in which God condescended to people and gradually revealed God over time. These mighty acts of God within history began with the call of Abram and led eventually to the coming of Jesus and the gift of the Spirit. It will then ultimately lead to the culmination of universal history at the end of time. The aim of God's actions in history, which the prophets announce, is "the knowledge of his deity," and therefore of God's nature (Pannenberg 1.238–9).

---

[2] Dulles, *Models of Revelation*, 205. See also the same point that is made by Stephen T. Davis, OHPT 35.

Whereas Hofmann and others, such as Ebeling, have thought that history needed the prophetic and apostolic word to interpret it as "God's history," and that the acts of God include God's addressing human beings directly and indirectly, Pannenberg has insisted that the events of history are self-interpreting and need no additional prophetic revelation. He also stresses, against the views of Barth and Bultmann and those significantly influenced by them (for example, Jüngel), that God's self-revelation is always indirect, at least until the final event of history at its "end," and that divine revelation is more than God's word of address to human beings. "God's revelation in Jesus Christ is indeed only an anticipation of the final event, which will be the actual revelatory event. And yet, we have the well-founded confidence that the final event will not bring anything decisively new that was not already anticipated in the resurrection of Jesus."[3] Pannenberg restates this position in his systematic presentation of Christian theology:

> Because the lordship of the one God is to be thought of as encompassing all occurrence, and world occurrence can be seen as a whole only in the light of its end, the deity of God in his rule over the world is manifest in Jesus only on the condition that in him the **eschaton** [end] of history is proleptically present. The reshaping of the idealistic view of universal history by relating it to biblical eschatology, to the end of history as the condition of its totality, made it possible to abandon the restriction of the historical self-demonstration of God to exceptional miraculous events. In the same way it became possible to overcome the antithesis between revelation as manifestation and a supplementary inspiration insofar as the dawning of eschatological reality in the coming and work of Jesus implies that the expectation of the final revelation of the deity of God to the whole world that is bound up with the eschatological future of history is already fulfilled in Jesus, although only by way of anticipation. (Pannenberg 1.229)

Like Hofmann, Pannenberg maintains that the greatest act of God in history, the resurrection of Jesus from the dead, is the revelation of the end of universal history that has occurred in the middle of history, but it will only be fully comprehended "at the end of history."[4] The resurrection of Jesus from the dead marks the end of God's revelation to human beings, as nothing more needs to take place, save the actual end of history that is

---

[3] Pannenberg, *Basic Questions in Theology*, 2. 44.
[4] For further comparison between Hofmann's understanding of "salvation history" and Pannenberg's understanding of "revelation as history," see Becker, *The Self-Giving God and Salvation History*, 22–5, 220–32, 244–57.

anticipated in Christ's resurrection. In the end, it will become apparent to all ("universal") that Jesus indeed is Lord over life and death. According to Pannenberg, the end of history is identical to God's essence, whereas all revelations of God prior to this end must remain indirect and incomplete.

One strength of this type of understanding of revelation is the recognition that divine revelation is historical in character. Those who hold this view understand that not everything within the Bible or church traditions is of the same theological weight. Indeed, they acknowledge that some earlier elements within the biblical revelation are now outdated, due to later historical-theological developments. For example, polygamy, slavery, and the subordination of women to men may have been acceptable elements within the earlier biblical revelation, but in light of the coming of Jesus and the gift of the Spirit, the gospel has eventually transformed our understanding of these matters so that they may be criticized and rejected.[5]

Despite this important stress on the historical character of divine revelation, this type does have difficulty acknowledging the verbal character of God's address to human beings through prophets and apostles in their historical circumstances. Contrary to Pannenberg's position, the divine word of address and the divine action to accomplish what the word promises are not so easily distinguished in the biblical materials. Hofmann and Ebeling were correct to hold the position that history is never self-interpreting. Historic events always require God's prophetic and apostolic word to interpret their deepest meanings. In this sense the prophetic and apostolic word is also revelatory speech.

In both the OT theophanies (see Exod. 3 for perhaps the most significant manifestation of the LORD to Moses), and in the manifestation of God through Jesus, there is a distinct disclosure of the nature of God. This disclosure was not merely a matter of action; it also involved words that reveal both the Son for who he is and the Father for who he is. Nor is this divine self-disclosure a single "all-embracing event of self-revelation" at the "end of history." It is indeed a two-fold revelation of law and gospel in the past, present, and future. (This distinction between God's "law" and "gospel" is particularly important for Lutheran Christians and will be discussed further in Chapters 10 and 11.)

While Christians believe that the Word of the Lord came to the Hebrew prophets and led them to say what they said, the incarnate Word was sent

---

[5] See especially the essay by Wolfhart Pannenberg, "Dogmatic Theses on the Doctrine of Revelation," in *Revelation as History*, ed. Wolfhart Pannenberg, 125–58.

from the Father and given a commandment about "what to say and what to speak... What I speak, I speak just as the Father has told me" (Jn 12.49–50). "No one has ever seen God. It is God the only Son, who is close to the Father's heart, who has made him known" (Jn 1.18). In light of these passages, it is clear that the incarnate Word directly makes God known through words and actions, each conditioning the other. It will not do to divorce God as author of the Word from "the content of the Word," as Pannenberg would have it (Pannenberg 1.243). To be sure, the fullest knowledge of God will only be given in the manifestation of God's glory "on the last day," but it is incorrect to assert that the knowledge of God will *only* occur at the end of the sequence of revelatory events. If this view were correct, then divine revelation has not (yet) really occurred in history, God has not really spoken a word that is self-disclosing through the prophets and the apostles, the divine wrath is not being revealed now (see Rom. 1.18), and the Son of God has not made and is not now making God known as merciful.

Contrary to Pannenberg's position, wherein the divine self-disclosure must still be coming and only fully present at "the end" of history, divine revelation is both historical event and divine address through prophets and apostles.[6] The address is as essential as the event, since the address interprets the historical events as events of God and announces God's judgment and grace on the basis of them. Apart from the address, the historical event referred to by the address is too ambiguous to be understood. The divine word is necessary to interpret the divine event, and that word speaks now. It now addresses contemporary people in words of divine judgment and grace.

(3) *Revelation as divine address in the present moment of proclamation.* The third type or way of understanding revelation stresses the contemporary dimension of divine address. God's self-revelation occurs fully now, in the present, when God addresses people with the Word. God is known in this address, which confronts people with the message about the incarnate Word. In this type, divine revelation is always God's word of judgment and grace to present human beings that invites their faithful and obedient response.

According to theologians in this group, such as Kierkegaard, Barth, Bultmann and, more recently, Gerhard Ebeling and Eberhard Jüngel, nothing that is conditioned by human beings, including the Bible and the

---

[6] Pannenberg, "Dogmatic Theses on the Doctrine of Revelation" (Theses 1 and 2), *Revelation as History*, 125ff.

church, can be directly identified with divine revelation. God is absolutely and qualitatively different from human beings. In God's self-revelation, God is immediately present but not directly discernible. God always uses a finite means that effectively "hides" God's presence behind it.

For Barth, the Word of God has a three-fold form: Christian proclamation of Christ, the Bible's witness to Christ, and the incarnate Christ himself (Barth 1/1.88–124); but the latter alone is the revelation of God and most properly "the Word of God." The other two forms only "become" the Word of God when they properly bear witness to Christ (Barth 1/1.117). In the case of Bultmann, Christian eschatology is not about the temporal end of history, which he maintains is mythological, but about the present moment of decision for or against faith in the word about Jesus that is proclaimed to contemporary people. Revelation occurs in that moment of preaching and in one's faithful response to the preaching.

All of the so-called "dialectical" theologians (especially Barth, Bultmann, and Tillich), despite their significant differences from one another, insist that Christian faith is not dependent upon the scholarly results of historical-critical investigation, and yet such an insistence has widened the gap between "the Christ of faith" (which could turn out to be an illusion) and "the Jesus of history." To compare Bultmann's historical-critical conclusions about Jesus with what he proclaimed about the Word is to find a real disconnect between "history" and "faith."

There is here then a theological problem with this third type, too. While Barth and Bultmann stressed that the Bible is not strictly the word of God, since it is thoroughly conditioned by human beings, it can become God's word of address when it bears faithful witness to Christ, the eternal Word of God. Likewise, while the church is to proclaim the gospel of Christ faithfully, the teaching of the church per se cannot be identified with divine revelation either. It must always be critically examined against the word of God as it is testified to by the prophets and the apostles.

But if, as especially Barth insisted, human beings are by nature incapable of receiving the word of God, is divine revelation really possible? If the Bible is understood as a thoroughly humanly-conditioned set of documents, how does it "become" the word of God that alone serves as judge and norm for the church's teaching and preaching and all things human? More significantly, divine revelation includes an additional revelation of God beyond the witness to Christ, since Paul indicates that the wrath of God is also being revealed by God apart from Christ. A further problem, underscored by Pannenberg and his circle, is that the dialectical model is really uninterested in divine revelation in "history," since for Barth and Bultmann revelation occurs only in the present proclamation of the word that bears witness to the Word of God who is Christ.[7] The eschatological future of all creation, and of God's final revelation in glory, collapse completely into the existential present moment.

It should be emphasized that the Hebrew word *Dabar*, which can be rendered either as "word" or "event," conveys this two-fold dimension within the divine revelation (see Ps. 33.6; Gen. 1.1; and Jer. 23.29; where the *Dabar* ["word"] of the Lord is described as being like "fire" and "a hammer which breaks the rock in pieces"). What Pannenberg, on the one hand, and Bultmann and Barth, on the other, tear apart must be kept together: Divine revelation is both historical event *and* the divine word of address that interprets the event and that summons the listener to trust the address as address from God in the present. The Roman Catholic *Constitution on Divine Revelation* that was formally received at the Second Vatican Council gets this issue correct. It strikes the right balance between "history" and "word of God":

> This plan of revelation is realized by deeds and words having an inner unity: the deeds wrought by God in the history of salvation manifest and confirm the teaching and realities signified by the words, while the words proclaim the deeds and clarify the mystery contained in them.[8]

---

[7] James Barr has criticized all attempts to link "revelation" and "history" in Christian theology. He stressed that the narratives within the OT cannot properly be described as "history" and are better understood in the category of "story." See James Barr, "Revelation through history in the OT and in modern theology," *Interpretation* 17 (1963), 193–205; and idem, "The Concepts of History and Revelation," in James Barr, *Old and New in Interpretation* (New York: Harper and Row, 1966), 65–102. Against Barr's views, one must note that the OT indicates a regard for "God's acts" and "deeds," and even tends to put these deeds into a kind of sequential order. Furthermore, against Barr's rejection of "revelation" as "a general term for man's source of knowledge of God," one must simply point to the Pauline teaching about the natural knowledge of God available to all human beings (Rom. 1.19). More significantly, Pannenberg has rightly criticized Barr and those influenced by him for giving up the category of "history" altogether in favor of "story" or "narrative": "Theology can honor the realistic intention of the biblical accounts only if it takes seriously their witness to the divine action in real events which come upon people and in part were fashioned by them, inquiring into the divine action in the reality of what we call history today. We may not be able to do this without taking a critical view of the historicity of many of the details and stories in the biblical texts, but if theology seeks God's historical action in the sequence of events which the Bible records, and as they appear to modern historical judgment and according to their reconstruction on the basis of historical-critical research, it will be closer to the spirit of the biblical traditions than if it treats the texts simply as literature in which the facticity of what is recorded is a subsidiary matter" (Pannenberg 1.231).

[8] *Dei Verbum*, "The Dogmatic Constitution on Divine Revelation," Chapter 1, Article 2, in Norman P. Tanner, ed., *Decrees of the Ecumenical Councils*, 2 vols (Georgetown: Sheed and Ward, 1990), 2.971ff.

(4) *Revelation as interior experience of God's grace or communion with God.* The fourth type of understanding views divine revelation neither as a collection of propositional truths nor as an historical series of events, but as an interior experience of God's grace or communion with God. In this type, God's revelation occurs within the interior soul of the one who is open to God's grace. This experience is a direct, unmediated encounter between God and the soul, not the communication of information or abstract church teaching.

In view of Kant's critique of religious knowledge, a strength of this fourth type is to stress that divine revelation exists in a different dimension from the sciences and thus provides a different kind of truth. As Tillich notes, "If myth and cult are considered to be the expression of the depth of reason in symbolic form, they lie in a dimension where no interference with the proper functions of reason is possible... Revelation does not destroy reason, but reason raises the question of revelation" (Tillich 1.81). (It should be noted that Tillich's approach to revelation does not fall neatly into this one type, but overlaps with the second and the fifth as well.)

The view of revelation as "interior experience," however, will be judged deficient by anyone who wants to take the primary and normative cues for divine revelation from the witness of the prophets and the apostles and not from subjective religious experience. Divine revelation cannot avoid a doctrinal dimension, and yet this model seems to suggest a content-less revelation of private individual experience. "By divorcing revelation from doctrine this model pays a price. It disappoints many of the expectations with which people ordinarily approach religion. It says in effect that there are no divine answers to the deep human questions about the origin and ultimate destiny of humanity and the world. A church that can acknowledge no revealed doctrine can hardly offer the kind of heavenly wisdom which revealed religion is commonly supposed to supply."[9]

(5) *Revelation as imaginative vision.* A final, fifth type holds that revelation expands or fulfills the consciousness of the human being in his or her world as it gives the human being a new perspective on God, the self, and the world. Revelation is mediated through revelatory events, which stimulate the human imagination and cause humans to work toward the creative transformation of the world. Lacking in specific content, revelation nonetheless allows the individual so enlightened to participate in God's

---

[9] Dulles, *Models of Revelation*, 79.

creative and redemptive activity that leads toward reconciliation among divided peoples and ultimate fulfillment in God's future.

While Dulles did not attend to liberationist (whether Latin American or Black) and feminist theologies in his typology, they clearly would be sub-categories of this final type, since, in their differing ways, these theologies also yearn for creative transformation of individual and social relationships, critical re-thinking of such categories as race, class, and gender, and the creation of more just communities. Some of these alternative theologians have, as in the later work of Mary Daly, definitely and defiantly abandoned any form of Christian teaching, but others have sought to retain a critical perspective from within Christianity and to articulate ways in which the Christian tradition is capable of reform and adjustment, whether in a feminist critique of Christian tradition (for example, Fiorenza, McFague, Chopp) or in a liberationist critique (for example, Gutiérrez).

Certainly this final type of understanding revelation allows for more flexibility in the interpretation of Scripture, including the need for criticism of elements within it that have traditionally been understood and used to oppress whole groups of people. This type encourages the re-visioning of church teaching and practices for the sake of positive, needed changes in theological understanding and praxis for the sake of justice and equality. For example, Jon Sobrino (b. 1938) argues that natural theologies, based on the general revelation of God, tend to distort the biblical knowledge of God by focusing on the goodness of creation and ignoring the realities of sin, evil, and human suffering. Such theologies thus ignore human poverty and suffering in the world, especially in so-called developing countries. Sobrino, like Luther, emphasizes that theology must take its orientation and content from the suffering of Christ and the special revelation that accompanies his crucifixion, and relate this to the real problems of human suffering and oppression in the world today.[10]

Despite the important contribution that liberation and feminist theologies make to contemporary theology, they too can run into theological problems, the chief of which is the tendency to blur a biblical understanding of salvation, including especially the liberation from sin and death and the judgment of God, with this-worldly political, economic, and social liberation. While indeed there are conditions and patterns of social injustice that ought to be criticized and changed by Christians and investigated critically,

---

[10] Jon Sobrino, *Christology at the Crossroads: A Latin American Approach*, trans. John Drury (Maryknoll NY: Orbis, 1978), 195–201.

there will always be ambivalences inherent in every liberation movement in this world. Christian theology thus "must always remain mindful of the fact that the deepest servitude of human beings is a servitude to the powers of sin and death from which we are freed only by the death of Christ, in faith in God and his kingdom..."[11] Revelation is *of God*, who remains transcendent to human action and history. Divine revelation cannot be uncritically equated with human creativity and ideologies, however promising they might otherwise appear to be. Every theology must remain open to criticism on the basis of the divine transcendence and in view of God's address of judgment and grace.

Although there are significant differences among the types of under-standing divine revelation within Christian theology, there are some common points of contact among most, if not all, of them. We may list these as follows:

- divine revelation is God's free action of self-disclosure to the world that is related to God;
- God's revelation, at least as understood by Christians, is finally and ultimately centered in Jesus, the incarnate Word of God;
- This self-revelation of God in Christ is normally accessed through the canonical Scriptures as proclaimed by the church;[12]
- The goal of divine revelation is its reception in faith;
- The self-disclosure of God is an unveiling of God's essential hiddenness.[13]

In what has preceded and what will follow this section, it should be clear that the position set forth here more fully accords with aspects of the first three of Dulles' models. Divine revelation is the self-disclosure of

---

[11] Wolfhart Pannenberg, *Christianity in a Secularized World* (New York: Crossroad, 1989), 55.

[12] Dulles, *Models of Revelation*, 117. Whereas Dulles reflects a Roman Catholic position when he states that "the normal way of access to revelation is through the Church which reads and proclaims the biblical message," I am here reflecting a Lutheran position that understands the divine word, testified to through prophets and apostles, as the creative source of the church and the abiding norm for the church's teaching and practice. In this sense, the Scriptures remain *above* the church, even as they are also read and proclaimed in the church.

[13] John Baillie has noted that the recovery of the Bible's emphasis on God's self-disclosure in God's actions within history is a key insight in theological understanding during the past century. This affirmation is in marked contrast to those who insist that divine revelation is the communication of supranatural doctrinal propositions within the Bible. See John Baillie, *The Idea of Revelation in Recent Thought* (New York: Columbia University Press, 1956), 28–9, 62. Nevertheless, as Baillie himself implies but does not develop, the divine self-disclosure has noetic implications. There is a content that is conveyed within the divine self-disclosure.

God in history, a self-giving that involves doctrinal content (even if that content cannot be strictly identified with every statement in the Bible), especially the teaching and proclamation of God's law and gospel, and that entails specific actions in the church (preaching, administration of the church's sacraments) that convey theological meaning. "It is thus fitting that the church has steadfastly insisted that the content of revelation includes both a *who* and a *what*, a someone as well as a something. Through God's work and word we do in fact know God" (BJ 1.202 [Sponheim]). This self-revelation thus involves a deep connection between certain historical events, ultimately the coming of Jesus, his life, death, and resurrection, and the prophetic and apostolic interpretation of these events in the Holy Scriptures, all for the sake of eliciting and strengthening faith in God.

Key Words

special revelation of God	Pontius Pilate
Jesus of Nazareth	faith
the Holy Spirit	gospel
theophanies	four canonical gospels
(theophany)	Avery Dulles
patriarchs	Dulles' five models of
matriarchs	understanding revelation
the law	magisterium
the prophets	*eschaton*
the apostles	

Reference literature

For a general orientation to the special revelation of God

EC 4:672–7 ("Revelation" [Antes, Sykes]); OHPT 30–53 ("Revelation and Inspiration" [Davis]); OHST 325–44 ("Revelation" [Quash]; RPP 11:165–75 ("Revelation III–V: Old Testament, New Testament, Christianity" [Kaiser et al.]).

For recent analysis of special revelation in the more important textbooks of dogmatics

SCF §§ 3–11; Aulén 30–65; Barth 1/2 §17; Elert §§2–5, 8, 22–5; Brunner
1:117–36; Tillich 1:106–59; Weber 1:199–227; Macquarrie 43–58; Rahner
44–71, 138–321; BJ 1:197–264 (Sponheim); Thielicke 2:1–258; Gilkey
39–107; Hall 1:402–27; 2:43–72; Pannenberg 1:63–257; Migliore 20–43;
Jenson 1:42–60; ICT 49–76.

For older understandings of the revelation of God

Aquinas 1a.2; 12.12; 2b.92–4; on Luther (Althaus 15–24; Lohse 196–218);
Calvin 1.43–69; on Lutheran Orthodoxy (Schmidt 21–38); on Reformed
Orthodoxy (Heppe 1–11).

Questions for review and discussion

1 How does the author define special revelation? Does he think it is the revelation of eternal, abstract truths? What gets "revealed" in special revelation?
2 What is the content of the gospel, according to Jesus, as presented in the Gospel according to Mark? What is the content of the gospel according to the apostle Paul? How is each understanding similar to the other? How are they different?
3 Why do Christians attach importance to Pontius Pilate?
4 How did Martin Luther define "the gospel"?
5 Be familiar with Dulles' five models of understanding revelation. What are the strengths and weaknesses of each model? Which model is more persuasive than the others? Why? Are there elements that all five models have in common?

Suggestions for further reading

On the special revelation of God

Paul Avis, ed., *Divine Revelation* (Grand Rapids: Eerdmans, 1997) [A selection of essays by international scholars that examine the biblical, historical, and contemporary-systematic understandings of revelation.]

John Baillie, *The Idea of Revelation in Recent Thought* (New York: Columbia University Press, 1956) [Classic account of mid-twentieth-century understandings of divine revelation.]

Matthew Becker, *The Self-giving God and Salvation History* (New York: T & T Clark, 2004) [This is the only book-length study in English of the life and theology of Johannes von Hofmann. He revised the doctrine of revelation to be about God's actions within history. According to Hofmann, the Bible is the monument to this history by pointing to the events of divine revelation within it.]

Rudolf Bultmann, "The Concept of Revelation in the New Testament," *Existence and Faith*, trans. Schubert Ogden (New York: Meridian, 1960), 58–91 [Controversial essay by the premiere New Testament scholar of the twentieth century. Bultmann thought that faith arises from the contemporary preaching of the gospel about Christ, and that Christ is revealed within that preaching of the gospel. Revelation occurs in the present moment of hearing the gospel and responding in faith. Revelation is not tied to Jesus as he was in history, but only to the word about him in authentic, contemporary Christian preaching.]

Dei Verbum, "The Dogmatic Constitution on Divine Revelation," in Norman P. Tanner, ed., *Decrees of the Ecumenical Councils*, 2 vols (Georgetown: Sheed and Ward, 1990), 2.971–81. [The landmark statement on revelation as understood within the Roman Catholic Church. Revelation is linked to participation in God's self-giving reconciliation offered and interpreted in the church.]

Avery Dulles, *Models of Revelation*, rev. edn (Garden City, New York: Doubleday, 1985) [A helpful overview of the principal options within contemporary Christian theology.]

Wolfhart Pannenberg, ed., *Revelation as History*, trans. David Granskou (London: The Macmillan Co., 1968) [Controversial and ground-breaking set of theses in which Pannenberg argues that divine revelation is not the disclosure of truths about God but the self-unveiling of God, which is indirect in historical events, and only fully direct at the end of history, when all preceding historical events and all of reality will be illuminated. This universal revelation is proleptically realized in Jesus of Nazareth and his resurrection from the dead.]

Paul Ricoeur, "Toward a Hermeneutic of the Idea of Revelation," *Harvard Theological Review* 70 (1977), 1–37 [Explores various types of biblical discourse, each of which belongs to specific theologies that reveal some aspect about God. The essay stresses the importance of poetic discourse for divine revelation, which can never be reduced to a systematic, rational set of beliefs.]

Christoph Schwöbel, *God: Action and Revelation* (Kampen, the Netherlands: Kok Pharos, 1992) [The second part of this book explores the concept of revelation in relation to human experience and faith. The author argues that a theology of revelation should not exclude the concept of experience nor should a theology of experience exclude the concept of divine revelation.]

Richard Swinburne, *Revelation: From Metaphor to Analogy*, 2nd edn (Oxford: Oxford University Press, 2007) [This major philosopher of religion thinks that, if God exists, God has good reasons for making God known. Swinburne moves from a consideration of how poetry can reveal metaphorical and analogical truth through a consideration of what would count as revelatory truth within a book or statement of faith and finally to a consideration of whether the Christian Bible and Christian creeds convey truth.]

Ronald Thiemann, *Revelation and Theology: The Gospel as Narrated Promise* (Notre Dame: Notre Dame Press, 1985. [Thiemann brings Luther into conversation with Barth's understanding of revelation and stresses the Barthian notion that knowing God is itself an act of divine grace.]

Dan O. Via, *The Revelation of God and/as Human Reception in the New Testament* (Harrisburg, PA: Trinity Press International, 1997) [Via's helpful analysis of several NT passages underscores that divine revelation is other than, and prior to, the human reception that it elicits, and yet divine self-revelation does not occur apart from its human reception.]

9

Themes in Special Revelation

The chapter briefly identifies key elements within the special revelation of God: God the Creator, the law, the gospel concerning Jesus, the Holy Spirit, the church and sacraments. The chapter emphasizes that the good message about Jesus is the central theme within Christian theology.

While summarizing all of the individual themes and topics within the divine self-revelation would take us well beyond the purpose of this book (if one wrote about each of them at length, one would end up producing something like a summary of Christian doctrine), a few of them, including the key theme, should be mentioned here so as to clarify further the special content of the subject matter of Christian theology. Together, these principal themes embrace the fullness of the subject of Christian theology, which includes both the general revelation of God (natural knowledge of God) and the special revelation of God (the knowledge that is given in the self-revelation of the triune God, the world, and human beings in the apostolic witness to Jesus the Christ).

The revelation of God the Creator

The first of these themes within the special revelation of God is that God is the one, almighty Creator and Lord of heaven and earth. This is the affirmation of the great Jewish *Shema*: "Hear, O Israel, the LORD, our God, is one LORD" (Deut. 6.4). Jesus also affirmed this teaching, as did his apostles (Mk 12.29). It is consistent with the **First Commandment**: "You shall have no other gods" (Exod. 20.3). Paul, too, insisted on this basic monotheistic point: "There is no other God but one" (1 Cor. 8.4). This is why Luther interpreted the First Commandment to mean, "We should fear, love, and trust God above all things" (*Small Catechism*, Ten Commandments, BC 351). Within the apostolic witness, **God the Creator** is the God of Israel, the One who made promises to Abram (Gen. 12) and to David (2 Sam. 7), who delivered the Israelites out of Egypt and gave them the Law (Exod. 1–20), who spoke through the biblical prophets, and, most significantly, who raised Jesus from the dead (Rom. 4.24; see Jenson 1.42). The gift of the Holy Spirit has been given to the world in order to bear witness to the salvation accomplished through Jesus' death and resurrection, to awaken faith in him, and to prepare creation for its ultimate consummation in the new creation.

We have already noted that the general revelation of God also reveals God as the Creator. But the special revelation of God goes beyond what is disclosed in that general revelation. How so? For starters, Jesus teaches that one can trust this Creator as a child trusts a loving parent. One is invited by Jesus to call upon the Creator as "Our Father." What does this mean?

While Robert Jenson has taught that this form of address, "Our Father…," is neither a straightforward nor a metaphorical predicate of God but "a term of address within a narrative construction" (Jenson 1.45)—one that identifies God as "Father, Son, and Holy Spirit" within an authentic and orthodox Christian community—the name of God so revealed in the apostolic witness is not completely identical to the gospel narratives. The latter bear witness to the former but cannot be fully equated with it. Jenson's position on the name of God does not completely remove the challenges that all finite human language encounters with respect to the incomprehensibility of the infinite God, nor does it eliminate the need for analogical understanding in all human reference to God. Moreover Jenson seems to minimize the tendency of human beings to misuse the names of God for their own selfish, sinful, and ideological ends. In light of these challenges and problems, some Christian theologians argue that one should use more inclusive language for God, such as "loving Parent," or allow for the use of both "Father" and "Mother" in reference to the Creator.[1] Masculine names and images for God are not the only ones that are legitimated in Holy Scripture. On occasion, motherly, feminine images for God are also set forth (Deut. 32.10–18; Ps. 61.4; Mt. 23.37). These references alone, in addition to the Second Commandment ("Do not misuse the name of the LORD, your God"), should give us pause with respect to naming the Creator. Understanding the various names for God is an ongoing task within Christian theology.

---

[1] This issue about the nature of language for God will be addressed again in Chapter 10.

Certainly the intent of Jesus' form of address to God ("Abba," "Dad"), which cannot fully avoid being a metaphorical predicate as well as a term of address, is to underscore God's loving care for all that God has created and redeemed through Christ, the Son of God (a term that also invites analogical interpretation), and that God can be addressed "boldly and with complete confidence, just as loving children ask their loving father" (*Small Catechism*, Lord's Prayer, BC 356). On the basis of Christ and his teaching Christians believe that God has created them "together with all that exists," that God provides for all of their needs, and protects and defends them, all because of "pure divine goodness and mercy" (*Small Catechism*, The Apostles' Creed, BC 354). In other words, one can count on God as "the source, ground, and sovereign of all that we are and experience" (Gilkey 69) or, as Gilkey's teacher put it, as "the originating, sustaining, and directing ground of the world" (Tillich 1.252–71).

In this contemporary, existential relation to God ("God has created me and everything else..."), the Creator is not merely the originating cause of all that is, but also the continuing Creator who brings novelty out of the old, "the power that gives us our past and preserves it, that creates and recreates our freedom, and that lures and calls us with new possibilities" (Gilkey 84). This idea has been classically expressed with the Latin phrase, "*creatio continua*," that creation is an ongoing project of God. In this view, God is also the goal of all that is, the one who calls people out of death into new life, the one who creates a new heaven and a new earth. Most Christians thus believe that ultimately God will recreate them into the image and likeness of the risen Jesus Christ and bring them into heaven, where they will know God more fully, "face to face" (1 Cor. 13.12).

The revelation of God the Creator has implications not only for one's understanding of the nature of reality—that it is, at least partly, an intelligible cosmos and not a wholly unknowable chaos—but also for one's understanding of God's relation to humankind and of the ultimate goal or purpose of the cosmos: that humankind has been created by God for relationship with God. The meaning of human life is to be discovered in one's relationship to God, as creature to Creator. The world itself is affirmed as the gift of God, the arena in which God is acting for the good of God's creatures, the place of human flourishing and moral responsibility. Other implications of the biblical witness to God the Creator include the affirmation that there is only one God who creates all that is, that God is distinct from that which God creates, that God creates in an orderly fashion, that God calls all that God creates "good," and that God blesses creatures, including human beings, and calls them to bring forth other creatures. God's purpose in creating is to bring forth new life and divine blessing.

The biblical witness stresses that human beings are special to God since they are created in God's "image and likeness" (Gen. 1.26–7), in **the image of God**. While biblical scholars and theologians have disagreed among themselves about the meaning of this affirmation, many conclude that this teaching implies that there is a fundamental unity of all human beings and that human beings are in some ways different from all other creatures. Certainly human beings are temporal, contingent, finite creatures like all other creatures, yet they are also called to reflect God's creative freedom, love, and responsibility within God's creation. Thus they have free "dominion" over the rest of creation that is both a condition of their moral responsibility toward the rest of creation but also a threat to the rest of creation because they can misuse their freedom in selfish, destructive, sinful ways. While human beings are called to care for God's creation, they tragically abuse and destroy creation in ways that are harmful to themselves, to other creatures, and to the planet as a whole.

The revelation of God the Creator includes this awareness that human beings are responsible to God and to the rest of creation. *There is thus a second theme in the self-revelation of God and this is the revelation of **the divine law***. Here God is known not only as the ground of the universe's rational order but as the cause and basis of the world's moral order. The self-revelation of God in the law is always a message of "You shall not..." or "You shall..." While it is sensed intuitively already by the individual in his or her conscience and within the specific customs, rules, and laws that arise from the way the world is, and that shape and order human interaction within and across cultures—wherever there are human beings, there are laws and rules—the Creator's law is revealed in the moral laws that are given in the Scriptures, most especially the so-called Ten Commandments (Exod. 20). These laws sharpen one's sense of right and wrong, of good and bad, of justice and injustice, of truth and falsehood, and they give a distinct form to what is often called "**the Golden Rule**," a rule that is found in one form or another in all of the major religions: "So whatever you wish that others would do to you, do so to them; for this is the law and the prophets" (Mt. 7.12). The intention of the divine law, at least in this respect, is to preserve and protect human community ("one's neighbors") and to create the limits within which human beings can care for one another and flourish.

This revelation of the divine law, which governs all aspects of human life and every relation to God and to others, also includes as a *third theme the revelation that human beings cannot keep the law as God intends.* The prophets and the apostles proclaim that the divine law confronts human beings in every aspect of their lives and yet reveals that they are unable to obey this law. They always fall short of the ideal. Human history is revealed to be a tragic history. Human efforts at creating their own immortality inevitably end in failure. As Ernest Becker (1924–74) has acknowledged through his social analysis of human beings, the most basic human behavior is self-justification that allows one to make oneself into a "god."[2] There are no atheists, for everyone thinks he or she is God, or they treat something or someone as "God" or their "ultimate concern" (Tillich). This conclusion accords with the basic sin that is revealed by the law: the sin of refusing to trust in the true and living God (unbelief) and of making a "god" of oneself.

Because of this self-focused idolatry, human moral accomplishments are always partial, limited, and ambiguous. True social justice remains elusive, even as standards of justice are continually violated. In all of these ways, the divine law condemns human beings as moral failures. The one who is guilty of failing the law in even one point is guilty of failing the law at every point (Jas. 2.10). The apostle Paul thus stated: "For no human being will be justified in his sight by works of the law since through the law comes knowledge of sin" (Rom. 3.20). While the law is a wonderful gift of the Creator to human beings, it is not a gift that can ultimately help them before God, since it continually points to the sinful condition and actions of every human being. Even the apostle Paul had to acknowledge that "nothing good" dwelt within him: "I can will what is right, but I cannot do it. For I do not do the good I want, but the evil I do not want is what I do" (Rom. 7.18–19). He was not here speaking only for himself; he was attempting to articulate a truth about all human beings.[3]

The revelation of the divine law is thus the revelation of *human beings as sinners before God.* Human beings may know what is right because of God's general revelation of the law, in their conscience and within their

---

[2] Ernest Becker, *The Denial of Death* (New York: Free Press, 1975).

[3] The so-called "new perspective" on Paul, linked with such scholars as Krister Stendahl, E. P. Sanders, James D. G. Dunn, and N. T. Wright, does not do justice to Paul's teaching about human sin as a radical hostility and rebellion against God. The "new perspective" downplays the centrality of justification by faith in Christ and re-visions Paul's central concern to be about the inclusion of Gentiles in God's original covenant with the Jews. But this shift minimizes the reality of human sin and its universality among all human beings, Jew and Gentile alike. When one minimizes the reality of sin, one minimizes the need for a crucified Christ before the divine judgment of God. For critical assessment of this "new perspective" on Paul, see the essays in *The New Perspective on Paul*, ed. David C. Ratke (Minneapolis: Lutheran University Press, 2012).

human society, but they inevitably do what is contrary to this law. Under the revelation of the divine law, human beings stand condemned:

- They are shown to lack true fear and trust in God their Creator;
- they are self-centered;
- they attempt to control, manipulate, and rule over others for their own advantage;
- they are born into sinful, guilty communities (e.g. family, society) which unavoidably shape and condition them toward sin and evil;
- they fail to act in true love toward others;
- they constantly try to justify themselves before others;
- their own consciences frequently accuse and condemn them as guilty for their decisions and actions—and for their failures to act rightly.

Human beings *should* do what is good, but they *inevitably* do what is sinful and even evil. Various classical and modern dragnets let no one escape. The classic **seven "cardinal" or "deadly" sins** are a temptation to everyone: lust, gluttony, greed, sloth, anger, envy, and pride.

The reality of sin also frustrates and distorts the revelation of God. This occurs both as a result of human ignorance or blindness to the Creator's power and will and as a result of human defiance of God's will in law and gospel. Because of the reality of sin and the human sense and experience of sin, the reality of God can be a terrifying experience. The prophets and the apostles refer to this experience of God's judgment as *the wrath of God or the anger of God, which serves as a fourth theme in the self-revelation of God.* Here the revelation of God's law is bound to be also the revelation of God's wrath or anger. "For the wrath of God is revealed from heaven against all ungodliness and wickedness of human beings who by their wickedness suppress the truth" (Rom. 1.18). Chief among the suppressions of the truth is replacing one's trust in the true and living God with trust in an idol of one's own making. Christian theology acknowledges that the root of all sin is the failure to keep the First Commandment: "You shall have no other gods."

While many modern theologians, not least Schleiermacher and Ritschl, have rejected as outmoded the biblical notion of God's wrath, this rejection does not accord with either the teaching of the prophets and the apostles or the actual experience of human beings before the hiddenness of God. An abiding challenge of contemporary Christian theology is to clarify the fullness of meaning attached to the biblical language about the wrath of God in relation to the nature of sin and the reality of death (there are nearly 40 occurrences of the expression "wrath of God" in the NT)—while at the same time giving priority to the biblical affirmation that "God is love" (1 Jn 4.8). The revelation of the wrath of God illumines the darkness of God's judgment against sin and human sinners (Rom. 2.5, *et passim*). Whereas sinful human beings want God to act according to human understandings of law and justice and to do to and for them what they think is right and reasonable, the revelation of the wrath of God is the illumination of God's judgment against human beings in their conscience, in the divine law, and in their death. It is a revelation that leads humans to fear, dread, and even hate God. Because of the reality of sin and the human experience of the hiddenness of God, there is enmity between God and human beings (Rom. 8:7), an enmity that only God can bring to an end.[4]

Contrary to theologies that see a continuity between divine grace and human nature, as in the optimistic vision of Aquinas, wherein "grace does not destroy nature but perfects it" (Aquinas 1a.8.8 et passim), Protestant theology maintains a discontinuity between sinful human beings, who lack the capacity to love God, and divine grace, which is entirely a gift of God's own self-giving. For many (but not all) Protestants, human beings come into the world lacking true fear and trust in God (see the second article of the *Augsburg Confession*).[5] They are ignorant of God's intention toward them

---

[4] Another recent theologian who seems to have minimized the reality of the wrath of God is Ronald Thiemann (1946–2012). See Ronald Thiemann, *Revelation and Theology: The Gospel as Narrated Promise* (Notre Dame: University of Notre Dame Press, 1985). While he undoubtedly was correct to have stressed the gospel as a narrated promise, a narrative that involves reference to actual historical events, he failed to give adequate weight to the reality of the hidden God and God's wrath as unbearable threat and terrible experience by sinners, unbelievers, and opponents of God (which Paul thought included every human being). As Robert Bertram (1921–2003) has cogently argued: Contrary to Thiemann's Barthian-influenced understanding of God's "hiddenness," wherein the hidden God is merely "unknown" beyond God's revelation and needs only to be identified with the Word of God incarnate in Christ, the hiddenness of God is indeed experienced and known as divine judgment apart from Christ. Conversely, the gospel promise is that Christ has so identified with unbelievers "that he not only assails their illusions about God but agreeably confirms their own worst fears. It truly is God, regardless of whatever else, from whom they need to be saved, and saved by being replaced—also in their noblest parts, their 'rationality'—by a whole new, plausible identity. Mercifully, this occurs as Godself in Christ acquires a new unprecedented identity of his own, not just as 'prevenient' or even 'gracious' but now, for the first time and forever after, as one of them, relieving them of that onus and reidentifying them as junior deities with a 'prevenience' of their own, faith, to which God in turn is now the pleased respondent. It is their faith in this promise of Jesus which renders them plausible—I mean, literally, pleasing—yet only if this new, self-reidentifying God, to the very core of the Trinity, has, in historical fact, become true" (Robert Bertram, "Review symposium on revelation and theology: *The Gospel as Narrated Promise* by Ronald Thiemann," *Dialog* 26 [Winter 1987], 70–1).

[5] Baptists and Methodists do not teach that infants come into the world adversely affected by sin or lacking true trust in God.

and manifest contempt for God and the divine will. There is no sin that is not simultaneously enmity against God. The principal sin of human beings is their inclination to create idols after their own image and desires. There is really no such thing as an atheist, for everyone has his or her gods and idols. Human beings do not fulfill the will of God. They lack the capacity to do so, and yet human beings should do the will of God and are held accountable when they do not do it. God demands what no sinful human being can do and executes the divine wrath against them because they fail to do what they should do. "You have no excuse, whoever you are" (Rom. 1.20; 2.1). The only hope for human beings in face of the revelation of the wrath of God is to fear it and flee from it. But flee to where? Under the revelation of the law and wrath of God, there is no escape for human beings, for wrath is revealed against the whole world (Rom. 3.6). According to Luther:

> It is obviously utterly repugnant to common sense, for God only to be guided by his own will when he abandons, hardens, and damns human beings, as if he enjoyed the sins and the vast, eternal torments of the unfortunate creatures, even though preachers praise the greatness of God's mercy and loving kindness. It seems that for this reason one must regard God as unfair and cruel, as unbearable. This repugnant thought has caused many distinguished people of all times to go to pieces. And who would not be offended? I myself was offended more than once, and brought to the very depth and abyss of despair, so that I wished I had never been born—until I learned how salutary this despair is, and how close it is to grace. (Luther, "Bondage of the Will," LW 33.109 [slightly modified to reflect the original, WA 18.719])

Without the gospel, the experience of the hidden God ends in despair, dread, and hatred of God. That is, without the gospel, one is left in unbelief.

The revelation of the gospel of God

While human beings cannot attain to God, and every effort on their part to do so ends in disaster and despair, God is confessed by Christians to have condescended to the level of human beings and to have uncovered God to them. God can bridge the chasm that exists between finite, sinful creatures and the infinite holiness of the transcendent God. The Holy One "who dwells in unapproachable light" (1 Tim. 6.16) is thus approachable through the promising word of mercy, the Word that became incarnate in Jesus. Here, in Jesus Christ, the Holy One is pure goodness and compassion. Here, in Jesus Christ, God's infinite majesty has condescended to humankind in love, has become familiar, intimate and, more to the point, merciful and forgiving. Here, in Jesus Christ, is God's great "nevertheless," God's promise of forgiveness for the ungodly, God's promise of eternal life for mortal sinners, God's promise of salvation for the condemned and the doomed. Such a promise makes life good, gives it ultimate meaning, provides a context for the responsible use of freedom, and renews one's hope for the future.

The sad reality of sin, evil, divine wrath, and death would spell ultimate disaster except that the prophets and the apostles also proclaim that God's fundamental, ultimate intention toward creation and the human community within creation is one of blessing and love, and not curse and wrath. While humanity cannot bring an end to their sinful condition, **the gospel** states that God promises to bring this condition to an end and has brought it to an end in Christ. The NT witness is that God's wrath and curse against sinners have been overcome by God's merciful love and grace. This outcome is the apostolic interpretation of the foundational promise to Abram in Genesis 12 (echoed in the Messianic promise of Ps. 72.17b), namely, that all the nations of the earth would be blessed through Abram and his family, a promise that is understood by Christians to have been fulfilled in the coming of Jesus, through whom God's ultimate blessing is given to the world. God's final revelation in Jesus thus presupposes a revelatory history that precedes and prepares for it and a universal focus that is aimed at all people. God's overall intention is to bless humankind in Jesus the Christ and to bring all people into the fullness of God's grace, love, and truth (1 Tim. 2.4). This has occurred in Jesus as the climax of a long process of revelation in the events of Israelite and Jewish history, as this was interpreted by the Hebrew prophets and further interpreted by the post-resurrection apostles. (The problem of the relationship between "the Jesus of history" and "the Christ of faith" will be analyzed in Chapter 10.)

Certainly Christians have spoken differently about Jesus and have understood his saving work in different ways, yet all orthodox Christians believe that Jesus is God's decisive act of salvation for the whole world, that in Jesus the gracious purposes in the mind of God are disclosed, and that in Jesus the new creation has dawned. "For the law was given through Moses; grace and truth have come through Jesus Christ" (Jn 1.17). *Thus a further theme in the special revelation of God is the key theme, namely, the self-revelation of God in Jesus as merciful and forgiving love,* a theme that is also articulated in the OT witness (see, for example, Exod. 34.6–7):

> Beloved, let us love one another, because love is from God; everyone who loves is born of God and knows God. Whoever does not love does not know God, for God is love. God's love was revealed among us in this way: God sent his only Son into the world so that we might live through him. In this is love, not that we loved God, but that he loved us and sent his Son to be the atoning sacrifice for our sins. (1 Jn 4.7–10 [NRSV])

The final sentence in the quotation above is one of the clearest articulations of the gospel, the good news of God's amazing grace and salvation, which is the basis and central focus of Christian faith and thus the central issue in the subject of Christian theology. Thinking about this salvation is called **soteriology,** a term that is based on the Greek word for "savior."

According to mainstream Roman Catholic and Lutheran teaching, this gospel:

> (a) was proclaimed by witnesses—apostles and others in the early Church; (b) was recorded in the NT Scriptures, which have a "normative role for the entire later tradition of the Church"; (c) has been made living in the hearts of believers by the Holy Spirit; (d) has been reflected in the "rule of faith" (*regula fidei*) and in the forms and exercise of church leadership; (e) has been served by ministers.[6]

While Roman Catholics and Lutherans are not yet in complete agreement regarding the actual content of the gospel (for example Roman Catholics reject the idea that justification is by faith *alone* and insist that it must include the grace-powered transformation of the individual believer), they agree that it does have a content, that this content is conveyed through the early witnesses to Jesus and summarized in what will come to be called "**the rule of faith**" (*regula fidei*), and that the abiding aspects of this content must be developed in the present situation. Although this apostolic witness cannot be expressed in a single formula nor stated in its entirety in one single moment, it can be summarized under what the apostle Paul calls "the truth of the gospel" (Gal. 2.5, 14). The gospel or "good message" is qualitatively different from all other messages and points directly to the "good" proclamation of the apostles about Jesus. As we will note below, Lutheran theologians stress that the promise of the gospel is properly received solely by faith alone, although they also insist that such faith is active in works of merciful, loving service to others.

---

[6] Paul C. Empie, T. Austin Murphy, and Joseph A. Burgess (eds), *Teaching Authority and Infallibility in the Church: Lutherans and Catholics in Dialogue VI*, "Common Statement," (Minneapolis: Augsburg, 1980), 15.

One must immediately acknowledge at this point that the apostolic and prophetic writings of the Scriptures articulate the gospel in various ways. Perhaps the principal articulation is the announcement of the divine forgiveness of sins and the promise of eternal life through the death and resurrection of Jesus (1 Cor. 15.1–8ff.). Human sinners, who cannot end their sinful condition or raise themselves from the dead, are thereby revealed in the gospel to be forgiven sinners, restored and renewed children of God in and through Christ. Their own death is thus revealed to be a judgment from God, but one that God has overcome in the resurrection of Jesus and through baptism, which connects individual people to the death and resurrection of Jesus (Rom. 6.1ff). This is a basic promise within the apostolic witness to the actual historical event in and through the person of Jesus, which includes Jesus' own gospel words of address (for example, Mk 1.14), which are themselves presented within the narrative gospels as God's address to those hearing it.

The apostolic gospel about Jesus Christ is articulated in other ways, too, even by the same apostle. Paul refers to the gospel as God's "word of **reconciliation**" (2 Cor. 5.19). This is the promise that in Christ all are reconciled to God and brought into a fundamental unity. "God was in Christ, reconciling the world to himself, not counting people's sins against them" (ibid.). The apostle thus enjoins his hearers: "Be reconciled to God!" (2 Cor. 5.20). The letter to the Ephesians articulates this reconciliation in terms of "unity" between God and all things: "For God has made known to us in all wisdom and insight the mystery of his will, according to his purpose which he set forth in Christ as a plan for the fullness of time, to unite all things in him, things in heaven and things on earth" (Eph. 1.9–10). Thus the gospel calls attention to an historical event, inclusive of the birth, life, death, and resurrection of Jesus, in which God has acted to reconcile the cosmos to God.

For Christian theology, the wrath of God and the love of God are intimately connected to the death of Jesus on the cross, where they meet in the most profound and ultimately inexplicable way. Human beings know the love of God precisely because God "laid down his life for us" (1 Jn 3.16) and removed the divine wrath against them. In some way God has overcome this wrath against sinners and sin by crossing it out in and through the crucified Christ. "For our sake God made [Christ] to be sin who knew no sin, so that in him we might become the righteousness of God" (2 Cor. 5.21). In other words, God damns and curses Jesus, making him the greatest sinner who has ever lived (Luther), even though he himself is called righteous and is said to have committed no sin. God has placed upon him the sins of the entire world, thus making him into a scapegoat, and in return God has given the goodness and perfection ("righteousness") of Christ as a free gift to sinners.

> There is now no condemnation for those who are in Christ Jesus. For the law of the Spirit of life in Christ Jesus has set you free from the law of sin and death. For God has done what the law, weakened by the flesh, could not do: by sending his own Son in the likeness of sinful flesh, and to deal with sin, he condemned sin in the flesh, so that the just requirement of the law might be fulfilled in us, who walk not according to the flesh but according to the Spirit (Rom. 8.1–4 [NRSV]).

The gospel promise also asserts that those who are baptized into Christ become "new creatures," no longer slaves to sin and enemies of God, but free children and heirs of God, dead to sin and alive to God. In this changed existence, which the apostles call "regeneration" or "new birth" (see Titus 3; Jn 3.1ff.), the fruits of the Spirit replace the works of the sinful self (Gal. 5.21ff.).

Still other ways in which the apostles articulate the gospel include the following:

- the message of God's grace and love for sinners and outcasts (especially through the words and actions of Jesus during his earthly ministry; see, for example, Lk. 19.1ff.);
- the atonement that has occurred in and through the person of Christ (Eph. 2.14ff.);
- the expiation of sin that has occurred through his sacrifice on the cross (1 Jn 2.2);
- the justification of the sinner before the court of God's judgment (Gal. 2.15–21; Rom. 5.1ff.);
- the redemption of sinners (Gal. 3.3);
- the triumph of Christ over the powers of sin, death, and evil (1 Cor. 15.55–6; 1 Jn 3.8);
- the hope of immortality that has dawned through the resurrection of Jesus from the dead (2 Cor. 5.1ff.).

Lutheran Christians especially emphasize the gospel as always a promise connected with the suffering and cross of Jesus Christ, which are proclaimed in the light of Christ's resurrection from the dead. For many Protestants, all genuine Christian theological knowledge is given in the suffering and death of Christ, where God is hidden. Here, in the crucified and risen Christ,

God attacks sin and accomplishes salvation. The word about this cross is "foolishness to those who are perishing" (1 Cor. 1.18), "but to those who are being saved it is the power of God" (ibid.). The reality of God, of God's grace, of salvation, of the Christian life, of the church itself—all these remain hidden in "the wisdom of the cross." The theology of the cross centers on the death cry of Jesus (Mk 15.34), its attack on human pretensions, and on the resurrection of Christ from the dead as the hope of the human being's own death and resurrection, entirely of God's doing, which then make a radical difference for one's standing before God in the present.

A "**theologian of the cross**" comes to know God through suffering, trials, pangs of conscience, the troubles and joys of daily life, being put to death daily with Christ and being raised anew in the promise of God's forgiveness and love. Contrary to "a **theologian of glory**," who seeks to know God by seeing through "the created world and the acts of God to the invisible realm of glory beyond it" and by "willing and working" one's way upward on "this glory road," a theologian of the cross will look for God in the story of Jesus' cross, to understand all things, including the realities of oneself before God, "through suffering and cross."[7] Even Moses, who desired to see God's glory (Exod. 33.18–23), was prohibited, since no one can see God's face and live. Moses was allowed only to see God's "backside," his posterior.

In the NT witness of the apostles, it is the suffering and crucified Jesus "that takes the place of God's backside."[8] "Because men misused the knowledge of God through works, God wished again to be recognized in suffering, and to condemn wisdom concerning invisible things by means of the wisdom concerning visible things, so that those who did not honor God as manifested in his works should honor him as he is hidden in his suffering" (Luther, "Heidelberg Disputation," LW 31.52–3). The "visible things" of God are God's incarnation in Jesus, God's weakness, condescension, humility, and foolishness. These are to be contrasted with "the glory" of the invisible God and with "the theologians of glory" who insist that one can approach this divine glory on the basis of human action ("works" and "human wisdom") and be justified before God by what one does in one's life.[9] With the apostle Paul, the theologian of the cross believes that God justifies God and the sinner precisely in the cross and resurrection

---

[7] Gerhard O. Forde, *On Being a Theologian of the Cross: Reflections on Luther's Heidelberg Disputation, 1518* (Grand Rapids: Eerdmans, 1997), 12–13.
[8] Ibid., 78.
[9] B. A. Gerrish, *Grace and Reason: A Study in Luther's Theology* (Oxford: Clarendon, 1962), 77.

of Jesus. "For this reason true theology and recognition of God are in the crucified Christ: ... 'No one comes to the Father, but by me,' 'I am the door,' etc." (Luther, "Heidelberg Disputation," LW 31.53). The theologian of the cross knows that, forgiven by God in Christ and dying to the old, sinful self, the one who trusts in Christ now lives in him and looks forward to being raised with him.

According to Luther, too, the gospel is always a counter-factual promise because the one so forgiven still experiences sin and senses mortality in this life. The one so loved still lives in a world of "fate" (*Schicksal*), of evil and injustice, in a world marked seemingly more by the absence of God and the realities of sin and evil and the universality of death than by God's gracious and uncanny presence. Not at all obvious in the world and its history is the Christian claim that God is love (1 Jn 4.8). It is certainly not obvious that God loves sinners and evil people. The world of nature and history is full of examples of evil and human tragedy, full of sin and suffering, ultimately full of death itself, all of which contradict this basic message that God is merciful and loving toward God's own enemies. Therefore the Christian, living by faith in that gospel promise, trusts it, contrary to all appearances— as we will now see and hear.

While the law of God is always (but not only or merely) accusatory against human beings, their sins, their self-assured arrogance, and ultimately against their efforts at setting themselves up as gods, the gospel is always and only a gracious promise of divine mercy and forgiveness for the sake of the crucified and risen Christ, with no apparent, visible support in the world of sense experience, save the preaching and announcing of that promise, which is also attached to Baptism and the Lord's Supper (and for Roman Catholic and Eastern Orthodox Christians also to other sacraments). Foundational in this regard is the ritual washing "in the name of the Father, the Son, and the Holy Spirit" (Mt. 28.19) that connects an individual to the saving work of God and brings the person into fellowship within the community that bears the name of Christ. Believers in Christ are not "solo," autonomous individuals, but they live and die within faith-sustaining communities.

The intended aim of the gospel promise is **faith** ("trust," "confidence" in God), since faith alone can receive the promise. According to Christian teaching, people are called to live by faith in God over against what they perceive with their senses, not by sight, since there is much that contradicts the message of the gospel in the world of appearances. Against appearances and doubts and, yes, even against the hiddenness of God, one trusts the divine promise, that it will be fulfilled eschatologically, in the end. In the meantime, within the community of faith, one comes to the certainty of faith in God only through spiritual trial and affliction, suffering and death and doubts, when all false supports for faith drop away. Nothing else is left but the radical promise of God's mercy in Christ, proclaimed in word and sacraments, which can be received only by faith. According to Luther, God has to shatter "the security we find in philosophical systems and to reduce us to nothing" with the help of spiritual trial, so that at this lowest point we might then hear his word of promise for faith.[10]

> The gospel constrains us to decide whether or not we know that we are meant by it. If we do know, then we do not doubt that we must not only decide in one way or in another, but that we have no other choice than to know that we are meant; for our decision is, after all, only the acknowledgment that we are meant. (Elert 77)

In this way faith is always a response to the gospel; it is always trust that the word of the gospel has hit its mark (Rom. 10.9). "Faith comes from what is heard, and what is heard comes from the preaching of Christ" (Rom. 10.17). Faith is trusting that the message pertains to oneself, that it is valid for one's life, that God is summoning one to trust in Christ through the gospel message about him.

Oswald Bayer makes use of John L. Austin's theory of speech acts, especially the latter's analysis of performative statements of promise, to underscore Luther's view that the divine promise in the gospel is the proper subject of Christian theology:

> In contradistinction to every metaphysical construct of the doctrine of God, God's truth and will therefore are not abstract properties but are a concrete promise, made orally and publicly, to a particular person in a particular situation. "God" is the one whose promise to us in the oral word is such that we can depend on him. God's truth lies in his faithfulness to the word that he speaks. Because he has bound himself to the promise that he made to us at our Baptism, we are emboldened and empowered through the oral word of the sermon, when we are spiritually attacked, to lay hold of him once again in that same promise. We are made confident that he will snatch us out of ourselves whether in pride (*superbia*) or in despair (*desperatio*). (Bayer 130–1)

---

[10] Thielicke, *Modern Faith and Thought*, 55.

In this view, Christian faith is both a "knowing" and a "trusting." It includes elements of knowledge, especially regarding an historical individual (Jesus), yet this knowledge is aimed at eliciting trust in God's mercy. As Luther has insisted, faith is primarily a matter of trusting in God's forgiveness for the sake of Christ, as proclaimed in the gospel. Agreeing essentially with Luther, Calvin defined faith as the "firm and certain knowledge of the divine goodwill toward us, based on the free promise in Christ, and both revealed to our minds and sealed on our hearts through the Holy Spirit" (Calvin 3.2, 7).[11] The apostolic witness to Christ is the admonition to be comforted by Christ, to be saved, atoned, reconciled, and redeemed by him. For Luther and Calvin, the opposite of faith is to think that God is against you, to conclude that God is one's enemy.[12] The divine summons is to trust in God's goodwill through faith in Jesus Christ. Through the work of the Holy Spirit people can be confident that God's ultimate intention toward them in Christ is love. "There is therefore now no condemnation for those who are in Christ Jesus... For I am convinced," the apostle Paul wrote, "that neither death, nor life, nor angels, nor rulers, nor things present, nor things to come, nor powers, nor height, nor depth, nor anything else in all creation, will be able to separate us from the love of God in Christ Jesus our Lord" (Rom. 8.1, 38–9 [NRSV]). This faithful confidence can be communicated and shared with anyone, anyone who will take the time to listen to the message and the promise it conveys. All who receive the promise are invited to trust in the trustworthiness of God to be merciful and forgiving for the sake of Christ. True "fear of God" allows God to be God in order to hear the word of promise. "If you, O LORD, should keep track of sins, LORD, who could stand? But with you there is forgiveness. Therefore you are feared" (Ps. 130.3–4). Even the righteous before God consider themselves to be standing in "fear of God, constantly in need of repentance and forgiveness, without which they would be lost."[13] Thus, "fear," "love," and "trust" mark the Christian life, but ultimately it is the divine summons to trust that

---

[11] This translation is by B. A. Gerrish, *Saving and Secular Faith: An Invitation to Systematic Theology* (Minneapolis: Fortress, 1999), 12.

[12] Gerrish, *Saving and Secular Faith*, 14. Gerrish agrees with Calvin that God's wrath is an "accommodated expression," one that is improper but not false. The classic Lutheran theologians of the sixteenth and seventeenth centuries stressed that God's wrath is not a human misperception. The wrath of God is real, so real that it was necessary for Christ to suffer it and remove it. Faith is trust and belief that God has reconciled one to God through Christ, that God is no longer one's enemy.

[13] Forde, *On Being a Theologian of the Cross*, 43. Forde (1927–2005) is here commenting on the seventh thesis of Luther's "Heidelberg Disputation": "The works of the righteous would be mortal sins if they would not be feared as mortal sins by the righteous themselves out of pious fear of God."

overcomes one's fears in this life, even one's fear of almighty God, whose judgments remain an ultimate mystery, but less so in view of Christ. In that faithful view, the summons to love as Christ has loved is also again possible to heed and to follow. Thus the Christian of today joins the apostle Paul in confessing: "I have been crucified with Christ; it is no longer I who live, but Christ who lives in me; and the life I now live in the flesh I live by faith in the Son of God, who loved me and gave himself for me" (Gal. 2:19b-20).

Living "by faith" does not imply that one has God and oneself completely figured out. Even believers in Christ do not always understand the ways of God in the world. While believers share, even now, in the promise of a new creation (2 Cor. 5.17), they are still called to struggle against sin and evil within themselves and in this present evil age that is dying away. In this life the new creation or the "new being" (to use Tillich's pregnant phrase) also remains hidden "with Christ in God" (Col. 3.3). Even the new life in Christ that one receives by faith must be believed and will only be fully revealed when God's glory is revealed in the end: "When Christ who is your life is unveiled, then you also will be unveiled with him in glory" (Col. 3.4).

The revelation of the church

What is true of the Christian as believer is also true of the new community that hears the voice of Christ and lives from his word, namely, *the church* (Greek: "*ecclesia*" = "called out ones"), *a further theme in the special revelation of God*. The church, too, is an article of faith, not a matter of clear visibility. "The church is hidden; the sanctified ones are concealed" (LW 33.89). While faith perceives the reality of the church on earth, due to the effective power of the proclaimed gospel and administered sacraments, the church will be visibly and clearly revealed for what it is only in the revelation of Christ in glory. For now, most Christians confess that they "believe in … one holy, catholic, and apostolic church" (The Nicene Creed). This one church of Christ is described theologically through several key NT metaphors and symbols: as the people of God, as those who serve the LORD, as the body of Christ, and as the community of the Holy Spirit. (See also Migliore 252–4.) Some theologians, such as Luther, have also spoken of the "marks of the church," that is, signs that point to the reality of the church. According to

---

The biblical support for this assertion includes the penitential psalms, the Lord's Prayer ("Forgive us our trespasses..."), and the vision of the righteous in Revelation 21.27.

Luther, there are seven such "marks" (see LW 41.141ff.): the preaching of the word of God, Holy Baptism, the Lord's Supper, the public and private reproving and forgiving of people's sins, the holy ministry, the public liturgy (singing, praising God, etc.), and the sacred cross. Wherever one hears or sees these *notae ecclesiae* ("marks of the church"), one can be certain that the one, holy, catholic, and apostolic church of Christ is there.

Rubbing against this faith in the one church of Christ, however, is the appearance of the empirical churches as disparate, flawed, and divided groups of Christians who do not all agree on the same points of doctrine and practice and who do not live as if they are among the sanctified. What Christians confess of the church is different from what it appears to be on earth. They long for the revelation of the reality in which they also believe. In the meantime they live by God's grace alone, within concrete fellowships of faith, hope, and love; they continue to celebrate the Eucharist as a foretaste of the heavenly banquet to come; and they work toward maintaining the fellowship in the bond of peace and toward overcoming those issues that currently divide the churches from one another.

For more than a century now, one of the principal tasks of theology has been to overcome the divisions among the divided churches and to call them to work toward greater unity in the gospel. The modern Ecumenical Movement has sought ways of furthering visible unity among the divided churches of Christ until the day of the revelation of Christ and those who belong to him. Thus **ecclesiology**, the study of the church as a theological entity, and **sacramental theology** (the study of the ritual actions within the Christian churches), also address elements within special revelation.

Until that final revelation of the church, when it will be revealed to be what the apostles have said it is, the church proclaims the gospel and administers the sacraments (especially Baptism, the Eucharist, and Holy Absolution [the formal proclamation of the forgiveness of sins])—all for the sake of calling people to faith, hope, and love and keeping them united with Christ and with one another in the one church of Christ. And where the gospel is proclaimed and the **sacraments** administered in accord with the gospel, there the church truly is. Indeed, the Holy Spirit acts through the word and the sacraments to call, gather, enlighten, and sanctify the whole Christian church *on earth* (the church is not a Platonic reality) and keep it united to Christ (Luther, *Small Catechism*, The Apostles Creed). Because of the power of the Spirit to create and preserve the church, even the gates of hell cannot prevail against it (Mt. 16.18).

This side of that ultimate revelation, Christians trust that the church truly exists on earth and the people of God are active in faith, hope, and love. Such trust is based on the visible means by which the church is created and sustained: the preaching of the gospel, the administration of Baptism and the Eucharist, the confession of sins, the announcement of forgiveness of sins on account of Christ, the singing of spiritual songs and hymns in praise of God through Christ, the mutual consolation and encouragement of the brothers and sisters in Christ, and the sign of Christ's cross (see LW 41.147ff.).

Finally, there are additional consequences that Christians make on the basis of what has been specially revealed through Jesus and the gift of the Holy Spirit. For example, most Christians believe that because the divine promise includes the statement that death itself cannot separate the human being from the love of God, God will bring them through death into eternal life ("heaven"). God's relationship to human beings cannot be frustrated by sin, death, or even the dissolution of "this present evil age." "Blessed be the God and Father of our Lord Jesus Christ! By his great mercy he has given us new birth into a living hope through the resurrection of Jesus Christ from the dead" (1 Pet. 1.3). Christians thus hope for God's future wherein God will transform mortal and sinful human beings and reveal them to be "the children of light" in the general resurrection of the dead "on the last day." In this "new heaven and a new earth" (Rev. 21.1ff.) God will no longer be known in part, that is, "by faith," but his "glory" will be revealed to all flesh (Isa. 40.5) and God will be known "face to face" (1 Cor. 13.12). Christian hope, however, is not merely a hope centered on the future of human beings, since Christians also long for "the restoration of all things" (Acts 3.21), the consummation of creation in "a new heaven and a new earth" (Rev. 21.1). Thus *eschatology, teaching about the end*—and about the present on the basis of the eschatological in-breaking of God's reign in Jesus and his resurrection from the dead—*is also a theme in the special revelation of God.* Eschatology is about both the "then" of the end and the "now" of the present.

The promise of the gospel as the principal theme in Christian theology

Given what has been said about God in this chapter and the previous two, it is clear that God encounters human beings in ways that are quite different, even irreducibly so. "In the midst of the contradictory and complementary ways in which God encounters us, which are laden with tension and conflict, the gospel stands out in its uniqueness as God's decisive, final word. The gospel, strictly speaking, is a promise without any demand, a pure promise (*promissio*), a gift" (Bayer 125). In the most basic and specific way, the proper theme of Christian theology is this promise. It is given in both the apostolic preaching about Jesus, that is, the **kerygma** or "proclamation" about him, which of necessity also includes reference to the Father and the Holy Spirit, and in the apostolic **parenesis** or "exhortation" that follows as a consequence of the gospel promise.

Both the development of **trinitarian theology** (thinking about **the Trinity**) in the first six centuries of the Christian church and the development of Christology and **pneumatology** (thinking about the Holy Spirit) in these and subsequent centuries must be understood in the context of the overall attempts by church leaders in these centuries to remain faithful to the gospel promise within the apostolic and prophetic witness to Christ for the sake of creating and sustaining faith in him. The concern within these dogmatic developments is both theological—seeking to preserve the identity of God in God's historical acts, as these have been shaped and attested in the biblical traditions—and soteriological (salvific)—endeavoring to keep the gospel promise as what it is, truly "good news." From this vantage point, whatever theological developments have occurred in the history of Christian theology need to be evaluated principally on the basis of the apostolic witness to the gospel promise and its effective articulation to later generations, while also attending to how the gospel promise was communicated in the languages and thought forms of these later generations.

Contemporary Christian theology must also keep its focus on the abiding truth within the apostolic witness—inclusive of both the *kerygma* and the *parenesis* in their service to the gospel promise—and on the complex world of present-day human beings, their language and concepts. What the abiding truth is in the apostolic witness to the gospel promise, of course, remains open for investigation, discussion, and re-articulation in the present situation of the theologian and his or her world, even as the historical development of Christian doctrine remains open for further investigation and assessment in light of this same gospel. The substantive content of Christian theology cannot be answered historically, as if one could merely repeat what previous theologians have said regarding the content of Christian teaching in the language and thought forms of their day and in view of their own problems and challenges. Rather, the subject of Christian theology is always in part dependent upon what the apostolic witness to the gospel promise means today, how that proclamation and consequent exhortation are to be understood and spoken in the present, and how that witness remains a valid witness today. The subject of Christian theology is also partially shaped by the significant criticisms that are leveled against it, not merely in the dominant voices of atheism and religious criticism, but also in the voices and claims of the other world religions.

What is the essential content of the apostolic witness? What within that witness is essential for the gospel promise to be the gospel? How does one articulate that promise today, so that it is meaningful for contemporary sinful human beings? How should one respond to criticisms of that promise that call it into question? These challenges are always inherent in the task of Christian theology, at least if it hopes to remain attentive to the historic apostolic witness to Jesus and to its immediacy for contemporary human beings. Christian theologians are always challenged to find that point within the content of Christian teaching which most immediately confronts contemporary individuals with the reality of its subject matter.

People from one generation to the next have discussed and analyzed the normative, abiding gospel content within the apostolic witness, yet the history of Christian theology shows that Christian theology is constantly changing, since the people so engaged in the theological task undergo change over time, as do the people addressed by its findings. In this way, too, Christian theology is often compelled to raise questions to the churches themselves, perhaps even to speak a critical word against them, when it appears that their beliefs and practices are running contrary to the abiding truth within the apostolic witness. "Theology reforms the church, not vice versa" (Elert 6). How one is to discern the abiding content within the apostolic witness to the gospel promise, and to understand it and teach it today, moves us into the next two chapters on the sources and norms of theology and the principles of biblical interpretation.

Key Words

First Commandment	theologian of glory
God the Creator	faith
the image of God	the church
the divine law	ecclesiology
The Golden Rule	sacramental theology
seven deadly/cardinal sins	sacraments
wrath of God	eschatology
the gospel	kerygma
soteriology	parenesis
the rule of faith (*regula fidei*)	trinitarian theology
reconciliation	the Trinity
theologian of the cross	pneumatology

Reference literature

For a general orientation to God the Creator

ABD 2:1041–55 ("God" [Scullion, Bassler]); EC 1:715–24 ("Creation" [Frey]); ER 5:3537–60 ("God" [Sperling et al.]); ODCC 688–91 ("God"); RPP 3:542–3 ("Creatio Continua") [Link]); RPP 3:543–5 ("Creatio ex nihilo" [Gross; Link]); RPP 3:545–57 ("Creation" [Friedli et al.]); RPP 5:459–75 ("God" [Zinser et al.]).

For a general orientation to law and gospel

EC 2:446–9 ("Gospel" [Stuhlmacher, Jäger]); EC 3:216–18 ("Law and Gospel" [Kolb]); ER 6:3640–2 ("Gospel" [Collins]); RPP 5:528–33 ("Gospel" [Koester, Beintker]); RPP 7:357–60 ("Law and Gospel" [Schwöbel]); TDNT 2:721–36 ("Euangellion" [Friedrich]); Lohse 257–76.

For a general orientation to Jesus Christ

ABD 3:773–96 ("Jesus" [Meyer]); EC 1:458–74 ("Christology" [Ritschl et al.]); EC 3:24–8 ("Jesus" [Holtz]); ER 7:4843–52 ("Jesus" [Allison]); RPP 2:643–8 ("Christology III: Dogmatics and Systematic Theology" [Gunton]); RPP 6:698–723 ("Jesus Christ" [Roloff et al.]).

For a general orientation to the Holy Spirit

EC 2:577–83 ("Holy Spirit" [Pratscher, Ritschl]); RPP 12:207–16 ("Spirit/Holy Spirit" [Stolz et al.]).

For a general orientation to the doctrine of the church

EC 1:477–502 ("Church" [Fahlbusch et al.]); ER 3:1763–79 ("Church" [Lynch et al.]); RPP 3:1–22 ("Church" [Wenz et al.]).

For a general orientation to the doctrine of the sacraments

EC 4:791–800 ("Sacrament" [Sattler]); ER 12:7954–64 ("Sacrament" [Jennings, Helwig]); RPP 11:354–66 ("Sacraments" [Köpf et al.]).

Questions for review and discussion

1   What are key aspects of the Christian teaching that God is the Creator?
2   What are some problems connected to the word "Father" in reference to God? Do you think it is appropriate that some Christian theologians insist on also using the word "Mother" in reference to God?
3   Many theologians criticize the notion of the "wrath of God." Others, like Luther, insist that the concept is both biblical and experiential. What do you think about the concept of the wrath of God? Are human beings really as badly off before God as the author indicates?
4   What are the common elements in the gospel as affirmed by both Roman Catholics and Lutherans?
5   How is the gospel a *promise*? What gets promised? Why do Protestant theologians insist that the gospel promise can be had only by faith?
6   How does a theologian of the cross differ from a theologian of glory?
7   Why is the church also a matter of divine revelation? When will that revelation take place? What are some of the reasons Christian churches are divided from one another today? Do you think that there will ever be visible unity among Christians on earth? Why or why not?
8   What are sacraments? Do all Christians practice the same number of

sacraments? How many do Roman Catholics observe and practice? How many do Lutherans?

9   What is eschatology? Do you think that the biblical reference to "the end of the world" should be understood mythologically (as Bultmann did) or do you think there will be an actual end of the world (as Pannenberg and others have argued)?

10   Not much is said about Christian ethics in this chapter. Is this a weakness of the chapter? What place does Christian ethics have in the special revelation of God?

Suggestions for further reading

God the Creator

Ian McFarland, ed., *Creation and Humanity* (Louisville: John Knox/Westminster, 2009) [An excellent collection of classic and contemporary readings on "creation" and "human beings" by Christian theologians.]

Jürgen Moltmann, *God in Creation: A New Theology of Creation and the Spirit of God*, trans. Magaret Kohl (New York: Harper and Row, 1985) [Moltmann's Gifford Lectures that set forth an "ecological doctrine of creation." He treats such topics as God the Creator, time and space, heaven, evolution, the image of God in human beings, and the eschatological future of creation.]

Michael Welker, *Creation and Reality* (Minneapolis: Fortress, 1999) [An important, if brief engagement with a contemporary theological understanding of the first two chapters in Genesis, with God as the Creator, the image of God in human beings, sin, "the fall," and the hope of creation.]

Gustaf Wingren, *Creation and Law*, trans. Ross MacKenzie (Philadelphia: Muhlenberg, 1961) [A classic study of creation, human beings, the divine law, sin, and the gospel, by an important Scandinavian Lutheran theologian.]

See also the bibliography on "science and theology" at the end of Chapter 15.

The law and the gospel

Gerhard Ebeling, *Luther: An Introduction to His Thought*, trans. R. A. Wilson (Minneapolis: Fortress Press, 1970), 110–24 [This chapter in Ebeling's book provides a clear and concise summary of Luther's understanding of the gospel.]

Werner Elert, *Law and Gospel*, trans. Edward Schroeder (Minneapolis: Fortress Press, 1967) [A key essay by a principal German Lutheran theologian who opposed Barth's reversal of "law and gospel" and who stressed the sharp distinction between the law, which always accuses human sinners, and the gospel, which promises them forgiveness and salvation.]

Gerhard Forde, *On Being a Theologian of the Cross: Reflections on Luther's Heidelberg Disputation 1518* (Grand Rapids: Eerdmans, 1997) [A classic treatise on the insights of Luther's "theology of the cross" for our contemporary world. Complements and slightly corrects the reflections of Hall's book below.]

Douglas John Hall, *The Cross in Our Context: Jesus and the Suffering World* (Minneapolis: Fortress Press, 2003) [Offers a brief, profound set of reflections on the meaning of Jesus' suffering within a North American context.]

Jürgen Moltmann, *The Crucified God: The Cross of Christ as the Foundation and Criticism of Christian Theology* (London: SCM Press, 1974) [A classic articulation of the theology of the cross by a leading German Reformed theologian. A seminal work, one of the most quoted texts in theology from the past century.]

Peter Stuhlmacher, *Reconciliation, Law, and Righteousness: Essays in Biblical Theology*, trans. Everett R. Kalin (Minneapolis: Fortress Press, 1986) [A set of essays by a major NT scholar who explores the nature of reconciliation as gospel within the apostolic witness to Jesus.]

Ecclesiology and sacramental theology

Louis Bouyer, *Word, Church, and Sacraments: In Protestantism and Catholicism* (San Francisco: Ignatius, 2004) [A brief but useful introduction to the differences between Roman Catholics and Protestants on the issues of "church" and "sacraments."]

Avery Dulles, *Models of the Church* (New York: Doubleday, 1974) [A classic study by an important American Roman Catholic theologian that sets forth five different models or ways in which people have understood the Christian church: as institution, mystical communion, sacrament, herald, and servant.]

See also the documents that emerged from the official North American dialogues between Lutheran and Roman Catholic theologians (1965–). The second through fourth official dialogues addressed differences and agreements on the doctrines of the church and the sacraments (Baptism, the Eucharist as Sacrifice, and Eucharist and Ministry).

10

Sources and Norms of Christian Theology

After briefly reviewing two different approaches to the problem of sources and norms in Christian theology with respect to the use of the Christian Bible, the chapter proceeds to discuss the distinction between the Word of God and the Bible, the principal source of Christian theology (the NT Scriptures), the second main source (the OT), subordinate sources, and the central norm (the gospel).

The preliminary sketch of Christian theological traditions in Chapters 2 and 3 has identified the principal methodological approaches to Christian theology. The description of the task of theology in Chapter 4, which is informed by the earlier sketch, indicates that theology involves critical and self-critical reflection on the revelation of God, the world, and human beings in the apostolic witness to Jesus Christ. Such reflection takes into account how that witness has been understood and believed in the Christian churches over time, but it also seeks to interpret that witness within the academic setting of a university. In this setting, theology has a four-fold goal: (1) to understand the content of the apostolic witness in the ecumenical and intellectual situation of the present; (2) to consider the nature of Christian faith as trust in the gospel promise that is given within the apostolic witness; (3) to identify weak or even false elements within that witness; and (4) to appropriate the possible truth and wisdom within the witness. This four-fold goal raises additional issues in theological methodology, especially concerning the authority and interpretation of the Christian Bible and its relation to other sources of theological knowledge. These issues will be explored more fully here.

All Christian theologians affirm that **the Bible** (Latin: *biblia* = "books") is central for the proper knowledge of God, but they have frequently disagreed among themselves about the extent and nature of its authority and about how best to interpret it in light of other knowledge and human experience. These disagreements about the Bible's authority and its use in theology make clear that not every Christian theologian follows the same methodology in theology.

If Christian theology in a university context is a discipline that invites critical and self-critical reflection on the revelation of God, the world, and of human beings in the apostolic witness to Jesus Christ, a revelation that has been mediated through historical documents and handed down through living communities of Christians, how should that enterprise be undertaken? Is the Bible the *sole* source of Christian theology or are there other sources? If there are additional *sources* of theology beyond the Bible, what is their proper relationship to the Bible and its contents? What *norms* or standards should one use to set forth the abiding content of Christian teaching? If there is more than one norm or guiding principle, then how does one navigate among those norms and principles when they conflict with one another, as can easily happen when one engages in Christian theology within a university setting? If the Bible remains the principal authority for Christian theology, which principles should guide one's interpretations of it?

The problem of sources and norms

As has already been indicated at the end of Chapter 3, contemporary Christian theology manifests two broad, conflicting tendencies regarding the sources and norms of theology.[1] On the one hand, there have been those theologians, like David Tracy, who argue that Christian academic theology *must* be guided by the same criteria that are used elsewhere in the university, for example, the scholarly criteria that are used in the modern natural and social sciences. The use of these criteria, external to Christian theology and its subject matter, does not necessarily provide theologians with a set of rules to follow but with a basic and normative way of doing theology that is always open to revision. Within this *revisionist* approach, one's understandings of the Bible and church traditions are always open to

---

[1] These tendencies are also described quite generally by Hans Frei in his posthumously published book, *Types of Christian Theology*, George Hunsinger and William C. Placher (eds) (New Haven: Yale University Press, 1992), 2–7.

criticism from external sources. It is always possible that one's theological understandings may need to be revised in light of other knowledge and experience. In this approach, the interpretation of the Bible occurs in the light of contemporary scientific knowledge and philosophical reflection, which are used to help explicate the Bible's contemporary meanings and applications. Such an approach to theology also utilizes modern scholarly methods for investigating the historical and literary dimensions of the Bible.

There is much to commend in this theological approach, especially its concern to explicate the content of Christian theology in a way that is meaningful for contemporary people and that takes into account knowledge from other university disciplines that has a bearing on theological under- standing. The actual execution of this method of theology, however, can potentially lead to the loss of the substance of the Christian faith if the particularities of Christian teaching and practice become subsumed under non-Christian criteria and explanations. In the effort to make Christian teaching meaningful and relevant, the fullness of orthodox Christian teaching can be explained away. Extra-Christian sources and norms might assume a superior role in the theological enterprise of translating Christian teachings into non-Christian categories within the context of the public discourse in the academy. In the process of translating Christian doctrine into contemporary categories, the distinctive content of Christian teaching, such as the dogmas of God and Christ, might easily get lost.

In contrast to the various forms of this kind of revisionist theology, there have been other theologians who have tended to understand Christian theology completely (or mostly) within the cultural or semiotic system that constitutes "Christianity" as a distinct religion and to articulate theology entirely (or mostly) according to the "grammar" or "internal logic" of "the Christian narrative," as it is authoritatively given in the Bible and summa- rized in the classic creeds and confessions of the Christian churches. In Chapter 3 we identified this approach as *post-liberal*. Its method is not transcendental or universal but quite specific to the internal language and grammar of the Christian faith that together form the self-description of Christian faith and practice. Of special concern is the perceived need to articulate and defend the particular Christian narrative and how that narrative shapes the life of the Christian within the church and the academy. According to this approach, Christian truth is entirely a matter of "coherence" within the world of the Bible, of how Christian beliefs and practices are interconnected into an integrated and coherent whole that provides the overarching framework of meaning for the individual Christian and his or her community of faith.

This model of post-liberal theology also has some significant weaknesses. For example, a follower of this approach could make the case that orthodox Christian theology has no legitimate place within a public university, since theology can only be guided and defined by sectarian criteria of faithfulness, truth, and orthodoxy. In the post-liberal view, theology should not be guided by any external criteria for judging evidence and argumentation. It should more or less operate according to its own parochial norms and standards. If followed consistently, however, such a method could end up with a form of theology that is quite sectarian and isolated from mainstream scientific knowledge and the central intellectual currents of the time. It is thus difficult to imagine that theologians who follow this method consistently are actually interested in learning from other academic disciplines when those disciplines might have something true and worthwhile to contribute to biblical and theological understanding. (It should be pointed out that the key post-liberal theologians, George Lindbeck, Hans Frei [1922–88], and Stanley Hauerwas, have allowed modern knowledge to inform their theological understandings, but such informing seems arbitrary and not really consistent with their basic methodological concerns.)

Within the American context, Protestant Fundamentalism takes an even more radical position when it comes to extra-biblical sources and norms for theology. For example, one early-twentieth-century Lutheran theologian, Francis Pieper (1852–1931), actually asserted that the Copernican Theory of a heliocentric solar system must be rejected as contrary to the clear teaching of the Bible, and thus contrary to the Christian truth and faith (Pieper 1.473). For Pieper, the Bible's "worldview" must be held to be absolute and inviolate. While he acknowledged in theory that the Bible is not a science textbook, he nevertheless insisted that when the Bible treats matters that the sciences also treat, the Bible's position (that is, Pieper's *interpretation* of the Bible's position) is the correct one, regardless of the evidence in the world "out there" and rational argumentation from the sciences that investigate that evidence. According to Pieper, since straight-forward statements in the Bible conflict with post-Copernican cosmology, a "Bible-believing" Christian must reject the latter theory and allow the first chapters in Genesis and all other geocentric statements in the Bible "to absorb" the universe (to use Lindbeck's metaphor). One can easily conclude that Pieper would support the post-liberal view toward the Bible and a coherence theory of truth, had he been around to learn of these, and it is not surprising that many of Pieper's theological heirs have done so. Like Pieper, other conservative Christians also affirm a "six-day" creation to be the clear teaching of Scripture and thus a basic element in the doctrinal content of the biblical texts. They thus reject the theory of evolution as contrary to the teaching of the Bible. Christians of this mindset do not allow any role for extra-biblical sources of knowledge to inform their understanding of the Bible and those of its statements that overlap with what the natural sciences also investigate. Data from outside of the Bible that conflicts with the interpretation of the Bible by these conservative Christians must be rejected. For them the Bible is the sole source and norm of faith and theology.

The theological method followed by Pieper and his heirs is simply unsustainable within an academic setting, at least one in which church authorities do not interfere with the pursuit of truth and knowledge. Few if any reputable scientists today would pay any serious attention to Pieper's theological assertions about the cosmos, and many would rightly judge his idea of biblical authority to be coercive and oppressive toward free academic inquiry. How many Christian theologians today are uninterested in learning from the non-theological disciplines, even when those disciplines present evidence and argumentation that directly relate to the theologian's own subject matter and that might require the theologian to modify his or her biblical interpretation and theological understanding accordingly? Those who follow Pieper's line of thinking would probably have a difficult time being self-critical about their theological understandings and biblical interpretations, however coherent they are with their other beliefs and practices.

Similarly, early Christian theologians have used the Bible in ways that later Christians find deeply troubling. For example, some Christians have used the Bible to justify institutions and structures that have enslaved whole groups of people. The Bible was used to keep people "in their proper place" and to support slavery, racial segregation, and the subordination of women in church and society, all within a coherent biblical framework of Christian belief and practice. In this regard as well, these earlier biblical interpreters had a difficult time discerning how the Bible might be wrongly used.

Despite the problematic use of the Bible within the history of Christianity, theologians today will continue to make use of the Bible as the principal source of Christian theology, at least if they desire to maintain the particular identity and integrity of Christian teaching. But the Bible cannot be the sole source of Christian theology. Other sources factor in to the theological task, even if they have only a subordinate role to play in the articulation of theological understanding. If post-liberal theologians are correct to stress that the Christian theologian must take his or her *primary* bearings from the particularities of the biblical revelation, especially the gospel promise, that revelation is never the sole factor in the theological enterprise.

We have already noted the importance of reckoning with the so-called general revelation of God that occurs apart from the Christian Bible, whose witness nevertheless includes reference to this extra-biblical revelation. This extra-biblical revelation is thus an aspect of the subject of Christian theology. The revelation of God apart from Christ, despite its ambiguities, is sufficient to indicate that Christian theology is about more than merely "what the Christian Bible teaches." The challenge of Christian theology within a university setting is to keep its proper subject matter in view, especially the promise of the Christian gospel and the distinctive "way of believing" (Schleiermacher) that comes from this "good message," while undertaking the scholarly investigation of that subject matter by means of academic criteria and methods that are operative in the other human and social sciences. In this way the problem of the sources and norms of Christian theology keeps open the dialectic between the subject of Christian theology and the ways in which that subject is critically and creatively investigated within the academy.

This approach is also consistent with the dominant stream of Christian theology wherein Christian thinkers have used specific philosophies to assist them in explicating the content of Christian faith for their contemporaries. The goal in this approach is to honor as primary the post-liberal concern to maintain the integrity of the Christian gospel while also striving to honor as secondary the revisionist concern to utilize the external criteria of scholarship within the academy and to follow the basic canons of academic civility.

Of course sorting out the competing and conflicting claims within the various sources of Christian theology requires careful attention to the issue of the prioritizing of sources and norms within theology and of discerning wherein the truth truly lies. Here the witness of the apostle Paul to "the truth of the gospel" is helpful (Gal. 2.5, 14). He acknowledged that even within the Scriptures themselves not everything is normative for contemporary Christian faith and practice, that even the key apostle of Jesus, namely, Peter, could err in a matter of faithful practice, and that the church itself could become corrupted and act contrary to the truth of the gospel. The gospel promise, then, really is the central focus for Christian theology, and the concern for it will always distinguish a properly conservative theology from those that deny or disregard it. A truly orthodox and conservative theology is concerned for the truth of the gospel and the sound teaching that flows from it; yet such a theology is also properly liberal in that it truly liberates individuals from sin, death, and the power of evil and liberates them for loving service in the world. While Christian, academic theology will take its primary cues from the biblical gospel, it will also be open to other insights, insofar as these overlap with its own proper concerns and goals and assist it in the task of clarifying the truth claims within its subject matter.

Sources and norms of Christian theology

The word of God and the Bible

There is no single passage or book in the Bible that makes reference to the Bible as a whole. The first person to refer to the writings of the OT and the NT collectively as "the Bible" seems to have been Chrysostom, who lived in the fourth century. There is no passage in the Bible that refers to the Bible as "**the word of God**." While the Bible contains passages that refer to "the word of the LORD" and even a few that make reference to "God-breathed" writings (2 Tim. 3.16; 2 Pet. 1.21), no one can be certain which "word" and/or writings are being referred to here. One cannot properly apply these passages to the Bible as a whole, since that book did not exist when these passages were first spoken and written. Other Scripture passages indicate that "the word of God" is not identical to written documents: "Forever, O Lord, your word is firmly fixed in the heavens" (Ps. 119.89). "The word of the Lord lasts forever" (1 Pet. 1.25). In light of these and similar passages, the word of God cannot be strictly and unconditionally identified with the Christian Bible per se, since the Bible will not last forever.

The biblical phrase "word of God" has at least four meanings: (1) the creative and active word of God (Gen. 1.1; Ps. 19.1–4; 33.6; 1 Pet. 1.23); (2) the proclaimed word of God (Am. 1.2; 3.1; 1 Pet. 1.24); (3) the incarnate Word of God (Jn 1.1ff., 1.14); and (4) the written word of God (2 Tim. 3.16; 2 Pet. 1.21). The Bible, then, is a witness to the word of God—given in these various ways. Human access to the word of God is normally through the Bible. It points beyond itself to the living word (the *Logos*) by which God created the universe, the word proclaimed through the prophets, the Word of God that became incarnate in Jesus the Christ, the Word that is "the same yesterday, today, and even forever" (Heb. 13.8). For Christians the abiding Word that remains sure and certain is Christ. While that living Word is mediated through the Holy Scriptures, which testify to the Word, the original Scriptural texts are not identical to the Word. Bibles wear out; they do not last; they are not eternal.

The Word that became incarnate in Jesus is also tied to the prophetic "word of the LORD" that was spoken in and to ancient Israel in its history. This "word of the LORD" is quite varied in content, but it can be summarized in terms of both judgment and grace, of law and promise, of wrath and mercy. On the one hand, the word of the LORD was a prophetic message of judgment against sin and injustice. This message was grounded in the moral vision of the Mosaic Law, summarized most definitively in "the ten words," the Ten Commandments (Exod. 20). On the other hand, the word of the LORD was also a message of blessing, a wonderful promise about the future, an encouraging and forgiving word of hope. This message was grounded in the divine promises to Abram (Gen. 12.3) and David (2 Sam. 7.16), a message about God's mercy and love and of God's future acts of salvation. According to the teaching of the apostles, both of these prophetic messages, equally called "the word of the LORD," must be distinguished from each other, and yet they both have their ultimate fulfillment, end, and resolution in Christ, the living Word of God.

Only in a qualified way may one refer to the Bible as "the word of God," and only then because it contains the authoritative apostolic and prophetic witness to the word of God in its varying forms and content. However central and important the Bible is for Christian faith and teaching, it is neither identical to God nor the same as Christ, the incarnate word of God, and it should not be treated as such. Nevertheless, the Bible is special and unique for Christians because it is for them God's means for drawing attention to the word of God in its multiple forms and content, and ultimately in its authoritative witness to Christ, the incarnate Word of God. Finally, one needs to note, too, that because of the differing contents in the Bible, the diversity of genres and literary forms in the biblical texts, as well as the differing degrees to which each book has been used in the history of all Christian communities, the biblical books do not have a uniform authority. Some books are more central and others less so, just as some sections in some books are more central and important than other sections.

Despite these important qualifications and limitations on the Bible's authority as a whole, the book that Christians call the Bible is treasured by them as the principal source of faith and the only clear witness to the living Word of God, Jesus Christ. Several NT passages underscore this point: According to John's gospel, Jesus once stated to his detractors, "You search the Scriptures for you think that in them you have eternal life and yet it is they that bear witness to me" (Jn 5.39). The Gospel of John itself was written so that the reader of it "would come to believe that Jesus is the Messiah, the Son of God," and that by believing in him such a person would have life in his name (Jn 20.31). According to Luke, the risen Christ opened the disciples' minds to understand the Scriptures in their witness to the suffering, death, and resurrection of the Messiah (see Lk. 24.45ff.). In light of these and similar passages, the authority of the Bible resides in its normative witness to Jesus Christ and to the Spirit's ongoing use of the prophetic and apostolic words that summon individuals to repent of their sins and to trust in Christ.

Despite the fact that the biblical writings are humanly conditioned by the time and circumstances in which they were first spoken, transmitted, and written down, Christian faith does not receive these prophetic and apostolic words "as the word of human beings, but as God's word" (1 Thess. 2.13; Gal. 1.11), a word that authenticates itself in the lives of those who hear it and trust it as a message for them. The word of God is a word that comes from beyond human beings and does not originate with them, their thoughts or wills or imaginations. It is a word that comes from God. It is a powerful word that leads people to change their understandings of themselves, of their world, and of God. "The Bible must therefore be treated with the devotedness, thoroughness and conscientiousness that accord with its authority, that is, its power to originate and further the coming of the Word of God and faith."[2]

Some Christians ground the authority of the Bible in a theory about the Bible's divine inspiration (for example, "verbal inspiration"). As we will see below, however, such an approach to biblical authority is fraught with problems and weaknesses. A more promising way of understanding the overall authority of the Bible is not by means of its divine inspiration but solely because of its faith-evoking and faith-strengthening witness to the word of God (in all of its variety) and centrally to Christ, the incarnate Word. This witness is used by the Spirit to make of the Scriptures a means of God's grace. In this view, Christians revere the Bible because of their

---

[2] Gerhard Ebeling, "Introductory Lectures on the Study of the Bible," *Word and Faith*, trans. James W. Leitch (London: SCM Press, 1963), 427.

reverence for Christ and the fact that he is the central content of the entire Scriptures.

The principal source: The Apostolic writings in the New Testament

As far as is known today, Jesus of Nazareth did not write anything down for posterity's sake, nor did he command his immediate followers to write anything down. If he did write something (see Jn 8.6), it has not survived to the present. The writings that Christians call "the New Testament" (NT) were written by a variety of Jesus' later followers, themselves dependent upon earlier oral traditions, and all these writings were passed on in Greek, the main common language of the eastern Mediterranean region in the wake of Alexander the Great (d. 323 BC). Although this language form was less polished and elegant than the classical Greek of the great Athenian poets and philosophers, it was at that time spoken by a large percentage of the population in areas conquered by Alexander, so that it communicated far more effectively than Hebrew (the original language of the OT writings) or Latin. Even many within the scattered Jewish communities in the eastern Mediterranean region after the time of Alexander relied upon a Greek version of the Hebrew Scriptures (the so-called Septuagint, which later was used by early Greek-speaking Christians as well). Whether or not Jesus knew this common form of Greek is unknown, but it seems likely that he and his initial followers originally spoke most often in a form of Hebrew ("Aramaic"), so that already in the NT itself there has been some translating of Jesus' original words into a different language.

Most of the twenty-seven books that are now included in the NT were composed during the half-century between about AD 50 and 100. Since Jesus died around the year 30, it was not until 20 years or so after his death that the first NT document was written, probably a letter that the apostle Paul wrote to a Christian congregation he founded in Thessalonica. This delay in Christian writing is important. The disciples of Jesus did not immediately begin to write down the message of the gospel. Instead, the teaching of Jesus and of his apostles was mainly transmitted orally and not initially through writing. It was proclamation (**kerygma**). This oral teaching and preaching carried authoritative weight in the early Christian communities. For example, Paul demonstrated his own dependence upon oral tradition when he passed on set teaching he had received regarding the Lord's Supper or Holy Communion, which was later called the Eucharist because of Jesus' action of giving thanks to God over the bread and the cup of wine ("Eucharist" = "thanksgiving"; see 1 Cor. 11.23; ODCC 570–2 ["Eucharist"]). This same dependence on oral tradition is evident in his set summary of the report about Jesus' resurrection from the dead (1 Cor. 15.1ff.). Even into the second century, oral tradition was still favored by some, such as Papias, who wrote, "I did not suppose that information from books would help me as much as the word of a living and surviving voice."[3] Even later, in the sixteenth century, Martin Luther stressed the proclaimed gospel as the living voice of God, in contrast to the "dead" letter of Scripture, and he remarked that the Christian church is a "mouth house" and not a "pen house" (WA 10/1.2, 48, 5 [*Kirchenpostille*, 1522]). Within this oral tradition, the authority of the words of Jesus, as remembered by his followers, was given special prominence. This is clear in several NT writings themselves (Acts 20.35; 1 Cor. 7.10; 1 Thess. 4.15) and among the writings of the second, third, and fourth generations of Christian disciples (for example, Clement of Rome, Polycarp, Justin Martyr).[4]

Following the deaths of the apostles, certain writings were treasured, copied, recopied, and passed on to later generations as authoritative and apostolic in character. These writings were understood to contain apostolic teaching that bore witness to Jesus. These writings served as the core of what would come to be called the Christian **canon** ("rule," "measuring rod," "guiding principle"; ODCC 279, 281–2). What was biblical would be canonical, and also vice versa.

Because the four NT gospels (Matthew, Mark, Luke, and John) contain the remembered teachings and actions of Jesus and were written by people who had the closest historical connection to him and the apostles, they gained an early acceptance among Christians in the second century as having Scriptural, apostolic, canonical authority. Prior to the late second century, when people first spoke of the four written gospels as a single collection, each gospel circulated independently, and most communities

---

[3] Papias, as quoted in Eusebius of Caesarea, *The Church History*, trans. Paul L. Maier (Grand Rapids: Kregel Academic, 2007), 3.29.4.

[4] See 1 Clement 13.2, 15.2, 24.5; and the Letter of Polycarp to the Philippians 2.3; 5.2, 7.2, 12.3 in *The Apostolic Fathers*, 2nd edn, trans. J. B. Lightfoot and J. R. Harmer, ed. Michael W. Holmes (Grand Rapids: Baker, 1989), 35–6, 42, 124–5, 127, 129. See also Justin Martyr, *First Apology* and *Second Apology*, in Justin Martyr, *The First and Second Apologies*, ed. Barnard, Leslie William (New York: Paulist, 1997).

likely used only one written gospel.[5] Irenaeus mentions, for example, how the Ebionites regarded the Gospel of Matthew as the only valid one.[6] That was true for Syrian Christians, too. Still other Christians, notably a few "elites" in Alexandria, primarily used a "secret" gospel of Mark. And later other Christian communities would use so-called apocryphal gospels, such as the Gospel of Peter, but these were criticized and rejected as heretical by key bishops and not used widely beyond fringe groups.[7] A late second-century document, the Muratorian Fragment, whose origin and authority suggests a connection with the bishop of Rome, indicates four gospels ought to be used, the last two of which are Luke and John. It is likely that this fragment, which is missing its opening lines, began with references to Matthew and Mark.[8] Eventually there came a time, certainly by the early third century, when these four gospels gained equal recognition among the churches that would be considered "orthodox" and "catholic."

But these four written gospels were probably not the first writings to be accorded the status of "Christian Scripture." Among the 27 documents that would eventually be included in most Christian Bibles after the fourth century, the letters of Paul were the first to gain this status (though not by means of any formal church decision, at least not during the first millennium of Christian history). While Paul had not been a follower of the historical Jesus and had actually been an opponent of the early Christian movement, he became a disciple and apostle after the revelation of Christ that he received (Gal. 1.1, 11–17), and his writings were the first to be treasured within early Christian communities. Initially each letter was a separate document that had been sent to a specific congregation of Christians. (When one reads the NT one is largely reading other people's mail!) These congregations preserved these letters carefully, read them regularly in their worship services; but also copied them so that they could be used by other Christian communities as well.[9] In Colossians 4.16 one reads: "And when this letter has been read among you, have it read also in

---

[5] C. F. D. Moule, *The Birth of the New Testament*, 3rd edn (New York: Harper and Row, 1982), 253.
[6] Irenaeus, *Against Heresies* 1.26.2 in Philip Schaff Philip and Henry Wace (eds), *Nicene and Post-Nicene Fathers of the Christian Church*. 2nd series, 14 vols (Peabody, MA: Hendrickson, 1995), 1.922.
[7] W. H. C. Frend, *The Rise of Christianity* (Minneapolis: Fortress Press, 1984), 251.
[8] For more on the Muratorian Fragment (also called the Muratorian Canon), see Bruce Metzger, *The Canon of the New Testament: Its Origin, Development, and Significance* (New York: Oxford University Press, 1987), 191–201.
[9] Kurt Aland and Barbara Aland, *The Text of the New Testament*, 2nd edn, trans. Erroll F. Rhodes (Grand Rapids: Eerdmans, 1989), 48.

the congregation of the Laodiceans; and see that you also read the letter from Laodicea." Even if Paul did not himself write this letter, this statement likely reflects the standard practice of reading, copying, and sharing Paul's letters and other writings in the early church—and having them read aloud during Christian worship services.

That Paul's letters gained an early acceptance among Christians is evident in the oldest Christian document outside of the NT, a letter from Clement, bishop of Rome, that dates to around the year 95. It contains statements from Paul's letter to the Romans, in addition to quotations from First Corinthians and Hebrews (1 Clem. 47.1–6). Eventually Paul's writings were grouped into a collection in various places (whose collections likely differed slightly in content from locale to locale). By the middle of the second century the author of Second Peter included Paul's letters as being among "the other Scriptures" (2 Pet. 3.16), although we cannot know for certain which of Paul's writings are being referred to here.

In the early church, up through the fourth century, each individual Christian community or cluster of communities (as in those under the authority of the bishop of Rome or those under the authority of one of the other patriarchs) had its own collection of prophetic and apostolic writings that were used in worship and instruction. While these collections varied from region to region, they did contain many of the same documents. Each church would have had its favored gospel or set of gospels, which would have been used alongside of writings from the OT, either in Hebrew or as they were handed down in Greek translation (the **Septuagint** version of the OT). Likewise the letters of Paul had a central authority in all of the Christian communities. While not every church seemed to have known or used First John and First Peter, they too had a more central status, as did the book of Acts (the second part of Luke's written gospel). Other writings, however, struggled for acceptance "but with unequal success."[10] These included James, Second and Third John, Second Peter, Jude, Hebrews, and Revelation.

Despite early mainstream Christian acceptance and use of the OT, already in the second century some Christians, especially those influenced by the teaching of Paul, questioned the authority of the OT. Some even rejected it outright. One such individual, **Marcion of Sinope** (c. 85–c. 160),

---

[10] Aland and Aland, *The Text of the New Testament*, 49.

totally rejected the OT writings, because they were in his view all about an inferior god who was different from the Father of Jesus. For Marcion the god of the OT was a god of war and anger and judgment. This evil god is responsible for the despicable creation, full of death and filth and sin. By contrast, the God of the NT, the Father of Jesus, is a God of love and mercy and forgiveness. Marcion maintained that there is no comparison between the God of Israel and the God of Jesus, so he rejected the whole OT as "unworthy" of being truly Scripture. He also rejected the written gospels, except for a version of Luke (edited in such a way as to remove its Jewish OT elements), and all of the other writings that would eventually be included in the NT, except the "true" letters of Paul, the ones that Marcion thought originally contained no quotations from the OT. Any Jewish elements in Paul's writings were edited out of Marcion's canon. Any reference to the God of the Old Covenant had to be an addition and not original to the writings of Paul or Luke.

Though we cannot know for certain if four gospels were already widely recognized by Christians at the time of Marcion (who then limited them to his edited version of Luke) or if his actions forced other Christians to argue for the inclusion of the three gospels that he rejected, he likely did lead people to become more aware of the need to define the limits of sacred Scripture. Nevertheless, it needs to be emphasized, at no point during these early centuries did any one group of Christians formally decide or determine those limits. That kind of formal decision did not occur until the sixteenth century, when the Roman Catholic Church at the Council of Trent formally identified which writings are to be used in Catholic churches. Instead, in the early church there was a general recognition in several locales that some writings (in addition to the Septuagint) ought to be used and accepted as Scripture. These NT writings included the four gospels, the letters of Paul, First John, and First Peter. These writings are called the **homologoumena**, a word meaning, "agreed upon things." Other writings that were not uniformly agreed upon and were "spoken against" are thus called the **antilegomena** ("spoken against things"). These writings that were questioned and even rejected by some, but later included in other canonical lists include Hebrews, James, Jude, Second John, Third John, Second Peter, Revelation, the Shepherd of Hermas, the Didache, the Letter of Barnabas, and several other documents.

The first person to identify the 27 writings that would eventually be included in most NT canons was Athanasius, whose 39th Festal Letter (written in AD 367) contains such a list. Nevertheless, that letter was not a formal decision. It merely indicates for those who read it which NT writings were in use among mainstream Christians in Egypt at that time.

While some of the antilegomena writings were eventually included in most post-fourth-century Christian canonical lists, such as we see in Athanasius' letter, they have a secondary, subordinate rank within the NT because of questions about their authorship and their contents. Still other antilegomena writings, including the so-called **Gnostic writings**, were completely rejected by mainstream Christian communities as contrary to the apostolic, normative, catholic, and orthodox gospel and thus not Scripture in any sense (save for those fringe groups that used them).

Some contemporary scholars think this rejection was either wrong or fairly arbitrary. Among the most well-known of these is Elaine Pagels, who has written several books that help to shed light on the competing versions of Christianity in the ancient world.[11] One of her principal assertions is the claim that the attacks on Gnostic texts by orthodox theologians in the second and third centuries were the result of institutional and political factors in the early church and not primarily a matter of theological disagreement and conflict. She is particularly troubled that women, who were accepted as spiritual leaders in Gnostic-Christian circles, were marginalized and subordinated within the emerging catholic orthodoxy of these early centuries. This marginalization, too, was the result of political factors and not the result of theological concerns.

Gerd Lüdemann and Bart Ehrman have argued along similar lines.[12] Like Pagels, they have built on the work of the German scholar Walter Bauer (1877–1960), who demonstrated that some early forms of Christianity, which were eventually deemed heretical at a later time, had been in fact quite popular in an earlier period.[13] What would come to be called "**orthodoxy**" at a later time might have been a minority view in the early decades of Christianity and what was "**heresy**" (false teaching) in later decades might have been quite popular in earlier times. The line between "heresy" and "orthodoxy" is thus blurred; what is "non-canonical" has just as much to tell us about "Christianity" as those writings in the traditional biblical canon. A few other scholars assert that there is no good reason

---

[11] See especially Elaine Pagels, *The Gnostic Gospels* (New York: Vintage, 1989).
[12] See Gerd Lüdemann, *Heretics: The Other Side of Early Christianity*, trans. John Bowden (Louisville: Westminster John Knox, 1996); and Bart Ehrman, *The New Testament: A Historical Introduction to the Early Christian Writings*, 5th edn (New York: Oxford University Press, 2011).
[13] Walter Bauer, *Orthodoxy and Hersey in Early Christianity*, Robert A. Kraft and Gerhard Krodel (eds), trans. Paul J. Achtemeier et al. (Minneapolis: Fortress Press Press, 1971).

to think that the stories about Jesus in the canonical, biblical gospels are any more historically reliable than the heretical versions.[14] For example, Lüdemann flatly asserts, "The heretics of the second century, men and women, are at least as close to Jesus as the orthodox, and must be welcomed back into the church."[15]

While there is much to learn about the complexity of early forms of Christianity from works like those written by Pagels and Ehrman, other scholars are not persuaded that the Gnostic Scriptures, with their alternative understandings of Jesus, are just as authoritative and normative and historically reliable as the central biblical texts. Even the Gospel of Thomas, which may, in very small part, be based upon early traditions about Jesus, strikes many as fundamentally at odds theologically with the teaching and narrative structure of the **synoptic gospels** (Matthew, Mark, Luke).[16] A careful theological comparison of the canonical texts and their stories with those that come from the later Gnostic and other **apocryphal** ("hidden") **writings** must lead one to make a choice: either the canonical or the apocryphal. They cannot be reconciled with each other since they present essentially contradictory portraits of Jesus and his significance. (Such a conclusion cannot and ought not minimize the significant differences between the portraits of the Jesus in the synoptic gospels, on the one hand, and the Gospel of John, on the other, but these differences do not approach the radical disjuncture that exists between the canonical portraits of Jesus and the presentation of him and his teaching in the non-canonical texts.)

Luke Timothy Johnson, a Roman Catholic scholar, takes a very different approach from Pagels, Lüdemann, and Ehrman.[17] Johnson begins with questions about "Jesus in the memory of the church," and how the earliest apostolic preaching about Jesus had a distinct and normative shape already in the earliest decades of the post-resurrection Christian community (see 1 Cor. 15.1ff. and the kerygmatic speeches in the Acts of the Apostles [e.g. 10.34ff.; 13.16ff.; 17.22ff.; 22.3ff.]). This apostolic shape is evident in the canonical gospels, despite the differences among them. After exploring

---

[14] See Timothy Miller, Book Review of *Alternative Christs*, ed. Olav Hammer (Cambridge: Cambridge University Press, 2009), *Church History* 80/1 (March 2011), 208.

[15] Lüdemann, *Heretics*, 219.

[16] These three written gospels are called "synoptic" ("view together with") because one can compare their basic outlines and see many similarities. By contrast, the Gospel according to John has many structural and essential differences from the synoptics.

[17] See Luke Timothy Johnson, *The Real Jesus: The Misguided Quest for the Historical Jesus and the Truth of the Traditional Gospels* (San Francisco: HarperOne, 1997); and idem, *Living Jesus: Learning the Heart of the Gospel* (San Francisco: HarperOne, 2000).

the canonical gospels and the problems attendant to them, Johnson moves on to discuss how early Christians rejected some texts that claimed to be Christian but were not, marginalized some texts that were not necessarily heretical but were not canonical, and accepted others that had been widely used and were viewed as having a continuity with that earliest apostolic proclamation.

Certainly there are good reasons to believe that the canonical stories about Jesus are generally more historically reliable than the stories in the Gnostic and apocryphal gospels ("hidden gospels," almost all with Gnostic emphases). For one thing, the canonical texts are much closer historically to the source about which they communicate, and their connection to places tied to authentic apostolic tradition is much firmer. Moreover, the exclusion of Gnostic and heretical writings from the biblical canon involved more than mere political decisions. There were both historical and theological factors at play in that process. The theological issues were particularly significant since these related to the nature of the gospel itself, as it had been delivered to the early church by the apostles and had been maintained by the faithful (see 1 Cor. 15.1ff.; 11.2, 23; a similar idea is present in 2 Thess. 2.15). These biblical texts provide the earliest of theological and historical traditions about Jesus.

Scholars who have investigated the development of the New Testament canon detect at least five principal criteria that were implicitly followed by early Christian communities to help them identify that which was in continuity with authentic apostolic teaching and that which conflicted with it.[18] These criteria may be labeled today apostolicity, antiquity, orthodoxy, catholicity, and episcopacy. Together they helped to define what would come to be orthodox and catholic understandings of the gospel about Jesus.

Apostolicity addressed the question of who wrote a given document. In order for a text to be considered authoritative it had to have been written or dictated by an apostle, or at least be understood to have continuity with the apostles' teaching. For example, in the late first or early second century, Papias of Hierapolis (in Phrygia) wrote about his memories of early Christian traditions that make reference to Mark's memories of what Peter proclaimed in Rome. Justin Martyr wrote about the gospels as "memoirs" of the apostles. The letters of Paul were treated with respect because they originated from one who had a recognized claim to the title "apostle."

---

[18] See especially Metzger, *The Canon of the New Testament*. See also ABD 1.837–61 ("Canon" [Sanders; Gamble]) and O'Collins, 247—50.

That was also true for First Peter and First John. The Gospel of Luke was favored because it was widely held to have been written by someone close to the apostle Paul or to traditions connected with Paul, one who himself indicated that he was dependent upon traditions passed down by those who were "eye-witnesses" to the words and actions of Jesus (Lk. 1.1–4).

A second criterion, closely related to the first, is the **antiquity** of a particular writing. The older, the better. Since all of the apocryphal gospels, with the exception of the Gospel of Thomas and the Infancy Gospel of James, were written after AD 180, they fall far short of being in close proximity to the apostolic witness to the words and deeds of Jesus. Even if a writing claimed to have been written by an apostle, as most of the apocryphal and antilegomena writings did as well, if a writing was not known before the middle of the second century (such as was the case, for example, with the NT writing called Second Peter), it ran into difficulties with the criterion of antiquity. Even a respected text like the Shepherd of Hermas was eventually excluded from the New Testament canon by many communities since it dated from the second century.

A third criterion was **orthodoxy** or correct doctrine, i.e. adherence to the *regula fidei* ("**rule of faith**") as handed down orally and in writing by those who were "eye-witnesses" and "hearers of the word" (Lk. 1.1–4). Unless a book could be shown to conform or fit with the recognized teaching of the apostles, it was rejected. Gnostics who claimed to be "Christian" ran afoul of other Christians because the former held that the God of the OT was an inferior God to the Father of Jesus, that the god who created the world was an evil god, that the world is an evil creation from which one's soul is to escape, that Jesus was merely a revealer of secret knowledge about the human soul ("a spark of the divine" inside of a human being), that Jesus is only concerned about saving this "spark" inside of people, and that Jesus was not really human, that he did not really die on the cross. Each of these teachings was rejected as contrary to authentic apostolic teaching.

A fourth criterion was **catholicity**, that is, how widespread was the usage of a text in worship, teaching, and spiritual edification. Some writings were accepted and used by nearly all who were called "Christian" in the first and early-second centuries (the letters of Paul, the synoptic gospels, the Gospel of John, First John, First Peter), whereas other writings (James, Hebrews, Revelation, Second Peter, Second John, Third John, Jude, and many others) were not as widely used. This lack of usage was itself often tied to doubts about the author(s) of these writings, about the antiquity of the writing, and about the content of their teaching. The apocryphal writings fell far short of being as widely used as Pagels and Ehrman seem to suggest.

A fifth criterion, related to the third criterion, is **episcopacy**, that is, the public succession of faithful bishops in certain key cities (Jerusalem, Antioch, Byzantium [later called Constantinople], Alexandria, and Rome) that became important in and after the second century. The early bishops in these key places were held to be a generally reliable means for transmitting apostolic texts and teaching (and the lists of authoritative Scriptures that were used in their churches), and to be reliable critics of alien texts, such as the apocryphal gospels, epistles, acts, and apocalypses. There were good reasons for why Gnostic texts did not win wide acceptance in early Christianity, for why the canonical texts are understood to be more historically and theologically authentic than later texts that claim to be apostolic and ancient, and for why the biblical canon that eventually developed the way it did generally looks the way it does.

Finally, if the apocryphal gospels are just as historically authentic (or inauthentic) as the canonical gospels, then why do nearly all scholars who investigate the problem of the historical Jesus limit themselves to the canonical texts, even in view of the notoriously difficult nature of the canonical gospels as primary sources for the historical Jesus? One preeminent scholar speaks for mainstream scholarship on this issue: "I share the general scholarly view that very, very little in the apocryphal gospels could conceivably go back to the time of Jesus. They are legendary and mythological. Of all the apocryphal material, only some of the sayings in the Gospel of Thomas are worth consideration. This does not mean that we can make a clean division: the historical four gospels versus the legendary apocryphal gospels. There are legendary traits in the four gospels in the New Testament, and there is also a certain amount of newly created material... Nevertheless, it is the four canonical gospels that we must search for traces of the historical Jesus."[19]

It is significant, too, that the first-century Jewish-Roman historian, Flavius Josephus (c. 37–c. 100), included a small paragraph about Jesus in his history of the Jews. Although we cannot know for certain what Josephus actually wrote about Jesus, since that particular paragraph was

---

[19] E. P. Sanders, *The Historical Figure of Jesus* (New York: Penguin Press, 1993), 64–5; see also the complementary discussion by John P. Meier, *A Marginal Jew: Rethinking the Historical Jesus*, 3 vols (New York: Doubleday, 1991–2009), 1.1–201, which takes one through the various sources for understanding the historical Jesus.

The 27 Documents in the New Testament[1]	Probable Date of Composition
The Gospel according to Matthew (H)	Late 80s to early 90s
The Gospel according to Mark (H)	Early 70s
The Gospel according to Luke (H)	Late 80s to early 90s
The Gospel according to John (H)	90s–100
The Acts of the Apostles (H)	Late 80s to early 90s
Letter to the Romans (H)	Late 50s
First Letter to the Corinthians (H)	Middle 50s
Second Letter to the Corinthians (H)	Middle 50s
Letter to the Galatians (H)	Middle 50s
Letter to the Ephesians (H)	80s
Letter to the Philippians (H)	Early 60s
Letter to the Colossians (H)	Middle 60s
First Letter to the Thessalonians (H)	Early 50s
Second Letter to the Thessalonians (H)	Early 50s
First Letter to Timothy (H)	90s–100
Second Letter to Timothy (H)	90s–100
Letter to Titus (H)	90s–100
Letter to Philemon (H)	Middle 60s
Letter to the Hebrews (A)	90s–100
Letter of James (A)	90s–100
First Letter of Peter (H)	90s–100
Second Letter of Peter (A)	140s–150s
First Letter of John (H)	90s–100
Second Letter of John (A)	90s–100
Third Letter of John (A)	90s–100
Letter of Jude (A)	90s–100
The Revelation of John (A)	90s–100

Figure 10.1

[1] H = Homologoumon; A = Antilegomenon

tampered with by Christian scribes at a later time, Josephus does provide corroborating testimony that locates Jesus in time and space (in relation to the Roman official Pontius Pilate), repeats the claims of others about Jesus' "wonders" and teaching, testifies to his crucifixion by Pilate (about whom Josephus wrote more than he did about Jesus), and summarizes the basic report of Jesus' followers about his resurrection. This limited information, recorded by a non-Christian historian who was a near contemporary of Jesus, generally fits with the central affirmations in the canonical gospels, namely, that Jesus was reported to have done miraculous deeds, that he taught people, that he was crucified under the authority of Pontius Pilate, and that his followers reported him to have been raised from the dead three days after his death.[20]

For Christians today, only the homologoumena writings in the NT serve as the principal source and norm of Christian teaching. These "agreed-upon" writings are the only authentic source for our knowledge of God's historical self-revelation in Christ, since this could only be certified authentically by eye- and ear-witnesses and second-generation "servants of the word" (Lk. 1.2; 1 Jn 1.1), and since we today have no access to the oral kerygma, but only to the literary testimony of these apostolic witnesses and their immediate followers. These writings articulate in a manifold way the one apostolic gospel concerning Jesus. These central apostolic writings, in their witness to the gospel concerning Christ, are the only norm for the church's total teaching, since the apostles themselves (via their reception of the Holy Spirit promised them by Christ) became organs for God's self-revelation, and because all subsequent events that happen in the church must be guided and shaped by this revelation. It is clear, however, that not everything within the NT writings, even the homologouma ones, is normative for all times and places, as Paul's teaching about the eating of food offered to idols and the eating of blood makes clear (in contrast to the statement of James in Acts 15 regarding these practices).

The normative authority of the antilegomena texts remains a theological problem for today's church, just as it did for the church of the second, third, and fourth centuries. Because there are legitimate concerns about

---

[20] Flavius Josephus, "Antiquities of the Jews," Book 18, Chapter 3, para. 3, in Flavius Josephus, *The Complete Works of Josephus*, trans. William Whiston (Grand Rapids: Kregel, 1981), 379. For the textual difficulties in this paragraph, see Sanders, *The Historical Figure of Jesus*, 50. "This paragraph, whose precise wording we do not know, is the best objective evidence of the importance of Jesus during his own lifetime" (ibid.). Josephus mentioned Jesus, but he gave more attention to Pilate, John the Baptizer, and other prophetic figures.

the canonical character of some biblical writings, the canons used by Roman Catholics, the Orthodox, and Protestants cannot serve as the "rule and guiding principle" of Christian theology, nor is the totality of any one of these canons "the pure, clear fountain of Israel" (BC 527 [*Formula of Concord*, Solid Declaration, Preface, 3]), as Martin Luther's prefaces to the biblical books also make clear (see LW 35.235ff.). Not every biblical book or biblical passage is of equal canonical, theological weight. Nevertheless, the canonicity of the majority of the NT writings is not in doubt.

One needs to underscore that for Protestants the post-apostolic church did not and does not today determine the canonicity of the NT. There was no "light from above" stating, "Choose and use these writings and not these." The Christian church has always been dependent upon the authority of the apostles, first in their oral teaching and witness and then in their written witness and the written witness of those who faithfully transmitted their teaching. Questions about the apostolic nature of some NT texts cannot be resolved by a decision of a church body. The church received its faithful teaching from the apostles, just as the apostles received their teaching from Christ through the power and revelation of the Holy Spirit. The decisive criterion for canonicity was the intimate bond between the content of a text and its origin: an apostolic text bears authentic and true witness to Christ, and an authentic, true witness to Christ originated from an apostle or the follower of an apostle. The authentically apostolic word stands over against the church. Some NT documents that claim to be apostolic and authoritative remain within the antilegomena and thus they are always open to the possibility that they are non-apostolic, non-canonical. In any case, the antilegomena are not central to Christian faith and teaching; they are subordinate to the homologoumena. The center of the canon, both historically and theologically, comprises the authentic letters of Paul, the synoptic gospels, the Gospel according to John (which was nevertheless disputed in some quarters because of its Docetic-leaning elements), First John, and First Peter (which is Pauline in content and character).

To be sure, some church groups have passed decrees at councils or meetings that define the biblical canon used in their church. The first time such an act was undertaken occurred in the sixteenth century at the Council of Trent. (See O'Collins 244–5, 250–1.) Here the Roman Catholic Church defined the biblical canon as coterminous with the Latin Vulgate translation, a list that contains some apocryphal writings. Likewise the Reformed churches developed their own list of canonical writings (Heppe 13). These decisions are problematic, however, because of the distinction between the homologoumena and the antilegomena.

While the Lutheran Church has refrained from identifying an authoritative list of canonical writings, it has been concerned to maintain the ancient and venerable distinction between the homologoumena and antilegomena and to keep open the question about the margins of the canon. One cannot avoid the fact that the antilegomena within the NT itself cannot shirk questions about their apostolicity, antiquity, catholicity, and especially their orthodoxy. It was because of questions about the latter that Luther famously passed judgment on some antilegomena books in the **OT Apocrypha** and in the NT (especially James, but also Jude, Hebrews, and Revelation). To be sure he did not exclude these antilegomena from his edition of the Bible, but it is interesting to note that his 1522 edition of the NT did not list these writings in the table of contents and these books themselves were put in the very back of the book on unnumbered pages! He clearly did not want people focusing on these writings, which he, like the ancient biblical scholars, thought contained teaching that was at least inconsistent with authentic apostolic teaching, if not outright contradictory to the gospel.

Consistent with mainstream judgments about the center of the biblical canon in early Christianity, Luther thought that the epistles of Paul, First Peter, First John, and the Gospel of John were "the true kernel and marrow of all the books" (LW 35.231), although he regularly preached on the synoptic gospels and many OT books. Despite his support for the historic **"canon within the canon"** (the gospel itself as a norm within the biblical canon) Luther did not think of excluding every antilegomenon from his translation or of rejecting the OT and the Apocrypha as Scripture, as seems to have been the case with Schleiermacher's judgment against the abiding authority of the OT for Christian theology (see SCF §27). But Luther did insist on the necessity of acknowledging a distinction between the central biblical writings and those on the margins that could be legitimately criticized.

Whereas most Lutheran and Reformed theologians since the sixteenth century have spoken about specific attributes of the Bible as whole, it is really more accurate to apply these traditional attributes only to the homologoumena writings of the NT and then, by extension, to the OT prophetic writings, which are interpreted by the apostolic writings of the NT. In relation to the purpose of these central biblical writings, their perfection resides in their *sufficiency*: they contain everything one needs to know in order to become knowledgeable of the nature and will of God, of the world as God's creation, of human beings as sinful creatures of God who have been redeemed by Christ Jesus, and of the new creation that has dawned in Christ. In other words, these apostolic and prophetic writings alone are able to instruct a person in everything necessary for salvation and of the blessed life. "For our faith rests upon the revelation made to the apostles and prophets, who wrote the canonical books..." (Aquinas 1a.1.8). In this sense, one may speak of the apostolic and prophetic writings as "the pure fount" from which flow all the articles of faith that together constitute the doctrinal content of the faith.

Likewise, the attribute of "*necessity*" also attaches to the homologoumena apostolic and prophetic writings, which are able to refute the errors of human beings with respect to the revealed truth of the gospel and the articles of faith that serve as corollaries to the gospel. "If we consider how slippery is the lapse of man's mind into forgetfulness of God, how great his proclivity for every kind of error, how great his passion for fashioning simultaneously new and fictitious religions, it will be easily revealed, how necessary such a sealing of heavenly doctrine has been, to prevent its extinction in oblivion, its disappearance in error or its corruption by man's presumption" (Calvin 1.6.3).

Finally, the homologoumena apostolic and prophetic writings are clear in their teachings about the essential content of the faith. In other words, the truth of the gospel is plainly and clearly revealed in these writings and may be understood by most everyone who pays careful attention to them. While the "*perspicuity*" of the apostolic and prophetic writings does not mean that everything within them is unambiguously clear or that one can avoid the need for careful historical-critical exposition of their contents, it does mean that the basic and essential teachings of the faith within these writings are not opaque. Whatever obscure passages are found in Holy Scripture are to be understood theologically in the light of the unambiguously clear ones that serve as a guide to "the rule of faith and love" (Heppe 34). This is the basis for the venerable interpretational principle, which will be further clarified in the next chapter, "Scripture interprets Scripture."

The second main source: The Old Testament

Whenever a writing in the NT canon refers to "Scripture," it is referring to the Hebrew Scriptures, which Christians traditionally call the Old

Testament (OT). The historical development of the OT was even more complex than that of the NT, although by the time of Jesus its basic contents had been determined. The central writings are the so-called "books of Moses" (Genesis through Deuteronomy) and the "prophets," inclusive of both the so-called "historical" books (Joshua through Chronicles), the major prophets (Isaiah, Jeremiah, and Ezekiel), the 12 minor prophets, the Psalms and the Proverbs. Other writings, including especially Esther and what would come to be called the OT Apocrypha, were questioned and "spoken against" and thus were not as central for most Jews and early Christians.

To refer to the OT as a "second main" source of Christian theology needs careful clarification. The only sacred Scriptures that Jesus knew and read were the Jewish Scriptures that were regularly used in Palestinian synagogues during the centuries prior to his birth. All of his initial followers read the same Scriptures. But with the destruction of Jerusalem in AD 70 and the subsequent rise of Gentile (non-Jewish) Christianity, the nature and application of the traditional Hebrew Scriptures changed within both Judaism and Christianity. Some significant portions of the Hebrew Scriptures that provided instructions and commentary on cultic ("worship") practices, especially relating to sacrifices, no longer could be strictly heeded in either Judaism or in Jewish Christianity after the destruction of the Jerusalem temple (where sacrifices had occurred). Other portions of the Hebrew Scriptures, again largely but not exclusively relating to cultic practices, were criticized by Jesus himself and later by Paul and other apostles; these were viewed by later Gentile Christians as no longer normative for their own faith and practice. Nevertheless, even these passages were often still interpreted by Christians in figurative, theological ways in reference to Jesus and his death on the cross.

Despite the many quotations from the OT in the NT, the OT is not the principal source of Christian theology. The main reason for this assessment is the fact that the apostolic NT witness is critical of some teachings and practices from the OT. In other words, apostolic criticism of the OT Scriptures and their non-binding authority upon Gentile Christians serves as a canon or norm over against the OT. Such criticism and abrogation of the Mosaic law is already evident in the Hebrew prophets themselves (compare Deut. 23.1–8 with Isa. 56.3–8), but becomes more explicit in the witness to Jesus' words and actions within the canonical gospels. The authority of Jesus over against the Jewish law is the central indication that the OT law would have a subordinate and even outdated authority for Christians, both Jewish and Gentile. Jesus did not always enforce or keep the Scriptural laws from the OT. For example, according to the witness of John, Jesus forgave the woman who was caught in adultery (Jn 7.53ff, compare with Deuteronomy 22, which clearly teaches that such a woman should have been killed) and, according to Mark, Jesus "declared all foods clean" and thus rightly edible (Mk 7; compare with the diet laws in Exod., Lev., and Deut., which list those foods that are not to be eaten). On occasion, Jesus himself broke the Mosaic law (= "making himself unclean") by talking with a Samaritan woman alone (Jn 4; compare with Lev. 15.19ff.), eating with sinners and tax collectors, touching lepers, and loving Gentile "enemies." On these occasions, Jesus did not "keep" or "fulfill" what the Jews understood to be the divinely given, clearly stated written Word of God in Leviticus and Deuteronomy. The statement in Matthew (5.17) about Jesus "fulfilling" the law can only mean that Christ has fulfilled the law by bringing it to an end or conclusion (as Paul states in Rom. 10.4). Now that Jesus has accomplished all things, the OT law *as law* has been abrogated and brought to its termination. In the words of John, "The OT law was given through Moses, but grace and truth have come through Jesus Christ" (Jn 1.17).

The authoritative apostolic writings—whose center remains the writings of Paul, First Peter (which is actually Pauline in character and content), First John, and the canonical gospels—teach that the OT law has now been set-aside for Gentiles. For example, Paul teaches that one does not sin by working on the Sabbath, that circumcision is unnecessary, and that one can eat whatever food is set before one without sinning, even though the OT clearly states that one is to keep the Sabbath laws, that circumcision is necessary, that some foods are unclean, and that one does in fact sin if one eats those foods. (See especially Gal. 3.25–6, Rom. 4.14–15, and Eph. 2.15–16. The verb that is used in this latter passage, *katargeo*, means "to invalidate, to make powerless, to cause something to come to an end or to be no longer in existence, abolish, wipe out, set aside" [BDAG 525–6].) "For freedom (from the OT law), Christ has set you free; don't be yoked again (to the Mosaic law)" (Gal. 5.1). Paul's whole argument in Galatians is against those who insisted that followers of Jesus must abide by the rules and laws that were given in the OT. See also Phil. 3.2ff., which was written against those who insisted upon the normative validity of the OT law of circumcision for Gentile Christians, and Colossians 2.20, which was written against those who insisted on obedience to Jewish regulations that are given in the OT. By faith in Christ one is "no longer under law but under grace" (Rom. 6.15). "You have died to the law through the body of Christ, so that you may belong to another, to him who has been raised from the dead in order that we may bear fruit for God" (Rom. 7.4). "We have been released from the law, dead to that which held us captive, so that we serve not under the old written code but in the new life of the Spirit" (Rom. 7.6). "Christ is the end of the law, that everyone who has faith may be justified" (Rom. 10.4). Through the law the Christian has died to the law, so that Christ may replace the law. "Now that faith has come, we are no longer under the law" (Gal. 3.25). Christ has "abolished [abrogated, destroyed] the law of commandments and ordinances in his flesh" (Eph. 2.15).

The normative authority of the OT for Christian theology is dependent upon the authority of the homologoumena writings in the NT. The apostolic preaching about Christ alone identifies what is normative for Christian faith within the OT prophetic and wisdom texts. One can speak of the prophetic writings of the OT, inclusive of all of the books within the Hebrew canon, as normative and as a source that is secondary to the apostolic preaching only because the apostolic witness to Christ, given in the apostolic writings, identifies what is normative within that OT witness for Christian faith. For Christian theology, the content of the OT is only understandable on the basis of the content of the apostolic witnesses: The God of Israel is the Father of Jesus Christ and the Scriptures of Israel contain promises about Christ. But not everything in the OT pertains to Christian faith, since much in the law of Moses was only directed to the original covenant people of ancient Israel in their historical situation of nationhood.

One must put forth a very important cautionary note at precisely this point. Already in the second century, Marcion and Gnostic Christians rejected the Hebrew Bible entirely. They asserted that the God of Israel is a different god from the Father of Jesus. Christian anti-Semitism throughout history has also disparaged and rejected the OT, just as it has led Christians to act violently toward Jews. For example, some racist, anti-Semitic "German Christians" (*Deutsche Christen*) in Nazi Germany called for the complete rejection of the OT, as have other theologians in the history of Christian thought.[21] The racist ideology of the nazified German Christians, which

---

[21] Not all Christians in Germany during the time of Hitler and Nazism were "German Christians" (*Deutsche Christen*). The latter sought to change the content and practice of the Christian faith to accord with Nazi nationalist and racist ideals. They combined the cross of Christ and the swastika of Hitler, they watered down the historic content of Christianity, and they worked against those Christians in Germany who opposed the introduction of Nazi ideology into the Protestant churches there.

attacked the OT and "the Jew Paul" and which falsified Jesus into an "Aryan" non-Jew, was used by Christians to attack European Jews, and it contributed to those factors that led directly to the Holocaust. This fact cannot be ignored or downplayed. Post-Holocaust Christian theology must be aware of these terrible connections, including the close connection between a negative decision against the Hebrew Scriptures and negative actions toward Jews in history.

Mainstream Christian theology is grounded in the Hebrew Scriptures, even if it is not entirely normed by those Scriptures. Marcion's view and the Gnostic disparagement of the OT were rightly rejected. The rejection of the OT by the "German Christians" has also been rightly condemned, as has their blatant racism and anti-Semitic hatred and violence. Christians today need to recognize *both* the integrity of the Hebrew Scriptures as Jewish Scriptures, because they bear witness to the one, true, living God, the Creator of all, *and* the important role that the Hebrew Scriptures play in bearing witness to the coming Messiah. On the one hand, the Hebrew Scriptures are normative in their revelation of the Creator and the Creator's divine law that is addressed to every human being and not merely to the ancient covenant people of Israel in their cultic life. On the other hand, whereas many Jews still await the promised Jewish Messiah, Christians believe he has already arrived. Thus Christians read the Hebrew Scriptures with a perspective that is shaped by the historic apostolic witness to Jesus as the fulfillment of the divine promise of the coming Messiah. So Christian theological understanding is grounded in the Hebrew Scriptures but normed by the apostolic witness to Jesus, a witness that also interprets key sections of the Hebrew Scriptures. What is normative for Christians within those Scriptures, especially the prophets and the psalms, provides a clarifying witness to God's self-revelation as Creator, Law-giver, and Messiah-sender.

Subordinate sources

The apostolic writings of the NT are the principal source of Christian theology and provide the sole norm of theology in their witness to the apostolic gospel. While the canonical writings of the OT, especially the psalms and the prophets, are the second main source of theology, there are several additional sources that serve and assist the theological task. The first and most important of these other sources is *church tradition*, which comprises the handing on of apostolic writings, the history of biblical interpretation, and the history of dogmatic decisions made at the ecumenical councils. While the essential doctrinal content of the Christian faith is grounded solely in the prophetic and apostolic writings of the OT and NT, it is nonetheless insufficiently articulated and clarified in these writings. The church has thus found itself in the position of having to define its faith, sometimes over against false teaching, as happened in and through the articulation and acceptance of the Nicene Creed (AD 325), and sometimes for the sake of brevity in a sacramental and liturgical context, as happened in and through early baptismal creeds and especially the Apostles' Creed.

The meaning of any biblical writing is in some sense contained within the history of its interpretation, and thus church history is a more or less implicit source of Christian theology insofar as it sheds light on how the church has understood the Scriptures over time. This is especially true since no one can honestly jump over two thousand years and become contemporaneous with the biblical writings themselves. The earlier wrestling with the biblical texts by principal thinkers in the Christian tradition helps to clarify how biblical doctrines have been understood and articulated over the centuries. While church councils and individual Christian theologians can and have erred and contradicted one another, their theological and interpretational decisions have had a profound influence on the formulation (and re-formulation) of church doctrine. These decisions invite repeated re-investigation.

Within the Lutheran tradition, the confessional writings of Luther and Melanchthon, especially Luther's catechisms and the *Augsburg Confession* and its *Apology*, have served as normative exposition of the doctrinal content of the Holy Scriptures for those churches that subscribe to these confessional writings. Within the churches of the *Augsburg Confession*, the Lutheran Confessional writings are not held to be on the same level of authority as the Holy Scriptures, but they are understood to be a faithful presentation of the doctrinal teachings of the whole of Holy Scripture in relation to the heart of the Scriptures, namely, their witness to the saving gospel of Christ. Moreover, these teachings are not understood to be the private perspective of Lutheran Christians, but the basic and universal teachings of the whole catholic and orthodox Christian church:

> Resting on Scripture as a whole, the Confessions aim to summarize the multiplicity of statements from Scripture in doctrinal articles directed against the errors of their day and designed for the protection of the correct proclamation then and for all time to come... This fact, that here the church

(not an individual) witnesses to the sum of Scripture (not an incidental exegetical discovery), is the basis for the claim of the Confessions that they are the norm according to which the thinking and speaking of the believers is to be tested and determined. Specifically, they claim to be the obligatory model of all of the church's preaching and teaching. This claim admits of no limits, either of time or of space.[22]

In the case of the churches of the *Augsburg Confession*, the claim is that the doctrinal articles in that particular Confession summarize the faith of the one, holy, catholic, and apostolic church and are not merely a sectarian statement of faith from the "Lutheran" church (a designation that is itself repudiated in the evangelical confessions themselves). A similar claim to "catholicity" and "orthodoxy" is also made by other churches in their catechisms and confessional writings.[23]

These confessions must be taken seriously and examined carefully and critically against Holy Scripture. The various confessional writings of the divided churches cannot be placed above the Scriptures, but must be investigated themselves to see if they accord with the theological content of the prophetic and apostolic Scriptures. Thus ecumenical discussion and attention to how Christian groups throughout the world understand the Scriptures, as summarized in their creeds, confessions, and catechisms, are essential aspects of theological understanding. These documents serve as ancillary sources of theology, since they seek to clarify the content of the Christian faith and the witness to the truth of the gospel. The intent of every engagement with a particular church confession, creed, or catechism ought to be to discern what is central and living within a church's faith, to celebrate agreement, and to engage in further dialogue on those matters about which there is still disagreement.

A further source is *the history of religions and cultures* that have affected and shaped both the content of the writings in the OT and NT and the formulation of Christian doctrine in the history of the Christian churches. Tillich was correct to stress that the biblical message cannot be understood and could not have been received had there been no preparation for it in human culture. Language, poetry, philosophy, religious concepts—all of these have had an effect on the expression of biblical ideas and thus are

---

[22] Schlink, *Theology of the Lutheran Confessions*, xvi–xvii.
[23] See, for example, *The Catechism of the Catholic Church*, the *Thirty-Nine Articles* of the Anglican Church, *The Book of Confessions* in the Presbyterian Church, and the *Twenty-Five Articles of Religion* in the Methodist Church.

important, though subordinate, sources/resources for the formulation of doctrine (see especially Tillich 1.34–40). To understand the biblical texts, it is necessary to consult other extra-biblical resources, which serve to clarify the meaning of the biblical texts. These extra-biblical sources of knowledge from the Ancient Near East help to eliminate false and inadequate understandings of the biblical texts. For example, they help to discern the various genres and forms in the biblical texts, which bear similarities to genres and forms in the non-biblical religious texts from the ancient world, and thus they help to avoid the misinterpretation of the Scriptures.[24]

A final source is *contemporary human experience*, including scientific knowledge and cultural interpretations of human experience, which shape and inform the language and thought forms that are used to articulate and effectively communicate the essential content of Christian faith in particular, temporal, cultural, social contexts. While the prophetic and apostolic texts alone serve as the judge and rule of doctrine and theology, Scripture is never alone: it is always interpreted in specific contexts, which themselves shape the formulation of doctrine and the expressions used in Christian theology. Every listener and reader of the Scriptures, even the most "anti-modern" and "fundamentalist" of Christians, is embedded in social, cultural, and theological contexts that shape and inform his/her listening and reading of the Scriptures and that shape the manner in which he/she articulates and communicates the essential content of Christian faith.

One example will demonstrate this point. Historical investigation of the biblical texts, coupled with an understanding of contemporary cosmological knowledge, serves to clarify the nature of the Christian doctrine of creation. In this light one must conclude that the Christian doctrine of creation does not entail the acceptance of biblical expressions of cosmology as literal descriptions of fact, such as the outdated view that the earth is immovable or that it rests on pillars or that the world was created over the course of six actual days in the recent past. The "limiting power" or "clarifying power" of these additional extra-biblical sources/resources thus shapes the formulation of church teaching.

---

[24] See especially, James L. Bailey and Lyle D. Vander Broek, *Literary Forms in the New Testament: A Handbook* (Louisville: Westminster John Knox Press, 1992).

The principal norm: The gospel of Jesus Christ

The apostolic writings in the NT make clear that *the principal norm of Christian faith is the gospel concerning Jesus the Christ*. All authentic Scripture bears witness to Christ alone in service to faith alone in him. All authentic Scripture turns about Christ as its authentic center. He is its proper and central content and the gospel about him is its norm. This is often called "the canon within the canon," since the gospel about Jesus Christ serves as the sole standard for the theological interpretation of Scripture. Thus all Scripture, both the OT and the NT, both the homologoumena and the antilegomena, must be interpreted in relation to Jesus Christ and the gospel about him. From the perspective of the apostles (Lk. 24), the entirety of the Scriptures is only understood in relation to Christ. While one cannot force a Christological interpretation on texts that cannot bear such a narrow interpretation, the essential content of any given section of Scripture is always properly defined in relation to Holy Scripture's overall basic witness to Jesus. Every authentic, homologoumena Scriptural book presents the clear gospel, yet not every biblical writing (inclusive also of the antilegomena) presents the gospel to the same extent or with the same clarity. Luther has given this gospel-norm its classic expression:

> All the genuine sacred books agree in this, that all of them preach and inculcate [German: *treiben*] Christ. And that is the true test by which we judge all books, when we see whether or not they inculcate Christ. For all the Scriptures show us Christ (Rom. 3.21); and St. Paul will know nothing but Christ (1 Cor. 2.2). Whatever does not teach Christ is not yet apostolic, even though St. Peter or St. Paul does the teaching. Again, whatever preaches Christ would be apostolic, even if Judas, Annas, Pilate, and Herod were doing it. (LW 35.396)

This gospel principle or "canon within the canon" was not Luther's invention. It is found already in the apostolic Scriptures themselves, especially the letters of Paul to the Galatians, the Philippians, and the Romans. Even Jesus himself seems to have operated with something similar, at least according to the apostolic witness. Within John's gospel, Jesus says to the biblical scholars of his day, "You search the Scriptures because you think that in them you have eternal life; and it is they that bear witness to me" (Jn 5.39). According to the apostolic witness, "To [Jesus] all the prophets bear witness that everyone who believes in him receives forgiveness through his name"

(Acts 10.43). "And Jesus interpreted to them the matters about himself in all the Scriptures. ...Then he opened their minds to understand the Scriptures, and he said to them, 'Thus it is written, that the Messiah is to suffer and rise from the dead on the third day, and that repentance and forgiveness of sins are to be proclaimed in his name to all nations...'" (Lk. 24.27, 45–7)

If a person comes to the Bible with any other issue in mind, beyond this one about preaching and teaching the righteousness of Christ for repentance and faith, then indeed the Bible remains opaque and unclear. It devolves into an oppressive book of laws, much like it had become in the use of the Hebrew Bible by some interpreters in the time of Jesus, or it becomes a mere collection of disparate historical documents from the ancient world. Apart from its use in witness to Christ and the good news about him, Scripture can easily be turned into a "wax nose," that is, its "face" can be changed and distorted in many ways by an arbitrary interpretation, even one that claims to be "historical" and "without illusion."

As has already been noted in previous chapters, the prophetic and apostolic writings actually teach and proclaim two basic, distinct messages from God, **the law and the gospel**. These two Scriptural messages are not identical and must be distinguished from each other. Both are valid and true; both come from God; both are found in both testaments; yet both are quite different from each other. The differentiation between the law and the gospel as a basic rule for the interpretation of Scripture is still another way of articulating "the canon within the canon," the norm or standard within the biblical writings that allows the writings to be properly understood in service to Jesus Christ as the living Word of God.

> The law commands and requires us to do certain things. The law is thus directed solely to our behavior and consists in making requirements. For God speaks through the law, saying, "Do this, avoid that, this is what I expect of you." The gospel, however, does not preach what we are to do or avoid. It sets up no requirements but reverses the approach of the law, does the very opposite, and says, "This is what God has done for you; he has let his Son be made flesh for you, he has let him be put to death for your sake..." For the gospel teaches exclusively what has been given us by God, and not—as in the case of the law—what we are to do and give to God. (LW 35.162)

The law thus accuses and judges sinners under the wrath of God, while the gospel forgives and acquits sinners for Christ's sake. For this reason the law is always God's "alien word" (*verbum alienum*), while the gospel is God's "proper word" (*verbum proprium*). While both words are found in both testaments, the law predominates in the Old and the gospel predominates in the New. Christ brings to light the hidden presence of the gospel in the OT and actualizes the gospel promises foretold in the prophets and OT writings. He makes clear that the law, sin, and death have met their match.

These two words of God, both true, nonetheless cannot remain at peace with each other in the life of the individual person. "The letter [RSV: "the written code"] kills but the Spirit gives life" (2 Cor. 3.6). The letter is not a good word, for it is the word of God's judgment and wrath against the sinner. The Spirit, however, is a good word, *the* good word, because it is the word of God's grace and forgiveness for the sinner because of Christ. There is thus conflict in the sinner/believer who hears both words. The one who hears them is caught in a struggle between the old age ("the age of the law") and the new age ("the age of grace"). The law says to sinners, "You are damned under the just judgment of God." The gospel, however, says, "You are forgiven for Christ's sake. I have damned him so that you might live. There is now no condemnation for those who are in Christ..." He—and he alone!—has put to death the accusing word of the law.

This conflict between "the letter that kills and the Spirit that gives life" results in several consequences. One consequence is a paradoxical under-standing of the human being before God. Under the law, the human being is a sinner and under the wrath of God; but under the gospel, in Christ, the person is righteous and full of the Spirit and under grace. To use yet another Augustinian phrase, the sinner in Christ is *simul justus et peccator* ("at the same time just and a sinner"), a total sinner and yet totally righteous at the same time. The distinction between the law and the gospel leads to a paradoxical anthropology: one and the same human being is both judged and forgiven by God.

Another consequence of this conflict is that these two words of God, the law and the gospel, must always be distinguished and never identified or confused in biblical interpretation, even though both messages might be tightly wound together in the same passage of Scripture. This is a most difficult task, to distinguish the law properly from the gospel, for the sake of creating and sustaining faith in Christ who has triumphed over God's just judgment. Ultimately the basis for Christian faith is that the word of the law is overcome by the message of the gospel, "the word of faith that we proclaim" (Rom. 10.9). This latter word of the Lord "lasts forever." "That word is the good news that was proclaimed to you" (1 Pet. 1.25).

There is also a consequence for Christian theology. The gospel is not merely one teaching among many others. Rather, the gospel is the key and central article of faith, which illumines all other articles. The gospel is the divine promise that for Christ's sake God will not ultimately judge and damn the sinner, but forgive the sinner and welcome the individual into God's family.

> Dealing with any doctrine in a formally correct manner is never enough unless we also express the proper distinction between law and gospel in the double nature of God's activity as well as our twofold relationship to God as people who are both judged and who have experienced mercy. Precisely here we become most clearly aware of the powerful dynamic that flows through Luther's theological work. At the same time we can now begin to see that the simple theoretical assertion that Scripture alone is the authority in theology says really very little. (Lohse 158–9)

Key Words

The Bible	synoptic gospels
the word of God	apocryphal writings
kerygma	apostolicity
canon	antiquity
the Septuagint	rule of faith (*regula fidei*)
Marcion of Sinope	catholicity
homologoumena	episcopacy
antilegomena	Old Testament Apocrypha
Gnostic writings	canon within the canon
orthodoxy	the law and the gospel
heresy	*simul justus et peccator*

Reference literature

For a general orientation

ABD 1:837–61 ("Canon" [Sanders; Gamble]); ABD 5:1017–56 ("Scriptural Authority" [Brueggemann et al.]); EC 2:713–16 ("Inspiration" [Williams]); ER 2:878–96 ("Biblical Literature I: Hebrew Scriptures" [Sarna]); ER 2:905–23 ("Biblical Literature II: New Testament" [Allison]); ER 3:1405–11 ("Canon" [Sheppard]); ER 12:8194–205 ("Scripture" [Graham]); ER 7:4509–11 ("Inspiration" [Carpenter]); OCCT 69–72 ("Bible" [Barton]); ODCC 200–2 ("Bible"); OHPT 11–29 ("Authority of Scripture, Tradition, and the Church" [Swinburne]); OHST 345–61 ("Scripture" [Fowl]); OHST 362–77 ("Tradition" [Williams]); OHST 394–412 ("Reason" [Moore]); RPP 2:1–7 ("Bible II: Old Testament" [Müller]); RPP 2:7–13 ("Bible III: New Testament" [Rydbeck]); RPP 2:13–17 ("Bible IV: Dogmatics" [Schwöbel]); RPP 2:353–54 ("Canon II: Church History" [Schindler]); RPP 6:505–9 ("Inspiration" [Koch et al.]); RPP 11:553–4 ("Scriptural Principle" [Steiger]).

For analysis of the authority and interpretation of Holy Scripture in the more important textbooks of modern dogmatics

SCF §§128–31; Aulén 359–70; Barth 1/1 §4.2; 1/2 §§19–21; Elert §§17–33; Brunner 1:14–49; Tillich 1:34–68; Weber 1:169–345; Rahner 369–88; Thielicke 2:184–258; BJ 1:61–78 (Braaten); HK 35–87 (Tracy et al.); Migliore 44–63; Pannenberg 1:189–257; Peters 51–63; ECT 11–49 (Grenz and Erskine).

For older understandings of the authority and interpretation of Holy Scripture

Aquinas 1a.1.8–10; on Luther (Althaus 35–42, 72–102; Bayer-L 68–92; Lohse 187–95); Calvin 1.69–96; on Lutheran Orthodoxy (Schmid §§6–12 [38–91]); Gerhard (Locus 1); on Reformed Orthodoxy (Heppe 12–46); on the Council of Trent (Denzinger Nr. 783–86).

Questions for review and discussion

1   The author argues that there are multiple sources for theology but only a single norm. Do you agree? What is the difference between a "source" of theology and a "norm" for theology? Is it always easy to distinguish these two resources in Christian theology?

2   At one end of the theological spectrum are various kinds of revisionist theologies (Tracy, Kaufman, Hodgson, McFague). At the other end of the spectrum would be the kind of Fundamentalist theology represented by Pieper. Toward which end of the spectrum do you lean? Why?

3   Describe how the author understands biblical authority. Do you agree or disagree with this position. From a conservative Protestant

perspective that leans in the direction of Pieper, the author's position on the authority of Scripture will likely be criticized as inadequate. Why might that be the case? How would you improve the author's position? What changes would be required? Do you agree or disagree with Augustine's statement that faith will stagger if the authority of the Sacred Scriptures wavers?

4   What are various meanings for the biblical expression "word of God"? Why does the author argue that the Bible cannot be strictly identified with "the word of God"? How does the author think the written Scriptures are related to the word of God in its multiple meanings? How do you understand this relationship?

5   What's the importance/significance of stressing the message of the gospel as primarily an oral message, not a written one? Why does the author insist that only the NT writings are the principal source of Christian theology and not the OT? Why does he insist that the gospel is the sole norm of Christian theology?

6   What role did Marcion play in the formation of the Christian biblical canon? Be familiar with the five criteria for canonicity. Are you surprised that "inspiration" apparently was not one of the criteria?

7   What is meant by the expression "canon within the canon?" How did Luther understand this concept? How might a Roman Catholic theologian respond to Luther's view that the canon within the canon is both a critical principle *vis-à-vis* the content of the Bible as a whole and a critical principle toward the church's own teachings and traditions?

8   Which of the secondary sources that are identified in the chapter is most important for contemporary theology? Why?

9   What are some of the differences between the divine law and the divine gospel? Why does the author insist on rightly or properly distinguishing between law and gospel?

10 What is meant by the expression "*simul justus et peccator*"? How does this expression reflect the difference between law and gospel as it applies to the Christian believer?

Suggestions for further reading

General reference works

Michael D. Coogan, ed., *The Oxford Encyclopedia of the Books of the Bible*, 2 vols (New York: Oxford University Press, 2011)

Daniel Master, ed., *The Oxford Encyclopedia of the Bible and Archaeology*, 2 vols (New York: Oxford University Press, 2013)

The Canon and Authority of Scripture

James Barr, *The Scope and Authority of the Bible* (Philadelphia: Westminster, 1980) [Helpful essays that espouse a view of biblical authority that complements the one presented in this chapter. Barr has been a strong critic of Fundamentalist understandings of biblical authority.]

Ernst Käsemann, "The New Testament Canon and the Unity of the Church," in *Essays on New Testament Themes* (London: SCM Press, 1964), 95–107. [Major essay that seeks to demonstrate through historical analysis that the NT canon contains several conflicting theological perspectives that do not establish the unity of the church but rather the diversity of theological confessions. Against this view, the present chapter argues that the apostolic gospel in the homologoumena is clearly defined and can serve as the norm for theological orthodoxy.]

David H. Kelsey, "The Bible and Christian Theology," *Journal of the American Academy of Religion* 48 (September 1980), 385–402 [A careful articulation of the place and use of Scripture in the theological task within the Christian church. He identifies the eschatological resurrection of Jesus as the "norming norm" within Christian theology.]

Bruce Metzger, *The Canon of the New Testament: Its Origin, Development, and Significance* (New York: Oxford University Press, 1997) [A classic work in the development of the New Testament canon. This is the place to begin one's study of this issue.]

Harold C. Skillrud et al. (eds), *Scripture and Tradition: Lutherans and Catholics in Dialogue IX* (Minneapolis: Augsburg, 1995) [A very brief summary of agreements between Lutherans and Catholics on the relationship between the Scriptures and church traditions.]

John Webster, *Holy Scripture: A Dogmatic Sketch* (Cambridge: Cambridge University Press, 2003) [Webster acknowledges the importance of textual and historical criticism, but affirms the centrality of a Reformed, Barthian understanding of the authority of Scripture that is grounded in the self-giving revelation of the triune God. This view provides a counter-perspective to the law-gospel approach set forth in the present chapter.]

11

Interpreting the Bible

After analyzing some unsatisfactory approaches to the interpretation of the Bible this chapter describes six basic principles of theological interpretation (hermeneutics). These principles can assist the person who seeks to understand the Bible both historically and theologically.

"Doesn't the Bible teach against evolution?" "I don't believe the Bible anymore because it puts women down and at one time it was used to sanction slavery?" "Just what does the Bible teach about homosexuality?" "The problem with contemporary Christians is they completely ignore the most important book in the Bible, namely, Revelation. It gives us the key to what is happening in the world right now and in the immediate future." One could multiply similar statements a million-fold.

The most controversial issues in the last half millennium of Christian theology surround the Christian Bible. Of course the major division that began in western Christendom in the sixteenth century was largely the result of disagreements over scriptural authority and interpretation vis-à-vis church doctrine and practice; yet, even among Protestant church bodies, divisions have occurred for the same or similar reasons. For example, the institutional conflict that occurred in the Lutheran Church—Missouri Synod (LCMS) in the 1960s and 1970s—was largely about the authority of the Bible and the proper ways of interpreting Holy Scripture in the contemporary world. Some have even used the expression "The Battle for the Bible" to describe that crisis.[1] Other church bodies have gone through, or are going through, similar crises (on such matters as the service of women in the church, the relationship between scientific knowledge and "what the Bible teaches," the issue of homosexuality, and other matters of Christian individual and social ethics). These ongoing discussions and disagreements

---

[1] See Harold Lindsell, *The Battle for the Bible* (Grand Rapids: Zondervan, 1976).

among Christians naturally lead to a fundamental question in theology: How should Christians understand the nature of biblical authority and how should the Bible be interpreted today?

For more than two centuries no doctrine has been more contentious within the Protestant churches than the doctrine of Holy Scripture.[2] No issue has been more central than the problem of interpreting the Bible for the present day. We usually refer to this as the problem of "**hermeneutics**."

The term "hermeneutics" is likely derived from the name of the Greek god, Hermes, who was the son of Zeus and Maia, the daughter of the Titan Atlas. The name "Hermes" itself appears to be derived from the early Greek word, "*herma*," which means "a pile of stones" that could be set up to mark a boundary."[3] So Hermes is the god of boundaries and roads. His main boundary is the one that divided the gods and human beings. His role was to cross that boundary and deliver and translate messages from the gods for human beings. Hence the Greek word for "interpreter" is "*hermeneus*." Hermeneutics is the art of interpretation or explanation. In a Christian context hermeneutics refers narrowly to the art of understanding Scripture. More broadly, it refers to the process of understanding the Christian tradition and all that it contains—other texts, images, liturgical forms, architecture, and icons. Hermeneutics also then entails the specific principles which one utilizes toward that goal of understanding.

In the wake of the Protestant Reformation and the rise of the modern sciences and critical scholarly disciplines, including history, philosophy, and philology (the study of words and their historical uses and meanings), the authority of the biblical writings has come to be questioned and even totally rejected. The entire tradition of Christian theology, including its treasured Bible, was subjected to critical examination on the basis of new principles of thought. This development has led to a variety of positions about the Bible and its authority that have been rightly criticized as inadequate. Before we examine helpful principles of interpretation that might help one to understand the Bible better, we should point out some positions toward the Bible

---

[2] Already more than 50 years ago Hermann Sasse (1895–1976) identified this doctrine as the most disputed one within the Lutheran Church. See his unpublished letter, "On the Doctrine De Scriptura Sacra," Letter Addressed to Lutheran Pastors, No. 14 (August 1950). While Sasse was critical of the inroads that Protestant liberalism had made into the Lutheran Church (e.g. minimizing the Scriptures as the written Word of God), he was especially critical of the inroads that Fundamentalism had made among American Lutherans (e.g. holding to the inerrancy of the Bible with regard to all matters it treats, even indirectly).

[3] Robin Hard, ed., *The Routledge Handbook of Greek Mythology* (London: Routledge, 2004), 158.

that have been shown to be problematic at best. These are extreme positions that one might want to avoid.[4]

Avoiding extremes

Biblicism

The first of these positions has been called **biblicism**, since it treats the Bible as a fully supernatural document, almost as if it fell out of heaven in its current shape and size, and as absolutely true and accurate on every matter which it addresses. This position, which came to prominence only after the sixteenth century (in Protestant Orthodoxy and conservative Roman Catholicism), largely as a reaction against the changed intellectual situation in the modern age, views the Bible as authoritative solely because of its divine origin and the complete inspiration of its every word. The Word of God is thus held to be identical to the entire contents of the Bible and these contents are, in their entirety, directly applicable to every time and place. The seventeenth-century Lutheran theologian, Johann Gerhard, provides a classic defense of this position:

> The divine authority of Scripture rises from and depends on the efficient principal cause of Holy Scripture, which is God. Because Holy Scripture has God as its author, by whose immediate inspiration the prophets, evangelists, and apostles wrote, it obtains its divine authority there from and therefore. Because it is God-breathed, published, and spread by divine inspiration, therefore it is credible in itself, having credibility from itself. It is important that the divine authority of Scripture be a well-built structure, for as Augustine rightly warns us: "Faith will stagger if the authority of the Sacred Scriptures wavers." (Gerhard 1.68)

Gerhard argued that every book, even the antilegomena, every chapter, every verse, every word, even the vowel points in the Hebrew words of the OT (which are not original to the text but were added in the early middle ages, c. AD 600–750), were divinely inspired and the direct result of God's supernatural operation. Gerhard acknowledged that the biblical authors were indeed human beings who wrote down the Scriptures, but they were like a flute that the Holy Spirit played. Such an idea was first developed in

---

[4] In the following section I am expanding on terms and analysis by Migliore, 47–50.

relation to the Hebrew Scriptures in the context of Hellenistic Judaism. The Hebrew Scriptures were believed to be qualitatively different from all other human writings because of their divine, supernatural origin. Some Jews even maintained that the books of Moses, the Torah ("instruction"), pre-existed in heaven before they were given to Moses directly on Mt. Sinai.

Certainly Gerhard and other Protestant theologians in the seventeenth and eighteenth centuries were right to tie the perfection of Scripture to its ability to instruct perfectly "about all things necessary for attaining salvation" (Gerhard 1.333; see Schmid 38–66), but subsequent theologians (such as Pieper, as noted in the previous chapter) wrongly extended its "perfection" to every matter about which it treats, even in passing.[5] If the Bible is not perfect and without error in every respect, Pieper maintained, then it cannot be trusted to convey God's word of truth. The guarantee of this "**inerrancy**" is the divine, **verbal inspiration** of the Biblical writings, that the Holy Spirit guided and governed the biblical writers in such a manner that they were kept from committing *any* error. In this view God literally spoke into the ears of the prophets and apostles the exact words they were to use, directly inspiring them, so that the biblical writers were more like passive secretaries who were only taking down God's dictation, or musical instruments through which the Holy Spirit played the divine tune. More moderating forms of verbal inspiration allow that the Holy Spirit did not override the biblical prophets and apostles with respect to their historical, social, and cultural limitations and allowed them more freedom to reflect their linguistic and cultural particularities. If the Bible is still confessed to be the inspired word of God, such inspiration did not do away with the human conditioning that leads to stylistic, linguistic, cultural, and even minor theological differences from one biblical writing to the next (and even within the same biblical writings).

A problem with this overall view of biblical authority as "inerrancy," however, is that one can end up with a solely mechanistic, miraculous understanding of the Bible's origin that downplays or even ignores the human, historical, and cultural conditioning that is clearly apparent within the biblical writings themselves. This view of inerrancy often ends up

---

[5] Even Aquinas came close to this position when he quoted Augustine's statement from his *Epistle to Hieronymus*, "Only those books of Scripture which are called canonical have I learned to hold in such honor as to believe their authors have not erred in any way in writing them. But other authors I so read as not to deem anything in their works to be true merely on account of their having so thought and written, whatever may have been their holiness and learning" (Aquinas 1a.1.8).

directly applying all of the Bible's statements to the present, as if there have been no historical changes since the days of the biblical writings (or historical and cultural changes from one biblical writing to another). This view also flattens out the variety of expressions within the Bible and gives them all an equal authority, as if the biblical assertion that "Nimrod was the first on earth to become a mighty fighter" (Gen. 10.8) is of the same theological value as the Johannine assertion, "For God so loved the world that he gave his only Son that whoever believes in him shall have eternal life" (Jn 3.16 [RSV]). In this way, theology is entirely based on biblical quotations and all the theologian need do is martial biblical passages into a sequence of the theologian's own making in order to present or attack dogmatic statements.

The problem with such an approach ought to be clear: Not every individual statement or assertion in the Bible is consistent with the gospel. Every reader of the Christian Bible ought to distinguish between what is incidental or peripheral within the Bible and what is essential and central to its overall message and purpose. The gospel about Christ, which is attested in diverse ways within the Scriptures, is the key that unlocks the meaning of the whole of Scripture and allows its individual parts to be understood in relation to that biblical whole.

The idea of verbal inspiration, as it has developed within Protestantism, is also problematic because it suggests that, unless one can rationally demonstrate the divine inspiration and perfection of the Bible first, one cannot submit to the Scriptural word. But how can one ever prove or demonstrate a writing to be "divinely inspired," especially when one considers that in the early church many writings that were purported to be inspired were in fact judged heretical or at least non-apostolic (and thus non-canonical)? In point of fact, Christian faith does not submit to the authority of the Bible because its divine authority has first been demonstrated, but because the power of the divine words, particularly the law and the gospel, authenticate themselves again and again in the present through the inner testimony of the Holy Spirit, which nevertheless remains always conditioned through human witnesses who spoke and wrote in different settings over the course of many centuries and who used many differing types of speaking and writing to convey the word of the LORD.

The authority of Scripture is not formal but is highly material and is content driven. It is the voice of its author, who gives; who allows for astonishment, lament, and praise; who demands and fulfills. Scripture can in no wise be confirmed as having formal authority in advance, so that the content becomes important only at a secondary stage of the process. The text in its many forms—particularly in the law's demand and the gospel's promise—uses this material way of doing business to validate its authority. (Bayer-L 69)

As another German theologian has put the matter:

The authority of Scripture can always and only be discovered in the validity of its substantive content. To cite one example, we do not believe in Christ because of the formal binding force of Scripture, but rather Scripture first becomes authority for us by and in the fact that it certifies Christ to us. (Elert 26)

Moreover, the Bible did not fall out of heaven as a complete document. It emerged gradually over time, and many, many human voices and hands were involved in its production and transmission. From one perspective, the Bible is in its entirety a collection of human documents. From another perspective, these diverse human writings are the means by which God continues to address human beings with his divine words of law, wisdom, and promise. In this sense, too, they reflect the humility and condescension of the living Word of God in Jesus himself, who also authoritatively addressed human beings. "These conditions under which the word of God exists cannot be improved or overcome by any kind of theories of inspiration, or by arguments that are designed to protect the Bible from its 'humanity.' Faith always discovers the revelation of God in 'secret,' in the human covering that hides it" (Aulén 365).

Likewise, there are significant problems with the position that the Bible is without error of any kind, a position that is actually a fairly recent development in the history of Christianity. Instead of seeing the authority of Scripture in its prophetic and apostolic witness to the truth of the gospel for the sake of creating trust in God, this position insists that Scripture is without error in all matters of which it speaks, even history and science. Whereas the Roman Catholic Church developed the doctrine of papal infallibility at the First Vatican Council (1870), some Protestants have developed the doctrine of biblical infallibility and inerrancy. To guarantee the truth and certainty of faith, one must first have a perfect and absolute authority in either the pope or the Bible. Those who hold the latter position often use the following syllogism: (1) God is the primary author of the Bible; (2) God cannot err; therefore, (3) the Bible is without error.

But this position of inerrancy does not stand up to careful scrutiny. First, it must be frankly acknowledged that the Bible does contain minor errors and contradictions. The writings of the prophets contain some errors of historical fact, since they were first spoken in various places and times, by individual prophets who were separated by time and space from other prophets, and only written down at a later time. If one compares the histories of the kings that are given in the OT books of First and Second Kings with the histories of the same kings that are given in the OT books of First and Second Chronicles, there are many apparent errors of historical fact that come to light. Frequently the high numbers of those involved in biblical events are literal errors and must be understood as hyperbole. Many of the reports about the same event in the canonical gospels conflict with each other and cannot be harmonized. For example, how many individuals did the women encounter when they came to the tomb of Jesus? One "angel" who is sitting on the stone, as in Matthew 28.2ff.? One "young man" who is not on the stone but inside the tomb, as in Mark 16.5? "Two men" who suddenly stood beside the women inside the tomb, as in Luke 24.4? In John's account (20.1ff.), only Mary Magdalene initially went to the tomb and she encountered no angel or young man or young men. There is no way to harmonize these four individual accounts of the same event. Where did Peter deny Christ? John's account cannot be squared with the accounts of the same event in Matthew, Mark, and Luke. The Gospel of Matthew (27.9) wrongly attributes a quotation to Jeremiah instead of Zechariah. The journey of Jesus described in Mark 7.31 is geographically impossible (suggesting that the author of the Gospel of Mark never lived in Palestine, let alone actually knew firsthand about Jesus' words and deeds). James 2.24 seemingly contradicts the clear teaching of Paul that a person is justified by faith "apart from works" (Gal. 2.16; Rom. 3.28; a teaching that is a consistent theme in the authentic letters of Paul). Hebrews 6.1–3 is contradicted by 1 John 1.9, which indicates that there is always an opportunity to repent of one's sins and seek Christ's forgiveness. From the perspective of modern cosmology, the Bible contains errant understandings of the physical universe. There is nothing in Scripture that teaches a heliocentric solar system. Many passages literally teach the immobility of the earth, and several teach the movement of the sun around the earth. Many biblical passages indicate the earth is founded on pillars or an immovable foundation. From the perspective of modern biology, Jesus' statement in Mark 4.31 ("...the mustard seed... is the smallest of all the seeds on the earth..."), is inaccurate. Many other such examples of tiny inaccuracies or errors in the Scriptures could be given. Then, too, one notes how contemporary individuals rightly object to some outdated teachings in the Bible that support the ongoing subordination of slaves to masters and of women to men, teachings that are contradicted by the gospel promise that is given in Gal. 3.28 and other biblical texts that support the full equality and dignity of human beings.

Second, the doctrine of the verbal inspiration and inerrancy of the Bible tends to level the biblical writings and to give them an equal importance. This "leveling" ends up turning the Bible into an absolute legal authority, whose commands and exhortations in their entirety are binding for all times and places. Not only does such a leveling downplay the distinction between the law and the gospel within the biblical writings, but it ignores the fact that some biblical passages of divine gospel "cross out" other biblical passages and open them up for alternative understandings and applications over time. Some biblical commands, for example, can no longer be understood and applied in the present because they presuppose a different social and political ordering from modern ones. Even many apostolic commands within the NT no longer have the same meaning or application as they had in the first centuries of the church. Slavery has been abolished. No one today talks about eating (or not eating) food "offered to idols." Christians today eat food with blood in it. Modern liberal democracy has done away with hierarchical understandings of political authority. Women have the same equal standing and spiritual responsibility before God as men, and so on. The ethical exhortations within the NT apostolic texts provide a pattern for contemporary reflection on how those exhortations might be understood and applied today in very different circumstances from the first-century church, but they cannot be viewed on the same level as the proclamation of the gospel and the promise of the new creation in and through the crucified and risen Christ. The ethical exhortations in the NT cannot be directly applied to contemporary situations without careful attention to the historical and cultural distance that exists between them and those situations.

One may certainly affirm the prophetic and apostolic Scriptures to be the only infallible rule of Christian faith and life, because they teach faithfully and with clarity the truth of the gospel which God wanted recorded for the sake of creating and sustaining faith in Christ, but the entirety of the Bible cannot serve as that infallible rule. If the Christian Bible is not a perfectly consistent set of documents, at least with respect to matters of history, science, and geography, and even in matters of theological teaching and ethical exhortation, most Christians insist that its basic, overall message is clear and consistent: God judges sin and sinners, yet God loves and forgives sinners for Christ's sake and will not let them go. In this respect, the Bible will not mislead one; it can be trusted to impart the truth of the gospel in a reliable manner (Peters 63; see also the similar position in Rahner 375–7).

Historicism

Another position on biblical authority that has also been criticized is sometimes called "**historicism**." This view treats the Bible only and entirely as a humanly constructed set of documents and denies or brackets out of consideration the theological, supra-historical dimension within these writings and their witness to divine revelation. Accordingly, historical events are entirely a matter of human actions, one is to be skeptical and critical toward claims of the miraculous, to be critical in discerning what really happened in the past and why, to weigh historical evidence, and to understand the historical, this-worldly connections and influences between Ancient Near Eastern cultures and the contents of the Christian Bible.

Ernst Troeltsch (1865–1923) has classically summarized the historicist perspective by stressing **three principles** of historical criticism that every historian ought to follow: (1) the principle of criticism or methodical doubt, which implies that historical reconstruction is always a matter of probability and not certainty; (2) the principle of analogy, which implies that every historical event bears some similarity to all other events and that what occurs today may serve as a reliable norm for what has occurred in the past; and (3) the principle of correlation, which implies that all historical events are interrelated within a chain of natural causes and effects.[6] Of course, if one applied these principles without qualification to the historical investigation of the Christian Bible one would have to deny (or at least bracket out) the possibility of a properly theological cause within history, including the possibility of any divine miracle within nature or history. The historicist's view of history, which is sometimes also called "historical positivism" (which rejects metaphysics and theism in the practice of historical science), "precludes that the Bible's own view of history could be true."[7]

To be sure, the apostolic witness to Jesus as the crucified and risen Christ invites critical reflection on the historical person of Jesus and on

---

[6] Ernst Troeltsch, "Historical and Dogmatic Method in Theology," in *Religion in History*, trans. James Luther Adams (Minneapolis: Fortress Press, 1991), 13–15. For a more recent articulation of a similar position in relation to Christian theology, see Van A. Harvey, *The Historian and the Believer: The Morality of Historical Knowledge and Belief* (Urbana, IL: University of Illinois Press, 1996).

[7] Edgar Krentz, *The Historical-Critical Method* (Minneapolis: Fortress Press Press, 1975), 61.

his reported words and actions. Such reflection, especially since the seventeenth century, has led to a greater awareness of the cultural and historical distance that exists between contemporary biblical interpreters and that which they strive to understand historically and make clear in the present. In light of this awareness the historical-critical method of biblical interpretation has contributed to new and lasting insights into the historical character of the biblical texts and their contents. The use of that method is one of the great developments within the history of Christian theology (Tillich 2.107).[8] It has helped to disclose the fact that the written sources for the historical figure of Jesus, to varying degrees, have been shaped by theological interests and perspectives that have more or less concealed Jesus "as he really was" behind "the Christ" as he has been proclaimed by the believing church. The method has thus helped to expose the tensions between the so-called "Jesus of history" (first-century Palestinian Jew) and the theological-dogmatic understandings of "the Christ of faith" (the significance of Jesus for Christian faith) that was gradually clarified and defined in the NT and early church creeds and confessions in the centuries after Jesus' life, and to seek to understand Jesus as he actually was in his original historical context. The method has also helped to highlight the tensions and contradictions that exist between the supernatural worldview(s) in the Bible and modern, scientific worldviews, and to wrestle with these differences.

Somewhat ironically, the use of the historical method to investigate the history of scholarly inquiries into the historical Jesus has itself disclosed how the presuppositions of historians often pre-determined the sort of "Jesus" the scholar set out to find. Nearly every historian in search of the historical Jesus, attempting to be rational and historical and free of illusion, discovered a Jesus that reflected the historian's own values and ideals.[9] The

---

[8] See also Gerhard Ebeling, "The Significance of the Critical Historical Method for Church and Theology in Protestantism," in *Word and Faith*, 17–61. While modern Protestants have used the historical-critical method since the seventeenth and eighteenth centuries, its use in the Roman Catholic Church has only been officially authorized by the Pope since 1943. See the papal encyclical, *Divino afflante spiritu* (Denzinger 3825–31 [754–7]).

[9] This is one of the abiding conclusions of Albert Schweitzer's classic investigation of the historical-critical study of Jesus. See Albert Schweitzer, *The Quest for the Historical Jesus*, ed. John Bowden, trans. William Montgomery and others (Minneapolis: Augsburg Fortress Press, 2001). Schweitzer's own ideals regarding the nature of the historical method and his understanding of Jesus as a failed apocalyptic prophet determined his own evaluation of the scholars he investigated. Schweitzer judges all of the figures in his book by how well they contributed to the liberation of the historical method from supernaturalism, to the recognition that the synoptic gospels are more valuable as historical sources than the gospel of John, and to the triumph of the eschatological view of Jesus

scholar looking for Jesus "behind" the apostolic writings ended up creating a Jesus after his or her own heart, all in the name of the strict canons of historical investigation, the principles of rational and historical criticism, and the denial of divine action within history.

One consequence of the historicist position is "the eclipse of the biblical narrative," when the supposed historical facts "behind" the biblical writings became more central than the biblical narrative itself.[10] The canonical gospels are not really historical sources that will give us a "life," much less a "biography" of the historical Jesus. That is not their purpose. The Jesus of history remains concealed behind the apostolic witness to his theological significance. Following the insights of the nineteenth-century biblical scholar, Martin Kähler (1835–1912), one has to note that the canonical gospels—from beginning to end—are not merely concerned with Jesus as he was in his historical time, but with Jesus as he now is, namely, the real and living, risen Christ who is decisively significant for Christian faith.[11] The gospels then are expansions of the apostolic kerygma into narrative forms, whose goal is the creation and sustenance of faith in the living Christ (Jn 20.31: "These are written so that you may believe that Jesus is the Messiah, the Son of God, and that by believing you may have life in his name.") This point was made by another nineteenth-century scholar, Johannes von Hofmann, who argued that historical criticism, at least in an historicist-positivist framework, does not allow the interpreter of the church's Scriptures to be open to the present experience of faith in the living, risen Christ, as confessed by the apostles, as formed in the historic divine liturgies, and as clarified in the dogmatic history of the church. In this regard, the canonical gospels share the apostles' kerygmatic goals and have as their presupposition an experience that goes beyond the bounds of the principles of historical positivism. This experience is itself the precondition for understanding the continuity between Jesus' preaching, the apostles' preaching of Jesus, the orthodox and catholic divine liturgies, and the development of Christological dogma in the history of the church.

---

over against the non-eschatological view. (For Schweitzer Jesus was a world-denying apocalyptic preacher whose announcement of the coming kingdom of God predicted the imminent end of the world.) See Matthew L. Becker, "Schweitzer's Quests for Jesus and Paul," *Concordia Journal* 28 (October 2002), 409–30.

[10] See Hans Frei, *The Eclipse of the Biblical Narrative* (New Haven: Yale University Press, 1974).

[11] Martin Kähler, *The So-called Historical Jesus and the Historic Biblical Christ*, trans. Carl Braaten (Minneapolis: Fortress Press Press, 1964).

It must be frankly stated, then, that "Jesus of Nazareth as he really was," as uncovered only by historical research, cannot be "the norm of what is Christian today," since that norm would inevitably be a modern construct of the historian's own making.[12] The essential significance of the homol-ogoumena and their theological meanings are tied to the apostolic witness which is thoroughly and without remainder a witness to the significance of Christ for Christian faith.

The scholarly overview of "the quest for the historical Jesus" by Albert Schweitzer (1875–1965) demonstrates that in the history of investigating the gospels many have been overconfident in the use of their reason to uncover historical facts behind the canonical writings. Perhaps contrary to Schweitzer's own historicist ideals, his narrative discloses that the truth of the gospel is of a different character than the truths that human reason is capable of discovering on its own. While the correct responses to Enlightenment rationalism and historicist positivism cannot be irrationalism or anti-rationalism or anti-historical inquiry, one's rational investigation of Holy Scripture ought to be humble and self-critical in the face of apparent facts and realities that go beyond the domain of the sciences and the strict canons of historical-critical investigation. Certainly, the principles of the Enlightenment ought not to be rejected in toto, but their limitations ought to be recognized.

The investigation of reported miracles in the apostolic witness, including the investigation into the claim of Jesus' resurrection from the dead, cannot presuppose from the outset that the divine reality is incapable of working beyond the normal course of secondary causes in nature, as if the universe is closed-off from God's ongoing, active involvement. While God usually works through natural means, God also intervenes in creation, according to the uniform testimony of the biblical prophets and apostolic witnesses. Because God is the Creator of nature and the general order of things (often called "the laws of nature"), God is responsible for them but is not always subject to them. God can act directly without the intervention of secondary causes (ODCC 1091 ["miracle"]).

---

[12] This sentence is directed against the contrary assertion by Lüdemann, *Heretics*, 207. "History" and "dogma" need not necessarily be mutually exclusive, especially since every understanding of "history" contains assumptions about what is true, real, and significant.

Aestheticism

Another position on biblical authority that also needs to be criticized is the one that views the Bible merely as a literary "classic." In this view, the Bible is understood only as a great piece of world literature. This position is "**aestheticism**," since it is concerned only with the artistic, literary qualities of the biblical writings and avoids understanding the writings as they were originally intended and as they continue to be read by the faith communities that treasure them and use them theologically.

Of course appreciating the Bible's aesthetic qualities is laudable and perhaps even necessary, given how many people in the western world today are unfamiliar with even the most basic of biblical stories and figures. The four-hundredth anniversary of the publication of the so-called King James Bible served as an opportunity for scholars to note the huge cultural influence, especially on English literature and the development of the English language, that that particular version of the Bible has had.[13] Other scholars, too, have provided helpful analysis of the literary and narrative aspects of the biblical texts.[14] These aspects are often unrecognized or unknown by many young people in the American context today.

While appreciating the Bible as great world literature, and underscoring its significant influence on the development of Western culture, art, and literature, are worthy endeavors, there are at least two problematic consequences from this approach. First, the historical dimensions of the Bible can easily be ignored in favor of merely understanding it as a collection of literary texts. Schweitzer's analysis of the thesis by David F. Strauss (1808–74), who held that the written gospels contain religious-mythic ideas that appear to be "historical" but are really the product of human imagination, and Schweitzer's criticism of the purely literary approaches of Bruno Bauer (1809–82) and William Wrede (1859–1906), should be a warning to those who want to adopt non- or anti-historical approaches to the gospels.[15] A purely literary approach to the gospels and other historical writings in the

---

[13] The anniversary year witnessed the publication of several important studies, but in general see Gordon Campbell, *Bible: The Story of the King James Version 1611–2011* (Oxford: Oxford University Press, 2010); and David Crystal, *Begat: The King James Bible and the English Language* (Oxford: Oxford University Press, 2010).

[14] The literature here is extensive, but in general see, for example, Robert Alter and Frank Kermode, eds., *The Literary Guide to the Bible* (Cambridge: Harvard University Press, 1990); and Robert Alter, *The Art of Biblical Narrative*, 2nd edn (New York: Basic Books, 2011).

[15] Bauer held that the Gospel of Mark was purely a literary invention of a single author who created the fictional character of Jesus. Likewise Wrede held that the so-called "Messianic secret" in Mark,

Bible, one that is unwilling or unable to address historical-critical questions, leads necessarily to consistent skepticism about Jesus as an historical figure. At least this is what Schweitzer's study demonstrates. Second, this aesthetic approach can lead people to downplay or even ignore the place of the Christian Bible within the Christian communities and the theological claims that are made there. Christian communities do not treat the Bible merely as literature but as a "normative witness to the acts of the living God for our salvation" (Migliore 50). The theological purpose of the Scriptures is to elicit and strengthen faith in Christ to the glory of God.

The living Jesus of the apostolic kerygma always escapes the grasp of the person who would attempt to understand Jesus purely historically or purely literarily, but at present it seems that the emphasis has shifted toward the literary end of the spectrum and thus there is the need to be reminded that the canonical gospels are witnesses to events that the disciples "saw and heard" (Acts 4.20). While everything in the gospels was *shaped* by the disciples' experience of the death and resurrection of Jesus, not everything in the texts is the *result* of that experience. Their experience of the risen Christ did not do away with their memories of Jesus prior to his crucifixion. It is a huge stretch to conclude that their memories were faulty or that their motives for speaking and acting were deceptive, especially when one considers the risks that the disciples took for such speaking and acting.

Subjectivism

A final problematic position regarding biblical authority can be labeled "**subjectivism**." This occurs when the individual treats the Bible in such a manner that it merely and completely confirms what he or she already holds to be true and valid. In that way, the Bible becomes merely a mirror of the self and of one's individualistic values and ideas, rather than that which also speaks over against the individual and calls the individual into question. Subjectivism holds that there is no external meaning within the biblical writings and that interpretation is really just a matter of the self who imposes meaning on the text or discovers a meaning that suits the autonomous individual who is beholden to no external authority.

To be sure, every interpreter of the biblical writings, whether that one is a Christian believer or not, brings his or her presuppositions to the Bible that

---

wherein Jesus tells his disciples not to tell anyone that he is the Christ, was a literary invention in the early church, thus also undermining Mark as a source for the historical Jesus.

shape and inform his or her understanding of the Bible. Bultmann rightly argued that every interpreter ought to come to the task of interpreting the Bible "without presupposing the results" of one's exegesis ("leading out" the meaning[s] of a biblical text), but he also noted that "no exegesis is without presuppositions, because the exegete is not a *tabula rasa* but approaches the text with specific questions or with a specific way of asking questions and thus has a certain idea of the subject matter with which the text is concerned." [16] One of the first to note this personal dimension within biblical interpretation was Hofmann, who articulated the necessity for an existential, personal relationship to the basic message of the Christian Bible and to the history of biblical interpretation within Christian communities. According to Hofmann, the interpreter cannot avoid a personal relationship with that which is interpreted, if he or she wishes to gain a fuller understanding of that "other." The question, then, is: which are the most appropriate hermeneutical presuppositions that are the conditions for proper theological understanding?[17] Those who think they interpret without Christian presuppositions have merely replaced those traditional presuppositions with some other kind of presupposition. While some historians have called for "the death of the self" in the quest for "objective" historical knowledge, Hofmann recognized that the self is inescapably part of theological understanding. The interpreter is not a *tabula rasa*, a blank

---

[16] Rudolf Bultmann, "Is Exegesis Without Presuppositions Possible?," in *New Testament & Mythology and Other Basic Writings*, ed. and trans. Schubert M. Ogden (Minneapolis: Fortress Press, 1984), 145. See also Werner Jeanrond, *Theological Hermeneutics: Development and Significance* (London: SCM Press, 1994), 137–48; and Hans-Georg Gadamer, *Truth and Method*, 2d edn, trans. J. Weinsheimer and D. G. Marshall (New York: Crossroad, 1989), 331–41.

[17] Hofmann's concern to articulate an adequate theological-biblical hermeneutic that takes seriously the presuppositions of the interpreter, especially the historicity and faith commitment of the interpreter, as well as the need to understand the history of the effects of the scriptural events/texts in shaping Christian self-understanding, is similar to concerns voiced in recent discussions of hermeneutics by and about Hans-Georg Gadamer and Paul Ricoeur. See Becker, *The Self-Giving God and Salvation History*, 59ff. For a cogent critique of Gadamer and Ricoeur that takes seriously the positive contributions of each thinker, see Werner Jeanrond, *Text and Interpretation as Categories of Theological Thinking* (New York: Crossroad, 1991), 64–72. See also Kathryn Tanner, *Theories of Culture: A New Agenda for Theology* (Minneapolis: Fortress Press Press, 1997), 131–5. Tanner is particularly critical of Gadamer's false assumption that "tradition" is an "object," i.e. that "traditional materials… are found, discovered, or received, and not constructed in a significant sense. Post-modern cultural theory makes the important claim that traditions are invented, meaning by that not merely that traditional materials are often new rather than old and borrowed rather than indigenous, but that they are always products of human decision in a significant sense" (ibid., 133). Gadamer and Hofmann acknowledge, however, that construals of "tradition" encompass an open-ended process of human decision-making that is always in need of revision. Furthermore, while "traditions" are the product of individual decisions, they are certainly also "trans-individual" and formative of individuals.

slate, on which the Bible can paint itself, but he or she enters into the process of interpretation as the one he or she is. Indeed, the process of interpretation is both a seeking to understand that which is other than oneself but also a seeking of self-understanding. In the end, one cannot properly speak of God theologically without being caught up in this speech with one's whole being.

This process of interpretation leads to what is commonly called "**the hermeneutical circle**." All interpreters find themselves within such a circle when they endeavor to understand a text: One has a pre-understanding or expectation of the text one is to understand which one cannot avoid bringing to the text.[18] Through one's encounter with the text, one discovers this pre-understanding confirmed to a certain degree, yet never to the point that one's pre-understanding is simply confirmed *in toto*.[19] It is this latter aspect, of allowing the biblical text to speak to the self, to question the self and its values and assumptions, and to place the self into a larger, transpersonal, theological framework that leads the individual away from subjectivism and solipsism.

The interpretational reflections of **Paul Ricoeur** are particularly helpful in this regard. According to Ricoeur, all interpretation moves through a circular process, from "guessing" to "validation," and then from "expla-nation" of the other to "self-understanding" by means of the encounter with a text that is other than one's self. More recently, Ricoeur has shown how all understanding follows an "arc" that begins with an initial pre-understanding of reality that we bring to the text, the restructuring and reconfiguring of this initial understanding of reality by the text, and the final intersection between the world configured by the text and the world of the interpreter.[20] This hermeneutical circle need not be "vicious" (imposing a narrative and theological order where there is not one) or tautological (merely confirming

---

[18] For a discussion of hermeneutical "pre-understanding," see Gadamer, *Truth and Method*, 265–307; Jeanrond, *Text and Interpretation*, 12–22; and Tracy, *Plurality and Ambiguity*, 16–27. "A person who is trying to understand a text is always projecting. He projects a meaning for the text as a whole as soon as some initial meaning emerges in the text. Again, the initial meaning emerges only because he is reading the text with particular expectations in regard to a certain meaning. Working out this fore-projection, which is constantly revised in terms of what emerges as he penetrates into the meaning, is understanding what is there" (Gadamer, *Truth and Method*, 267). Of course, the challenge is: "How can a text be protected against misunderstanding from the start?" (ibid., 268).

[19] See Paul Ricoeur, "Explanation and Understanding," in *Interpretation Theory: Discourse and the Surplus of Meaning* (Fort Worth: Texas Christian University Press, 1976), 71–88.

[20] Paul Ricoeur, *Time and Narrative*, 3 vols, trans. Kathleen Blamey and David Pellauer (Chicago: University of Chicago Press, 1984–8), 1.52–87.

what one already knows about oneself and another), but a dialectical process that leads to new understanding of the self and others and opens up a responsible ethic of speaking and acting.[21]

The goal of authentic biblical interpretation must remain *exegesis* (pronounced "ex-uh-jesus"), of leading out the meanings that the biblical texts themselves have for the individual and, beyond the individual, the message that the Scriptures have for others and for the whole world. What one ought to avoid is *eisegesis* (pronounced "ice-uh-jesus"), that is, "reading into" the Bible the individualistic, private meanings one wants to find there that merely confirm what one already values and believes. *Eisegesis* always results in the twisting and distorting of biblical passages to suit one's own ends, which are often synonymous with an extra-biblical ideology. One merely uses the Bible to make it say what one wants it to say without any regard for what the passage likely meant in the past and how it has been understood over time. To avoid this kind of subjective distortion in one's reading of the Bible, there have developed over time certain basic principles of biblical interpretation, the use of which in communities of faith and scholarship can help to ward off interpretive error and mistaken uses of the Bible (as when the Bible is used to oppress people).

Theological hermeneutics

The apostolic Scriptures are the principal source of Christian theology and the sole norm of theology in their witness to the gospel, and the canonical writings of the OT are the second main source, yet these Scriptures are always in need of careful interpretation so that their normative meaning(s) emerge(s) more clearly. Because of the historical and cultural distance between the Scriptures and contemporary interpreters of the Scriptures, there is a need for clear interpretive principles or **hermeneutics**. Hermeneutics thus refers to these interpretive principles that have been defined through the centuries and assist the process of "translating" texts, "interpreting" them, "explaining" them. These principles

---

[21] Paul Ricoeur, *Oneself as Another*, trans. Kathleen Blamey (Chicago: University of Chicago Press, 1992). See also Ricoeur's own execution of the interpretation of specific biblical texts in *Figuring the Sacred: Religion, Narrative, and Imagination*, ed. Mark I. Wallace, trans. David Pellauer (Minneapolis: Fortress Press, 1995), 129ff., and in Paul Ricoeur and André LaCocque, *Thinking Biblically: Exegetical and Hermeneutical Studies*, trans. David Pellauer (Chicago: University of Chicago Press, 1998).

have received special attention, however, in the wake of the changed intellectual situation of the modern period. In a broader sense "hermeneutics" also refers to the process of understanding itself. Below are some of the more important hermeneutical principles that are typically followed in Christian theology.

A *primary hermeneutical principle* is that **Scripture interprets Scripture** (*Sacra scriptura sui ipsius interpres*). This principle implies first that the clearer passages in Scripture are to shed light on the less clear. The clarity or perspicuity of Scripture does not mean, however, that everything in Scripture is clear and plain to all, only that what is essential to salvation, namely the gospel and faith, are clearly and plainly taught in the apostolic writings (Schmid 69). While the "perspicuity of Scripture does not exclude its need for exposition" (Heppe 33), the teaching/preaching of the apostles is always clear witness to Christ and to what he has done for us for the sake of eliciting faith. This is what makes the teaching of an apostle "apostolic." This is why gospel passages in the apostolic writings are the "clearest" passages in the NT. The "clearest" biblical passages are always passages of gospel promise/proclamation.

This initial hermeneutical principle also means that the biblical text itself "causes one to pay attention" (Bayer-L 68), that the text itself has a priority over the interpreter, that it makes a claim upon the interpreter, and that it persists as an infallible norm while changing those whom it interprets. "It is not the interpreter who makes sense of the text or makes the text understandable. The text itself needs to say what it has to say for itself" (Bayer-L 69). This engagement is not a matter of oppressing the interpreter but of revealing who the interpreter is before God, of interpreting the interpreter, of opening that one up to the promise of the gospel.

A *second fundamental hermeneutical principle* involves what has traditionally been called "**the analogy of faith**" (*analogia fidei*) and "the rule of Christian love": a passage cannot be so interpreted that it goes contrary to the clear and essential content of Christian faith, that is, faith in the gospel promises of God and the dictates of Christian love. Thus, the second hermeneutical principle is a correlative of the first: the analogy of faith is identical to faith/confidence in the clearly promised gospel and the clearly taught "faith that is active in love" (Gal. 6). This principle implies that the normative meaning of any scriptural text is only discerned in relation to the hermeneutical-theological task of properly distinguishing God's law from God's gospel promise and of underscoring the mercy and love of God that is the basis for one's love of the neighbor. "Whoever thinks that he understands the divine Scriptures or any part of them so that it does not build the double love of God and of our neighbor does not understand it at all."[22]

Through the two-fold focus on "faith apart from works of the law" and "faith that is active in love" one keeps central the teaching that the prophetic and apostolic writings authenticate themselves in the life of an individual via "the internal witness of the Holy Spirit" (*testimonium spiritus sancti internum*). The Scriptures are authenticated precisely in their actions upon individuals and groups of individuals: acting as God's word of law that reveals that one is a sinner; acting as God's word of gospel that promises forgiveness, life, and salvation in Christ alone; and acting to summon the forgiven sinner to allow his or her faith to be active in love toward others. This hermeneutical principle thus acknowledges that biblical interpretation is always about making proper distinctions. The Scriptures in their totality cannot be identified as the truth of the gospel since the Biblical canon bears witness to the law of God and to apostolic exhortations that are based on the gospel but not identical to the gospel. The varying messages of God that are communicated and revealed in the Scriptures must be sharply distinguished from each other in order to arrive at a normative interpretation of a scriptural text. To confuse the law and the promise is to misunderstand and misapply the Scriptures; to confuse gospel and apostolic exhortation on the basis of the gospel is to misunderstand and misapply the Scriptures. Although law, gospel, and apostolic exhortation originate in God and relate to all of creation, the gospel message "contradicts" and "out-criticizes" the other messages by means of God's critical work on the cross of Jesus. The proclamation of the gospel "crosses out" the communication of judgment and invites all the ungodly to trust and believe that they are forgiven and acceptable to God for the sake of Christ crucified. The truth of the gospel, which overcomes the truth of the law, is the hope and life of Christian faith and the focal point of the interpretation of Scripture and the discipline of theology. The truth of the gospel always then leads to exhortations about Christian love, but even these exhortations should not be confused with the truth of the gospel itself. The gift of gospel freedom is to be lived in freedom, only not in a way that serves the sinful self (Gal. 5.13). "Freedom is found not in the law, not in the individual, not in escape from the world, but in the

---

[22] Augustine of Hippo, *On Christian Doctrine*, trans. D. W. Robertson (New York: Liberal Arts Press, 1958), 30.

love of Jesus Christ that we receive, which through faith in him becomes in turn the love we show to others."[23]

Since both law and gospel are bound tightly together in the Scriptures, it is easy to mix them up in such a way that the gospel promise gets lost. The legal dimension of the Scriptures is always about the commending of good works and love, whereas the promissory dimension is always about the commending of God's mercy because of Christ, his work, and his love. The challenge of contemporary biblical interpretation is to keep God's law and gospel in their original, divinely-intended order: the divine law as subordinate and sub-dominant; the divine gospel as ultimate and dominant. While both the law and the gospel are divine truths that are in tension with one another, God intends the promise always to have the final say.[24] Whenever the divine law has the last word, the divine promise gets displaced, left out, or worse, totally abandoned. To end up with the law, in all of its threatening power, is to make a shipwreck of faith. For the sake of faith, God subordinates the divine, accusing law to the divine gospel promise. In this way God reconciles God's wrath and mercy in Jesus Christ, crucified and risen for the sake of sinners. This law-gospel ordering is a basic key to the interpretation of Holy Scripture.

A third principle is the need to pay attention to how a given Scriptural passage has been interpreted in the history of the church and how the narratives within the Scriptures have been understood within the communities of biblical faith, inclusive of both Judaism and Christianity. The Christian Scriptures are the church's book. The normative meaning of a scriptural text is therefore partially dependent on the history of the interpretation of that scriptural text within the history of Christian traditions. This involves also listening to how the Bible has been, and is being, understood within communities that are far removed from one's local setting and even one's immediate faith tradition. Such listening is not merely a matter of ecumenical engagement with biblical interpretations from beyond one's confessional tradition, it also involves listening to how people in Africa, South America, Asia, and other non-Western cultures read the Bible with their sets of eyes and ears, especially when their understandings challenge

---

[23] Gerhard Ebeling, *The Truth of the Gospel: An Exposition of Galatians*, trans. David Green (Minneapolis: Fortress Press Press, 1985), 243

[24] No one recently has stressed this point more fully than Robert Bertram (1921–2003). For example, see Robert W. Bertram, "How a Lutheran Does Theology: Some Clues from the Lutheran Confessions," in *Lutheran-Episcopal Dialogue: Report and Recommendations*, William G. Weinhauer and Robert L. Wietelman (eds) (Cincinnati: Forward Movement Publications, 1981), 73–87.

the comfortable readings of the Bible by western, affluent Christians and draw attention to how the Bible has been used oppressively against women, the poor, and marginalized people from other cultures. Then, too, as a result of such listening, the Christian theologian cannot help but be affected in his or her theological understanding by this engagement with the world, its problems, and sufferings. Dietrich Bonhoeffer (1906–45) refers to this changed perspective that came to him and fellow conspirators through their experiences of suffering and oppression, a change that certainly had implications for how Bonhoeffer himself interpreted the Bible and articulated theological understanding:

> It remains an experience of incomparable value that we have for once learned to see the great events of world history from below, from the perspective of the outcasts, the suspects, the maltreated, the powerless, the oppressed and reviled, in short from the perspective of the suffering. If only during this time bitterness and envy have not corroded the heart; that we come to see matters great and small, happiness and misfortune, strength and weakness with new eyes; that our sense for greatness, humanness, justice and mercy has grown clearer, freer, more incorruptible; that we learn, indeed, that personal suffering is a more useful key, a more fruitful principle than personal happiness for exploring the meaning of the world in contemplation and action. But this perspective from below must not lead us to become advocates for those who are perpetually dissatisfied. Rather, out of a higher satisfaction, which in its essence is grounded beyond what is below and above, we do justice to life in all its dimensions and in this way affirm it.[25]

While church tradition and the history of biblical interpretation in the various Christian communities and their contexts help to inform contemporary interpretation and theological understanding in one's own context, the former cannot rigidly determine the latter. If church tradition, including the history of biblical interpretation, is indeed a source of theological understanding, it cannot finally be a norm. This issue remains a point of contention between Protestants, who insist on the priority and sufficiency of Scripture to interpret itself, and Roman Catholics, who teach that the Scriptures are to be interpreted authoritatively by the church's teaching office, ultimately centered in the office of the papacy. Augustine stressed that not only had the orthodox and catholic church decided what is and is

---

[25] Dietrich Bonhoeffer, "After Ten Years" [1942], in *Letters and Papers from Prison*, 52.

not Holy Scripture, this authoritative church alone provided the authentic interpretation of those Scriptures. "I would not believe the Gospel unless the authority of the Catholic Church moved me."[26] While Aquinas held that Christian theology is always a mix of biblical argument, correct opinions of the church fathers, and true propositions from Aristotle, the Roman Church alone establishes and guarantees the normative character of official Church doctrine over against theological errors. Even Ockham, who was otherwise on occasion critical of the pope and his errors, finally appealed to the Roman Church as the one arbiter of true doctrine: "I submit myself and my words to the correction of the Catholic Church."[27] Gabriel Biel (1420–95) echoed Ockham when he stated that there could never be any real opposition between statements in Holy Scripture and the official doctrines of the Roman Church. For each of these theologians the truth which Holy Mother Church defines as catholic and orthodox is to be believed with the same respect and devotion as the truth expressed in the Holy Scriptures. Opposition or tension, let alone contradiction, between sacred Scripture and the authority of the Roman Church is simply out of the question. The true meaning of Scripture had to be compatible within the total context of the Church's doctrinal teachings and decisions and had to be interpreted in harmony with them.[28]

Martin Luther's experience led him to a very different conclusion. The church, comprised of fallible individuals, could indeed develop errant theological understandings, as could even the Pope. Luther's investigations into the history of dogmatic developments within the church led him to see a wide gap between "what Scripture teaches" and "what the Roman Catholic Church teaches." While technically Rome's position on papal infallibility did not achieve dogmatic status until the First Vatican Council (1870–1), the argument that Johann Eck (1486–1543) set forth against Luther was consistent with that doctrinal trajectory wherein the pope is Christ's official representative on earth and thus the final earthly authority for what constitutes catholic doctrine. Eck's arguments forced Luther to assert that the authority of the Roman Church is subordinate to the authority of the canonical Scriptures themselves. If Luther had ever heard the old one-liner,

---

[26] Augustine, *Against the "Foundation Letter" of the Manichees*, 5 in *Corpus scriptorum ecclesiasticorum latinorum* (Vienna, 1866–), 25.197.

[27] Quoted in Gerrish, "The Word of God and the Words of Scripture," *The Old Protestantism and the New*, 53.

[28] Bernhard Lohse, *Martin Luther: An Introduction to His Life and Work* (Minneapolis: Fortress Press Press, 1986), 154.

"Is the Pope Catholic?," he would have responded, at least in reference to the papacy of his day, "No, he might not be 'catholic.' What is 'catholic' is what is apostolic and what is apostolic is what is Scriptural, canonical. What is ecclesial, traditional, institutional, and 'papal' may conflict with what is biblical."

Protestants insist that the teaching of the apostles is securely grounded in the biblical canon, yet such grounding does not imply that future church leaders and bishops, including the bishop of Rome, are incapable of committing theological and ecclesial errors against that biblical teaching under any circumstance. The sole reliable means and sole authority for preserving and transmitting the truths of God's Word rest in the biblical canon alone ("*sola Scriptura*," "Scripture alone"), although of course the biblical canon is never alone in actual practice. Every human being is unreliable when it comes to preserving and passing along the truth of God's Word. This human unreliability necessitated the development of the biblical canon in the first place, to serve as an external norm for church leaders and communities.

More recently, statements have emerged from official Lutheran-Roman Catholic dialogues that rightly stress the primacy of Scripture as the principal source and ground of authentic church tradition. Nevertheless, there is still ongoing tension between the two church groups regarding the critical function of Scriptural teaching over against perceived errant doctrinal developments within church tradition. It must be frankly acknowledged that throughout history church councils and leaders have made false and contradictory judgments about the doctrinal content of Christian faith, as have individual interpreters of the biblical texts. In light of this complex history, one must insist that every post-apostolic judgment about the essential content of Christian faith and the interpretation of biblical teaching must always be tested against the original apostolic witness itself. Indeed, every subsequent event in the history of the Christian church must be evaluated on the basis of this apostolic norm. "All interpretation, whether private or official, is measured against the truth of the subject matter, which is not decided by any one expositor but in the process of expository debate" (Pannenberg 1.15). "The content and truth of dogma [theology] do not rest, then, on the consensus of the church. Instead, knowledge of the subject matter of Scripture produces consensus" (Pannenberg 1.16).

A fourth hermeneutical principle, which is in tension with the third principle, is that the modern method of historical criticism ought to be used to uncover the historic meaning(s) in the biblical writings and to address the historical distance that exists between the ancient biblical writings and all contemporary interpreters. The use of the **historical-critical method** takes seriously the historical particularity of divine revelation and helps the interpreter to avoid projecting onto the biblical texts meanings that the historical dimension of those texts will not allow. The use of this methodology also allows the theological traditions that have developed within the history of the Christian communities to be continually evaluated in light of the historical biblical witness. The historical-critical method involves determining what the original biblical text likely was (weighing the many textual variants that emerged through the process of editing, copying, and transmitting the biblical writings); ascertaining the ancient literary form of the biblical text (more on this below); discovering, so far as possible, the original context(s) and setting(s) of the biblical text, its author(s), editor(s), hearers, and readers, and their historical circumstances; apprehending the meaning which the words had for the original author(s), hearers, and readers; and understanding the biblical passage in the light of its total context and of the background out of which it emerged.

While the use of the historical-critical method will undoubtedly shed light on passages that seem initially opaque and whose meaning(s) seem uncertain, one must also acknowledge that many biblical passages resist conclusive determination of their meaning(s). Just one example among dozens will suffice: What did Jesus mean when he told one would-be follower, who wanted first to do his duty to his father by burying him, "Let the dead bury the dead; but as for you, go and proclaim the kingdom of God" (Lk. 9.59–60)? The jury is still out on that one.

A fifth hermeneutical principle is that the normative meaning of a scriptural text only becomes clear in relation to the language and narrative structure that give literary shape to the text. The interpreter must take seriously the literary character of the biblical writings, including the fact that the biblical writings were originally written in ancient Hebrew, Aramaic, and Greek. While modern, scholarly translations effectively convey the basic and central meanings of the biblical writings, important nuances are often lost in translation. Thus, the college student who does not know the biblical languages ought to rely upon several good scholarly editions of the Bible, and not limit himself or herself to just one translation.

A couple of other principles fall under this one. Whenever possible one should affirm **the literal sense** (*sensus literalis*), that is, the straightforward, plain sense that the words seem to have, although a deeper figurative or spiritual meaning is allowable and perhaps even necessary if the passage or story states something that at the literal level is contrary to the nature of God, goes against the analogy of faith or the truths of the law and the gospel, or conflicts with obvious sense experience. With respect to biblical metaphors for God, the principle developed by Augustine, the Cappadocians, and Aquinas ought to be heeded: on the basis of a literal understanding of biblical metaphors for God we can come to an understanding of what God is not (*apophatic* or negative theology); but arriving at true comprehension of what God is is highly difficult, if not impossible. All analogies for God are always "inexpressibly surpassed" by God's nature:

> We are talking about God; so why be surprised if you cannot grasp it? I mean, if you can grasp it, it isn't God. Let us rather make a devout confession of ignorance, instead of a brash profession of knowledge. Certainly it is great bliss to have a little touch or taste of God with the mind; but completely to grasp him, to comprehend him, is utterly impossible.[29]

One should also note that the literal meaning of a biblical text might not necessarily be the meaning that finds the greatest degree of agreement within the Christian church, as the experience of Luther and other Reformers demonstrates.

Likewise, the biblical interpreter must reflect carefully about the type of literature ("**genre**") to which a given Scriptural text or passage belongs. Is it prose or poetry? Is it an address, a prayer, a monologue, a treaty, an edict, a letter? Is it an oracular saying, an invective, a lament, a liturgy, a proverb, a parable, a creed, a hymn? The biblical writers made use of many literary forms and devices (hyperbole, parable, simile, allegory, metaphoric language, fable, personification, stylized or re-created speech, e.g. Paul's speeches in Acts). The genre of a text only becomes clear in relation to other kinds of writing that are similar in form and content to the text that is being interpreted. For example, most adults instinctively make interpretive adjustments when they move from reading history to poetry, or from reading a parable to reading a novel, or from reading a trial transcript to reading a comic strip. People learn to recognize genres and to interpret them accordingly. By sensing similar features from one text to the next, one is helped to understand the nature of the text and the nature of the claims a text is making. Clear thinking about genre and rhetorical structures within texts

---

[29] Augustine of Hippo, Sermon 117, in *Sermons, The Works of St. Augustine: A Translation for the 21st Century*, Part 3, vol. 4, ed. John E. Rotelle, trans. Edmund Hill (Brooklyn, NY: New City Press, 1992), 211.

keeps the interpreter focused on the truth(s) of the genre and the purposes of the text. Clear thinking about genre and rhetorical structures keeps the interpreter from taking interpretive routes that force the text into a genre or form of writing that is foreign to the text. To misunderstand the genre of a text is to misunderstand that text. To avoid such misunderstanding, extra-biblical sources of knowledge help to eliminate false and inadequate understandings of the genres of the biblical texts. For example, the genres present in the first eleven chapters of Genesis become clearer as the stories contained in these chapters are compared with other, similar "stories of origin" from the Ancient Near East (e.g. Babylonian creation myths, the stories of Gilgamesh, extra-biblical flood stories, etc.). Discerning the genre of a text keeps the interpreter of this text from forcing it into a genre that is foreign to it. Thus, the stories in the first chapters of Genesis are not "pure myth" (as in "false story"), nor are they "historical report" (as you would find in a modern history textbook), nor do they fit within the modern genre of "scientific treatise." The texts in Genesis 1–11 make profound claims to truth without necessarily being understood as either "false story" or "pure historical description" or "scientific treatise." When encountering a text like Genesis 1–3, people might be tempted to go after its truth by reading it as a kind of history similar to the Patriarchal narratives (Gen. 12–50), but with the rise of modern science (geology, astronomy, biology, etc.) seeking the truth/meaning of Genesis 1–3 in a literal-historical reading for the *how* of creation leads to a dead end. When one identifies these chapters as "a story of origin," like the Babylonian creation myths or the Gilgamesh Epic, then Genesis 1–3 becomes accessible as a serious, profound narrative about *the what* and *why* of the origin of the cosmos as God's creation and of the enigma (mystery) of humanity's place in it.

The example of Matthew 5.27–30 may also prove illustrative. What kind of writing is this? In its context(s), what did it mean? What does it mean now? Some individuals have taken the passage quite literally, as did the college student who admitted himself to the hospital because he was missing an eye. When asked what had happened, he responded that because of Matthew 5.27–30 he had gouged out his eye after looking at pornography. "Since my eye caused me to sin, I gouged it out…" Did this young man understand these words of Jesus correctly? Would Jesus really want us to gouge out our eyes or cut off our hands? What about his statement that sin comes "from within," "out of the heart," and thus is not something that can be adequately handled merely by some external action (e.g. cutting off one's hand or gouging out one's eye)? Or what about his actions to heal people, which indicate his concern for health and physical wholeness? Most likely, this Matthean passage is hyperbolic, an exaggeration to make a point. Surely Jesus is concerned about the health and well-being of human bodies and would not want people actually to harm themselves in this way. But the more pertinent point: sin comes from the heart. Jesus' statement here is an example of his preaching of "the law," to warn and admonish his hearers out of his concern for their eternal welfare—about the urgency and seriousness of cutting out this deadly, diseased tumor of the heart. Only repentance and faith, in response to the gospel, can bring about the death of sin, not the gouging out of one's eye or the cutting off of some other body part.

A sixth and final hermeneutical principle is that one must always balance "what a text has meant in the past" with "what a text means today."[30] The awareness of the historical and cultural distance between the biblical texts and all contemporary interpreters, coupled with the awareness that the Christian churches have themselves undergone some change in theological understanding over time, leads one to be open to the possibility that a given Scriptural text may mean something different today from what it has meant in the past. For example, the statements in the Bible that reflect a pre-Copernican worldview are not understood in the same way today as they were prior to the seventeenth century. These are now understood figuratively, whereas before they were likely understood as straightforward descriptions of nature that supported a geocentric worldview. Much of the OT law has been set aside with the coming of Christ and is no longer binding on Christians. The statements in the NT about "honoring the emperor," or about slaves being submissive to their masters, or of women being subordinate to men, no longer have the same meaning today as they did in the centuries before the rise of modern democracy and the awareness of basic human rights. As Krister Stendahl (1921–2008) has noted, the new freedom that has been given in Christ was neither perfectly comprehended nor fully actualized in the early church. It took time for the new and radical teaching about individual and social equality and freedom in the words and actions of Jesus and Paul to become more fully realized.[31] While there are key insights into this new freedom in the NT, it has taken Christians many

---

[30] This point is nicely made in the Report of the Commission on Theology and Church Relations of the Lutheran Church—Missouri Synod, *A Lutheran Stance toward Contemporary Biblical Studies* (St. Louis: CTCR, 1967), 10.

[31] Krister Stendahl, *The Bible and the Role of Women: A Case Study in Hermeneutics* (Minneapolis: Fortress Press, 1966).

centuries to flesh out the implications of the gospel and Christian love on the relation of slave and free, men and women, within the new creation that has dawned in Christ. Sixteenth-century Christians, like Luther, did not worry about eating blood sausage or food from strangled animals, even though the apostles clearly forbade such practices. Likewise most modern Christians do not think Christian women sin if they have short hair (or no hair) or if they go out in public without a veil (contrary to the literal sense of 1 Cor. 11). Very few American Christians understand Ephesians 6.5–9 in the way that a majority of pre-Civil War Americans did, and very few contemporary preachers will expound on this text as if nothing has changed since the first century, let alone since 1865 or 1965. The same is true with regard to biblical passages that reflect outmoded understandings of the relationship between men and women in church and society.

It is important to stress that these are "principles," not "rules" that if followed correctly will automatically lead to the "right" or "true" interpretation of a given biblical passage. There are no pure *a priori* or timeless principles that will lead ineluctably to a faithful understanding and contemporary application of biblical teaching. Rather, biblical interpretation is always a matter of wrestling with the scriptural text, of wrestling ever again with how it is interpreting the one who reads it and how it interprets the world. The challenge of reading the Bible is always to come ever anew to an understanding of the material contents of the Scriptures in their witness to Christ, to the divine law, to the gospel promise, to apostolic and prophetic exhortation.

> A lifelong relationship develops, in fact a love relationship is formed, between the biblical text that is at hand for study, with its freeing authority, and those who interpret it, within the freedom that is granted them; it is also within certain confines that they examine the text critically, this very text that interprets them and gives them understanding... It hardly needs mentioning that this love relationship cannot last for a short time only; it describes a faithful relationship that lasts a lifetime. (Bayer-L 91–2)

Luther's final words, written on a scrap of paper two days before he died, ought to give pause to everyone involved in the pursuit of biblical understanding:

> No one can understand Virgil in the *Bucolics* and the *Georgics* unless he has been a shepherd or a farmer for five years. No one can understand Cicero in his letters—so I feel—unless he has spent forty years in a prominent office of state. No one should suppose that he has even an inkling of an understanding

of the authors of Holy Scripture, unless he has governed the churches for a hundred years, together with the prophets. Thus John the Baptist, Christ and the apostles represent an immense miracle. "Do not lay hands upon the divine *Aeneid*, but bow down and honor its tracks" [the Latin poet Statius]. We are beggars. That is true.[32]

Key Words

hermeneutics	the hermeneutical circle
biblicism	Paul Ricoeur
inerrancy of Scripture	exegesis
verbal inspiration	eisegesis
historicism	Scripture interprets Scripture
Ernst Troeltsch	the analogy of faith
Troeltsch's three principles of	historical-critical method
historical criticism	the literal sense
aestheticism	genre
subjectivism	

On contemporary theological hermeneutics

EC 2:237–43 ("Exegesis, Biblical" [Smend, Roloff]); EC 2:531–39 ("Hermeneutics" [Boraas et al.]); ER 2:870–8 ("Biblical Exegesis II: Christian Views" [Rowland]); ER 6: 3930–6 ("Hermeneutics" [Harvey]); OCCT 295–7 ("Hermeneutics" [Bühler]); RPP 2:58–64 ("Biblical Criticism" [Wacker et al.]); RPP 4:731–4 ("Exegesis IV: Bible" [Seidl, Schnelle]); RPP 4:734–9 ("Exegesis V: Church History" [Bienert et al.]); RPP 6:87–8 ("Hermeneutics II: Old Testament [Dohmen]); RPP 6:88–9 ("Hermeneutics III: New Testament" [Schunack]); RPP 6:91–3 ("Hermeneutics V: Fundamental Theology" [Jeanrond])

---

[32] WA 48, 241, 2ff. [1546]; cf. WA (Table-Talk) 5, nos. 5468, 5477. The exact text has not been preserved. See Martin Brecht, *Martin Luther*, 3 vols (Minneapolis: Fortress Press, 1985–92), 3.374–5.

Questions for review and discussion

1   What is meant by "hermeneutics"? Why do people disagree about the interpretation of the Bible? Why is this such a big problem in Christian theology? In addition to the questions that appear in the first paragraph of this chapter, can you identify some other issues on which Christians disagree in their interpretation of the Bible?

2   Why is the author critical of the idea of biblical "inerrancy"? Do you agree with the author's criticisms? Why or why not?

3   What are Troeltsch's three principles of historical criticism? Why have these principles created problems for contemporary Christians? Do you agree with the author's criticisms of historicism? Why or why not?

4   Many people merely interpret the Bible as great literature. What does the author see as problematic in this approach?

5   Do you agree that the Bible has contents that we are to try to uncover or do you really think people can legitimately make the Bible say whatever they want it to mean?

6   What is meant by the distinction between "the Jesus of history" and "the Christ of faith"? Can you identify some tensions between "Jesus as he really was in the first century" and "Christ as he came to be believed in by later Christians"? Or do you think that this might be a false antithesis? What has Albert Schweitzer demonstrated about the presuppositions of all who have sought to find Jesus "behind" the apostolic witness to Jesus?

7   What is meant by "the hermeneutical circle"? How do the principles of theological interpretation that are set forth at the end of the chapter influence the hermeneutical circle?

8   What is the difference between exegesis and eisegesis? Do you really think it is possible not to read into the Bible meanings you want to find there? Or do you think that exegesis is really possible? Which presuppositions do you yourself bring to the task of understanding the Biblical writings?

9   Which of the hermeneutical principles that are outlined in the chapter do you think is most important for properly understanding the biblical writings? Which of the principles is the most difficult to practice? Why?

10 How do Lutherans and Roman Catholics differ on the understanding of the relationship between "Scripture" and "church"? What are the

strengths and weaknesses of each church body's position on this relationship?

Suggestions for further reading

General reference works

A. K. M. Adam, ed. *Handbook of Postmodern Biblical Interpretation* (St. Louis: Chalice, 2000) [Offers a helpful overview of basic postmodern approaches to biblical interpretation.]

Michael D. Coogan et al. (eds), Oxford Biblical Studies Online. [A comprehensive online resource for the study of the Christian Bible and biblical history. An excellent place to begin one's research of any topic relating to the Bible.]

Frederick W. Danker, *Multipurpose Tools for Bible Study*, 2nd edn (Minneapolis: Fortress, 1993) [Helpful overview of resources for the scholarly study of the Christian Bible.]

John Hayes, ed., *Dictionary of Biblical Interpretation*, 2 vols (Nashville: Abingdon, 1998) [Excellent initial resource for finding basic information on Bible scholars and theories.]

Steven McKenzie, ed., *Oxford Encyclopedia of Biblical Interpretation*, 2 vols (New York: Oxford University Press, 2013)

Richard N. Soulen, *Handbook of Biblical Criticism*, 3rd edn (Louisville: Westminster John Knox, 2001) [Defines all the major terms in biblical studies and summarizes the work of the major figures.]

W. Randolph Tate, *Interpreting the Bible: A Handbook of Terms and Methods* (Peabody: Hendrickson, 2006) [Helpful resource that complements Soulen's edition.]

Scholarly editions of the Bible

A. Alt et al., *Biblia Hebraica Stuttgartensia*, 4th edn (Stuttgart: Deutsche Bibelgesellschaft, 1990) [Scholarly edition of the Hebrew Bible.]

Alfred Rahlfs, ed., *Septuaginta*, 2nd edn (Stuttgart: Deutsche Bibelgesellschaft, 1979) [Scholarly edition of the Septuagint.]

Eberhard Nestle et al., *Novum Testamentum Graece*, 28th edn (Stuttgart: Deutsche Bibelgesellschaft, 2012) [Scholarly edition of the Greek New Testament.]

Kurt Aland, ed., *Synopsis of the Four Gospels* (New York: United Bible Societies, 1982) [Gives both Greek and English versions of the four canonical gospels in parallel columns in order to compare and contrast individual units of material (pericopes).]

Scholarly editions of the Bible in English

The Catholic Study Bible, 2nd edn, New American Bible Revised Edition (Oxford: Oxford University Press, 2011) [Includes study notes that reflect a Roman Catholic theological perspective.]

HarperCollins Study Bible, New Revised Standard Version, rev. edn (San Francisco: HarperOne, 2006) [A major ecumenical study Bible that includes notes by reputable international scholars.]

The Learning Bible, Contemporary English Version (New York: American Bible Society, 2000) [Includes exhaustive notes, charts, and maps that help to explain cultural and historical aspects of the ancient biblical texts.]

The NIV Study Bible, New International Version (Grand Rapids: Zondervan, 2011) [Includes study notes that reflect an American Evangelical theological perspective.]

New Oxford Annotated Bible with Apocrypha, 4th edn, New Revised Standard Version (Oxford: Oxford University Press, 2010) [The major ecumenical study Bible that includes notes by reputable international scholars from a variety of religious backgrounds.]

The Oxford Study Bible, Revised English Bible with Apocrypha (Oxford: Oxford University Press, 1992) [Includes study notes that reflect an Anglican theological perspective.]

Concordances of the English Bible

The NRSV Concordance Unabridged, ed. John R. Kohlenberger III (Grand Rapids: Zondervan, 1991) [Provides all of the English words that appear in the New Revised Standard Version, which is the key scholarly translation of the Bible in the English language today.]

Strong's Exhaustive Concordance of the Bible (Nashville: Abingdon, 1890) [This is a classic reference work for the King James Version of the Bible. It is still useful today because of its analytical features which allow one to find all occurrences of a given Hebrew or Greek word without knowing either language.]

Bible dictionaries

David Noel Freedman, ed., *The Anchor Bible Dictionary*, 6 vols (New York: Doubleday, 1992) [The major scholarly Bible dictionary in the English language. Exhaustive entries with scholarly bibliographies. This is a key reference work for college students doing work in biblical studies.]

Mark Allen Powell, ed., *HarperCollin's Bible Dictionary*, rev. edn (San Francisco: HarperOne, 2011) [A good single-volume reference work.]

Katharine Doob Sakenfeld, ed., *The New Interpreter's Bible Dictionary*, 5 vols

(Nashville: Abingdon, 2009) [Less scholarly than the ABD edition above, but equally useful for the student who wants to read entries that are oriented toward the context of Christian communities and church leaders.]

Bible atlases

Adrian Curtis, ed., *Oxford Bible Atlas*, 4th edn (Oxford: Oxford University Press, 2009) [The major scholarly Bible atlas in the English language. More than just a collection of maps, it provides a lot of cultural and historical information on the biblical world.]

James B. Pritchard, ed., *The HarperCollins Concise Atlas of the Bible* (San Francisco: HarperCollins, 1997) [An inviting resource that has easy-to-read maps and charts and a lot of cultural and historical information.]

Lexical aids

G. Johannes Botterweck et al. (eds), *Theological Dictionary of the Old Testament*, 15 vols (Grand Rapids: Eerdmans, 2006) [A major reference work for theological study of the Old Testament.]

D. J. A. Clines, *Concise Dictionary of Classical Hebrew* (Sheffield: Sheffield Academic Press, 2009) [Standard reference work for interpreting Hebrew terms in the OT.]

Frederick W. Danker, ed., *A Greek-English Lexicon of the New Testament and other Early Christian Literature*, 3rd edn, trans. William F. Arndt et al. (Chicago: University of Chicago Press, 2000) [The standard lexicon for English-speaking scholars.]

Gerhard Kittel and Gerhard Friedrich (eds), *Theological Dictionary of the New Testament*, 10 vols, trans. Geoffrey W. Bromiley (Grand Rapids: Eerdmans, 1964) [German-based scholarly entries on all the key Greek words in the NT. Although somewhat dated, this reference work still provides useful information and insights.]

Ludwig Koehler et al. (eds), *The Hebrew and Aramaic Lexicon of the Old Testament*, 2 vols (Leiden: Brill, 2002)

Ceslas Spicq, *Theological Lexicon of the New Testament*, 3 vols, ed. and trans. James Ernest (Peabody: Hendrickson, 1994)

Biblical interpretation and hermeneutics

Rudolf Bultmann, *New Testament and Mythology & Other Basic Writings*, ed. and trans. Schubert M. Ogden (Minneapolis: Fortress Press Press, 1984) [This collection of essays set forth Bultmann's understanding of the interpretation of the NT and his project of de-mythologizing it.]

Hans Conzelmann and Andreas Lindemann, *Interpreting the New Testament: An Introduction to the Principles and Methods of N.T. Exegesis*, 8th edn, trans. Siegfried S. Schatzmann (Peabody, MA: Hendrickson, 1988) [Introduces students to the principal methods of historical criticism through actual exegetical exercises and activities.]

Gerhard Ebeling, "The Significance of the Critical Historical Method for Church and Theology in Protestantism," *Word and Faith*, trans. James W. Leitch (London: SCM Press, 1963), 17–61 [Classic Protestant defense of the need for historical-critical methods in the study of the biblical texts.]

Gerhard Ebeling, "Word of God and Hermeneutics," *Word and Faith*, 303–32 [Ebeling's essay stresses the importance of hermeneutics in the process of theological understanding.]

Elisabeth Schüssler Fiorenza, *Searching the Scriptures: A Feminist Introduction* (New York: Crossroad, 1993) [A basic introduction to feminist hermeneutics.]

Robert M. Grant and David Tracy, *A Short History of the Interpretation of the Bible* (Minneapolis: Fortress Press Press, 1984) [An excellent overview of the history of Biblical interpretation from the early church through postmodernism.]

Roy A. Harrisville and Walter Sundberg, *The Bible in Modern Culture: Baruch Spinoza to Brevard Childs*, 2nd edn (Grand Rapids: Eerdmans, 2002) [This book provides helpful summaries and analyses of the principal interpreters of the Bible since the seventeenth century.]

Werner G. Jeanrond, *Text and Interpretation as Categories of Theological Thinking*, trans. Thomas J. Wilson (New York: Crossroad, 1988) [Brief introduction to theological hermeneutics from a Roman Catholic scholar. Tends to downplay or ignore several key figures—Hofmann, for one—but it gives a good introduction to many other figures and developments.]

André LaCocque and Paul Ricoeur, *Thinking Biblically: Exegetical and Hermeneutical Studies*, trans. David Pellauer (Chicago: University of Chicago Press, 1997) [Presents six dialogues between Ricoeur, one of the most important scholars of philosophical hermeneutics from the past century, and LaCocque, a major scholar of the Hebrew Bible, on six OT stories.]

Robert Morgan with John Barton, *Biblical Interpretation* (Oxford: Oxford University Press, 1988) [A good summary of the main scholarly developments in twentieth-century theological hermeneutics and the interpretation of the Bible.]

Paul Ricoeur, *Figuring the Sacred: Religion, Narrative, and Imagination*, trans. David Pellauer, ed. Mark I. Wallace (Minneapolis: Fortress, 1995) [This collection of essays is the best entry into the study of Ricoeur's theological hermeneutics.]

Paul Ricoeur, *Essays on Biblical Interpretation*, ed. Lewis S. Mudge

(Minneapolis: Fortress Press, 1980) [Earlier collection of essays that present Ricoeur's initial examination of theological hermeneutics, including his engagement with Bultmann's program of de-mythologizing.]

David Tracy, *Plurality and Ambiguity: Hermeneutics, Religion, Hope* (San Francisco: Harper and Row, 1987) [Tracy sets forth a practical approach to theological hermeneutics that is based on the models of conversation and critical argument.]

Ernst Troeltsch, "Historical and Dogmatic Method in Theology," in *Religion in History*, trans. James Luther Adams (Minneapolis: Fortress, 1991), 11–32. [Classic essay that explains Troeltsch's understanding of the difference between a historical-critical approach to the biblical writings and a dogmatic-theological one. He sets forth the three key principles of historical criticism in this essay.]

Francis Watson, *Text, Church and World: Biblical Interpretation in Theological Perspective* (Edinburgh: T & T Clark, 1994) [Watson is critical of historical-criticism and stresses the need to recover a properly theological approach to the Scriptures on the basis of a kind of post-liberal approach.]

Francis Watson, *Text and Truth: Redefining Biblical Theology* (Edinburgh: T & T Clark, 1997) [Stresses the Bible as the sacred Scripture of the church first and foremost and is critical of academic approaches that distort or subvert this basic position.]

Hebrew Bible/Old Testament studies

Bruce Birch et al., *A Theological Introduction to the Old Testament*, 2nd edn (Nashville: Abingdon, 2005) [Provides classic and contemporary engagement with key theological themes, issues, and problems within the Old Testament from the perspective of Christian faith.]

Walter Brueggemann and Tod Linafelt, *An Introduction to the Old Testament: The Canon and Christian Imagination*, 2nd edn (Louisville: Westminster John Knox, 2012) [Perhaps the best one-volume introduction to the Old Testament in the English language.]

John Collins, *A Short Introduction to the Hebrew Bible* (Minneapolis: Fortress Press, 2007) [Designed especially for undergraduate students, this book offers a standard, up-to-date historical-critical introduction to the OT.]

Michael Coogan, *A Brief Introduction to the Old Testament: The Hebrew Bible in Context*, 2nd edn (Oxford: Oxford University Press, 2011) [Also written for the undergraduate student, this book is by one of the leading scholars of the OT in the United States.]

Jan Christian Gertz et al., *T&T Clark Handbook of the Old Testament* (New York: T & T Clark, 2012) [Provides a useful introduction to the sources, methods, history, religion, literature, and theology of the OT.]

New Testament studies

Raymond Brown, *An Introduction to the New Testament* (New Haven: Yale University Press, 1997) [Excellent historical-critical introduction by an esteemed Roman Catholic scholar.]

Rudolf Bultmann, *Theology of the New Testament*, 2 vols, trans. Kendrick Grobel (New York: Scribners, 1951, 1955) [Classic statement of theological themes in the New Testament by the most important NT scholar of the twentieth century.]

Bart Ehrman, *The New Testament: A Historical Introduction to the Early Christian Writings*, 5th edn (New York: Oxford University Press, 2011) [Standard and popular college-level historical-critical introduction to the NT by a leading scholar.]

Luke Timothy Johnson, *The Writings of the New Testament*, 3rd edn (Minneapolis: Fortress Press, 2010) [Student-friendly introduction to the NT by a leading American scholar. Emphasizes the deep relationship between the NT texts and living Christian communities in the early church.]

Pheme Perkins, *Reading the New Testament: An Introduction*, 3rd edn (New York: Paulist, 2012) [Also a standard in the field by a leading Roman Catholic scholar.]

Robert Spivey et al., *Anatomy of the New Testament*, 7th edn (Minneapolis: Fortress Press, 2013) [Standard, venerable, college-level introduction to the NT that utilizes both historical-critical and literary-critical approaches to the texts.]

The historical Jesus

Martin Kähler, *The So-called Historical Jesus and the Historic Biblical Christ*, 2nd edn, trans. Carl Braaten (Minneapolis: Fortress Press, 1988) [Major attempt to stress the canonical gospels through and through as theological interpretations of the risen Jesus and not as sources for Jesus as he was in the first century.]

John P. Meier, *A Marginal Jew: Rethinking the Historical Jesus*, 3 vols (New York: Doubleday, 1991–2009) [Perhaps the most thorough scholarly investigation into the historical Jesus.]

Wolfhart Pannenberg, *Jesus—God and Man*, 2nd edn, trans. Lewis L. Wilkins and Duane A. Priebe (Philadelphia: Westminster, 1977) [A basic and widely read introduction to issues in Christology.]

Jaroslav Pelikan, *Jesus through the Centuries: His Place in the History of Culture* (New Haven: Yale University Press, 1999) [An accessible survey of basic understandings of Jesus in key periods of church history.]

E. P. Sanders, *The Historical Figure of Jesus* (London: Penguin, 1993) [This is the best one-volume introduction into the historical problems and probabilities regarding Jesus of Nazareth. An excellent place to begin one's engagement with the issues.]

Albert Schweitzer, *The Quest for the Historical Jesus*, trans. William Montgomery, J. R. Coates, Susan Cupitt and John Bowden, ed. John Bowden (Minneapolis: Fortress, 2001) [Still unsurpassed as an analytical survey of all of the major and many minor attempts to uncover the Jesus "behind" the church's written gospels.]

N. T. Wright, *Simply Jesus: A New Vision of Who He Was, What He Did, and Why He Matters* (San Francisco: HarperOne, 2011) [Wright is one of the leading figures in contemporary scholarly discussions about who Jesus was—and is. His account is shaped by equal concerns to take the findings of historical-critical research seriously and to affirm the basic apostolic, orthodox claims regarding the death and resurrection of Jesus.]

Part III

Christian Theology within the University

12

The Shape of Christian Theology as a University Discipline

This chapter begins by situating Christian theology within the broad history of the development of the university as an institution. The chapter then explains the purpose and genre of theological encyclopedia and summarizes how some theologians have divided theology into several sub-disciplines.

Placing Christian theology in a university

Christian theology has been an integral scholarly discipline within universities since the earliest ones were founded in Europe in the twelfth and thirteenth centuries. Their formation was itself a further development of an older Christian institution, the so-called "cathedral school," that had been established through educational reforms during the reign of Charlemagne at the end of the eighth century. These changes led to a closer interaction between Christian theology, wisdom from other religious traditions (particularly Judaism and Islam), and the other scholarly disciplines that had grown out of classical antiquity (Greece and Rome). Prior to the Carolingian reforms, theological study took place in monasteries and the households of individual Christian bishops and priests.

Medieval universities carried these traditions forward when they established theology as one of the **higher faculties**, alongside law and medicine. These three higher disciplines were themselves based on the **lower faculties**, the arts and letters, which equipped students to think carefully and logically, to read critically, to write well, and to speak persuasively. This preliminary "arts course" would ideally liberate a person from ignorance and prejudice and equip him to become a free citizen. The seven **liberal arts** defined this education: grammar, rhetoric, logic [the *trivium*]; and arithmetic, geometry, music, and astronomy [the *quadrivium*]). Upon completion of that preliminary arts course, a student of theology would undertake a course of study that typically lasted a further eight or more years.[1]

Within this medieval setting scholars like Aquinas argued that Christian theology is a science, at least in the Aristotelian sense, since it aspires to set forth a rational presentation of the content of divine revelation. According to Aquinas, scholarly theology has its proper grounding in divine revelation, which serves as its basic or axiomatic principle, yet one may rationally investigate that revelation and articulate its content in accordance with Aristotelian philosophical categories. In the view of medieval theologians who were influenced by Aquinas, this rational presentation gives theology its scientific or scholarly character.

The historical research of Walter Rüegg confirms that core Christian beliefs served as the most important presuppositions of the medieval university itself. They included beliefs about God the Creator of the universe, about human beings who are created in the image of God and who can investigate the divinely created order of the universe through their God-given reason, about human sin and divine redemption, and about the connection between knowledge, wisdom, virtue, and faith. These basic Christian beliefs helped to make medieval universities places where people could pursue certain fundamental goals:

- the rational investigation of God's creation;
- the cultivation of basic ethical principles and the intellectual virtues of humility, reverence, and self-criticism;
- the fostering of respect for the dignity and freedom of the individual human being;
- the encouragement of rigorous public arguments that appeal to demonstrated knowledge and the rules of evidence;

---

[1] For the rise of medieval universities in the shadows of the great cathedral schools, see David Knowles, *The Evolution of Medieval Thought*, 2nd edn, D. E. Luscombe and C. N. L. Brooke (eds) (London and New York: Longman, 1988), 139–66. For an overall history of the institution of the university in Europe, see Walter Rüegg, ed., *A History of the University in Europe*, 4 vols (Cambridge: Cambridge University Press, 1992–2011).

- and the pursuit of knowledge as a public good in and of itself that cannot be reduced to mere economic value.[2]

While other rationales have replaced the Christian theological underpinnings of these medieval principles (at least in secular, public universities), many institutions of higher education still pursue the goals themselves.[3]

Despite its historic place within the oldest universities, Christian theology has become more and more marginalized in higher education over the past four hundred years. That process had already begun prior to the Protestant Reformation as humanism and interest in classical antiquity supplanted medieval scholasticism and forms of philosophical (Aristotelian) theology that seemed esoteric and far removed from human life. Instead of debating metaphysical questions, such as how many angels can dance on the head of a needle, scholars (often outside of authoritarian and church-controlled universities) began to study the world and human beings for their own sakes and to be critical of ecclesiastical control of human educational institutions. That process of marginalizing theology in intellectual life only intensified in subsequent centuries. The principal reasons for this further development have already been identified in earlier chapters.

Not only has Christian theology played a negative role in suppressing and attacking legitimate scientific knowledge (think of how medieval religious leaders reacted to Galileo's defense of the theory of Copernicus or how some Christian theologians have attacked the Darwinian theory of evolution), but it has also allowed itself to be guided by ecclesial, authoritarian interests that have run contrary to truly open, scholarly inquiry. "All too often the church and theology have closed themselves to the progress of scholarly knowledge and have suppressed the truth until the artificial dam bursts again and the stream of true insight can no longer be stopped" (Ebeling, 81–82).

One response to this sad state of affairs was the radical solution of eighteenth-century French revolutionaries who tried to abolish all Christian-based universities in France. They attempted to establish new academic institutions grounded entirely on their ideological conceptions of secular reason. In Germany at that time, Johann Fichte (1762–1814) argued that the new University of Berlin, which he helped to found in 1810, should also exclude theology in favor of disciplines that are entirely guided by

---

[2] Walter Rüegg, "Themes," in *A History of the University in Europe*, 1.32ff. These themes are summarized in David Ford, *Christian Wisdom: Desiring God and Learning in Love* (Cambridge: Cambridge University Press, 2007), 307.

[3] Ford, *Christian Wisdom*, 308.

rational scientific inquiry and scholarly methods of research.[4] Only through the persuasive argument of another key founder, Schleiermacher, did that university include theology as one of the professional, practical disciplines. Nevertheless scholars in the tradition of Fichte have continued to question the place of theology in any university.

Authoritarian churches and poor theologies are not entirely to blame for this criticism and the marginalization of theology as an academic discipline. Skepticism about religious knowledge, including the theology of Christianity, has also been a factor within a broader **secularization** that has been taking place within universities (if not entirely in Western cultures) since the time of the Enlightenment. Over the past two hundred years a very narrow definition of what constitutes "knowledge" has been put forth within academic communities and this, too, has led not only to strong criticisms of religious ideas, including specifically Christian theology, but also to the marginalization of the humanities, philosophy, and the arts within many institutions of higher learning. In this view "knowledge" is only that which can be empirically verified, mathematically measured, and humanly controlled. Such knowledge is valuable only to the extent that it serves individual, economic, utilitarian gain. It is frequently divorced from larger questions about wisdom, truth, human understanding, and the common good. This narrowing of the notion of what constitutes knowledge has coincided with the expansion of ever narrowing fields of study.[5] This development further fits with a mindset that views college or university as providing people with the basic minimum they need to know in order to get a degree, so that they can become more marketable in business or some other practical vocation, such as engineering, nursing, or education. The humanistic disciplines, including philosophy and theology, often do not factor favorably into that view of higher education. Not surprisingly, since 1970, the more higher education has expanded in America, the more the humanities have contracted in relation to all other disciplines. Because of market, economic pressures, not only have colleges and universities become big companies with brand names, they have become largely vocational training centers for these practical jobs or careers.

---

[4] See Johann G. Fichte, *Introductions to the Wissenschaftslehre and Other Writings*, ed. and trans. Daniel Breazeale (Indianapolis: Hackett, 1994).
[5] In the United States a university student may now major in such "academic fields," as "parks, recreation, and leisure," "fitness studies," and "beverage management."

Despite the numerous efforts since the eighteenth century to remove Christian theology from modern universities—Fichte's attempt is illustrative—it continues to be a recognized scholarly field among the higher faculties in many contemporary universities (divinity schools), seminaries, and graduate institutions. The principal European universities still support separate theology faculties (a few exclusively Protestant or Catholic and several that are more ecumenical) and they prepare future church leaders for service in churches that value well-educated clergy, some of which have historically been supported by the state. Schleiermacher's model for the University of Berlin is still largely in place throughout Europe. Such a model, which has also significantly influenced American universities, values academic freedom in all university disciplines and understands the university itself to be a place of interdisciplinary teaching and research in the arts, humanities, and the sciences. It treasures and passes on what is important and valuable from the past, while striving to be open to innovation and advances in knowledge and understanding. Unlike the model of the university in revolutionary France, the Berlin model "tried both to do justice to reason and to engage constructively with religion as it was found in Prussia at the time."[6]

In America, where constitutional issues regarding "church and state" come into play (often quite confusedly and awkwardly), Christian theology also remains an important academic discipline, if mostly in private divinity schools and church-related colleges and seminaries. Still, even in America, academic theology also takes place in public, non-religiously-affiliated institutions of higher education. In fact, despite widespread secularization that has occurred in American higher education over the past 150 years, the presence of Christian theology in public universities is more noticeable today than it was even two decades ago.[7] This is the case both formally (for example, in optional courses in religious studies, psychology of religion, sociology of religion, philosophy of religion) and informally (for example, when students and faculty raise properly theological issues in courses or research or in relation to on-campus religiously based student activities). That religion has not gone away in Western culture, that it has undergone transformation and renewal in ways that were largely unexpected two and three decades ago among sociologists, that it remains a vital force to be reckoned with in the world, and that it is still a "live option" on college

---

[6] Ford, *Christian Wisdom*, 312.
[7] See Jacobsen and Jacobsen, *No Longer Invisible*, 3–15.

campuses—all of these developments have led many to reassess earlier theories about "inevitable secularization."[8] Students from all over the world are flocking to American universities and they are bringing their religious beliefs, practices, and understandings with them. These often clash in creative ways with other religious (and non-religious) beliefs, especially when students talk about matters of "ultimate concern," truth, the way things are, and the way they should be. Recent surveys of college and university faculties further indicate the importance that knowledge about God ("theology") or "a Higher Power" and spiritual matters has among educational leaders, even if most try to keep these views private or concealed from others.[9] The persistence of religious practices, of religious questioning and questing, of pursuing spiritual and theological answers within the context of learning, suggests that thinking about these matters will continue to remain an aspect of American higher education, both public and private, for the foreseeable future.

But the inclusion of academic theology in undergraduate higher education should not be based merely on sociological data. The discipline itself is worthy of scholarly investigation for reasons that were set forth in Chapters 1 and 4. Within undergraduate institutions, whether public or private, Christian theology fits within the larger framework of the **humanities**, which seek to further human self-understanding and the cultural understandings that have been transmitted by human beings.[10] The place of

---

[8] See especially Peter Berger, *The Desecularization of the World* (Grand Rapids: Eerdmans, 1999).

[9] A 2004–5 UCLA survey of more than 40,000 faculty members at 421 colleges and universities indicates that 64 percent of them consider themselves to be "religious" (29 percent to some extent, 35 percent to a great extent) and 81 percent consider themselves "spiritual." For additional data, see Neil Gross and Solon Simmons, "The Religious Convictions of College and University Professors," in *The American University in a Postsecular Age*, Douglas Jacobsen and Rhonda Hustedt Jacobsen (eds) (New York: Oxford University Press, 2008), 19–29.

[10] The term "humanities" has had different meanings since the days when Cicero first used the term "*humanitas*" to refer to the education of a public official. In the second century Aulus Gallius identified this term with the Greek concept of *paideia*, the liberal education that prepared an individual for citizenship and public service. Hence "encyclopedia," the circle of learning that was necessary for such preparation. Fifteenth-century Italian humanists revitalized this understanding, as did other European humanists in the following century. This notion persisted through the eighteenth century. In the nineteenth century the "humanities" were viewed in opposition to the natural sciences. In Germany at that time a distinction was developed between the "*Geisteswissenschaften*" (literally the "spiritual" or "intellectual sciences," that is, the "human sciences") and the *Naturwissenschaften*, "the natural sciences." The former were understood to be beyond the reach of the latter. More recently, scholars have distinguished between a narrower definition of "the humanities" and the "social sciences." While in our time the natural and social sciences are looking to explain fully everything, including everything human, others point out that the natural and social sciences themselves have had a history, that human ideologies have

theology here fits within the overall concern to investigate human beings, their histories/stories, their creative and cultural achievements, their self-understandings and social organization. But this placement of theology within the humanities also reflects the fact that Christian theology is more than merely "the study of God," as Christians understand God, and includes reflection on human self-understanding, human religious experiences, the study of world religions (in dialogue with Christian theology), and the transmission of human religious traditions and practices.

As has already been suggested in Chapter 1, theology has often been subsumed under the category of **religious studies** within the humanities. Some scholars of religion see no real difference between theology and this broader discipline since for them all religious phenomena are to be studied according to the same critical methods that are used to study any other natural and human phenomena. Others try to maintain a sharp distinction between theology and religious studies, since the former is about matters of ultimate truth, the reality of God, and the world as it is given, while religious studies is about the religions, however they are finally defined, and how they are interpreted through lenses and theories from human-centered disciplines such as psychology, sociology, anthropology, and biology. Within the American context, especially in public universities, the actual practice of theology is almost entirely subsumed under these human-centered disciplines. Still other scholars argue that the two disciplines are not the same yet need each other to offer important corrections and limitations to their specific methods and scholarly understandings.

This latter approach has advantages, for it recognizes an important relationship between theology and religious studies while seeking to maintain the distinctive approach and concerns of each. Within public, non-church-related institutions, Christian theology would most likely have to be a sub-discipline of religious studies and could itself be further divided into specific theological or metaphysical traditions of reflection. Within church-related schools, which would likely have a preferred religious tradition, religious studies and theology could actually be two different, if closely-related departments. Whether as a separate department or as a

---

significantly shaped their execution, and that there is more to human beings and their culture than can be fully explained by the natural and social sciences. For our purposes here I am using the term "humanities" quite broadly to refer to humankind's creative, cultural legacy that has been handed down through the visual arts (including painting, sculpture, photography and film), music, the performing arts, architecture, literature, poetry, the religions, philosophy, theology, and history (at least as a literary form).

sub-discipline within religious studies, theology would welcome, explore, and argue about questions of ultimate truth and meaning, and it likely would not try "to explain them away" by means of those primary scholarly methods used within religious studies and other humanistic disciplines. Such a view would allow for Jewish theology within Jewish Studies, Muslim theology within Islamic Studies, and so on. In this way the particularities of specific theologies and practices are allowed to stand on their own as subjects of study without necessarily transposing them into an overarching and problematic theory of "religion" and explaining them away in purely naturalistic and humanistic terms.

Regardless of where Christian theology is finally located within the humanities, how it is structured and organized as a university discipline, is a further important question. What are the constitutive elements of Christian theology and how do they relate to each other as a unified whole? These questions have traditionally been answered by Christian theologians, under the category of "theological encyclopedia."

Theological encyclopedia

Humanist scholars in the fifteenth century created the Latin word "**encyclopedia**," which itself is based on a Greek phrase, the "circle of learning" (*enkyklios paideia*), that referred to "the circle of arts and sciences considered by the Greeks as essential to a liberal education" (OED 512). A young Greek would have to pass through this "circle" before he could undertake more specialized studies or become a public official. As we have already noted, within the medieval period, especially under the influence of Augustine, the development of the so-called "liberal arts" provided the foundation for the further study of one of the "higher disciplines," namely, theology, medicine, or law. This conception of a foundational, preparatory "circle [of learning] for young people" was already at work in the theology of Clement of Alexandria, who sought an all-embracing knowledge of everything known in his day, which included especially the knowledge of the *Logos* of God (*theologia*).

Later, the term "encyclopedia" was used to describe introductory accounts of all the known knowledge in a given academic field. Within the medieval period the synthesis of Greek philosophy and Christian theology provided an encyclopedic orientation to Christian theology, a synthesis that was still evident in the writings of Renaissance humanists and post-Reformation

Christian humanism. Some contemporary scholars have wryly noted that Aquinas might have been the last human being who was able to organize in his head all the known knowledge of his day, both scientific and philosophical/theological. Goethe's Faust represents the end of that illusion: "I've studied now, to my regret, philosophy, law, medicine and—what is worse—theology from end to end with diligence, yet here I am, a wretched fool and still no wiser than before."[11]

During the Enlightenment several efforts were made to compile a comprehensive account of all human knowledge, which either excluded or criticized that which was deemed superstitious or outmoded, such as religious knowledge and theology. Perhaps the most famous example of this approach is the eighteenth-century *Encyclopédie* by Diderot and his associates, whose anti-Christian animosity appears throughout its pages. Hegel's nineteenth-century *Encyclopaedia of the Philosophical Sciences*—which still had a theological flavor to its contents, since its author thought that learning was incomplete without understanding theology—might very well be the last attempt by a single thinker to try to summarize the whole of human knowledge. Hegel and his contemporary Schelling still reflected the ideal of Clement. Today, all such projects are criticized as much for their partiality and incompleteness as for their authors' biases, hubris, and short-sightedness—despite their best efforts at comprehensiveness. Even the modern editors of the *Encyclopedia Britannica*, which includes many articles of a theological nature, frankly acknowledge the essential, temporal, and spatial limitations of their work. These same limitations are evident in the standard encyclopedia of religious studies, the 4th edition of the 13-volume *Religion Past and Present*. Its 15,000 entries (over 8 million words) nevertheless provide helpful introductions to the basic topics in this large and complex academic field, at least as of the year 2000 or so.

While most scholars acknowledge that it is simply impossible to gather all human religious and theological knowledge, let alone all contemporary human knowledge, into one set of books or even into one internet database, many now affirm that academic knowledge cannot perforce exclude religious and theological understandings. Religious studies and theology are to be found within the circle of arts and sciences as critical, humanistic,

---

[11] Johann Wolfgang von Goethe, *Faust I and II*, in *Goethe: The Collected Works*, vol. 2, ed. and trans. Stuart Atkins (Princeton: Princeton University Press, 1984), Part I, lines 355–9 (translation slightly altered).

interdisciplinary fields of study—"critical" in the methodological sense of this term, which gained currency through Kant's philosophy.

Already in the eighteenth century, when the complexity of the study of theology began to be felt more acutely, there developed in Europe a distinct genre of theological reflection, which is usually called "**theological encyclopedia**," whose purpose is not to give an alphabetized summary of the various bits and pieces of theological knowledge but to provide a rationale for the discipline as a whole within the academy, to offer an introduction to its branches or sub-disciplines, and to highlight ongoing problems within the discipline.[12] Works of this kind in North America have been few in number and all have been oriented toward graduate-level theological education of future church leaders. The dearth of such resources for undergraduate students is unfortunate, since beginning students of theology are often confused and bewildered by the large and complex range of resources within the diverse sub-disciplines of Christian theology. They could benefit from a general description of its essential and basic shape, a description, which, by definition, is a severe restriction and limitation of theological knowledge, but one which is necessary so that the beginning student has a basic framework in which to begin. One has to start somewhere. One does so, recognizing that every attempt at describing theology as an academic discipline, including the one set forth in this book, is partial, incomplete, and inevitably somewhat subjective.

Since the rationale for theology as an undergraduate academic discipline has already been given in earlier chapters, the focus of this chapter is on the second problem addressed by a theological encyclopedia, namely, the structure of Christian theology as an academic discipline. On the one hand, Christian theology is aimed toward the past, since it takes its basic orientation from the revelation that has occurred in relation to the apostolic witness to Jesus Christ. This past orientation means that theology cannot uncritically allow the present situation to undermine or even eliminate the basic claims within the historical revelation of God, the world, and human beings in the apostolic witness to Jesus. On the other hand, Christian theology is aimed toward the contemporary ecumenical and intellectual situation in which the claims of a Christian theology of revelation are analyzed and evaluated. This orientation toward the present situation means that theology cannot merely repeat what Christians have said in the past without attending to changes

---

[12] See especially Farley, *Theologia*, 73–124; and Howard, *Protestant Theology and the Making of the Modern German University*, 303–23.

in the cultural and intellectual situation between present believers and all past manifestations of Christian faith and theology. Furthermore, within a university context, Christian theology is also undertaken in view of all other academic disciplines, including especially those that overlap its own subject matter or whose methods, such as those used in history, psychology, and sociology, are also used by scholars of theology. In this undergraduate setting, Christian theology is naturally done in ecumenical conversation with people from the major branches of the Christian tradition, people from other religious traditions, and people from intellectual traditions that are critical of "religion" and metaphysics. This academic and ecumenical orientation also impacts the theological task and its execution.

The division of Christian theology into sub-disciplines thus follows from *both* the subject matter of theology, which demands attention to past and present understandings of the revelation of God, *and* the comprehensiveness of theology, which leads to a division of responsibilities and the use of multiple methods and resources within the theological task.

Dividing theology

We noted in Chapter 3 that already in the ancient world a Stoic philosopher, Panaetius (d. 110 BC), had divided philosophical theology into three distinct parts or functions: (1) mythological theology, which maintained and interpreted the stories about the gods from ancient Greece; (2) natural theology, which reasoned about God or the gods on the basis of the world or universe, and was often critical of the ancient myths as fictional and unethical; and (3) civil theology, which served to understand and perform the rites and ceremonies in the cult of the Caesars, and often to justify the political regime.

Several Christian theologians in the early church, such as Tertullian and Augustine, adapted this three-fold division for their own purposes, but obviously the distinctions among the parts were understood differently. Generally, the first division focused on biblical interpretation, the second offered philosophical exploration of Christian teaching, and the third was oriented toward the practical arts of Christian ministry (spiritual care, preaching, sacramental theology, and so on). Despite this three-fold distinction, most early Christian theologians typically referred to theology as a single intellectual enterprise that uncovered the truth and wisdom of God, that cultivated holiness, and that aimed toward the salvation of human beings.

This understanding of theology as a unitary intellectual discipline persisted into the medieval period. At the University of Paris, Aquinas spoke of theology as "sacred doctrine" (*sacra doctrina*) or sacred teaching. Augustine had used these words as well. Three hundred years after Aquinas, at the University of Wittenberg, Melanchthon called theology "the doctrine of the gospel" (*doctrina evangelii*). Throughout these medieval centuries, theology was often called "the queen of the sciences," alongside the liberal arts and the higher faculty of law. In this context, university theology was guided by reigning philosophical conceptions about knowledge and methodology, largely of an Aristotelian nature. As a result, theological inquiry was freely undertaken apart from the interference of church officials, but its goal was still the same as it had been since the time of the apostles, namely, the pursuit of divine wisdom and saving knowledge. This was the model of university theology, both Roman Catholic and Protestant, until the end of the seventeenth century.[13]

The division of theology into academic sub-disciplines or specialties is a post-eighteenth-century phenomenon, occasioned by those who wanted to give a scholarly account of theological encyclopedia for university students in the wake of Enlightenment critiques of religion, the rise of the modern sciences, and the historical-critical investigation of Christian sources (apart from the influence and control of church officials). As noted in Chapter 3, post-Enlightenment university professors (like Semler) began to study the Christian Scriptures like all other ancient documents and to use universal and historical-critical principles to study the origins of Christianity as a purely historical set of phenomena. Within a short period of time, all aspects of the Christian religion were being studied with the same presuppositions and scholarly tools that were brought to other university disciplines. The challenge for Christian theologians after the Enlightenment has been to explain how theology still belongs within a university that is governed by modern scholarly ideals of dispassionate inquiry, relevant evidence, and rational argumentation, and that is not responsible to any institutional religious authority.

The most significant modern ordering of the theological disciplines was done by **Schleiermacher**, whose ground-breaking *Brief Outline for the Study of Theology* has informed all later descriptions (see SBO). This work marked a significant turning point within the larger Christian tradition,

---

[13] See especially Farley, *Theologia*, 1–39.

not merely because it offered a creative defense of Christian theology as a university discipline, but also because it set in motion a distinctively Protestant manner of understanding the nature of the theological task and the relation of the various theological sub-disciplines to one another. Although Schleiermacher's little book was not the first of its kind to be written in the modern period, or even the one most studied by students in the nineteenth century, it has served as the classic model for all subsequent attempts in the genre.

For Schleiermacher, theology is to be divided into **three sub-disciplines**: *philosophical* theology, which essentially examines the form and content of the particularities of Christian religious conviction; *historical* theology, which concentrates upon biblical interpretation, church history, and the history of doctrine; and *practical* theology, which teaches people the necessary skills to undertake ministry within Christian communities. These internal divisions of theology flow from the concept of Christian theology itself and each is integrally related to that concept. Nevertheless, in Schleiermacher's view, the final branch of theology, the practical, provides the discipline with its overarching goal as a university subject, since the other two branches are actually carried out by means of non-theological philosophical and historical methods, and since the real purpose of theology as a university discipline is to provide the (state) church with well-educated clergy. Moreover, Schleiermacher held that academic theology arises from a personal and communal conviction about the truth of God that can neither be proved nor demonstrated. In this way Christian theology is "a positive science," that is, a scholarly activity that describes a particular, empirical way of believing, that ultimately is oriented toward the cultivation of practical skills among those preparing for public service as church leaders. The study of theology, in this view, is thus a lot like the study of civil law. One studies materials that are empirically given and one does so for the sake of preparing oneself for public service, either as a pastor (in the case of theology) or a lawyer (in the case of law). For Schleiermacher, the challenge of academic theology is to reconcile the tradition of biblical and creedal doctrines with a distinctively modern, scientifically informed account of Christian faith in service to a practical goal. Although he presented the disciplines in the order he did (philosophical, historical, practical), the methods and results of each are intimately and dialectically related to those of the others. Thus the *Brief Outline* frequently draws attention to correlations and cross-references among the three branches.

Because Schleiermacher held that human beings are religious by nature and that they find their religious meaning within specific religious communities, the task of philosophical theology is to locate the Christian church in space and time and to articulate the essential character of the way of *Christian* believing that is commonly held within that community. What is the essential content of the (Protestant) Christian way of believing? How has that content been defined over time within the Christian community? These are the main questions within philosophical theology. Thus the starting point of theology for Schleiermacher involves inquiry into the nature of the Christian religious consciousness ("faith") and its basis within a specific, empirical community ("the Protestant Church"). The concern of the theologian is to investigate how this specific community is located within history ("in relation to Jesus of Nazareth") and how its faith has been transmitted over time.

If the task of philosophical theology is to delineate the reality of the church and to define the essence of Christianity, *historical theology* explores the unfolding of that essence in every period of church history, from the time of the apostles to the present. Within the *Brief Outline* this section is by far the largest. "Since historical theology attempts to exhibit every point of time in its true relation to the idea of Christianity, it follows that it is at once not only the founding of practical theology but also the confirming of philosophical theology" (SBO §27). The essence of Christianity that is disclosed by philosophical theology is thus examined historically. Such historical investigation of the essence of Christianity is not merely interested in ascertaining historical facts; it is also interested in the disclosure of the historical meanings of relevant facts and in making judgments about what is truly authentic (consistent with the essence of Christianity) and inauthentic in the history of Christianity. Historical theology is further divided into biblical theology (exegesis), church history, and dogmatics, which collectively explore the essence of Christianity in chronological sequence from earliest period (the apostolic) to the latest (present understanding of dogmatic teaching). Although the earliest, apostolic sources provide a normative understanding of the essence of Christianity, not everything in those sources is necessarily normative for the contemporary church, and everything within the biblical texts requires attention to hermeneutical, i.e. interpretational issues. Contemporary articulation of church doctrine is grounded upon its historical development and shaped by philosophical (and scientific) considerations that inform the interpretative process. The challenge of dogmatics is to form a coherent articulation of the contemporary teachings of the Christian church and not merely the private opinions of the individual theologian. While many critics of Schleiermacher have accused him of completely historicizing Christian dogmatics, and thus of preparing the way for its diminishment over time, he himself thought that dogmatics always reflects the theological convictions of the communities of faith within each successive epoch of history. Consequently, dogmatics must be undertaken anew by each generation.

It needs to be underscored that Schleiermacher broke with previous orderings of theology by placing dogmatics within historical theology:

> In the usual arrangement of theology the chief points are exegetical theology, historical theology, systematic theology, and practical theology. Only two of these, historical and practical, are acknowledged here and the exegetical and the dogmatic are both subordinated to the historical. Dogmatics thus appears as a part of historical theology, while it usually appears as coordinated with historical theology. The same holds for exegetical theology, about which far fewer objections have been made. (SBO 182–3)

In this way, dogmatics remains closely tied to the historical conditions of the church and its development through time. It remains attentive to the historical conditioning of church teachings, both past and present, and takes its cues from the historical confessions of faith that have been produced throughout the history of Christianity. Clearly, in order to carry out the tasks of theology, one must have a strong sense of history. The theologian is called upon to respect the church's past and its authentic traditions that have been handed down to the present. (In Schleiermacher's case, the preeminent confessions are the Protestant ones from the sixteenth century.) Nevertheless, the theologian also has the responsibility to speak critically of those teachings and traditions that are inconsistent with the essence of Christianity or that contradict it. Likewise, the theologian has the responsibility of defending those teachings that are consistent with the essence and that manifest that essence in the past and the present. Historical theology thus seeks to avoid biblicism, which fails to acknowledge the historical and cultural distance between the apostolic writings and contemporary Christians and the historical developments that followed the apostolic age. On the other hand, historical theology also seeks to avoid an individualist philosophy of faith that fails to acknowledge the manifestations of Christian teaching in the long history of the church. In other words, Christian theology must avoid uncritical biblicism, on the one hand, and ahistorical rationalism and subjectivism, on the other.

Practical theology, as the crown of the theological disciplines, implements the results of the other two theological disciplines in the life of a congregation through pastoral leadership. If philosophical theology is a *critical* discipline and historical theology is an *empirical* discipline, practical theology is a *technical* discipline wherein the "arts of ministry" are used in "the care of souls" within a congregation. Such ministry requires the requisite basic knowledge of both philosophical and historical theology but also the necessary skills to communicate the truth of Christian faith to the contemporary religious community. While no one single person "can perfectly possess the full compass of theological knowledge," one must "master the basic features of [the three theological disciplines]," if one is "to deal with any one of the theological disciplines in a truly theological sense and spirit" (SBO §§14, 16). The challenge of practical theology is to balance concern for the church and the "care of souls" (an "ecclesial interest") with a scholarly understanding of Christianity (a "scientific spirit"). Those who do this balancing job best are truly "princes of the church."[14]

In the aftermath of the *Brief Outline*, works of this kind were produced by many German Protestant theologians who wanted to further Schleiermacher's goals, even if they disagreed with him about how to reach them. Among the more successful of these later encyclopedias of theology was the one by **Karl R. Hagenbach** (1801–74), his *Encyclopedia and Methodology of the Theological Sciences*, which was published in 1833. Unlike Schleiermacher, Hagenbach divided theology into **four sub-disciplines**: exegetical (biblical interpretation), dogmatic, historical, and practical. He emphasized that the first sub-discipline, the exegetical, was the most important, since all of Christian (Protestant) theology is grounded in the biblical revelation and exegesis is closest to that normative foundation.

But not everyone agreed with Hagenbach's four-fold division and his prioritizing of exegesis above the other sub-disciplines. For example, **Hofmann**, who had studied under Schleiermacher, delivered lectures on theological encyclopedia over the course of 30 years of teaching at Erlangen University.[15] He adopted Schleiermacher's innovative **three-fold structure**

---

[14] See B. A. Gerrish, *A Prince of the Church: Schleiermacher and the Beginnings of Modern Theology* (Eugene, OR: Wipf and Stock, 2001).
[15] These lectures were published posthumously as *Encyklopädie der Theologie, nach Vorlesungen und Manuscripten*, ed. H. J. Bestmann (Nördlingen: C. H. Beck, 1879). See Becker, *The Self-Giving God and Salvation History*, 31–58; and idem, "The Shape of Theology as a University *Wissenschaft*: Schleiermacher's Reflection in Hofmann's *Theological Encyclopedia*," *Papers of the Nineteenth-Century Theology Group*, 37 (American Academy of Religion) (November 2006), 103–27.

for the organization of theology and attempted to articulate the essence of Christian faith as a unity of both his own personal Christian experience of faith and the historical development of the church. Nevertheless, he also tried to distance his taxonomy from the one set forth by his more famous teacher. For example, he did not think the first branch should take its orientation from philosophical methods, as he thought had been the case in the *Brief Outline*. The theologian should simply strive to systematize the essence of Christianity by providing a coherent summary of contemporary Christian teaching. For this reason, he labeled that first branch "*systematic theology*," not "philosophical theology." Likewise, he was critical of what he perceived to be Schleiermacher's inattention to historical details in the Christian tradition, which for him also included the anticipatory events narrated in the OT. He thus, highlighted the centrality of biblical exegesis, though he still located it within *historical theology* as Schleiermacher had done. Hofmann also agreed with his teacher by stressing that not everything the biblical scholar uncovers is normative for contemporary faith. In this way, he acknowledged that exegesis must also be guided by the results from both systematic and practical theology. More significantly, he thought that a strictly formal approach to theology, as both Schleiermacher and Hagenbach represented, was inadequate to the task of a theological encyclopedia. He wanted to give a material accounting of the various disciplines, always in relation to the object of one's personal, existential faith and the risks that it involves. In other words, Hofmann included within his encyclopedia attention to the personal, existential dimension of faith and its relation to specific doctrinal teaching, drawn from the Scriptures. His theological encyclopedia is accordingly about three times as long as Schleiermacher's. Finally, while Hofmann rejected Schleiermacher's attempt to ground the unity and integrity of theology in a practical, clerical goal, he did agree that the third sub-discipline is *practical theology* (which concerns church leadership and other matters relating to the pastoral care of people and congregations). Unlike Schleiermacher, Hofmann thought academic theology should be solely grounded in its unique object of study (God and the individual Christian), in the peculiar mode of knowing that object (Christian faith), and in the particular method by which that object is understood and expressed as a unified whole, a method that correlates personal faith and historical investigation.

While Hofmann acknowledged the correctness of Schleiermacher's concern to avoid dogmatic biblicism, on the one hand, and an ahistorical rationalism and subjectivism, on the other, he and others have been troubled that Schleiermacher's own approach would lead to the complete historicizing and relativizing of Christian teaching. This outcome is perhaps most obvious in the theological work of **Troeltsch,** who sharpened Schleiermacher's theological method to be more historical. Troeltsch severely limited what is included in the content of faith.[16] Following Troeltsch, others have also insisted that Christian doctrine is entirely a matter of historical factors that are distinct from divine revelation and "churchly" theology. For these scholars, only the historical method provides a truly scientific theology. In this view, the study of Christianity is entirely a scholarly matter of investigating the history of religions. The challenge for theologians after Schleiermacher and Troeltsch has been to affirm the positive results of the introduction of modern historical-critical methods into theology without losing the object of theology or its abiding theological claims on present individuals and communities.

One tendency among theologians after Troeltsch has been to retreat from the university setting altogether into a narrower context that is entirely ecclesial. **Karl Barth's** theology has given support toward that movement of theology away from other university disciplines. Despite his own university appointment, Barth himself emphasized that Christian theology is entirely a matter of the revelation of God in Jesus Christ that the church has received from God. The title of Barth's multi-volume *Church Dogmatics* underscores his position, as does the title of a three-volume theological encyclopedia by one of his associates, *Theology as Ecclesial Science.*[17] While Christian theology is a scholarly discipline, it is an ecclesial/churchly discipline first and foremost, one which takes its entire orientation from the revelation of God in Jesus Christ. The task of theology is to serve the task of preaching within the church.

The problem with this Barthian approach, however, is that it presupposes the special and unique character of Christian theology, over and against all other religions and university disciplines. Because Barth insisted that scholarly theology is entirely determined by the unique object it studies, it is easy to see how theology could become completely isolated from all other scholarly disciplines. Already in Barth's own time, his former

---

[16] See Walter E. Wyman, Jr., *The Concept of* Glaubenslehre: *Ernst Troeltsch and the Theological Heritage of Schleiermacher,* AAR Academy Series 44 (Chico, CA: Scholars Press, 1983). The classic essay by Troeltsch that treats the differences between historical and theological approaches to Christian theology is "Historical and Dogmatic Method in Theology," in *Religion in History,* 11–32.
[17] Hermann Diem, *Theologie als kirchliche Wissenschaft,* 3 vols (Munich: Kaiser, 1951–63).

teacher, Adolf von Harnack, warned that Barth wished "to transform the theological professor's chair into a pulpit."[18] Less than a decade after Barth's death, another important theologian, namely, Pannenberg, leveled similar criticism:

> What means has theology of justifying its claim to be automatically in a different and privileged position when the truth of its statements is challenged? Any such claim can be no more than an empty assertion. Even if claims of this sort are made on the theological side with disarming innocence, it is understandable, to say no more, if in other quarters they give an impression of immense arrogance on the part of a discipline which can ultimately, as a discipline, be no more than human. (PTPS 19)

Pannenberg's own approach is better suited for an undergraduate university context in which the theologies of the world's religions are investigated critically and evaluated systematically with respect to their particular, historical, and theological truth claims. Accordingly, in this context, the Christian theological disciplines must engage the questions and provisional solutions that arise from all other university disciplines insofar as they also impact on a contemporary understanding of the subject matter of Christian theology. Christian theology must be especially attentive to the critical perspectives and insights from the history of religions, the philosophy of religion, psychology of religion, sociology of religion, and the phenomenology of religion.

Most works in theological encyclopedia for a North American audience have not taken these other disciplines into account. The primary audience for most introductions to Christian theology tend to be students at church-related institutions, seminaries, and professional divinity schools. In these contexts Christian theology is undertaken mostly by Christians who are preparing for leadership positions within Christian communities and who share certain Christian presuppositions. Within these contexts the four-fold division of theology has been dominant: Biblical theology (exegesis) is the initial sub-discipline, followed by historical theology, systematic theology, and practical theology (developing skills necessary to be a priest or a pastor). In this scheme, all four branches approach the same object, namely, "Christianity," but they approach it through differing methods (historical, psychological, sociological, church-practical) and concentrate on differing

---

[18] Adolph von Harnack, "Open Letter to Karl Barth," in *The Beginnings of Dialectical Theology*, ed. James M. Robinson, trans. Keith Crim (Richmond: John Knox, 1968), 171.

sources or materials (Bible, church history, the care of souls in contemporary congregations). Following Schleiermacher's taxonomy, the unifying goal of the four sub-disciplines is the practical training of future pastors or church leaders.

Unfortunately, a consequence of this division has been the fragmentation of theology into disparate, autonomous, specialized disciplines that have little or nothing in common with the others and are often only tenuously related to other, non-theological academic disciplines (especially psychology and sociology). Frequently, the theological dimension may be neglected altogether within a given sub-discipline, especially within the historical study of the Christian Scriptures and the Christian church and the teaching of those practical techniques that are necessary for church leadership. While the practical training of future pastors and priests may help to unify the sub-disciplines at the graduate level, this practical goal often does not apply at the undergraduate level, where many students are not preparing for a leadership position in a church and some may not be Christian. At all levels, at least in explicitly Christian-based institutions, most students of theology may take "a little exegesis" and "a little church history" and "a little systematic theology," but never wrestle with the unity among these different courses or grapple with the interrelationships of the sub-disciplines. Even if some students have the professional goal of becoming a church leader, lost in the curricular shuffle is the material unity that is given in the object of theology itself, which becomes subordinate to the scholarly foci and methods within each of the sub-disciplines. This problem is exacerbated at the undergraduate level, where the practical goal is likely not a factor for most students or their instructors.

The four-fold division and its practical aim are not without further problems, especially at the undergraduate level. By dividing theology into the four-fold pattern, one could easily assume that each discipline is independent and autonomous from the others, when in fact each sub-discipline interacts with the others and influences the others in relation to the single object of theology. This is especially prone to happen in the four-fold structure that separates biblical theology (exegesis) from historical theology. Since biblical exegesis is guided largely by historical and philological methods that are also used by historians, it best fits as a sub-discipline under historical theology. By stressing the relation of exegesis to the other areas of historical theology, one underscores the intimate connection between present interpretations of Scripture and the history of the interpretation of those same Scriptures. In this way, too, one avoids minimizing the interpretational challenges that have resulted from the temporal and cultural distance that exists between past biblical authors/communities and present interpreters. Not everything within Scripture is normative for contemporary Christian faith.

As Chapter 11 aimed to make clear, biblical exegesis is not undertaken in isolation from either historical theology or systematic theology. Historical theology wrestles with the historical origins of the biblical writings, evaluates the canonical status of each writing in relation to historical and theological factors, and makes critical judgments about the historical claims within the biblical documents and the history of biblical interpretation (which includes attention to errors that have arisen within biblical interpretation). Systematic theology, which is operative in all of the sub-disciplines to one degree or another, discloses that not every statement in Scripture is binding upon contemporary Christians, that not every Scriptural word or message is addressed to contemporary people, that some Scriptural teachings are outdated and others are more central. Systematic theology includes the task of comparing the results of contemporary interpretation of the biblical texts with those that have emerged within the history of biblical interpretation and the history of doctrine and of evaluating their theological claims. Thus, systematic theology has an impact on biblical interpretation and the history of Christian doctrine. Furthermore, systematic theology provides historical theology and practical theology (especially ethics) with the perspective for distinguishing what is important from what is unimportant in the biblical writings as well as in church history and the history of doctrine. Without this differentiation biblical exegesis would be mere philology (the study of words and their meanings), church history would be completely indistinguishable from secular history, and ethics would be no different from philosophical ethics.

Systematic theology thus raises questions about the contemporary meaning of biblical passages (do they mean the same as they did in the past?) and about the practical application of biblical passages in present situations that are different from past contexts. Have not some biblical texts themselves become null and void in the wake of the gospel and the dictates of Christian love? So systematic theology addresses itself to potential differences between past and present meaning(s) of biblical texts. It hopes always to articulate a contemporary understanding of Christian faith. And it does so in relation to contemporary knowledge and cultural circumstances. Finally, too, systematic theology has a critical task over against the church itself. Systematic theology wants to develop the essential content of the church's own faith in the present, to criticize the church and its history when it deviates or has deviated from that essential content, and to call the church back to its own immovable center, namely, Jesus the Christ, the Word (the *Logos*) of God. So, systematic theology reminds the church and all individuals within the church, including especially theologians, that they do not have an authority above or independent from that center.

Given these concerns, the overall goal of systematic theology is to provide the other two disciplines with a systematic presentation of their own results, insofar as they are significant for an understanding of what is essential in Christian doctrine, and to develop a theological summary of that essential content. This is the abiding insight of Schleiermacher, namely, that the systematic task of theology is the key to understanding each of the theological sub-disciplines. Thus, the intent of systematic theology is not to defend Christian documents per se (either Scripture or church confessional writings) as authoritative products of the past, but to set forth what they contain as valid for the present. It hopes to answer the question, "What does the historic witness to Christ mean for today? How does one make sense of the manifold content of that witness for contemporary human beings and their world?" Because the systematic task of theology is the key to the others, it ought to be discussed first in any taxonomy of Christian theology.

Nevertheless, while systematic theology will have a crucial impact on the execution of historical theology (including biblical exegesis), so historical theology will have an influence on systematic theology. Especially through its investigations of the normative sources of Christian teaching, historical theology discloses when particular systematic expositions of Christian faith have not taken into sufficient account some historical detail that is of abiding importance to Christian teaching. The historical theologian is thus in a position to correct flawed systematic presentations or flawed applications of Christian teaching in present, practical situations.

Perhaps the greatest weakness of both Schleiermacher's encyclopedia and the four-fold structure, at least at the undergraduate level, is their common assertion that practical theology is the crown and goal of theology. Such a view, at all levels of theological education, can easily lead to what Farley has called "the clerical paradigm," in which theology is merely a practical matter of educating future church leaders and providing them with "skills" for "public ministry." Farley and others lament that such a practical focus can minimize how the discipline engages people with certain basic *theological* questions: truth about God, the world, and human beings.

As an undergraduate academic discipline, Christian theology is not oriented toward the practical aim of clergy education or the education of church leaders. Rather, in this context, theology is primarily about the pursuit of truth, the cultivation of wisdom, and theological knowledge of God, one's self, and the world. While there is a place for practical theology at the undergraduate level, its focus is largely a matter of Christian ethics, the pursuit of justice, and the study of church structures and institutions (congregations, trans-denominational organizations, missions, Christian service, Christian public theology and political actions). Like the other two sub-disciplines, practical theology also invites critical and self-critical reflection on the revelation of God, the world, and human beings in the apostolic witness to Jesus Christ for the sake of the pursuit of wisdom, especially as it informs personal and social-political ethical action. In this way, the question of the truth of theological claims remains fundamental in each of the sub-disciplines, also practical theology. Accordingly, the unity of the sub-disciplines at the undergraduate level is given in the object of theology itself, the revelation of God, the world, and human beings in the apostolic witness to Jesus Christ.

Still another, related reason why practical theology is not the crown of the theological disciplines resides in the fact that systematic and historical theology have a responsibility to criticize the church and its practical traditions when these conflict with the truth of the object of theology. In other words, theology has the task of always putting the church and its beliefs and practices into a position of being questioned and examined. While none of the theological disciplines can disregard the reality of the churches and their situations, systematic and historical theology are neither to promote the church nor protect it from criticism, especially if the historical development of the churches and their present situation call for it (see Elert §2). Theology ought not to be fundamentally guided by the perspective of a practical, pragmatic, ecclesial utility. Too often theology devolves into a kind of "ghetto" operation when its sole focus is on the church and its practical life rather than the more encompassing arenas of the academy, human societies, and larger questions about truth, wisdom, and justice. The concerns for truth and the promise of the gospel are more basic to the theological task, and these concerns could lead the theologian to be critical of the church (or a church body), its beliefs, and its practices. When theological correction is required within Christian communities, the theologian has the responsibility to bring that criticism. "Discernment begins within the household of faith" (1 Pet. 4.17). Such criticism is, of course, in service to the church and its mission; academic theology cannot avoid the reality of the church, but it is not necessarily the advocate of the church and its practical life. It can do its work properly only if it is not encumbered by thoughts about defending or promoting the church and its practical activities.

Key Words

higher faculties	Karl Barth
lower faculties	Hagenbach's four
seven liberal arts	sub-disciplines
secularization	Ernst Troeltsch
humanities	Hofmann's three
religious studies	sub-disciplines
encyclopedia	systematic theology
theological encyclopedia	historical theology
Schleiermacher's three sub-	practical theology
disciplines	

Reference literature

For a general orientation to the issues and challenges in theological encyclopedia

ER 4:2782–5 ("Encyclopedias" [Stuckrad]); RPP 4:436 ("Encyclopedia" [Kronauer]); RPP 12:610–17 ("Theological Education" [Meireis et al.]); RPP 12:643–6 ("Theology: Theological Encyclopedia" [Schwöbel]).

For analysis of the divisions within theology in the more important textbooks of modern dogmatics

Aulén 3–22; Barth 1/1:3–44; Elert §§1–5; Tillich 1:28–34; Grenz 1–25; ICT 12–24; McGrath 104–10.

Questions for review and discussion

1   Walter Rüegg and others have noted how the medieval university was premised on core Christian beliefs. What are these beliefs? To

what extent are these beliefs still central to the institution of modern, secular universities?

2   According to the Lutheran theologian, Gerhard Ebeling, "All too often the church and theology have closed themselves to the progress of scholarly knowledge and have suppressed the truth until the artificial dam bursts again and the stream of true insight can no longer be stopped." The author refers to the Galileo affair and to the rejection of Darwinian evolution by many American Christians. Can you think of other examples that fit Ebeling's description?

3   How do religion, Christian theology, and theological issues continue to surface in contemporary public universities in the United States?

4   Where does Christian theology fit in a modern university? The author very briefly notes how some have understood the relationship between "theology" and "religious studies." Which way is most persuasive to you? Why?

5   What is the difference between an encyclopedia (like *Religion Past and Present*) and a theological encyclopedia, like Schleiermacher's *Brief Outline*? On what basis did Schleiermacher defend the place of Christian theology in a university over against Fichte's proposal to exclude it?

6   Why is academic Christian theology typically divided into sub-disciplines?

7   Schleiermacher divided theology into three sub-disciplines (philosophical, historical, and practical), as did Hofmann (systematic, historical, and practical). Hagenbach divided the discipline into four (exegesis, historical, systematic, and practical). How did each of these theologians understand the purpose of each of the main sub-disciplines?

8   Why does the author think Hofmann's and Pannenberg's respective approaches are more suited to an undergraduate liberal arts setting than the approach of Barth? Do you think that Barth's approach is less suitable for an undergraduate setting? Why or why not?

9   The author is critical of those who orient Christian theology toward a practical goal. Why? Do you agree or disagree with this criticism?

10   Do you think Christian theology can or should be studied as an academic discipline within a religious studies department in a North American public (secular) university? Why or why not?

Suggestions for further reading

The place of Christian theology within a university

David Ford, *Christian Wisdom: Desiring God and Learning in Love* (Cambridge: Cambridge University Press, 2007) [Professor Ford's focus is on the British scene, but his reflections apply to other university settings, both graduate and undergraduate. His book has significantly influenced the present chapter.]

David Knowles, *The Evolution of Medieval Thought*, 2nd edn, D. E. Luscombe and C. N. L. Brooke (eds) (London and New York: Longman, 1988) [Excellent historical survey of the rise of medieval universities and how they brought together earlier classical and Christian traditions of learning.]

D. L. Bird and Simon G. Smith (eds), *Theology and Religious Studies in Higher Education* (New York: Continuum, 2009) [This set of essays by scholars from around the world sets forth some of the current issues and debates regarding the tensions, conflicts, and agreements between the academic disciplines of "religious studies" and "theology."]

Theological encyclopedia

Matthew Becker, "The Shape of Theology as a University *Wissenschaft*: Schleiermacher's Reflection in Hofmann's *Theological Encyclopedia*," *Papers of the Nineteenth-Century Theology Group* 37 (American Academy of Religion) (November 2006), 103–27 [Provides a description and analysis of Schleiermacher's and Hofmann's contrasting views on theological encyclopedia.]

Richard Crouter, "Shaping an Academic Discipline: the Brief Outline on the Study of Theology," in *The Cambridge Companion to Friedrich Schleiermacher*, ed. Jacqueline Mariña (Cambridge: Cambridge University Press, 2005), 111–28 [A helpful analysis of Schleiermacher's ground-breaking theological encyclopedia.]

Gerhard Ebeling, "Discussion Theses for a Course of Introductory Lectures on the Study of Theology," in *Word and Faith*, trans. James W. Leitch (Minneapolis: Fortress Press Press, 1963), 424–33 [Provides a further defense of the need for all of the theological sub-disciplines to take their orientation from the theological subject that is studied hermeneutically.]

Gerhard Ebeling, "Theology as a Whole," in *The Study of Theology*, trans. Duane A. Priebe (Minneapolis: Fortress Press, 1978), 1–11 [Underscores the need to keep the properly theological character of theology as a whole in view of its potential and real disintegration into sub-disciplines and specialities.]

G. R. Evans, *Old Arts and New Technology: The Beginnings of Theology as an Academic Discipline* (Oxford: Oxford University Press, 1980) [Provides a complementary and partly contrasting account of the rise of medieval universities and the place of Christian theology within them from the ones offered by Ford and Knowles.]

Schubert Ogden, "What is Theology?" in *On Theology* (Dallas: Southern Methodist University Press, 1986), 1–21 [The most important example of theological encyclopedia by an American theologian in the last century. Ogden's presentation is informed by his engagement with Bultmann and modern process philosophy.]

Wolfhart Pannenberg, *Theology and the Philosophy of Science*, trans. Francis McDonagh (Philadelphia: Westminster, 1976), 346–440 [The most important German example of theological encyclopedia in the past century. Like Ogden's essays in the above volume, Pannenberg's are oriented toward a graduate-level audience.]

Karl Rahner, ed., *Encyclopedia of Theology: The Concise Sacramentum Mundi* (New York: Crossroad, 1982) [Major reference work in Roman Catholic theology.]

Friedrich Schleiermacher, *Brief Outline of Theology as a Field of Study*, trans. Terrance N. Tice (Lewiston: Edwin Mellen, 1988) [The most important Protestant analysis of the nature and tasks of Christian theology, as it was conceived for students at the University of Berlin in the early nineteenth century. This book has had a decisive influence on subsequent attempts in theological encyclopedia, including the one set forth in this book.]

13

The Sub-disciplines of Christian Theology

This chapter divides undergraduate theology into systematic theology (fundamental theology and doctrinal theology), historical theology (biblical theology, history of theology, and the history of Christianity), and practical theology (ecclesial studies and ethics).

In light of the concerns raised in Chapter 13, a better way of structuring Christian theology at the undergraduate level is the three-fold pattern set forth by Johannes von Hofmann: **systematic theology** (inclusive of fundamental and doctrinal theology), **historical theology** (inclusive of biblical interpretation, the history of Christian theology, and church history), and **practical theology** (inclusive of ecclesial studies and ethics). Although systematic theology appears first in the taxonomy, since its hermeneutical and methodological reflections provide an essential and normative understanding of the subject matter of theology in the present situation, the methods and results of each sub-discipline are intimately and dialectically related to those of the others (as in Schleiemacher's view). Systematic theology explores the most pressing methodological issues in Christian theology and endeavors to set forth a coherent summary of the principal doctrines or teachings of Christian theology in and for the present situation. Historical theology investigates the historical meaning(s) of statements within the NT and OT writings, the history of church doctrine and theology (which includes the study of church confessions), and the history of the church. Practical theology is divided into ecclesial studies (liturgics, homiletics, sacramental theology, missions, para-church activities, and ecclesial and liturgical art and architecture) and ethics. Since ecclesial studies examine the practical life of the present-day churches, it is most closely related to the sub-discipline of church history in historical theology. Since ethics is also partially oriented to theological principles for the present situation, it is most closely related to doctrinal theology within systematic theology. At the undergraduate level, where students are pursuing basic, foundational knowledge in all academic disciplines and are not directly pursuing professional training, most attention is given to the first two branches of theology and to ethics in the third branch.

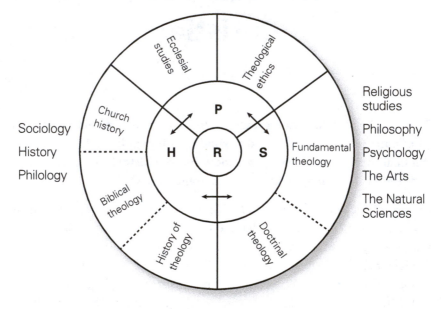

R = Revelation S = Systematic theology

H = Historical theology P = Practical theology

Figure 13.1

Systematic theology

Fundamental theology

Fundamental theology (not to be confused with Protestant Fundamentalism or biblicism) is a sub-discipline in systematic theology that desires to provide a scholarly defense of the place of theology within the academic disciplines and to discern what can be known of God through human reasoning and through reflection on the nature of divine revelation. While the roots of fundamental theology go back to the time of the Reformation, when several Roman Catholic theologians tried to defend their church and its teachings as the authentic form of Christianity over against perceived Protestant deviations, works in fundamental theology have been more common since the age of the Enlightenment. In view of the challenges posed by modern critics of the Roman Church, nineteenth-century Roman Catholic fundamental theology put forth a defense of religion against atheism, argued for the superiority of Christianity over other world religions, and maintained the truth of Catholicism over against the errors of heretics (such as Luther and his followers). While Roman Catholic fundamental theology had consistently focused upon the relation of philosophy to theology and had fostered a lively interest in metaphysics, during the past century it has focused more and more on the relation of theology to modern thought forms and toward the knowledge that has come from the sciences. In these ways, modern Catholic fundamental theology has tried to navigate between intellectual developments in the secular university disciplines and the normative character of the Roman Catholic Church as both the product of divine revelation and the normative means of that revelation. Since the Second Vatican Council, however, Catholic fundamental theology has shifted away from the attempt to set forth a rationalistic defense of that particular church and its teaching and toward interreligious and interdisciplinary dialogue and the problems that have arisen from thinking about divine revelation, epistemology, metaphysics, hermeneutics, and theological method. Contemporary Catholic fundamental theology continues to discuss such issues as the relationship between revelation and reason, the authority of Church tradition, the relationship between faith and human experience, the problems of language and historical understanding, the relationship between theory and social-political-ecclesial praxis, the relation of scientific knowledge to church teaching, and the appropriate form of a Catholic theology of the world's religions.[1]

Because Protestant theologians have traditionally been suspicious of all attempts to provide a supposedly rational, objective basis and defense of Christian faith, and because of their distrust of ecclesial institutions and their power to corrupt Scriptural teaching, Protestants did not develop a tradition of fundamental theology, in the Roman sense, until the twentieth century. While issues treated within Roman Catholic fundamental theology have also been important for Protestant theologians since the Reformation, these have typically been addressed only within the introductory section of works in dogmatic theology, usually under the heading of "theological

---

[1] See especially, O'Collins, *Rethinking Fundamental Theology*.

prolegomena" ("the first principles of theology"). These first principles set forth typically Protestant understandings of divine revelation, the use of philosophy in theology, the relationship of reason and faith, the nature of biblical authority, and the principles of biblical interpretation. Nevertheless, just as post-Reformation Catholic fundamental theology defended Catholicism and its particular understandings of church, tradition, authority, reason, and faith, so also traditional Protestant prolegomena have tried to defend Protestant positions on the primacy of the oral and written word of God over against church tradition and the primacy and centrality of faith alone in the Scriptural gospel of Christ alone over against human philosophy and the sinful condition of all things human, including human reasoning. One must underscore that the analysis and presentation of these "first principles" in Protestant theology occurred almost entirely within a church setting and within works of dogmatics that were written for future Protestant pastors. Because of these self-imposed limitations, pre-Enlightenment Protestant dogmatic theology was frequently unrelated to the problems that would surround Christian theology as an academic discipline in post-Enlightenment universities.

In the wake of the collapse of the older Protestant position on the inspiration of the Bible and various attempts to move beyond the subjectivist turn in the liberal Protestant tradition that was begun by Kant and Schleiermacher, contemporary Protestant fundamental theology has focused on the problems of theological hermeneutics and the challenge of speaking of the word of God as divine revelation. Protestant fundamental theology continually hunts for theological truth, especially concerning the reality of God and of God's revelation, in relation to all other claims to truth. Protestant fundamental theology thus "has the tendency to embrace everything in theology methodologically oriented to the question of contemporary validity and to the testing of the claim to truth."[2] Fundamental theology wants to engage all disciplines of human inquiry in relation to Christian theology and its truth claims. This present book is an attempt at articulating a Protestant understanding of issues in fundamental theology from a Protestant (Lutheran) perspective.

---

[2] Ebeling, *The Study of Theology*, 126.

Doctrinal theology

Doctrinal theology is a sub-discipline in systematic theology that tries to provide a contemporary, coherent, ordered, and systematic summary of Christian teaching that is attentive to the results of fundamental theology and that draws upon material that is uncovered by historical theology. It is also systematic in that it engages the object of Christian theology in such a way that the teaching is presented properly, that is, to thematize the truth of the Christian gospel message. Sometimes called "dogmatics" (Greek "*dogma*" = "that which seems [good]," "opinion," "thought" [OED 464]), doctrinal theology presents the big picture of Christian doctrine (Latin "*doctrina*" = "teaching"), i.e. what present-day Christians "believe, teach, and confess" (to use language from the Lutheran *Formula of Concord*). It does so on the basis of the biblical injunction: "Always be ready to give an answer to anyone who demands from you an explanation for the hope that is in you; yet do it with humility and respect" (1 Pet. 3.15–16). If Christian doctrine is the teaching that God intends people to receive and believe regarding divine revelation and the truth of the gospel, and "dogmatics" refers to the whole of that instruction, doctrinal theology clarifies the content of that teaching. "It has as its task, then, the comprehensive and coherent presentation of the doctrinal content of scripture and the articles of faith (*articula fidei*), in the sense of both positive restatement and learned argumentation" (Pannenberg 1.18).

Although doctrinal theology is clearly related to the history of Christian doctrine/dogma, it is different from that sub-discipline of historical theology because of its concern to provide a *contemporary, systematic* account of Christian teaching. To fulfill that task the doctrinal theologian must take into account the changed intellectual and cultural situation in which he or she stands in relation to previous situations or epochs in the history of Christianity. To be sure, the doctrinal theologian strives to bring forward into the present whatever is unchangeable in theology and unaffected by the passing of epochs, but doctrinal theology is not simply the passing on of past theological understandings *in toto*. Doctrinal theology changes over time precisely because the people engaged in it change over time. It cannot be burdened with aspects or content which are no longer necessary, if they ever were. Not every problem in the history of Christian theology is of abiding importance, and novel problems arise for which easy solutions are not available from the past. Doctrinal theology aspires only to comprehend, to test, and to articulate the essential and necessary content of Christian teaching, though to be sure a critical understanding of Christian doctrine also requires an understanding of biblical exegesis and the history of doctrine.

Because of this basic task of comprehending, testing, and articulating the essential and necessary content of Christian teaching on the basis of the results of all three sub-disciplines, systematic theology has the task of setting forth the subject matter of theology in its full complexity. It does this on behalf of the other two sub-disciplines. Only in the perspective of systematic theology, with its carefully thought through understanding of the total content of Christian theology, do the distinctive tasks of historical theology (biblical exegesis, church history, and the history of church doctrine) become clearer in relation to the scholarly disciplines of history and philology. Only in the perspective of systematic theology do the distinctive tasks of practical theology (ethics and ecclesial studies) become clearer in relation to philosophical ethics, psychology, and sociology. Systematic theology continually raises the question of the subject matter of Christian theology as a whole. It does so on behalf of the other theological disciplines and in conversation with those university disciplines whose foci intersect with that subject matter.

Because all theologies, including Christian systematic theology, are constantly confronted with the question of contemporary validity, they must be undertaken ever anew. Christian theologians in the second and subsequent centuries could fulfill their tasks as theologians as little as could the apostles by merely reciting a monotonous formula or using the same language as previous believers. The challenge in every age is to set forth the substance of the apostolic gospel by also taking into account the diverse people to whom that gospel promise is addressed and how best to convey it within new situations.

Moreover, any attempt at a coherent, systematic presentation of theology is always in need of revision. One cannot avoid returning again and again to the sources of that theology and to the perennial questions that have given rise to it. In this way, questions in theology remain open, and the answers to them provisional. This understanding of theology should be sufficient to ward off criticism that systematic theology is merely the authoritative transmission of an uncritical orthodoxy. Systematic theology must take the lead in constantly putting Christian faith and practice into a position of being questioned. It must also question any and all forms of dogmatism, whether of the believing kind frequently found within religious communities or the insufficiently grounded, skeptical kind often found within academic communities. Unsubstantiated skepticism is just as far removed from true learning as is unsubstantiated dogmatism. Critical theology is opposed to both, even as it wants to be self-critical in relation to its subject matter.

Within Christian systematic theology there is the explicit awareness that all human knowledge, including the theological, remains incomplete and imperfect (1 Cor. 13.9) until "the end of time." For this reason, too, doctrinal theology must be understood as not referring to a static, closed system, but to an interpretative, hermeneutical stance for engaging the questions of understanding, wisdom, and truth within theology—also in relation to the person who is by nature "without faith." While some Christians will undoubtedly find this approach to theology intellectually challenging, and even uncomfortable, especially if cherished beliefs are held up to critical scrutiny, one cannot and should not avoid such challenges, that accompany every academic subject. "Just like every other academic investigation, theology distinguishes itself from the witches' kitchen of alchemy by the fact that it may at all times grant others an insight into its mode of operation, but academic discipline demands also that we wait until its fruits have matured" (Elert 20).

While doctrinal theology is guided by strict academic standards and methods and the concern for truth and accuracy, it is also shaped by existential commitments:

> To engage in systematic theology in this way is quite compatible with personal confidence in the ultimate truth of the Christian doctrine, even more so than on the basis of a prior commitment to authority. A Christian should be ready to leave it to God himself to prove definitely his reality, and he or she should be content to perceive but vaguely and to adumbrate the infinite wealth of the truth of God. But certainly, we need to be reassured of that truth, and precisely there is the place for systematic theology.[3]

Finally, doctrinal theology is theology only to the extent that it wrestles with the abiding problems of theology as these have emerged from history, problems that are posed for theology by its own historical location and its relation to the past of theology. Since the task of systematic theology is to investigate the content that is given within the revelation of God, the world, and human beings in the apostolic witness to Jesus, and to inquire about its sufficient basis and abiding nature, the task of systematic theology is necessarily informed by historical inquiry. This historical dimension of systematic theology is further explored within the sub-discipline of historical theology.

---

[3] Pannenberg, *An Introduction to Systematic Theology*, 18.

Historical theology

Historical theology investigates historical developments within "Christianity." It is "theology" only to the extent that it participates in the investigation of that which systematic theology also investigates, namely, the object of Christian theology. With regard to its method, historical theologians use the same tools and principles that all other historians use, and thus historical theology stands in close proximity to the academic disciplines of history, the history of religions, the philosophy of history, sociology, and the humanities. Historical theologians utilize historical-critical methods for investigating past phenomena within Christianity, they follow the scholarly principles that Troeltsch has classically formulated (criticism, analogy, and correlation), and they seek to be rid of (religious or anti-religious) prejudice and bias.[4]

On the other hand, to the extent that they are guided by theological principles, norms, and concerns, historical theologians do address matters of *theology* that take them beyond mere historical-critical study. Not only are historical theologians interested in the distinctiveness and uniqueness of Christianity as a collection of phenomena within world history, they also cannot avoid addressing their own theological judgments regarding Jesus the Christ and his relation to all subsequent historical phenomena, a perspective that undoubtedly shapes and informs their attempt to understand past events within the history of Christianity. For example, what is the relation of the Jesus of history to the Christ of faith? Did Jesus found "the church?" Are the so-called "Gnostic" Christians just as legitimate as those who attacked them and labeled them "heretics"? Which historical-critical and theological judgments does the scholar make about other turning points in the history of Christianity? Do the developments of early "catholicism" and the Constantinian "revolution" mark legitimate continuations of apostolic Christianity, or are they essentially discontinuous? Were the reforms of Luther legitimate or illegitimate? Historical theologians, to the extent that they are indeed involved in theology, cannot avoid these kinds of normative, theological questions, that often enter into historical theology as an academic discipline.

---

[4] For Troeltsch's principles of historical investigation, see Chapter 11.

Biblical theology

As noted in the previous chapter, **biblical theology** is best understood, not as a separate branch of theology (as in Hagenbach's four-fold division), but as a sub-discipline in historical theology. Its placement there is due to the fact that the interpretation of the Bible is guided largely by the same historical and philological methods that are used by secular historians. Furthermore, by stressing the relation of biblical interpretation (exegesis) to the other areas of historical theology, one underscores the intimate connection between present interpretations of Scripture and the history of the interpretation of those same Scriptures. In this way too one avoids minimizing the interpretative, hermeneutical challenges that have resulted from the temporal and cultural distance that exists between past biblical authors/communities and present interpreters. That not everything is normative in the Bible today becomes clearer if one keeps biblical theology firmly placed in historical theology.

Biblical theology investigates the historical origin of the Christian Scriptures and their historical meaning(s) in the history of their interpretation. What distinguishes theological interpretation of these writings from the historical investigation of all other historical writings is the degree to which the interpreter allows the theological subject matter of the texts to address him or her and others with an authoritative *theological* claim. This claim is itself premised on a theological engagement with the questions regarding the nature of the biblical canon and the extent of those Scriptures that are deemed to be truly prophetic and apostolic. Because the biblical theologian comes to these Scriptures with the expectation that they attest to the authoritative word of God, the scholar will make use of all methods and means which are appropriate to an ancient text that has been used to pass on historical tradition as normative. The scholar will strive to remain open to the theological content of these Scriptures, to give complete attention to all details in the texts, and to use the most rigorous scholarly methods for the sake of making clear how the word of God has been expressed and understood through them over time.

Given that the collection of early-Christian literature is large and complex, and contains a wide variety of different types of writing with differing theological claims, the biblical theologian must attend first to the problem of the development of the biblical canon within early Christianity (and to the abiding theological significance of the distinction between the homolegoumena and the antilegomena), to the hermeneutical challenges involved in the interpretation of the Scriptures, and to the problem of the relation between the writings of the OT and of the NT. As noted in Chapter 11, the biblical theologian is guided by certain hermeneutical principles *vis-à-vis* the interpretation of these texts. Not only must the biblical theologian master the original biblical languages (Hebrew, Aramaic, Greek) and learn about the historical contexts of the biblical writings, but that person must also attend to the literary character of the Bible and to the process by which the biblical books have been gathered into a canonical whole. The goal of biblical theology is to uncover and explain the historical meaning(s) of the biblical texts—what they "meant" "then and there"—to criticize and ward off false or inappropriate understandings, and to maintain a posture of self-criticism in view of the many possible ways in which biblical interpreters can deceive themselves in the process of their interpretations. Since "the word of God" is by its very nature not simply and only a written, once-upon-a-time word ("Scripture"), but also a living and incarnate Word (one that exercises an uncanny claim on the reader/hearer and is proclaimed and understood in the present), biblical theology provides faithful exposition of the ancient biblical writings in service to that present proclamation and understanding.

History of Christian theology

This sub-division of historical theology investigates the development of theological ideas in the course of the history of Christianity. The study of this development is not limited to formal expressions of church teaching (as if it were merely a sub-discipline of church history) but includes the reflections of individual theologians and religious philosophers (who might have a tenuous relationship to Christianity) on key themes in Christian theology. Thus **the history of theology** focuses on the main dogmatic issues in the history of Christianity (the doctrine of God, theological anthropology, the person and work of Jesus Christ, church sacraments, and so on) and how these issues have been understood theologically over time. Attention is given, for example, to the development of the various creeds and confessions in church history, both those that developed in the context of the church's liturgy (baptismal creeds) and those that developed in conflict over true and false teaching (creeds that developed in opposition to specific heresies, such as the Niceno-Constantinopolitan Creed which condemns Arianism). Following the crucial conclusion of the eighteenth-century historian, Semler, historical theologians over the past two centuries have stressed the need to attend to the ways in which the theological language and thought-forms of earlier Christian thinkers have been shaped by the historical and social situations in which these thinkers lived and moved and had their being. The use of historical-critical methods for investigating that history is central to the discipline, even if there is also widespread awareness today regarding the need to investigate the historical theologian's own intellectual presuppositions and social-cultural location.

While the principal methods and goals of the sub-discipline of historical theology are the same as those in history and the social sciences, what distinguishes the history of theology from all other historical and social investigations of intellectual history is the degree to which the historian allows the theological subject matter within the historical sources to persist and even become prominent. The goal here is not merely to understand past Christian sources as intellectual artifacts of the history of Christianity, as important as those artifacts might be in their own right, but to analyze those sources theologically and critically and to draw from them those insights that can be brought forward into contemporary systematic theology (and to criticize those aspects that are outdated, flawed, or insignificant). "It is not sufficient, then, for historical theology to reconstruct the meaning of texts in their historical setting, to observe changing conceptions from one generation to another, and to note the differences between those who lived in former ages and ourselves" (NHCT 229 [Wilken]). Historical theology must continually inquire after the theological subject matter that unifies the discipline of theology as a whole.

If biblical theology strives to allow the canonical biblical writings to speak theologically to the present, the history of Christian theology seeks to identify the significant Christian voices from the past that still have something important to say today. One thinks in particular of early-church conciliar decisions (e.g. Nicaea, Chalcedon) and of the writings of those "doctors of the church" (at least the ones prior to the fifteenth century, whose importance Protestants also acknowledge), whose reflections continue to be an influence upon contemporary understandings of the key themes in Christian theology. One also thinks of other "classic" thinkers in the tradition, such as the sixteenth-century Reformers and those significant nineteenth- and twentieth-century figures whose writings continue to provide important insights to all who are thinking about theology today. So the history of Christian theology is also an important component in the bridge between historical theology and contemporary systematic theology. It aims to show how both of these sub-disciplines pursue the formulation of Christian teaching at the present time.

The history of Christian theology also helps to address the widespread ignorance that many university students seem to have about the development of Christian thought between the first century and the present, a development that has significantly shaped the course of Western civilization and that is even now shaping large areas of the contemporary world. By following the trains of thought in the classic figures in the history of Christian theology, by thinking with them, one can learn how the basic concepts within Christian theology have grown out of the circumstances in which they were first formulated. What were the rationales that were given for specific theological positions in Christian history? What were the authoritative judgments that these figures made about what is central and peripheral, normative and heretical, abiding and transitory in the history of Christian thought? What can and should we learn from past theologians?

History of Christianity

This sub-discipline, classically called **church history**, investigates the development of the Christian institutions as social and political phenomena. The academic discipline of the history of Christianity seeks both historical and theological understanding, but what distinguishes it from the historical investigation of all other social and political institutions is the degree to which the scholar allows properly *theological* issues, judgments, and claims to be raised. If this connection between theology and the history of Christianity (church history) is not properly grasped, then both church history and the other theological disciplines suffer. "The dissociation of theology from church history is a symptom and source of bad theology."[5]

What is the theological significance of the history of Christianity? What is the relation of the churches as social and political entities to the formulation of theological understanding or misunderstanding? While church history is not a primary source of theological knowledge, it does inform the theological task in central ways. For example, the meaning of Christian Scripture is in some sense tied to the history of its interpretation (or misinterpretation), and thus church history helps to show how churches have understood and applied the Scriptures in the past. Church history also explores the development of church traditions and their applications in the

---

[5]Gerhard Ebeling, "Discussion Theses for a Course of Introductory Lectures in the Study of Theology," in *Word and Faith*, 429.

life of the churches. Much of this history is a history of conflict over the nature of church traditions, and thus the historian has the duty of uncovering the underlying causes of these tensions and disagreements. What is all the fuss about? Or what was it all about? Such questions invite repeated investigation.

Moreover, the history of Christianity, as an academic discipline, provides a critical service over against contemporary (mis)understandings of the churches, their teachings, and practices. For this reason it is perhaps better to speak of "the history of Christianity" rather than "church history," since much of that history involves more than merely "the church" (as an ideal construct) or "the churches" (as individual instances of Christian community in the world). This shift in focus from "church" to "Christianity" is evident in the history of the publication of the principal North-American academic journal in this field. There one detects a movement away from broad topics and themes in "church history" to narrower, more specialized studies of issues, problems, and figures in the history of Christianity and its historic manifestations in diverse cultures.[6] Focusing on the manifold character of "Christianity" rather than merely on the ideal concept of "church," one will be led to uncover aspects of the "tradition" that have been lost or forgotten or not widely known in the first place. Recent scholars, for instance, have uncovered forgotten voices and lives in the history of Christianity—women, for example—and have allowed them to speak to the present.[7] Thus scholarly conclusions in this sub-discipline often disabuse people of their wrong notions of the church, its history, its teachings, and its practices. The execution of this scholarly discipline has a way of disrupting comfortable understandings of "church" or at least complicating them. It demonstrates that there never has been a time when *one* unambiguously demonstrable church has ever existed. There has always been a plurality of churches, and this fact complicates a theological understanding of "church." While Christian theology in North America still remains largely Eurocentric and North-American in nature, the study of the history of Christianity reveals how the diversity of the world's cultures has influenced the shape and content of Christian theology in global contexts.

---

[6] See *Church History: Studies in Christianity and Culture*, a quarterly journal that has been published by the American Society of Church History since 1911. The sub-title was added in the 1990s to reflect this change of focus beyond merely the Christian "church."

[7] See especially Barbara J. MacHaffie, *Her Story: Women in Christian Tradition*, 2nd edn (Minneapolis: Augsburg, 2006) and Nicola Denzey, *The Bone Gatherers: The Lost Worlds of Early Christian Women* (Boston: Beacon, 2007).

Other, non-theological factors can become central in the history of Christianity and the history of Christian thought. In other words, the history of Christianity as an academic discipline "combats the illusion that theology has only to do with theology."[8] Can one, for example, understand the development of the fourth-century Niceno-Constantinopolitan Creed without appreciating the political complexities within the Roman Empire of that time and how they affected that development? Can one understand the theology of Augustine of Hippo without attention to the political and social factors of fourth- and fifth-century Milan and North Africa? Can one even begin to understand the Protestant Reformers' criticism of papal authority in the sixteenth century without first appreciating the crisis that developed for the Roman Church when the humanist scholar Lorenzo Valla demonstrated that the Donation of Constantine was in fact a forgery? Can one understand the theological development of the various Protestant groups in sixteenth-century Europe without attention to geo-political, economic, and social factors? Investigation into the history of Christianity will uncover the "mishmash of error and power" (Goethe) that often lurks behind theological decisions and the exercise of church authority. Such investigation will probe more deeply into the well-known and not-so-well-known scandals in that history. Furthermore, it will wrestle with the interaction between what is perceived to be "essentially Christian" with what is not. Insofar as properly theological issues surface within the study of the history of Christianity, one will be led back to questions regarding the relation of Jesus (understood to be the origin of "the one, holy, catholic, and apostolic church") to all later phenomena within that historical development.

As in the study of biblical theology so also in the study of the history of Christianity as a *theological* discipline, the scholar will continually wrestle with hermeneutical, interpretive, and theological issues. These issues are not limited to problems of understanding in the history of biblical interpretation or to applications of biblical teaching in the history of Christian communities. The church historian also desires to interpret biographies of Christians, institutions, liturgies (forms of worship), programs, the actions of individuals and communities (and the theological motivations for those actions, if any can be detected), suppressions of truth, persisting theological expressions across the centuries, and human suffering and lived human experience in relation to Christianity. When the historian of Christianity

---

[8] Ebeling, ibid., 429.

seeks to understand such phenomena he or she cannot help but be shaped by properly theological concerns. These theological concerns arise when one struggles to make sense of historical phenomena in relation to the truth claims of Christian faith, specifically the claim that the eternal *Logos* of God has become incarnate in Jesus of Nazareth and that this claim has significant consequences for one's understanding of reality as a whole. In this way the interrelation of "truth" and "history" remains open to repeated investigation.

The theological dimension of the history of Christianity, as an academic discipline, also arises when one explores one's own faith commitments and theological presuppositions in relation to one's scholarly work as an historian of Christianity, when one's faith provides a perspective or insight upon one's interpretation of relevant historical phenomena, when basic questions of faith remain open to further investigation, and when one attempts "to reflect theologically upon Church history using historical approaches."[9] No one approaches the history of Christianity as an empty computer. There is no such creature as a presuppositionless historian of Christianity.

Precisely because of the immensity and diversity of material in the history of Christianity, much of which remains ambiguous and open to multiple interpretations, one needs to recognize that no individual scholar or even group of scholars can possibly master its breadth and complexity as a whole, even if one's theological commitments lead one to make judgments about that "whole" and about specific individual parts or pieces within that historical whole. There is thus the need for humility, openness to correction, repeated attentiveness to the primary source materials, and respectful engagement with the work of other scholars who are investigating the same phenomena. Because this field of study is so large and complicated, the beginning student would do well to focus on the one-volume surveys of church history that are listed in the bibliography at the end of the chapter. These provide an initial, broader picture in large frameworks. These resources are a good place to begin one's historical study of Christianity, before moving on to appreciate how the picture changes in its details as a result of more specialized study.

---

[9] Euan Cameron, *Interpreting Christian History: The Challenge of the Churches' Past* (New York: Blackwell, 2005).

Practical theology

Practical theology investigates the actions of Christians within their various congregational-communal-social settings and inquires into the theological reasons for those actions. It is "theology" only to the extent that it also participates in the investigation of that which systematic theology investigates, namely, the subject of Christian theology. Practical theology continually inquires about the relation of that subject to actual **praxis** (action) within specific communities of Christian faith. While the scholarly character of practical theology has been criticized over the past two centuries as being too focused on "the church" (and thus many have wondered if it really belongs within a *university* curriculum), its position within the circle of the theological disciplines can be defended as long as it maintains its relationship with the other two sub-disciplines and underscores their relationship to the actual lived experiences of Christians in their congregational and social settings. With regard to method, practical theologians are particularly guided by the social sciences, although they also engage the other sciences that shed light on human behavior and on the beliefs and motivations that are related to that behavior.

Practical theology within academic communities, whether undergraduate or graduate, often occurs informally outside of the academic curriculum as members of the community undertake actions that are related to Christian faith. Most obviously this might take place in the context of a university or seminary chapel, its worship services, and its extra-curricular activities. For example, many students will reflect upon their personal faith (or the faith of others) in relation to the social actions they undertake as students (e.g. raising money for the poor, giving food to the hungry, building homes for the homeless, seeking to end racial inequality, etc.). Or they will inquire about the theological understanding of preaching or the sacraments or other Christian ritual actions. Or they will wonder about appropriate ethical action in relation to some significant problem or set of problems. They will thus engage in political theology and the praxis that is related to it.

Within a curricular setting, however, practical theology at the graduate or professional level looks different from what it is at the undergraduate level. In a graduate context, practical theology tends to focus on the training of church leaders for their specific practical tasks within a congregational setting or in the context of a church-related institution or program. Here practical theology is largely about teaching people basic objectives, skills, and techniques for their practical administration of Christian communities. Thus it often tends to be mostly a matter of pastoral theology, of educating and training individuals for their role of "shepherding" a congregation, or serving as a leader in a church-related or para-church ("alongside the church") organization. So graduate or seminary students learn to develop and lead Christian worship services, to preach, to administer church sacraments, to provide pastoral care and counseling, and to be involved in community organizing. More recently, practical theology at this professional level has both broadened and sharpened its focus to include reflection on the actions of communities of faith within their particular social-historical setting and on the need for transformative praxis (action) in the world. Feminist and liberation theologians have been at the forefront of this reformation within practical theology. They have continued to maintain the vision of Schleiermacher, wherein practical theology is the crown and goal of the theological disciplines.

Practical theology at the undergraduate level takes a slightly different shape and does not serve as the goal of the theological disciplines. Here it is less oriented toward equipping future pastors or church leaders for their practical vocation within the actual life of a Christian congregation or church-related organization, though it may include this. It is more broadly focused on the practical impact of Christian theology upon an individual's "vocation(s)" or "calling(s)" in the world, callings that may have very little to do with preaching, administration of sacraments, pastoral care and counseling, or even community organizing. Practical theology at the undergraduate level focuses less on the preparation of clerical professionals and their vocation of equipping others for Christian action in the world than it does on the study of the complex experiences of Christians within their own vocation (in the broader sense of calling to responsibility in their communities and world), within their congregations and communities, regarding their actions and endeavors, and their understandings and applications of personal and social ethics. While practical theology at this undergraduate level will also examine the social-historical context of Christian communities of faith and learn from the insights of liberation and feminist theologians, it will seek to engage individuals in reflection on their own vocations of faith, their own callings in the world, whatever these might be or become, and upon the social and communal aspects of their faith. As at the graduate level, so also at the undergraduate level, practical theology critically appropriates insights and findings from the various social sciences and engages in theological reflection on human action.

Certainly all three sub-disciplines of theology have a relationship to the present, to current understandings of reality, and to contemporary domains of life (politics, economics, social phenomena such as family structures, the environment). Yet practical theology is especially focused on the present situation of the church and its activities, and upon the vocation and ethical actions of individual Christians in their world; and it is concerned to understand and evaluate those activities and actions in light of theological principles and findings from the other two sub-disciplines.

So practical theology does, in fact, belong in the undergraduate curriculum after all, precisely because it focuses on the theological idea of "vocation":

> Vocation, because it involves on the one hand matters of identity and destiny, questions of who we are and why we are here and what we might become, belongs to the discourse of liberal education. But because vocation also involves a summons to particular kinds of work in the world, it belongs as well to the discourse of the professions. Indeed, the idea of vocation, rightly understood, cuts across the domains of the social sciences and humanities, the performing arts, and the learned professions. . . Vocation has the capacity to imbue those who are called with a sense of responsibility, with an ethical dimension to their actions in the world; the liberal arts have the potential to render action in the public domain reasonable, articulate, and effective.[10]

Practical theology assists the liberal arts by constantly returning to the theological roots of the idea of "vocation," to the examination of Christians and the communities in which they live out their vocations, and to the theological aspects of personal and social ethics.

Ecclesial studies

Ecclesial Studies, a sub-division of practical theology, investigates Christian institutions and activities as they exist or occur at the present time. Although such study may examine individual Christian congregations as social phenomena, this sub-division explores what is church-wide, ecumenical, trans-denominational, and occurs even beyond the organized churches or para-church organizations. Thus the name "ecclesial studies" is

---

[10] Mark Schwehn, "Lutheranism and the Future of the University," *The Cresset* 73 (December 2009), 8–9.

more appropriate than "congregational studies," which term is simply too parochial and narrow.

Ecclesial studies seeks both sociological and theological understanding of contemporary church-related phenomena. Such study could focus quite narrowly on a local congregation, its demographics, its church practices and activities. For example, one might explore theological understanding of a particular church's liturgy (forms of worship), ritual actions (sacraments), homiletics (preaching), liturgical art and architecture, or congregational programs. What is the theological meaning of Christian liturgy?[11] What are a congregation's "stories and structures," and how do they help to embed a congregation in its social setting?[12] How is Christ mediated to the world through the activities of empirical churches? How does the church communicate the gospel in the present moment? One might also compare the activities of a given church, its proclamation of the word and administration of grace through sacramental means, its educational programs, its visual arts, with those of a church from a different confessional or theological background.

More broadly, ecclesial studies also address larger "macro-church" or "para-church" institutions and activities. For example, one could focus on the theological, social, and political actions of the worldwide ecumenical organizations such as the Lutheran World Federation or the World Council of Churches, or one could focus on current missionary activities in one part of the world or another. Or one might look at a cluster of complex social, economic, and political issues that affect Christian communities in their present local settings. What is their role in "faith-based" initiatives or community activities? Still further, one might explore the theological understandings of health and healing as these relate to church-operated hospitals and health clinics. The list of possible areas of study are as broad and complex as the extent of Christian involvement in the world.

In any case, regardless of what aspect of the Christian church one investigates, what distinguishes this kind of ecclesial study from purely social-scientific analysis and criticism or aesthetic criticism (in the case of liturgical art and architecture) is the degree to which properly *theological*

---

[11] The range of literature in "liturgical studies" is large, but a good place to begin is the important study by Gordon W. Lathrop, *Holy Things: A Liturgical Theology* (Minneapolis: Augsburg Fortress, 1993). See also Marva J. Dawn, *Reaching Out without Dumbing Down: A Theology of Worship for This Urgent Time* (Grand Rapids: Eerdmans, 1995).

[12] One of the best explorations of this aspect of practical theology is James F. Hopewell, *Congregation: Stories and Structures* (Minneapolis: Fortress Press, 1987).

issues, judgments, and claims are allowed to factor in to one's investigation. To one degree or another, every instance of ecclesial phenomena points beyond itself to its historical origin and to properly theological questions: Is this phenomenon consistent with the normative sources of Christian theology? What is the faith dimension of this particular empirical reality or action? How is this a manifestation of the church as "the body of Christ?" in the world? What is the relationship of this phenomenon to the present mission of the church? What is appropriate within the contemporary church's life and mission?

Like the discipline of historical theology, ecclesial study examines the church as a social phenomenon (or set of phenomena), but it focuses more directly on the present situation of the church and not on past developments. Like systematic theology, ecclesial study has the challenge of constantly calling the church and its practices into question. It, too, is concerned with making judgments about what is peripheral and central in the Christian community, what is normative and what is subject to negative criticism within the present existence of the church and its involvement with the world.

Theological ethics

The place of **theological ethics** or moral theology within Christian theology is a matter of dispute. Some scholars see it as a sub-discipline within systematic theology since it addresses the *principles* of Christian moral theology in the world today. Others view it as a sub-discipline within practical theology since its goal is the *practical application* of the principles of Christian moral theology in the actual lives of Christians and their communities of faith in the world today.

While systematic theology concerns the underlying doctrines and teachings that serve as the foundation for how Christians should live, practical theology addresses how those teachings should be applied in specific, actual situations. While most scholars rightly distinguish "ethics," which is concerned with theory, from "morals," which address specific behaviors or actions, in the execution of theological ethics this distinction is not always clear nor can it always be maintained. Indeed, this overlapping of "ethics" and "morals" also makes the place of Christian theological ethics within a theological encyclopedia ambiguous. Certainly, while Christian doctrine cannot be separated from the practical concerns of Christian ethics or moral theology, it must be distinguished from the latter for the sake of properly distinguishing faith in the gospel promise from the good deeds that flow as a consequence of that promise. Even Barth acknowledged this when he clearly distinguished the themes of Christian doctrine/dogmatics from those of Christian ethics within his overall dogmatics. He, too, acknowledged that Christian faith is entirely a matter of passive reception, as do most other Protestants out of concern for the gospel promise (which can only be received by faith), and not something that is identical to human action or behavior. The gospel does not have the character of law, which addresses human beings in their activity. Systematic theology is not always practical. "Theology as such is not ethics" (Ebeling 149). Its principal focus must always be a theoretical concern for the truth of Christian theology and for the centrality of the promise of the gospel. Practical theology, on the other hand, is always focused on a pragmatic concern to apply Christian teaching in the lives of Christians and to explore how that teaching intersects with the needs of the world. Consequently, theological ethics is best placed within practical theology although it is always closely related to the other two sub-disciplines, especially systematic theology.

Christian ethics is to be distinguished from all other religious and philosophical ethics to the extent that it allows the subject of Christian theology to shed light on one's understanding of the questions, "How should I live?" "How should we live as a society?" "How should we live as a human community on this fragile planet?" Within a theological context, these questions multiply into many others: "How does God want me/us to live and act? What is the will of God in this particular, concrete situation? How am I to live before God? What am I to do now, given my Christian understanding of God, the world, and myself?" Thus ethical discussion within Christian theology is constantly oriented toward the ethical and moral consequences of one's faith in God. Its focus is on the present and the future. What is the relation between Christian faith in God or understanding of God, on the one hand, and Christian moral action, on the other? What do I understand about myself as a child of God and about all other people? For what am I responsible? For what are we responsible? To whom are we responsible? What are my/our duties? How does one address the moral failures of others and of oneself? In view of the connectedness of "fate," responsibility, and human freedom to make ethical choices, what is the nature of the human consciousness of fault, of guilt, of shame, of sin (which is entirely a religious/theological concept)? How does one make theological sense of ethical situations in which one cannot avoid guilt, regardless of one's chosen course of action? What is the nature of Christian love?

How about situations in which people pride themselves on their moral accomplishments and somehow think they count positively toward their good standing before God? Jesus had some rather harsh words for people who arrogantly thought they were religiously and ethically perfect. Both the moral weakness of human nature, and the moral strength of human beings, comes under criticism within Christian theological ethics. In many respects, such ethics complicates philosophical ethics by raising questions that point toward the limits of a purely philosophical approach to ethics and that underscore the religious and theological dimensions of ethical life and one's reflection upon it.

To be sure, the Christian ought to make use of ethical insights from beyond the circle of Christian theology, to be attentive to lasting insights from the history of philosophical ethics that began with Aristotle. The modern Christian is especially concerned to analyze and criticize conceptions of human freedom and autonomy in philosophical ethics and to explore their potential continuity and discontinuity with Christian theological anthropology. The history of Christian ethics demonstrates that theological ethics is intertwined with the history of philosophical ethics and of efforts to base human action on non-theological, entirely rational (universal) presuppositions. One needs only to mention the influence of Stoicism on early Christian ethics and the respective influences of Aristotle's *Nicomachean Ethics*, Kant's moral philosophy, and Marxist and feminist social analysis on contemporary forms of Christian ethics, to show this intertwining. Of course, each of these influences is contested among Christian theologians, and all of them have come under fire from one quarter or another because they are perceived to be in contradiction to central assumptions of Christian faith and understanding. Nevertheless, contemporary Christian ethics does not occur in isolation from the larger context of philosophical ethics. It is concerned to analyze and interpret the same existential, ethical realities that all human beings face in their lives and communities.

Despite its openness to the valid ethical insights and analysis from beyond the circle of Christian theology, Christian ethics takes its fundamental orientation from the gospel promise, which is received by faith, and from the concrete character of Christian love. According to Paul, "faith" is "to be active in love" (Gal. 5.6). Thus Christian theological ethics will evaluate human behavior on the basis of these two normative foci and within that perspective try to assist people to make good decisions about their future courses of action. Of course, finding this good and right course of action is the great challenge, given the complexities and ambiguities of life, and the ethical demands that come upon us. A challenge, too, is how to commend the doing of good actions without losing the gospel promise that is received by faith. From the perspective of Christian faith the gift of God's own goodness and righteousness to the individual provides that person with the proper starting point for ethical reflection. That grace of God provides a necessary context for discerning ethical demands and making ethical choices. It is central to the ethics of those who live from the promises of God.

Key Words

systematic theology	history of theology
historical theology	history of Christianity
practical theology	church history
fundamental theology	praxis
doctrinal theology	theological ethics
biblical theology	ecclesial studies

Reference literature

On systematic theology

ER 4:2381–5 ("Doctrine" [Comstock]); ER 13:9134–42 ("Theology: Christian Theology" [Congar]); NHCT 469–74 ("Systematic Theology" [Macquarrie]); OCCT 700–2 ("Theology" [Hastings]); RPP 4:134–7 ("Dogma" [Herms]); OHST 1–15 ("Introduction: Systematic Theology" [Webster]); RPP 4:141–52 ("Dogmatics" [Herms; Lange]); RPP 5:280–7 ("Fundamental Theology" [Jeanrond et al.]); RPP 12:608–10 ("Theologia" [Cancik]); RPP 12:617–46 ("Theology" [Schwöbel]); RPP 12:449–53 ("Systematic Theology" [Schwöbel]).

On historical theology

ER 2:83–9 ("Biblical Theology" [Janowski; Welker]); ER 2:870–8 ("Biblical Exegesis: Christian Views" [Rowland]); NHCT 225–30 ("Historical Theology" [Wilken]); RPP 3:96–112 ("Church History/Church Historiography" [Markschies et al.]); RPP 4:137–41 ("Dogma, History of" [May]); RPP 12:646–50 ("Theology, History/Historiography of" [Köpf]).

On practical theology

ER 3:1650–7 ("Christian Ethics" [Curran]); ER 3:1660–741 ("Christianity" [Pelikan et al.]); ER 3:1763–79 ("Church" [Lynch et al.]); NHCT 375–7 ("Practical Theology" [Polk]); RPP 3:1–22 ("Church" [Wenz et al.]); RPP 4:577–98 ("Ethics" [Herms et al.]); RPP 10:273–8 ("Practical Theology" [Grethlein; Meyer-Blanck]).

Questions for review and discussion

1   What is systematic theology? What are its goals? Do you agree that systematic theology ought to be discussed first in any theological encyclopedia? Why does the author think so?

2   Many theologians will want to make biblical theology a separate sub-discipline of theology and not include it under "historical theology"? Why does the author place biblical theology where he does? Do you agree with this placement? Why or why not?

3   Why does the author prefer the designation "history of Christianity" rather than "church history"?

4   Why might some Christians argue that "Christian doctrine" or Christian teaching does not have "a history"? In other words, why might some Christians argue that Christian doctrine does not change over time? Do you agree with the author that Christian doctrine (or at least the theological understanding of that teaching) does in fact change over time? Why or why not?

5   Why does the author constantly insist on the properly *theological* character of each of the sub-disciplines of theology and their own sub-branches?

6   Why is the author critical of viewing "practical theology" as the goal of academic theology at the undergraduate level? Do you agree or disagree with the author on this point?

7   The term "ecclesial" comes from the Greek word for "church." Why does the author stress that "ecclesial studies" studies more than merely "the church" or "Christian congregations"? Can you identify a couple of "para-church" organizations (i.e. organizations that are not a "church" but are largely organized by Christians and have a "Christian" basis or background)?

8   How might theological ethics be different from so-called philosophical ethics?

9 What are the most important ethical questions of today? How might Christian teaching and practices address these questions? What is meant by the term "praxis"?

10 Which of the three sub-disciplines most interests you for further study? Why? Which least interests you? Why?

Suggestions for further reading

Systematic theology

Roman Catholic fundamental theology

Hans Küng, *Does God Exist?: An Answer for Today*, trans. Edward Quinn (New York: Crossroad, 1991) [Exhaustive treatment of theism and atheism by a leading Roman Catholic theologian of the last 60 years.]

Bernard Lonergan, *Method in Theology* (New York: Herder and Herder, 1972) [Sets forth his transcendental method in Roman Catholic fundamental theology.]

Gerald O'Collins, *Rethinking Fundamental Theology: Toward a New Fundamental Theology* (New York: Oxford University Press, 2011) [An excellent Roman Catholic introduction to the nature of Christian faith, general and special revelation, Jesus, ecclesial tradition, the Bible, and the church. Provides a contrary perspective on some similar issues treated in the present book.]

Karl Rahner, *Foundations of Christian Faith*, trans. William V. Dych (New York: Crossroad, 1978) [Still the best entry into Rahner's understanding of the basis for Christian faith within a progressive Roman Catholic framework. Like the present book, Rahner begins with analysis of human religious experience and then proceeds to explicate this on the basis of Christian symbols.]

David Tracy, *Blessed Rage for Order: The New Pluralism in Theology* (Minneapolis: Winston-Seabury, 1975) [Sets forth Tracy's Tillichian model of mutual-critical, correlational, revisionist theology.]

David Tracy, *The Analogical Imagination: Christian Theology and the Culture of Pluralism* (New York: Crossroad, 1981) [Ground-breaking work that analyses the social situation of the theologian and its impact on the theological task.]

Protestant fundamental theology

Gerhard Ebeling, "Fundamental Theology," in *The Study of Theology*, 153–65 [Ebeling's understanding of fundamental theology has significantly shaped the presentation in this chapter.]

Wolfhart Pannenberg, *Theology and the Philosophy of Science*, trans. Francis McDonagh (Philadelphia: Westminster, 1976) [Pannenberg's massive effort to situate Christian theology within the sciences and humanities in a typical German university. The final section of the book sets forth his understanding of the key sub-disciplines.]

Roman Catholic doctrinal theology

Francis Schlüssler Fiorenza and John P. Galvin, *Systematic Theology: Roman Catholic Perspectives*, 2nd edn (Minneapolis: Fortress Press, 2011) [Excellent introduction to key theological topics and themes by leading Roman Catholic theologians.]

Gregory Higgins, *Christianity 101: A Textbook of Catholic Theology* (New York: Paulist, 2007) [A very basic introduction to Roman Catholic doctrinal theology. Start here before moving on to the more challenging Fiorenza and Galvin edition.]

Protestant doctrinal theology

Rebecca S. Chopp and Mark Lewis Taylor (eds), *Reconstructing Christian Theology* (Minneapolis: Fortress, 1994) [An exploration of key themes and issues in contemporary Christian theology by leading North American theologians. Emphasizes alternative ways of understanding traditional topics, especially feminist, liberationist, and post-liberal theologies.]

Douglas John Hall, *Christian Theology in a North American Context*, 3 vols (Minneapolis: Fortress, 1991–6) [A significant examination of Christian theology by a leading North-American Lutheran theologian. Hall approaches topics through an interpretive lens that favors liberation and social themes.]

Bradley Hanson, *An Introduction to Christian Theology* (Minneapolis: Fortress Press, 1997) [A standard textbook of Christian theology for undergraduate students. Written from an American-Lutheran, post-liberal perspective.]

Alister E. McGrath, *Christian Theology: An Introduction*, 5th edn (Oxford: Wiley-Blackwell, 2011) [A leading textbook of Christian theology for undergraduates and graduate students by a major evangelical theologian from Britain.]

Daniel L. Migliore, *Faith Seeking Understanding: An Introduction to Christian Theology*, 2nd edn (Grand Rapids: Eerdmans, 2004) [Mainstream textbook of Christian theology for a seminary audience. Written from a Reformed Protestant perspective that is also ecumenical.]

Wolfhart Pannenberg, *Systematic Theology*, 3 vols, trans. Geoffrey W. Bromiley (Grand Rapids: Eerdmans, 1991–8) [The culmination of a life-time of study and research by one of the most important Christian [Lutheran] theologians of the last half century. This is Pannenberg's restatement of all major themes in Christian theology.]

Richard J. Platinga, Thomas R. Thompson, and Matthew D. Lundberg, *An Introduction to Christian Theology* (Cambridge: Cambridge University Press, 2010) [An excellent textbook for undergraduate students that reflects issues and concerns in the Reformed theological tradition.]

Dorothee Sölle, *Thinking about God: An Introduction to Theology* (Philadelphia: Trinity Press International, 1990) [An engaging entry into theological issues as understood by one of the most important Protestant feminist theologians of the past half-century. These were originally public lectures to a general audience of German citizens.]

The principal academic journals for systematic theology

Calvin Theological Journal, Dialog, Harvard Theological Review, International Journal of Systematic Theology, Journal of the American Academy of Religion, Journal of Religion, Modern Theology, Pro Ecclesia, New Blackfriars, Scottish Journal of Theology

Historical theology

Biblical theology

In addition to the following, see the list of suggested readings at the end of Chapters 10 and 11.

Jean Bethge Elshtain et al. (eds), *The Bible and Christian Theology*, a special issue of *The Journal of Religion*, vol. 76, no. 2 (April 1996) [Explores the study of the Christian Bible in the context of a modern university.]

Church history

See the list of suggested readings at the end of Chapter 2.

The history of Christian doctrine

See the list of suggested readings at the end of Chapter 3.

The principal academic journals for historical theology

Biblica, Catholic Biblical Quarterly, Church History, Interpretation, Journal of Biblical Literature, Journal of Ecclesiastical History, Journal for the Study of the New Testament, Journal for the Study of the Old Testament, Lutheran Quarterly

Practical theology

Ecclesial studies

Gregory Dix, *The Shape of the Liturgy*, 2nd edn (New York: Continuum, 2003) [Classic study of the historical development of the Eucharist. Has influenced liturgical studies for more than half a century.]

James F. Hopewell, *Congregation: Stories and Structures* (Minneapolis: Fortress Press, 1987) [Engaging sociological analysis of how Christian congregations function.]

Gordan Lathrup, *Holy Things: A Liturgical Theology* (Minneapolis: Fortress, 1993) [An excellent theological analysis of what Christians do—or ought to do—when they gather to worship God.]

Gordon Lathrup, *Holy Ground: A Liturgical Cosmology* (Minneapolis: Fortress, 2003) [A marvelous book that explores how Christian worship "may help us to imagine, understand, care for, and live in the world."]

David Truemper et al. (eds), Institute of Liturgical Studies, *Occasional Papers* (Valparaiso, IN: Institute of Liturgical Studies, 1981–) [Ongoing studies of Christian liturgy and other aspects of congregational life.]

Geoffrey Wainwright, *Doxology: The Praise of God in Worship, Doctrine, and Life* (New York: Oxford University Press, 1980) [An engaging account of themes in systematic theology on the basis of reflection on Christian worship life.]

James F. White, *Protestant Worship and Church Architecture: Theological and Historical Considerations* (Oxford: Oxford University Press, 1964) [Classic study of the connection between Christian theology and church architecture.]

Ethics

James M. Childs, Jr., *Ethics in the Community of Promise: Faith, Formation, and Decision* (Minneapolis: Augsburg Fortress, 2006) [An important contribution to ethical reflection by a Lutheran ethicist.]

Roger H. Crook, *An Introduction to Christian Ethics*, 6th edn (Upper Saddle River, NJ: Pearson, 2012) [This is a good place for the college student to begin the study of Christian ethics. Offers summaries and assessments of a wide variety of Christian ethical positions.]

Charles Curran, *The Catholic Moral Tradition Today: A Synthesis* (Georgetown University Press, 1999) [Provides an overview of the Roman Catholic moral tradition and its re-assessment by a major Catholic ethicist.]

Stanley Hauerwas, *The Peaceable Kingdom: A Primer in Christian Ethics* (South Bend: Notre Dame Press, 1991) [A helpful introduction to ethical reflection by a leading post-modern Christian theologian and ethicist.]

Robin W. Lovin, *An Introduction to Christian Ethics: Goals, Duties, Virtues* (Nashville: Abingdon, 2011) [Discusses various theological possibilities within Christian ethics so as to lead students to reflect on how they would think and act morally. Provides a number of test cases with which to test out ethical options.]

Gilbert Meilaender, *Bioethics: A Primer for Christians*, 3rd edn (Grand Rapids: Eerdmans, 2013) [A very helpful introduction to basic issues in bioethics by a Valparaiso University professor of ethics.]

Gilbert Meilaender and William Werpehowski (eds), *The Oxford Handbook of Theological Ethics* (New York: Oxford University Press, 2007) [The standard reference work for Christian theological ethics in the English language.]

Anders Nygren, *Agape and Eros*, trans. Philip Watson (New York: Harper and Row, 1969) [A major, controversial study of "the Christian idea of love" by an important Lutheran theologian.]

Servais Pinkaers, *The Sources of Christian Ethics*, 3rd edn (Baltimore: Catholic University Press, 1995) [Widely-used textbook in Roman Catholic moral theology. An excellent resource for theological ethics from a Roman Catholic perspective.]

Trutz Rendtorff, *Ethics*, 2 vols, trans. Keith Crim (Minneapolis: Fortress, 1986–9) [The first volume examines theological principles that shape and inform ethical reflection from a Lutheran perspective. The second volume examines several ethical challenges and situations.]

The principal academic journals for practical theology

International Journal of Practical Theology, Journal of Pastoral Theology, Journal of the Society of Christian Ethics, Journal of Religious Ethics, Studies in Christian Ethics.

14

Christian Theology and the Humanities

The next two chapters sketch ways in which Christian theologians seek interaction with other university disciplines. After briefly describing H. R. Niebuhr's classic typology for possible ways of relating Christian theology to other domains of knowledge and culture, this chapter proceeds to highlight a dialectical, correlational way of relating theology to the humanities and the arts. The next chapter does the same for the sciences.

As we have noted in previous chapters, some theologians have argued that Christian theology is a kind of science or scholarly discipline (German: *Wissenschaft*) in the university. Aquinas thought of theology as a theoretical science that presents a rational exposition of its guiding principles that are grounded in divine revelation and aided by Aristotelian philosophy. In his day, some theologians developed the view that Christian theology is "the queen of the sciences," since it addresses the first principles upon which all the other sciences are premised. Since Aquinas' day, other theologians have also defended the notion that Christian theology is a "science," although they have differed among themselves as to its character. Some have defined it as the science of divine revelation (Hegel), others as the science of the divine Word (Barth), still others as the science of the Christian religion (Schmid), or the science of God (Pannenberg).

Already in Aquinas' day people were beginning to call into question the scientific character of Christian theology. As the natural sciences became more and more oriented toward empirical reality, and capable of being understood without recourse to God, those who studied nature became less and less concerned with metaphysical and theological speculations. These scholars desired to be free from the bondage to external authorities, especially religious and political ones.

In view of the growing criticism of theology's scientific character that had already begun in the fourteenth century, theologians took a different tack by trying to defend theology in the university as a practical science, one that focused not so much upon theoretical knowledge about God as upon matters of practical wisdom that would lead human beings to see God as their highest goal in life, and after death. Within the period of Protestant Orthodoxy (seventeenth and eighteenth centuries) theologians debated among themselves whether theology was more of a speculative, theoretical science or a practical wisdom for living in the light of God. As we noted in Chapter 3, John Gerhard tried to keep both of these aspects together when he stressed that theology "continually occupies itself with God and teaches how everything has its basis in him, how everything has received its origin from him and how everything finds its goal in him, in order finally to rest in him" (Gerhard 1: Preface, § 29). Schleiermacher modified this view when he spoke of the task of academic theology as providing a scholarly, scientific (*wissenschaftliche*) self-representation of the Christian-religious consciousness for the sake of the practical goal of educating and training future church leaders in the Prussian state church. Here, too, the theoretical and practical interests of academic theology remained in tension with each other.

Although medieval scholars referred to Christian theology as the queen of the sciences, it has not always been so understood. Already under the influence of Augustine, some theologians in the early and medieval church regarded theology primarily as "wisdom" (*sapientia*) and not as "science" (*scientia* [PTPS 8–10]). For Augustine, the sciences sought to understand the world and its temporal things, whereas theology, true *sapientia*, attempted to understand the eternal God as the highest good of all things. While wisdom and science did not exclude one another, the goal of the sciences was the pursuit of knowledge of temporal things for the sake of the larger pursuit of wisdom. All temporal, worldly knowledge is to be oriented toward God, who is the highest good. This is a definition that fits with Gerhard's seventeenth-century understanding as well.

That medieval vision of education is mostly gone in our world. Nevertheless, some contemporary scholars are calling for greater educational "wholeness," "integration," and "interdisciplinary cross-fertilization" within undergraduate higher education. They seek to keep together "science" and "divine wisdom," despite not fully knowing how to achieve that goal, given the loss of the philosophical and theological coherence that allowed the university disciplines some measure of commonality in ages past. There is a growing awareness of how the fragmentation of knowledge and greater specialization within the disciplines threaten "long-term intellectual, cultural and spiritual ecology."[1] Such cries for **interdisciplinarity** (if we can invent such a term) in both teaching and research help to highlight the ongoing importance of paying attention to theological perspectives from the religions, including Christianity, and to what light they might shed on a broad range of fields within the academy.[2] Such a theological approach would keep open the possibility that at least some theological understandings provide plausible ways of making sense of the universe and of the human beings within it. The very fact that the discipline of Christian theology is included in a university setting offers the greater likelihood that interdisciplinary encounters will occur between theology and the other university disciplines, that they will have to take into account each other's scholarly findings and perspectives, and that the whole of human knowledge and wisdom is greater than the individual bits and pieces of information that get generated in the separate disciplines.

Whether such interdisciplinary encounters occur within the context of religious studies, wherein the theology of Christianity is investigated like that of any other theology or spiritual tradition, or within a separate theology faculty, which may give preference to a particular tradition of Christian theology, the goals should likely be the same: the pursuit of wisdom and insight, the furthering of personal intellectual growth and cultural literacy, the greater illumination of the interconnectedness of all legitimate knowledge, and greater clarity about matters of the common good. While academic theology will engage the knowledge and insights that come from other scholarly approaches, methods, and theories relating to its own subject matter, it will also seek to keep open those questions regarding the reality of God and the insights and understandings that come from its own theological approaches to that subject.

---

[1] Ford, *Christian Wisdom*, 349.

[2] On the need for further "interdisciplinarity" within universities, see Ford, *Christian Wisdom*, 333ff.; and Mike Highton, *A Theology of Higher Education* (New York: Oxford University Press, 2012). Within the American context, see especially George Marsden, *The Outrageous Idea of Christian Scholarship* (New York: Oxford University Press, 1997). See also Warren A. Nord, "Taking Religion Seriously in Public Universities," *The American University in a Postsecular Age*, 167–85.

Christian theology within the humanities

Not surprisingly, many Christian scholars also underscore the need to integrate "faith and scholarship," "love and learning," "hope and research," "scientific knowledge and wisdom," although they disagree among themselves about how this is best achieved or what such "integration" actually looks like.[3] What one believes about God, the world, and human beings, does affect what one believes about the connections or relations between theology and other university disciplines. Certainly, the understanding that one has about God will undoubtedly shape one's perspective on a whole host of intellectual matters. "One might expect it to have a bearing on some of the most sharply debated issues in academia today."[4] Despite disagreements about how best to relate one's religious and theological insights to the much larger world of the academy and the still larger contexts of one's society and the planet as a whole, Christian scholars tend to agree that bracketing one's religious commitments and perspectives leads to a short-sighted, narrow range of vision. Many argue that the above pairings, however they are finally related or ordered, allow for a multitude of voices (often a cacophony, never a chorus) to be heard on a variety of academic subjects that are more or less related to the flourishing of humankind (at least one hopes), and to the pursuit of truth and happiness, insight and wisdom, beauty and goodness, and to informed, intelligent discussion about matters of the common, public, global good.

We have already defined the academic discipline of Christian theology in Chapter 4, so we need not say anything further here about the distinctive contribution that the subject of Christian theology makes to the academy. Study of the revelation of God, the world, and human beings in the apostolic witness to Jesus, in order to appropriate the possible truth and wisdom within that witness, is a worthwhile intellectual pursuit for its own sake. But critical and self-critical inquiry into that witness also invites engagement with other disciplines, whose interests and subject matters overlap with that which Christian theology likewise investigates. Such engagement occurs in

---

[3] See Douglas Jacobsen and Rhonda Hustedt Jacobsen, with essays by others, *Scholarship and Christian Faith: Enlarging the Conversation* (New York: Oxford University Press, 2004).

[4] Marsden, *The Outrageous Idea of Christian Scholarship*, 4 (quoted also by Nord, "Taking Religious Seriously in Public Universities," 170).

relation to the arts, the humanities, and the sciences, which raise religious, philosophical, and theological questions about God, the world, and human beings.

Before turning to these interdisciplinary encounters between Christian theology and the other university disciplines, however, one should note that Christian scholars have disagreed among themselves about the inter-disciplinary character of Christian theology and of its relation to so-called secular or "worldly" learning. A now classic typology that still provides insight into possible ways of relating "Christ" and "culture" is by the American Protestant theologian, **H. Richard Niebuhr** (1894–1962).[5] His study of "the problem of Christianity and civilization" suggests that there have been **five basic ways** or types in which Christians have tried to relate these two aspects of their lives: their "faith" (symbolized by "Christ"), on the one hand, and "civilization" (symbolized by "culture"), on the other. While both the terms "Christ" and "culture" are ambiguous, as Niebuhr himself acknowledged, and the typology is clearly somewhat artificial, Niebuhr's study does help one to get at least a preliminary picture or map of several possible ways that Christian thinkers have related Christian theology to human culture and worldly knowledge and learning. (One must always keep in mind that a "map" is not the same as the "territory" it depicts!)

The first type Niebuhr labeled "*Christ against culture.*" This type empha-sizes an opposition between Christ and culture. Whatever human beings create and achieve, whatever is maintained by "the world," is sinful, corrupt, opposed to Christ, and thus contrary to authentic Christian faith. In this view, the Christian is called to leave the world, its truths, its values, and to follow only Christ. The Christian's loyalty is solely to him, not to any human cultural society. This position is very "cut and dried," "black and white." The world is entirely evil and devoid of anything truly good, right, and beautiful. It is soon going to pass away and come under the judgment of God, and so the true Christian should forsake the world, its cultural artifacts, and be devoted solely to Christ and his word. There can be no compromise with "the world."

In this type, higher education is more or less rejected, since such education is too involved in the world and its cultural values. Tertullian best exemplified this attitude when he asked rhetorically, "What has Athens to do with Jerusalem?" In other words, "What has pagan learning to do

---

[5] H. Richard Niebuhr, *Christ and Culture* (New York: Harper and Row, 1951).

with the teaching, death, and resurrection of Jesus?" "Absolutely nothing!,"
was Tertullian's implied position, although it should be pointed out that
he himself made good use of his classical pagan education. The other
illustrative example that Niebuhr linked to this first type is Leo Tolstoy
(1828–1910), who late in life was mostly critical toward human art and
the sciences. He attacked the prevailing culture of his day and stressed a
peasant's obedience to the Sermon on the Mount as the best example of
authentic human life. Kierkegaard's "attack upon Christendom" also fits
here, as do all those Christian groups that separate themselves more or less
from "the world." Less extreme forms of this type operate in contemporary
Fundamentalist Protestant schools whose curricula oppose every teaching
that is contrary to their interpretations of the Bible.

The second type, which Niebuhr calls *"the Christ of culture,"* is the
opposite of the first. This type stresses a basic and essential agreement
between Christ and culture. There is no opposition. Whatever is good,
right, and true about Jesus is identical to that which is good, right, and
true within human civilization. Those who fit within this type sense no
great tension between their Christian faith and the world. "On the one
hand they interpret culture through Christ, regarding those elements in it
as most important which are most accordant with his work and person; on
the other hand they understand Christ through culture, selecting from his
teaching and action as well as from the Christian doctrine about him such
points as seem to agree with what is best in civilization."[6] So they harmonize
Christianity and whatever is dominant within their given culture.

In this type, higher education is unconditionally affirmed as being fully
consistent with the Christian faith. There can be no real tension or contradiction between Christ and what is set forth in universities and academies.
For Niebuhr, the so-called Gnostic Christians best represent this view, since
they sought to reconcile Jesus with the reigning Greek philosophy of their
day, but he also points to the medieval Abelard and the nineteenth-century
German Lutheran, Albrecht Ritschl, as additional examples. A particularly
negative example, one that Niebuhr does not provide, is the transformation
of Jesus into an Aryan German by Christians in Nazi Germany. They tried to
make Christianity completely compatible with their racist ideology. Within
the history of higher education, this type has often led to the blending of
Christ and culture in such a way that "Christ" is completely subsumed

---

[6] Ibid., 83.

under secular knowledge and even lost altogether. One needs only to point to the history of formerly church-related institutions (e.g. Harvard, Yale, Princeton, Brown) that have now become almost totally secularized.

The other three types, which Niebuhr placed in the center of Christian tradition, acknowledge in one way or another that Christ or Christian faith are not identical to human culture but neither are they totally opposed to the world. What distinguishes these three types from each other is how they combine the two poles and understand their respective authority.

The third type, which Niebuhr calls *"Christ above culture,"* seeks to blend Christ and culture in such a way that authentic human achievements point toward Christ as their true and ultimate perfection and completion, but neither Christ nor culture can be fully identified with the other. This third type stresses the incarnational and sacramental presence of God in the world that is full of suffering and injustice. The world is God's creation and the object of God's love and grace, which seek to transform and perfect the world. In this view, higher education is affirmed and celebrated, but it is authentic and has lasting value only in relation to Christ who completes and fulfills all knowledge and learning.

The classic example of this third type is Aquinas. Although he was a monk who rejected the secular world (like the first type), he lived in a culture that was entirely shaped by the medieval Catholic Church. The civilization was a "Christian civilization." With Christ as its head, the church governed and shaped every aspect of human life and culture. In that situation, one could stress, as Aquinas did, that human culture—the arts, philosophy, civic life, the classical and Christian virtues—has an integrity all its own but its benefit to human beings is limited. Human culture takes a person only so far. While it cannot be regarded as the realm of godlessness, human beings and their culture must nevertheless be perfected by divine grace. "Grace does not destroy nature; it perfects it." There is, thus, a continuity between human culture and the grace of Christ, though the latter is hierarchically superior to the former. This hierarchical, Christ-above-culture view is probably best exemplified in Aquinas' medieval synthesis of Aristotelian philosophy and orthodox Augustinian theology. Another example, not mentioned by Niebuhr, would be the vision of John Henry Cardinal Newman (1801–90), whose "idea of a university" is based on the Thomistic principle that grace fulfills and perfects nature, that knowledge and reason are servants to faith.[7]

---

[7] John Henry Newman, *The Idea of a University Defined and Illustrated*, ed. I. T. Ker (Oxford: Clarendon Press, 1976), Preface, 6.

The fourth type, "*Christ and culture in paradox*," acknowledges the authority and integrity of both "Christ" and "culture" and seeks to uphold each, which in its own way, has an independent authority for the Christian. People of this type "seek to do justice to the need for holding together as well as for distinguishing between loyalty to Christ and responsibility for culture."[8] While a Christian's ultimate faith and obedience are oriented toward Christ, he or she is called to live and act and think within the world and to embrace it as the arena in which God the Creator is working, even apart from Christ. In this view, the world is not entirely pagan and the Christian cannot really be separated from it. Moreover, God in Christ has forgiven the sinner who lives in the world by faith. Freed from the need to justify oneself before God and others, the forgiven sinner can be creative within the world, the arena in which to act in loving service to others. This "duality" of the Christian life, wherein the forgiven, sinful creature is simultaneously a sinner and a saint, creates an inevitable tension or polarity within the Christian, who lives fully by faith "in Christ" and lives fully "in the created/fallen world" at the same time. This side of heaven and eternity, the tension and polarity remain together, in a kind of paradox. This paradox concerns both the individual sinner/believer and God the creator and redeemer, who acts in two distinct, though related, ways in the world (the two reigns of God through law and gospel). Given this paradoxical view, one trusts that God is ultimately merciful toward sinners, that God continues to preserve creation and restrain evil, and that God has endowed God's creatures "with a reasonable degree of common sense and civic responsibility."[9]

This fourth type is best reflected in the theology of Luther, a university professor, who struggled with faith in a merciful God and lamented the

---

[8] Niebuhr, *Christ and Culture*, 149.

[9] Richard Solberg, "What Can the Lutheran Tradition Contribute to Higher Education?," in *Models for Christian Higher Education*, Richard T. Hughes and William B. Adrian (eds) (Grand Rapids: Eerdmans, 1997), 74. See also Sydney E. Alhstrom, "What's Lutheran about Higher Education?—A Critique," *Papers and Proceedings of the 60th Annual Convention* (Washington, DC: Lutheran Educational Conference of North America, 1974), 8–16. Ahlstrom identifies three streams within the larger Lutheran tradition that have shaped Lutheran higher education: the scholastic (Lutheran Orthodoxy), the pietistic (Pietism), and the critical (Rationalism, Enlightenment). All three have been important, but in the context of 1974, when the faculty of a North-American Lutheran seminary, Concordia Seminary, St. Louis, was under attack by religious and cultural conservatives, Ahlstrom thought that the critical aspect needed to be highlighted. "Can an institution, a college, seminary, or university, regard itself as an embodiment of the western tradition of higher learning if it abrogates the freedom of investigation? Can a Lutheran institution of any of these types maintain its intellectual health and credibility if it neglects or denies its own critical tradition?" (ibid., 16).

fallen condition of sinful humanity (including especially his own), but who celebrated the good gifts of the Creator, including music, Greek and Roman literature, and his wife's beer and wine. Luther encouraged the pursuit of creaturely knowledge in the university where he taught. He and Melanchthon and their fellow academic colleagues were committed both to the truth of the gospel that is revealed in Holy Scripture and to the use of human reason that is fully capable of uncovering legitimate knowledge within the natural order. Their version of "Christian humanism" endeavored to keep both of those terms in tension and creative interaction with each other. It is worth being reminded now and then that proponents of this type, German Lutherans for the most part, founded and developed the important principle of academic freedom.[10]

The fifth and final type, the one that Niebuhr himself preferred, agrees that human beings and their creative works are fallen or perverted (a position reflected also in types one and four), and thus human culture is in some way to be opposed, but Christ is viewed as One who converts human beings and their culture away from sin and toward God now. This "conversionist" type, which Niebuhr labeled "*Christ transforming culture*," stresses the sovereignty of God over all creation. Since almighty God encounters the Christian in Christ in the present, the Christian "does not live so much in the expectation of a final ending of the world of creation and culture as in awareness of the Lord to transform all things by lifting them up to himself... This is what human culture can be—a transformed human life in and to the glory of God."[11] Christ thus transforms culture in a way that a type-four person thinks can only happen when Christ comes again.

John Calvin is perhaps the preeminent figure in type five, since he worked toward the transformation of this fallen world into the kingdom of God on earth, although Niebuhr tries to make a case that Augustine's mature view of "culture" also fits within this model. Proponents of this type understand Christ as the regenerator of human beings in their culture, of changing them from being self-centered to being Christ-centered; the so-called "Puritans," who helped to found the English colonies in the seventeenth and eighteenth centuries, were guided by this type of thinking. They attempted to make their communities into a model kingdom of Christ on earth. Their governments were thus entirely shaped by Christian principles. Within higher education, this model operates in Christian universities that

[10] Ahlstrom, "What's Lutheran about Higher Education?—A Critique," 14.
[11] Neibuhr, *Christ and Culture*, 195–6.

seek to transform all knowledge into service of Christ. They often operate on explicitly Reformed-Christian principles, as is the case at Wheaton College or Calvin College.

Each of Niebuhr's types has problems and challenges within an academic setting, even if each also has something important to contribute to a conversation about the place of Christian theology within the humanities and about the relation of theology to other university disciplines. While the first type warns us that Christ and culture are not identical, it too neatly makes a separation between the two. Such a dualistic view can lead Christians to be judgmental toward those who are not like themselves and to think that somehow they are free of the corrupting power of sin and the temptation to evil. Then, too, such a view does not acknowledge that even Christians make use of human reasoning and that God is working within creation, even apart from Christ and his followers, to bring about justice and love, goodness and beauty. Likewise, this first type often ends up with a very sectarian view of the church that is cut off from the rest of Christendom and the larger ecumenical world. This, too, restricts its vision and leads toward its isolation from both church and the academy.

If the second type rightly acknowledges a continuity between Christ and culture and a frank acknowledgment that Christians need not be opposed to authentic truths and insights from non-Christian sources, it does not fully appreciate the contrast and/or tension between them, that all human beings are sinful, that "the world" often rejects "Christ," and that Christ offers a word of promise that cannot be fulfilled by "the world." The second type often runs into problems with the First Commandment, especially when proponents of this type completely eliminate "Christ" from any positive or critical consideration, or when they transform the Christian faith into something that it is not. The second type can easily lead to the loss of Christian integrity within the academy or to the creation of a theological perspective that many Christians would no longer recognize as truly "Christian."

Although the third type is appealing to Christians who want to maintain a synthesis between their faith and the world in which they live and move, who highlight the ways in which their faith has shaped even this present "secular age," and who want to cooperate with all, believer and non-believer alike, in the pursuit of the common good, others point out that this type tends to be inherently conservative, authoritarian, and incapable of appreciating how Christ might be doing a new thing in human history and culture. While this type is not the only one which may succumb to the interference of the church within the university (e.g. when it dictates to the disciplines what their conclusions ought to be), it does seem prone to that danger.

The fourth type, which has also sometimes led to cultural conservatism, has a different danger. Its position has contributed to a sharp separation between "Christ" and "culture," as if each has its own separate domain and set of standards (similar to type one) that are largely unrelated. This type has, perhaps unwittingly, contributed to the further marginalization of theology within the academy, since most academic disciplines can seemingly get along just fine without theology sticking its nose into their work. Nevertheless, the fourth type has often been praised as one of the main ways in which Christian theology can function with integrity in a university alongside of other disciplines that also have their own integrity.

Although Niebuhr himself thought the fifth type was the best because its goal is the transformation of all things in the service of Christ, it too has often led to a kind of "theocracy" or "Christocracy" in the domain of culture that many would judge to be oppressive toward both scholarship and the critical understanding of Christian faith. Must everything in human culture, including ideas that are generated within the university, be made captive to the mind of Christ? If so, does that process not necessarily jeopardize the integrity of culture?

One's position on the relation of Christ to culture will largely determine what one will say about the relation of Christian theology to the humanities, the arts, and the sciences within the university. Some Reformed scholars, such as George Marsden, for example, insist that their Christian faith causes them to see matters within the university differently from their non-Christian counterparts and this difference leads to distinctively Christian forms of scholarship that are dissimilar to non-Christian forms. In this view Christian theology or reflection on one's Christian faith have a priority above secular learning and a responsibility to bring all knowledge under the sovereignty of God and into the service of Christ. But other scholars might wonder if such a view does not inevitably lead to unnecessary conflict between Christian and non-Christian scholars and their work. Surely there is not something like "Christian mathematics" or "Christian astronomy" or "Christian physics," is there? Must every intellectual pursuit within the academy ultimately be governed by "Christian principles," or viewed in relationship to the lordship of Jesus Christ, even if at the end of the day one acknowledges that there is something divine about mathematics and chemistry and even history, as implied in the Christian teaching about creation? Is not the world, as fallen as it is, still

God's creation that can be studied on its own terms in distinction from the kingdom of Christ that is both present and not yet fully here? Admittedly, these are Lutheran questions, but they at least point toward some of the challenges that attend to the Reformed perspective.

Still other scholars insist that one must maintain a strict separation between Christ and the secular academy. Here one encounters many examples from the first two types within Niebuhr's paradigm: At one end of the spectrum, the academy becomes completely Christianized, because the secular pursuit of knowledge has nothing to do with Christ and must be rejected in favor of a purely Christian worldview (type one). Nothing that is contrary to this worldview, based as it is on very particularistic readings of the Bible, is allowed its say or its own integrity. Many so-called "Bible colleges" take this position, since they reject most Enlightenment scholarly presuppositions and the knowledge that has been generated by their use, especially in the natural sciences. Other schools, particularly from the Mennonite tradition, are less extreme in their rejection of Enlightenment ideals and emphasize the centrality of radical discipleship to Christ that transforms all learning. For them, Christian discipleship is more than mere "head knowledge," since it involves practical action and "service learning." At the other end of the spectrum, the academy becomes completely secularized, because whatever is "secular" and worldly fits completely with "Christ" and thus the ideals of the Enlightenment are totally congruous with the ideals of Christianity (type two). This view, which minimizes the tensions and contradictions between Christ and culture, has likely contributed to the transformation of some formerly Christian-based colleges and universities into religiously unaffiliated institutions. But do not both of these types, with their respective one-sided restrictions either in favor of "Christ" or "culture," short-change what the other, subordinated pole is able to contribute to human knowledge and understanding? Though both types at least formally weaken or lessen the tensions and contradictions between the two poles, do they not in fact contribute to a narrower range of vision when it comes to knowledge of God, the world, and human beings?

The strength of types three and four within an academic setting is the concern to study the world "as it is," not imposing upon it or upon one's study of it a particular Christian "worldview" or perspective, and then "to bring that world into dialogue with the Christian vision of redemption and grace."[12]

---

[12] Richard T. Hughes, "Introduction," *Models for Christian Higher Education*, 6–7.

This approach allows one to take seriously the religious and cultural pluralism that is found within the world without immediately trying to transpose them into Christian categories or to bring them under the sovereignty of God in service to Christ. Both types (three and four) acknowledge that the Christian is "not of this world," yet he or she is called to live within the world as a follower of Christ. Both types also acknowledge the sacramental presence and gifts of God that are mediated through created means and which form the people of God into a spiritual community. Likewise, both types allow the tensions and even contradictions between "Christ" and "culture" to remain in place, at least for the time being. The difference between types three and four is how they understand the resolution of those tensions and conflicts. Whereas type three stresses continuity between grace and reason, between faith and scholarship, between Christ and culture, type four emphasizes their ultimate discontinuity, since faith in Christ alone is what receives the promise of salvation. Type four is much more open to the notion that secular disciplines within the academy have an intrinsic secularity that can be fully comprehended "within reason alone." While both types underscore the need for academic freedom and the responsible pursuit of the truth, type three tends to be less critical of formal ecclesiastical control and authority of academic institutions and will stress the ultimate harmony between authentic truth and what the church "believes, teaches, and confesses." There is, then, perhaps less danger of absolute secularization occurring under type three than type four, although both types acknowledge that God is at work in the *saeculum*, the world, in ways that are also distinct from Christ. Finally, both type three and type four emphasize the role of theology within the whole of the university disciplines. This role is especially central for the interdisciplinary integration of knowledge, the critical dialogue or dialectical conversation between "faith and reason," the pursuit of ethical responsibility within the world, and the bringing of a theological perspective to bear within the university.[13] The brief sketches below and in the final chapter are premised on a view that is consistent with emphases in types three and four. These types seem a more fruitful way for pursuing interdisciplinary encounters between theology and other university disciplines

---

[13] Pope John Paul II, *Ex Corde Ecclesiae*, sec. 19, as given in *Catholic Universities in Church and Society: A Dialogue on* Ex Corde Ecclesiae, ed. John P. Langan (Washington, DC: Georgetown University Press, 1993), 236.

Christian theology, the humanities, and the arts

Because Christian theology is located within **the humanities** (religious studies, history, philosophy, visual arts, performing arts, music, literature), either as a sub-discipline within religious studies or as its own independent discipline, it is understandable that it would emphasize dialogue with scholars from these academic subjects that are its closest neighbors. One of the challenges and joys of college theology is the opportunity to bring theology into dialogue with these other university disciplines.

Christian theology and religious studies

Since Christian theology seeks insight and understanding about God, the world, and human beings on the basis of a particular religious tradition, it cannot avoid engaging other religious traditions that also make reference to God, the world, and human beings. Christian theology ought to be open to the investigation of other religious traditions, to gain insight and wisdom from them about matters that theology also addresses, and to pursue inter-religious dialogue as a way of clarifying both consensus and areas of disagreement among the religions. Moreover, since scholars of **religious studies** also investigate Christianity as a world religion, Christian theologians need to be attentive to modern theories about religion, to modern methods of studying religions, and to ways of encouraging students to be both critical and self-critical about their own religious tradition in relation to other religious traditions. The need for inter-religious and ecumenical dialogue is perhaps even greater today since the distances between differing religious traditions have become smaller and smaller in the modern, technological age in which we are living. We also know that the level of conflict and serious disagreement among and within the world's religions remains dangerously high.

Christian theology cannot avoid the historical influences of ancient religions upon the biblical revelation and how that revelation is conditioned historically. Its revelation is interwoven with terms, beliefs, and practices from the history of ancient religions. Moreover, Christian theology cannot avoid the religious pluralism that defines our global scene. The history of Christianity reveals the manifold ways in which Christians have interacted with other religions in the world, mostly negatively and critically, though not always. Over the past century many Christian theologians have worked to understand the history of religions as a way of engaging religions more positively. While ecumenical discussions among Christian churches and groups will remain a necessity as long as those who call upon the name of Christ are divided among themselves (contrary to the straightforward prayer for unity by Christ in John 17), there is an equally great need for comparative theology and further discussions among representatives of the major religions. Christian theology plays a role here by being informed by scholarly descriptions and interpretations of the other religions, by seeking points of consensus and agreement, and by raising critical questions of its own on the basis of its concern for the truth of the gospel.

But the critical methods used in religious studies within universities can also call Christian theology into question since those methods are guided by scholarly presuppositions that tend to bracket out questions regarding the reality and truth of the object(s) of devotion and study within Christianity. The various approaches within religious studies—history, phenomenology, philosophy of religion, psychology of religion, sociology of religion—are inherently reductive in nature and often quite critical of traditional Christian assumptions and perspectives.[14] Christian theology has the responsibility to respond to these critical questions and positions that emerge from religious studies regarding Christian teaching and practices. It does so on the basis of its own subject as this becomes clear through its own sub-disciplines: to return again and again to the reality and essential truth of that subject (the exploration of religious experience and natural theology within funda-mental theology), to articulate Christian teaching ever again for each new situation in light of knowledge from the other religions (doctrinal theology, ethics), to investigate the history of Christianity to check other interpreta-tions of that same history (historical theology), and to explore through

---

[14] See, for example, J. Samuel Preus, *Explaining Religion: Criticism and Theory from Bodin to Freud* (New Haven: Yale University Press, 1987). Preus interprets all religions in exclusively naturalistic terms and thus necessarily excludes "theology" from "religious studies." In his view, "religious studies" is scientific, while theology is most definitely not. Unfortunately, Preus fails to consider, on the one hand, that academic theology is a "critical" discipline, one that is guided by scholarly modes of inquiry that are appropriate to its subject matter, and, on the other hand, that scholars within "religious studies" cannot avoid being motivated by prior personal commitments, apologetic interests, and political and metaphysical convictions. They too occasionally operate with biases and certain metaphysical presuppositions about the nature of reality, the subject matter(s) within every religion, and religious phenomena. His claim that only religious "outsiders" are qualified to explain "religion" truthfully and accurately is thus open to debate.

practical theology the present dynamics of actual Christian communities, their beliefs and actions.

Over the past half century in debates about the nature of modernity, scholars have stressed that all theories about the religions (or about any academic subject, for that matter) are socially and historically located and necessarily involve commitments to certain values, concepts, assumptions, and methods. In other words, all data that one would study and account for are "theory laden" and more or less interpreted on the basis of one's presuppositions, values, and commitments. Marxist and feminist scholars of history, the religions, and literature, and also philosophers of science, have been the primary contributors to this on-going discussion. It is not surprising, then, to discover interpreters of the religions who explicitly study religions on the basis of their own particular religious understandings and commitments. In contrast to the biases and presuppositions of those who study the religions on the basis of naturalism and a modern disbelief in the transcendent, these scholars interpret religions on the basis of a particular theology.

One need not agree with Barth's radical rejection of all the religions, including Christianity, as products of human sin, idolatry, and disillusionment. Other Christian theologians, such as Tillich, Tracy, and Küng, have taken a more positive approach to the other religions and have attempted to make correlations between Christian teaching and other religious traditions. These scholars not only make explicit their own Christian presuppositions regarding the claims of Christianity, but they also involve themselves in the difficult task of inter-religious dialogue. Similarly, Wilfred Cantwell Smith (1916–2000), who spent a lifetime studying the world's religions, argued that scholars of the religions ought to attend carefully to the unique self-understanding of the representatives of the religious traditions and not give in to prejudiced and simplistic understandings of them. A Christian theological approach toward the other religions seeks to take seriously the truth claims of each particular religion and to relate those claims to the faith/truth claims within Christian teaching. While Christian theology cannot avoid making normative judgments in the study of the religions, it also cannot avoid repeatedly testing those normative judgments in light of knowledge that arises from within the study of the religions. It does so according to established rules and customs for scholarly work: concentrated inquisitiveness, openness to all relevant knowledge and data, clear and considered judgment, a desire for scholarly objectivity and accuracy, honesty, humility, the avoidance of proselytizing, and accountability to the community of scholars in one's university and beyond.

Christian theology and philosophy

We have already given a brief overview of how Christian theologians responded to the origin of theology within ancient Greek philosophy (see Chapter 3). We noted there that Christian thinkers have disagreed among themselves about the importance of non-Christian philosophy for Christian thinking. Some have followed Niebuhr's first type and have radically rejected any and all forms of non-Christian knowledge as unimportant. Tertullian is the classic example of this approach. Others have allowed non-Christian philosophy to more or less shape their understanding and presentation of Christian teaching. For or example, the second-century Apologists saw no real distinction between philosophy, "the love of wisdom," and theology, "thinking about God."

The history of Christian theology can be instructive to a person who wants to understand the history of Western philosophy and vice versa, since the history of Western civilization demonstrates a partnership between the two. Already in the apostolic witness there are indications that Paul was influenced by Stoic philosophy and that John was working with terms and concepts from Platonic philosophy. The theologies of Augustine and the Cappadocians are incomprehensible apart from a knowledge of Neo-Platonic philosophy, just as the theology of Aquinas is significantly shaped by Aristotelian philosophy. Much of nineteenth- and early-twentieth-century Protestant theology is incomprehensible apart from an understanding of critical philosophy (Kant), German Romanticism (Schleiermacher), and German Idealism (Hegel), just as European Existentialism influenced mid-twentieth-century Protestant and Catholic articulations of theology. In every one of these situations philosophy was taken into service for the shaping of theological truth. It is this use of philosophy by theologians that illuminates the medieval judgment that philosophy is "the handmaiden of theology."

This same history of Western philosophy/Christian theology provides numerous examples of how theologians wanted to make Christian ideas intelligible on the basis of the reigning philosophical system of their day, only to have their own theology become dated as that system was found wanting, for one reason or another. Not surprisingly, since the days of late-medieval Scholasticism and the Protestant Reformation, the disciplines of Christian theology and philosophy have become more and more distinct and independent of each other, often accompanied by a mutual distrust and criticism of the other, despite some notable efforts (Hegel, Rahner,

Pannenberg) to overcome their antitheses. Within the most recent period of intellectual history one notes a heightened awareness among scholars about the incompleteness of all worldviews and the need for vigilant criticism of all attempts at intellectual comprehensiveness.

Despite this historic distrust and conflict between Christian theology and secular philosophy, both disciplines cannot fully avoid the other. Scholars within each of them will encourage renewed attempts at positive interaction and partnership. This encouragement is especially necessary today when some theologians are dismissive of the use of critical philosophy within theology and when some philosophers are altogether dismissive of theological questions and issues. While theology and philosophy address some of the same questions (the reality of God, philosophical theology, the nature of human beings, the problem of meaning, the nature of evil, the limits of human reasoning), they do so on very different bases or sources and by means of different methods, and these differences have led to greater and greater separation between scholars in each discipline, as has the fact that scholars define each discipline differently *vis-à-vis* the other.

Questions about the subject matter of philosophy, the subject matter of theology, and the degree to which they overlap, remain open questions that invite on-going discussion. At the very least, both students of theology and students of philosophy ought to be encouraged to return repeatedly to classic sources within their respective disciplines, to examine how past thinkers have engaged the questions that are common to both disciplines (for example, the questions about the reality of God and the problem of evil), and to learn by instructive example when the subject matter of each discipline has been distorted by inappropriate intrusion of the one upon the other.

Christian theology ought to involve clear thinking, careful argument, and attention to the meanings of terms and their usage within the discipline. Both disciplines benefit from insightful analysis of initial judgments and hidden assumptions, just as they are deepened by critical reflection on the supposed logical character of their complex arguments. "As long as philosophy remains in contact with its own origin—in any case without this it would give up its character as philosophy—theology retains its partner. To be in conversation with philosophy in one way or another must serve to further the truth" (Ebeling 66).

How Christian theology seeks to further the truth may bring it into conflict with philosophy or at least some forms of philosophy. This is because Christian theology, despite its common ground with historic Western philosophy, cannot avoid insisting upon a theological interpretation of reality in the light of the reality of God. Christian theology remains grounded within a particular, historical tradition that interprets all of reality through this manifold revelation of God and the ultimate witness to the truth of the gospel. Here, too, in its relation to philosophy, Christian theology cannot avoid making normative judgments in the light of that particular truth.

Christian theology, the arts, and the other humanities

Christian theology explores a living legacy. This broad tradition includes more than mere writing, speaking, and thinking. Visual art, music, architecture, and the performing arts (for example, dance) are also integral elements of the Christian heritage, even if the history of Christianity reveals important Christian individuals and movements that have been critical and dismissive of them.

Without question the Christian tradition has been "the single most important factor" in the development of art, architecture and music in the Western world over the past 2,000 years (EC 1.65 [Pickstone]). A few hours in any major art museum, a summer's journey to the most important European cathedrals, and a season's worth of classical music will be sufficient to demonstrate this claim about the close relationship between the arts and Christianity. Some knowledge of the latter is therefore necessary for one to appreciate more fully the former's rich heritage. At the very least Christian theology can help to make people more literate about the explicitly Christian aspects within much of Western art, literature, and music and of how people through the centuries have used these art forms to symbolize matters of Christian faith. Engagement with Christian theology will also help to disclose how Christianity has shaped the development of art, architecture, music, and literature. Often details within Western art and literature are incomprehensible without retrieving forgotten stories and ideas within the Christian tradition. Entire books have been written, for example, to help people interpret the great cathedrals of the world, such as the one at Chartres with its intricate sculptures and carvings and heavenly stained-glass windows. Even today people are still entranced by Gregorian chant or spiritually uplifted through German chorales. In view of the challenges of appropriating insights from the past, Christian theology may help to uncover unknown or forgotten theological dimensions within the arts, literature, and music and to offer informed interpretations of them. At the very least theology may help the student of cultural history to understand better the artifacts of Christian faith that are scattered among the art, literary, and architectural treasures of the past. Perhaps, too, theology can help to highlight how these objects continue to communicate the presence of God to people today.

But Christian theology may also provide a perspective on the arts and music that underscores the mystery of human creativity in relation to the mystery of the divine. Take the encomium to music by Luther, who himself was a musician and a composer:

> I would certainly like to praise music with all my heart as the excellent gift of God, which it is, and to commend it to everyone. But I am so overwhelmed by the diversity and magnitude of its virtues and benefits, that I can find neither beginning nor end nor method for my discourse. As much as I want to commend it, my praise is bound to be wanting and inadequate. For who can comprehend it all? And even if you wanted to encompass all of it, you would appear to have grasped nothing at all. First then, looking at music itself, you will find that from the beginning of the world it has been instilled and implanted in all creatures, individually and collectively. For nothing is without sound or harmony. . . Music is still more wonderful in living things, especially birds, so that David, most musical of all kings and minstrel of God in deepest wonder and spiritual exultation, praised the astounding art and ease of the song of birds. . . Philosophers for all their labor cannot find the explanation; and baffled, they end in perplexity, for none of them has yet been able to define or demonstrate the original components of the human voice, its sibilation and, as it were, its alphabet in the case of laughter to say nothing of weeping. They marvel, but they do not understand. Music deserves the highest praise. She is a mistress and governess of those human emotions—to pass over the animals—which as masters govern people or, more often, overwhelm them. No greater commendation than this can be found, at least not by us. For, whether you wish to comfort the sad, to terrify the happy, to encourage the despairing, to humble the proud, to calm the passionate, or to appease those full of hate—what more effective means than music could you find. The Holy Spirit himself honors her as an instrument for his proper work when in his holy scriptures he asserts that through her music, his gifts were instilled in the prophets. Thus it was not without reason that the fathers and prophets wanted nothing else to be associated as closely with the word of God as music. Therefore we have so many hymns and

psalms where message and music join to move the listener. While in living beings, or when played on instruments, music remains a language without words. Finally, when education is added to all this, and artistic music, which corrects, develops, and refines the natural music then at last it is possible to taste and wonder God's absolute and perfect wisdom. Here it is most remarkable that one single voice continues to sing the tenor, while at the same time many other voices trip lustily around it, exulting and adorning it in exuberant strains and, as it were, leading it forth in a divine dance, so that those who are the least bit moved know nothing more amazing in the world. But any who remain unaffected are clodhoppers indeed, and are fit to hear only the words of horseshit poets and the music of pigs. Amen. (LW 53.321–4)[15]

And, of course, Luther knew nothing of his spiritual descendent, J. S. Bach, or of any of the other great composers of the last 250 years! Nor is he the only Christian theologian to have reflected on the theological dimensions of music. For example, Barth offered an insightful theological analysis of Mozart's music, as did Jaroslav Pelikan on Bach.[16]

How have Christian faith and artistic creation come together in the history of Christianity? Even the non-Christian may wonder about what early Christians were doing when they had images painted on catacomb walls or what Michelangelo was trying to depict on the ceiling and walls of the Sistine Chapel or what Eastern Christians were trying to reveal through their church mosaics, icons, and Byzantine chanting. What is conveyed through Grünewald's *Isenheim Altarpiece* (connecting the dying Christ with those who suffer illness), or Caravaggio's *The Calling of St. Matthew* (tying together the Christian notions of "new creation," vocation and discipleship), or Rembrandt's *The Return of the Prodigal Son* (one of the best paintings ever of love, forgiveness, and reconciliation)? Or what are the theological implications of the placement of Christ in *The Flagellation of Christ* by Piero della Francesca, a work of art that the poet Seamus Heaney (1939–2013) has

---

[15] The copyrighted material cited here from *Luther's Works* is used by permission of Fortress Press.

[16] See Barth 3/3.472 (one among many references in his dogmatics that could be cited); Karl Barth, *Wolfgang Amadeus Mozart*, trans. Clarence K. Pott (Grand Rapids: Eerdmans, 1986); and Jaroslav Pelikan, *Bach among the Theologians* (Minneapolis: Fortress Press, 1986). With respect to more recent popular music, there is the insightful commentary by Jeffrey Symynkywicz in his book, *The Gospel according to Bruce Springsteen* (Louisville: Westminster John Knox, 2008). Eric Alterman also hits some properly theological notes in his analytical work, *It Ain't No Sin to Be Glad You're Alive: The Promise of Bruce Springsteen* (Boston: Back Bay Books, 2001).

described as having "the aura of the uncanny; a sense of Christian iconography, but defamiliarised."[17]

"In the beginning was the Word..." (Jn 1.1). That theological assertion has relevance for any theological engagement with beautiful words. What are the theological implications within Dante's *Divine Comedy*, Milton's *Paradise Lost*, or Dostoevsky's great novels? What theological understanding emerges from readings of poetry by Donne, Herbert, Hopkins and other great artists? Many scholars have devoted themselves to theological issues and themes in "religion and literature," to explore tensions and agreement between a Christian theological understanding and understandings that emerge from the great literature of the world (from Greek tragedy to contemporary novels). For example, how do the characters and worlds in Shakespeare intersect with the world(s) and characters envisioned in Christian Scripture? That same "intersection" may be explored in so many other literary creations (e.g. Tolkien's Middle-earth, Lewis' Narnia Tales, the world of Harry Potter, and the list goes on). Is not one's self-understanding deepened by the correlation between these "classics" and the vision given in Scripture? Why do such "classics" persist across time and space? Could it be that they help us to understand ourselves, and our world, better? Might they even "read" us better than we can ourselves on our own?[18] One is not the same as he was before he read a collection of essays like those in Christian Wiman's *My Bright Abyss: Meditations of a Modern Believer*.[19] The reader "gets read" here, too, as he or she is imaginatively brought into the poet's struggles with doubt and his Christian faith, with illness and joy, love and fear, sorrow and hope. Great themes in world literature lead the theologically attuned toward theological engagement with those themes, even as the literature itself cannot help but impact one's theological understanding.

Who cannot be deeply moved by the intimate connection between word and music in the passions of Bach or his *B-Minor Mass*, in Haydn's *Creation*, or in Beethoven's *Requiem Mass* or the one by Cherubini (which Beethoven thought superior to Mozart's)? These experiences of music reveal

---

[17] Seamus Heaney, "Seven Wonders," Interview by Maggie Fergusson, *Intelligent Life Magazine* (January/February 2013), 24.

[18] "I define a 'classic,' in literature, in music, in the arts, in philosophic argument, as a signifying form which 'reads' us. It reads us more than we read (listen to, perceive) it... Each time we engage with it, the classic will question us" (George Steiner, *Errata: An Examined Life* [New Haven: Yale University Press, 1997], 19).

[19] Christian Wiman, *My Bright Abyss: Meditations of a Modern Believer* (New York: Farrar, Straus & Giroux, 2013). For the past decade Wiman has been the editor of *Poetry* magazine.

a meaningful theological vision.[20] Many of the scenes from the gospels (the annunciation to Mary, the visit of Mary with Elizabeth, the birth of Jesus, the deaths of the holy innocents, Jesus' baptism, his sermon on the mount, his miracles, his entry into Jerusalem, the Last Supper, his crucifixion, resurrection, and ascension) and the Acts of the Apostles (the gift of the Holy Spirit at Pentecost, the revelation of the risen Jesus to Paul) are variously and beautifully and often disturbingly (as in Nicholas Serrano's *Piss-Christ*) rendered in visual art and music down the centuries. The rich, complex theological themes in these and other great works of Western art call for theological interpretation of their subject matter and the cultural assumptions that have shaped them, as well as aesthetic appreciation of their truth and beauty.

While we could focus more on the relation of Christian theology to music, literature, architecture, we shall limit ourselves to a few further comments about the visual arts. The history of Christianity shows that Christian thinkers have been divided among themselves over the visual arts. Some have highlighted the importance of the visual arts to convey theological truth, only to be countered by others who decry all such visual creations as idols that are contrary to the prohibition on "graven images" (Exod. 20.4). Certainly some early Christians, influenced by this Jewish prohibition, have been "anti-image," yet others borrowed classical forms, such as the figure of Apollo, to depict Jesus as the Good Shepherd or as a wise teacher or as a worker of miracles. Later, a serious conflict arose in early-eastern Christianity over the use of visual **icons** to depict Christ and individual saints and martyrs. During the eighth and ninth centuries it seemed the whole of the eastern Roman Empire was embroiled in controversy regarding the proper use of symbols and images within the church. This controversy, which occurred in a context that included Jewish and Muslim criticism of all images, led to serious reflection on the relation of theological understanding to the use of icons within the church. It was an argument about Christian tradition, which was ambiguous regarding images. While both sides in the **Iconoclastic Controversy** accepted the belief that the *Logos* of God had entered into the material world and had become incarnate in Jesus, and that in the Eucharist the bread becomes an image of the body of Christ, and that therefore the invisible God had made God known in and through material, visual things, one side insisted that only Christ could be depicted in images

---

[20] For extended discussions of this point, see especially Jeremy S. Begbie, *Voicing Creation's Praise: Towards a Theology of the Arts* (New York: T & T Clark, 1991).

while the other side affirmed that Mary, other saints, and the martyrs could be depicted as well. On the one side were the **iconoclasts**, those who held icons to be idols and thus contrary to authentic Christian worship. On the other side were the **iconophiles**, those who defended the veneration of icons in the divine service and their reverence in the devotional life of Christians. This latter position eventually won out as the official position of the Eastern Orthodox Church, largely due to its deep-seated practice within the eastern tradition, but also because of the theological reflections of theologians like John of Damascus, who clarified the nature of icons as a means by which the faithful could be drawn to contemplate the archetype which the icon depicts or symbolizes. The icon is neither an idol nor is it identical to that which it represents, but it follows from the Scriptural teaching that the eternal Son of God is "the image of the invisible God" (Col. 1.15) and that Adam was "made in the image of God" (Gen. 1.27). In the eastern tradition icons are meant to portray the reality of the history of Christ and his church, which is similar to the use of stained-glass windows in Western Christian traditions (save for some forms of Protestantism, such as mainstream Calvinism, that reject all use of images). This conflict over icons had run its course within the eastern churches by the end of the ninth century, although arguments about symbols and images continued to be made in response to further Jewish and Muslim iconoclastic opposition.

Throughout the history of the western church there have appeared various iconoclastic movements and positions as well. Despite their common commitment to the priority of the proclamation of the word for the sake of creating faith in Christ alone, Calvin and his spiritual ancestors attacked the use of images within the church, while Luther and Lutherans have generally, if not universally, allowed stained-glass windows, wood cuts, sculptures, and other visual arts to convey biblical truths within their sacred spaces and within their published versions of the Bible. One reason for this Protestant divide about the arts might be the fact that Calvin made the Mosaic prohibition on "graven images" as a separate commandment, while Luther interpreted it as merely an example of how one could break the First Commandment. But another reason is the one given by Niebuhr in the description of his fourth type: For Luther, visual, creaturely art is not inherently demonic or idolatrous; it could be used for good purposes within the church, to depict law and gospel or some other truth about God and human beings, as in the biblical woodcuts and paintings by Lucas Cranach Sr. (1472–1553), Albrecht Dürer (1471–1528), and other artists who were influenced by the German Reformer.

Within twentieth-century Christian theology we also find similar disagreements about symbols and images, that hearken back to the debates within the Iconoclastic Controversy. Although Barth had a copy of the crucifixion scene from the *Isenheim Altarpiece* hanging above his desk, he opposed the presence of images within Protestant churches and was generally negative toward a theological use of the visual arts. He was convinced that the splendor of visual art and material objects will likely lead people astray into idolatry. Other Christians, mindful of medieval and Thomistic discussions about art and beauty, have built on an incarnational and sacramental theology that sees objects of beauty as the means by which God conveys and manifests the divine presence and glory. One particularly fruitful example of such an approach is the seven-volume theological aesthetics by the Roman Catholic theologian, Hans Urs von Balthasar (1905–88), who was inspired by Barth's discussion of "glory" in his *Church Dogmatics* and by Aquinas' understanding of the analogy of being, in which all created being participates in eternal being (a notion that Barth fully rejected).[21] Similarly to the position of Aquinas, other theologians stress that the arts are capable of drawing individuals beyond themselves to the contemplation of the transcendent God. "The art object and practice of art are not thought of as theological in any direct sense. What is important is the divine joy and beauty these might evoke" (OHST 595 [Dryness]). Such a view fits well with Niebuhr's third type, since proponents of this position see art as drawing the individual to a vision of God or heaven, the so-called beatific vision, beyond the transitory material world. Art gives expression to human desires for the divine. For contemporary Orthodox theologian David Bentley Hart (b. 1965), beauty is intimately connected to every moment of "the Christian story" and is identical with its truth.[22]

By contrast, Tillich and those influenced by him, such as Langdon Gilkey and John Dillenberger, have stressed the importance of the arts, especially the visual arts, for disclosing or illuminating the depths of theological meaning, including the realities of sin and evil and human brokenness, as well as divine grace and love. Following Schleiermacher's positive appraisal of artistic beauty and aesthetic experience, which he thought was akin to faith in God the creator, they have insisted that the Christian theologian

---

[21] Hans Urs von Balthasar, *The Glory of the Lord: A Theological Aesthetics*, 7 vols (New York: Crossroad, 1982–9).
[22] David Bentley Hart, *The Beauty of the Infinite: The Aesthetics of Christian Truth* (Grand Rapids: Eerdmans, 2003), 4.

needs to be open to engaging secular, creaturely works of art, architecture, and music, since these too may become the means by which God is revealed within human religious experience. The goal of this revelation may be the transformation of self and the world. Important truths about human beings, their world, and God may be revealed through one's experience of a painting or a photograph or a film or some other revelatory, meaningful piece of art. In this way theology approaches human creativity and the human imagination as providing the conditions for divine revelation of God, human beings, and their world.[23] Creative "symbols" "open up dimensions of reality which cannot be grasped any other way."[24] What can art teach us about God and also about ourselves and our world?

Although many conservative Christians are convinced that artistic culture is inherently evil and must be condemned and avoided altogether, other Christians will take a more nuanced, critical position about the nature of the arts, however corrupted they might be by the powers of sin and evil. They will view the arts as potentially providing insight into the revelation of God as creator and of human beings as creatures and sinners before God—or as drawing people to the contemplation of "the beauty of the infinite." There is the need for discernment about what is good and evil, about what is profound and what is trivial, about what is true and false, and about what is beautiful and what is not. Christian theology may help to respond creatively to questions of aesthetics and to issues of truth, goodness, and beauty.

Near the end of his letter to the Christians in ancient Philippi, the Apostle Paul provides a scriptural basis for thinking about such matters: "Finally, beloved, whatever is true, whatever is honorable, whatever is just, whatever is pure, whatever is pleasing, whatever is commendable, if there is any excellence and if there is anything worthy of praise, think about these things" (Phil. 4.8). Perhaps more than any other verse in the NT, this one has reminded Christians that they, too, should be concerned to uphold what is "good, true, and beautiful." These ideals are not contrary to Christian faith. Indeed they "formed the triad of transcendental ideals that the Christian tradition inherited from the classical age and appropriated for

---

[23] Cecilia González-Andrieu, who builds on the reflections about "revelation" by Dulles (see Chapter 8 above), stresses the transformative character of art in her insightful book, *Bridge to Wonder: Art as a Gospel of Beauty* (Waco: Baylor University Press, 2012).

[24] Paul Tillich, "Visual Arts and the Revelatory Character of Style," in Paul Tillich, *On Art and Architecture*, ed. John Dillenberger (New York: Crossroad, 1987), 133.

its own uses."[25] They are still worth appropriating today, however difficult that process may be.

The task of Christian theology in relation to the other humanities is to discern the theological subject matter within them and to allow it to become prominent. The goal here is not merely to understand Christian art, literature, music, and architecture from the past as artifacts in the history of Christianity, as important as those artifacts might be in their own right, but to analyze them theologically and critically and to draw from them those insights that can be brought forward into contemporary theology. Nor is the goal to be merely critical of so-called secular art, literature, film, and music, whether contemporary or not, as if it has nothing to do with matters about which Christian theology also speaks. It is difficult, for example, to miss the Christian symbolism and theological meanings within a film like *Flight*, which is at least partly about the bondage of sin and the power of divine grace to transform an individual, or to avoid engaging the metaphysical problems (the problem of evil, the reality of God) in so many other great films of the past century.

How do the arts and humanities deepen, complicate, and revitalize one's understanding of Christian theology? How does Christian theology help to interpret religious and theological symbols that are conveyed through the arts and the humanities? How do art and theology mutually inform the other's manifestation of the sublime and the beautiful? What is the connection between the beauty of art and the truth of the gospel? Between the metaphors that are used of the triune God, Christ, the Spirit, the church, creation and the metaphorical beauty that is found in creation and in imaginative works of art? What, for example, is the connection between the truth of the message about the cross of Christ, which makes foolish the wisdom of the world (1 Cor. 1.20ff.), and the power of art to disclose truth and beauty? Within theological anthropology, the question that is raised in Psalm 8.4 is especially significant since great art, music, and literature continually raise this question and similar ones and provide creative visions about human beings and their world, about God, evil, suffering, and salvation. To what extent are those visions similar or complementary to the biblical revelation of God, the world, and human beings? To what extent do they differ? These are among the basic questions that arise in a theological investigation of the arts and the humanities.

---

[25] Daniel J. Treier, Mark Husbands, and Roger Lundin, "Introduction," *The Beauty of God: Theology and the Arts*, Daniel J. Treier, Mark Husbands, and Roger Lundin (eds) (Downers Grove, IL: InterVarsity, 2007), 7.

Key Words

interdisciplinarity	religious studies
H. R. Niebuhr	icon
Niebuhr's five types of	Iconoclastic Controversy
relating Christ and culture	iconoclasts
the humanities	iconophiles

Reference Literature

For a general orientation to the relationship of Christian theology with the humanities and the arts

EC 1:65–77 ("Arts" [Pickstone]); ER 1:493–506 ("Art and Religion" [Apostolos-Cappadona]); OHST 561–79 ("The Arts" [Dyrness]); RPP 1:398–418 ("Art and Religion" [Krech et al.]); RPP 6:326–7 ("Humanities" [Gander]); 7:527–35 ("Literature and the Christian Tradition" [Auerochs]).

Questions for review and discussion

1   How do one's understandings of God shape one's perceptions about intellectual matters? Do you think one's Christian faith should cause one to view an academic discipline differently from someone of another religion (or no religion)? What difference, if any, does Christian faith make to the study of mathematics, physics, or biology?

2   Review H. Richard Niebuhr's five types of relating Christian faith and culture. Which type best describes your understanding? Which type did Niebuhr himself favor? Why does the author think types three and four are better suited to an undergraduate university setting? Do you agree or disagree with the author on this point? Why?

3   The relationship between religious studies and Christian theology has surfaced at several points in the book. How do you think theology and religious studies are similar? How might they be different?

4   How have Christian theologians disagreed about the role of philosophy in theology?

5   What are two examples of a question that both philosophers and

theologians address? How does a philosopher deal with those questions? How does a Christian theologian?

6   Are you more inclined to take a negative position with regard to the role of philosophy in theology (as Tertullian, Luther, and Barth have taken) or a more positive position that emphasises the importance of philosophy for theology (as Aquinas, Hegel, and Pannenberg have taken)?

7   The chapter offers some representative examples of how the Christian faith has impacted art, architecture, and music in the history of western civilization. Can you think of some additional examples that were not mentioned?

8   Christian theologians have disagreed among themselves about the visual arts, most notably in the so-called Iconoclastic Controversy. Do you side with those theologians who have been critical of visual representation (as did the iconoclasts) or with those who have encouraged the creative arts and view them as potentially revelatory (as did Luther, Tillich, and several more recent Christian thinkers)? Be familiar with the theological arguments that have been given for and against visual art within the Christian tradition.

9   What is your favorite film? Can you identify any religious or theological dimensions in that film? How might a Christian theologian understand that film theologically?

10   Can you think of some other ways, beyond the ones mentioned in the chapter, in which the arts and humanities deepen, complicate, and revitalize one's understanding of Christian theology?

Suggestions for further reading

The interdisciplinary character of Christian theology

David F. Ford, *Christian Wisdom: Desiring God and Learning in Love* (Cambridge: Cambridge University Press, 2007) [Ford offers a way of relating a distinctively Christian form of wisdom in dialogue with other religions and other academic disciplines.]

Mike Highton, *A Theology of Higher Education* (New York: Oxford University Press, 2012) [An engaging critique of higher education by a British Christian theologian. Highton argues for the importance of theology within every good university. Not only can theology serve an important role in helping to form intellectual virtues, but it can also help to contribute to the vibrancy of a university as a center of academic inquiry and it can help to serve the public good.]

Roger Lundin, ed., *Christ Across the Disciplines: Past, Present, Future* (Grand Rapids: Eerdmans, 2013) [A set of lectures to commemorate the sesquicentennial of Wheaton College. These essays, written by scholars from mostly Reformed, Evangelical, and Catholic backgrounds, provide historical, theological, and philosophical inquiry into the nature and purpose of Christian higher education.]

George Marsden, *The Outrageous Idea of Christian Scholarship* (New York: Oxford University Press, 1997) [Suggests that Christians will in fact approach academic disciplines differently from non-Christians.]

H. Richard Niebuhr, *Christ and Culture* (New York: Harper and Row, 1951) [Niebuhr's classic examination of five different ways of relating Christian faith to secular culture and civilization.]

Wolfhart Pannenberg, *Theology and the Philosophy of Science*, trans. Francis McDonagh (Philadelphia: Westminster, 1976) [A significant effort to engage the natural sciences and the philosophy of science on the basis of Christian theology, "the science of God."]

Ted Peters et al., "Theology and the Arts and Sciences," in *The Modern Theologians*, ed. David F. Ford (Oxford: Blackwell, 1997), 645–719 [These essays summarize basic positions regarding the relationship of Christian theology to the natural sciences, the visual arts, music, and the social sciences.]

Christian theology and religious studies

See the bibliography at the end of Chapter 1.

Christian theology and philosophy

See the bibliographies at the end of Chapters 3, 5, 6, and 7.

Christian theology, the arts and the other humanities

Jeremy Begbie, ed., *Beholding the Glory: The Incarnation Through the Arts* (Grand Rapids: Baker, 2000) [Marvelous and rich exploration of the artistic imagination in relation to the central Christian theological affirmation that the Word of God became incarnate in Jesus.]

Jeremy S. Begbie, *Voicing Creation's Praise: Towards a Theology of the Arts*

(New York: T & T Clark, 1991) [Ground-breaking work on the arts, especially music, from a Christian theological perspective that takes its starting point in orthodox Christology.]

Bruce Birch Brown, *Religious Aesthetics: A Theological Study of Making and Meaning* (Princeton: Princeton University Press, 1989) [Demonstrates how the aesthetic dimensions of religious experience can shed light on theological meaning.]

Northrop Frye, *The Great Code: The Bible and Literature* (New York: Harcourt Brace Jovanovich, 1981) [A strictly aesthetic approach to the importance of the Christian Bible in western culture and to its power to create a visionary poetic perspective that enriches scientific perspectives.]

Giles B. Gunn, *Interpretation of Otherness: Literature, Religion and the American Imagination* (New York: Oxford University Press, 1979) [Penetrating study of the importance of literary criticism within religious studies by examining several representative American authors.]

Rowan Williams, *Dostoevsky: Language, Faith, and Fiction* (Waco: Baylor University Press, 2011) [An extraordinary theological interpretation of the major novels by the great Russian author. A major example of how theology contributes to both literary criticism and human understanding.]

The principal academic journals for Christian theology, the arts, and the humanities

Christianity and Cultural Studies, Christianity and Literature, The Cresset, Cross Currents

15
Christian Theology and the Sciences

This chapter sketches ways in which Christian theologians seek interaction with the sciences in the university.

One of the most basic questions in any introduction to Christian theology is the relation of Christian faith to the practice of human reasoning. Since the middle of the last century that question has been reformulated in terms of the relationship between Christian faith/theology and the human, social, and natural sciences. Because Christian theology is about the revelation of God, the world, and human beings in the apostolic witness to Jesus Christ, its subject matter overlaps with that which the sciences investigate as well. Despite this overlapping, however, the claim of Christian theology is that the objects which the sciences investigate do not exhaust reality as a totality. Instead, the reality of the revelation of God remains central to a theological understanding of the world and human beings, indeed to a fuller understanding of the nature of reality itself. It is precisely this concern for the truth of God that defines theology's task within the larger pursuit of knowledge, truth, and wisdom that marks the overall purpose of a liberal arts university.

Inquiry into the relationship between Christian theology and the sciences occurs within all three branches of theology, but it is especially important to systematic theology and the sub-discipline of ethics within practical theology. How do Christian understandings of God, creation, and human beings relate to understandings of nature that have been set forth in the natural and social sciences? How do scientific understandings of nature affect Christian theological understandings? How does one go about responsibly engaging Christian theology in relation to scientific knowledge and vice versa? How might Christian theology impact knowledge in the sciences and mathematics, as happened, for example, when the Russian mathematician, Nikolai Luzin (1883–1950), a Russian Orthodox believer, was able to shed light on the mathematical question of infinity as a result of his theological understanding of the name of God.[1]

Christian theology seeks conversation with scientists about their work, especially when that work touches upon metaphysical or theological issues, or when scientists make metaphysical or theological judgments that theologians find intriguing and questionable. Such engagement by theologians is particularly significant in view of an implicit atheistic ideology or implied metaphysical presuppositions that a scientist makes about the nature of reality as a whole and about human beings within that reality. For example, anti-theistic accounts of evolution are found in Stephen Jay Gould's metaphysical assertion that all religions are the product of human imagination and stem from the need to create "some warm and fuzzy meaning" to life that is "just a story"; in Richard Dawkins' metaphysical assertion that the universe has "no design, no purpose, no evil or good, nothing but blind, pitiless indifference"; in William Provine's metaphysical assertion that "modern science directly implies that there are no inherent moral or ethical laws, no absolute guiding principles for human society"; and in E. O. Wilson's metaphysical assertion that all behaviors (including religious and cultural ones) have only a genetic basis and are merely the object of natural selection.[2] If these metaphysical extrapolations were actually inherent to the theory of evolution, then indeed Christian theology would be critical of it. That such a theory need not include such atheistic metaphysical assumptions and speculations is quite clear from reading other scientific and theological descriptions of evolution, ones that seek to refrain from metaphysical speculation or that remain open to some form of divine action, as in versions of **theistic evolution**, where God and evolution are distinct but related causes in nature.

When a scientist confidently maintains that science provides all the knowledge that we human beings can know, it would not be surprising if

---

[1] See Jean-Michel Kantor and Loren Graham, *Naming Infinity: A True Story of Religious Mysticism and Mathematical Creativity* (Cambridge, MA: Harvard University Press, 2009).

[2] Stephen Jay Gould, *Rocks of Ages: Science and Religion in the Fullness of Life* (New York: Ballantine, 1999); Richard Dawkins, *The Blind Watchmaker* (New York: W. W. Norton & Company, 1996); William Provine, "Scientists, face it! Science and religion are incompatible," *The Scientist* (September 5, 1988) [online]; and E. O. Wilson, *Consilience* (New York: Knopf, 1998). For a caustic, atheistic critique of "creationism" and "theistic evolution," see Frederick C. Crews, "Saving Us from Darwin," *The New York Review of Books* (October 18, 2001). Crews presupposes that evolution implies the rejection of God and of any kind of divine action in the world.

a theologian would attempt to show how that might not be the case. We have already noted in Chapter 7 how several philosophers of religion and scientifically-informed theologians have responded to atheistic "**scientism**" (the rejection of religious knowledge as knowledge) and "**scientific imperialism**" (the transformation of religious knowledge into purely naturalistic, materialistic knowledge), to use Ted Peters' helpful descriptions.[3] While these atheistic positions insist that there is only one reality, the natural, over which science alone has a monopoly of knowledge, other scholars resist the elimination of religious knowledge or its transformation into purely naturalistic, materialistic categories.[4] Christian theology will likely join that effort by insisting on the reality of its subject matter—the revelation of God, the world, and human beings—and attempting to keep open the question about God as the ground and source of all that is. It will show that human reasoning is not able to discover on its own all that is real and true. At the very least, it will strive to demonstrate that the reality of God is not irreconcilable with modern scientific knowledge of nature and that purely naturalistic assumptions and conclusions about human beings do not exhaust all of the possible ways of interpreting them. According to Pannenberg, one of the leading Christian theologians in the area of science and theology:

> There is more to nature than simply what the scientists, working within the confines of the established disciplines, have been able to report. The reality of God is a factor in defining what nature is, and to ignore this fact leaves us with something less than a fully adequate explanation of things. The recognized contingency within natural events helps us perceive the contingency of nature's laws, and this cannot be accounted for apart from understanding the whole of nature as the creation of a free divine creator… Our task as theologians is to relate to the natural sciences as they actually exist. We cannot create our own sciences. Yet we must go beyond what the sciences provide and include our understanding of God if we are properly to understand nature.[5]

---

[3] Ted Peters, "Science and Theology: Toward Consonance," in *Science and Theology: The New Consonance*, ed. Ted Peters (Boulder, Colorado: Westview Press, 1998), 13.

[4] Alvin Plantinga is quite right to identify the grounds for whatever conflicts exist between theism and science as residing in the unwarranted atheistic and naturalistic presuppositions of some scientists rather than in an actual conflict between "science" and "theism." He locates the real conflict as occurring between "naturalism" (implying the non-reality of God and a worldview which denies the reality of God or anything like God), on the one hand, and science and theism, on the other. See Alvin Plantinga, *Where the Conflict Really Lies: Science, Religion, and Naturalism* (New York: Oxford University Press, 2011).

[5] Wolfhart Pannenberg, "The Doctrine of Creation and Modern Science," in Wolfhart Pannenberg,

So, for example, when the great mathematician and cosmologist Stephen Hawking (b. 1942) wrote a book in which he claims that because "there is a law such as gravity, the Universe can and will create itself from nothing" and that "[s]pontaneous creation is the reason there is something rather than nothing, why the Universe exists, why we exist," one should not be surprised that theologians will point out the fallacy of such assertions.[6] George L. Murphy (b. 1942), another leading thinker in science and theology, was among several who highlighted how Hawking involved himself in a number of logical contradictions. "Hawking's claim is incoherent. 'Because there is a law such as gravity'—i.e. because there is something—'the Universe can and will create itself from nothing.' It takes no scientific expertise to see that this sentence is self-contradictory. Religious leaders should be willing to rethink their teachings in the light of scientific discoveries, but they should also be prepared to refute obvious errors."[7]

Certainly, the natural and social sciences *do* present many challenges and problematic issues for Christian theology, and these challenges/issues need to be engaged critically and constructively by Christian theologians in the university. For example, the physical data of evolution by natural selection and mutation have led many modern people to reject the idea of divine Providence and the notion of a gracious, loving God who makes good promises for all of creation. What about the extinction of the vast majority of animals that have ever lived on the planet in its multibillion-year history? How does God act in the universe? Does God intervene in nature? How does evolution affect theological understanding of human beings? In such a framework, what constitutes the uniqueness of human beings?[8] How do the social and human sciences shed light on the nature of human beings, their religious experiences, unjust social orderings, and how ought theology to engage this knowledge constructively?

As we noted in Chapter 6, recent work in the cognitive sciences, still in its infancy stages, lends some support to a phenomenological understanding of religious experience by endeavoring to uncover and explain the neural

---

Toward a Theology of Nature: Essays on Science and Faith, ed. Ted Peters (Louisville: Westminster John Knox, 1993), 48.

[6] Stephen Hawking and Leonard Mlodinow, *The Grand Design* (New York: Random House, 2010), 180.

[7] George L. Murphy, Letter to the Editor, *The Christian Century* (October 27, 2010) (online) [accessed on December 1, 2012]

[8] Many of these issues and themes are identified in the writings of Langdon Gilkey. See especially, Langdon Gilkey, *Maker of Heaven and Earth: The Christian Doctrine of Creation in the Light of Modern Knowledge* (New York: Anchor Books, 1965) and idem, *Message and Existence*, 69–107.

basis for such experience. Research in this area has led some scholars to conclude that religion is an integral aspect of human experience, that it has a biological basis, and that this biological basis is at least part of the reason why religions have not disappeared in scientifically informed cultures. Work in this area is by definition inter-disciplinary since it involves scientists, scholars of religious experience, and theologians ("neurotheology") who are seeking to understand the nature of religious experience.

As we noted in Chapter 7, a number of scholars, including several former atheists, think that the complex conditions necessary for the evolution of life make better sense in a theological framework that allows for an infinite Intelligence rather than a purely materialistic, atheistic framework that only allows for random, chance accidents. The fine-tuning that is evident in the laws of nature, the complex arrangements in DNA, the evolution of very complex and intricately-organized organisms, including the evolution of purpose-minded human beings and their consciousness—all fit better with the theological affirmation about God as the underlying Creator and sustainer of the universe.

In this chapter we will give more attention to theology and the natural sciences, but certainly theology is open to engagement with the social sciences and has been significantly impacted by their theories and findings. For example, recently theologians and religious psychologists have been interested in analyzing the religious and theological presuppositions that are often implicit in sociological and psychological theories. Scholarly work in this area has led some to conclude that there are important theological reasons for maintaining a skeptical outlook toward the metaphysical assumptions that sometimes get expressed by social (and natural) scientists:

> All too often, the sciences become reductionistic in their attempts to chart reality. Must not our quest for scientific understanding be tempered by humbly acknowledging that the buzzing, blooming manifold of experience, and the criteria of thinking itself, transcend a total conceptualization, either through [contemplation or action]? Theologically speaking, the greatest peril of the university, with all its various disciplines, is the attempt to establish—by whatever means—an encyclopedic "God's-eye" view of reality, walking by sight, not by faith.[9]

---

[9] Mark Mattes, *The Role of Justification in Contemporary Theology*, Lutheran Quarterly Books (Grand Rapids: Eerdmans, 2004), 179. While Mattes is surely correct to identify how frequently claims to "scientific knowledge" become anti-theistic arguments for an alternative faith with a quite different "deity," the thesis of his book cannot be understood to be supportive of an ignorant or anti-intellectual posture toward basic physical data and argumentation in the natural and social sciences.

One need not accept the rather stark "either/or" that **John Milbank** (b. 1952) presents regarding a choice between accepting the presuppositions of the modern social sciences, which he argues are entirely premised on anti-Christian principles, or his version of Anglo-Catholic Christianity, in order to agree with him that many social scientists do in fact assume and operate with completely secular, anti-religious perspectives that replace one set of theological presuppositions with another.[10] Milbank is correct to highlight how aspects of "modernity," including dominant social theories in the modern social and human sciences, are indeed wrapped up with theological presuppositions that often favor atheism and nihilism.[11] Other scholars of religious psychology and Christian theology have in addition noted how various psychological theories also make religious and theological assumptions about human beings and their perceptions of reality.[12] Christian theology is thus especially interested in the sociology and psychology of religion for the sake of engaging these disciplines on such matters as the interpretation of the human condition, the nature and character of human beings as social creatures, issues that arise in Christian practical theology (ecclesial studies that involve the social sciences and theological reflection upon social ethics), theologies of social and political liberation, and the criticism of de-humanizing and inhumane religious understandings. Theology will always seek to maintain that human beings are more than merely economic and political creatures, that they do engage transcendent, ultimate, spiritual questions, and questions of personal and social identity.

Indeed, his criterion of "walking by faith, not by sight" applies to those who try to prove through empirical data the supposed "scientific" and "historical" truthfulness of the stories in Genesis 1–11 (literalistically interpreted).

[10] John Milbank, *Theology and Social Theory: Beyond Secular Reason* (Oxford: Blackwell, 1990).

[11] Milbank goes too far, however, when he reduces the social sciences to theologies that are alternative to his version of Platonic-Aristotelian-Augustinian-Thomistic orthodoxy. As in the natural sciences, so also in the social sciences, theology can be a partner in the pursuit of truth and justice and it can become a mutual critic of inhumane and unjust behaviors and social orderings in church and society. God is at work in human societies, even apart from Christian communities, and not everything that occurs in secular life is necessarily idolatry.

[12] For example, Terry D. Cooper's works on Tillich, Reinhold Niebuhr, and Don Browning, and their interactions with psychology, show how these theologians identified theological and metaphysical assumptions about human beings and their perceptions of reality within psychological theories. See Terry D. Cooper, *Paul Tillich and Psychology: Historic and Contemporary Explorations in Theology, Psychotherapy, and Ethics* (Macon: Mercer University Press, 2006); idem, *Reinhold Niebuhr and Psychology: The Ambiguities of the Self* (Macon: Mercer University Press, 2009); and idem, *Don Browning and Psychology: Interpreting the Horizons of Our Lives* (Macon: Mercer University Press, 2011).

Since the broad topic of "science and religion" has become a very important area of scholarly interest over the past two decades, we shall focus our final attention on theology and the natural sciences. While most Christians will insist that those who practice "scientism" and "scientific imperialism," to use Ted Peters' descriptive terms, are wrong to reject the reality of God, some Christians have unfortunately reacted to the atheistic, metaphysical positions of some scientists by merely appealing to church authorities or to the authority of the Bible. These so-called "creationists" or "scientific creationists" insist that only the authority of the church or the authority of the Bible ought to be followed in scientific matters.[13] If church tradition, or one's particular reading of biblical cosmology, conflicts with scientific findings, then too bad for those finding.

We saw in an earlier chapter how Francis Pieper is an example of this **creationist** approach. Not only did he reject Darwinian evolution because it conflicts with Pieper's literal reading of the "six days" of creation in the first chapter of Genesis, but he also rejected the Copernican view of the solar system, since it conflicts with his literal reading of those biblical statements that speak of the earth being founded on an immovable foundation and of the sun moving around the earth. (Pieper's position to the contrary, most Christians today interpret Psalm 19.1–4a and Joshua 10 differently from pre-Copernicus Christians since they know that the sun does not actually "run" its "circuit" around the earth. Prior to Galileo's time, nobody interpreted these and similar verses the way modern Christians do. After Galileo, Christians had to adjust their interpretation of Scripture, though indeed many Christians continued to think the sun orbits the earth and some still thought the earth flat.) More recently, some creationists have asserted that God purposely put dinosaur or other fossils in the geological layers "to test one's faith," i.e. to test whether or not one will hold to a literal interpretation of the early chapters of Genesis. Another speculative assertion that has been expressed by some creationists is that God purposely made the universe to look mature or old, even though it is really young (around 6,000 years old).[14] Those who call themselves "scientific creationists" try to demonstrate

---

[13] For a historical analysis of the rise of "scientific creationism" in twentieth-century Protestant Fundamentalism, see Ronald L. Numbers, *The Creationists* (Berkeley: University of California Press, 1993). For a classic example of a creationist position in Lutheranism, see John W. Klotz, *Genes, Genesis, and Evolution* (St. Louis: Concordia Publishing House, 1955), which defends a universal flood, a young earth, and a six-day creation.

[14] Philip Henry Gosse (1810–88) appears to have been the first one to put forth the theory that God made the earth to look old.

from appeals to very selective scientific knowledge (and criticism of other knowledge) that a literal reading of the first chapter of Genesis (God creating the world over the course of six 24-hour days several thousand years ago) fits quite well with the scientific data.

Each of these positions of "**creationism**" or "**scientific creationism**" has been rightly criticized by scientists and theologians alike. Why would God try to deceive us in these ways, for example, by making the universe 6,000 years ago or, as others have suggested, just a millisecond ago, complete with all our memories, but then give it the appearance of 13.7 billion years? If God did this, would not such a deception make God deceptive? Is not such a deception in nature contrary to what Scripture teaches us about the reliability of nature (e.g. Ps. 19.1ff; Rom. 1–2), not to mention the reliability of God? This recent and innovative speculation about a "mature-looking but really young universe" has only one concern, to maintain a treasured, literalistic reading of the first chapter of Genesis, since the theological starting point is the unquestioned assumption that God made the universe over the course of six twenty-four hour days a short time ago. A problematic consequence of this view is that God is deceptive and cannot be reliably trusted in the realm of nature. Why would God play such silly games? While creationists stress that scientists can make mistakes, they do not often admit that sinful, limited human beings, interpreting the first chapters in Genesis and other cosmological passages, could also possibly make a mistake in their interpretations. Of course, a "young earth" created to look mature is scientifically indistinguishable from the 4.55 billion-year-old earth that scientists study today![15]

More recently, some individuals have tried to poke holes in standard naturalistic accounts of Darwinian evolution by appealing to features in nature that appear to be "irreducibly complex" or to have been "intelligently designed" by direct divine causation.[16] It is important to note that those who support "**Intelligent Design**" generally accept the scientific consensus regarding the age of the universe and the age of the earth. Moreover, they

[15] That the universe is approximately 13.7 billion years old has been scientifically confirmed in several ways, particularly through the measurement of the distances that light has had to travel from stars to reach the earth. The speed of light is constant and has been shown not to slow down over time. The concordat agreement of several different types of radioisotope testing has led to the scientific consensus that the earth is approximately 4.55 billion years old.

[16] For the major texts that present versions of the theory of "Intelligent Design" (ID theory), see especially Philip Johnson, *Darwin on Trial* (Washington, DC: Regnery Gateway, 1991); Michael Behe, *Darwin's Black Box* (New York: The Free Press, 1996); and William Dembski, ed., *Mere Creation* (Downer's Grove, IL: InterVarsity Press, 1998).

do not attempt to fit all the scientific data into a literal interpretation of the early chapters of Genesis. For example, Michael Behe (b. 1952) argues that there are biological structures that could not possibly have been produced by the natural process of evolution since they are "too complex." He appeals to a supernatural Intelligent Designer as the direct cause of these "irreducibly complex" structures. His goal is to undermine the Darwinian theory, since Darwin claimed that if it could be shown that any complex organ existed that "could not possibly have been formed by numerous, successive, slight modifications," then his theory would collapse. Behe thinks he has found such complexity in flagella and mitochondria. In point of fact, however, many of the examples of so-called "irreducible complexity" that Behe used in his argument have been shown to be the result of natural causes.[17] Many critics of ID theory thus think that if it is taken seriously it would undermine scientific investigation of the natural causes of things. Why look for a natural, empirical, rational explanation for mysteriously complex phenomena when the whole point of the ID theorists' appeal to "complexity" is to argue that it could not have arisen through natural means and could only be the result of direct action by a transcendent Intelligence? One needs to underscore that just because something is mysterious or apparently complex does not mean that God is the direct cause of that mystery or complexity. The sciences may eventually uncover a fully natural, empirical, and rational explanation that needs no recourse to a direct super-natural cause. The sciences should indeed avoid appealing to God as the explanation for the gaps in our scientific knowledge of nature.

Of course, as we saw in Chapter 7, it is perfectly rational to infer from one's overall impression of an underlying, mathematical order and complexity in nature that there is an Intelligent Creator of the universe, but this inference is itself further grounded in special revelation and properly expressed as an article of religious faith ("I believe that God has made me and all things..."). A practicing scientist, however, will not use such an inference to attempt an explanation for some specific matter in nature that appears to be divinely designed or so complex that only a supernatural cause is sufficient to explain it. Truly scientific explanations for natural phenomena reside at the natural, empirical, and rational level of the inves-tigation of nature. Theological inferences about God the Creator and about

---

[17] For a helpful critique of Behe and Intelligent Design Theory in general, see Kenneth Miller, *Finding Darwin's God: A Scientist's Search for Common Ground between God and Evolution* (New York: HarperCollins, 1999).

the universe as God's creation reside at a different level, a kind of "second-order" level that embraces the former, natural level but transcends it as well.

One of the classic early scientists, Johannes Kepler (1571–1630), who was himself a practicing Lutheran Christian, alluded in a prayer to this distinction between first-order and second-order causes in nature: "[O God], . . .deign graciously to cause that these [scientific] demonstrations may lead to thy glory and to the salvation of souls, and nowhere be an obstacle to that. Amen." Kepler refrained from appealing to God as a sufficient explanation for specific natural processes, but he allowed that the demonstrations themselves might lead people to acknowledge the glory of God.

What Luther said in his explanation to the first article of the Apostles' Creed (on God the Creator) about human reason and senses is apropos: "I believe that God has created me... God has given me *and still preserves* my body and soul; eyes, ears, and all limbs, and senses; *reason and all mental faculties...*" (*Small Catechism*, BC 354, emphasis added). Like most other academic Christian theologians, Luther had high regard for the power of human reason and human senses to uncover reliable knowledge in nature. By contrast, six-day creationism implies that human observation and reasoning about nature are unreliable and that the interpretation of biblical passages that deal with cosmology must be literal, even though such a literal interpretation directly conflicts with what the sciences have correctly uncovered regarding the age of the universe and the natural history of the earth. Such a creationist approach to the interpretation of Scripture has neglected the important hermeneutical principle that has been articulated by Augustine and other venerable Christian scholars, namely, that facts of nature, discovered by the reliable means of human observation and reasoning, have a direct bearing on the careful interpretation of those scriptural passages that also concern nature. The true sense of Scripture about creation will agree with established natural fact, something Christian theology has been affirming since the days of the Christian Apologists (second century), the Cappadocians (fourth century), and Augustine (fifth century), but which has had to be relearned after Copernicus, Darwin, and Hubble.

Scripture itself indicates that we can trust the facts of nature and need not try to re-interpret their "speech" to us, even if such "speech" apparently conflicts with our particular interpretations of Scripture. If there is an apparent conflict between natural data and a straightforward, literal interpretation of Scripture, then the interpreter needs to re-examine his or her interpretation of Scripture and keep an open, humble posture towards the self-correction of scientific theories within science itself. We need not try to re-interpret the data of nature to fit with a non-critical reading of biblical cosmology. God does not deceive us in the realm of nature, God's creation. Indeed, the scientific data discovered in nature assists us toward an appropriate understanding of Scriptural passages that also speak of nature. While self-correction within the sciences may be assisted by criticism from within the philosophy of science and by reflection on the metaphysical and theological issues that arise from within the practice of science, merely citing Scripture and/or church tradition to reject scientific knowledge is inconsistent with Christian academic theology.

Augustine has perhaps underscored this point best:

Usually, even a non-Christian knows something about the earth, the heavens, and the other elements of the world, about the motion and orbit of the stars and even their size and relative positions, about the predictable eclipses of the sun and moon, the cycles of the years and the seasons, about the kinds of animals, shrubs, stones, and so forth, and this knowledge he holds to as being certain from reason and experience. Now, it is a disgraceful and dangerous thing for an infidel to hear a Christian, presumably giving the meaning of Holy Scripture, talking nonsense on these topics; and we should take all means to prevent such an embarrassing situation, in which people show up vast ignorance in a Christian and laugh it to scorn. The shame is not so much that an ignorant individual is derided, but that people outside the household of the faith think our sacred writers held such opinions, and, to the great loss of those for whose salvation we toil, the writers of our Scripture are criticized and rejected as unlearned men. If they find a Christian mistaken in a field which they themselves know well and hear him maintaining his foolish opinions about our books, how are they going to believe those books in matters concerning the resurrection of the dead, the hope of eternal life, and the kingdom of heaven, when they think their pages are full of falsehoods on facts which they themselves have learned from experience and the light of reason? Reckless and incompetent expounders of Holy Scripture bring untold trouble and sorrow on their wiser brothers when they are caught in one of their mischievous false opinions and are taken to task by those who are not bound by the authority of our sacred books. For then, to defend their utterly foolish and obviously untrue statements, they will call upon Holy Scripture for proof and even recite from memory many passages which they think support their position, although they understand neither what they say nor the things about which they make assertions.[18]

---

[18] Augustine of Hippo, *The Literal Meaning of Genesis*, 2 vols, trans. John Hammond Taylor (New York: Newman, 1982), 1.42–3. Mark Noll uses this quotation from Augustine for a purpose similar to mine. See Mark Noll, *The Scandal of the Evangelical Mind* (Grand Rapids: Eerdmans, 1994), 202–3.

Of course figurative, non-literalistic interpretations of the stories in the early chapters of Genesis and of other stories that have cosmological implications do entail some revision in one's articulations of the Christian doctrines of creation, anthropology, and sin, and many Christians are deeply uncomfortable with such a prospect. This discomfort is at least as great as the discomfort many sixteenth-century Christians must have felt in view of the revision to traditional teaching that the Copernican Theory entailed. As then, however, so also now: such modification would not necessarily undermine an orthodox understanding of creation, human beings, sin, and grace. Such revision would need to address such issues as the nature of God's good creation prior to the evolution of human beings, the nature of suffering and physical death as a part of that good creation prior to human evolution, and the origin and nature of sin. The scientific data about the reality of physical death in the animal and plant kingdoms prior to origin of human beings (for example, fossils of animals that lived long before the origin of human beings) must lead those who interpret the Bible in light of scientific knowledge to restate the nature of God's good creation prior to the advent of human sin. Such a good creation must have included the reality of death prior to the existence of human beings. Likewise, the character of the historical origin of sin must be reinterpreted. While the advent of sin is to be traced to the first hominids who disobeyed God's will, it is not necessary to trace that origin to "Adam and Eve" having eaten from a tree in an actual place called "the Garden of Eden" several thousand years ago.

Unfortunately, a whole generation of theologians, many influenced by the work of Barth, declined to engage in discussion about the impact of scientific knowledge on theological knowledge and vice versa. Such disengagement contributed to the separation of theology from the sciences and to the charge by many scientists that theology is pseudo-knowledge and merely a matter of subjective values. Such a view has led some to develop what Ted Peters and others have called a **"two-language theory"** of the relation of science and theology. In this view, theology speaks only one language, that of "values," while science speaks only one language, that of "facts," and the two languages are incommensurate with one another. Each language needs to be restricted to its respective domain and should not interfere with the language and operations of the other. The American paleontologist, **Stephen Jay Gould** (1941–2002) called this the NOMA principle, i.e. "nonoverlapping magisteria." Each discipline has its own separate, magisterial domain that should not be infringed upon by the other.[19]

> NOMA is a simple, humane, rational, and altogether conventional argument for mutual respect, based on non-overlapping subject matter, between two components of wisdom in a full human life: our drive to understand the factual character of nature (the magisterium of science) and our need to define meaning in our lives and a moral basis for our actions (the magisterium of religion).[20]

A similar position has also been supported by some Christian theologians, such as **Langdon Gilkey**, who held that science talks about proximate data while religion deals with existential and ultimate questions. Science addresses questions of "how" and theology addresses those of "why."[21]

While "a wall of separation" between theology and the sciences was perhaps necessary for a time, in order to advance both science and theology beyond the "warfare" model, such a metaphor has itself created problems for both disciplines and has been shown to be an impossible ideal.[22] For example, this view of the relation of science to theology implies that there can be no shared understandings between science and theology; but many today are attempting to show that such common understandings are possible and needed. Furthermore, the two-language theory tends to ignore that theology also attempts to speak of "facts" and "knowledge," just as scientists often find themselves properly running into problems of "values," ethics, and an overall metaphysical worldview. The sciences, too, operate with foundational, yet undemonstrated faith assumptions about reality and our rational perceptions of it.[23] Just as in theology, so also in the sciences, mystery about reality will undoubtedly always remain contested. If there

---

[19] See Gould, *Rocks of Ages*, Chapter 2.

[20] Ibid., 175.

[21] Langdon Gilkey, *Creationism on Trial* (San Francisco: Harper, 1985), 49–52; 108–13.

[22] For a very distorted historical account of the supposed "warfare" between science and Christian theology, see Andrew D. White, *A History of the Warfare of Science with Theology in Christendom*, 2 vols (New York: D. Appleton & Co., 1896). For essays that provide contrary accounts of the history of the interaction between scientific knowledge and Christian theology, see David C. Lindberg and Ronald L. Numbers (eds), *God and Nature: Historical Essays on the Encounter between Christianity and Science* (Berkeley: University of California Press, 1986). As indicated above, the modern sciences emerged in a theological context that assumed basic Christian affirmations about the nature of reality and human reasoning.

[23] Langdon Gilkey has been one of the more forceful theologians to identify the faith assumptions within the sciences regarding the nature of reality. See, for example, Langdon Gilkey, *Religion and the Scientific Future* (San Francisco: Harper and Row, 1970).

is no longer any mystery to reality, then neither the sciences nor theology would be necessary. Yet "ultimate" questions (Tillich) will continue to haunt all academic disciplines. In view of these connections and commonalities between theology and the sciences, the "nonrelational coexistence" of theology and the sciences is neither accurate nor helpful.[24]

A more promising theological approach to the sciences is one that allows the sciences to operate as if God is not a given in nature and then seeks to identify areas of convergence or **consonance** between theology and the sciences. In this way, theology does not appeal to God as an explanation for our gaps in scientific knowledge nor does it appeal to biblical authority or church tradition to trump well-established scientific theories and conclusions; rather, theology seeks to show a correspondence between what the sciences tell us about nature (including human beings) and what Christian theology affirms when it speaks about nature as God's creation and about human beings who are created in "the image of God." This approach invites positive, cooperative contributions from scholars in both theology and the sciences.

A key attribute of this approach is for both theologians and scientists to seek to remain open to insights from both sets of disciplines. For example, scientific advances in physics and astronomy regarding Big-Bang **cosmology** have raised questions about the reality of God as the transcendent origin of the cosmos. Likewise, scientific advances in chemistry, biology, and genetics regarding evolutionary theory have led theologians to articulate versions of theistic evolution, wherein the basic natural data and theory of evolution are affirmed, but within a theistic framework, and to raise questions about the character of God's creation as an on-going creation that produces novelty. Philosophical and metaphysical reflection on knowledge from the natural sciences, especially regarding evolutionary theory, have led to questions about God in relation to suffering, animal extinction, and the problem of natural evil.

These issues remain in the forefront of discussions among theologians and scientists today. The global ecological crisis has intensified efforts to bridge scientific knowledge regarding climate change and religious, ethical reflection on the world as God's creation, and on the nature and place of human beings within God's creation. This same crisis raises questions about the economic forces that transform all aspects of human life into

---

[24] Pannenberg, "God and Nature," in *Toward a Theology of Nature*, 51.

marketable commodities. It also forces people to think about potential ways of reforming human communities to be sustainable, more humane, and responsible for the future of the planet as a whole. As a part of that discussion, Christian theology invites people to think about the promise of God's new creation that they believe has been inaugurated in Jesus and on ways in which the vision of that future can positively impact on hopeful, responsible action in view of serious global environmental problems, which have been exacerbated by some advances in science and technology and by wrong notions about God, human beings, and the future.[25]

There are some excellent examples of Christian theologians who follow the approach of seeking convergence between what the sciences tell us about reality and what theology teaches about God and creation. We will end by merely mentioning two. **Arthur Peacocke** (1924–2006), a biochemist and a Christian theologian, has argued that theology "needs to be consonant and coherent with, though far from being derived from, scientific perspectives on the world."[26] **John Polkinghorne** (b. 1930), a mathematician, physicist, and Christian theologian, has sought to show the compatibility between scientific truths about nature and Christian theological affirmations and faith commitments regarding God the creator and redeemer. In his view both scientific reasoning and Christian faith seek truth and not illusion. Although faith "goes beyond what is demonstrable," "it is capable of rational motivation. Christians do not have to close their minds, nor are they faced with the dilemma of having to choose between ancient faith and modern knowledge. They can hold both together."[27] Obviously that means that the Christian doctrine of creation must accept what the sciences tell us about the origin of the universe from the Big Bang and the evolution of life on the planet, but likewise the sciences ought to remain open to Christian theological insights about metaphysics, the reality of God, the

---

[25] Among the first modern American theologians to focus special attention on issues in ecology and faith was Joseph Sittler (1904–87). See Joseph Sittler, *The Ecology of Faith* (Philadelphia: Muhlenberg, 1961); idem, *Care of the Earth and Other University Sermons* (Minneapolis: Fortress Press, 1964); and idem, *Evocations of Grace: The Writings of Joseph Sittler on Ecology, Theology, and Ethics*, Steve Bouma-Prediger and Peter Bakken (eds) (Grand Rapids: Eerdmans, 2000). Since his pioneering work, many theologians publish writings every year that address matters of "theology and ecology" and "theology and the environmental crisis."

[26] Arthur Peacocke, *Theology for a Scientific Age*, 2nd edn (Minneapolis: Augsburg Fortress, 1993), 10. Before his death, Peacocke taught at Cambridge and Oxford universities and was active within the Society of Ordained Scientists.

[27] John Polkinghorne, *The Faith of a Physicist*, 5. Polkinghorne has been a member of the Royal Society and a professor at Cambridge University.

nature of God's ongoing involvement in creation, the origin of life, the nature of human life, and the nature of faith commitments in the sciences and theology.[28] Then, too, there is the promise of the gospel that Christians believe is the hope not merely for human beings, but also for the whole of creation.

Key Words

theistic evolution
scientism
scientific imperialism
John Milbank
creationism/creationist
"scientific creationism"
Intelligent Design Theory
Stephen Jay Gould

Langdon Gilkey
two-languages theory
  (NOMA)
cosmology/cosmological
consonance
Arthur Peacocke
John Polkinghorne

Reference literature

For a general orientation to the relationship of Christian theology with the sciences, see EC 4:873–79 ("Science and Theology" [Padgett]); ER 12:8180–92 ("Science and Religion" [Peters]); OHST 543–60 ("Natural Science" [Murphy]); RGG 10:45–55 ("Natural Sciences" [Evers et al.]); RGG 11:534–37 ("Science" [Enskat])

Questions for review and discussion

1   How does one's understanding of God shape one's perceptions about the natural sciences? How do metaphysical assumptions manifest themselves in supposedly scientific statements about the meaning of reality as a totality?

---

[28] Other important Christian theologians who have been engaging the natural sciences include Pannenberg, Ian Barbour, Robert John Russell, Nancey Murphy, Philip Hefner, and Ted Peters.

2   What difference, if any, does Christian faith make to the study of chemistry, physics, paleontology, biology?

3   What is the difference between "scientism" and "scientific imperialism?" Why is the author critical of these positions?

4   What is the difference between "creationism" and "theistic evolution?" Why is the author critical of creationism? Do you agree or disagree with this criticism? Why?

5   What is "Intelligent Design Theory"? Why is the author critical of ID theory? Do you agree with this criticism? Why or why not?

6   Is there is an important difference between appealing to "God" as the divine cause for some unknown mystery or complexity in nature and inferring that there is a Creator of the universe because of the presence of complexity and apparent design in nature?

7   Do you think that the theory of evolution is inherently "atheistic" or do you think a Christian could accept evolution within a theistic framework (theistic evolution)?

8   Why is the author critical of the so-called "two-languages theory" for discussion of the relation between science and theology? Why have some supported this theory? Do you think science and religion "speak" different languages?

9   Do you think there can be a "consonance" or harmony between science and Christian theology? What would be necessary for that to occur?

10   The chapter ends by identifying two recent figures who are experts in both Christian theology and their respective scientific discipline. Can you identify some other recent individuals who are interested in bridging both science and Christian faith?

Suggestions for further reading

Christian theology and the sciences

Ian Barbour, *Religion and Science: Historical and Contemporary Issues* (San Francisco: Harper San Francisco, 1997) [A very good summary of past and recent efforts to bridge theology and the natural sciences. Barbour, who earned advanced degrees in both physics and Christian theology, has been a leading contributor to bridge-building between the sciences and theology.]

John F. Haught, *God after Darwin: A Theology of Evolution* (Boulder: Westview, 2000) [A major attempt by an American Roman Catholic theologian at demonstrating consonance between a process-theological understanding of Christian faith and modern evolutionary theory.]

Philip Hefner, *The Human Factor* (Minneapolis: Augsburg Fortress, 2000) [A major theological analysis of human evolution by a leading North American Lutheran theologian of the past half century.]

Alister McGrath, *Science and Religion: An Introduction* (Oxford: Blackwell, 1999) [This is a good place for the college student to begin further exploration of the issues in science and theology.]

John Milbank, *Theology and Social Theory: Beyond Secular Reason* (Oxford: Blackwell, 1990) [Controversial, critical analysis of the theological presuppositions within the social sciences and how those assumptions are at odds with Orthodox Anglo-Catholic theology.]

George L. Murphy, *The Cosmos in the Light of the Cross* (Harrisburg: Trinity Press International, 2003) [Engages the problems of natural theology and issues within the natural sciences that have theological import from the perspective of the suffering and death of Jesus. This is an excellent summary of a Lutheran theology of the cross in relation to matters of the natural sciences.]

Nancey Murphy, *Reconciling Science and Religion: A Radical Reformation Perspective* (Oakland, CA: Pandora, 1997) [A brief, very readable argument for a positive, complementary understanding of "science" and "religion." Murphy, who teaches at Fuller Seminary, is an ordained minister in the Church of the Brethren. She has written widely in the area of science and Christian theology.]

Wolfhart Pannenberg, *Toward a Theology of Nature: Essays on Science and Faith*, ed. Ted Peters (Louisville: Westminster John Knox, 1993) [Provides a good introduction to Pannenberg's engagement with the natural sciences. Includes essays on questions that theologians have for scientists, creation and modern science, and contingency and natural law.]

Arthur Peacocke, *Theology for a Scientific Age: Being and Becoming—Natural, Divine, and Human* (Minneapolis: Fortress Press, 1993) [Peacocke's process metaphysic is not persuasive to many, but his theological engagement with issues in biochemistry is stimulating.]

Ted Peters and Gaymon Bennet (eds), *Bridging Science and Religion* (Minneapolis: Fortress, 2003) [Contains essays by many of the leading figures in "science and religion." Explores methodological issues in science and religion, specific topics in the science and theology (natural law and divine action, biological evolution, genetics, and the neurosciences), and inter-religious perspectives on a host of other matters.]

John Polkinghorne, *Belief in God in an Age of Science* (New Haven: Yale

University Press, 1998) [Provides a metaphysic that is contrary to the process one of Peacocke. Polkinghorne seeks to show how one can believe in God and accept what the natural sciences tell us about nature.]

John Polkinghorne, *Faith of a Physicist* (Minneapolis: Fortress Press, 1996) [This is a good way to see how a practicing mathematician and physicist understands the basic theological affirmations in the Nicene Creed.]

Murray Rae, Andrew, Hilary Regan, and John Stenhouse (eds), *Science and Theology: Questions at the Interface* (Grand Rapids: Eerdmans, 1994) [Each of the six sections of the book contains a principal essay by a leading scholar on a given theme (natural theology, the reality of God, scientific methodology, natural and divine truth, relativity, creation and divine action) and then two responses by other scholars.]

W. Mark Richardson and Wesley J. Wildman (eds), *Religion and Science: History, Method, Dialogue* (New York: Routledge, 1996) [A great resource that offers a collection of essays from a variety of perspectives on key topics within the broad field of natural science and religious studies/theology.]

The principal academic journals and other resources for Christian theology and the sciences

In addition to the journals of systematic theology that are listed at the end of Chapter 13, see *Zygon*; Center for the Study of Theology and the Natural Sciences (http://www.ctns.org/) [accessed 30th June 2014]; Zygon Center for Religion and Science (http://zygoncenter.org/) [accessed 30th June 2014]

Afterword

Martin E. Marty

Matthew Becker is not interested in simply assigning blame for the way in which modern Christianity became represented, or let itself be represented at the margins of the higher academy. He shows more interest in what scholarly and ecclesiastical representatives of the Christian faith might do to address the situations that have developed in recent centuries. Once upon a time, as he imagines it and implies, specifically Christian elements were integral to the university, to which they helped give birth. In our time, as he can detail, and about which he can be explicit, those who care about relating Christianity to life and thought in the centers where intellectual transactions most consistently occur are at best permitted restricted roles. At worst, they are ignored or disdained.

Christians do not, or at least they need not, think that all phases of their marginalization were the result of Christian mistakes, yet they do well to regard creative responses to them as scientists do when they have to pick up the pieces after there have been mistakes in experiments. As Lewis Thomas, the great physician and commentator on the world of medicine, has written, when for some reason or other "results come in [and] something is obviously screwed up, ... then the action can begin." Thomas continues that the "misreading" or whatever else is wrong, "is not the important error; it opens the way." The next step, he says, is when the investigator or someone says, "But even so, look at that!" Then the new finding, "whatever it is, is ready for snatching. What is needed, for progress to be made, is the move based on the error."[1]

Becker's book is an exercise in urging "even so, look at that," as he looks at the great achievements and the failures, self-inflicted or as the result of actions by others in higher education, as Christians address it. All 15 chapters in this book have pointed: "Even so, look at that!" But Becker's

---

[1] Quoted from Lewis Thomas, *The Medusa and the Snail: More Notes of a Biology Watcher*, in Edward Rothstein, Herbert Muschamp, and Martin E. Marty, *Visions of Utopia* (New York: Oxford, 2003), 49–50.

mission is not fulfilled by that pointing; the question now is what readers are to do by way of looking and acting. One way to put the issue is in question form, "Where do we go from here?"

While traces of nostalgia appear when Becker traces the history of higher education and (mainly Western) Christian fates within it, he shows that he knows that people of today could not go back into Christendom and its universities before the Enlightenment and modernity, whatever all we mean by that word. He also knows that we readers cannot do much without realizing from where we came. I find the act of tracing clearer when I reference three Latin phrases, as voiced by Eugen Rosenstock-Huessy in his essay "Farewell to Descartes." First, the university was born of the impulse summarized thus: "Truth is divine and has been divinely revealed—*Credo ut intelligam.*" But while that affirmation is at the base of the university, it did not begin to guide or charter or judge other impulses and themes of the university. So higher education needed Descartes and what he represented: "Truth is pure and can be scientifically stated—*cogito ergo sum.*"

Rosenstock-Huessy, a front-rank European and then American intellectual, would not ignore or disdain the great achievements of the modern scientific-based university. But he was writing after World War I, when people of intellectuality and spirit counted the cost or looked at the ruins that came with skeptical reason if it had ruled unchallenged and faced no complementary vision. So Rosenstock-Huessy added a third—dare we now call it "post-modern"?—affirmation, "Truth is vital and must be socially represented—*Respondeo etsi mutabor* (I respond although I will be changed)."[2]

It is impossible and in any case limiting to seek to "go back" to the ways of the university "pre-Descartes," but, as we "look at that," and hear Eugen Rosenstock-Huessy's critique and his urging for something to be added to the first two motifs, we can locate the larger context in which the Christian interpretation begins to find its place:

> . . . Among men, in society, the vigorous identity asked of us by the "*cogito ergo sum*" tends to destroy the guiding Imperative of the good life. We do not exist because we think. Man is the son of God and not brought into being by thinking. We are called into society by a mighty entreaty, "Who art thou, man, that I should care for thee?" And long before our intelligence can help

---

[2] Eugen Rosenstock-Huessy, *I Am an Impure Thinker* (Norwich, Vermont, Argo Books, 1970), 2. I have accepted *respondeo etsi mutabor* as the guiding image for my own scholarly work (and the rest of life as well).

us, the newborn individual survives the tremendous question by his naïve faith in the love of his elders. We grow into society on faith, listening to all kinds of human imperatives. Later we stammer and stutter, nations and individuals alike, in the effort to justify our existence by responding to the call. We try to distinguish between the many tempting offers made to our senses and appetites by the world. We wish to follow the deepest question, the central call which goes straight to the heart, and promises our soul the lasting certainty of being inscribed in the book of life.[3]

If *credo ut intelligam* is received and perceived as the only perspective for higher education, the accent will be on the vertical dimension of reflection and learning. If *cogito ergo sum*—the main affirmation of those who make up the modern university—holds the unique place in respect to learning, the accent would be on the horizontal dimensions. *Respondeo etsi mutabor,* in Rosenstock-Huessy's elaboration, provides an intellectual and spiritual framework for inquiry, experiment, and action in the kind of university about which Matthew Becker is speaking.

"Where do we go from here?"

Chapter 1: "Ways into Theology" bids readers to regard the reflective element, "thinking about God," as being central for dealing with "human questions, situations, and phenomena," as Rosenstock-Huessy also brought them to mind. Here the focus is not on these in a self-referential way. The context instead is "theology—thinking about God." Where we go from here is not to try to backtrack and re-convert universities to a theology-dominated (by at least implicit force inside Christen-*dom)* domain wherein the Western universities were born. Any impulse to strive to re-impose, as if by force, Christian meanings on and boundaries around all the "human questions, situations, and phenomena" presumably addressed in the literal readings of Scriptures, summas, and canons would be limiting and unfair to the genre of those sacred texts.

"Academic theology," on which Becker concentrates, is only one way of reflecting in a Christian context. Conversation, discourse, prayer, mystical experience, hymnody, and patterns of human action beyond formal theology also occur or can occur in university settings. But formal academic theology has to be, well, academic, with no favors asked from other disciplines or ways.

Chapter 2: "Traditions of Christianity". Where do we go from here? In Becker's vision it is certainly possible and valid for any number of reasons

---

[3] *Ibid.* pp. 9ff. Rosenstock-Huessy's "men" is easily translatable to "humans."

to privilege one strand of what is "handed down"="tradition" within a tradition. No one expects Hebrew University to privilege Zen Buddhist texts, or Japanese Universities deliberately to claim that only one tradition is sufficient for the schools in Japan. One comes to know a tradition best when it is regarded as a tradition, possessing a particular subject matter and ethos which differs from those of others. The university, in Becker's picture, does not fulfill its mission unless a tradition is well explored. In his book on tradition, Jaroslav Pelikan tells of the assignment given Jerome Robbins as he worked on what became *Fiddler on the Roof.* "If it's a show about tradition and its dissolution, then the audience should be told what that tradition is."

In the university where a tradition is expounded, "where do we go from here?" The epigraph to Pelikan's book is from Goethe's *Faust,* translated: "What you have as heritage, Take now as task; For thus you will make it your own!" Becker does not presume or picture that the classrooms and halls of a university will be made up of people who have inherited and agreed on one version of the Christian tradition (or, of course, of any particular religion in isolation, or of religion at the expense of everything else.) But Pelikan, and here also Becker, advocates attention to the varied contents, practices, and nuances associated with any religion which is to be subjected to study. So the university wherein significant faculty teach Christian theology combines an intense focus on one tradition in relation to other traditions which do or should beckon for attention.

Chapter 3: "Traditions of Christian Theology" simply (simply?) carries over into academic theology the formal heritage, thought patterns and texts of a religious community, as practiced. If the second chapter alerted readers to contemporary manifestations of tradition, here Becker reaches into history and helps readers learn to see all their work on texts and issues which appear at specific times and places, at least some of which must be addressed, and in advanced learning even somehow mastered.

Chapter Four: "What is Christian Theology?" Where do we go from here with two main new themes Becker introduces here? The first is his stress on the context of "other academic disciplines" When Rosenstock-Huessy promoted the theme *respondeo etsi mutabor,* he pointed to the social context of learning, as Becker begins to do here. It would take another, different, and longer book to flesh this out by reference to the ever-expanding array of disciplines. Becker does put the topic on the agenda and helps the reader sample and picture implications of this social approach to truth. The solitary scholar in a cell or on an island could, if texts were made available there, go far in treating on purely isolated terms something of an awareness of what their other disciplines have to offer, in challenge and enrichment. However, and emphatically, we have universities and colleges (etymologically related to "reading together") to help shape vivid, dynamic, and personal traditions.

The other fresh idea here is that of "witness." It begins, of course, for Becker or anyone dealing with Christianity, with the ancient apostolic witness. But its testimony also thrives and is transmuted in our time. The Christian into our own time, for example, witnesses even among prisoners who are artificially separated from their communities because of their faith commitment. We know that most such witness died when the witnesses were imprisoned or executed, but the university library is also full of exceptional and surviving witnesses as books. The more these are encountered—where do we go from here?—the more students will find their lives enriched, thanks to empathy, identification with others, and commitment. Witnesses can also go astray or can distort, and Becker includes a reminder and a strategy for dealing with weak, faltering, misleading, and lethal forms of witness.

Looking at the next three chapters (God as a problem, the natural knowledge of God, and philosophical theology), I wonder. Where do we go from here? Half way through, Professor Becker turns specialist about the general. From here on in I am diffident about suggesting direction after hearing the question, "Where do we go from here?" While I learned much from those initial three chapters in this second part, they belong to disciplines which I think of as philosophical. I have great interests in philosophy, especially as it relates to theology. But to make informed comment, I should have taken one of Becker's courses in philosophical theology. I somehow managed to pass through five years of pre-seminary education in a denominational school and then through theological seminary, plus four more years for Master's and Doctoral work, without ever having taken a course in philosophical theology. For two or three years I roomed with a philosopher, and learned much from him, but would not trust myself to try to show expertise.

So I made a mistake by not doing well in the fields where discussion of the "general revelation of God" or the "natural knowledge of God" was systematically treated. Here I should follow the Lewis Thomas picturing and blurt, "But, even so, what then?" I have historical, theological and, I suppose, political reasons to stand back and let others take over. The problem: as I read and tell the stories of Christian theology I find that what one regards as "general" or "natural" tends to come pretty close to what an advocate of a tradition expounds as "specific" or "supernatural." Thus, when Roman Catholics talk about "the natural method of birth control," I find that it matches formal Catholic teaching on the subject—which well-reasoning Catholics will also notice, as they go from observing the natural.

Most scriptures, including the New Testament of the Christian tradition, do bear witness to "general revelation" as a basis for determining why non-believers deserve judgment, and I would expect that a good university with a good department and good scholars like Professor Becker should take this up. It does have some practical consequences beyond law-giving, one of which is taken up in Chapter 6, namely, addressing the challenge of "the New Atheists." As I listen to them I hear that they picture believers being believers because they can prove the existence of God. The atheist, in many cases, claims that she has disproven the existence, or proven the non-existence, of God. I've not met anyone yet—including Thomas Aquinas—who could do that. People are Christian on a variety of grounds, and "proofs" are only one of them.

When I was a pastor instructing adults I would spend a little time on Proofs for the Existence of God but would hurry past the Ontological Argument and all the others. I thought I was pooh-poohing these proofs, or at least suggesting that those in the class would be disappointed with what they yielded. Yet almost always someone would come forward and say that this or that "proof" spoke to exactly what had been bothering her, so it helped her in her faith or her quest for faith. More power to the prover, the proof, and the proven to! I stand ready to learn, and this book at least outlines why universities ought to care and to do well with this subject. Where do we go from here? To a philosophical theology course at a good university.

Chapters 8 and 9: "The Special Revelation" and "Themes in Special Revelation." Here Matthew Becker is very helpful. Christians cannot evade witness to "special revelation," because within its context one encounters the texts which witness to the God of Christian faith. One cannot sit at home and decide to invent a religion and come up with anything as surprising, particular and, yes, "offensive" or "scandalous," in biblical terms as what is in the special revelation in the Scripture and corollary texts. Almost a century ago the most prominent Protestant thinker in Europe, Karl Barth, showed more than mild disdain for the writings of his near-peer and fellow Swiss teacher, Emil Brunner. Brunner had presented intelligent defenses of natural law and natural revelation and natural theology. Barth read it and felt a need to respond at book length. The title? *Nein!* No! That approach would not serve students well or deepen friendships in the faculty lounges of Switzerland. But it did stimulate a generation's worth of valid debate that belongs in universities where Protestant theology is a familiar subject.

If Barth stifled thought on general revelation, he gave great impetus to the study of special revelation, and wrote a 13-volume (unfinished!) *Church Dogmatics* which was rich in witness to the Bible and theological texts drawn on it. "Even his footnotes had footnotes," it was said. And many observers found that much Protestant opposition to the "natural" religion of totalitarians, in his case, Nazis, came from witness to God's special revelation. Becker has no trouble convincing us that "the natural" deserves its place in university-theology (though the place for university theology remains complex, as the author knows and shows).

The problem of "special revelation" in the university is difficult because by its nature it exemplifies "the scandal of particularity." One finds this in interfaith relations, where debates are constant about prayer on public occasions. Pray in the name of Jesus Christ and you may well offend fellow citizens who do not believe in him. So they will say be "general," and yet the generalized language sounds quite particular to, say, Buddhist students in public schools or ceremonies. We do not have to solve that issue here. The point for now is that, if Christianity has a place in the university, it can serve as a launching point for valuable discussions about life in a pluralist society.

Chapter 10: "Sources and Norms in Christian Theology." Where do we go from here? Into lively discussion; here is one topic which will draw out from students of all creeds, or none, good debates about what God speaks and with what authority we are to regard what is heard (and read). Picture a typical university classroom in religious studies where conservative evangelicals who are inspired by campus Christian groups sit next to students who have low levels of biblical literacy, or who profess interest in "poetic interpretations," and more. Soon there will be questions about tradition, about authoritative teaching, and corollary topics. We need say little: the "sources and norms" as they are located in the minds and hearts of students will take care of themselves.

Chapter 11 might offer ways for students to sort out conflicting interpretations of these venerable biblical texts. It, too, will lead to scholarly areas (not least a library) further afield.

Chapters 12 and 13: "The Shape of Christian Theology as a University Discipline" and "The Sub-disciplines of Christian Theology." In a way this is a summary of the issues in the whole book, yet it also brings much to the point. In a tax-supported state university the "shape" will be very different from what it will be in a Catholic university or a mainline Protestant one—though in both cases the population will be quite diverse. Only a small minority of students and, often, of faculty and policy-makers will be Episcopalian at an Episcopalianly-chartered school and, for that matter, Catholics and Lutherans are likely to be minorities at Catholic or Lutheran schools. I am not sure that Matthew Becker has had the last word or even his own last word on this subject, so dynamic and volatile are the situations of today's public, secular, vestigially Christian or Jewish and even explicitly confessionally based universities that the resolutions of one decade or even year will be changed in the light of new circumstances.

Where do we go from here, after Matthew Becker's final two chapters on the interdisciplinary orientation of theology? We go to the library, the curriculum committee, the classroom, the lab, the settings where faculty-student conversations are open and intense, and, for believing theologians, to the chapel. This is not to be done in the cynical sense of the old two-liner:

It's nice to have Old Trinity
To remind us of Divinity.

Yes, the artifacts of a world acknowledged to have been shaped by theology surround participants in modern university life. They are there in the libraries, "on-line," in the architecture of many a campus, in rituals of Commencements, *Alma Mater* songs, and more. But theologians, Becker's world, are not to be satisfied with being reduced to status befitting archaeological or museum interests. There is no way to get agreement on exactly what that location of theology in the university will be. Even most Roman Catholic universities regard that situation or status as problematic in a pluralistic culture. One can specialize in Hindu or Buddhist studies on many a Catholic campus. But one can conclude from Becker's approach that, metaphorically, theology has moved from the medieval picture of being the "queen of sciences" to having become the "handmaiden to the various fields of learning."

If that sounds humiliating, Christian theologians, if true to their craft, do well to point out that being humble is more congruent with the Gospels, which are normative for them, than with the hubristic "queen" status. There was something illusory about the claim that it was "queen" when university leaders could refer to it thus without stirring controversy. The more we know of the curricular map of the medieval "Christian" university, we can see anticipations of modern studies of chemistry or physics, though they bore other names. So theology is a handmaiden, an aide, a correlating ally— closer to Becker's term—and not a dominator? Fine. "Get over it," Becker implicitly counsels, and then he moves on with helpful comment.

His use of H. Richard Niebuhr's *Christ and Culture* is helpful as he uses it, which means as a map. But academics remember that "a map is not a territory," so he explores some ways of being an inquirer in the midst of a territory. At one point he seems a bit uneasy about the fact that fulfilled theology has—has to have?—a practical dimension. Heirs of Aristotle, who should have something to say about learning in any age, ancient, medieval, modern, or post-modern, honored "practical reason." In the modern world British philosopher Michael Oakeshott, in *Experience and Its Modes*" after discussing *science*, whose differentia is measurement and *history*, whose differentia is "the past," speaks of "religion," to say nothing of "theology," about which Becker says much, as "practical." The details of this categorizing are too complex to be entertained in a paragraph or two here.[4] I cite this as but one instance of high-level philosophy which wrestles with what engrossed Becker. He comments on a variety of approaches.

Whichever "mode of experience" higher educators who have religious or theological interests entertain, I think they will take from Becker's book implied counsel not to wallow in nostalgia for "good old days" when theology ruled, or to mope because they no longer "run the show," if they ever honestly did, but to enjoy the correlating role (and others Becker mentions) and be intelligent, respectful, open to dialogue, and faithful in the pursuit of their exciting discipline. There will be clashes among the doctrinaires and over the "doctrines" within and among the disciplines, but this book in its final chapter evokes the spirit of Alfred North Whitehead, who observed and taught that "a clash of doctrines is not a disaster—it is an opportunity."

G. K. Chesterton once said that, if you have and want to keep a white fence, you will be very busy re-whiting it. Mud, dirt, animal refuse, and erosion will work their effects. So it is with conserving, conservatism, or tradition, and as it will be when you are debating issues of modernity and post-modernity. Odds are, however, that in any discussion of the place one particular tradition—Christianity—and one discipline—theology—have in the mix, the conversations and deliberations will be much more promising and productive if the participants have engaged and been engaged by Matthew Becker's wonderful ponderings and systematic presentations.

Martin E. Marty
Emeritus
The University of Chicago

---

[4] Michael Oakeshott, *Experience and Its Modes* (Cambridge: Cambridge University Press, 1933).

Appendix

An excerpt from Martin Luther's "Preface to the Wittenberg Edition of Luther's German Writings" (1539)[1]

Moreover, I want to point out to you a correct way of studying theology, for I have had practice in that. If you keep to it, you will become so learned that you yourself could (if it were necessary) write books just as good as those of the fathers and councils, even as I (in God) dare to presume and boast, without arrogance and lying, that in the matter of writing books I do not stand much behind some of the fathers. Of my life I can by no means make the same boast. This is the way taught by holy King David (and doubtlessly used also by all the patriarchs and prophets) in the one hundred and nineteenth Psalm. There you will find three rules, amply presented throughout the whole Psalm. They are *Oratio* [prayer], *Meditatio* [meditation], *Tentatio* [spiritual crisis, turmoil, and trial].

Firstly, you should know that the Holy Scriptures constitute a book which turns the wisdom of all other books into foolishness, because not one teaches about eternal life except this one alone. Therefore you should straightway despair of your reason and understanding. With them you will not attain eternal life, but, on the contrary, your presumptuousness will plunge you and others with you out of heaven (as happened to Lucifer) into the abyss of hell. But kneel down in your little room [Matt. 6.6] and pray to God with real humility and earnestness, that he through his dear Son may give you his Holy Spirit, who will enlighten you, lead you, and give you understanding.

Thus you see how David keeps praying in the above-mentioned Psalm, "Teach me, Lord, instruct me, lead me, show me," and many more words

---

[1] An excerpt from Martin Luther's "Preface to the Wittenberg Edition of Luther's German Writings," trans. Robert R. Heitner, in LW 34: 285–8. Some of the translator's footnotes have been omitted. This copyrighted material from the American Edition of *Luther's Works* is used here by permission of Fortress Press.

like these. Although he well knew and daily heard and read the text of Moses and other books besides, still he wants to lay hold of the real teacher of the Scriptures himself, so that he may not seize upon them pell-mell with his reason and become his own teacher. For such practice gives rise to factious spirits who allow themselves to nurture the delusion that the Scriptures are subject to them and can be easily grasped with their reason, as if they were *Markolf*[2] or Aesop's Fables, for which no Holy Spirit and no prayers are needed.

Secondly, you should meditate, that is, not only in your heart, but also externally, by actually repeating and comparing oral speech and literal words of the book, reading and rereading them with diligent attention and reflection, so that you may see what the Holy Spirit means by them. And take care that you do not grow weary or think that you have done enough when you have read, heard, and spoken them once or twice, and that you then have complete understanding. You will never be a particularly good theologian if you do that, for you will be like untimely fruit which falls to the ground before it is half ripe.

Thus you see in this same Psalm how David constantly boasts that he will talk, meditate, speak, sing, hear, read, by day and night and always, about nothing except God's Word and commandments. For God will not give you his Spirit without the external Word; so take your cue from that. His command to write, preach, read, hear, sing, speak, etc., outwardly was not given in vain.

Thirdly, there is *tentatio*, *Anfechtung* [spiritual crisis, turmoil, and trial]. This is the touchstone which teaches you not only to know and understand, but also to experience how right, how true, how sweet, how lovely, how mighty, how comforting God's Word is, wisdom beyond all wisdom.

Thus you see how David, in the Psalm mentioned, complains so often about all kinds of enemies, arrogant princes or tyrants, false spirits and factions, whom he must tolerate because he meditates, that is, because he is occupied with God's Word (as has been said) in all manner of ways. For as soon as God's Word takes root and grows in you, the devil will harry you, and will make a real doctor of you, and by his assaults [*Anfechtungen*] will teach you to seek and love God's Word. I myself (if you will permit me, mere mouse-dirt, to be mingled with pepper) am deeply indebted to my papists

---

[2] The very popular medieval legend of Solomon and Markolf was treated in a verse epic, pamphlets, dialogues, and farces. The figure of Markolf, a sly and unprincipled rogue, was known in Germany as early as the tenth century.

that through the devil's raging they have beaten, oppressed, and distressed me so much. That is to say, they have made a fairly good theologian of me, which I would not have become otherwise. And I heartily grant them what they have won in return for making this of me, honor, victory, and triumph, for that's the way they wanted it.

There now, with that you have David's rules. If you study hard in accord with his example, then you will also sing and boast with him in the Psalm, "The law of thy mouth is better to me than thousands of gold and silver pieces" [Ps. 119.72]. Also, "Thy commandment makes me wiser than my enemies, for it is ever with me. I have more understanding than all my teachers, for thy testimonies are my meditation. I understand more than the aged, for I keep thy precepts," etc. [Ps. 119.98–100]. And it will be your experience that the books of the fathers will taste stale and putrid to you in comparison. You will not only despise the books written by adversaries, but the longer you write and teach the less you will be pleased with yourself. When you have reached this point, then do not be afraid to hope that you have begun to become a real theologian, who can teach not only the young and imperfect Christians, but also the maturing and perfect ones. For indeed, Christ's church has all kinds of Christians in it who are young, old, weak, sick, healthy, strong, energetic, lazy, simple, wise, etc.

If, however, you feel and are inclined to think you have made it, flattering yourself with your own little books, teaching, or writing, because you have done it beautifully and preached excellently; if you are highly pleased when someone praises you in the presence of others; if you perhaps look for praise, and would sulk or quit what you are doing if you did not get it—if you are of that stripe, dear friend, then take yourself by the ears, and if you do this in the right way you will find a beautiful pair of big, long, shaggy donkey ears. Then do not spare any expense! Decorate them with golden bells, so that people will be able to hear you wherever you go, point their fingers at you, and say, "See, See! There goes that clever beast, who can write such exquisite books and preach so remarkably well." That very moment you will be blessed and blessed beyond measure in the kingdom of heaven. Yes, in that heaven where hellfire is ready for the devil and his angels. To sum up: Let us be proud and seek honor in the places where we can. But in this book the honor is God's alone, as it is said, "God opposes the proud, but gives grace to the humble" [I Pet. 5.5]; to whom be glory, world without end, Amen.

Glossary of Names

Individuals whose names are typically connected to a locale are normally alphabetized by first name (e.g. *Ambrose* of Milan), unless the locale is widely regarded as the family name (e.g. Thomas *Aquinas*; Nicolas von *Zinzendorf*). All others are alphabetized by their family name or common nickname (e.g. John *Chrysostom*).

Peter Abelard (1079–1142/3) Professor of philosophy and theology at the University of Paris. He used logic and dialectic to set forth rational understandings of church teachings that sometimes conflicted with traditional positions.

Julius Africanus (160–240) Christian historian. His dating of the birth of Jesus, though incorrect, led to the development of the standard Christian reckoning of time (BC/AD). He miscalculated the death of Herod the Great and thus was incorrect in fixing the probable year of Jesus' birth. He was off by about four years.

Albert the Great (Albertus Magnus; c. 1195–1280) Professor of science, philosophy, and theology at the University of Paris, where he helped to introduce the writings of Aristotle to his students, including Thomas Aquinas.

William P. Alston (1921–2009) American philosopher who specialized in the philosophy of language, epistemology, and the philosophy of religion. He was especially interested in the nature of religious experience. Founding editor of the journal *Faith and Philosophy*.

Ambrose of Milan (c. 339–97) Bishop of Milan. Famous for his preaching, he was instrumental in helping Augustine to become a baptized Christian. Ambrose wrote treatises on the sacraments and Christian ethics. He also stressed the importance of monasticism.

Anselm of Canterbury (c. 1033–1109) Archbishop of Canterbury and the major figure in early–medieval scholastic theology. He sought to provide a rational basis for the being of God (the so–called "ontological argument") and a scholarly rationale for the incarnation of the divine *Logos* (apart from reference to biblical and patristic sources).

Thomas Aquinas (c. 1224–74) Professor of philosophy and theology at the University of Paris. Member of the Dominican Order. He is the major theologian of the medieval period. He used Aristotelian philosophy to understand and explicate the content of revealed faith. His two main theological works are the *Summa Theologica* ("summary of theology" for university students), which remained unfinished at his death, and the *Summa contra Gentiles* ("summary against the non–Christians"), a defense of the truth of Christian faith over against Jewish and Muslim objections.

Aristotle (384–322 BC) Greek philosopher. Student of Plato. Major influence on the development of western medieval theology, especially the thought of Aquinas. Like Plato, Aristotle understood theology to be mainly criticism of Greek myths ("stories").

Arius (256–336) Priest in Alexandria. He was condemned as a heretic for teaching and preaching that "there once was when the *Logos* was not" and "before the *Logos* was begotten he was not." These statements were condemned at the first ecumenical council of Nicaea in AD 325. Arianism held that the *Logos* was the first creature of God and thus not fully divine or eternal as the Father.

Jacobus Arminius (1560–1609) Dutch Reformed theologian who later rejected Calvin's teaching about predestination.

Athanasius (c. 296–373) Bishop of Alexandria. Major defender of orthodox trinitarian theology over against Arianism. One of the major eastern (Greek) theologians.

Augustine of Hippo (354–430) Bishop of Hippo and the major western (Latin) theologian. His ideas shaped theological discussions in the western church for more than a millennium, down to the Protestant Reformation. He wrote essays and books on all of the major theological topics, including especially the doctrine of the Trinity, the nature of sin and grace, and the theology of history.

Averroes (1126–98) Medieval Muslim philosopher and scientist. His commentaries on Aristotle influenced Thomas Aquinas and other medieval Christian theologians.

Avicenna (980–1037) Muslim philosopher and physician from Persia. Influenced by Aristotle's philosophy, Avicenna's writings also influenced early–medieval Christian theologians.

Johann S. Bach (1685–1750) Lutheran composer and organist. Little appreciated in his lifetime, Bach has become one of the most celebrated creative geniuses. His oratorios, passions, and B–minor Mass are considered by many to be among the most beautiful sacred music ever created.

Hans Urs von Balthasar (1905–88) Swiss Roman Catholic theologian. Influenced by the eastern Fathers, Augustine, Karl Barth, and the Swiss mystic, Adrienne von Speyr, von Balthasar sought to broaden the basis of theology in relation to what is true, good, and beautiful.

Karl Barth (1886–1968) Swiss Reformed theologian. One of the two or three major Protestant theologians of the twentieth century. Educated within liberal Protestant theology, Barth came to criticize aspects of that tradition in favor of the revelation of the Word of God "from above." His commentary on Romans, published shortly after the end of the First World War, emphasized the otherness of God and God's judgment against human sin. His major work was the unfinished thirteen–volume *Church Dogmatics*, the most ambitious summary of Christian teaching since Johann Gerhard's *loci Theologici*.

Basil of Caesarea (c. 330–79) Greek theologian and bishop of Caesarea. One of the three so–called "Cappadocian Fathers," which also included his brother Gregory of Nyssa and Gregory Nazianzus. These theologians were particularly influential in their writings about the doctrine of the Trinity, especially on the role of the Holy Spirit.

Bruno Bauer (1809–82) German philosopher and historian. He argued that the Gospel of Mark is a work of fiction on which all other written gospels are founded. Thus, in his view, Jesus was a fictional, non–historical character.

Walter Bauer (1877–1960) German theologian who set forth the thesis that heresy flourished in many regions of early Christianity before becoming supplanted by later orthodox positions. He was also the author of a Greek lexicon that has become a standard scholarly reference work. (See the entry for BDAG in the list of abbreviations.)

Oswald Bayer (b. 1939) German Lutheran theologian. He has stressed the nature of the gospel as a divine promise to which humans are invited to respond in faith.

Ernest Becker (1924–74) American cultural anthropologist. His most important work is *The Denial of Death*, which explores the human tendency to deny mortality and the problems that this denial creates within human societies.

Peter Berger (b. 1929) Austrian–born American sociologist and Lutheran theologian. He has written extensively on the process by which human beings create their understandings of reality through interaction with social institutions.

Bernard of Clairvaux (1090–1153) Latin theologian and abbot of Clairvaux. His most important work is a series of sermons on the Song of Songs. In these sermons and in other writings he stressed that God should be loved simply and merely because God is God.

Robert Bertram (1921–2003) American Lutheran theologian. His theology was deeply shaped by his engagement with Martin Luther's 1535 commentary on Galatians and the need for contemporary preachers and theologians to distinguish properly God's accusing law from God's promising gospel.

Gabriel Biel (c. 1420–95) German medieval theologian. One of the last of the scholastic theologians. His theology of justification stressed that as long as one "did one's best" "to do what is in one's power to do," then God will grant his grace so that the individual will be able to do more good works.

Bonaventure (c. 1217–74) Franciscan professor of theology. His most important work was *The Mind's Road to God*, in which he describes how God provides mystical illumination to the prayerful Christian. Like other medieval Latin theologians, he also wrote a commentary on Peter Lombard's *Sentences*.

Dietrich Bonhoeffer (1906–45) German Lutheran theologian. Influenced by Karl Barth, Bonhoeffer was very involved in the ecumenical movement. He later directed an illegal seminary of the Confessing Church, which opposed the nazification of the German Protestant Church. He was executed by the Nazis for his participation in a plot to assassinate Hitler.

Bono ([Paul David Hewson] b. 1960) Irish musician and lead singer for the band U2. Raised by Anglican and Catholic parents, he is one of the great humanitarians of the past quarter century. Many of his songs contain Christian symbols and imagery.

Ernest Boyer (1928–95) American educator. He wrote several influential reports on the need for reforms in undergraduate education.

Don Browning (1934–2010) American Protestant theologian. He was particularly interested in interdisciplinary study that brought together insights from Christian theology, psychology, and the social sciences.

Emil Brunner (1889–1966) Swiss Reformed theologian. Like Karl Barth, Brunner was critical of liberal Protestant theology, but unlike Barth he thought that there is a human "point of contact" that allows human beings to respond to the general revelation of God. The latter then is the larger context for God's saving revelation in Jesus Christ.

Rudolf Bultmann (1884–1976) New Testament scholar and German Lutheran theologian. Along with Karl Barth and Paul Tillich, Bultmann is one of the most influential Protestant theologians of the twentieth century. An early supporter of Barth's dialectical theology, Bultmann later developed his program of "de–mythologizing" the New Testament, which Barth criticized.

John Calvin (1509–64) French–born Swiss Reformer and theologian. His *Institutes of the Christian Religion* is a classic statement of Reformed Protestant theology.

Cappadocians See the entries for Basil of Caesarea, Gregory Nazianzus, and Gregory of Nyssa.

Catherine of Sienna (c. 1347–80) Dominican theologian. All of her writings, mostly letters and prayers, stress the centrality of the crucified Christ and his blood, which she interpreted as the sign of God's love for human beings.

Martin Chemnitz (1522–86) German Lutheran theologian. A student of Philip Melanchthon, he was a great defender of Luther's teaching of the real presence in the Lord's Supper. In addition to his classic work on the two natures of Christ, he wrote a lengthy critique of the decrees of the Council of Trent.

Rebecca Chopp (b. 1952) American theologian and academic administrator.

She has written extensively about liberation and feminist theologies and issues of social justice.

John Chrysostom (c. 347–407) Bishop of Constantinople and major eastern (Greek) theologian. He was especially well-known for his preaching ("Chrysostom" = "Golden-mouth") and personal holiness.

Clement of Alexandria (c. 150–c. 215) Egyptian theologian. He was especially interested in cultivating a positive relationship between Greek pagan philosophy and Christian teaching.

Francis Collins (b.1950) American physician, chemist, and geneticist. He was the co-director of the Human Genome Project and currently serves as the head of the National Institutes of Health. His book, *The Language of God*, sets forth his understanding of the compatibility between his Christian faith and modern scientific knowledge.

Lucas Cranach Sr. (1472–1553) German painter. He created visual art that supported Martin Luther's reform efforts.

Oscar Cullmann (1902–99) French–born Lutheran theologian. He rehabilitated the idea of "salvation history" (*Heilsgeschichte*), first developed by Johannes von Hofmann, as the key way of understanding the biblical view of time and history. *Heilsgeschichte* is a narrow stream of revelatory history in the middle of secular history that provides insight into the meaning of all history.

Cyprian of Carthage (c. 200–58) Bishop of Carthage and a leading western (Latin) theologian. He wrote mainly about the unity of the catholic church and the role of bishops in maintaining that unity.

Cyril of Alexandria (378–444) Bishop of Alexandria and a leading eastern (Greek) theologian. He opposed Nestorius' Christology and wrote treatises that defended the two natures in Christ.

John Nelson Darby (1800–82) Member of the Plymouth Brethren and later of a group called the "Darbyites." He is the father of modern "Dispensationalism," which holds that human history can be divided into several periods or dispensations and that we are living in the last days of that history. Darby was the first to teach a "secret rapture," whereby Christ would secretly remove the elect from the trials and tribulations of the last days. Darby's millennial ideas are reflected in the *Scofield Reference Bible* and the "Left Behind" stories and accepted by many Fundamentalist Christians.

Richard Dawkins (b. 1941) British evolutionary biologist and author. A professor at Oxford University, he has written many books in the area of evolution and the natural sciences. In this role he has been one of the more out-spoken defenders of scientific materialism and atheism and has been a strong critic of all religious belief.

Dorothy Day (1897–1980) American journalist and Catholic social activist. She co-founded the Catholic Worker movement.

Jacques Derrida (1930–2004) French philosopher. Leading figure in post-modern deconstructionism.

René Descartes (1596–1650) French philosopher. Often called the father of modern philosophy, he emphasized the role of methodical doubt, "rejecting everything in which one can imagine the least doubt." He developed his own version of the ontological argument for the existence of God, similar to Anselm's.

Duns Scotus (c. 1265–1308) English philosopher and theologian. He taught at Oxford and then at Paris. He wrote insightful commentaries on Peter Lombard's *Sentences* and on works by Aristotle and Porphyry. His theology offers a synthesis of Aristotelian philosophy and Augustinian theology. He stressed the primacy and centrality of Christ as the supreme revelation of God's love.

Albrecht Dürer (1471–1528) German painter and engraver. He served as an important bridge between Italian art and Northern German art. He was lauded by both Catholic humanists, such as Erasmus, and by Protestant reformers, such as Martin Luther.

Avery Dulles (1918–2008) American Catholic theologian. His most important writings set forth "models of revelation" and "models of the church."

Gerhard Ebeling (1912–2001) German Lutheran theologian. Influenced by the theologies of Bonhoeffer and Bultmann, Ebeling wrote numerous books and essays on the historical Jesus, faith, hermeneutics, and Christian theology. He was the first Protestant theologian in Germany to work on problems in fundamental theology.

Johann Eck (1486–1543) German Catholic theologian. He was the leading Catholic theologian in opposition to Martin Luther's theology and reform efforts.

Jonathan Edwards (1703–58) American Reformed theologian. He was the major theologian of his century. His writings and preaching contributed to the so-called "Great Awakening." A strict Calvinist, he opposed the theology of Arminius.

Bart Ehrman (b. 1955) American scholar of the New Testament. He has written extensively on issues within textual criticism of the New Testament and has furthered the thesis of Walter Bauer regarding the interaction between heresy and orthodoxy in early Christianity.

Werner Elert (1883–1954) German Lutheran theologian. Elert stressed the sharp distinction between God's law and gospel for the sake of grounding faith in the gospel promise alone. Because of his concern for classic Lutheran distinctions between law and gospel and the two kingdoms, Elert became a fierce critic of Karl Barth's theology, which he thought undermined these important themes.

Mircea Eliade (1907–86) Romanian-born philosopher and scholar of religions.

He was particularly influential in his phenomenological interpretations of religious experience and symbols.

Eunomius (d. c. 394) An Arian theologian and bishop. He held that God is a simple, supreme Substance that is absolutely intelligible. He taught that Son was the first creature that God created. Eunomius' writings were criticized by the Cappadocian Fathers.

Emil Fackenheim (1916–2003) German-born Jewish philosopher and rabbi. He became a professor of philosophy at the University of Toronto. He famously asserted that Jews had the responsibility not to give Hitler any posthumous victories by giving up their Jewish faith and way of life.

Edward Farley (b. 1929) American Presbyterian (Reformed) theologian. He has written several books in the areas of fundamental theology and theological education. He has been one of the leading revisionist Protestant theologians of the past half century.

Ludwig Feuerbach (1804–72) German philosopher. One of the leading atheist thinkers of the nineteenth century. He developed a psychological understanding of religion in which he asserted that the belief in God is the result of human projection of people's internal desires and ideals.

Johann G. Fichte (1762–1814) German philosopher. Co–founder of the University of Berlin, he argued against Schleiermacher that Christian theology did not belong in the university.

Elisabeth Schüssler Fiorenza (b. 1938) New Testament scholar and American Catholic theologian. She has been particularly concerned with feminist interpretation of the Bible, hermeneutics, and theology.

Francis Schüssler Fiorenza (b.1941) American Catholic theologian. His primary interests include fundamental theology, hermeneutics, and Catholic systematic theology.

Antony Flew (1923–2010) British philosopher. He was an articulate critic of theism and a defender of atheism for most of his professional life. Later he became a convinced deist.

Gerhard Forde (1927–2005) American Lutheran theologian. Concerned to keep classic Lutheran themes at the forefront of theology, he wrote extensively on the nature of the Christian gospel as justification by faith alone in Jesus Christ alone.

George Fox (1624–91) English dissenter and founder of the Society of Friends (Quakers).

Hans Frei (1922–88) German-born American Reformed theologian. Along with George Lindbeck, he was one of the key "post–liberal" theologians in the second half of the twentieth century. He wrote especially about Christology, biblical hermeneutics, and theological method.

Sigmund Freud (1856–1939) Austrian neurologist and the founder of psychoanalysis. He regarded religion as an illusion based on infantile needs.

Hans–Georg Gadamer (1900–2002) German philosopher. He was a major contributor to discussions about philosophical and theological hermeneutics in the second half of the twentieth century.

Clifford Geertz (1926–2006) American anthropologist. He was the most significant cultural anthropologist in the last third of the twentieth century. His definition of religion as a cultural system of symbols has been very influential.

Johann Gerhard (1582–1637) German Lutheran theologian. He wrote a nine-volume textbook of dogmatics that is unsurpassed as a summary of orthodox Lutheran teaching.

Brian Gerrish (b. 1931) British-born Reformed theologian. For several decades he taught historical and systematic theology at the University of Chicago. He has been a leading scholar of the theologies of Luther, Calvin, and Schleiermacher.

Langdon Gilkey (1919–2004) American Protestant theologian. Gilkey was a major interpreter of the theologies of Reinhold Niebuhr and Paul Tillich and was a key proponent of Protestant revisionist theology in the second half of the twentieth century.

Billy Graham (b. 1918) American conservative-evangelical (Baptist) evangelist. He became famous for his "stadium campaigns" as a key aspect of his evangelism efforts.

Robert Grant (b. 1917) American scholar of the New Testament and early Christianity. He wrote many books and articles on a variety of topics in early Christianity, including Gnosticism and the formation of the New Testament canon.

Gregory of Nazianzus (also known as Gregory Nazianzen) (329–89) Greek theologian. One of the three so-called "Cappadocian Fathers." He was a key interpreter of Origen's theology. He was a great defender of Nicene orthodoxy. His "Five Theological Orations" offer extensive analysis of the person and work of the Holy Spirit.

Gregory of Nyssa (c. 330–c. 395) Greek theologian and bishop of Nyssa. One of the three so–called "Cappadocian Fathers." He was the younger brother of Basil of Caesarea. A strong defender of Nicene orthodoxy, he was a well–regarded preacher. Influenced by Origen's theology, he wrote several important works against Arianism and sought to provide a rational understanding of the Trinity, the incarnation, salvation, and the sacraments.

Gustavo Gutiérrez (b. 1928) Peruvian Catholic (Dominican) theologian. His key book, *A Theology of Liberation*, is a classic contribution to liberation theology.

Karl Hagenbach (1801–74) German Protestant scholar of historical theology. In addition to writing a textbook on the history of Christian doctrines, he wrote a classic theological encyclopedia in which he set forth a four–fold pattern of the sub–disciplines: exegetical, historical, systematic, and practical.

David Bentley Hart (b. 1965) American Orthodox theologian. He is a leading interpreter of eastern Orthodox theology in North America. He is particularly interested to bring insights from classic patristic sources (such as Gregory Nyssa) into conversation with contemporary figures and issues.

Charles Hartshorne (1897–2000) American philosopher and theologian. He articulated a modified version of Anselm's ontological argument for God. Influenced by the process philosophy of Alfred North Whitehead, Hartshorne became a leading figure in process theology.

Stanley Hauerwas (b. 1940) American Methodist theologian and ethicist. He is a leading figure in post–liberal, narrative theology.

Vaclav Havel (1936–2011) Czech playwright and poet and the first president of the Czech Republic. Many of his plays and essays raise metaphysical and even theological questions.

Stephen Hawking (b. 1942) British mathematician and cosmologist. He has not only been a leading theoretician in his field, but he has done much to popularize important findings in modern physics and cosmology (see, for example, *A Brief History of Time*).

Georg Hegel (1770–1831) German idealist philosopher. Heavily influenced by Lutheran theology, his philosophical system interprets religious symbols and ideas as figurative representations of philosophical truths.

Martin Heidegger (1889–1976) German existentialist philosopher. His most famous and influential work, *Being and Time*, is a complicated analysis of the historical and temporal character of human being.

Henry VIII (1491–1547) King of England. Instrumental in separating the Church of England from the Roman Catholic Church. He named himself Supreme Head of the Church of England.

Heinrich Heppe (1820–79) German Reformed theologian. He authored a definitive textbook of Reformed dogmatics.

Herbert of Cherbury (1582–1648) English philosopher and poet. He was a leading deist who thought that all religions had five common features: (1) that God exists; (2) that God ought to be worshipped; (3) that virtue is the main way to worship God; (4) that one must repent of one's sins; and (5) that God will reward and punish individuals in the afterlife.

Hesiod (eighth century c. BC) Greek poet. His *Theogony* tells of the birth of the cosmos and of the Greek gods.

Hilary of Poitiers (c. 315–67) Western (Latin) theologian and bishop of Poitiers. A convert from paganism, he became the leading Latin theologian of his time and a strong opponent of Arianism.

Hildegard of Bingen (1098–1179) Western (Latin) theologian and abbess of Rupertsberg. She understood herself to be a prophetess, who wrote about several mystical visions she experienced that shed light on the nature of human beings and their salvation in Christ.

Christopher Hitchens (1949–2011) British-born American journalist and author. He often criticized institutional religion and described his own position as antitheist.

Peter Hitchens (b. 1951) British journalist and author. A former atheist, he is a conservative member of the Church of England and a critic of atheism. He is the younger brother of Christopher Hitchens.

Peter Hodgson (b. 1934) American liberal Protestant theologian. His work explores both historical theology (for example, the theology of Hegel) and contemporary systematic theology (for example, liberation theology, revisionist theology). He describes his own theological approach as revisionist in character.

Johannes von Hofmann (1810–77) German Lutheran theologian and scholar of the Bible. He interpreted the Bible as a witness to God's acts of salvation in history (*Heilsgeschichte*). In addition to writing a commentary on the whole of the New Testament, he wrote many books and articles on biblical interpretation and theological encyclopedia.

David Hume (1711–76) Scottish philosopher and historian. His *Dialogues Concerning Natural Religion* offer a critical appraisal of various views toward the existence of God. Hume himself was skeptical about that reality.

John Hus (c. 1372–1415) Czech Catholic priest, reformer, and forerunner to the Protestant Reformation. He taught philosophy and theology at the University of Prague. Deeply critical of clerical corruption within the church of his day, Hus was burned at the stake at the Council of Constance. He had supported Wycliffe's ideas about reforming the church and set forth his own proposals that were met with criticism and official condemnation.

Thomas Huxley (1825–95) British biologist. He was a major spokesman for the defense of Charles Darwin's theory of evolution by natural selection. He coined the term "agnosticism" to describe his own uncertainty about the existence of God.

Irenaeus of Lyons (c. 130–c. 200) Bishop of Lyons and one of the first truly systematic Christian theologians. He was a major opponent of Gnosticism. Not only did he stress the fundamental unity between God the Father and Jesus, the Son of God, but he emphasized the centrality of the incarnation of the *Logos* of God. His opposition to Gnosticism and his defense of the essential unity of the four canonical gospels also furthered the development of the orthodox and catholic biblical canon.

William James (1842–1910) American pragmatist philosopher and scholar of psychology. He argued for the practical usefulness and benefits that come from the deliberate decision to believe in God. His Gifford Lectures, published as *The Varieties of Religious Experience* (1902), is a classic examination of religious conversion and the dynamics of religious psychology.

Karl Jaspers (1883–1969) German existentialist philosopher. He held that certain basic human experiences and questions lead one to reflect more deeply about one's life as a whole and upon matters that have the effect of calling one's life into question. These are "boundary questions" because they push one beyond trivial knowledge toward what he called "the transcendent." Jaspers stressed the limitations of science to deal with these boundary questions.

Robert Jenson (b. 1930) American Lutheran theologian. A major interpreter of Karl Barth's theology, Jenson has been a leading Lutheran theologian in the United States. Along with his close friend, Carl Braaten, he has been especially interested in fostering ecumenical discussions on key issues that divide Lutherans, Roman Catholics, and the Orthodox. His two-volume *Systematic Theology* is an impressive articulation of church doctrine from the perspective of ecumenical evangelical-catholicism.

Jerome (c. 345–420) Western catholic scholar of the Bible. His most significant achievement was translating the entire Bible into Latin (the Vulgate). He wrote many commentaries on biblical writings. His judgment that the OT canon should be restricted to the 39 books in the Hebrew canon (and thus excluding the Apocrypha) was later accepted by the Protestant reformers in the sixteenth century. He was a fierce critic of Arianism, Pelagianism, and Origenism, and a strong proponent of asceticism.

Jesus of Nazareth (born c. 6 BC and crucified c. 30) Acclaimed the Christ by his followers, Jesus was an itinerant preacher, teacher, and healer. According to the synoptic gospels, he announced the coming kingdom of God. According to early non-Christian sources (Josephus, Tacitus, Suetonius, and Pliny), he was condemned by the Roman prefect, Pontius Pilate, and crucified. His followers later reported that Jesus had been raised from the dead. Christians believe him to be their Lord and Savior, the living Word, and eternal Son of God.

Wilfried Joest (1914–95) German Lutheran theologian. For nearly thirty years Joest taught systematic theology at the University of Erlangen. For forty years he was the editor of *Kerygma und Dogma*, the leading journal of confessional Lutheran theology in Germany. Along with Gerhard Ebeling, he was particularly interested in issues of fundamental theology, which he addressed from the perspective of Martin Luther and modern Lutheran confessional theology.

Pope John XXIII (1881–1963) Elected Pope in 1958. He called for the Second Vatican Council (1962–5), which significantly reformed the Catholic Church. He was particularly interested in fostering greater ecumenical relationships between Rome and other churches.

John of Damascus (ca 655–c. 750) Major Eastern Orthodox theologian and doctor of the church. He is among the most influential of eastern theologians. He not only set forth a comprehensive summary of the teachings of the Greek fathers on the central doctrines of the church, but he was a strong defender of the use of icons in the church.

Pope John Paul II (1920–2005) Second longest-serving Pope in history. A Polish priest, university chaplain and professor of theology, he eventually was made a bishop, archbishop, and cardinal. After his election as Pope in 1978, he traveled extensively throughout the world. His pontificate has been interpreted as having fostered conservative catholic orthodoxy and taken critical steps against perceived false teachings and practices outside of the church (atheism, materialism, Communism) and within Catholic circles (women's ordination, liberation theology).

Luke Timothy Johnson (b. 1943) American Catholic scholar of the New Testament and early Christianity. He has written extensively on Luke-Acts, the letters of Paul, and the letter of James.

Mark Johnston (b. 1954) American professor of philosophy. His work in the philosophy of religion centers on his arguments for anti-supernatural religious naturalism. He has been critical of the so–called "New Atheists."

Flavius Josephus (c. 37–c. 100) Jewish-Roman historian. His *Antiquities of the Jews* provides significant information on historical figures that are mentioned in the NT (John the Baptist, Pontius Pilate, Jesus of Nazareth, and others). His writings were well-regarded and used by early Christian theologians, such as Jerome.

Julian of Norwich (c. 1342–c. 1416) English anchoress, mystic, and spiritual writer. Her *Showings* or *Revelations of Divine Love* has had a great influence, especially among contemporary feminist theologians. This work demonstrates her profound theological understanding of God's love and suffering in Christ.

Eberhard Jüngel (b. 1934) German Lutheran theologian. He was significantly influenced by the theology of Karl Barth and the hermeneutics and theology of Rudolf Bultmann and Bultmann's students. Along with Pannenberg, Jüngel is the most well-known German Lutheran theologian of the past half century. He has been particularly influential in the areas of theological hermeneutics and trinitarian theology.

Justin Martyr (c. 100–c. 165) Christian apologist who sought to defend the moral and theological intelligibility of Christian teaching to those who criticized it. In his work he made extensive, positive use of pagan philosophy.

Martin Kähler (1835–1912) German Lutheran theologian. He wrote extensively on Christian dogmatics, but his most influential writing was his little booklet, *The So–called Historical Jesus and the Historic, Biblical Christ*, which stressed that the gospels do not give us a means of reconstructing the historical Jesus as he was in the first century, since they are thoroughly shaped by the post-resurrection faith of the early disciples of Jesus. The real, living Christ encounters us in the *kerygma* or preaching about Jesus by the apostles that is given in the NT documents.

Immanuel Kant (1724–1804) German Enlightenment philosopher. He wrote ground-breaking books in the areas of epistemology, metaphysics, ethics, and religion. He was critical of the traditional arguments for the existence of God. Nevertheless he postulated the existence of God (along with freedom and immortality) as a necessary presupposition for "moral reason." God is necessary to apportion happiness in the afterlife in accord with the level of one's virtue in this life. For Kant, religion is essentially reduced to matters of ethics.

Gordon Kaufman (1925–2011) American Mennonite theologian. He was a major revisionist systematic theologian who understood God as "the profound mystery of creativity" and interpreted the theological task as one in service to nonviolence, justice, and human creativity. Kaufman made significant contributions to conversations about religion and science.

David Kelsey (b. 1932) American Presbyterian theologian. He has written widely in the areas of theological education, fundamental theology, and theological anthropology.

Johannes Kepler (1571–1630) German astronomer. He was also a practicing Lutheran Christian who discerned continuity between the Christian doctrine of God the creator and the scientific order within the universe.

Søren Kierkegaard (1813–55) Danish Lutheran philosopher and theologian. He attacked the institutional state church for accommodating itself to non–biblical ideals and was a sharp critic of Hegelian philosophy. His philosophical writings would later influence several European existentialist thinkers. His sharp contrast between God and all things finite would later be developed by Barth and other dialectical theologians.

Martin Luther King Jr. (1929–68) American Baptist pastor and civil rights leader. His sermons, addresses, and writings are a significant example of Christian theology in service to social justice. He was awarded the Nobel Peace Prize in 1964.

Hans Küng (b. 1928) Swiss Roman Catholic theologian. He has written on all major topics in Christian theology and has been a major contributor to ecumenical discussion and inter-religious dialogue. He was among the principal theologians of reform (over against traditionalists) at the Second Vatican Council. After the council, he was attacked for his criticism of papal infallibility, enforced clerical celibacy, and contraception.

Gerardus van der Leeuw (1890–1950) Dutch Reformed scholar of religion. He was among the first to use a phenomenological (descriptive) method to describe religious experience.

Gottfried Leibniz (1646–1716) German Lutheran philosopher, mathematician, and theologian. He helped to found the Prussian Academy in 1700. His major work in theology is on the problem of evil in relation to God's goodness. He defended the traditional arguments for the existence of God.

Leo I (c. 400–61) "Leo the Great," Pope after 440. He sought to strengthen the church by centralizing power and administrative control through a strengthened papacy. His "Tome" (449) was accepted at the Council of Chalcedon (451) as setting forth orthodox Christological doctrine about the two natures of Christ.

C. S. Lewis (1898–1963) British literary scholar and Christian apologist. His spiritual autobiography, *Surprised by Joy*, describes his gradual conversion from agnosticism to orthodox Anglican belief. Some of his radio addresses in defense of Christian faith were later published as *Mere Christianity*.

George Lindbeck (b. 1923) American Lutheran theologian. He is a leading "post–liberal" and ecumenical theologian who has taught at Yale University.

John Locke (1632–1704) English philosopher. Well known for his treatises on epistemology and government, he was a major voice for religious toleration in the seventeenth Century. His writings on Christianity set forth what he considered a rational understanding of Christianity that is premised on the acceptance of the miracles reported about Jesus and the belief that his life is a fulfillment of Jewish prophecies about the Messiah.

Bernard Lonergan (1904–84) Canadian Roman Catholic theologian. A Jesuit, he published books on theological method that have been influential, especially among revisionist-minded theologians. He was particularly interested in describing the various mental acts of the theologian that are necessary in the process of "doing theology."

Gerd Lüdemann (b. 1946) German scholar of the New Testament and early Christianity. Deeply skeptical about orthodox understandings of Jesus and the New Testament, he has attempted to follow a strictly positivist method of historical criticism to attempt to uncover what he thinks is authentically historical behind the NT witness.

Martin Luther (1483–1546) German Augustinian friar, university scholar of the Bible, translator, and principal reformer in the sixteenth–century. Educated in scholastic philosophy and later excommunicated by the Pope (1520) because of his criticisms of church practices (e.g. the sale of indulgences) and the papacy, Luther was the key figure in a movement of church reforms that swept Northern Europe. The traditional starting-point of the Protestant Reformation was the publication of Luther's *95 Theses* in October 1517. The center of his later theology is the Pauline-Johannine teaching of justification by faith (alone) and the distinction between the divine law and the divine gospel.

Nikolai Luzin (1883–1950) Russian mathematician and Orthodox Christian. His Christian theological understanding of the divine infinity provided him with creative insight into the mathematical problem of infinitesimals within modern calculus.

Jean Francois Lyotard (1924–98) French philosopher, literary theorist, and sociologist. He was a key interpreter of postmodernism and its influence within western cultures.

Alisdair MacIntyre (b. 1929) Scottish-born Roman Catholic philosopher and theologian. His work has been instrumental in using insights and arguments from Aristotle and Aquinas to articulate a post–Enlightenment moral philosophy, one that is critical of the Enlightenment's rejection of moral ends. He has taught at a wide number of universities in Britain and the United States and has published numerous works in ethics, philosophy, and theology.

Maimonides (1135–1204) Spanish-Jewish philosopher. One of the most influential Jewish thinkers. He sought to show continuity between Aristotelian philosophy and Jewish religious ideas.

Norman Malcolm (1911–90) American philosopher. A close friend of Wittgenstein, he articulated a revised version of Anselm's ontological argument for the reality of God.

Marcion of Sinope (c. 85–c. 160) Religious thinker from Asia Minor. The son of a Christian bishop, Marcion set forth a religious system in which the God of the OT is different from the Father of Jesus, the law is sharply separated from the gospel, and the OT God's wrath is totally rejected in favor of the love revealed in the gospel of Jesus. His decision to include only an edited version of Luke and some of Paul's letters in his biblical canon helped to compel other Christians to articulate standards for what would come to be the orthodox biblical canon.

George Marsden (b. 1939) American historian of American evangelicalism and fundamentalism. An expert on the life and thought of Jonathan Edwards, Marsden has also written on Christianity in higher education and religion in American culture.

Martin E. Marty (b. 1929) American historian of American religions and a Lutheran theologian. Marty has written and edited dozens of books on such topics as the history of Protestantism, modern American religions, religious fundamentalism, religion in American public life, and Martin Luther. Marty taught at the University of Chicago for 35 years and served as a senior editor of the *Christian Century* magazine.

Karl Marx (1818–83) German philosopher and social revolutionary. He asserted that religions function like an opiate to keep the masses content with their status quo.

Sallie McFague (b. 1933) American Protestant theologian. A leading feminist theologian, her most significant book, *Models of God*, criticizes traditional, patriarchal models of God for contributing to the degradation of the planet. Similar to Gordon Kaufman, McFague understands theology as a creative, constructive enterprise that must develop better models and metaphors for God, such as her preferred model of the world as "God's body."

George McGovern (1922–2012) US representative, US senator, and Democratic Party presidential nominee (1972). A member of the Methodist Church, McGovern was especially concerned with issues of poverty, hunger, and nutrition.

Alister E. McGrath (b. 1953) Irish-born Anglican theologian. He has written and edited many books on the history of Christian theology and evangelical systematic theology. An atheist as a youth and young adult, McGrath converted to Christianity and later studied for the Anglican priesthood. He has been critical of the "new atheists" and has worked tirelessly to set forth a robust understanding of orthodox Anglican Christianity, one that is engaged in positive, constructive dialogue with the sciences and contemporary culture.

Philip Melanchthon (1497–1560) German humanist and Lutheran theologian. A close friend and colleague of Martin Luther, Melanchthon taught a variety of courses in theology and the classics at the University of Wittenberg. He was the author of the *Augsburg Confession* (1530) and its *Apology* (1531), two of the most important documents in the German Protestant Reformation. His *Loci Communes* (1521) is the first systematic theology that reflects the theological understandings of Luther.

Daniel Migliore (b. 1935) American Presbyterian theologian. He has taught at Princeton Seminary. His book, *Faith Seeking Understanding*, has been widely used by colleges and seminaries as a basic introduction to the Christian faith.

John Milbank (b. 1952) Anglican theologian. The leading figure in the theological movement known as "Radical Orthodoxy," he resists the idea that modern secular ways of understanding reality should set the agenda for Christian theology. His most significant work, *Theology and Social Theory*, exposes the theological and anti-theological assumptions within the modern social sciences and their dominant paradigms. He has written widely in the areas of religion, ethics, and Christian systematic theology.

William Miller (1782–1849) American Baptist minister. He tried to calculate the timing of Christ's Second Return based on his interpretation of biblical prophecies. Miller helped to found Adventism.

Jürgen Moltmann (b. 1926) German Reformed theologian. An atheist as a youth, Moltmann became a Christian following his experiences as a German soldier and a prisoner in a prisoner-of-war camp. His early writings on hope revitalized Christian eschatology and the expectation of the coming kingdom of God. His work on the crucified Christ was instrumental in awakening a political theology that is oriented toward God's loving solidarity with those who suffer. Moltmann has also made significant contributions to contemporary discussions about the Trinity.

George L. Murphy (b. 1942) American Lutheran theologian. He has written several important books in the area of science and theology.

John Henry Cardinal Newman (1801–90) Anglican theologian who later became a leading Roman Catholic theologian and Cardinal. He was the principal figure among those Anglicans who sought greater closeness with the Roman Church. Initially interpreting the Anglican Church as a "middle way" between Catholicism and Protestantism, he later became convinced that the Roman Catholic Church represented the true development of apostolic doctrine and practice.

H. Richard Niebuhr (1894–1962) American Reformed theologian. A professor at Yale University, he wrote widely in the areas of systematic theology and ethics. He was an articulate defender of monotheism over against many forms of idolatry (treating as God that which is not God). His book, *Christ and Culture*, sets forth five classic types of relating Christian faith and contemporary civilization.

Friedrich Nietzsche (1844–1900) German classicist and philosopher. The son of a Lutheran pastor, Nietzsche later moved in the direction of atheism and he became a fierce critic of Christianity.

Gerald O'Collins (b. 1931) Australian Roman Catholic theologian. For more than three decades he taught at the Pontifical Gregorian University in Rome. He has written widely in the areas of fundamental theology, Christology, and Catholicism.

Schubert Ogden (b. 1928) American Methodist theologian. He taught at the University of Chicago for several years and at Southern Methodist University for 34 years. He has written on theological method, Christology, the doctrine of God, and Buddhist–Christian dialogue.

Graham Oppy (b. 1960) Australian philosopher. He has written widely in the area of the philosophy of religion. Raised as a Methodist, he later became an atheist.

Origen (c. 185–c. 254) Egyptian Bible scholar and theologian. He wrote extensively on the Bible, helped to develop the allegorical approach to biblical interpretation, and sought to reconcile Platonic philosophy and Christian teaching. His most important work, *De Principiis*, which exists almost entirely in an unreliable Latin translation, examines a wide range of theological topics. Because of later controversy about some of his speculative ideas, his place within the Christian tradition has been ambiguous. Nearly all of his theological writings have been lost. He must be counted one of the most creative and significant theologians in the early Christian church. He was particularly influential upon the Cappadocians.

Rudolf Otto (1869–1937) German Lutheran theologian and scholar of comparative religions. His most important work, *The Idea of the Holy*, examines the role of the numinous, that is, non-rational, non-sensory experience or feeling of the Holy or the Divine within religious experience. His work draws insights from the theological reflections on religious experience of Luther and Schleiermacher.

Elaine Pagels (b. 1943) She has written extensively on Gnostic writings within early Christianity. Influenced by the thesis of Bauer, she has highlighted the role of women in these marginalized Christian documents and has suggested an important connection between Christian Gnosticism and traditions within Buddhism.

William Paley (1743–1805) English philosopher and Christian apologist. His most important books, *Evidences of Christianity* and *Natural Theology*, sought to defend orthodox Anglican beliefs against the intellectual challenges presented by Deism, the Enlightenment, and the French Revolution. He is most noted for his argument for the reality of God on the basis of apparent design in nature.

Panaetius of Rhodes (c. 185–110 BC) Greek Stoic philosopher. He was the first to divide pagan philosophical theology into three divisions: (1) mythological theology, which maintained and interpreted the stories about the gods from ancient Greece; (2) natural theology, which reasoned about God or the gods on the basis of the world or universe (and was often critical of the ancient myths as fictional and unethical); and (3) civil theology, which served to understand and perform the rites and ceremonies in the cult of the Caesars (and often to justify the political regime).

Wolfhart Pannenberg (b. 1928) German Lutheran theologian. He is one of the most prolific and influential of Protestant theologians in the second half of the twentieth century. He first came to prominence through his thesis that divine revelation only occurs at the end of time, when God will make clear how he had acted proleptically in Israel and Jesus to redeem the world and bring it to its consummation. In addition to writing about revelation, history, and faith, he has written extensively on Christology, ethics, and the relationship of theology to the sciences. His three-volume *Systematic Theology* provides a robust understanding of the Christian doctrine of the Trinity and careful reflection on all of the major issues in Christ theology.

Parmenides (c. 515–445 BC) Greek philosopher. Often called "the father of western metaphysics," he viewed differences in nature as illusory and held that true reality is unchanging, invisible, indivisible, and intelligible. He was thus the first to insist on a distinction between the world as it appears to human beings and reality as it "really is."

Blaise Pascal (1623–62) French scientist, mathematician, and Roman Catholic theologian. After two religious conversion experiences, one in 1646 and the other, more definitive one, in 1654, he sharply distinguished the God of Abraham, Isaac, and Jacob from that of which scientists and philosophers speak. His scattered notes, sayings, and aphorisms were gathered together and published posthumously as the *Pensées*, which was intended as a defense of Catholic Christianity.

Paul of Tarsus (c. 10–c. 65) Apostle to the Gentiles. Born a Jew and educated as a Pharisee, Paul was an opponent of early Christians. While he apparently never encountered Jesus during the latter's earthly ministry, he later claimed to have received a revelation of the risen Jesus. Paul was baptized and later understood himself as a slave of Jesus and an apostle to the Gentiles. His authentic letters (Rom., 1 Cor., 2 Cor., Gal., Phil., 1 Thess., and Phil.) help to define the center of the NT canon. His missionary activities are depicted in narrative form within the Acts of the Apostles, the second part of the Gospel according to Luke. He was likely martyred in Rome during the reign of Nero.

Arthur Peacocke (1924–2006) British biochemist and Anglican theologian. He taught biochemistry at Oxford University and later taught theology there and at the University of Cambridge. He wrote several important and influential books and essays in the area of science and Christian theology.

Jaroslav Pelikan (1923–2006) American historian of Christian history and doctrine. Baptized as a Lutheran (his father was a Slovak Lutheran pastor in Chicago), he received his M.Div. (from Concordia Seminary, St. Louis) and his Ph.D. (from the University of Chicago) in the same year (1946), when he was 22. His five-volume *The Christian Tradition*, based on his study of original Christian sources in their native languages, offers a comprehensive description and analysis of the development of Christian teaching from the time of the apostles to the Second Vatican Council. He taught at Valparaiso University, the University of Chicago, and Yale University.

Peter (d. 64) Apostle to the Jews. Peter is always named first in the lists of apostles in the NT. His primacy has been understood differently by Roman Catholics, Orthodox, and Protestants.

Ted Peters (b. 1941) American Lutheran theologian. He has written widely in the areas of systematic theology, theology and the natural sciences, and Christian ethics.

Philo of Alexandria (c. 20 BC–AD 50) Egyptian Jewish philosopher. His allegorical method for reconciling Jewish teaching with Platonic philosophy was influential upon later Christian thinkers, notably, Origen and Augustine.

Francis Pieper (1852–1931) German-born American Lutheran theologian. Born Franz A. O. Pieper in Pomerania, he was educated in American Lutheran seminaries of the Wisconsin and Missouri synods. His three-volume *Christian Dogmatics* has been a standard textbook and reference work for conservative Lutherans in the United States.

Pontius Pilate (d. c. 37–38) Fifth Roman prefect of the Province of Judaea (AD 26–36). As prefect he served under the Emperor Tiberius. Pilate authorized the crucifixion of Jesus of Nazareth.

Alvin Plantinga (b. 1932) American philosopher and Reformed theologian. One of the most prolific of American Christian philosophers, he has taught at Calvin College and the University of Notre Dame. He has written extensively in the areas of the philosophy of religion, metaphysics, and Christian theology. He has defended a version of the ontological argument and has analyzed the implications of theistic and atheistic presuppositions within epistemology.

Plato (427–347 BC) Greek philosopher. Often called the father of western philosophy, Plato's early dialogues treat primarily ethical issues, while two of his later writings, *Timaeus* and *Laws* (Book 10), address some theological matters (for example, creation) and questions of metaphysics. Later platonic philosophy had a profound influence on the development of Christian theology (for example, on Augustine).

Plotinus (205–270) Egyptian Neoplatonist philosopher and mystic. His metaphysical and theological ideas owe much to Plato's philosophy, although scholars debate among themselves the degree to which they tend toward pantheism rather than theism. In his view, the goal of intellectual, contemplative mysticism and physical asceticism is the union of the individual soul with God.

John Polkinghorne (b. 1930) British theoretical physicist, mathematician, and Anglican theologian. Before his retirement, he taught mathematical physics at Cambridge University. His scientific work focused on elemental particles in physics. In more recent years, especially after becoming an Anglican priest, he has written many significant books that explore the interface between the sciences and Christian theology. He is one of the foremost proponents of dialogue between practicing scientists and contemporary Christian theologians.

Proclus (c. 412–85) Greek Neoplatonist philosopher. The last head of Plato's Academy, Proclus provided extensive analysis and commentary on the Neoplatonic metaphysics of Plotinus in his book, *Elements of Theology*. This work influenced a number of Christian theologians, including Augustine.

Johannes Andreas Quenstedt (1617–88) German Lutheran philosopher and theologian. The nephew of Johann Gerhard, Quenstedt taught geography, logic, metaphysics, and theology. Quenstedt was an irenic theologian who represents a scholastic form of Lutheran theology (Lutheran Orthodoxy) that also shares important aspects of later Lutheran Pietism. His most important textbook, *Theologia didactico-polemica sive systema theologicum* (1685; 2nd edn, 1715), influenced many subsequent Lutheran theologians in Germany and North America.

Karl Rahner (1904–84) German Roman Catholic theologian. Rahner was one of the most influential and prolific theologians of the twentieth century. Much of his literary output was in the form of journal articles and essays, although he also wrote several books. Many of his essays were later published in a multi-volume edition, *Theological Investigations*. He served as an editor or co-editor of several standard reference works in Catholic theology. His theological reflections had an impact on the deliberations that occurred at the Second Vatican Council. His *Foundations of Christian Faith* (1978) offers his analysis and exposition of Christian doctrine.

Paul Ricoeur (1913–2005) French philosopher and Reformed theologian. Ricoeur is perhaps the most influential Christian philosopher of the twentieth century. His reflections on phenomenology and hermeneutics have been especially important for contemporary Christian theologians and interpreters of the Bible. His myriad writings explore myths, symbols, biblical exegesis, psychoanalysis, metaphors, and narrative theory. He taught at universities in France and at the University of Chicago.

Albrecht Ritschl (1822–89) German Lutheran theologian. He was the leading systematic theologian in Germany in the second half of the nineteenth century. As such he represents the last main figure in liberal Protestant theology. His thought combined elements from Kant's moral philosophy, Schleiermacher's understanding of the church as community, and nineteenth–century historians of Christianity. His three-volume study of justification and reconciliation remains a classic exposition of these central Christian teachings.

Richard L. Rubenstein Jr. (b. 1924) American rabbi and Jewish theologian. He has written widely on the holocaust, ethics, and Jewish-Christian relations. His book, *After Auschwitz* (1966), sets forth a Jewish "death-of-God" theology in which he argues that God's providential direction of history and God's special relationship with the Jewish people must be rejected "after Auschwitz." He stresses that people must accept the cold fact that they live in an indifferent and absurd universe.

Rosemary Radford Ruether (b. 1936) American Roman Catholic theologian. Ruether is a leading feminist theologian who has been a strong critic of the patriarchal character of traditional Christianity. In addition to her works of feminist theology (for example, *Sexism and God-Talk* [1993]), she has also written about the Israeli–Palestinian conflict, American nationalism, and the theology of ecology.

Friedrich D. E. Schleiermacher (1768–34) German Reformed theologian and philosopher. Schleiermacher is perhaps the most significant Christian theologian of the past half millennium. A leading figure in German Romanticism, he helped to found the University of Berlin and defended the role of theology as an appropriate university discipline. His dogmatics, *The Christian Faith*, is the classic liberal Protestant account of Christian teaching. In this work he defines faith as an elemental feeling or intuition of being in relationship with God. He sought to move theology beyond the moralism and rationalism of Kant and the intellectual dogmatism of seventeenth-century Protestant Orthodoxy. Schleiermacher's theological encyclopedia, *The Brief Outline for the Study of Theology*, is the classic Protestant description of the three principal sub-disciplines in theology (philosophical, historical, and practical). His revisionist theology has influenced all subsequent Christian theologians, even those who were otherwise quite critical of him (such as Barth).

Edmund Schlink (1903–84) German Lutheran theologian. Schlink is the most significant and influential confessional Lutheran theologian of the second half of the twentieth century and one of the leading figures in the modern Ecumenical Movement. He taught for several decades at Heidelberg University and helped to make that institution a center for ecumenical theology. He was a Protestant observer at the Second Vatican Council and the official spokesperson for all non-Catholic observers. In addition to his ecumenical writings, he wrote a major dogmatics work, *Ecumenical Dogmatics*, which received high praise from Protestants, Catholics, and Orthodox theologians.

Heinrich Schmid (1811–85) German Lutheran theologian and historian. His classic book, *Doctrinal Theology of the Evangelical Lutheran Church*, provides a summary of sixteenth- and seventeenth-century Lutheran Orthodoxy. He also wrote an influential history of Lutheran Pietism.

Albert Schweitzer (1875–1965) Alsatian Lutheran theologian, philosopher, medical missionary, renowned organist, and Bach expert. Schweitzer earned advanced degrees in theology, philosophy, and medicine. He wrote classic works on the history of research into the historical figures of Jesus and Paul. Schweitzer himself held that Jesus ought to be understood as a failed apocalyptic prophet who announced the imminent end of the world. At the age of 33 Schweitzer left his European academic and cultural world to become a physician at a village in Gabon (then French Equatorial Africa). In 1953 he was awarded the Nobel Peace Prize of the previous year.

Johann S. Semler (1725–91) German Lutheran theologian. He rejected the Pietism of his youth in favor of rational historical–critical investigation of the Bible and church origins.

Sargent Shriver (1915–2011) United States statesman and activist. As a member of the Kennedy administration, he was the leading force behind the creation of the Peace Corps and its first director. He also founded the Jobs Corps and Head Start programs. As a Roman Catholic layman, he attended mass daily.

Joseph Sittler (1904–87) American Lutheran theologian. He taught at the University of Chicago and at the Lutheran School of Theology in Chicago. He was particularly interested in relating Christian theology and ethics to ecological issues.

Wilfred Cantwell Smith (1916–2000) Canadian scholar of world religions and a pastor in the United Church of Canada. An expert in Islam, Smith became a leading figure in religious studies in North America.

Jordan Howard Sobel (1929–2010) American-born philosopher. Educated at universities in the United States, he taught philosophy at the University of

Toronto. He was a leading figure in the philosophy of religion and a major critic of theism.

Jon Sobrino (b. 1938) Born in Basque, Sobrino has been a Catholic (Jesuit) theologian in El Salvador for most of his adult life. He helped to found the University of Central America in San Salvador. He has been a leading Latin–American liberation theologian and a vocal supporter for peace and justice.

Benedictus Spinoza (1632–77) Dutch Jewish philosopher. Spinoza's thought is complex but it is clear he held some form of pantheism (all things as part of God). The highest activity of human beings is the loving contemplation of God through the use of human reason. He had a major influence on the development of historical-critical interpretation of the Bible. His philosophical reflections were especially influential on several key nineteenth-century thinkers (for example, Hegel and Schleiermacher).

Krister Stendahl (1921–2008) Swedish Lutheran theologian and scholar of the New Testament. He taught at Harvard Divinity School for many years.

David F. Strauss (1808–74) German Protestant theologian and historian. Strauss' most famous work, the first edition of *The Life of Jesus* (1835), criticized both rationalist and conservative understandings of the historical Jesus. For Strauss, the written gospels contain miraculous elements that appear to be "history" but are really non-historical religious ideas that have been shaped by the unconsciously inventive power of legend, and embodied in a historic personality. While many have criticized this thesis, Schweitzer notes how central Strauss's controversial work has been to further the quest for the historical Jesus.

Richard Swinburne (b. 1934) British philosopher of religion. He has taught at Keele University and at Oxford. For more than half a century he has been one of the most significant philosophers to articulate arguments for the reality of God and in defense of the Christian faith.

Kathryn Tanner (b. 1957) American Episcopalian theologian. Tanner has taught at Yale University and the University of Chicago. Her work creatively engages feminist theology, social theory, and hermeneutics.

Charles Taylor (b. 1931) Canadian Roman Catholic philosopher and historian. One of the most important Christian philosophers of the past century, Taylor taught at McGill University. He has been a careful critic of philosophical naturalism and a major contributor to hermeneutical theory. He has written important books on Hegel, the "sources of the self" in western culture, and the abiding presence of the sacred in western civilization.

Frederick R. Tennant (1866–1957) British science teacher and Anglican priest and theologian. Tennant sought to defend Christian faith by demonstrating its harmony with modern scientific understandings. His most important book, *Philosophical Theology* (2 vols, 1928ff.), contains his version of the argument for the reality of God on the basis of the overall apprehension of design within the natural world as a whole.

Teresa of Ávila (1515–82) Spanish Roman Catholic (Carmelite) nun and mystic. She was a great practical reformer in the Catholic "counter-reformation" in Spain. She is one of three female "doctors of the church" and thus one of the most important theologians in the Christian tradition. Her writings on mystical theology are particularly significant for what they say about prayer and spiritual ecstasy.

Mother Teresa of Calcutta (1910–97) Albanian-born Roman Catholic nun who lived most of her life among the poorest of the poor and sick in Calcutta, India. She founded the Missionaries of Charity, a Roman Catholic religious congregation that is active today in more than 130 countries. She was given the Nobel Peace Prize in 1979.

Tertullian (c. 160–225) North African theologian and church father. Raised as a pagan in Carthage, Tertullian received a good classical education. He later converted to Christianity. He wrote numerous essays on key Christian themes and practices and he sought to defend Christianity against pagan criticisms. He was particularly influential in the development of Latin terms in western Christian theology (for example, the term "Trinity"). Eventually he joined the Montanists, a heretical group.

Ronald Thiemann (1946–2012) American Lutheran theologian. Educated at Yale University, he taught for many years at Harvard Divinity School. Influenced especially by the theology of Barth and post-liberal theologians at Yale, Thiemann sought to bring Lutheran theology into conversation with Barthian themes and post-liberal narrative theology.

Paul Tillich (1886–1965) German–born Lutheran theologian who taught at Union Seminary in New York City, Harvard University, and the University of Chicago. He is one of the two or three most important and influential Protestant theologians of the twentieth century. As a religious socialist and critic of National Socialism, Tillich was forced out of Germany in 1933. Upon his arrival in the United States he quickly established himself as the leading Lutheran theologian in the country. His model of "correlational" theology is sharply distinct from Barth's revelational model. Tillich's most important work remains his three-volume *Systematic Theology* (1951–64).

Matthew Tindal (1655–1733) Anglican theologian and later leading Deist. His most important and influential book, *Christianity as Old as the Creation* (1730), sets forth his particular rationalist, anti–superstitious account of Christianity.

John Toland (1670–1722) Irish-born English Deist. He wrote several treatises against what he perceived to be the superstitious corruptions within orthodox Christianity and in defense of his version of authentically "rational" Christianity. He was one of the most influential Deist writers.

David Tracy (b. 1939) American Roman Catholic theologian. Tracy taught mainly at the University of Chicago. Influenced especially by Tillich and process theologians, Tracy has been one of the most influential Roman Catholic theologians of the past half century. He has made important contributions to discussions about theological method, hermeneutics, and inter-religious dialogue.

Ernst Troeltsch (1865–1923) German historian, philosopher, and theologian. He wrote numerous important essays on the historical development of modern European Christianity and theology. He was among the first to use sociological tools to analyze the development of social teachings within Christianity. He also studied the principles of historical criticism and the problems they create for theological understanding (for example, historical relativism).

Miroslav Volf (b. 1956) Croatian-born Protestant theologian. He has taught at a seminary in his native Croatia, at Fuller Seminary in Pasadena, and teaches presently at Yale Divinity School. Influenced especially by Moltmann, Volf has written important works on the Trinity, Christian understanding of other religions, and theological hermeneutics.

Charles Wesley (1707–88) Anglican priest, hymn writer, and later a member of the Oxford Methodists. Unlike his brother John, Charles Wesley opposed those who sought to separate themselves from the Church of England.

John Wesley (1703–91) Anglican missionary and later the founder of the Methodist movement. Educated at Oxford, he formed a group that became known as the Methodists. They included his brother Charles and George Whitefield. He later broke with Whitefield over the latter's Calvinist view of election. Wesley stressed justification by faith (which he learned from Luther) and the pursuit of holiness or Christian perfection.

George Whitefield (1714–70) Methodist missionary and evangelist. At Oxford he came under the influence of the Wesley brothers. He was a gifted orator and organizer. He later broke with the Wesleys over the doctrine of election. He made several visits to the United States, where his preaching led to a revival of activity within many churches and helped to prepare the way for the Great Awakening.

Elie Wiesel (b. 1928) Romanian-born American Jewish humanities scholar. A Professor at Boston University, he has written more than 57 books. Among them is *Night*, which recounts his experience as a young boy in Nazi concentration camps. He was awarded the Nobel Peace Prize in 1986.

A. N. Wilson (b. 1950) British novelist, historian, and newspaper columnist. As a young man he studied for the Anglican priesthood, but then became a devout atheist. For nearly 30 years he was a leading English skeptic. In 2009 he wrote a public essay in which he indicated he had once again become a practicing Christian.

Ludwig Wittgenstein (1889–1951) Austrian-born mathematician and philosopher. He taught at Cambridge University and eventually became a British citizen. His chief works in philosophy explore the relationship between the use of language and one's understanding of the structure of the world.

William Wrede (1859–1906) German Lutheran theologian and scholar of the New Testament. His scholarly work on the Gospel of Mark undermined that gospel as a source for the historical Jesus.

Xenophanes (c. 570–c. 480 BC) Greek philosopher. He attacked traditional conceptions of the gods among the Greeks. He was particularly critical of anthropomorphism (depicting the gods as human beings) and polytheism.

John Milton Yinger (1916–2011) American sociologist. The son of Methodist ministers, Yinger wrote many books in the areas of sociology and anthropology.

Nikolaus von Zinzendorf (1700–60) German Protestant pastor and community leader. He founded the Christian colony of Herrnhut ("the Lord's Keeping"), which attracted many persecuted Moravians. He later became the Bishop of the Moravian Brethren. He wrote more than 100 spiritual books and pamphlets.

Glossary of Terms[1]

A posteriori Latin: "from what comes after." In the context of philosophical theology, a posteriori arguments for the reality of God proceed from effects to causes (inductive reasoning). The five ways of Thomas Aquinas are an example of this kind of argument.

A priori Latin: "from what is before." In the context of philosophical theology, a priori arguments for the reality of God proceed from causes to effects (deductive reasoning). Anselm's ontological argument and Kant's moral argument are examples of this kind of argument.

Abbess Female head of a community (abbey) of nuns.

Abbot Male head of a community (abbey) of monks.

AD see **Anno Domini**

Adiaphora "Greek: "indifferent things." This term has been used by Christians to refer to teachings or practices that are neither commanded nor forbidden in Holy Scripture, to matters that are either peripheral or non-essential to the Christian faith.

Agnosticism/Agnostic Greek: "not knowing." An agnostic does not know with any certainty whether or not God exists. Some agnostics are convinced that all knowledge of God cannot be known.

Analogy of Faith The hermeneutical principle in Christian theology that states a biblical passage cannot be so interpreted that it goes contrary to the clear and essential content of Christian faith, that is, faith in the gospel promises of God and the dictates of Christian love.

Anfechtung/Anfechtungen German: "spiritual crisis/crises." Martin Luther used this German term to describe his complex experience of doubt, spiritual attack from the Devil, and his troubled conscience before God.

Anno Domini (AD) Latin: "In the year of the Lord." This expression and its abbreviation have been used by Christians since the sixth century to identify the years since the birth of Jesus.

Anthropomorphism Ascribing human features or attributes to the gods or God.

---

[1] For additional information about any of these terms, see the pertinent entries in ABD, BDAG, EC, ER, ODCC, and RPP. See also Orlando O. Espín and James B. Nickoloff (eds), *An Introductory Dictionary of Theology and Religious Studies* (Collegeville, MN: Liturgical Press, 2007).

Antilegomena Latin: "spoken against." This term refers to those Christian writings that were "spoken against" in the early church because of doubts regarding their apostolic authorship and because of questions about their contents. These writings were not widely used in early Christianity. Within the NT canon, there are seven antilegomena: Hebrews, James, Second Peter, Second John, Third John, Jude, and Revelation.

Apocalyptic Greek: "revelatory." This adjective describes a genre of writing that is found in the Old Testament (e.g. Daniel, parts of Isaiah), second-temple Judaism (e.g. First and Second Ezra), and the New Testament (Mk 13; The Revelation of John). This type of writing is highly symbolic, deeply pessimistic about the present world, and yet hopeful for a new creation from God. Apocalyptic literature "reveals" or "discloses" the hidden plan of God to destroy the forces of evil (e.g. Satan and his angels) and to create a new and better creation.

Apocrypha Greek: "hidden things (hidden writings)." The Apocrypha are those books that appear in the Greek canon of the OT (the Septuagint) but are not included in the Hebrew Bible. Their authority was often disputed by early Christians, although they were included in most early forms of the Christian Bible. They have a status similar to the antilegomena in the NT.

Apologetics Greek: "defense." Within Christian theology, apologetics seeks to defend the truth of the Christian faith and to criticise false or misleading ideas in theology.

Apostle Greek: "one who is sent." The term was first used as a title for each of the 12 men whom Jesus called to follow him. In the lists of apostles that appear in the NT, Peter is always listed first. Although he was not among the twelve, Paul used and defended the title for himself and for others beyond the 12 (including at least one woman, Junia). Sometimes the term is also used of later missionaries who first bring the gospel to a country.

Apostles' Creed see **Creed**

Apostolic Succession The teaching that the current spiritual authority of bishops and priests derives from the authority of the apostles, that has been transmitted to them through a succession of bishops and priests that go back to the original apostles. The succession is said to be maintained by an historical series of bishops.

Ascension The teaching that Jesus, after his resurrection, "ascended into heaven" (Lk. 24:51; Acts 1.9–11).

Aseity Latin: "from himself." This term is used in systematic theology to describe God's self-existence or God's "necessary being" in contrast to the "contingent being" of creation.

Atheism/Atheist Atheism is the confident belief that God and/or the spiritual are not real. An atheist is one who is convinced by the truths of atheism.

Atonement Within Christian theology this term is used to describe God's redeeming action to reconcile the world to God through Jesus Christ.

BC "Before Christ." A Christian abbreviation that refers to years before the birth of Jesus.

BCE "Before Common Era." A more neutral abbreviation than "BC" this is frequently used by scholars to refer to the years before the birth of Jesus.

Baptism Greek: "washing." Baptism is held by many Christians to be a sacrament of initiation into the Christian church and thus a means of divine grace. Some churches practice what is often called "believers baptism," in which baptism is the external sign of an inward conversion to the faith.

Baptist The principal Protestant tradition in North America. Baptists insist on believers baptism.

Bible The English word "Bible" comes from the Greek word "Biblia," which means "books." The Christian Bible is a collection of books that were written over many centuries and gradually collected together into authoritative versions. For most Protestant Christians, the OT contains 39 separate books and the NT 27. Roman Catholic, Lutheran, and Orthodox Christian Bibles contain the OT apocrypha in addition to the 39 OT books.

Biblical Theology A sub-discipline of historical theology that seeks to understand the theological content of the Christian Bible.

Biblicism This term describes the view of the Bible by those who insist on the complete verbal inspiration and inerrancy of the Christian Bible and upon their literalistic interpretations of certain chapters in it (for example, the stories in Gen. 1–11).

Bishop One who provides spiritual oversight and leadership to Christians in a given locale.

Boundary Questions According to the philosopher Karl Jaspers these are questions that arise from human experience that have the force of calling one's life as a whole into question. For example, what is the meaning of my life? To whom am I responsible in my life?

CE "Common Era." A more neutral abbreviation than "AD" that is used by scholars to refer to the years following the birth of Jesus. See **AD**.

Canon Greek: "measuring rod." In biblical studies, this term refers to the collection of biblical writings that served as the norm or rule for Christian teaching in a given place or tradition.

Canon within the Canon Within Christian theology, this expression refers to the norm of the gospel within the biblical canon. This internal norm of Scripture serves as the key for interpreting the rest of the contents within the Bible and for making theological judgments about biblical teachings that are no longer valid or binding upon contemporary Christians. Those who work with this hermeneutical principle trace its origins back to the critical position that Jesus, Paul, and the apostle John took over against the OT biblical law.

Canonical Gospels The gospels of Matthew, Mark, Luke, and John.

Catholic/catholicity Greek: "of the whole" or "according to the whole" (universal). The term "catholic" (with a small "c") refers to the whole church of Christ, inclusive of all believers. The term "Catholic" (with a large "C"), which should be modified with the term "Roman," refers to a specific church group, the Roman Catholic Church, whose head is the bishop of Rome. Within biblical studies, catholicity refers to the degree to which a biblical book was widely used in the early church.

Chalcedon Place of the fourth ecumenical council (AD 451). The Formula of Chalcedon states that Jesus is truly God and truly human, having two natures in one person "without division, without separation, without confusion, without change."

Christ see **Messiah**

Christian One who believes that Jesus is the Messiah and who follows his teachings.

Christology Thinking and speaking about the person of Jesus as the Christ. Christology focuses principally on the question, "Who is Jesus?"

Church Greek: "Ecclesia" = "called out". In the New Testament the "ecclesia" is the assembly or congregation of believers, who are also routinely called "saints" in the letters of Paul. In this view the "church" is the congregation of people. Later, the term "church" will be used to refer to a building where the congregation gathers for worship and prayer. "Ecclesiology" is the study of the church, its traditions, its polity or organization, and its activities.

Comparative Theology see **Ecumenical Theology**

Consonance This refers to the degree of agreement between theologians and scientists on a given issue or problem that they have in common.

Contextual Theologies Forms of thinking about God that are especially shaped by the local and concrete human situations in which that thinking occurs. Examples are political theology, liberation theology, and feminist theology.

Contingent Being Within philosophical theology contingent refers to all things that are dependent for their being upon something else. Unlike "necessary being," contingent beings do not have to be or exist.

Cosmology/Cosmological Thinking about the order of the universe. The cosmological argument for the reality of God arises from reflection on the perceived order within the universe and concludes that God is the cause of that order.

Creatio ex nihilo Latin: "Creation from nothing." This phrase has been used by Christian theologians to underscore that everything that is or exists is distinct from God the Creator and totally dependent upon God for its creaturely being. The phrase emphases that creation is not eternal with God nor did it come from matter that is co–eternal with God. Only God is eternal, while all being is contingent upon God for its being.

Creationism/Creationist Creationism is a minority movement in Christianity that insists the stories in the first chapters of Genesis are to be understood as historical narratives that summarize an actual sequence of events in the not-too-distant past. Creationists typically insist that the age of the universe is less than 10,000 years old.

Creed Latin "Credo" = "I believe." A creed is a short, formal, and authoritative summary of the key elements of religious teaching or belief. Within Christianity there is one creed that is used by a majority of Christians, namely, the Niceno-Constantinopolitan Creed (sometimes just called "the Nicene Creed"), which has remained unchanged since the fourth century in the East but which was modified in the west after the fifth century (adding the so–called "filioque," the Holy Spirit proceeds from "the Father and the Son"; the original creed refers to the procession of the Spirit solely "from the Father"). Within western Christianity there are many additional creeds, the most frequently used of which is the so-called "Apostles' Creed," which developed from an old Roman baptismal creed after the second century. The so-called "Athanasian Creed," which was not written by Athanasius (despite its traditional name), is a western, Latin creed that likely originated in Gaul in the sixth century.

Deism This term refers to a seventeenth-century intellectual movement that affirmed God as the creator of the universe but rejected God's further involvement in the created order. Deists often compared God to a watchmaker who created the intricate, machine–like universe, wound it up, and let it operate on its own without any further divine intervention .

Demystification The process of explaining (away) by rational means matters that were formerly mysterious and understood in a superstitious way.

Denomination A separate group or sect of Christians.

Deus Absconditus see **Hidden God**

Dialectical In the context of theology this term refers to a way of critical reasoning that oscillates between contrasting truths in order to arrive at a more accurate understanding. In other words, dialectical thinking examines paradoxes (for example, that the kingdom of God is both a present reality and a future reality or that God is both "hidden" and "revealed" or that the word of God is both "law" and "gospel").

Dialectical Theology A movement within early twentieth–century German Protestantism associated primarily with the theology of Karl Barth and Rudolf Bultmann. This group of theologians emphasized the qualitative difference between God and creation and the "dialectic" that results from both negating creation under God's judgment and affirming it under God's grace.

Dispensational Churches Protestant churches influenced by the ideas of John Nelson Darby. Christians in these churches believe that the history of the world, as recounted in the Bible, unfolds in a series of dispensations or eras.

Christians in these churches interpret the book of Revelation as a blueprint for end-time events and the second–coming of Jesus. This is the dominant view among Fundamentalist Protestants in the United States.

Distanciation Within the hermeneutical reflections of Hans–Georg Gadamer and Paul Ricoeur, distanciation refers to the critical distancing of the interpreter from that which is interpreted. Ricoeur stresses how a given text stands at a distance from the interpreter who treats it as a distinct object.

Doctor of the Church One recognized by the Roman Catholic Church as particularly outstanding teachers in the church. Among the most important western *Doctores Ecclesiae* are Gregory the Great, Ambrose, Augustine, and Jerome.

Doctrine Latin: "that which is taught." Normally in Christian theology this term refers to specific teaching that comprises an article of faith, such as "the doctrine of the church," or the doctrine of Baptism. See **Dogma**

Doctrinal Theology A sub-discipline of systematic theology that sets forth the contemporary content of Christian teaching.

Dogma Greek: "opinion." In Christian theology a "dogma" is an official doctrine or teaching that has been formally defined at an ecumenical council in order to set forth the orthodox understanding of whatever is presented in the dogma. The most important dogmas are those set forth by the first seven ecumenical councils, which focused on a correct understanding of God and the person of Jesus Christ. There are thus two central dogmatic foci in the Christian tradition: the Trinity and Jesus Christ. While Roman Catholic theologians stress that dogmas are truths revealed through divine revelation and authoritatively taught by the church's magisteria, Protestant theologians hold that all dogmatic formulations in the church's tradition are in principle open to revision.

Eastern Orthodox Churches A group of churches, situated mainly in Eastern Europe (especially Greece and Russia), that share the same Orthodox Christian faith, are in communion with one another, and honor the primacy of the Patriarch of Constantinople.

Ecclesial Studies Greek: "Ecclesia" = "congregation" or "church". A sub-discipline in practical theology that examines Christian congregations and other Christian organizations. It is sometimes called "ecclesiology." See "Church."

Ecclesiology see **Ecclesial Studies**

Ecumenical Council The term "ecumenical" comes from a Greek word that means "of the whole household." Within Christianity the term refers to the whole church throughout the world. The first ecumenical council met in Nicaea in AD 325 to address the Arian controversy. Subsequent to that first council there were six others that the western Catholic Church and the eastern Orthodox churches acknowledge as "ecumenical." The Roman Catholic Church acknowledges 14 additional councils, but these are not recognized by either the Orthodox Church or Protestant churches.

Ecumenical Theology Sometimes also called "comparative theology," this form of theology intentionally seeks positive engagement with theological understandings across the spectrum of church groups and denominations.

Eisegesis Greek: "leading into." This term refers to reading into a Scriptural passage an understanding that is not supportable by the text.

Elder see **Presbyter**

Encylopedia Greek: "circle of learning." The term initially referred to that course of instruction that a person would follow to become an educated citizen. Later the term referred to a collection of books whose editors sought to summarize all known human knowledge. Within Christian theology, the term refers to a short analysis of the sub–disciplines or branches within the academic discipline of theology.

Eschaton/Eschatological Greek: "the end"/"speaking about the end times." Within Christianity the eschaton refers to "the last day." Eschatology addresses "end things," especially the resurrection of the body, divine judgment, the consummation of creation, and eternal life. When the apostles spoke of the end of the world and the second coming of Jesus, their statements are "eschatological."

Ethics A sub-discipline in practical theology (although some place it within systematic theology) that addresses moral principles and conduct.

Eucharist Greek: "thanksgiving." After Baptism, the most central sacrament for many Christians. Sometimes called "the Lord's Supper," "the Mass," "The Divine Liturgy," or "Holy Communion," the NT indicates this sacrament was instituted by Christ at his final meal with his disciples on the night of his betrayal. At its institution Christ "gave thanks." The majority of world Christians believe that this sacrament conveys the body and blood of Christ for the forgiveness of sins to those who receive the consecrated bread and wine.

Evangelical First used by Martin Luther and his supporters, the term comes from the Greek word that means "good message" or "good report" (see Mk 1.15–16 and 1 Cor. 15.1ff.). Luther stressed that his theology was "*evangelisch*" ("evangelical"), that is, "oriented toward the good news or gospel." Since the sixteenth century, many Lutheran churches and some other Protestant churches have understand the term "evangelical" to be synonymous with "Protestant" or "Lutheran," especially in Germany. Many Lutheran churches that follow the teachings of Luther also use the word "evangelical" in the sense that he gave it. But after 1942, with the founding of the National Association of Evangelicals, this word began to take on a different meaning. It now was used to define those American Protestants and their denominations which opposed the "modernist," liberal, and ecumenical Federal Council of Churches (later called the National Council of Churches). In this context an "evangelical" is a conservative Protestant

Christian who has undergone a conversion experience ("being born again") and who affirms the inerrancy of the Bible, the miracles it reports, the blood atonement of Jesus, his physical resurrection, and his Second Coming. Most evangelicals also oppose the theory of evolution and, at least since the 1950s, have generally supported conservative, Republican political causes.

Exegesis Greek: "leading out." Within biblical theology, this term refers to the process of discerning the meaning of a biblical text and drawing it out from Scripture.

Existentialist Theology This form of theology, influenced especially by key ideas from Kierkegaard, Kant, Luther, and modern existentialist philosophers, focuses upon the human situation, human freedom, and the divine summons to live by faith/trust in God. Key figures in this movement are Bultmann, Tillich, and Ebeling.

Explanation According to Paul Ricoeur, within the process of interpretation explanation is the initial effort to understand what a text says.

Faith A key concept within Christian theology. Some theologians stress the cognitive aspect of faith ("faith as knowing"). They maintain that that faith is acquiesence to a body of teaching ("doctrines"), authoritatively set forth in Scripture and taught by the Church. The Latin expression for this understanding of faith is "*fidei quae creditur*," namely, "the faith that is believed." Other theologians stress the personal, existential aspect of faith ("faith as trusting"). These theologians maintain that faith is first and foremost a person's confident trust in God. The Latin expression for this understanding of faith is "*fidei qua creditur*," "the faith by which one trusts."

Feminist Theology A contextual theology that is critical of male-dominated forms of theology and church practice, that seeks to highlight the experience of women and their struggle for equality and justice, and that transforms theology to be more attentive to feminist concerns.

Filioque Latin: "and from the Son." This phrase was added to the original Niceno-Constantinopolitan Creed by western theologians in the sixth century. The original creed confessed the procession of the Holy Spirit "from the Father." The western interpolation confesses the Spirit to proceed "from the Father and the Son." This addition contributed to theological disagreement between eastern and western theologians and was one of the reasons for the official schism between the Eastern Church and the Western Church in AD 1054.

Final Cause According to Aristotle, a final cause is the end toward which a thing naturally develops or toward which it aims.

The Five Ways According to Thomas Aquinas there are five ways by which one can rationally move from observing phenomena in this world to positing the reality of God. In each way one observes phenomena in this world of sense experience and then moves from such sensing to the conclusion that God exists. The first of these ways is motion, the second is causation, the third is contingency, the fourth is degrees of perfection, and the fifth is purpose.

First Commandment According to Exodus 20.2, the first words that the LORD spoke to Moses on Mt. Sinai, after the Exodus from Egypt, were: "I am the LORD your God, who brought you out of the land of Egypt, out of the house of slavery; you shall have no other gods before me."

Forgiveness The Christian gospel or "good news" centers on God's free and graceful act to forgive sinners their sins on account of Christ's death and resurrection. This forgiveness is received by faith. As a consequence to the gospel, Christians are called to forgive and love others.

Fundamental Theology A sub-discipline in systematic theology that seeks to provide a scholarly defense of the place of theology within the academic disciplines and to discern what can be known of God through human reasoning. While fundamental theology has long been a Roman Catholic concern, especially with regard to the relationship between metaphysics and theology, Protestant theologians have also addressed issues in this sub–discipline, usually within theological prolegomena.

Fundamentalism A movement within American Evangelical Protestantism that began in the 1920s and that expressed itself in a series of pamphlets called "the Fundamentals." Among the teachings defended by these Protestants are the verbal inspiration and inerrancy of the Bible, the virgin birth of Jesus, the blood atonement of Christ, his bodily resurrection, and his Second Coming. As an attitude or mindset, "fundamentalism" appears in most religions.

General Revelation According to Paul and John, all human beings, even those who worship other gods, have some knowledge of the one, true God and are thus without excuse when they do not worship or serve God and instead serve other gods. This natural knowledge of God is often called "general revelation." It is distinct from special revelation, which is grounded solely in the historical self–giving of God in and through specific events as these are attested to in Holy Scripture.

Gentile A biblical term that refers to a non-Jew.

Glaubenslehre German: "teaching of faith." This term was used by Schleiermacher to describe his systematic theology as setting forth the Protestant "way of believing." Since justification by grace through faith alone is the central "Protestant principle" (Tillich), the doctrine of faith or teaching about faith permeates every aspect of a properly Protestant dogmatics.

Glory of God An important biblical concept that describes the awesome presence of God manifested in the mighty acts of God in ancient Israel. In the NT God's glory is revealed in and through Jesus, his miracles, and especially his death and resurrection.

Gnosticism/Gnostic Based on the Greek word for "knowledge," Gnosticism was a broad religious movement of "secret" or hidden knowledge that came to prominence within early Christianity in the second, third, and fourth centuries. A Gnostic was one who believed in the secret knowledge of a "divine spark" imprisoned within the body that would be released from the body at death to return to a higher, spiritual level. All Gnostics devalued the physical, material world, including the physical body of human beings. Gnosticism was rejected as heretical by mainstream catholic and orthodox Christianity.

God Within Christian theology "God" is both a proper noun (and thus always capitalized) and an abstract noun that refers to the nature of the divine as the absolute cause of the universe. Christians confess and teach that God is "triune," consisting of "three persons in one substance," the Father, the Son, and the Holy Spirit. See **God the Father, the Holy Spirit**, and **the Son of God**

God the Father Within orthodox and catholic trinitarian theology, God the Father is the One source of all that is, the One who loves the Son from all eternity and who has sent the Son into the world to love the world and to redeem it from sin, death, and the power of evil.

Golden Rule A specific ethical teaching that is found (in varying forms) within all of the major world religions. Jesus taught it as follows: "Do unto others what you would have them do to you."

Gospel Greek: "good message" or "good report"; Old English: "godspel" or "good news." According to the synoptic gospels, Jesus taught that the "gospel" is his announcement that "the time is fulfilled" and "the kingdom of God has come near" (see Mk 1.14–15). The apostle Paul defined "the gospel" as the death and resurrection of Jesus for the forgiveness of sins (see 1 Cor. 15.1ff.). After the first century, the canonical gospels were each given the title of "gospel" because they set forth the one gospel concerning Jesus ("The Gospel according to Mark," "The Gospel according to Matthew," and so on). (The title of "gospel" was also given to much later documents, called collectively "the apocryphal gospels," but these were rejected as non-apostolic and heretical within early Christianity.) Within mainstream Christianity, the gospel is first and foremost the proclamation of the divine forgiveness of sins on account of Christ's death and resurrection. A corollary to this teaching is the Pauline emphasis that a sinner is justified before God by divine grace through faith in Jesus Christ. This gospel or good news, which is also expressed in other terms within the OT and NT, is the central teaching within Christianity.

Grace Latin: "favor" or "a favorable act." A central teaching within Christianity since it expresses the divine favor that God has toward all sinners and the divine act to overcome the estrangement between God and sinners. While all Christians confess that God's free and unearned grace is absolutely essential to their salvation, they disagree about how one is to think about this unearned act of God and how it overcomes sin in the life of the Christian believer. For example, Catholic Christians understand grace as a sacramental power that works in the believers to make them holy and acceptable to God, whereas Protestant Christians understand grace as God's act of forgiving and accepting sinners solely on account of their faith (trust) in Christ.

Hebrew Bible Hebrew: "Tanakh." This collection of Jewish Scriptures, most but not all of them written in Hebrew, refers to the TaNaKh: "the **T**orah" (the Law), "the **N**ebiim" ("the Prophets"), and the "**K**ethubim" ("the Writings"). The terms "Hebrew Bible" or "Tanakh" are often used by scholars in an interfaith or scholarly setting to avoid making a theological judgment about that canon, as the Christian designation of it as "Old Testament" does. The Hebrew Bible closely corresponds to the canon of the Old Testament in most Protestant Bibles but differs from the Old Testament canon in Catholic and Orthodox Bibles. See **Old Testament**

Heilsgeschichte German: "salvation history" or "history of salvation" or "narrative of salvation." This term was invented and used by German scholars, including most importantly Johannes von Hofmann, who comprehended the Bible's essential content as a witness to God's saving actions in history. In this view the Bible is neither a collection of dogmatic statements nor a set of ancient writings to be understood merely historically and philologically. Instead the Bible presents a basic canonical narrative that reveals God's "self-giving" in history. This narrative begins with the promise to Abram, unfolds in the history of ancient Israel, and culminates in the coming of Jesus and the eschatological gift of the Spirit. The "center" of this history is Jesus, toward whom the history of Israel was moving and through whom all history is brought to its fulfillment.

Henotheism Greek: "one God." Henotheism is a modern term for describing the ancient belief that there is only one true God ("the LORD") among the many other real gods in the surrounding nations. In contrast to monotheism, which holds that there is only one true and living God, henotheism acknowledged the reality of the other gods but considered them to be inferior to their particular God. Some scholars maintain that henotheism was the original form of ancient Israelite religion that eventually gave way to strict monotheism.

Heresy/heretic Greek: a (false) "choice." The term "heresy" comes to be used in early Christianity to refer to those who choose a teaching that is contrary to central and essential tenents within orthodox and catholic teaching, usually concerning the nature of the triune God and the person and work of Christ. Later the term refers to teaching that members of a given church body deem to be contrary to the teachings of their church.

Hermeneutics Greek: "to interpret." Within Christian theology, hermeneutics refer to venerable principles of biblical interpretation (the methods of "exegesis") and to the process of theological understanding that arises from the use of those methods by the contemporary interpreter.

Hermeneutical Circle A metaphor for the process of interpreting any object. One way of describing the circle is as follows: The interpreter has an initial pre-understanding of an object (a work of art, a novel, a biblical story, etc.), but then, in the process of critically engaging the object, the pre-understanding is partly confirmed and partly corrected or modified. This new understanding then becomes a new pre-understanding for the next engagement with the object. Philosophers and theologians from Schleiermacher to Gadamer and Ricoeur have understood the "circle" differently, but all have noted the circular character of all authentic interpretation.

Hermeneutical Theology Forms of Christian theology that pay special attention to the role of hermeneutics in theological understanding. Many theologians, such as Bultmann and Ricoeur, regard hermeneutics, rather than metaphysics, as the central task of Christian theology.

Hidden God A biblical notion that expresses the experience of the absence or radical transcendence of God. Martin Luther emphasized this notion, based on his close reading of the Psalms (many of which lament the absence of God or heighten the awareness of God as a divine threat to one's well being), Isaiah (e.g. "You are truly a God who hides himself"), the suffering of Job, and the suffering and death of Jesus ("My God, my God, why have you forsaken me?").

Higher Faculties Within medieval universities, these referred to the disciplines of law and theology. Later medicine was added to them as well.

Historical Critical Method Sometimes called "historical criticism" or "higher criticism," this refers to a set of academic methods used by scholars to understand the historical, literary, and social contexts of the biblical writings, the world "behind" the text. The method assumes that the Bible can be studied like any other ancient set of documents, using the same historical and critical approaches that other scholars use to understand documents and artifacts from the past.

Historical Criticism see **Historical Critical Method**

Historical Jesus This phrase is used by scholars to refer to the Jesus "behind" the written gospels, to Jesus "as he really was" in the first century, or to Jesus as he can be "uncovered" through modern historical-critical tools and methods (which is never identical to Jesus "as he really was"), in contrast to Jesus as he is presented in the gospels and interpreted within the dogmatic tradition of the Christian church.

Historical Theology A sub-discipline of theology that examines biblical theology, the history of Christian theology, and the history of Christianity.

Historicism Within Christian theology, historicism refers to a philosophical or metaphysical perspective that views the Bible only and entirely as a humanly-constructed set of ancient documents, and denies or brackets out of consideration the theological, supra-historical dimension within these writings and their witness to divine revelation.

The Holy Spirit Within orthodox and catholic Christianity, the Holy Spirit is the third person of the Trinity, who proceeds from the Father (Eastern Orthodoxy) or from the Father and the Son (western Catholicism and Protestantism) and is the bond of union between the Father and the Son.

Homolegoumena Greek: "Agreed upon (things)." Within the history of Christianity, this term refers to those biblical writings that were nearly universally agreed-upon as sacred Scripture, in contrast to those writings that were "spoken against" (the antilegomena).

Homoousion Greek: "of the same being"; "of one substance." A non-biblical term used by some ancient Christians to stress the identity of the *Logos* with God. The term was debated at Nicaea in AD 325 in the context of arguments about the position of Arius regarding the *Logos*. The term was eventually incorporated into the creed that was accepted by the majority of bishops at that council. The creed underwent further modification at the next ecumenical council in Constantinople (AD 381). This Niceno–Constantinopolitan Creed states that the *Logos* of God is "God from God, light from light, true God from true God, begotten, not made, of one being ["*homoousion*"] with the Father, by whom all things were made… ." See **Creed**.

Humanities Within liberal arts universities the humanities refer to those academic disciplines that study history, literature, the visual and performing arts, architecture, music, drama, philosophy, world religions, and theology.

Icon Greek: "likeness," "image." An icon is a flat painting, often on wood but also on other materials, that represents Christ, the Virgin Mary, or another saint. Icons are used and venerated within the Eastern Orthodox Church.

Iconoclast Greek: "image-breaker." One who opposes the use of icons.

Iconoclastic Controversy A controversy over the use and veneration of icons in the Eastern Orthodox Church during the eighth and ninth centuries. At this time Christians who tended to downplay the humanity of Christ and his incarnation also tended to be critical of the use of images in the church. Those who defended the use of icons (iconophiles) often met with violent opposition from those who objected to their use (iconclasts). Many Christian iconoclasts were influenced by Jewish and Muslim polemics against icons, which they viewed as idolatrous. Many iconophiles were martyred because of their defense of icons. Eventually the eastern church officially endorsed the use and veneration of icons and strongly rejected the iconoclastic position.

Iconophile Greek: "image-lover." One who defends the use of icons.

Image of God Genesis 1.26 and other Scripture passages indicate that human beings are created in the image and likeness of God. Theologians have disagreed among themselves about what these terms ("image," "likeness") mean. Irenaeus and Origin distinguished between the two: "image" referred to the original state of humans before the fall into sin, and "likeness" referred to their final state in glory. Other theologians saw the terms as synonyms. Many interpreted the terms to refer to the moral freedom of human beings, or to their ability to reason, or to a quality of their soul (e.g. immortality). Protestant reformers generally held that the image was entirely lost due to the power of sin and human depravity and is only restored through Christ, whereas Roman Catholics and other theologians hold that the image has been distorted but not totally destroyed.

Incarnation of the Word The Christian teaching (based on Jn 1.14 and other passages) that the eternal Word (*Logos*) became a human being through Mary, his human mother. The incarnated Word is thus at once fully divine (from eternity) and fully human (born of Mary).

Inerrancy of Scripture The teaching that the Bible contains no errors. Some theologians understand the inerrancy of Scripture to be synonymous with its infallibility, that is, it will not mislead a person in the essential matters of faith. Others, particularly Protestant Fundamentalists, insist that the Scriptures (properly understood) contain no errors of any kind. Still others hold that while the Bible contains some errors, these are of little significance to the central teachings of Christianity.

Infallibility This term has been used in western Christianity in two different ways. On the one hand, some Christians have used it in reference to the authority of the Bible, that is, the Bible will not mislead a person in the essential matters of faith and morals. On the other hand, Roman Catholic theologians have developed an understanding of the term in relation to the authority of the pope. As a result of the First Vatican Council the Pope is said to be infallible when he speaks authoritatively from his bishop's chair on matters of faith and morals. See **Inerrancy of Scripture**

Intelligent Design Theory A modern view that infers the reality of a divine Intelligence or Deity on the basis of the observation of apparent "design" or "complexity" within nature. This theory has been criticized because of its appeal to God as a direct, supernatural cause of apparent design or complexity in nature as opposed to understanding such matters scientifically, that is, as the result of natural, material causes in nature.

Interdisciplinarity The quality of some academic disciplines (philosophy, theology, the humanities, etc.) to be related to and engaged with other academic disciplines.

Israel (ancient Israel) Hebrew: "he who struggles with God." The term is used in the Bible to refer initially to the patriarch Jacob (Gen. 32.28) who wrestled with a mysterious figure at Peniel. He is given the new name "Israel" after this experience. Jacob's 12 sons also receive this name collectively, as do the 12 clans/tribes that bear the names of these sons of Jacob. Later the term "Israel" refers to just the 10 northern tribes, in contrast to the two southern tribes that are called "Judah" (after the larger of the two). Elsewhere in the OT and NT the term refers to the whole people of God or (in the NT) to the Christian Church.

Judaism The religion of the Jewish people that developed after the time of the Babylonian exile (after 586 BC). The term derives from the larger of the two southern tribes in ancient Israel, Judah.

Justification A legal term used within the NT (especially by Paul) to refer to God's gracious forgiveness of sinners, their pardoning before God's condemning judgment on account of Christ, and their being declared righteous by faith in him. The doctrine of justification has been the major issue that has divided Roman Catholic theologians and Protestant theologians. Melanchthon called the doctrine of justification "the article on which the church stands or falls."

Kerygma Greek: "proclamation." In the NT this term refers to both the act of preaching the gospel as well as the content of that proclamation.

Law The Law of God is understood in three basic ways in the Christian tradition. First, the law is equated with God's eternal will for human beings, which God reveals through the human conscience and enforces through civil laws that protect human beings and punish evil doers. Some Christian theologians, but not all, discuss aspects of this initial understanding of the divine law under the categories of "natural law" and/or "the civil/political use of the law." Second, the law of God is identified with the specific biblical legislation that has come through Moses and the legal traditions of ancient Israel (the OT Mosaic law in the time of ancient Israel's nationhood). This Mosaic law is summarized in the Ten Commandments (which overlap with civil law, e.g. the laws against murder, stealing, etc.). Third, within the NT, "the law of Christ" or the law of Christian love (the love of God and the love of others, including one's enemies) is distinct from both the Mosaic law and the divine law that works in the conscience and through civic law. According to Paul, because all human beings have fallen short of what God expects of them in his eternal will, the law of God "brings wrath"; it exposes them as sinners under the judgment of God. According to Luther, the principal use of the law is theological, namely, to drive sinners to Christ, since the law (however it is experienced) always accuses them before God and can only be silenced by faith in Christ. Luther stressed that Christ frees the sinner from the law and places him or her under the guidance of the Spirit, whose gifts take one beyond the demands of the law and fulfill "the law of Christ," the law of love. For Calvin, whose position differs from Luther's, the law of God does not always condemn the Christian (who remains a sinner unto death), but principally serves as a positive guide to the Christian life. For Calvin, the Christian is to be obedient to the law of God joyfully and freely.

Lex orandi, lex credendi Latin: "the law of praying, the law of believing." This expression seeks to summarize the connection between what one prays and what one believes. For example, what one believes about God shapes the language one uses in prayer and the liturgy, just as the language one uses in prayer and the liturgy conveys what one believes about God.

Liberation Theology A broad theological movement of human social liberation that emerged in South America and elsewhere after the late 1960s. All liberation theologies are contextual, that is, they get articulated within specific socioeconomic, political, and cultural contexts. Such theologies seek to respond critically against social and political oppression and to struggle for social justice on the basis of God's "preferential option for the poor," the prophets' and Jesus' criticisms of the rich and powerful, and the promise of God's coming kingdom.

Literal Sense The sense or meaning that the words (patterns of letters) have in a biblical text.

Liturgy Greek: "public service." Within Christianity the liturgy refers to the contents and shape of the divine service, culminating in the celebration of the Eucharist. It includes the invocation, prayers, hymns, psalms, Scripture readings, often a sermon or homily, and usually the Eucharist.

Logos (the *Logos*) Greek: "Word," "reason," or "speech" According to John 1.1ff., "in the beginning was the Word and the Word was with God and the Word was God... And the Word became flesh and dwelt among us, full of grace and truth." The concept of the *Logos* was central to the development of Christology in the early Christian church. Jesus the Christ was acknowledged to be "the Word of God." Debates centered on the relationship between the divine *Logos* and the human nature in Jesus.

LORD see **YHWH**

Lord's Supper see **Eucharist**

Love Within the Christian tradition a central teaching, perhaps the central teaching, is that God *is* love (1 Jn 4.7–8). The Christian good news has been summarized as God's self-giving love and mercy for unlovable, undeserving sinners. "For God so loved the world that he gave his only Son that whoever believes in him should not perish but have eternal life" (Jn 3.16). Christians are called by Christ and His Spirit to love others with the same love by which God loves the world in Christ, a self-giving love that serves the needs of others. Christ Jesus made the love and forgiveness of one's enemies the key aspect of authentic love.

Lower Faculties Within the medieval university, the lower faculties were the seven liberal arts that were divided into the trivium (grammar, logic, rhetoric) and the quadrivium (arithmetic, geometry, music, astronomy). These disciplines prepared on for the higher faculties (law, theology, and, later, medicine).

Lutheran Church A confessional movement within the western catholic tradition that subscribes to the *Augsburg Confession* (1530), the *Small Catechism* of Martin Luther, and other writings contained in the *Book of Concord* (1580).

Magisterium Latin: "magister" = "teacher." This term refers to the teaching office of the pope and bishops in the Roman Catholic Church.

Marks of the Church These refer to signs by which one is able to recognize the character of the church as belonging to Christ, as being "one, holy, catholic, and apostolic," to use the classic language from the Niceno-Constantinopolitan Creed. Historically and traditionally, such "marks" or "signs" have included the teaching of the apostles as authoritatively contained in the prophetic and apostolic Scriptures, the rule of faith as summarized in catholic and orthodox baptismal creeds and ecumenical decrees/creeds, orthodox bishoprics (especially those of the five central Christian patriarchs), orthodox liturgies, the sign of the cross, and the use of the Lord's Prayer. The Lutheran Reformers in the Sixteenth Century taught that "the one, holy, catholic, and apostolic church" is present "wherever the gospel is proclaimed and taught in its truth and purity" and the sacraments (of Baptism and the Lord's Supper) "are administered in accord with the gospel." So the gospel is itself the chief mark of the church. Some Reformed Christians expanded that Lutheran understanding to include church discipline (excommunication) as a further mark.

The Matriarchs (of the Old Testament) These were the great women figures in the early traditions of ancient Israel: Sarah (wife of Abraham), Rebekah (wife of Isaac), Leah and Rachel (wives of Jacob).

Messiah Hebrew: "anointed one." The Greek equivalent, "Christos," also means "anointed one." In the OT a messiah was one who was set apart for a special divine task (e.g. a priest or a king). Later the term was used more specifically for the king. After the collapse of the Davidic dynasty, there developed within ancient Israel the expectation of a future Davidic king, "the Messiah," who would deliver the Jewish people from their oppressors and establish God's reign. In the NT Jesus is identified as this Messiah or the Christ.

Metanarrative Any attempt to provide a single narrative or story to account for the whole of reality. Within postmodern philosophy, people tend to be skeptical toward all such attempts since they tend to favor the powerful to the exclusion of the marginalized.

Metaphysics Greek editors of the works of Aristotle gave this term to what he called "First Philosophy," that deals with the study of "being" as "being." Within the history of western philosophy metaphysics explores the nature of ultimate reality or the first principles within reflection upon reality as a whole. Christian theology also addresses metaphysical questions but on the basis of special revelation.

Method of Correlation This way of doing systematic theology, classically expounded in the twentieth century by Paul Tillich (although he argued that theologians had been using this method since the time of the Apostle Paul), dialectically relates "questions" and problems that arise from within one's individual life and social setting ("the human situation") with "answers" and "solutions" that come from divine revelation ("the Christian message"). The Roman Catholic theologian, David Tracy, has modified Tillich's method by referring to the need for "mutually critical correlation," wherein both "the situation" and "the message" criticize and inform each other. See **Revisionist Theology**

Methodism That branch of Christendom that developed from the teaching and organizational efforts of John and Charles Wesley and their followers in the eighteenth century and later.

Ministry Greek: "diakonia" = "service"; Latin: "ministerium" = "service." Within the Christian tradition the ministry of Christ to a hurting and sinful world is the basis for all other Christian service. Everyone who is baptized into Christ is called to serve others in faithful love, bearing witness to Christ and the gospel in word and deed. According to Paul, the Holy Spirit gifts individuals with varying gifts of ministry/service: some are called to be apostles, others pastors and teachers, still others workers of miracles, and so on. What was dynamic and Spirit-oriented in the early years of Paul's apostolic ministry later became more institutionalized and stable: specific offices of ministry developed in continuity with apostolic leadership, such as bishop/overseer, pastor/teacher/priest, deacon. These offices developed differently in Eastern and Western Christianity, especially regarding the authority of the bishop of Rome (papal primacy) and the marriage of priests, but both streams of Christian tradition insisted that "valid ordination" (validly setting authorizing) was necessary for public service in the church as a deacon, priest, and bishop. Within Protestantism, the principal form of ordained ministry remains the office of pastor, who is authorized to preach the gospel and administer the sacraments in accord with the gospel.

Modern Theology This term has been used to describe many different forms of Christian theology since the time of the Protestant Reformation but in general it applies to any theology that positively engages philosophical and scientific developments since the seventeenth century. "Modern" forms of theology tend to be critical of religious traditions that do not stand up to careful scrutiny and to be supportive of the use of one's reason to uncover legitimate knowledge. Such forms of theology generally seek to allow the modern sciences to inform their theological understandings.

Classic examples of twentieth-century modern Christian theologians are Tillich and Bultmann. See **Method of Correlation**, **Post-liberal Theology**, **Post-modern Theology**, and **Revisionist Theology**

Monk Greek: "solitary one." Within Christianity a monk is a man who has taken the vows of chastity, poverty, and obedience and lives according to them within a monastic community. The term is most accurately applied to a hermit within a monastic community. His principle duty is to pray.

Monotheism A modern term to describe the belief that there is only one, true and real God. All other gods are either idols of human invention or entities that are not truly God.

Moral Argument This argument for the existence of God has been set forth classically by Immanuel Kant. He held that moral reason requires the reality of God (along with freedom and immortality) so that each person's level of virtue can be properly adjudicated in the afterlife by the divine justice. Because wicked people often get away with their wickedness in this life, and because righteous people often suffer at the hands of evil people, God is necessary to properly mete out justice in the afterlife.

Myth Greek: "story." Within popular usage a myth is an untruth, a false story, a legend, or an errant account of something. Within religious studies, however, a myth is simply a story about a god or gods or some religious matter that requires careful interpretation. Provided the genre is understood properly, a myth may convey profound spiritual or religious truth about human beings and their world.

Natural Knowledge of God The knowledge of God the Creator that is given through creation itself and human reflection upon it. This "natural knowledge" is the result of general revelation in distinction from special revelation. The natural knowledge of God may properly be described as philosophical theology, since it seeks to talk about God on the basis of nature, and human reasoning about God on the basis of nature.

Natural Theology Thinking about God on the basis of general revelation apart from special revelation. Natural theology is the way people think about the natural knowledge of God given through creation itself and human reflection upon creation (general revelation).

Necessary Being That which must exist or whose non-existence is inconceivable. Within Anselm's so-called ontological argument, God is the one necessary being whose non-existence is inconceivable. All other beings that truly exist are contingent or dependent upon God for their being. According to Anselm a necessary being, whose non-existence is inconceivable, is "greater than" a contingent being, whose non-existence is conceivable. Since for Anselm God is "that than which nothing greater can be conceived," God must exist, since necessary being is greater than contingent being.

Neurotheology A relatively new academic discipline that seeks to understand how human physiology and brain activity mediate (or perhaps create) religious beliefs and practices. Neurotheology seeks to explore the connections among physiology, the brain, spirituality, and religious belief.

New Testament A "testament" is a will or written disposition, as in "last will and testament." Within Christianity the expression "new testament" refers first to the statement of Jesus at his final meal with his disciples: "This is my blood of the new testament given and shed for you for the forgivness of sins" (Mt. 26.28 var.). The author of Hebrews thus refers to Christ as "the mediator of a new testament" (better than "covenant"), since Christ as testator simply declares that those who believe in him will inherit the forgiveness of sins and eternal life (see Hebrews 9.15ff.) As with a last will and testament, it only takes effect upon the death of the testator. In another sense, the writings that bear apostolic witness to Christ as this mediator of a new testament (or new covenant) are also called "The New Testament," in contrast to the Hebrew Scriptures ("the Old Testament" or "old covenant").

Nicaea Site of the first ecumenical council (AD 325). The creed that emerged from this council declares the *Logos* that became incarnate in Jesus to be "God from God, light from light, true God from true God, begotten, not made, of one being with the Father, by whom all things were made..." See **Homoousion**

Niceno-Constantinopolitan Creed The title that is given to the creed that was first set forth at the first ecumenical council in Nicaea (AD 325) and then further developed at the second ecumenical council in Constantinople (AD 381). Usually this creed is simply called "The Nicene Creed." See **Creed** and **Homoousion**

Non-denominational Churches Independent Christian churches that have no external, formal relationship with any other Christian church body.

Nun In a general sense a nun is a woman who is a member of a Christian religious order. In a more specific sense a nun is a woman who has taken a vow of chastity, poverty, and obedience and who lives in an enclosed religious order in which outsiders are not permitted.

Old Testament The traditional term that Christians use for the Hebrew or Jewish Bible (which, for the Orthodox and Roman Catholic communities, also includes the OT Apocrypha). For Protestant Christians the Old Testament is normally limited to the 39 books that are found in the Hebrew Bible. See **Hebrew Bible**

Omnipotence A traditional attribute of God that affirms God to be "all powerful" or having power and authority over all things. This attribute, as Christians understand it, does not mean God is the direct cause of every event or the cause of evil, nor does it mean that God can do what is self-contradictory.

Omniscience A traditional attribute of God that affirms God to be "all knowing" or having perfect knowledge.

Ontological Argument The a priori argument of Anselm to demonstrate the existence of God on the basis of the definition of God as "that than which nothing greater can be conceived." This argument presupposes that for God to be "perfect being" God must exist, since to exist would be more perfect than not to exist.

Orthodox/Orthodoxy Greek: "correct praise" or "correct teaching." The term "orthodox" within Christianity refers to that which is correct or true, in contrast to that which is heretical or false. Orthodoxy generally refers to those Eastern churches that are in communion with the patriarch of Constantinople (Istanbul).

Pantheism Greek: "all is God" or "God is everything." This position affirms that everything as a totality is God or one with God. This position conflicts with orthodox Christian theology that teaches that God is distinct from created reality and transcendent to it.

Paraclete Greek: "advocate" or "defense attorney." This is the term that is used in the Gospel of John for the Holy Spirit.

Parenesis Greek: "exhortation" or "counsel." NT scholars use this term to refer to the moral exhortations that are found in the apostolic writings.

Parousia Greek "coming" or "presence." This term is used in the NT in reference to the future coming of the risen Christ, when he will come again to judge the living and the dead.

Pastor Latin: "shepherd." This is a term used by Lutheran Christians and some other Protestants to refer to their clergy.

Patriarch Greek: "father." This is the title that is used for the bishops of the five chief centers of early Christianity: Jerusalem, Antioch, Constantinople, Alexandria, and Rome.

The Patriarchs (of the Old Testament) These were the three great forefathers in ancient Israel: Abraham, Isaac, and Jacob. The term also applies to the twelve sons of Jacob and their tribes.

Patristics Greek: "fathers." That branch of historical theology that examines Christian, post–apostolic thinkers from the second century into the early medieval period.

Pentecostal Churches Churches founded in the twentieth century whose members believe in the on–going gifts of the Holy Spirit that were poured out initially "on the day of Pentecost" (Acts 2.1ff.). They especially focus on spontaneous worship and the gifts of "speaking in tongues," spiritual healing, exorcism, and prophecy.

Phenomenology Greek: "appearance." The term was first used by Kant to refer to the "science of phenomena," that which appears to the senses. Later is it was used by Hegel to refer to the process by which Spirit develops from sense experience to absolute knowledge. More recently, the term was employed by Edmund Husserl and those influenced by him (e.g. Ricoeur) in reference to the discovery and analysis of essences and essential meanings.

Philosophical Theology Broadly speaking, philosophical theology addresses questions that arise in the philosophy of religion and metaphysics (for example, the question of God, the nature of evil, the question of human freedom, and so on). For Schleiermacher philosophical theology is that branch of theology which delineates the reality of the Christian church and defines the essence of Christian faith. Within the present book philosophical theology is undertaken within the sub-discipline of systematic theology called fundamental theology.

Pluralism Within religious studies "pluralism" refers to the diversity of religious groups, beliefs, truth claims, and practices within the world and to the tensions and contradictions that arise when one compares and contrasts specific religious beliefs, truth claims, and practices with other specific religious beliefs, truth claims, and practices.

Pneumatology The theological investigation into the person and work of the Holy Spirit.

Pope Latin: "father." A title that was used in early Christianity for bishops. In the east it was eventually restricted to the Bishop of Alexandria. In the west it was eventually restricted to the Bishop of Rome. Among Roman Catholics, the Pope is the supreme head of the universal church on earth. That claim is rejected by both Eastern Orthodox and Protestant Christians.

Post-liberal Theology The name given to a theological movement that was influenced by Karl Barth and centered at Yale Divinity School and Duke Divinity School (after the mid-1980s). This movement criticized the liberal Protestant orientation to human religious experience and emphasized the priority of the biblical narratives to frame theological understanding.

Post-modern Theology This term has been used to describe many different forms of Christian theology since the last decades of the twentieth century, but in general it applies to any theology that is critical of the intrusion of philosophy into Christian theology, skeptical regarding the positive contributions of the sciences to Christian theological understanding, and convinced that the notion of "autonomous reason" is an illusion. Post-modern theology might best be described as an attitude that is skeptical regarding all truth claims, pessimistic about technological advances, keenly atuned to the abuses of power by human beings in their interactions with others, and suspicious of all "grand narratives." Post–liberal theology is but one example of post-modern theologies. See **Method of Correlation**, **Post-liberal Theology**, **Post-modern Theology**, and **Revisionist Theology**.

Practical Theology That sub–discipline of theology that addresses how theology is to be applied in the life of the church. In this book, it addresses ecclesial studies (specific Christian communities and their impact in the world) and theological ethics.

Praxis Greek: "practice." Within recent Christian theology praxis refers to the mutual interaction between theory and practice, thinking and action in relation to specific contextual problems. Praxis has played a key methodological role in Liberation Theology, which stresses the concrete, practical consequences of theology in relation to social and political oppression and God's "preferential option for the poor," rather than theoretical theological understandings articulated in isolation from social realities.

Prayer The practice of communicating with God. Within a Christian context, prayer takes many forms, both individual and communal. Christians pray the psalms in the OT and they regularly pray the prayer that Jesus taught his followers, usually called "The Lord's Prayer." Christians pray to confess their sins to God, to cry in lament to God, to make their needs and the needs of others known to God (petition and intercession), and to call upon God in praise and thanksgiving.

Presbyter (Elder) Greek: "old man." The earliest Jerusalem church was governed by a board of presbyters or elders. The Apostle Paul appointed elders in the churches he founded. As such, they seem to have been identical to the "overseers" or bishops in those places. Later the term bishop was used only of the president of these boards of elders or presbyters.

Priest The term is a contraction of the Greek word "presbyter." See above. In the OT a priest is one who makes sacrifices. Within ancient Israelite religion the High Priest alone could enter the Temple on the Day of Atonement to make sacrifice for the people. In the NT Jesus is presented as a type of High Priest since his sacrifice on the cross makes atonement between God and sinners. After the second century there developed in Christianity the idea that a presbyter who celebrates the Eucharist offers a sacrifice and thus the term "priest" was applied to a presbyter.

Process Theology A twentieth-century theological movement, influenced by the philosophical reflections of Alfred North Whitehead and modern evolutionary science, which stresses the changing nature of human beings and the world and maintains that God is also undergoing development and change through God's responsive relationship with the world.

Prophet One who claims to speak for God. In the OT one finds seers (who know the future) and ecstatics (who speak divine words that are not their own). In later Israelite prophecy stress is laid on the intelligible word or message of God that is delivered through the authentic and true prophets. False prophets speak on their own authority and their words do not come to pass. The NT claims that Jesus is the fulfillment of the OT prophecies about the Messiah. The NT itself bears witness to prophets in early Christianity, both men and women.

Q A hypothetical, as yet undiscovered source document (mostly sayings of Jesus) for the gospels of Matthew and Luke (but not Mark). It is called "Q" (short for "*Quelle*," the German word for "source"), since German scholars first developed the four–source theory: the authors/editors of Matthew and Luke used Mark and Q as their principal sources and then each drew upon additional materials, a third source, labeled "M" (for material only in Matthew) and a fourth source, labeled "L (for material only in Luke).

Reconciliation This refers to one way in which the Christian gospel is presented in the NT. "God was in Christ reconciling the world to himself, not counting people's sins against them" (2 Cor. 5.19). Within the Roman Catholic Church "reconciliation" is a recent way of labeling the sacrament that used to be called "penance."

Redemption see **Salvation**

Reformed Although Martin Luther and others were important sixteenth–century reformers in the western catholic Church, the term "Reformed" usually refers to the Protestant tradition that traces its heritage back to John Calvin and his reforms. The term "Reformed" is usually used today instead of "Calvinist."

Regula Fidei see **Rule of Faith**

Religion A notoriously difficult term to define, the word "religion" was coined in the seventeenth-century. In general it refers to complex phenomena connected to peoples' worldviews, ultimate meanings, symbolic expressions, communal myths and rituals, "moods and motivations" (Geertz), ethical behaviors, beliefs, and practices. Some religions are theistic, others not. All religions have a communal aspect, which a possible etymology for the term religion (religare = "to bind together") suggests.

Religious Experience Any human experience that gives rise to religious feeling, thought, and behavior.

Religious Pluralism see **Pluralism**

Religious Studies An academic discipline that studies world religions, religious experience, and other religious phenomena. While the discipline may involve comparative theology (comparing and contrasting ideas and practices across multiple religions), religious studies tends to bracket out all particular theological commitments in favor of the pursuit of neutral observation and description.

Repentance This refers to the act of turning back or returning to God (as in the OT understanding) or changing one's mind to get in line with the coming kingdom of God (as in the NT preaching of Jesus). Throughout the history of Christianity repentance involves human contrition for sin and the desire for divine forgiveness and mercy. The biblical presupposition of repentance is human sin and alienation from God and the need for sinners to repent. The divine response to repentance is forgiveness, mercy, and love.

Resurrection Christians believe that God raised the enfleshed, crucified Jesus from the dead as a vindication of his life and ministry and to make him Lord over all creation. On the basis of the NT witness to the resurrection of

Jesus, Christians believe in "the resurrection of the dead" (as the Niceno-Constantinopolitan Creed states) or "the resurrection of the body" (as the Apostles' Creed states). This teaching is different from the Greek philosophical idea of the immortality of the soul, which focuses on disembodied souls. Traditional Christian teaching about the bodily resurrection, based on the witness to Jesus' own resurrection, holds the promise that God will raise people from the dead and give them new life in God's new creation. This teaching seeks to affirm the abiding significance of embodied human beings and, by extension, God's love and compassion for all material being (the whole of creation).

Revelation see **General Revelation** and **Special Revelation**

Revealed Theology see **Special Revelation**

Revisionist Theology Forms of theology, either Roman Catholic (e.g. David Tracy) or Protestant (e.g. Paul Tillich, Gordan Kaufman), that seek to keep theology always open to revision in light of new knowledge and experience.

Roman Catholic Church While Roman Catholics trace their church heritage back to Jesus through the church that was founded at Rome and led by the bishop there (the head of the western catholic church), the Roman Catholic Church embraces all those Christians who are in communion with the bishop of Rome (the Pope) and who adhere to all of the conciliar decisions of this hierarchical church, especially those from the Council of Trent and the two Vatican councils.

Rule of Faith Latin: regula fidei. A second-century phrase that describes the essential and normative content of Christian faith as taught and handed down by the apostles. Within early Christianity this rule helped Christians to interpret the prophetic and apostolic writings that would eventually be included in the OT and NT and to criticize understandings that were held to be heretical.

Sacraments The term "sacrament" (Latin: "public oath" or "public act") is not found in the Christian Scriptures. It is a word that comes to be used first in the western catholic tradition and then in Eastern Orthodoxy. It refers to special rites or rituals that convey God's grace. Augustine defined a sacrament as a visible sign of an invisible grace. Both the Roman Catholic and Eastern Orthodox traditions will come to recognize seven sacraments: Baptism, the Eucharist, confession of sins (called "penance" in the medieval Catholic Church and today called "reconciliation"), confirmation, marriage, holy orders, and the anointing of the sick and dying with oil. Most Protestant churches acknowledge only two sacraments: Baptism and the Eucharist (or Lord's Supper). Some Lutherans also refer to confession and absolution as a sacrament.

Salvation The Christian term for what Christ Jesus accomplishes for sinful human beings. The western catholic tradition emphasizes that Christ "saves" people from their sins, from death, from the judgement of God, and from the power of Satan. The eastern Orthodox tradition emphasizes that Christ saves people from death and eternal judgment.

Schism Greek: "tear" or "rent." This is formal or willful exclusion or separation from the church.

Scholasticism A medieval way of academic inquiry into biblical teaching by means of questioning, criticizing, and debating theological opinions. Sixteenth-century humanists criticized this method for its academic narrow-mindedness ("how many angels can dance on the head of a needle?") and favored a more literary and historical approach to traditional theological matters.

Scientific Imperialism A term coined by Ted Peters to refer to the view that the natural sciences can explain all of reality (including religious beliefs and practices) fully on the basis of a naturalistic, materialistic, anti–theological method.

Scientism This is a view similar to scientific imperialism. It holds that science alone can uncover what is true about reality.

Scripture Latin: "writing." The term "scripture" within Christianity refers to writings that are held to be sacred and authoritative for faith and life.

Scripture Interprets Scripture This classic phrase sets forth the important hermeneutical principle that clearer passages in the Bible ought to be used to shed light on less clear passages. For Lutheran Christians, the clearest passages of Scripture are those that teach the gospel concerning Jesus the Christ.

Secularization Latin (*saeculum*): "world." This refers to the process of human cultures and human beings becoming more "worldly," independent, free, and autonomous in the wake of the Enlightenment.

Self-revelation of God The Christian teaching that God shares himself and even gives himself through his Word (the *Logos*) and Spirit to be trusted, loved, and followed by human beings. The self-revelation of God is God's self–giving, which Christians believe has occurred most decisively in and through the person of Jesus, the Word of God incarnate.

Septuagint This is a term used for various versions of the Hebrew Bible in Greek translation.

Seven Deadly Sins A medieval list of mortal or deadly sins: pride, covetousness, lust, envy, gluttony, anger, and sloth.

Seven Liberal Arts A medieval grouping of academic disciplines which formed the basis for university education. They were divided into the trivium (grammar, rhetoric, and dialectic) and the quadrivium (arithmetic, geometry, music, and astronomy). It was only after completing a degree in the liberal arts that one could proceed to the higher faculties of law or theology (or, later, medicine).

Sin Within Christian teaching sin refers to both a human condition (original sin) and to specific acts of human beings (actual sin) that are contrary to the eternal will of God. The will of God is expressed through the divine law, which is experienced by every human being, principally through their conscience and moral sense. The classic summary of this law is the Ten Commandments, which Jesus summarized as "love of God" and "love of neighbor." Sin manifests itself in various ways in human life and society (see **Seven Deadly Sins**) but all sin can be traced back to a basic and fundamental distrust of God, which leads to despair or pride before God. The Christian message summons people to repent of their sins, to confess them to God, and to trust in the mercy and forgiveness of God through the salvation accomplished by Jesus.

Son of God A title that is used of several biblical figures (e.g. Adam), but especially of Jesus.

Son of Man A biblical designation that appears in the OT but is especially applied to Jesus in the NT.

Soteriology Greek (soteria): "salvation." Soteriology is the study of the doctrine of salvation in Christian theology.

Special Revelation In contrast to general revelation, which is the natural knowledge of God that the NT teaches all people have on the basis of creation and their reasoning about it, special revelation is the knowledge of God that comes from God's historical self-giving. This knowledge comes through specific historic events and figures, culminating in the coming of Jesus, the Word of God made flesh, as these are attested to in Holy Scripture.

Subjectivism A view in theology and philosophy which maintains that all knowledge is merely personal and relative.

Succession of Bishops see **Apostolic Succession**

Synoptic Gospels Greek (synopsis): "view together with." The Gospels of Matthew, Mark, and Luke. If one views these three gospel narratives alongside each other one sees that they generally follow the same outline and contain a number of the same pericopes (frequently modified from one gospel to the next). Approximately 90 percent of the material in the Gospel of John is unique to John, so it is not a synoptic gospel.

Synoptic Problem The modern and contemporary problem for explaining why the three synoptic gospels (Mark, Matthew, and Luke) have so much in common, in many cases verbatim agreement, and yet are so different from one another. The most common solution to this problem has been the so-called four-source theory. According to this theory, Mark was composed first and later served as the basic outline for the other two synoptic gospels, Matthew and Luke. They in turn drew upon a source they had in common (see **Q**), while also drawing upon material that appears only in Matthew ("M Source") and only in Luke ("L Source").

Systematic Theology Systematic theology explores the most pressing methodological issues in Christian theology and seeks to set forth a coherent summary of the principal doctrines or teachings of Christian theology in and for the present situation. It is further divided into fundamental theology (which examines the methodological issues) and doctrinal theology (which articulates a systematic account of contemporary Christian teaching).

Teleological Argument The argument for the reality that is made on the basis of the detection of purpose, design, and order in the universe. This is also called "the argument from design."

Theism The general belief in God (Greek: "theos").

Theistic Evolution The view that God the creator in some way is involved in the mechanisms that drive evolution in nature.

Theodicy This term combines the Greek word for "God" ("theos") with the Greek word for "justice" ("dike"). The term, coined by the Lutheran theologian Leibniz in the early eighteenth century, has been used in the modern period to refer to various attempts to justify God in view of suffering and evil. These attempts have been responses to the classic question of theodicy, namely, "If God is perfectly good and perfectly omnipotent, why is there evil and suffering in the world?"

Theologian One who thinks and speaks about God and about everything else in relation to God.

Theologian of the Cross One who thinks about God on the basis of reflection on the suffering and death of Christ on the cross. This expression was made popular by Martin Luther in his Heidelberg Debate (1518). Luther contrasted a theologian of the cross, who believes and understands God in accord with God's self-giving revelation in the cross of Christ, with a theologian of glory, who he thought speculates about the nature of God apart from this revelation of God in Christ. Luther accused most medieval Catholic theologians of being theologians of glory.

Theologian of Glory see **Theologian of the Cross**

Theological Anthropology A theological understanding of human beings, their nature and condition, and their goal in God's plan of salvation.

Theological Encyclopedia This term is used in two different ways in Christian theology. On the one hand, it refers to a brief account of the theological disciplines and their problems. On the other hand, it refers to multi–volume projects that seek to give a complete account of issues and topics in theology. This book is an example of an attempt at the former, while the multi–volume *Religion Past and Present* is an example of the latter.

Theology (Theologia) Greek: "speaking or thinking of God" ("theos" = god; "*logos*" = "word, speech, thought"). Theology is any reflection on God or gods. Christian academic theology seeks to develop a systematic, historical, and practical understanding of God as revealed in the apostolic witness to

Jesus Christ. Theology properly is "thinking about God," but theolog thinks about other matters (e.g. human beings, the world) in relation to or "under the aspect of God" (Aquinas).

Theology of the Cross see **Theologian of the Cross**

Theophany Greek: "appearance of God." An example of a theophany in the Christian Bible is the manifestation of God (or God's "backside") to Moses in the OT.

Tradition Within Christian theology this refers to the "handing on" or "passing over" of Christian teaching and practices. See 1 Cor. 15.1ff., where Paul defines the gospel about Jesus' death and resurrection as a tradition. Roman Catholics and Protestants disagree about the role of "tradition" in theological reflection, but both of these Christian traditions acknowledge the importance of "tradition" in Christian teaching.

Transcendence A term that the philosopher Karl Jaspers used in place of "God" to refer to that dimension of human existence that raises questions about one's life as a whole. More recently the American sociologist of religion, Peter Berger, has used the term to refer to that which is beyond this world without necessarily restricting it to "God." In Christian theology, the transcendence of God means that God is beyond that which God creates.

Trinity A central Christian affirmation about God is that God is "triune." There is only one God and yet this one God has revealed himself to be the Father who sends forth his *Logos* (the Son of God) into the world, who bears witness to the Father and who promises the gift of the Holy Spirit, "whom the Father will send in my name." The dogma of the Trinity developed over a long period of time, as Christians reflected upon the life and teachings of Jesus, his witness to God the Father, and the experience of the gift of the Holy Spirit at Pentecost (Acts 2). Christian theologians make a distinction between the "economic Trinity," which refers to the Father, the Son, and the Holy Spirit in their work of creation and salvation, and the "immanent Trinity," which refers to the Father, the Son, and the Holy Spirit in their eternal and essential relationship with one another "from all eternity."

Two Books of Nature and Scripture The traditional Christian view that God reveals himself both through the natural world and through Scripture and that these two revelations, properly understood, complement each other. Each can be understood to be like a book that one interprets. On the one hand, nature or the universe is understood and interpreted to be the orderly, intelligible, substantial creation of God. On the other hand, the Scriptures bear witness to God's creative and redemptive activity in history. Moreover, the knowledge that one receives from the study of nature can be brought into creative relationship with the knowledge of God that is given through Scripture, and vice versa.

Two-language Theory of Science and Religion This is a view of the relationship

...ween science and religion which holds that religion speaks about about values" and "morals," and science speaks about "facts." Such speakings are understood to be two different languages that may or may not be translatable into the language of the other. Recent thinkers who have set forth this theory include the theologian Langdon Gilkey and the paleontologist Stephen Jay Gould.

Uncaused Cause A philosophical phrase that is used for God in arguments based on the distinction between contingent being and necessary being. God alone is uncaused cause of contingent being.

Unmoved Mover Another philosophical phrase that people use for God in arguments based on the observation of motion. According to Aquinas' first way, nothing is completely the source of its own movement or change. From this, Aquinas believed that ultimately there must have been an unmoved Mover who first put things in motion. This is God.

Verbal Inspiration The teaching that the very words of Scripture are divinely inspired ("God–breathed").

Word of God see **Logos**

Wrath (Divine Wrath) The biblical teaching that God is angry with sin and judges it with divine judgment.

YHWH ("The LORD") The so-called "tetragrammaton" (four-letter word) is the Hebrew word for the proper name of God. Normally Jews and Christians do not attempt to say this name out of respect for it and in view of the Second Commandment ("Do not take the name of the LORD your God in vain."). Instead when they come across this name in Scripture they will say another word, the Hebrew word for "Lord." In most Christian Bibles this divine name is rendered as "LORD."

Select Bibliography

Aland, Kurt and Barbara Aland. *The Text of the New Testament*. 2nd edn. Translated by Erroll F. Rhodes. Grand Rapids: Eerdmans, 1989.

Alexander, Eben. *Proof of Heaven*. New York: Simon and Schuster, 2012.

Alhstrom, Sydney E. "What's Lutheran about Higher Education?—A Critique." *Papers and Proceedings of the 60th Annual Convention*, 8–16. Washington, DC: Lutheran Educational Conference of North America, 1974.

Alston, William P. *Perceiving God: The Epistemology of Religious Experience*. Ithaca: Cornell University Press, 1991.

Alter, Robert. *The Art of Biblical Narrative*. 2nd edn. Basic Books, 2011.

Alter, Robert and Frank Kermode (eds). *The Literary Guide to the Bible*. Cambridge: Harvard University Press, 1990.

Alterman, Eric. *It Ain't No Sin to Be Glad You're Alive: The Promise of Bruce Springsteen*. Boston: Back Bay Books, 2001.

Althaus, Paul. *The Theology of Martin Luther*. Translated by Robert C. Schultz. Minneapolis: Fortress Press, 1966.

Anselm of Canterbury. *Basic Writings*. 2nd edn. Translated by S. N. Deane. Introduction by Charles Hartshorne. La Salle, IL: Open Court Classics, 1962.

d'Aquili, Eugene G. and Andrew B. Newberg. *The Mystical Mind: Probing the Biology of Religious Experience*. Minneapolis: Fortress, 1999.

Aquinas, Thomas. *The Summa Theologica*. Translated by the Fathers of the English Dominican Province New York: Benziger Brothers, 1947.

—*The Summa contra Gentiles*. Translated by Anton Pegis. South Bend: University of Notre Dame Press, 2001.

Aristotle. *Metaphysics*. Translated by W. D. Ross. In *The Basic Works of Aristotle*. Edited by Richard McKeon. New York: Random House, 1941.

Ashbrook, James and C. R. Albright. *The Humanizing Brain: Where Religion and Neuroscience Meet*. Cleveland: Pilgrim, 1997.

Augustine of Hippo. *On Christian Doctrine*. Translated by D. W. Robertson. New York: Liberal Arts Press, 1958.

—*The Literal Meaning of Genesis*. 2 vols. Translated by John Hammond Taylor. New York: Newman, 1982.

—*The City of God*. Translated by Henry Bettenson. New York: Penguin, 1984.

—*Confessions*. Translated by Henry Chadwick. New York: Oxford University Press, 1991.

—*The Trinity*. The Works of St. Augustine: A Translation for the 21st Century. Translated by Edmund Hill. Brooklyn: New City Press, 1991.

—*Sermons*. The Works of St. Augustine: A Translation for the 21st Century. Part 3. Vol. 4. Edited by John E. Rotelle. Translated by Edmund Hill. Brooklyn, NY: New City Press, 1992.

Aulén, Gustav. *The Faith of the Christian Church*. 4th edn. Translated by Eric H. Wahlstrom and G. Everett Arden. Philadelphia: Muhlenberg, 1948.

Bailey, James L. and Lyle D. Vander Broek. *Literary Forms in the New Testament: A Handbook*. Louisville: Westminster John Knox Press, 1992.

Baillie, John, ed. *The Idea of Revelation in Recent Thought*. New York: Columbia University Press, 1956.

—*Natural Theology: Comprising "Nature and Grace" by Professor Dr. Emil Brunner and the reply "No!" by Dr. Karl Barth*. Translated by Peter Fraenkel. Eugene, OR: Wipf & Stock, 2002.

von Balthasar, Hans Urs. *The Glory of the Lord: A Theological Aesthetics*. 7 vols. Various translators. New York: Crossroad, 1982.

Barbour, Ian. *Religion and Science: Historical and Contemporary Issues*. San Francisco: Harper San Francisco, 1997.

Barr, James. "Revelation through history in the OT and in modern theology." *Interpretation* 17 (1963), 193–205.

—*The Scope and Authority of the Bible* (Philadelphia: Westminster, 1980) [Helpful essays that espouse a view of biblical authority that complements the one presented in this chapter. Barr has been a strong critic of Fundamentalist understandings of biblical authority.]

—*Old and New in Interpretation*. New York: Harper and Row, 1966.

Barrett, David, George Kurian, and Todd Johnson (eds). *World Christian Encyclopedia*. 2nd edn. 2 vols. New York: Oxford University Press, 2001.

Barth, Karl. *The Epistle to the Romans*. Translated by Edwyn C. Hoskyns. 6th ed. London: Oxford University Press, 1933.

—*Church Dogmatics*. 13 vols. Translated by G. W. Bromiley. Edinburgh: T & T Clark, 1936–9.

—*The Word of God and the Word of Man*. Translated by Douglas Horton. New York: Harper & Row, 1957.

—*Evangelical Theology: An Introduction*. Translated by Grover Foley. Grand Rapids: Eerdmans, 1979.

—*Wolfgang Amadeus Mozart*. Translated by Clarence K. Pott. Grand Rapids: Eerdmans, 1986.

Bauer, Walter. *Orthodoxy and Heresey in Early Christianity*. Edited by Robert A. Kraft and Gerhard Krodel. Translated by Paul J. Achtemeier et al. Minneapolis: Fortress Press Press, 1971.

Bayer, Oswald. *Theology the Lutheran Way*. Edited and translated by Jeffrey
    G. Silcock and Mark C. Mattes. Lutheran Quarterly Books. Grand Rapids:
    Eerdmans, 2007.
—"A public mystery." *Lutheran Quarterly* 26 (Summer 2012), 125–41.
Becker, Ernest. *The Denial of Death*. New York: Free Press, 1975.
Becker, Matthew L. "Schweitzer's quests for Jesus and Paul." *Concordia Journal*
    28 (October 2002), 409–30.
—*The Self-Giving God and Salvation History: The Trinitarian Theology of
    Johannes von Hofmann*. New York: T & T Clark, 2004.
—"Werner Elert in retrospect." *Lutheran Quarterly* 20 (Autumn 2006),
    249–302.
—"The Shape of Theology as a University *Wissenschaft*: Schleiermacher's
    Reflection in Hofmann's *Theological Encyclopedia*." *Papers of the Nineteenth-
    Century Theology Group* 37 (American Academy of Religion) (November
    2006), 103–27.
Begbie, Jeremy S. *Voicing Creation's Praise: Towards a Theology of the Arts*.
    New York: T & T Clark, 1991.
—*Beholding the Glory: The Incarnation through the Arts*. Grand Rapids: Baker,
    2000.
Behe, Michael. *Darwin's Black Box*. New York: The Free Press, 1996.
Bellah, Robert. *Religion in Human Evolution*. Cambridge: Harvard University
    Press, 2011.
Berger, Peter. *The Sacred Canopy: Elements of a Sociological Theory of Religion*.
    Garden City, New York: Doubleday & Company Inc., 1967.
—*A Rumor of Angels: Modern Society and the Rediscovery of the Supernatural*.
    New York: Anchor, 1970.
—*The Desecularization of the World*. Grand Rapids: Eerdmans, 1999.
Bertram, Robert. "How a Lutheran Does Theology: Some Clues from the
    Lutheran Confessions," in *Lutheran-Episcopal Dialogue: Report and
    Recommendations*. Edited by William G. Weinhauer and Robert L.
    Wietelman, 73–87. Cincinnati: Forward Movement Publications, 1981.
—"Review symposium on revelation and theology: *The Gospel as Narrated
    Promise* by Ronald Thiemann." *Dialog* 26 (Winter 1987), 69–71.
Betz, Hans Dieter et al. (eds). *Religion Past and Present*. 13 vols. New York:
    Brill, 2009–2013.
Bird, D. L. and Simon G. Smith (eds). *Theology and Religious Studies in Higher
    Education*. New York: Continuum, 2009.
Bonaventure. *The Mind's Road to God*. Translated by George Boas. Upper
    Saddle River, NJ: Prentice Hall, 1953.
Bond, Helen, Seth Kunin, and Francesca Murphy (eds). *Religious Studies
    and Theology: An Introduction*. Washington Square, New York: New York
    University Press, 2003.

Bonhoeffer, Dietrich. *Letters and Papers from Prison*. Edited by John W. De Gruchy. Translated by Isabel Best and others. Vol. 8 of Dietrich Bonhoeffer Works, edited by Victoria J. Barnett and Barbara Wojhoski. Minneapolis: Fortress, 2010.

Boyer, Ernest. *College: The Undergraduate Experience in America*. New York: Harper and Row, 1987.

Braaten, Carl E., and Robert W. Jenson (eds). *Christian Dogmatics*. 2 vols. Minneapolis: Fortress Press, 1984.

Brecht, Martin. *Martin Luther*. 3 vols. Minneapolis: Fortress Press, 1985–92.

Brondos, David A. "On the vital role of theology today." *Dialog* 50 (Fall 2011), 221–2.

Brown, Frank Burch. *Religious Aesthetics*. Princeton: Princeton University Press, 1989.

—*Good Taste, Bad Taste, and Christian Taste: Aesthetics in Religious Life*. New York: Oxford University Press, 2000.

Browning, Don S. *Reviving Christian Humanism: The New Conversation on Spirituality, Theology, and Psychology*. Minneapolis: Fortress, 2010.

Bruce, F. F. *The Canon of Scripture*. Downer's Grove, IL: Intervarsity Press, 1988.

Brunner, Emil. *Dogmatics*. 2 vols. Translated by Olive Wyon. Philadelphia: Westminster, 1950, 1952.

Buckley, Michael J. *At the Origins of Modern Atheism*. New Haven: Yale University Press, 1990.

Bultmann, Rudolf. *Kerygma and Myth*. 2 vols. Edited by Hans Werner Bartsch. Translated by Reginald H. Fuller. London: SPCK, 1957, 1962.

—*New Testament & Mythology and Other Basic Writings*. Edited and translated by Schubert M. Ogden. Minneapolis: Fortress Press Press, 1984.

—*Faith and Understanding*. Edited by Robert W. Funk. Translated by Louise Pettibone Smith. Minneapolis: Fortress Press, 1987.

—*What is Theology?* Edited by Eberhard Jüngel and Klaus W. Müller. Translated by Roy A. Harrisville. Minneapolis: Fortress, 1997.

Burtchaell, James T. *The Dying of the Light: The Disengagement of Colleges and Universities from their Christian Churches*. Grand Rapids: Eerdmans, 1998.

Calvin, John. *Institutes of the Christian Religion*. Four books in two volumes. Edited by John T. McNeill. Translated by Ford Lewis Battles. The Library of Christian Classics. Philadelphia: Westminster, 1960.

Cameron, Euan. *Interpreting Christian History: The Challenge of the Churches' Past*. New York: Blackwell, 2005.

Capps, Walter. *Religious Studies: The Making of a Discipline*. Minneapolis: Augsburg Fortress Press, 1995.

Chopp, Rebecca and Sheila Davaney (eds). *Horizons in Feminist Theology: Identity, Tradition and Norms* Minneapolis: Fortress Press, 1997.

Clark, Kelly James and Justin L. Barrett. "Reidian religious epistemology and the cognitive science of religion." *Journal of the American Academy of Religion* 79/3 (September 2011), 639–75.

Collier, Andrew. *Critical Realism.* London: Verso, 1993.

Collins, Francis. *The Language of God: A Scientist Presents Evidence for Belief.* New York: Free Press, 2006.

Conee, Earl and Theodore Sider. *Riddles of Existence: A Guided Tour of Metaphysics.* Oxford: Clarendon, 2005.

Connolly, Peter. *Approaches to the Study of Religion.* New York: Continuum, 2001.

Cooper, Terry. *Paul Tillich and Psychology: Historic and Contemporary Explorations in Theology, Psychotherapy, and Ethics.* Macon: Mercer University Press, 2006.

—*Reinhold Niebuhr and Psychology: The Ambiguities of the Self.* Macon: Mercer University Press, 2009.

—*Don Browning and Psychology.* Macon, GA: Mercer University Press, 2011.

Craig, Edward, ed. *Routledge Encyclopedia of Philosophy.* 10 vols. New York: Routledge, 2000.

Craig, William Lane and J. P. Moreland (eds). *The Blackwell Companion to Natural Theology.* Oxford: Blackwell, 2009.

Cross, F. L. and E. A. Livingstone (eds). *The Oxford Dictionary of the Christian Church.* 3rd rev. edn. Oxford: Oxford University Press, 2005.

Cunningham, Lawrence S. and John Kelsay. *The Sacred Quest: An Invitation to the Study of Religion.* 3rd edn. Upper Saddle River, NJ: Prentice Hall, 2002.

Danker, Frederick William, ed. *A Greek–English Lexicon of the New Testament and other Early Christian Literature.* 3rd ed.. Based on Walter Bauer's *Greichischdeutsches Wörterbuch zu den Schriften des Neuen Testaments und der frühchristlichen Literaur.* 6th edn. Translated by William F. Arndt, F. Wilbur Gingrich, and Frederick W. Danker. Chicago: The University of Chicago Press, 2000.

Darwin, Charles. *Life and Letters.* 2 vols. Edited by Francis Darwin. London: Murray, 1888.

—*The Autobiography of Charles Darwin 1809–1882.* Edited by Nora Barlow. London: Collins, 1958.

Davies, Brian. *The Thought of Thomas Aquinas.* Oxford: Clarendon, 1992.

Davies, Paul. *The Mind of God.* New York: Touchstone, 1993.

Dawkins, Richard. *The Blind Watchmaker: Why the Evidence of Evolution Reveals a Universe without Design.* New York: W. W. Norton, 1994.

—*The God Delusion.* Boston: Houghton Mifflin, 2006.

Dawn, Marva J. *Reaching Out without Dumbing Down: A Theology of Worship for This Urgent Time.* Grand Rapids: Eerdmans, 1995.

Dembski, William, ed. *Mere Creation*. Downer's Grove, IL: InterVarsity Press, 1998.

Dennett, Daniel. *Breaking the Spell: Religion as a Natural Phenomenon*. New York: Viking, 2006.

Denzey, Nicola. *The Bone Gatherers: The Lost Worlds of Early Christian Women*. Boston: Beacon, 2007.

Denzingner, Henricus and Peter Hunermann (eds). *Enchiridion Symbolorum: Definitionum et Declarationum De Rebus Fidei et Morum*. 43rd edn. Freiburg: Herder, 2010.

Derrida, Jacques. *Aporias*. Translated by D. Dutoit. Stanford: Stanford University Press, 1993.

Descartes, René. *Meditations on First Philosophy* [1641]. Cambridge Texts in the History of Philosophy. Edited by John Cottingham. Cambridge: Cambridge University Press, 1996.

Dulles, Avery. *Models of Revelation*. Revised edn. Garden City, New York: Doubleday, 1985.

Dunn, James D. G. "The new perspective on Paul." *Bulletin of the John Rylands University Library of Manchester* 65 (1983), 95–122.

Ebeling, Gerhard. *Word and Faith*. Translated by James W. Leitch. London: SCM Press, 1963.

—*The Study of Theology*. Translated by Duane A. Priebe. Minneapolis: Fortress Press, 1978.

—*The Truth of the Gospel: An Exposition of Galatians*. Translated by David Green. Minneapolis: Fortress Press Press, 1985.

Elert, Werner. *The Christian Faith: An Outline of Lutheran Dogmatics*. Translated by Martin Bertram and Walter Bouman. Columbus: Lutheran Theological Seminary, 1974.

Eliade, Mircea. *The Sacred and the Profane: The Nature of Religion*. Translated by Willard Trask. New York: Harcourt Brace Jovanovich, 1959.

Ellwood, Robert S. and Barbara A. McGraw. *Many Peoples, Many Faiths: Women and Men in the World Religions*. 7th edn. Upper Saddle River, NJ: Prentice Hall, 2002.

Empie, Paul C., T. Austin Murphy, and Joseph A. Burgess (eds). *Teaching Authority and Infallibility in the Church: Lutherans and Catholics in Dialogue VI*. Minneapolis: Augsburg, 1980.

Eusebius of Caesarea. *The Church History*. Translated by Paul L. Maier. Grand Rapids: Kregel Academic, 2007.

Fackenheim, Emil. *The Jewish Return into History: Reflections in the Age of Auschwitz and a New Jerusalem*. New York: Schocken Books, 1978.

Fahlbusch, Erwin et al. (eds). *The Encyclopedia of Christianity*. 5 vols. Translated by Geoffrey W. Bromiley. Grand Rapids: Eerdmans, 1998–2008.

Farley, Edward. *Theologia: The Fragmentation and Unity of Theological Education*. Minneapolis: Augsburg Fortress, 1983.

—"The Place of Theology in the Study of Religion." *Religious Studies and Theology* 5 (September 1985), 9–29.

—*The Fragility of Knowledge: Theological Education in the Church and the University*. Minneapolis: Fortress Press, 1988.

Ferguson, Everette, ed. *Encyclopedia of Early Christianity*. New York: Garland, 1990.

Feuerbach, Ludwig. *The Essence of Christianity*. Translated by George Eliot. New York: Harper & Row, 1957.

Fichte, Johann G. *Introductions to the Wissenschaftslehre and Other Writings*. Edited and translated by Daniel Breazeale. Indianapolis: Hackett, 1994.

Fiorenza, Francis Schüssler and John P. Galvin (eds). *Systematic Theology: Roman Catholic Perspectives*. 2nd edn Minneapolis: Fortress, 2011.

Flew, Antony and Gary R. Habermas. "Exclusive Interview with Antony Flew." *Philosophia Christi*. Vol. 6, no. 2 (Winter 2004), 197–212.

Flew, Antony and Roy Abraham Varghese. *There is a God: How the World's Most Notorious Atheist Changed His Mind*. New York: HarperOne, 2007.

Ford, David, Ben Quash, and Janet Martin Soskice (eds). *Christian Wisdom: Desiring God and Learning in Love*. Cambridge: Cambridge University Press, 2007.

Ford, David F. et al. (eds). *Fields of Faith: Theology and Religious Studies for the Twenty-first Century*. Cambridge: Cambridge University Press, 2004.

Forde, Gerhard O. *On Being a Theologian of the Cross: Reflections on Luther's Heidelberg Disputation, 1518*. Grand Rapids: Eerdmans, 1997.

Forell, George. *The Protestant Faith*. Minneapolis: Fortress Press, 1962.

Fredericks, James L. *Faith among Faiths: Christian Theology and Non-Christian Religions*. New York: Paulist, 1999.

Freedman, David Noel, ed. *The Anchor Bible Dictionary*. 6 vols. New York: Doubleday, 1992.

Frei, Hans. *The Eclipse of the Biblical Narrative*. New Haven: Yale University Press, 1974.

—*Types of Christian Theology*. Edited by George Hunsinger and William C. Placher. New Haven: Yale University Press, 1992.

Frend, W. H. C. *The Rise of Christianity*. Minneapolis: Fortress Press, 1984.

Freud, Sigmund. *The Future of an Illusion*. Translated by W. D. Robson-Scott and revised by J. Strachey. Garden City, NY: Doubleday Anchor Books, 1964.

—*Moses and Monotheism*. New York: Vintage, 1967.

Frye, Northrop. *The Great Code: The Bible and Literature*. New York: Harcourt Brace Jovanovich, 1981.

Gadamer, Hans-Georg. "The Future of the European Humanities," in

Hans–Georg Gadamer on Education, Poetry, and History: Applied Hermeneutics. Edited by Dieter Misgeld and Graeme Nicholson. Translated by Lawrence Schmidt and Monica Reuss. Albany: State University of New York Press, 1992.

—Truth and Method, 2d edn. Translated by J. Weinsheimer and D. G. Marshall. New York: Crossroad, 1989.

Geertz, Clifford. "Religion as a Cultural System," in *Reader in Comparative Religion: An Anthropological Approach*. 4th edn. Edited by William A. Lessa and Evon Z. Vogt. New York: Harper and Row, 1979.

Gerhard, John. *On the Nature of Theology and Scripture*. Vol. 1 of *Theological Commonplaces*. Translated by Richard Dinda. St. Louis: Concordia, 2006.

Gerrish, B. A. *Grace and Reason: A Study in Luther's Theology*. Oxford: Clarendon, 1962.

—*The Old Protestantism and the New*. Edinburgh: T & T Clark, 1982.

—*Saving and Secular Faith: An Invitation to Systematic Theology*. Minneapolis: Fortress, 1999.

—*A Prince of the Church: Schleiermacher and the Beginnings of Modern Theology*. Eugene, OR: Wipf and Stock, 2001.

Gilkey, Langdon. *Maker of Heaven and Earth: The Christian Doctrine of Creation in the Light of Modern Knowledge*. New York: Anchor Books, 1965.

—*Naming the Whirlwind: The Renewal of God-Language*. Indianapolis: Bobbs-Merrill, 1969.

—*Religion and the Scientific Future*. San Francisco: Harper and Row, 1970.

—*Message and Existence*. New York: Seabury, 1981.

—*Creationism on Trial*. San Francisco: Harper and Row, 1985.

Gilpin, W. Clark. *A Preface to Theology*. Chicago: University of Chicago Press, 1996.

Gingerich, Owen. *God's Universe*. Cambridge: Harvard University Press, 2006.

Glazier, Stephen D., ed. *Anthropology of Religion*. Westport, CT: Greenwood, 1997.

Goethe, Johann Wolfgang von. *Faust I and II*. In *Goethe: The Collected Works*. Vol. 2. Edited and translated by Stuart Atkins. Princeton: Princeton University Press, 1984.

González-Andrieu, Cecilia. *Bridge to Wonder: Art as a Gospel of Beauty*. Waco: Baylor University Press, 2012.

Gould, Stephen Jay. *Rocks of Ages: Science and Religion in the Fullness of Life*. New York: Ballantine, 1999.

Grant, Robert M. *Heresy and Criticism: The Search for Authenticity in Early Christian Literature* Louisville: Westminster John Knox Press, 1993.

Grenz, Stanley J. *Theology for the Community of God*. Grand Rapids: Eerdmans, 2000.

Grenz, Stanley J. and Roger E. Olson. *Who Needs Theology? An Invitation to the Study of God*. Downers Grove: Intervarsity, 1996.

Gunn, Giles B. *Interpretation of Otherness: Literature, Religion and the American Imagination*. New York: Oxford University Press, 1979.

Gutiérrez, Gustavo. *A Theology of Liberation*. London: SCM Press, 1973.

Hall, Douglas John. *Thinking the Faith: Christian Theology in a North American Context*. Minneapolis: Fortress, 1991.

Hanson, Bradley C. *An Introduction to Christian Theology*. Minneapolis: Fortress, 1997.

Harnack, Adolf von. *History of Dogma*. 7 vols. Translated by Neil Buchanan. New York: Dover, 1961.

Harris, Sam. *The End of Faith: Religion, Terror, and the Future of Reason*. New York: W. W. Norton & Company, 2004.

Hart, David Bentley. *The Beauty of the Infinite: The Aesthetics of Christian Truth*. Grand Rapids: Eerdmans, 2003.

Hartshorne, Charles. *Man's Vision of God*. New York: Harper and Row, 1941.

—*Anselm's Discovery*. La Salle, IL: Open Court Publishing, 1965.

Hartshorne, Charles and William L. Reese (eds). *Philosophers Speak of God*. Chicago: University of Chicago Press, 1953.

Harvey, Van A. *The Historian and the Believer: The Morality of Historical Knowledge and Belief*. Urbana, IL: University of Illinois Press, 1996.

Hastings, Adrian, ed. *A World History of Christianity*. Grand Rapids: Eerdmans, 1999.

Hauerwas, Stanley. *Against the Nations: War and Survival in a Liberal Society*. Minneapolis: Winston, 1985.

Haught, John F. *God after Darwin: A Theology of Evolution*. Boulder: Westview, 2000.

Havel, Vaclav. *Disturbing the Peace: A Conversation with Karel Hvizdala*. Translated by Paul Wilson. New York: Random House, 1990.

Hawking, Stephen and Leonard Mlodinow. *The Grand Design*. New York: Random House, 2010.

Heaney, Seamus. "Seven Wonders." Interview by Maggie Fergusson. *Intelligent Life Magazine* (January/February 2013), 24.

Hefner, Philip. *The Human Factor*. Minneapolis: Augsburg Fortress, 2000.

Hegel, Georg F. *Lectures on the Philosophy of Religion*. 3 vols. Edited by Peter C. Hodgson. Translated by R. F. Brown and others. Berkeley: University of California Press, 1984–5.

Heppe, Heinrich. *Reformed Dogmatics*. Revised and edited by Ernst Bizer. Translated by G. T. Thomson. New York: Harper & Row, 1950.

Herling, Bradley L. *Beginner's Guide to the Study of Religion*. New York: Continuum, 2008.

Hick, John. *Arguments for the Existence of God*. New York: Seabury Press, 1971.

Highton, Mike. *A Theology of Higher Education*. New York: Oxford University Press, 2012.

Hillerbrand, Hans, ed. *Oxford Encyclopedia of the Reformation*. 4 vols. New York: Oxford University Press, 1996.

Hitchens, Christopher. *God is Not Great: How Religion Poisons Everything*. New York: Twelve, 2007.

—*The Portable Atheist: Essential Readings for the Nonbeliever*. Philadelphia: Da Capo Press, 2007.

Hitchens, Peter. *The Rage Against God: How Atheism Led Me to Faith*. Grand Rapids: Zondervan, 2010.

Hodgson, Peter C. *Christian Faith: A Brief Introduction*. Louisville: Westminster John Knox, 2001.

Hodgson, Peter C. and Robert H. King (eds). *Christian Theology: An Introduction to Its Traditions and Tasks*. 2nd edn. Minneapolis: Fortress Press, 1985.

Hopewell, James F. *Congregation: Stories and Structures*. Minneapolis: Fortress Press, 1987.

Howard, Thomas Albert. *Protestant Theology and the Making of the Modern German University*. New York: Oxford University Press, 2006.

Hughes, Richard T. *How Christian Faith Can Sustain the Life of the Mind*. Grand Rapids: Eerdmans, 2001.

Hughes, Richard T. and William B. Adrian (eds). *Models for Christian Higher Education*. Grand Rapids: Eerdmans, 1997.

Hume, David. *Dialogues concerning Natural Religion*. Edited and with an introduction by Norman Kemp Smith. Indianapolis: Bobbs-Merrill, 1977.

—*Writings on Religion*. Edited by Antony Flew. La Salle, IL.: Open Court, 1992.

Husserl, Edmund. *Ideas*. Translated by Boyce Gibson. New York: Macmillan Company, 1931.

Huxley, Thomas Henry. *Agnosticism and Christianity and Other Essays*. Amherst, NY: Prometheus Books, 1992.

Irvin, Dale T. *Christian Histories, Christian Traditioning: Rendering Accounts*. Maryknoll: Orbis, 1998.

Jacobsen, Douglas. *The World's Christians: Who They Are, Where They Are, and How They Got There*. Oxford: Wiley-Blackwell, 2012.

Jacobsen, Douglas and Rhonda Hustedt Jacobsen. *Scholarship and Christian Faith: Enlarging the Conversation*. New York: Oxford University Press, 2004.

—(eds). *The American University in a Postsecular Age*. New York: Oxford University Press, 2008.

—*No Longer Invisible: Religion in University Education*. New York: Oxford University Press, 2012.

James, William. *The Varieties of Religious Experience*. New York: Collier Books, 1961.

—*The Will to Believe and Other Essays in Popular Philosophy*. Cambridge, MA: Harvard UniversityPress, 1979.

Jaspers, Karl. *Philosophy*. 3 vols. Translated by E. B. Ashton. Chicago: University of Chicago Press, 1969–71.

Jeanrond, Werner. *Text and Interpretation as Categories of Theological Thinking*. New York: Crossroad, 1991.

—*Theological Hermeneutics: Development and Significance*. London: SCM Press, 1994.

Jenkins, Philip. *The Lost History of Christianity*. San Francisco: HarperOne, 2008.

Jenson, Robert. *America's Theologian: A Recommendation of Jonathan Edwards*. New York: Oxford University Press, 1992.

—*Systematic Theology*. 2 vols. New York: Oxford University Press, 1997–9.

Johnson, Luke Timothy. *The Real Jesus: The Misguided Quest for the Historical Jesus and the Truth of the Traditional Gospels*. San Francisco: HarperOne, 1997.

—*Living Jesus: Learning the Heart of the Gospel*. San Francisco: HarperOne, 2000.

Johnson, Philip. *Darwin on Trial*. Washington, DC: Regnery Gateway, 1991.

Johnston, Mark. *Saving God: Religion after Idolatry*. Princeton: Princeton University Press, 2009.

Jones, Lindsay, ed. *Encyclopedia of Religion*. 2nd edn. 15 vols. New York: Thomson Gale, 2004.

Josephus, Flavius. *The Complete Works of Josephus*. Translated by William Whiston. Grand Rapids: Kregel, 1981.

Jüngel, Eberhard. *God as the Mystery of the World*. Translated by Darrell L. Guder. Grand Rapids: Eerdmans, 1983.

Kähler, Martin. *The So-called Historical Jesus and the Historic Biblical Christ*. Translated by Carl Braaten. Minneapolis: Fortress Press Press, 1964.

Kant, Immanuel. *Critique of Practical Reason*. Translated by Lewis White Beck. New York: Macmillan, 1956.

—*Religion within the Limits of Reason Alone*. Translated by Theodore M. Greene and Hoyt H. Hudson. New York: Harper and Row, 1960.

—*The Critique of Pure Reason*. Translated by Norman Kemp Smith. New York: St. Martin's Press, 1965.

Kantor, Jean-Michel and Loren Graham. *Naming Infinity: A True Story of Religious Mysticism and Mathematical Creativity*. Cambridge, MA: Harvard University Press, 2009.

Katz, Stephen. *Mysticism and Language*. New York: Oxford University Press, 1992.

Kaufman, Gordon. *Theology for a Nuclear Age*. Philadelphia: Westminster John Knox, 1985.

—*God-Mystery-Diversity: Christian Theology in a Pluralistic World*. Minneapolis: Fortress, 1996.

Kelly, Joseph, ed. *Perspectives on Scripture and Tradition: Essays by Robert M. Grant, Robert E. McNally, and George H. Tavard*. Notre Dame, IN: Fides, 1976.

Kelsey, David H. *To Understand God Truly: What's Theological about a Theological School*. Louisville: Westminster John Knox Press, 1992.

—*Between Athens and Jerusalem: The Theological Education Debate*. Grand Rapids: Eerdmans, 1993.

Kim, J., and E. Susa (eds). *The Blackwell Companion to Metaphysics*. Oxford: Blackwell, 1995.

Kittel, Gerhard and Gerhard Friedrich (eds). *Theological Dictionary of the New Testament*. 10 vols. Translated by Geoffrey W. Bromiley. Grand Rapids: Eerdmans, 1964.

Knowles, David. *The Evolution of Medieval Thought*. 2nd edn. Edited by D. E. Luscombe and C. N. L. Brooke. London and New York: Longman, 1988.

Kolakowski, Leszek. "Concern about God in an Apparently Godless Age," in *My Correct Views on Everything*. Edited by Zbigniew Janowski. South Bend: St. Augustine's Press, 2005.

Kolb, Robert and Timothy J. Wengert (eds). *The Book of Concord: The Confessions of the Evangelical Lutheran Church*. Translated by Charles Arand et al. Minneapolis: Fortress, 2000.

Krentz, Edgar. *The Historical-Critical Method*. Minneapolis: Fortress Press Press, 1975.

Küng, Hans. *Eternal Life: Life after Death as a Medical, Philosophical, and Theological Problem*. Translated by Edward Quinn. New York: Doubleday, 1984

—*Does God Exist? An Answer for Today*. Translated by Edward Quinn. New York: Crossroad, 1991.

Langan, John P., ed. *Catholic Universities in Church and Society: A Dialogue on Ex Corde Ecclesiae*. Washington, DC: Georgetown University Press, 1993.

Lathrop, Gordon W. *Holy Things: A Liturgical Theology*. Minneapolis: Augsburg Fortress, 1993.

Leeuw, Gerardus van der. *Religion in Essence and Manifestation*. 2 vols. New York: Harper and Row, 1963.

—*Sacred and Profane Beauty: The Holy in Art*. Translated by David A. Green. New York: Oxford University Press, 2006.

Leith, John H., ed. *Creeds of the Churches*. 3rd edn. Atlanta: John Knox, 1982.

Lewis, C. S. *The Abolition of Man*. New York: Macmillan, 1947.

—*Mere Christianity*. Revised edn. New York: Macmillan, 1952.

Lewis, Hywell David. *Our Experience of God*. New York, Macmillan 1959.

Lindbeck, George. *The Nature of Doctrine: Religion and Theology in a Postliberal Age*. Philadelphia: Westminster, 1984.

Lindberg, David C. and Ronald L. Numbers, (eds). *God and Nature: Historical Essays on the Encounter Between Christianity and Science*. Berkeley: University of California Press, 1986.

Livingston, James C. *Modern Christian Thought*. 2 vols. 2nd edn. Upper Saddle River, NJ: Pentice-Hall, 1997–2000. *Anatomy of the Sacred: An Introduction to Religion*. 5th edn Upper Saddle River, NJ: Prentice Hall, 2005.

Lohse, Bernhard. *Martin Luther: An Introduction to His Life and Work*. Minneapolis: Fortress Press Press, 1986.

—*Martin Luther's Theology: Its Historical and Systematic Development*. Translated by Roy A. Harrisville. Minneapolis: Fortress Press, 1999.

Lonergan, Bernard. *Method in Theology*. New York: Seabury, 1972.

—*Philosophy of God and Theology*. London: Darton, Longman & Todd, 1973.

Lüdemann, Gerd. *Heretics: The Other Side of Early Christianity*. Translated by John Bowden. Louisville: Westminster John Knox, 1996.

Ludwig, Theodore M. *The Sacred Paths: Understanding the Religions of the World*. 4th edn. Upper Saddle River, NJ: Pearson Prentice Hall, 2005.

Lundin, Roger, ed., *Christ across the Disciplines: Past, Present, Future*. Grand Rapids: Eerdmans, 2013.

Luther, Martin. *Luther's Works* (American Edition). 55 vols. Edited by Jaroslav Pelikan and Helmut T. Lehmann. St. Louis and Minneapolis: Concordia and Fortress Press, 1955–86.

Lyotard, Jean François. *The Postmodern Condition: A Report on Knowledge*. Translated by Geoff Benington and Brian Massumi. Minneapolis: University of Minnesota Press, 1984.

MacCulloch, Diarmaid. *Christianity: The First Three Thousand Years*. New York: Penguin, 2011.

MacHaffie, Barbara J. *Her Story: Women in Christian Tradition*. 2nd edn. Minneapolis: Augsburg, 2006.

MacIntyre, Alasdair. *Whose Justice? Which Rationality?* Notre Dame, IN: University of Notre Dame Press, 1988.

MacIntyre, Alasdair and Paul Ricoeur. *The Religious Significance of Atheism*. New York: Columbia University Press, 1969.

Macquarrie, John. *Principles of Christian Theology*. 2nd edn. New York: Charles Scribner's Sons, 1977.

Malcolm, Norman. "Anselm's Ontological Arguments." *Philosophical Review* 69 (1960), 41–62.

Marsden, George. *The Soul of the American University: From Protestant Establishment to Established Nonbelief*. New York: Oxford University Press, 1994.

—*The Outrageous Idea of Christian Scholarship*. New York: Oxford University Press, 1997.

Marshall, Bruce. *Trinity and Truth*. Cambridge: Cambridge University Press, 2000.

Marty, Martin. *A Nation of Behaviors*. Chicago: University of Chicago Press, 1977.

—*Protestantism*. New York: Doubleday, 1995.

—*Education, Religion, and the Common Good: Advancing a Distinctly American Conversation about Religion's Role in Our Shared Life*. San Francisco: Jossey-Bass, 2000.

Marx, Karl and Friedrich Engels. *Marx and Engels on Religion*. New York: Schocken, 1964.

Mason, Richard. *The God of Spinoza: A Philosophical Study*. Cambridge: Cambridge University Press, 1997.

Mattes, Mark. *The Role of Justification in Contemporary Theology*. Lutheran Quarterly Books. Grand Rapids: Eerdmans, 2004.

McFague, Sallie. *Models of God: Theology for an Ecological, Nuclear Age*. Minneapolis: Fortress Press, 1987.

McGinn, Bernard. *The Doctors of the Church: Thirty-three Men and Women Who Shaped Christianity*. 2nd edn. New York: Crossroad, 2009.

McGrath, Alister E. *Science and Religion: An Introduction*. Oxford: Blackwell, 1999.

—*The Open Secret: A New Vision for Natural Theology*. Oxford: Blackwell, 2008.

—*A Fine-Tuned Universe: The Quest for God in Science and Theology*. Louisville: Westminster John Knox, 2009.

Christian Theology: An Introduction. 5th edn. Oxford: Wiley-Blackwell, 2011.

McManners, John, ed. *The Oxford Illustrated History of Christianity*. New York: Oxford University Press, 1990.

Meier, John P. *A Marginal Jew: Rethinking the Historical Jesus*. 3 vols. New York: Doubleday, 1991–2009.

Melanchthon, Philip. *Loci Communes* (1521). Edited and Translated by Charles Leander Hill. Boston: Meador, 1944.

—*Loci Communes* (1555). Edited and translated by Clyde Manschreck. New York: Oxford University Press, 1965.

—"On the Distinction between the Gospel and Philosophy," in *Philipp Melanchthon: Orations on Philosophy and Education*. Edited by Sachiko Kusukawa. Translated by Christine F. Salazar. Cambridge Texts in the History of Philosophy. Cambridge: Cambridge University Press, 1999.

Migliore, Daniel L. *Faith Seeking Understanding: An Introduction to Christian Theology*. 2nd edn. Grand Rapids: Eerdmans, 2004.

Milbank, John. *Theology and Social Theory: Beyond Secular Reason*. Oxford: Blackwell, 1990.

Miller, Eddie LeRoy. *God and Reason: An Invitation to Philosophical Theology*. 2nd edn. Englewood Cliffs, NJ: Prentice–Hall, 1995.

Miller, Kenneth. *Finding Darwin's God: A Scientist's Search for Common Ground between God and Evolution*. New York: HarperCollins, 1999.

Moltmann, Jürgen. *Theology of Hope*. Translated by James W. Leitch. London: SCM Press, 1967.

Morris, Brian. *Anthropological Studies of Religion*. New York: Cambridge University Press, 1987.

Moule, C. F. D. *The Birth of the New Testament*. 3rd edn. New York: Harper and Row, 1982.

Murphy, George L. *The Cosmos in the Light of the Cross*. Harrisburg: Trinity Press International, 2003.

Murphy, Nancey. *Reconciling Science and Religion: A Radical Reformation Perspective*. Oakland, CA: Pandora, 1997.

Musser, Donald W. and Joseph L. Price (eds). *A New Handbook of Christian Theology*. Nashville: Abingdon, 1992.

Nagel, Thomas. *Mind and Cosmos: Why the Materialist Neo-Darwinian Conception of Nature is Almost Certainly False*. New York: Oxford University Press, 2012.

Neville, Robert Cummings. *Behind the Masks of God: An Essay Toward Comparative Theology*. Albany: State University of New York Press, 1991.

Newberg, Andrew B. *Principles of Neurotheology*. Surrey, England: Ashgate, 2010.

Newberg, Andrew, Eugene D'Aquili, and Vince Rause. *Why God Won't Go Away: Brain Science and the Biology of Belief*. New York: Ballantine, 2001.

Newman, John Henry. *The Idea of a University Defined and Illustrated*. Edited by I. T. Ker. Oxford: Clarendon Press, 1976.

Newport, Frank. *God is Alive and Well: The Future of Religion in America*. Berkeley: Gallup, Inc., 2012.

Niebuhr, H. Richard. *Christ and Culture*. New York: Harper and Row, 1951.

Nietzsche, Friedrich. *Thus Spoke Zarathustra*. Translated by Walter Kaufmann. New York: Viking, 1966.

—*The Gay Science*. Translated by Walter Kaufmann. New York: Random House Vintage Books, 1974.

—*Human, All Too Human: A Book for Free Spirits*. Translated by R. J. Hollingdale. Cambridge: Cambridge University Press, 1986.

Noll, Mark. *The Scandal of the Evangelical Mind*. Grand Rapids: Eerdmans, 1994.

Numbers, Ronald L. *The Creationists*. Berkeley: University of California Press, 1993.

—*Rethinking Fundamental Theology: Toward a New Fundamental Theology*. New York: Oxford University Press, 2011.

O'Collins, Gerald. *Fundamental Theology*. New York: Paulist, 1981.

Ogden, Schubert M. *The Reality of God and Other Essays*. New York: Harper and Row, 1963.

—*On Theology*. Dallas: Southern Methodist University Press, 1992.

Oliver, Dianne L. "Religion as 'Truth-Claims,'" in *Introduction to Religious Studies*. Edited by Paul O. Myhre. Winona, MH: Anselm Academic, 2009.

Oppy, Graham. *Arguing about Gods*. Cambridge: Cambridge University Press, 2006.

Otto, Rudolf. *The Idea of the Holy*. Translated by John W. Harvey. London: Oxford University Press, 1923.

Paley, William. *Natural Theology: Selections*. Edited with an introduction by F. Ferré. Indianapolis: Bobbs-Merrill, 1963.

Pals, Daniel L. *Seven Theories of Religion*. New York: Oxford University Press, 1995.

Pannenberg, Wolfhart, ed. *Revelation as History*. Translated by David Granskou London: The Macmillan Company, 1968.

—*Theology and the Philosophy of Science*. Translated by Francis McDonagh. Philadelphia: Westminster, 1976.

—*Basic Questions in Theology*. 2 vols. Translated by George H. Kehm. Philadelphia: Westminster, 1983.

—*Christianity in a Secularized World*. New York: Crossroad, 1989.

—*An Introduction to Systematic Theology*. Translated by Philip Clayton. Grand Rapids: Eerdmans, 1991.

—*Systematic Theology*. 3 vols. Translated by Geoffrey W. Bromiley. Grand Rapids: Eerdmans, 1991–8.

—*Toward a Theology of Nature: Essays on Science and Faith*. Edited by Ted Peters. Louisville: Westminster John Knox, 1993.

Parks, Sharon Daloz. *Big Questions, Worthy Dreams: Mentoring Young Adults in Their Search for Meaning, Purpose, and Faith*. San Francisco: Jossey-Bass, 2000.

Pascal, Blaise. *Pensees*. Translated by A. J. Krailsheimer. New York: Penguin, 1966.

Peacocke, Arthur. *Theology for a Scientific Age*. 2nd edn. Minneapolis: Augsburg Fortress, 1993.

Pelikan, Jaroslav. *The Christian Tradition: A History of the Development of Doctrine*. 5 vols. Chicago: University of Chicago Press, 1971–89.

—*Bach Among the Theologians*. Minneapolis: Fortress Press, 1986.

—*The Vindication of Tradition: The 1983 Jefferson Lecture in the Humanities.* New Haven: Yale University Press, 1986.

—*The Idea of the University: A Reexamination.* New Haven: Yale University Press, 1992.

—*Christianity and Classical Culture.* New Haven: Yale University Press, 1993.

—*Fools for Christ: Essays on the True, the Good, and the Beautiful.* Minneapolis: Fortress Press, 1995.

Peters, Ted, ed. *God—The World's Future: Systematic Theology for a Postmodern Era.* Minneapolis: Fortress, 1992.

—*Science and Theology: The New Consonance.* Boulder, Colorado: Westview Press, 1998.

Peters, Ted and Gaymon Bennet (eds). *Bridging Science and Religion.* Minneapolis: Fortress Press, 2003.

Peterson, Gregory R. *Minding God: Theology and the Cognitive Sciences.* Minneapolis: Fortress, 2003.

Piepkorn, Arthur Carl. *Profiles in Belief.* 3 vols. New York: Harper and Row, 1977–9.

Placher, William C., ed. *Essentials of Christian Theology.* Louisville: Westminster John Knox, 2003.

Plantinga, Alvin. *Warrant: The Current Debate.* New York: Oxford University Press, 1993.

—*Warrant and Proper Function.* New York: Oxford University Press, 1993.

—*Warranted Christian Belief.* New York: Oxford University Press, 2000.

—*Where the Conflict Really Lies: Science, Religion, and Naturalism.* New York: Oxford University Press, 2011.

Plantinga, Richard J., Thomas R. Thompson, and Matthew D. Lundberg. *An Introduction to Christian Theology.* Cambridge: Cambridge University Press, 2010.

Plato. *The Republic.* Translated by Tom Griffith. In *Plato: The Republic.* Edited by G. R. F. Ferrari. Cambridge Texts in the History of Political Thought. Cambridge: Cambridge University Press, 2000.

Polkinghorne, John. *Faith of a Physicist.* Minneapolis: Augsburg Fortress, 1996.

—*Belief in God in an Age of Science.* New Haven: Yale University Press, 1998.

Preus, J. Samuel. *Explaining Religion: Criticism and Theory from Bodin to Freud.* New Haven: Yale University Press, 1987.

Proclus. *Elements of Theology.* Translated by Thomas Taylor. Wiltshire, England: Prometheus Trust, 1994.

Proudfoot, Wayne. *Religious Experience.* Berkeley: University of California Press, 1985.

Putnam, Robert D. and David E. Campbell. *American Grace: How Religion Divides and Unites Us.* New York: Simon and Schuster, 2010.

Quinn, Philip L. and Charles Taliaferro (eds). *The Blackwell Companion to the Philosophy of Religion*. Oxford: Blackwell, 1997.

Rae, Andrew, Hilary Regan, and John Stenhouse (eds). *Science and Theology: Questions at the Interface*. Grand Rapids: Eerdmans, 1994.

Rahner, Karl. *Foundations of Christian Faith: An Introduction to the Idea of Christianity*. Translated by William V. Dych. New York: Crossroad, 1978.

—*Hearer of the Word*. Translated by Joseph Donceel. New York: Continuum, 1994.

Rahner, Karl and J. B. Metz. *Spirit in the World*. New York: Continuum, 1994.

Ratke, David C., ed. *The New Perspective on Paul*. Minneapolis: Lutheran University Press, 2012.

Richardson, W. Mark and Wesley J. Wildman (eds). *Religion and Science: History, Method, Dialogue*. New York: Routledge, 1996.

Ricoeur, Paul. *The Symbolism of Evil*. Translated by Emerson Buchanan. Boston: Beacon Press, 1969.

—*Interpretation Theory: Discourse and the Surplus of Meaning*. Fort Worth: Texas Christian University Press, 1976.

—*Time and Narrative*. 3 vols. Translated by Kathleen Blamey and David Pellauer. Chicago: University of Chicago Press, 1984–8.

—*Oneself as Another*. Translated by Kathleen Blamey. Chicago: University of Chicago Press, 1992.

—*Figuring the Sacred: Religion, Narrative, and Imagination*. Edited by Mark I. Wallace. Translated by David Pellauer. Minneapolis: Fortress Press, 1995.

Ricoeur, Paul and André LaCocque. *Thinking Biblically: Exegetical and Hermeneutical Studies*. Translated by David Pellauer. Chicago: University of Chicago Press, 1998.

Robinson, James M., ed. *The Beginnings of Dialectical Theology*. Translated by Keith Crim. Richmond: John Knox, 1968.

Rubenstein Jr., Richard L. *After Auschwitz*. Indianapolis: Bobbs–Merrill, 1966.

Rüegg, Walter, ed. *A History of the University in Europe*. 4 vols. Cambridge: Cambridge University Press, 1992–2011.

Russell, Bertrand. *Why I am Not a Christian and Other Essays on Religion and Related Subjects*. New York: Simon and Schuster, 1957.

Saler, Benson. *Conceptualizing Religion*. Leiden: Brill, 1993.

Sanders, E. P. *The Historical Figure of Jesus*. New York: Penguin Press, 1993.

—*Paul and Palestinian Judaism: A Comparison of Patterns of Religion*. Minneapolis: Fortress Press, 1977.

Schaff, Philip and Henry Wace (eds). *Nicene and Post-Nicene Fathers of the Christian Church*. 2nd series. 14 vols. Peabody, MA: Hendrickson, 1995.

Schippe, Cullen and Chuck Stetson. *The Bible and Its Influence*. 2nd edn. New York: BLP, 2011.

Schleiermacher, Friedrich. *The Christian Faith*. 2nd edn. Translated by H. R. Mackintosh and J. S. Stewart. Edinburgh: T & T Clark, 1928.

—*Brief Outline of Theology as a Field of Study*. Translated by Terrance N. Tice. Lewiston: Edwin Mellen, 1988.

Schlink, Edmund. *The Theology of the Lutheran Confessions*. Translated by Paul F. Koehneke and Herbert J. A. Bouman. Minneapolis: Fortress Press Press, 1961.

Schmid, Heinrich. *Doctrinal Theology of the Evangelical Lutheran Church*. 3rd edn. Translated by Charles A. Hay and Henry E. Jacobs. Minneapolis: Augsburg, 1889.

Schwehn, Mark. "Lutheranism and the Future of the University." *The Cresset* 73 (December 2009), 6–14.

Schweitzer, Albert. *The Quest for the Historical Jesus*. Edited by John Bowden. Translated by William Montgomery et al. Minneapolis: Augsburg Fortress Press, 2001.

Segal, Robert A., ed. *The Blackwell Companion to the Study of Religion*. Oxford: Blackwell, 2006.

Silverman, Allan Jay. *The Dialectics of Essence: A Study of Plato's Metaphysics*. Princeton: Princeton University Press, 2002.

Simpson, J. A. and E. S. C. Weiner (eds). *The Compact Oxford English Dictionary*. 2nd edn. Oxford: Oxford University Press, 1991.

Sittler, Joseph. *The Ecology of Faith*. Philadelphia: Muhlenberg, 1961.

—*Care of the Earth and Other University Sermons*. Minneapolis: Fortress Press, 1964.

—*Evocations of Grace: The Writings of Joseph Sittler on Ecology, Theology, and Ethics*. Edited by Steve Bouma-Prediger and Peter Bakken. Grand Rapids: Eerdmans, 2000.

Sobel, Jordan Howard. *Logic and Theism: Arguments For and Against Beliefs in God*. Cambridge: Cambridge University Press, 2004.

Sobrino, Jon. *Christology at the Crossroads: A Latin American Approach*. Translated by John Drury. Maryknoll, NY: Orbis, 1978.

Spinoza, Benedict, "The Theological-Political Tractate." in *Spinoza: Complete Works*. Edited by Michael L. Morgan. Translated by Samuel Shirley. Indianapolis: Hackett, 2002.

Steiner, George. *Errata: An Examined Life*. New Haven: Yale University Press, 1997.

Stendahl, Krister. "The Apostle Paul and the Introspective Conscience of the West." *Harvard Theological Review* 56 (1963), 199–215

—*The Bible and the Role of Women: A Case Study in Hermeneutics*. Minneapolis: Fortress Press, 1966.

Stenger, Victor. *The Comprehensible Cosmos: Where Do the Laws of Physics Come From?* Amherst: Prometheus Books, 2006.

Stone, Howard R. and James O. Duke. *How to Think Theologically*. 3rd edn. Minneapolis: Fortress, 2013.

Swinburne, Richard. *The Coherence of God*. Revised ed. Oxford: Oxford University Press, 1993.

—*The Existence of God*. 2nd edn. Oxford: Oxford University Press, 2004.

—*Is There a God?* 2nd edn. Oxford: Oxford University Press, 2010.

Symynkywicz, Jeffrey. *The Gospel according to Bruce Springsteen*. Louisville: Westminster John Knox, 2008.

Tanner, Kathryn. *Theories of Culture: A New Agenda for Theology*. Minneapolis: Fortress Press Press, 1997.

Tanner, Norman P., ed. *Decrees of the Ecumenical Councils*. 2 vols. Georgetown: Georgetown University Press, 1990.

Taylor, Charles. *A Secular Age*. Cambridge: Harvard University Press, 2007.

Tennant, Frederick R. *Philosophical Theology*. 2 vols. Cambridge: Cambridge University Press, 1928–30.

Teresa of Calcutta (Mother Teresa) and Brian Kolodiejchuk. *Come Be My Light: The Private Reflections of the Saint of Calcutta*. New York: Doubleday, 2007.

Thielicke, Helmut. *The Evangelical Faith*. 3 vols. Edited and translated by Geoffrey W. Bromiley. Grand Rapids: Eerdmans, 1974–81.

—*Modern Faith and Thought*. Translated by Geoffrey W. Bromiley. Grand Rapids: Eerdmans, 1990.

Thiemann, Ronald. *Revelation and Theology: The Gospel as Narrated Promise*. Notre Dame: University of Notre Dame Press, 1985.

Tillich, Paul. *Systematic Theology*. 3 vols. Chicago: University of Chicago Press, 1951–63.

—*On Art and Architecture*. Edited by John Dillenberger. New York: Crossroad, 1987.

Tracy, David. *Blessed Rage for Order: The New Pluralism in Theology*. Minneapolis: Winston-Seabury, 1975.

—*The Analogical Imagination: Christian Theology and the Culture of Pluralism*. New York: Crossroad, 1981.

—"Theology, Critical Social Theory, and the Public Realm," in *Habermas, Modernity, and Public Theology*. Edited by Don S. Browning and Francis Schlüssler Fiorenza. Chicago: University of Chicago Press, 1992.

—*Plurality and Ambiguity: Hermeneutics, Religion, Hope*. Chicago: University of Chicago Press, 1994.

Treier, Daniel J. et al. (eds). *The Beauty of God: Theology and the Arts*. Downers Grove, IL.,: Intervarsity, 2007.

Troeltsch, Ernst. *Religion in History*. Translated by James Luther Adams and Walter F. Bense. Fortress Texts in Modern Theology. Minneapolis: Fortress Press, 1991.

Volf, Miroslav. *Allah: A Christian Response*. New York: HarperOne, 2011.

—ed. *Do We Worship the Same God: Jews, Christians, and Muslims in Dialogue*. Grand Rapids: Eerdmans, 2012.

Voskamp, Ann. *One Thousand Gifts*. Grand Rapids: Zondervan, 2010.

Ward, Keith. *Why There Almost Certainly is a God: Doubting Dawkins*. Oxford: Lion Books, 2008.

—*God and the Philosophers*. Minneapolis: Fortress, 2009.

Weber, Otto. Foundations of Dogmatics. 2 vols. Translated by Darrell L. Guder. Grand Rapids: Eerdmans, 1981–3.

Webster, John, Kathryn Tanner, and Iain Torrence (eds). *The Oxford Handbook of Systematic Theology*. Oxford: Oxford University Press, 2007.

White, Andrew D. *A History of the Warfare of Science with Theology in Christendom*. 2 vols. New York: D. Appleton & Co., 1896.

Wiesel, Elie. *All Rivers Run to the Sea: Memoirs*. New York: Schocken, 1995.

Williams, Rowan. *Dostoevsky: Language, Faith, and Fiction*. Waco: Baylor University Press, 2011.

Wilson, A. N. "Why I Believe Again." *New Statesmen* (April 2, 2009).

Wilson, E. O. *Consilience*. New York: Knopf, 1998.

Wiman, Christian. *My Bright Abyss: Meditations of a Modern Believer*. New York: Farrar, Straus & Giroux, 2013.

Wolpert, Lewis. *Six Impossible Things before Breakfast: The Evolutionary Origins of Belief*. New York: W. W. Norton & Company, 2006.

Wright, N. T. "New Perspectives on Paul." 10th Edinburgh Dogmatics Conference (August 25–28, 2003).

—*Simply Jesus: A New Vision of Who He Was, What He Did, and Why He Matters*. San Francisco: HarperOne, 2011.

Wuthnow, Robert. *The Re-structuring of American Religion*. Princeton: Princeton University Press, 1990.

Wyman Jr., Walter E. *The Concept of* Glaubenslehre: *Ernst Troeltsch and the Theological Heritage of Schleiermacher*. AAR Academy Series 44. Chico, CA: Scholars Press, 1983.

Biblical Index

Index of Persons

Index of Subjects

CATALONIA

Nation Building Without A State

KENNETH MCROBERTS

OXFORD
UNIVERSITY PRESS

OXFORD
UNIVERSITY PRESS

70 Wynford Drive, Don Mills, Ontario M3C 1J9
www.oup.com/ca

Oxford University Press is a department of the University of Oxford.
It furthers the University's objective of excellence in research, scholarship,
and education by publishing worldwide in

Oxford New York

Auckland Bangkok Buenos Aires Cape Town Chennai
Dar es Salaam Delhi Hong Kong Istanbul Karachi Kolkata
Kuala Lumpur Madrid Melbourne Mexico City Mumbai Nairobi
São Paulo Shanghai Singapore Taipei Tokyo Toronto
and an associated company in Berlin

Oxford is a trade mark of Oxford University Press
in the UK and in certain other countries

Published in Canada by Oxford University Press

Canadian Cataloguing in Publication Data

McRoberts, Kenneth, 1942–
Catalonia : nation building without a state

Includes bibliographical references and index.
ISBN 0-19-541481-0

1. Catalonia (Spain) – Politics and government – 20th century.
2. Catalonia (Spain) – History – 20th century.   3. Nationalism – Spain – Catalonia.
I. Title.

DP302.C68M32 2001   946'.7   C00-933068-2

Cover Design: Brett J. Miller

2 3 4 – 04 03 02
This book is printed on permanent (acid-free) paper ∞.
Printed in Canada